OneStream Advanced Reporting and Dashboards

Roy Googin, Jessica Toner, Andrea Tout

OneStream™ Press

Published in 2023 by OneStream Press.

ISBN: 978-1-8382528-2-3

OneStream Press has endeavored to provide trademark information about all the companies and products mentioned in this book by the appropriate use of capitals. However, OneStream Press cannot guarantee the accuracy of this information. OneStream Press is an imprint of Play Technologies (England) Limited. 6 Woodside, Churnet View Road, Oakamoor, ST10 3AE, United Kingdom.

www.OneStreamPress.com

Disclaimer

While the advice and information in this book is believed to be true and accurate at the date of publication, OneStream Press, the authors, and OneStream Software LLC do not guarantee the accuracy, adequacy, or completeness of any information, and are not responsible for any errors or omissions or the results obtained from the use of such information.

OneStream Press, the authors, and OneStream Software LLC make no warranty, express or implied, with respect to the material contained herein, and hereby disclaim any liability to any party for any loss, damage, or disruption caused by errors or omissions, whether such errors or omissions result from negligence, accident, or any other cause.

Note: Any Files provided for Exercises in this OneStream Press Book are for the use of Customers and Partners in an On-Premise environment and are not supported by the OneStream Support Team.

About the Authors

Roy Googin is OneStream's Vice President of Presales Operations. Since joining the company in 2015, he has served in the implementation services, presales consulting, and demo engineering organizations. With over 25 years of experience in the field of corporate performance management (CPM), Roy has helped guide some of the world's largest and most complex organizations in the selection and implementation of multidimensional planning, forecasting, financial reporting, and profitability analysis solutions.

To my OneStream colleagues and friends, who constantly amaze me with their talent, creativity, and imagination. And, especially, to my wonderful wife Diane, who makes everything matter.

Jessica Toner is a Lead Solution Consultant on the OneStream Demo Architecture team. She joined the OneStream Software services team in 2017, where she played a vital role in the successful implementation of OneStream's inaugural Federal customer solution. In 2020, she shifted her focus to Partner Enablement as a Partner Engagement Manager, providing partner implementation support and project management for the OneStream Public Sector practice. Jessica currently manages the OneStream Public Sector Practice Demo Assets and provides technical build support throughout the organization. Prior to joining OneStream in 2017, she amassed over a decade of experience in accounting and finance across diverse industries, enabling her to acquire a deep understanding of the complex financial challenges that many organizations face. Jessica currently resides in Royal Oak, Michigan.

To my fiancé, Eric. I couldn't have asked for a better partner – you are my rock.

Andrea Tout joined OneStream in 2015 with the services team, where she spent five great years working with amazing consultants and clients. Andrea's OneStream career began with building reporting tools, and she hopes this book will inspire others to tackle something new in OneStream, think about the end-user when designing, and pass it on to others who need the knowledge and support! Andrea is grateful to her team of Technical Education Consultants, Technical Writers, Product Advocates, and Release Enablement Managers for their hard work and support of the community on Product Knowledge. Most of all, she is extremely grateful to the OneStreamers who dedicated so much time to helping her learn the product and still put up with her to this day.

To my husband, Justin, who encouraged me to write this book. Thank you for always pushing me to do things I am afraid to try, supporting me when I need it, and channeling some of my wild ideas into a reality.

Technical Reviewers

Peter Fugere is recognized as a leader within the corporate performance management (CPM) community, where he has been working to deliver world-class solutions for the past 25 years. He has worked extensively with Oracle Hyperion Financial Management, Oracle Hyperion Planning, Oracle EPM Cloud Financial Consolidation and Close, Oracle Hyperion Financial Data Quality Management, Hyperion Enterprise, Upstream, and SAP BPC (Business Planning and Consolidation) before leaving Hyperion in 2004 to help build another consulting practice. He has published books and written whitepapers on the topic of implementation and best practices. He joined OneStream in 2013, is currently OneStream's Chief Solution Officer, and is responsible for OneStream's "Architect Factory".

John Rodgers is based in Manchester, UK, and joined OneStream in 2016, having previously spent several years in the Oracle-Hyperion space. Since joining OneStream, John has worked in the Remote Consulting and Education organizations before moving into Solutions Consulting, aka Presales. In his various roles, John has provided training and enablement to hundreds of OneStream colleagues, customers, and partners over the years. As Director of POC Architecture, John has a passion for creating sophisticated consolidation, planning, and reporting & analytics solutions.

Errata

Despite best efforts, mistakes can sometimes creep into books. If you spot a mistake, please feel free to email us at **errata@OneStreamPress.com** (with the book title in the subject line).

The errata page for this book is hosted at **www.OneStreamPress.com/Dashboards**

Version Updates

The OneStream platform is constantly evolving, with each release bringing new features and capabilities. The material in this book is based on Platform Version 7.3.1, which was current at the time of writing. As new releases become available, information about Dashboarding and Reporting updates can be found at: **www.OneStreamPress.com/Dashboards**

Accompanying Download

An accompanying file containing sample material is available for this book. To download this file, visit: **www.OneStreamPress.com/Rad**

25% OFF VOUCHER

Certification

Validate your technical competence and gain industry recognition with OneStream Software.

In purchasing this book, you are eligible to claim a 25% discount on any OneStream Certification Exam.

To request your voucher, open a case with Credentialing via the ServiceNow Support Portal (https://onestreamsoftware.service-now.com/). Include proof of purchase that contains your name and address, the book title, date of purchase, and proof of payment.

Terms & Conditions:
One (1) certification exam voucher per book. All vouchers per receipt must be claimed at one time; if a receipt is for the purchase of 10 books, all 10 vouchers must be claimed at the same time. Vouchers are valid for post-beta production exams only. This offer is only valid for one year from the purchase date on the invoice or receipt.

 onestream

Table of Contents

1

Getting Started

Think of the last time you boarded a plane. If you glanced to your left – into the cockpit – you probably noticed a spectacular collection of glass panels, levers, knobs, and switches covering nearly every square inch of space. Pilots dedicate years of study and practice learning how to operate these marvels of modern engineering.

Now, think of the last time you stopped at an ATM, perhaps to withdraw some cash or deposit a check, or just review your account balance. Even if you have never been to this particular bank and have never seen this make or model of ATM, it will no doubt take you mere seconds to familiarize yourself with the device, perform your transaction, and go on with your day.

Both of these experiences – piloting a state-of-the-art airliner and operating an ATM – require a human-facing interface to control very complex processes behind the scenes. But the requirements of the people using these interfaces are very different. A well-designed cockpit will be comprehensive, with every control and information source that the pilot will ever need in any phase of flight or unexpected circumstance. And although nearly all aircraft conform to certain fundamental standards of cockpit layout, each individual make and model will have its own unique nuances, design decisions, features, capabilities, and specialized controls required to operate that specific machine safely and efficiently. Needless to say, it is well worth the time and effort required to train the pilots that will be flying these planes.

On the other hand, a well-designed ATM must be intuitive, self-explanatory, and require no training at all. Only the most common transactions will be supported, but that is a fine trade-off for the users of this machine – no one will expect anyone to refinance their mortgage by pushing a few buttons on an ATM.

The corporate performance management (CPM) systems of large and complex organizations support many interrelated processes and must meet the needs of very diverse communities of end-users. Like airline pilots, some users will require a comprehensive and sophisticated user interface providing efficient access to multiple, complex, and highly specialized capabilities to perform their duties. Other users, like the customer at the ATM, will be much better served by a front-end that simplifies their experience, presenting them with only the information they need and the controls they are likely to use.

These differing needs usually depend on various factors, such as the user's role within the organization, CPM experience and proficiency, and so on. For example, a seasoned system administrator or controller with ten years of CPM experience, who is in the system every working day, will typically need more application access than your average end-user planner who just wants to log in and complete a forecast once a month.

The OneStream platform provides the best of both worlds. With a well-designed implementation, the navigation, Workflows, Dashboards, and Reports that any one User sees will be well-aligned with how that User will be interacting with the application and what capabilities are most important to them.

Why It Matters

As you plan, deploy, maintain, and extend your OneStream implementation, you will, of course, pay close attention to the data sources and dimensionality, Business Rules and Member Formulas, User security, Confirmation Rules, Workflow approval processes, and all the other fundamental architectural aspects that make your application whole. But, along the way, to ensure a world-class implementation, you should also keep in mind the day-to-day experiences of the ultimate End-Users of your application. The best set of KPI Calculations ever created will be of very little use to the financial analyst who needs them if that analyst doesn't know (or doesn't remember) they are there! No process efficiency improvements will be achieved if the time-consuming manual efforts your implementation is hoping to eliminate are simply replaced by time-consuming hunting-and-pecking as Users try to remember how to access the amazing functionality they were introduced to several weeks (or months) ago but haven't revisited since.

If an End-User's Experiences while interacting with an application are confusing, inefficient, unnecessarily complex, or even just plain unattractive, no matter how well the underlying business model was designed or how perfectly the functionality meets the organization's requirements, the actual User will have a negative view of the application. Or perhaps worse… they will avoid using it at all.

In the pages that follow, you will learn how to design and configure User Experiences that meet the needs of your diverse community of End-Users, balancing the varying levels of front-end simplicity, functional completeness, and ease of use that these Users need and deserve. We will explore the various tools and techniques available to you, the best ways to design and deploy your application's User Experiences, and walk through multiple detailed examples, from the very simple to the very sophisticated, always with the requirements, skill sets, and objectives of your End-Users in mind.

2
Keeping The User in Mind

The OneStream platform can be home to a nearly unlimited set of distinct but interrelated processes – Financial Close, Account Reconciliations, Reporting and Analysis, Budgeting, Forecasting, Sales and Operational Planning, plus many more. Even within the specific context of any one of these processes, different Users will have different interests, skills, responsibilities, and frequency of interaction.

For any User community and process, the 'right' User Experience will be the one that provides the correct balance between functionality, time to train, and ease of use. So, let's consider, for example, a typical annual operating plan process.

There will probably be a small number of individuals responsible for managing this process. They might be responsible for seeding the Base-level version of the plan and managing the global assumptions and drivers. They will be monitoring Workflow completion statuses as each individual department head approaches their deadlines, locking plan Scenarios as they are completed, and more.

From an application administration perspective, these responsibilities primarily involve defining and assigning tasks and their associated due dates and dependencies; scheduling or manually running Business Rules, Data Management sequences, and Consolidations; verifying the successful completion of various Workflows; and other tasks that, by definition, involve managing the Planning process as a whole. These Users won't have much need for the kind of granular data entry, financial reporting, and variance analysis functionality that will be required by the department heads and operational Planners who are responsible for building the detailed, bottom-up plan.

And, by the very nature of an 'annual' process, our hypothetical Planning Process Managers will most likely be laser-focused on these duties for a few weeks or months, and then, when the Planning cycle is complete, move on. It may be close to a year before they revisit the system.

What would be the ideal User Experience for them? Preferably, they would be able to see – at a glance – the status of the process as a whole. They will also need to easily review any areas of concern, identifying missed deadlines or incomplete tasks. From a data perspective, they will need to easily initiate and verify the successful completion of data integrations, top-down allocations, Consolidations, and other global actions that impact the entire plan.

Based on these requirements, when these Users sign on to the application, they would be best served by a home page with relevant statistics about the progress of the overall Planning process, with clearly marked buttons to launch the background tasks they are responsible for, and intuitive navigation to the more detailed information they will need to monitor the timeliness and successful completion of the full Planning cycle.

Let's also think about how much time a User spends with the application. As we tailor the User Experience to balance the appropriate mix of functionality and ease of use, we need to consider the varying patterns of usage that different processes require throughout the year. Some Users will have relatively short periods of very intense activity for a few weeks or months, and then have very little interaction for long periods of time – say, a Manager who is responsible for contributing to an annual operating plan, or a Sales Executive who revises a Revenue Forecast once a quarter. Other Users will return to the application every month or week or even every day – for example, the Users who are responsible for the monthly Financial Close, or those who monitor daily bookings versus plan.

A User who spends a great deal of time in the application will often prioritize efficiency over simplicity. These highly active, frequent Users will probably be willing to spend a little more time learning to navigate a set of content-rich screens that provide 'one-stop shopping' in order to access the multiple Workflows and Reports they access every day.

On the other hand, their colleagues who interact with the system only a few times a year will probably appreciate a simpler interface, with large, clearly-labeled buttons providing self-explanatory navigation.

Your Users' Interactions: How Complex, and How Often?

We can think of these two fundamental aspects of End-User interaction – the complexity of the tasks our Users are performing, and the frequency of those interactions – as two axes on a chart. We can plot our application's various processes in their relative positions on this chart, with highly complex, frequently occurring processes in the upper-left and simpler, more sporadic interactions in the lower-right. Here's a possible example:

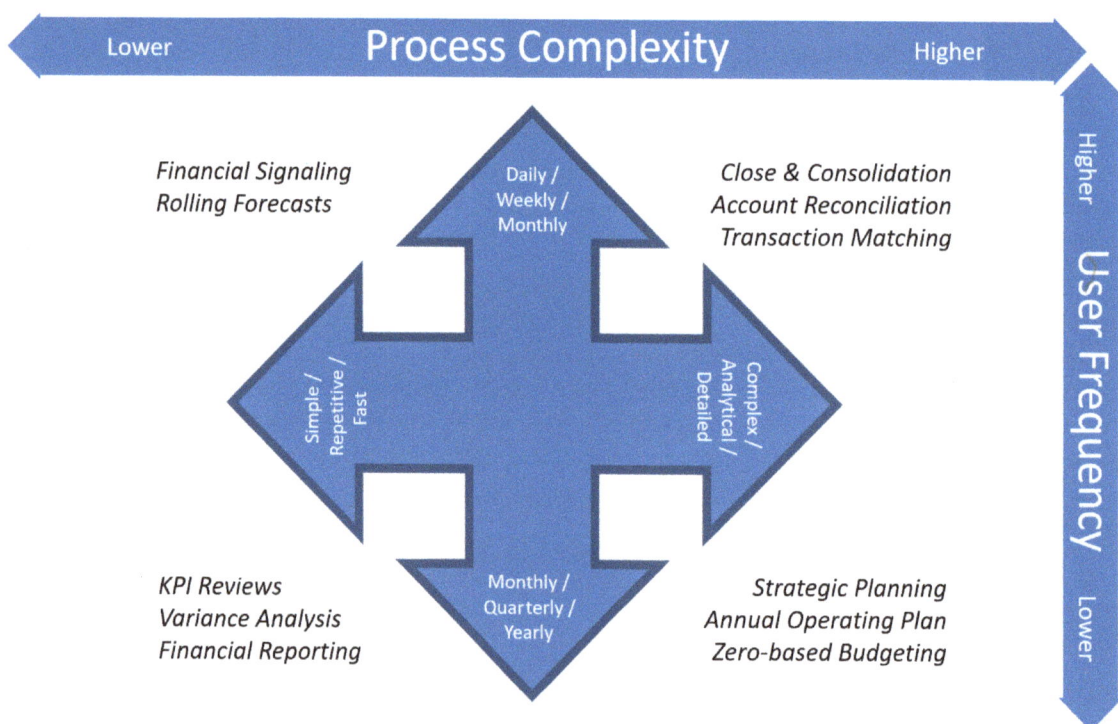

Figure 2.1

Sketching out a chart like this can help give us a sense of what our priorities should be when planning the User Experiences for each of these processes (and, if appropriate, for the various User roles within each of these processes).

As an example, we might be implementing a Rolling Forecast process, with largely pre-loaded, automatically-generated data provided by source system integrations and Business Rules. Our Forecast Users in our Sales organization will typically make a few manual adjustments or explanatory comments each week or month, then mark their Workflow complete.

For this process, we will design a User Experience that prioritizes efficiency, so the User can easily navigate to the handful of Forms that might require attention this month, and make their adjustments with as few clicks as possible. We can accomplish this by including as much of the most frequently updated information as possible on the User's home screen. Since this is a familiar part of the User's monthly routine, we won't take up valuable screen real estate with instructions, navigation buttons, etc. For this User, we might provide a home page that looks something like Figure 2.2.

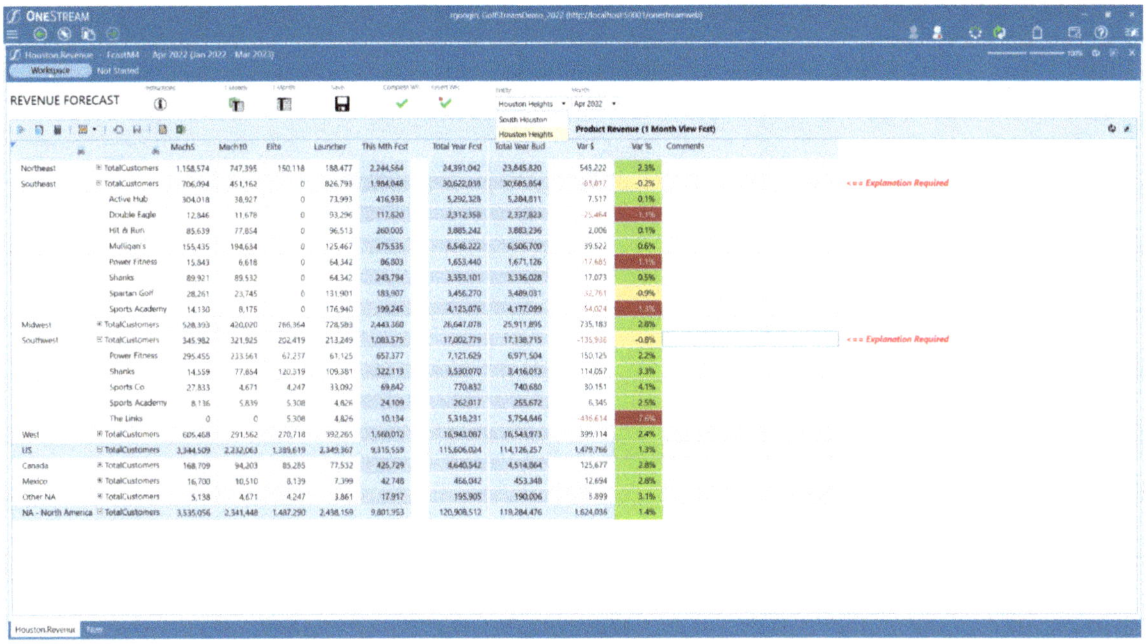

Figure 2.2

On the other hand, preparing the Annual Operating Plan might require much more User interaction across a broad assortment of interrelated but functionally distinct moving pieces. Product- and region-level revenue planning, cost center expenses, capital expenditures, headcount and salary planning, and many other components of the total plan will each have their own requirements, levels of granularity, purpose-driven productivity helpers, and Workflows. On our scale of process complexity, this might score very high. But on the scale of User frequency, this will be very low – our Planners will have a lot to do, much of it quite complex, but they will only be active with these parts of the application once a year.

For a process like this, we should design a User Experience that prioritizes ease of use, with self-explanatory navigation, function-specific data entry Forms appropriate to each of the components of the plan, and strategically-placed explanatory labels to guide the User through multiple steps. And, while we design this User Experience, we will need to be sensitive to the confusion, frustration, and even eye strain that can result from trying to fit everything on one screen. For this User, we might provide a home page that looks something like Figure 2.3.

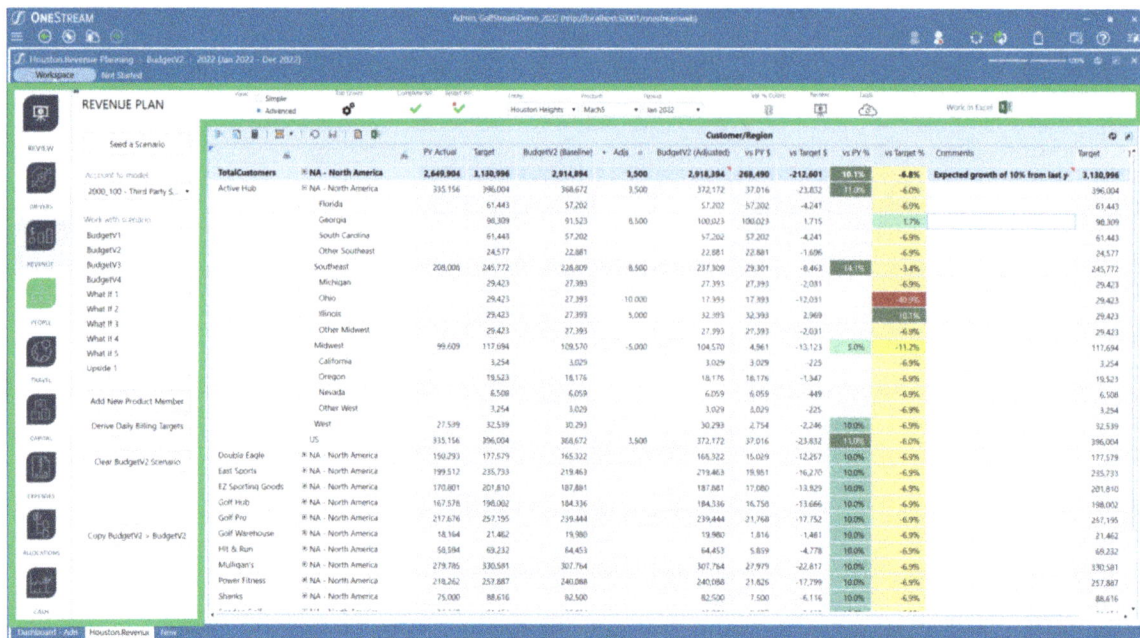

Figure 2.3

Notice that in this example, although the process is functionally similar to the Rolling Forecast, our Annual Operating Plan Users are provided with many additional controls, navigation buttons, and links to relevant reporting and modeling tools (outlined above in green). With this additional functionality, the Planning Process User Experience – while more detailed and time-consuming than the Forecast – will be just as intuitive and efficient.

It's clear that we will need to provide *different* User experiences based on the varying requirements of our multiple User communities. Let's step back and think about how we will accomplish this.

The OneStream Platform

As we mentioned earlier, OneStream is a true 'platform', and this platform provides remarkable flexibility and capabilities that can be leveraged when tailoring a User Experience. By 'platform', we mean that virtually anything an End-User sees or does can be configured to look, feel, and behave exactly as you want.

Out-of-the-box, OneStream provides a powerful, well-thought-out, feature-rich, standard User Interface. A large, complex implementation incorporating multiple concurrent daily, weekly, monthly, and yearly processes, such as the Financial Close cycle, Strategic Planning, environmental, social and governance reporting, profitability analysis – and countless others – can and should live side by side. They should share the Components they have in common, with each process configured to meet their own precise, specific business requirements.

OneStream's platform provides a comprehensive set of Components that can be easily configured to handle nearly any required User Interaction for any of these processes. Cube Views are used whenever you need to present multidimensional information in rows and columns, and can display this information in a multitude of formats – data entry Forms, real-time spreadsheet retrievals, highly-formatted Reports, and more. Workflows are defined to guide and control processes with multiple Users collaborating across the organization, ensuring the completeness and quality of the information that is being collected, derived, and shared. Data Management sequences, Business Rules, Report Books – all of these highly-configurable Components (and more) are available to address the unique requirements of your organization.

We'll get into much more detail on these Components in later chapters, but for now, just keep in mind that these Components, and the standard User navigation provided out-of-the-box by the OneStream platform, can *almost certainly* meet any functional requirements you will encounter.

But there's more.

The Magic of OneStream Dashboards

One of the most powerful tools provided by the OneStream platform is the ability to create your own custom-designed Dashboards.

First, a word about terminology. Through your experiences with other software, you may be familiar with the concept of 'dashboards' as User-facing screens providing real-time information through reports, charts, graphs, gauges, traffic lights, and other visualizations. With OneStream, you can (and probably will) create this type of 'Business Intelligence' Dashboard, too – and these are among the most popular and useful Dashboards in many implementations.

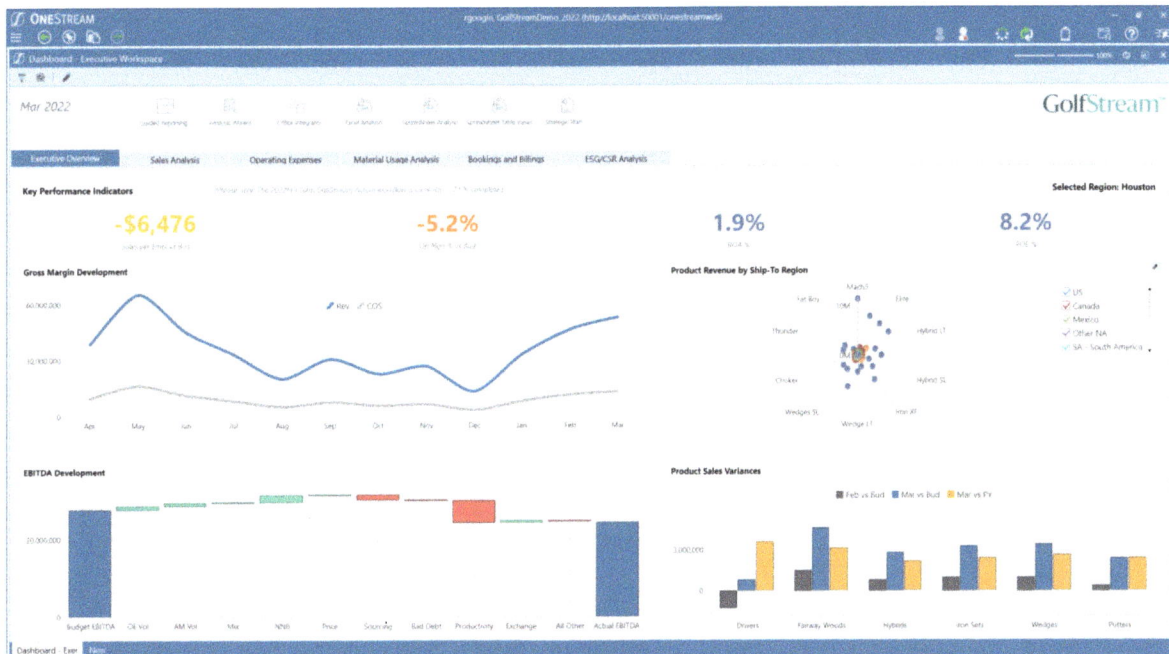

Figure 2.4

What we call 'Dashboards' in OneStream, though, go far beyond this. Yes, with OneStream Dashboards, you can configure attractive, intuitive screens to present information in formats appropriate to Users at any level in the organization, but OneStream Dashboards also give you the power to control the look and feel of any aspect of the End-User experience.

With these Dashboards, we can provide clean, professional home pages with big buttons, simplified navigation, and gorgeous Executive KPI reviews. We can give our Users mission-specific data entry screens with powerful, custom-configured User-productivity tools a mouse-click away. We can surface and highlight the application controls that are most important to a specific community of Users, without cluttering their screens with controls they are unlikely to need or use.

It is with these Dashboards that we provide Users with the 'ATM experience' where appropriate, the 'Airline Cockpit' experience where needed, and virtually any other User Experience our application might require.

In addition, OneStream also provides numerous Dashboard templates and reference examples via online channels such as OneStream University training classes and the OneStream Solution Exchange, which means that – more often than not – you have a starting point and don't always have to begin your dashboarding journey from scratch.

In the next chapter, we will dig deeper into the concepts and capabilities behind these Dashboards, as well as Cube Views, Reports, Spreadsheets, and the many other moving pieces available to you in this powerful platform, and see how they come together in your application to form truly world-class User Experiences!

3
The Moving Pieces

This chapter will take a deeper look at the reporting aspect of the User Experience.

Picture this: you have just taken the time to determine your requirements for creating your OneStream application, and you have it all jotted down in a beautiful requirements matrix. Now you are getting ready to design how your OneStream application will look and create something sleek and effective for your End-User. So, you… build 1,000 Cube Views!

Just kidding, let's back up for a minute.

We have fully vetted the Users we are building for, and know what will make their experience effective (be aware there will be some back and forth as that happens); the next thing to do is take an inventory of the tools at your disposal at OneStream, to try to visualize what will get the job done.

If you want to feel prepared going into any OneStream design, then having a well-rounded view of what OneStream has to offer will allow you to visualize what you can do, plus give you some peace of mind. Taking an inventory of what OneStream has to offer with out-of-the-box functionality and knowing *when* and *why* to use these solutions/methodologies will prepare you for almost anything that can get thrown at you. That may sound like I just said, "It's easy! You just have to know EVERYTHING", but having a rough demonstration of common use cases for a wide variety of things is all you need to get started. Even if you don't know how to use a specific tool just yet, there is probably someone in your network that does.

Let's get into the reporting aspect. OneStream has an abundance of tools at your disposal that can help you satisfy your reporting requirement: Cube Views, Excel Add-in/Spreadsheet, and Dashboards, to name a few. Deciding which tool handles which requirements is what sets you up for success on your project, and creates the most unique and rewarding User Experience. You already know that we want to think about the User when designing their experience, but when it comes to reporting we also want to think about two other things:

1. The types of data we are pulling
2. Metadata design

Interestingly, these two things create a bit of a 'chicken or the egg?' situation. Data and metadata requirements impact your Report design, and reporting requirements also tend to impact your metadata design. Clear as mud? Don't worry; we'll get you there!

Types of Reports

There are myriad reporting tools and User Experiences that we will discuss in this book. OneStream not only has the capability to present a wide variety of data in many flexible and interactive ways, but it also has built-in capabilities to Report on administration states (Workflow statuses, Task Activity, etc.) and granular audit trails. Two of the most common (and important!) types of reporting we see in OneStream are Financial Reporting and Management Reporting. Let's take a closer look.

Financial Reporting

Financial reporting is a great place to start our reporting journey. I find the associated requirements to be truly indicative of what *almost every client* will be faced with delivering at some point in their OneStream journey.

Typically, these reporting requirements are the focal point of your Financial Consolidation projects, but they are also commonly addressed during Financial Planning implementations. This is where we see many of our clients spend the bulk of their development hours in phase one implementations. I have seen many Planning projects where some sort of effort is required to get these Reports up and running, even if the data is simply loaded and used for variance analysis.

Typical Financial Reports are Income Statement, Balance Sheet, and Statement of Cash Flows. It's likely that there will be a combination of both summary and detailed iterations of each of these Reports, and varying columns of dimensionality used to explain the Account structure along the way. The overarching goals of these Reports tend to be the same for all businesses: to illustrate the financial performance and standing of the business. There is little variability in these Reports, as they are widely adopted and required as part of reporting compliance.

Every project and client is different, but these types of Reports tend to be a little more run-of-the-mill; they are standardized, and something you will quickly grow comfortable with building. They're also great for someone who is getting their feet wet with OneStream implementation and administration.

If Financial Reports were an outfit, I would say they are a nice black dress or suit. Almost everyone has one; they are usually your go-to when you want to dress up or look professional, and they are easy to pull off. Don't be fooled, though. Even though they are simple, we want them to be sleek, elegant, professional, flawless, and dynamic. Before you pour yourself a martini, you better watch out for those deodorant marks and get that lint roller ready!

First, the *formatting* for financial Reports is essential. You will almost certainly use row/column formatting, consistent headers and footers, and simple Calculations. More advanced Reports may add charts, buttons, and complex Calculations and variances. Also, most of these Reports will require some form of User prompt (known as a **parameter**) which helps Users make their dimensional selections and guides them to the right data.

The second challenge you are going to encounter is the sheer number of Reports you will have to configure. There are typically multiple versions of your financial Reports, so – when faced with this situation – you must think of two things: maintenance and speed. The last thing you want is a situation where you must change many Reports in a hurry; this is where **templates** become critical in building an efficient solution that is easy for anyone to maintain.

Figure 3.1 shows an example of the formatted PDF version of a Cube View. This Cube View is being used in a PDF Report Book that is meant to compile our fictional demo example company *GolfStream*'s Financial Statements. We will talk about Report Books in OneStream a bit more in this chapter and later ones.

GolfStream™ Income Statement
Book

	Mar 2022	Mar 2021
60000 - Operating Sales	204,691,245	0
60200 - Returns & Allowances	8,533,520	0
60999 - Net Sales	196,157,725	0
41000 - Operating Cost of Goods Sold	116,289,849	0
42000 - IC Cost of Goods Sold	216,304	0
43000 - Cost of Goods Sold	116,506,153	0
61000 - Gross Income	79,651,573	0
50300 - Total Employee Compensation	57,884,154	0
51099 - Total Utilities	756,230	0
51199 - Total Professional Services	200,613	0
52099 - Marketing & Advertising	25,982,323	0
52199 - Travel & Entertainment	632,314	0
52299 - Total Facility Expense	913,810	0
52399 - Total HR Expenses	81,611	0
52499 - Total Equip Expense	675,828	0
53099 - Total Telecom	169,770	0
53199 - Total R&D Expenses	1,577,282	0
54099 - Depreciation & Amortization Expense	62,206	0
54199 - Total Other Operating Expenses	1,889,479	0
54400 - Total Operating Exp Before Allocation	90,825,618	0
54350 - Total Allocations	0	0
54500 - Total Operating Expenses	90,825,618	0
62000 - Total Operating Income	-11,174,045	0
62100 - Exchange Rate Gain/(Loss)	-883,471	0
62200 - Gain/(Loss) on Sale of Assets	-440,395	0
62500 - Unrealized Gain/(Loss) on Investments	-2,757,290	0
62600 - Other Rev/(Exp)	-1,203,468	0
62999 - Total Other Income (Expense)	-5,284,624	0

Figure 3.1

Management Reporting

Management reporting's goal is to provide the leadership team with key information to monitor performance and operations. This is what Managers need to see to make important business decisions. Typically, we can expect to see a combination of financial and operational information in these Reports, and they come in a variety of shapes and sizes.

This is where our Report tools can really start to flex. Because we are trying to create something that helps people quickly see, gauge, and assess the performance of the business, we want to be paying extra attention to our User. Is this User an Executive who wants a Dashboard that flashes everything they need to see quickly? Do they need to drill in further to see underlying data and details in OneStream? Are they using this to build presentations to display to stakeholders? How often is this data expected to change? All these questions are useful in designing delightful Management Reports.

If financial reporting is a black dress, management reporting is high fashion! We can start to design customized Reports with wild features and a ton of flair. This is where we want to start introducing things like interactive Dashboards, flashy charts that you can click into and see more detail, gauges, and more – whizz, bang, boom, POP! Something that tells a story in a quick second but keeps the information at your fingertips and serves as a one-stop shop for all the information the intended target User needs.

The challenge that we have to cross with this style of reporting is choosing between the many reporting options in OneStream. You will get the chance to see what we are talking about in later chapters, but it can require you to think outside the box in the creation of these Reports. Budget a few extra hours in your project plan dedicated to exploring, iterating, and learning how to design and build management Reports. If you are not going to administer the Reports once built, try to simplify the design and keep the Reports maintainable for the next person. This requires designing with both the customer and Administrator in mind.

Data model design is the next management reporting challenge. Management Reports typically use lots of data from many sources – multiple Cubes, Extensible Dimensionality, or even Analytic Blend. Striking a careful balance between performance and design is a skill you must hone over time. It may sound daunting to orchestrate these systems, but OneStream has the tools and options you'll need to give Users beautiful Reports chock full of the data they need.

Reporting Tools

The Reporting Tool: Cube View

Now – for your most common Report – what is more fitting than a Cube View? Here it is, the moment we have all been waiting for, the first time we talk about Cube Views. We will get into this a little more later, but right now, I am literally picturing a Cube View descending a staircase with dramatic music playing in the background as if it's a starring cast member in the original Dynasty soap opera.

If you have not heard about them just yet, a Cube View is exactly what it sounds like: a picture of Cube data. Not everyone thinks this way, but my advice to anyone starting any Report development is to start with a Cube View. My reasoning is that a Cube View can turn into anything, so why not start here? Typically, they will be your best way to handle most of your financial reporting requirements because they respond well to the challenges I laid out in the prior section:

1. They are easy to build and maintain.
2. They can be heavily formatted.
3. They are *typically* the most performant option.
4. They can be easily accessed across the application.

Figure 3.2 shows a simple but highly-formatted Cube View in the Data Explorer View (or Grid).

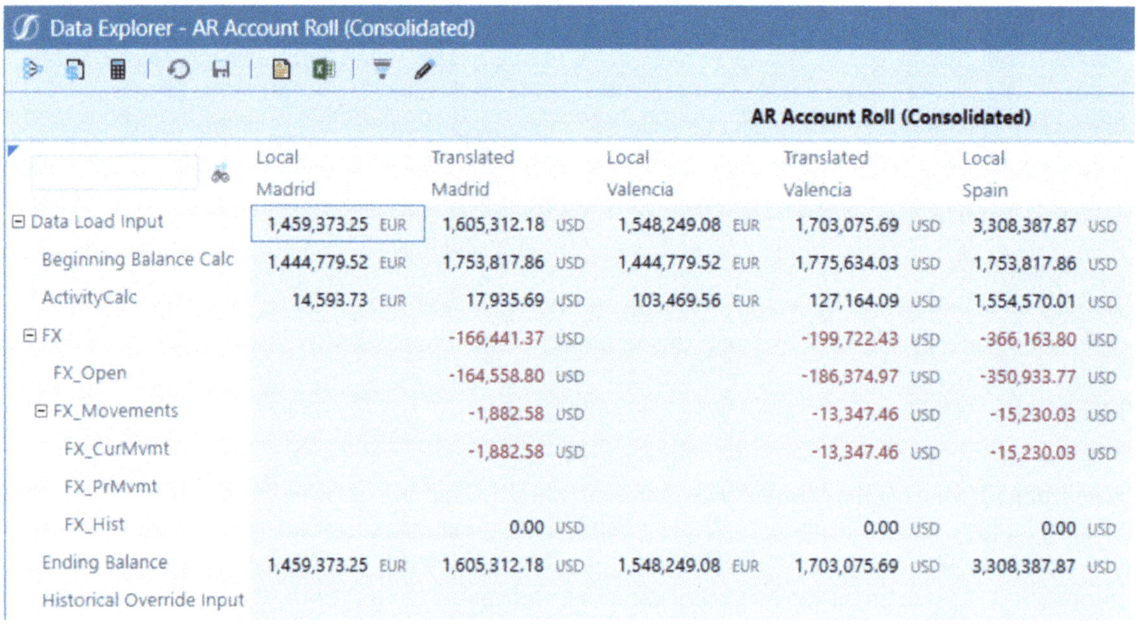

	Local Madrid	Translated Madrid	Local Valencia	Translated Valencia	Local Spain
⊟ Data Load Input	1,459,373.25 EUR	1,605,312.18 USD	1,548,249.08 EUR	1,703,075.69 USD	3,308,387.87 USD
Beginning Balance Calc	1,444,779.52 EUR	1,753,817.86 USD	1,444,779.52 EUR	1,775,634.03 USD	1,753,817.86 USD
ActivityCalc	14,593.73 EUR	17,935.69 USD	103,469.56 EUR	127,164.09 USD	1,554,570.01 USD
⊟ FX		-166,441.37 USD		-199,722.43 USD	-366,163.80 USD
FX_Open		-164,558.80 USD		-186,374.97 USD	-350,933.77 USD
⊟ FX_Movements		-1,882.58 USD		-13,347.46 USD	-15,230.03 USD
FX_CurMvmt		-1,882.58 USD		-13,347.46 USD	-15,230.03 USD
FX_PrMvmt					
FX_Hist		0.00 USD		0.00 USD	0.00 USD
Ending Balance	1,459,373.25 EUR	1,605,312.18 USD	1,548,249.08 EUR	1,703,075.69 USD	3,308,387.87 USD
Historical Override Input					

Figure 3.2

They are Easy to Build and Maintain

Cube Views have a lot of properties. This may sound daunting, but rest assured, this just demonstrates the possibilities of how intricately you can format your Reports. They are not difficult to stand up quickly. I bet if you knew the dimensionality and data in an application, I could get you to stand up a halfway decent Cube View in under five minutes.

When teaching someone to build their first Cube View, I always start with setting your Cube View POV, rows, and columns. Once you have that lined up, you are ready to tweak and tinker until you have every requirement beautifully fulfilled. Because of this, whenever you are tasked with building 30-400 Reports, I would recommend you make the majority of them a Cube View.

Building a Cube View is excellent for anyone getting started with reporting. If you think about it, what better place to start than the end result? It's even better to get someone on the client side (like an Admin or a Power User) to get involved early on. This goes beyond needing more hands to accomplish the amount of work, as a Cube View builder gets great exposure to the dimensionality of the system. It is also how you learn the data model of your application, and being hands-on will help someone learn how to troubleshoot data validation issues or Calculations.

The real reason why it is great to get someone from the client team involved in building your Cube Views is our cardinal rule of *driving the End-User Experience*; they know the End-User better than anyone external, and they may be one of the Report's consumers. Who better to empower and enable on your team than the person who will be the most passionate about getting it right?

Early in my career, I was one of the Cube View builders, and I had my client sit me down and say, "Okay, I am going to tell you the story of these Reports." It stuck with me. She was so passionate about how the Users needed every single Report and how they would use them.

> **Note:** There is a lot of pressure in our field to feel like you know everything, but you can't. And leaning on someone else's experience and fostering that team environment between Clients/Consultants/End-Users is how you truly create the best result together. There are people who know more than you in the room; let yourself be vulnerable, and don't be afraid to ask questions. It will make you more creative and open to ideas!

Alright, I got a little dramatic for a second there; sorry about that. Building and maintaining should always go hand-in-hand with anything in your implementation. Not just for your own sanity, but for the sanity of whoever must own what you create after you leave (and that may be you, depending on your role in the project). The art of building and organizing Cube Views is something that requires a bit of upfront planning. So, 'take the time to take some time' and nail down things like common formatting, common prompts, headers and footers, and whatnot ahead of time.

Once you have your bearings, here are a few tactics you can use when building Cube Views to reduce your maintenance:

1. Start with a template.
2. Share rows and columns.
3. Use your groups and profiles wisely.
4. Employ Literal Value Parameters and conditional formatting.
5. Think of your metadata; use dynamic expansions such as `.Children` and `.Base`.

I am sure that people can come up with a lot more than that. But we will take a deeper dive in the Cube View section of this book. Lucky you!

They can be Heavily Formatted

A significant portion of reporting is creating something visually appealing to the User community that resonates with their business branding and mission. Usually, with financial reporting, we are hoping for a polished and professional PDF. Cube Views have the inherent capability of allowing you to configure the displayed format of the Data Explorer Grid, Excel, and PDF export versions, all separately. And, if you employed my advice of setting up your formatting ahead of time, you can create a consistent look and feel throughout all Reports that are easy to maintain and repeatable.

Whenever I start my Cube View formatting, I remember my order of operations:

1. Application Properties (there is a tab in there for standard Report options)

2. Defaults and page formatting

3. Column header/cell formatting

4. Row header/cell formatting

You will want to start with your standard formatting, and you can override this at various points as you move down the order of operations list. Therefore, it is important to get the discussion going with formatting as soon as possible; to reiterate my point once more, set yourself up for success early on, so you don't have to chase things down later. Starting with a template is a great way to tinker with all those properties for your FIRST Cube View only. Then, you can create copies and share rows and columns as you move forwards.

On the other side of this is the granularity of how a Cube View can be formatted. There are always a few problematic Cube Views that take a little more love than we hoped. But that's okay; that's why we have things like:

1. Row/Column overrides: Can be used to bypass the natural order of operations to grant you the capability to perform more granular cell-by-cell formatting and/or querying.

2. Cube View Extender Rules: A type of Business Rule that can be written on the Business Rules page – or directly on the Cube View – to write complex, intricate formatting on the PDF version of the Cube View that cannot be done in your typical settings (e.g., header/footer control, logo control).

3. Conditional Formatting: Can be applied for more dynamic formatting based on the data or the Components of the Cube View (e.g., if the cell is greater than 100, color the background red; or color the even number rows gray).

4. XFBR (Or `DashboardStringFunctions`): A type of Business Rule that grants you more flexibility than your typical parameters.

5. Custom Member Lists: A type of Finance Business Rule to create your own Member Lists if the existing Member Expressions don't meet your requirements.

These items are great tools to get familiar with in order to take your Cube Views to the next level! But the one thing you can always do with Cube Views is integrate them into other reporting options easily:

1. Cube Views can be data adapters in Dashboards.

2. Cube Views can be Components in Dashboards.

3. Cube Views can be added to Report Books.

4. Cube Views can be pulled into Extensible Documents.

5. Cube Views can be added to the Excel Add-in and Spreadsheet tool through Cube View Connections.

6. Cube Views can be linked together via Navigation Links.

Performance

Cube Views are our most performant option when creating Reports. We typically think of performance in two spaces: our Consolidation performance, and our reporting and general navigation performance. Each is extremely important when creating our End-User Experience. It is a simple fact of life that no one likes to wait, especially in the tech space. I can get frustrated when I have to wait and remember a time when I was in the OneStream office furiously clicking around on my laptop. I had way too many things open and was expecting everything to work instantaneously. Someone had to shout, "Okay, Clicky! Calm down over there!" to get me to snap out of it.

Now, I may not be the most patient person, but if *I know that* then I KNOW someone out there will be the same (and probably worse). So, do your best to remove the frustration and design for performance; you are really designing for *your* User Experience when you think about it.

Cube Views are a great default option when you want to pull larger amounts of Cube data. However, we typically recommend that you keep your eyes peeled should a Cube View run for more than five seconds. When that starts happening, we recommend effectively using your **Sparse Row Suppression** settings, limiting the number of dynamically-calculated items in the Cube View. In a worst-case scenario, consider breaking up the Cube View. You can learn more about these options in the Cube View chapter of this book, and the reporting chapter in the OneStream Foundation Handbook.

Easily Accessible Across the Application

The final item that makes Cube Views great is that they are very easy to bring to our User. Cube Views themselves are a particularly viable tool, and because of their flexibility and intricate formatting, they are often great on their own. Cube Views have the additional capability to be added to other pages in the application through Cube View Groups and Profiles. This allows us to bring Cube Views directly to the User through the OnePlace tab, into the Workflow, and many other places. We will cover this concept in detail in a later section.

Cube Views don't just have to stand alone; they can also be incorporated into Extensible Documents, Spreadsheet/Excel Add-in, Dashboards, Form Templates, and Report Books. We will talk about this concept a lot, but don't be surprised when our little Cube View follows you wherever you need to go!

The Reporting Tool: Excel/Spreadsheet

The Excel Add-in is a fan favorite. A lot of our clients are extremely comfortable in Excel and even have in-depth exposure to other software's Excel Add-ins. But if you have not had a chance to hear of ours, or work with it, the OneStream Excel Add-in is an option that allows you to query real-time OneStream data from the comfort of Excel!

OneStream also has a tool called **Spreadsheet** that is almost exactly the same but gives you the ability to take the Excel Add-in's functionality – as well as the functionality of Excel itself – and place it within the OneStream application. This is handy if you don't want to go all the way to Excel or want to bring that comfort into your Forms and Dashboards. It's also nice if you are like me, and constantly forgetting to upgrade your Excel Add-in, and you need a second option!

So, what are the best things about the Excel Add-in/Spreadsheet?

1. Allows you to grow your population of builders.
2. Multiple options with how you want to query data.
3. Greatest flexibility with formatting and Calculations.

Figure 3.3 shows the **Spreadsheet** tool within the OneStream Windows application when it is first opened.

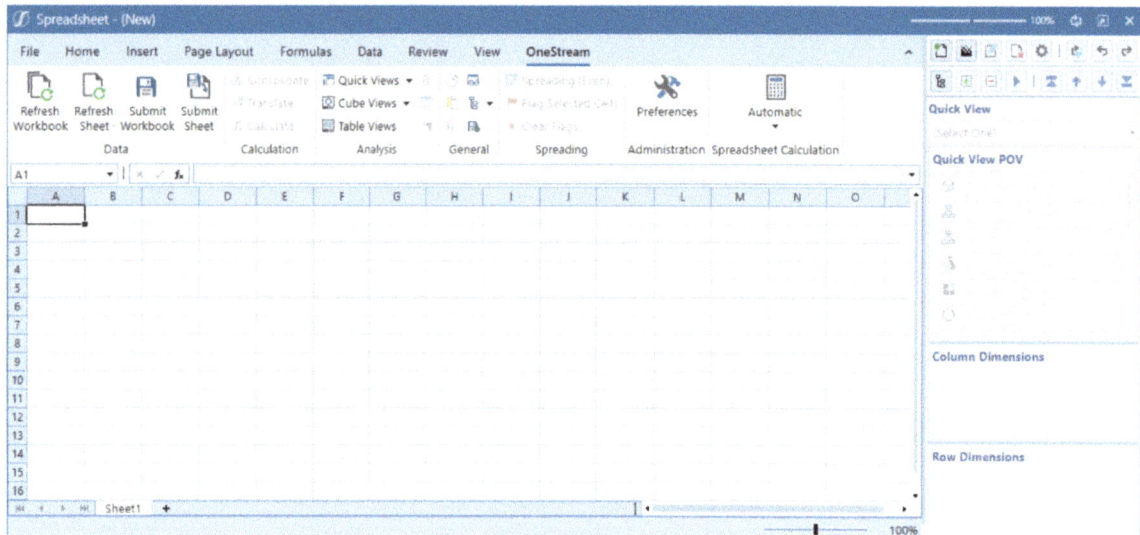

Figure 3.3

Allows You to Grow Your Population of Builders

Now, this is a tricky space for us. Typically, in our implementations, we try to encourage people not to rely on Excel as much as they possibly can. Our reasoning behind this is that if the software can do it for you… let it! You have a flashy new piece of technology; you should be enjoying it and removing as many of the manual aspects of your old life as possible.

But Excel is something that many people in the Accounting and Finance Department live in, and it is powerful and flexible. So, it is important to enable your Users to work with Excel and OneStream in ways that will allow them to create their self-serviced Reports and queries.

This brings us back to our cardinal rule – *know your User*. I always take some time with my clients on the project team to get them playing in Excel as early as possible. The first reason I do this is because it is a great tool for validating data, an important phase of the project that should be owned by the client as much as possible. The second reason is that your client will be able to champion this side of the project and get your End-Users into OneStream. If you are an Implementor, no matter how well you know Excel and the Excel Add-in, your client will know how their population uses it and how to create training and messaging that makes them comfortable and enables them to get going with their new tool. Make it easy on them and yourself.

The nature of Excel, paired with these tricks, means that you can get a lot of people building quite quickly. Not only is it easy to use and frequently in the comfort zone of a lot of people, but the Excel Add-in does not reside in the Application tab, meaning that it is something many people can build and play with; the only security rights required are access to the data.

I typically recommend the Excel Add-in when trying to query any data ad hoc, or when building variations of Reports used by only a small subset of the End-User population. Although Cube Views are not hard to update, if you are an Administrator and you have Users within your business who are constantly requesting updates to the Cube Views that you or your Consultant have created, you may want to empower your End-Users. It doesn't work for everyone, but if you are weary of giving security access to updating Cube Views, and you are finding more people saying, "Can I just do it? Let me at it!" then the Excel Add-in may be a nice way to complement your Report-creation endeavors.

Multiple Options

The other great side of the Excel Add-in is that you have more than one option for querying data. Whenever I start any training on the Excel Add-in, I always open with the fact that you have three options when querying data: Quick Views, Retrieve Functions, and Cube View Connections. These options give you a few different ways to query your data, which allows your Users to determine how they want to pull data out of OneStream.

Quick Views are usually where people want to dive in, because they are basically like simple Cube Views. Quick Views allow you to set your Quick View POV, rows, and columns to 'quickly' pull some data. There are some formatting options, but typically they don't have to be gorgeous if you don't want them to be. These are great for no-nonsense pulls of data.

Retrieves are a bit different. These are your `XFGetCell` formula-based functions that allow you to pull data – cell by cell – into Excel. But the magic doesn't stop there; you can also use functions to retrieve Member properties like text properties, descriptions, local currency, and so much more. I typically recommend retrieves for data validation, but they can potentially be used for final printed Reports as well. They can be easily integrated into your Report Books and Dashboards, too.

Cube View Connections are a nice third option if you are trying to adjust an existing Report or want to use it as a launching point. Cube View Connections allow you to pull a live connection of an existing Report into the Excel Add-in. The other great option for Cube View Connections is working them into your data entry options as well.

Greatest Flexibility with Formatting and Calculations

This section is going to shine a little light on **Retrieve functions**, specifically. Before I dive in, I want to point out one thing, retrieves do not exhibit as good a performance as your Cube Views. However, one thing that may drive you to consider building a Report out of retrieves (instead of Cube Views) could be limitations in your Calculations and formatting options. These situations are usually few and far between, but because files can still be added to Dashboards, Extensible Documents, and Books, this is not a bad option to pull out on some of your more cumbersome Reports.

One of the things that can greatly hurt the performance of your Cube Views is to add a lot of dynamically calculated (calc on the fly) cells. This is because these data points are actually generated when the Report is run. This is common in our Reports, and we want to avoid having too many overcomplicated Calculations in one Cube View Report. It can hurt the performance of the Report, and it can really hurt your maintenance as well. Think about it, unwinding a very complex Calculation with multiple overrides or rules will likely jeopardize your Report's shelf life.

To prevent this, a great option could be to write this Report in the Excel Add-in. There are a lot of simple Calculations, summations, and averages that you can easily do in the Excel Add-in that can relieve the performance pressure and maintenance on your Cube View. I usually suggest this option as a last-case scenario, though, because Cube Views are very powerful.

Another consideration could be some hands-down formatting requirements that may be more BU- or business line-specific. Trying to tear about a Cube View can be a maintenance nightmare, when this may be an easy Report to pass to the User, which they can maintain.

All of these considerations should be evaluated on a case-by-case basis, but when it comes to creating a User Experience, it is best to *learn our tools* as best you can and try a few things. That's the finest way way to get the ideas flowing within your project team.

The Reporting Tool: Dashboards

Now things are really going to get interesting; Dashboards are in the picture! If I picture a Cube View elegantly descending a staircase, I picture a Dashboard busting through a wall like the Kool-Aid man. Dashboards seem to be the object of everyone's deepest fears and desires. Clients want them, Consultants want to build them, but there is a shocking number of people afraid to attempt them.

The reason behind the fear makes logical sense; there are a lot of pieces that go into building Dashboards, and people put a lot of pressure into learning every single nugget to be successful. My advice – learn how to build one Dashboard at a time. The reason being that they have so many use cases and so many directions they can go. Each Dashboard can look 100% different from another and serve a completely different purpose from an entirely different User's perspective. After all, how wild can you really get with a Cube View?

But really, let's think about this. You can use a Dashboard to create a cool landing page for your Users, control the various Consolidations/Calculations that Admins need to run, build a fun Form that gives your Users more flexibility, show stylish charts and grids to display KPIs and ratios, display a full SKU Report, or perform ad hoc analyses on non-Cube data. Heck, all of our MarketPlace solutions are made using Dashboards, so they can go from simple pivot grids/printed Reports to full-blown Workspaces.

No wonder people can get intimidated! But if you are new to Dashboards, the reality is you have to start somewhere. Because they have so many use cases, I recommend you take them one at a time, as that will make the experience feel more manageable. But don't forget our rules: know your tools and know your User.

Knowing your tools is where Dashboards get tricky since there are so many options. Start by pulling apart existing Dashboards or MarketPlace solutions. Get into the guts and pull out the pieces you like, and see what can work for your situation.

No matter how they are used, Dashboards have a few key benefits that you will want to keep in the back of your head when deciding if they are the right answer to your requirement:

1. They allow you to integrate multiple reporting/data entry options.

2. Are necessary when querying non-Cube data.

3. Can run "jobs".

They Allow You to Integrate Multiple Reporting Options

Dashboards have a definite 'wow' factor; that is why so many clients want them incorporated into their applications. But the decision to use a Dashboard should be based on more than wanting 'something pretty.' Just like everything you design into your OneStream application, your Dashboard Components should have a purpose.

We typically break Dashboards into two categories: **Dashboard Workspaces** and **Dashboard Reports**. Your Dashboard Workspaces are what people normally picture. They incorporate buttons that can run data management jobs (Consolidations, custom calculates, exports, copies, etc.), interactive charts that link to various other Report types, grids, logos, combo boxes – you name it. Basically, a number of combinations of Dashboard Components (or items if you are using BI Viewer) to create a multi-faceted User Experience. They remind me of your quintessential Dashboard on your car, or an airplane if things really go wild!

But Dashboards don't always have to be huge. Enter your Dashboard Reports. I consider these more like Dashboards that only have one or two Components. They can be things like your Book Viewer for Report Books, File Viewer, Cube Views, Reports (formerly known as Studio), large data pivot grids, Grid View, and/or Data Explorer Reports.

Are Necessary When Querying Non-Cube Data

Dashboards are a great option if your OneStream application is using **Analytic Blend**, which many of them do. Remember, Analytic Blend is the act of reporting on data stored in the Cube with data stored outside the Cube. Basically, if you are trying to query any data that is not in the Cube, then you NEED a Dashboard!

Even if you are not using BI Blend itself, if you are using any MarketPlace solutions like People Planning, Thing Planning, OneStream Financial Close, or if you would like to query things like Stage data, you likely have some Dashboard Reports you are already using. Many of these Reports come built for you from the MarketPlace, but you have the ability to modify them using the Dashboard Maintenance Unit / Report Designer, or you may even find you would like to create your own. The Dashboard Report Component, large data pivot grids, Grid Views, and more are great tools to get you going.

Can Run "Jobs"

Now Dashboards are not just all flash; they have quite a bit of substance too. A common use case for a Dashboard is for data entry and Admin Workspaces. That's because they don't just give you that cool cockpit feel, but because they can run data management jobs, as well, meaning that an

Admin User can do things like easily trigger sequences of 'heavy lifting' processes with the click of a button.

When thinking of data entry, specifically, Dashboards are a common answer for Budget and Forecast requirements. This is because you may want to layer things like allocations, driver-based Calculations, and seeding into your data entry Forms. A simple Dashboard button can allow you to run these items and keep everything your Planning Users need at their fingertips.

The Reporting Tool: Extensible Documents

If you have never heard of Extensible Documents or if you have never implemented them, I recommend just giving them a try. They are probably the most mysterious of your reporting options, but they are really very easy to configure. Extensible Documents allow you to create a PowerPoint, Excel, and/or Word document that can display real-time OneStream data, Cube Views, Charts, or Excel Reports, and which can even refresh based on User selection.

If that didn't make sense, let me illustrate a world where you are the envy of all because you know how to make an Extensible (or XF) Document. Picture yourself strutting into a conference room, laptop in hand, flinging open your laptop, plugging in to display on the large screen, and you have your typical Monthly Presentation projecting trends, KPIs, etc. But this time is different. On this occasion, you have spent no time preparing a slide deck; this time, you're not displaying any ordinary PowerPoint; you are displaying an Extensible Document. And this PowerPoint has been configured to update all data, graphs, charts, even titles based on your OneStream Dimension Member selections. On top of it, you know this data is correct because it was pulled freshly out of OneStream right when you made your selections.

Extensible Documents tend to be used for specific purposes; that's why I recommend giving them a try so you know when they can get you out of a pinch. There is really one primary reason why you may choose Extensible Documents: their ability to integrate with PowerPoint, Word, and Excel.

When to Use Extensible Documents

We are going to break this one down a little differently to the other reporting tools. I am going to walk you through why you may want to use each type of Extensible Document: PowerPoint, Word, or Excel. We already illustrated the common reason to use PowerPoint Extensible Documents in the prior section.

Let's start with Excel since it tends to have a more elusive set of benefits. You may be thinking: we have the Excel Add-in; why would we need an Excel Extensible Document? Well, the one thing that Extensible Documents add is the ability to incorporate **parameter** and **substitution variables** into your Excel Workbooks. Technically, you could do this when using a Cube View connection, but in a regular Excel Add-in you don't have the luxury of referencing these items in your retrieve formulas. You could make a prompting Excel Report using Extensible Documents.

The reason why I start with Excel is because these Extensible Documents tend to be used differently to Word or PowerPoint. They can stand alone as a sheet or Workbook, but they are commonly used to feed your Word and/or PowerPoint Extensible Documents. Both options have the ability to take an image (yes, any image!), and when that image is run through OneStream it will transform to potentially display a sheet or named range of the Excel Extensible Document. In summary, there are two good reasons to use Excel Extensible Documents – to create dynamic Excel Reports, or to elevate your Word/PowerPoint Extensible Documents.

Word Extensible Documents work nicely with Report Books (covered in the next section). A common use case for them is to create a cover letter for your financial reporting packages. You can easily reference data points that can refresh based on the data changing or upon prompts that you can set once and never update. You can even reference XFBR strings if you need to home in on what you want to display as well. You may want to spice up these letters with a live Cube View or Dashboard Chart; what have you!

The Reporting Tool: Report Books

I think of Report Books and Extensible Documents as great tools for collecting and integrating your reporting options. Report Books are excellent if you are trying to create financial or managerial reporting packages. And they are so easy to use; if you have never built one, I would suggest cracking open a OneStream application and giving it a try!

The biggest thing I want to point out on Report Books is that we are not usually doing them instead of another reporting option. It's okay if you have to build this Report as a Dashboard Report or Excel file because you can still package it up with all the Cube Views. See? Very handy!

So, here are some great pros when entertaining Report Books on your project:

1. You can add flexibility to your reporting options.

2. They can be 'shipped' via email to Users through the Parcel Service solution.

Flexibility with Reporting Options

Report Books can seem a little enigmatic at first, but they are really easy to make. One cool thing about them is that – depending on how they are built and saved – you can choose if you want them to be a zipped Book, PDF Book, or an Excel Book. So perhaps you have a polished financial package with a beautiful cover letter as one output, or a multi-tabbed spreadsheet with Planning data per cost center; whatever the case, neither of these things are configured drastically differently from the other. You can easily impress your friends with your repertoire of Report Books early in your learning journey.

When I started learning about them, the first thing I explored was how to add various items to them. From the Report Book page, you can add files, Cube Views, Excel export items, and Dashboards. Your Cube Views and your Excel export items are basically you deciding if you want to add a Cube View to the Report Book or the Excel-exported version of the Cube View (this is for Excel or "xl" Books).

Figure 3.4 shows the Report Book page from the Application tab. This page looks simple, but you can create your Report Books and add all of the items we discussed using the + sign icon.

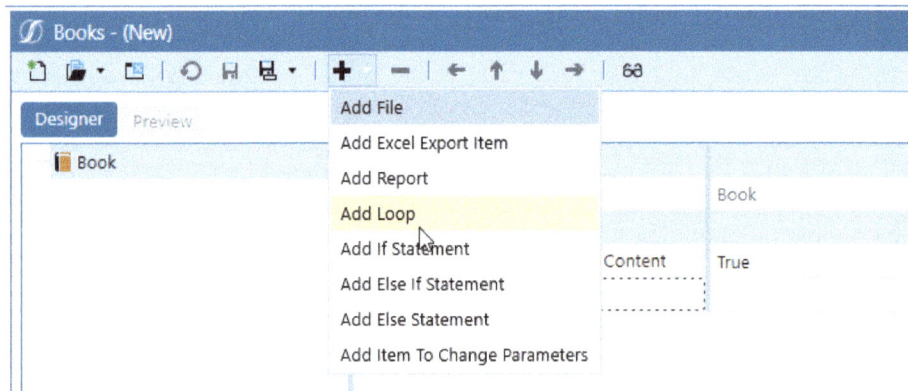

Figure 3.4

Files are where things get interesting because a file can mean a million things. You can get really creative with this (if that meets your requirements), and the two most common things I see here are if you are exploring the occasionally retrieved Report and that needs to be added to a Book. That is where you can use a file quite easily. The other thing that can really kick things up a notch is that files are the means to add Extensible Documents to our Books. One common use case for this would be to have a nice cover page added to your Report Book or a letter to your stakeholders. Remember, Extensible Documents allow you to pull real-time Cube Views, data, Dashboard charts, Dashboard Reports, and Excel Reports into them as well. This can be very dynamic!

Finally, you can add Dashboard Reports (formerly known as **Studio Reports**) and charts to your Report Books as well. If you are using any form of Analytic Blend, or you want to integrate your Application Standard Report into your reporting package, this is the feature for you!

The other side of your Report Book configuration is the tools you can use to manipulate your Reports within the Report Books. This is where your If/Else If/Else statements, Loops, and items to Change Parameters come into play. Loops are very common; this is where you can essentially say, "I want 20 versions of this same Report for all of my Entities." This is a fantastic, low-maintenance (because you SHOULD be using a Member Expansion… right?) way to generate all the Reports you need.

If/Else If/Else Statements usually go hand in hand with your Loops to allow you to omit or add Reports based on the Loop criteria. For example, when we loop through `E#Texas.base`, when you reach `E#HoustonHeights` you can also print off an additional file or Report. Report Books can also incorporate XFBRs (if you are a fan of Business Rules) that can allow you to do things like suppress a Report if it has no data.

Figure 3.5 shows the Preview tab of the Book Designer, where we can look through our Book and make sure all the pages are displaying as we expect. The file shown here is actually an Excel Extensible Document file which has been rendered as a nice clean PDF in the Book.

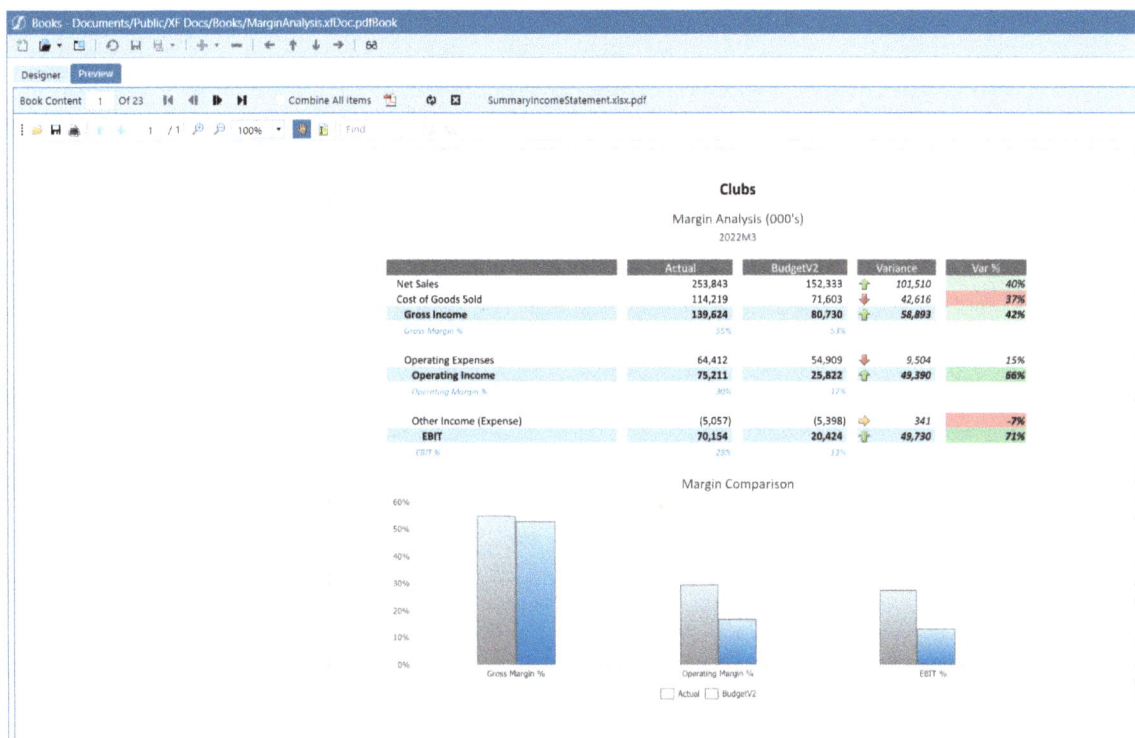

Figure 3.5

Report Distribution

This may not be the case in the larger community, but whenever we discuss the development of any learning on Report Books, we always ask ourselves, "How do we Address Parcel Service?" **Parcel Service** is a MarketPlace solution that can be easily downloaded and brought into your OneStream application. It is very easy to configure, and I know a lot of implementation Consultants that have read the instructions in a short amount of time and been on their way.

If you have never heard of this solution, Parcel Service can be used to 'ship' reporting packages outside the OneStream application. You can email them to people that do (or do not) have a OneStream license or even push them to a file repository. They give you the flexibility to adjust your various parameters (and whatnot) so you can ship the Report Books differently to different audiences (or locations).

I find this solution to be commonly misunderstood; heck, I did when I first heard about it. I had a client, once, who had very large Report Books. They were taking a while to run since they were using a lot of Loops, Cube Views, XF Docs, and even some Dashboard Reports. It was one big, beautiful dream of all the reporting tools! However, because it was so large, it took a while to run. I started scurrying around the Rochester, Michigan, headquarters to see what other people were doing. And after I clip-clopped up the blue metal stairs to my first victim, I was quickly met with "Parcel Service will definitely do that!" You can set up and even automate those packages to ship, and you just go about your day; no need to wait for something to spin, run, save, etc. Just let the Parcel Service deliver it to your 'door', aka inbox.

Conclusion

We have lightly touched on OneStream's many tools that can help you satisfy your reporting requirements: Cube Views, Excel Add-in/Spreadsheet, Extensible Documents, Report Books, and Dashboards. Each tool provides a unique experience for the User, but remember, we don't just worry about the consumer but the Administrator as well. You already know that we want to think about the User when designing their experience, but when it comes to reporting we want to also think about two other things: the types of data we are pulling and our metadata design.

The rest of this book will go through some of these tools and how you can use them, based on some interesting requirements we have seen. But knowing the User and the tool will set you up to handle anything that gets thrown your way.

The next section will take you *beyond* reporting, specifically, and look a little more at some of the out-of-the-box basics. After all, reporting is not the only part of your End-User Experience with OneStream.

4

OnePlace / Out-of-the-Box Basics

OnePlace is the default landing page for all Users when they log into an application. It is where they navigate and complete Workflow tasks, and interact with the application, as well as other Users within the application. As the chapter title suggests, OnePlace truly is out-of-the-box and serves as the default home page. I like to think the clue is in the name; Users don't have to go looking very far or ask their Administrators for anything they need because "Everything is in One Place."

There are four sub-menus within OnePlace:

1. Workflow

2. Cube Views

3. Dashboards

4. Documents

Configuring your application appropriately is dependent on knowing your User community and understanding their needs; this concept applies to every aspect of OneStream as Users drive *what* and *how* you configure various Components within the application.

In broader terms, I like to categorize the OnePlace sub-menus into two buckets:

1. Workflow

2. One-stop shop

I say this because Workflow is the collection point of everything necessary for a User to 'do', while the one-stop shop provides a repository of Reports, Dashboards, and documents that Users can access on-demand based on their User security profile.

This is not to say the User does not *need* the other sub-menus, but rather that a well-designed Workflow should include the relevant Components within each Workflow task to guide the User without needing to navigate away from the Workflow process.

So, back to bucket number two – the one-stop shop.

You have implemented OneStream and wonder how you should configure your Users' OnePlace experience. Think of everything non-Workflow related as à la carte options. Organizing Cube View Profiles and Dashboard Profiles is the key to ease of maintenance and User adoption. Why? Because once you have established role-based security, the User roles you have defined are used to assign access and maintenance rights by User type rather than individual Users, allowing for ease of administration. In other words, you can simply change the security access settings on any given Cube View, Dashboard, or Document Component to grant or revoke access to the appropriate Users within a User role group.

This chapter will explain the purpose of each sub-menu, how they work together, and some tips on how to configure them to provide a tailored User Experience, which will ultimately increase confidence and efficiency.

Workflow

Each of the reporting tools described in Chapter 3 are used to enhance the User Experience in Workflow progression. Let us take a deeper dive into the default Workflow steps and find out how each step can enhance the User Experience.

Import

Importing data into OneStream is an extremely powerful piece of any Workflow; this is where the magic happens! The most common use of the import step is to bring data into the Stage tables and transform the data into meaningful dimensional intersections. I like to think of sorting dirty laundry at this point; arranging the data fields using data source mapping is like making sure that fancy black dress does not shrink, and those white socks do not turn pink.

So, what exactly does this mean in terms of enhancing the User Experience? In addition to data validation, supplemental Dashboards for training can be assigned to each Workflow step to provide in-role refreshers as you go through your Workflow steps.

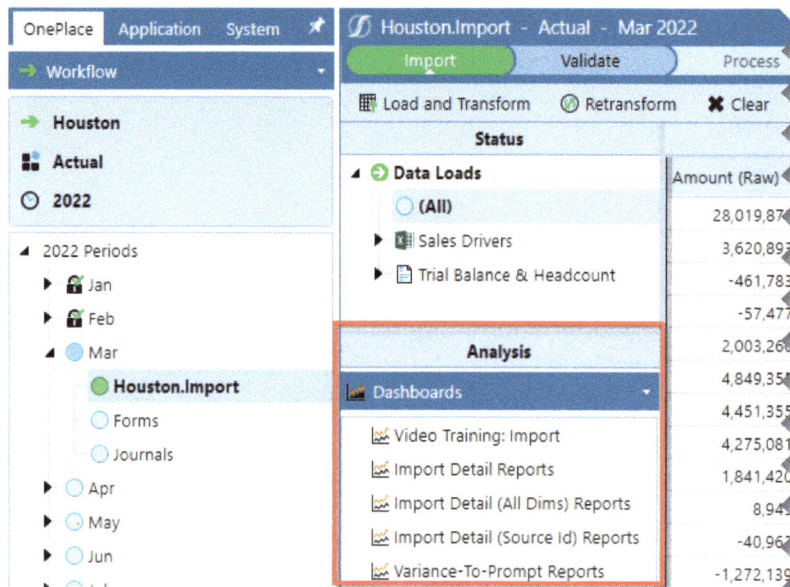

Figure 4.1

When designing the Workflow, it's important to know where the source and target data reside to leverage data collection upfront for additional uses that may or may not be anticipated. Make it a habit to capture unmapped data fields, and you'll set yourself up for success. To do this, you'll need to enable the attributes by Scenario Type from the Cube Integration settings.

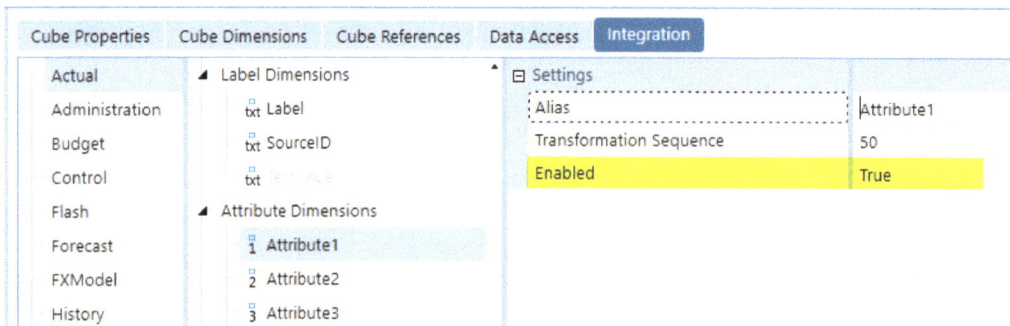

Figure 4.2

In the Dashboards section of this chapter, we will address how Stage tables can enhance the User Experience by querying the source data and effectively eliminating the need to navigate to external sources or files.

Forms

Data entry Forms are used to collect supplemental data, whether financial, statistical, or more granular data tie-out, commonly used to accelerate footnote generation.

In Figure 4.3, we are tracking headcount by cost center. Our prior period headcount import file tells us we had a headcount of 159; however, in the current period, we now have 162. How do we resolve the difference? We do not necessarily need to resolve but explain. We explain the difference using a Cube View with a calculated column to identify where cost center variances exist, so we can quickly adjust for headcount fluctuations. Notice the Parameters drop-down selector at the top of the Form. This indicates that the underlying Cube View's POV has been parameterized, which allows the same Cube View template to be used for any Entity or other specified Dimension.

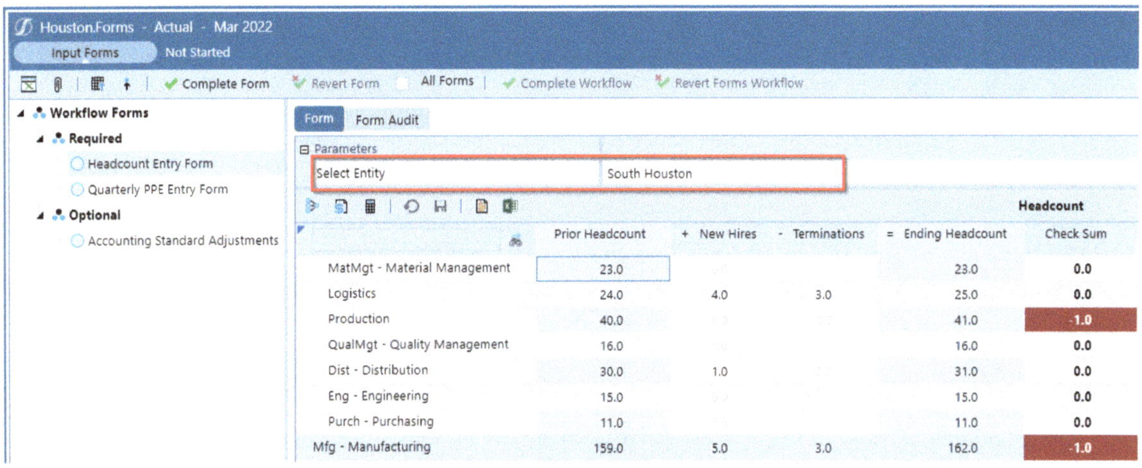

Figure 4.3

Another common use of data entry Forms is to collect roll-forward detail. Like the Headcount Form, Figure 4.4 shows another Form that is also parameterized to reduce the maintenance of Cube Views and then utilize the same settings between Entities.

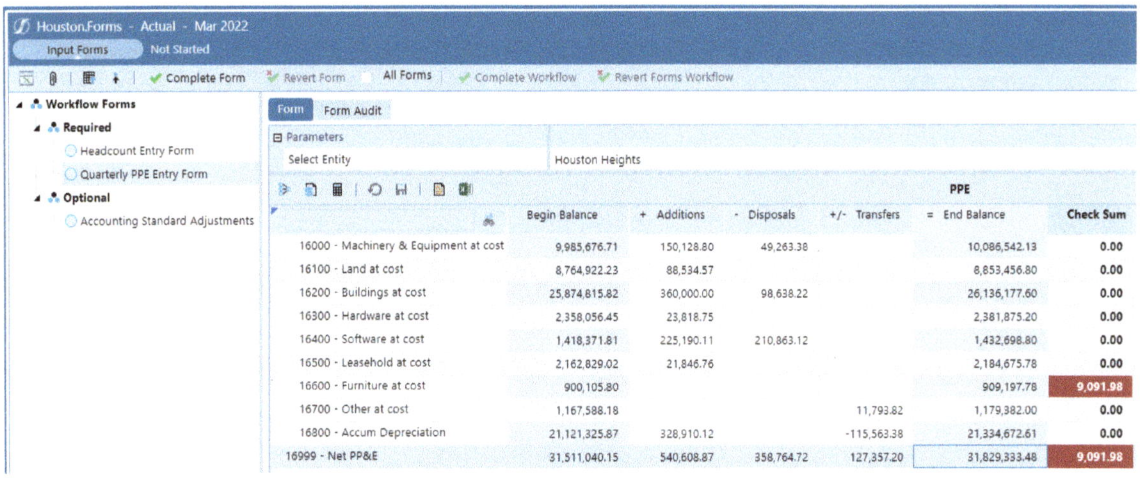

Figure 4.4

Now, to take this one step further, the Cube View in Figure 4.4 has been formatted for the Data Explorer Grid *and* PDF output. What does that mean for you? It means you can display the Form in PDF format to see how the footnote would appear in your financial reporting package.

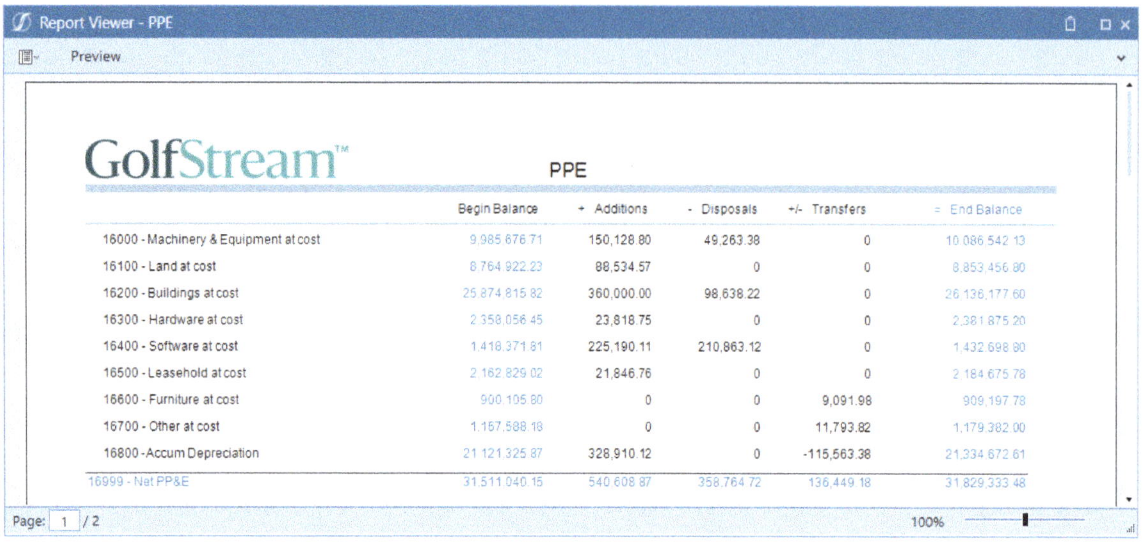

Figure 4.5

Adjustments

Adjustments are used in the Financial Close process but can also be used in Budget formulation and really any functional process, as this is dependent on Users' requirements. I love adjustments – correcting, adjusting, allocating, you name it – the accountant in me is a huge fan of cleaning up and organizing data. Unfortunately, most people do not find adjustments as exciting as I do, that is until they see just how much efficiency they gain when creating **Journal templates**.

Journal templates allow you to create standards based on the type of adjustment, frequency, and if/how much you want to allow your Users to modify any given entry. Do you have required monthly tax accruals? Quarterly PPE entries? What about discretionary or dependent adjustments? Figure 4.6 shows an example of required versus optional Journals for month-end. The optional Journal templates are available to the User for adjustments as necessary, while the required Journal template indicates that an entry must be made to complete the Workflow.

Journal templates are by no means required to enter adjustments; Users could enter Journals from scratch if the available templates do not align with the necessary adjustment.

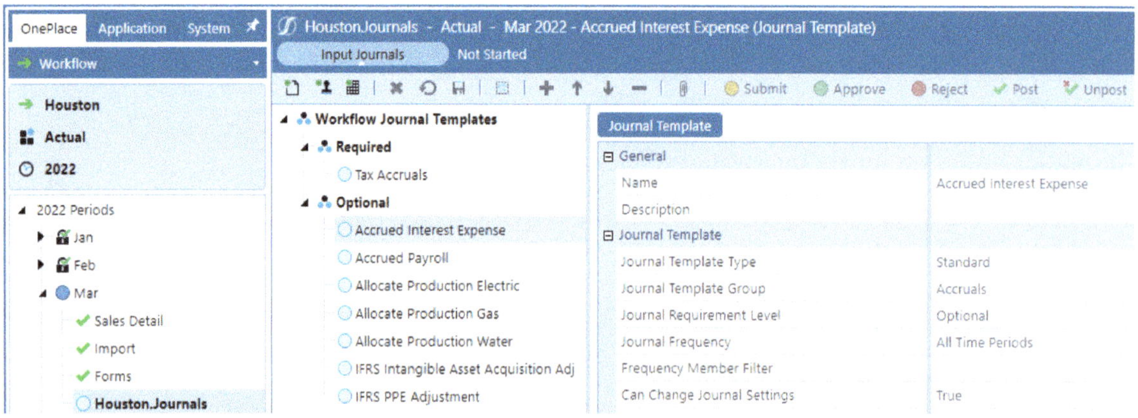

Figure 4.6

Review

Base Input Workflows are the Parent of Workflow tasks and are configured according to the level of review and approvals in the Workflow structure. Hence, this is the review phase of a standard Workflow.

Out-of-the-box Workflows for review include the following options, with varying combinations available for selection.

- Process

- Confirm

- Certify

- Workspace

Workflow Settings	
Cube Name	Houston ⊕
Workflow Name	Process, Confirm, Certify ▾
Workspace Dashboard Name (Custom Workflow)	Certify
Base Input Settings	Process, Certify
Load Overlapped Siblings	Process, Confirm, Certify
Data Quality Settings	Workspace, Process, Confirm, Certify
Cube View Profile Name	Process, Workspace, Confirm, Certify
Process Cube Dashboard Profile Name	Process, Confirm, Workspace, Certify
Confirmation Profile Name	Workspace
Confirmation Dashboard Profile Name	Workspace, Certify

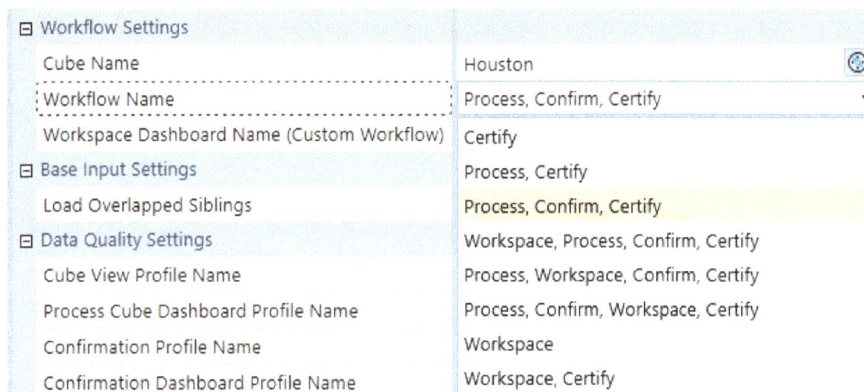

Figure 4.7

Process, Confirm, Workspace, Certify is my personal favorite Workflow because it makes the most sense in terms of data validation and the flow of certification.

Process can be a variety of methods for updating your data as needed. It may be a simple Calculation on a single Entity, or a Consolidation if multiple Entities have been loaded and need to roll-up data to common Parents.

Confirmation consists of rules defined by the User's process to evaluate activity, balances, annotation requirements, and any other validations that accelerate the process by marking Entities as passing or failing. The confirmation step tells the User what passes the validation and is designed to guide the User into taking corrective action.

Workspaces are incredibly flexible since they are any Dashboard that can be layered on a Workflow to provide more granular review and drill back capabilities.

Certify is always used at any review level; however, there is an option for just 'Workspace only.'

Why wouldn't all Workflows use all the review steps? The short answer is that not all steps are always applicable. Imagine three Entity-specific Workflows with import, Forms, and adjustments. In theory, each Entity would certify their Workflow and even validate data using Confirmation Rules. But now, imagine that individual Entities cannot independently validate data and – rather – the Confirmation Rules apply to the *consolidated* numbers. Confirmation Rules may not be relevant to the individual Entities and the option for 'Process, Certify, only' stands.

Cube Views

OnePlace

Cube Views are the drivers behind all functions in OneStream. They are used for Forms, Reports, Tables, and Dashboards. Due to the nature of expansive usage, **Cube View profiles** are available in various areas throughout the platform, making it easy to configure the application to display and securitize data effectively. Think of a Cube View profile as a cluster of Cube Views, which can comprise one or more groups.

Cube View profiles can be made visible in any of the following application areas:

- Forms

- Excel

- Dashboards

- Workflow

- OnePlace

Figure 4.8 shows a specific User with only two profiles visible in the OnePlace pane, based on security. Profiles and visibility are tailored to meet User needs and simplify the task at hand. You may be thinking, why not give them more profiles for the purpose of analysis? But bigger is not always better; in fact, by broadening the profiles that you make visible to a User, you could be creating confusion in the form of data overload.

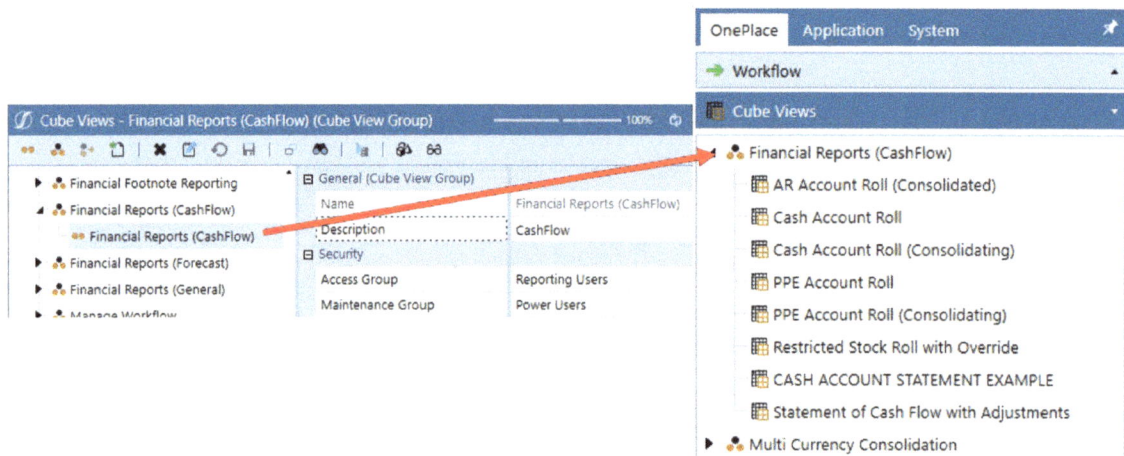

Figure 4.8

Cube View Groups

Cube View groups are where Cube Views are created and organized in OneStream; a Cube View group must be created before a Cube View can be created. Depending on the design of your application, you could have just a handful of groups or (more likely) you'll have a lot of groups to organize Cube Views (relative to when and where they need to be displayed or used).

Cube View Profiles

Cube View profiles allow Cube View groups to be combined or grouped within various areas of the application. Profile assignment is critical in designing a guided Workflow to provide ease of use and give the User insight into the data at each step.

Below, we see a Cube View profile with one Cube View group; notice that the profile and group have different security Access Groups assigned. Why would they be different? Think about this in terms of reduced maintenance; you may have different groupings of Cube Views for organizational purposes, but you might want to filter what Users see while not needing two profiles.

In this case, the profile is visible to Everyone, but the User would need to be in the Reporting Users Security Group to see the Cube View. To add a little complexity, let's say you added another Cube View group to the profile, and you want all Users to have access to it. By leveraging the existing profile, you can reduce profiles to be managed simply by narrowing security rights by each group.

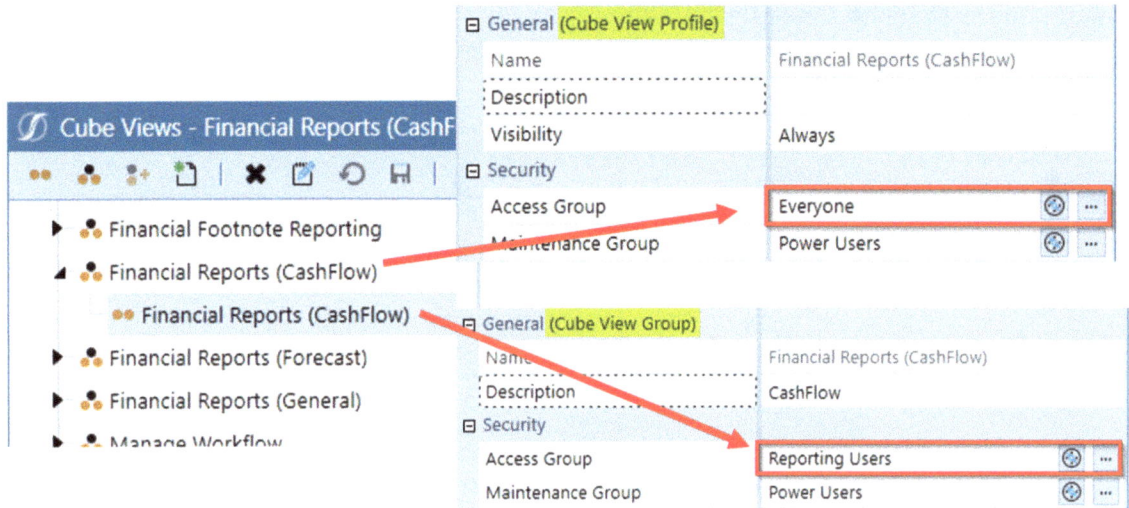

Figure 4.9

Vary Cube View Profiles by Workflow

OneStream's out-of-the-box Workflow functionality allows the User Experience to align with the goals they are trying to achieve at each step in the process. As the User progresses through the Workflow, we are able to display relevant data and Reports to guide the User to key data and validation.

In this example, we are showing that Cube Views for the import step are limited to trial balance data. Why? Because, at this point, the User's goal is to validate that the imported trial balance data is balanced and review any anomalies that may need to be adjusted in the subsequent steps of the Workflow.

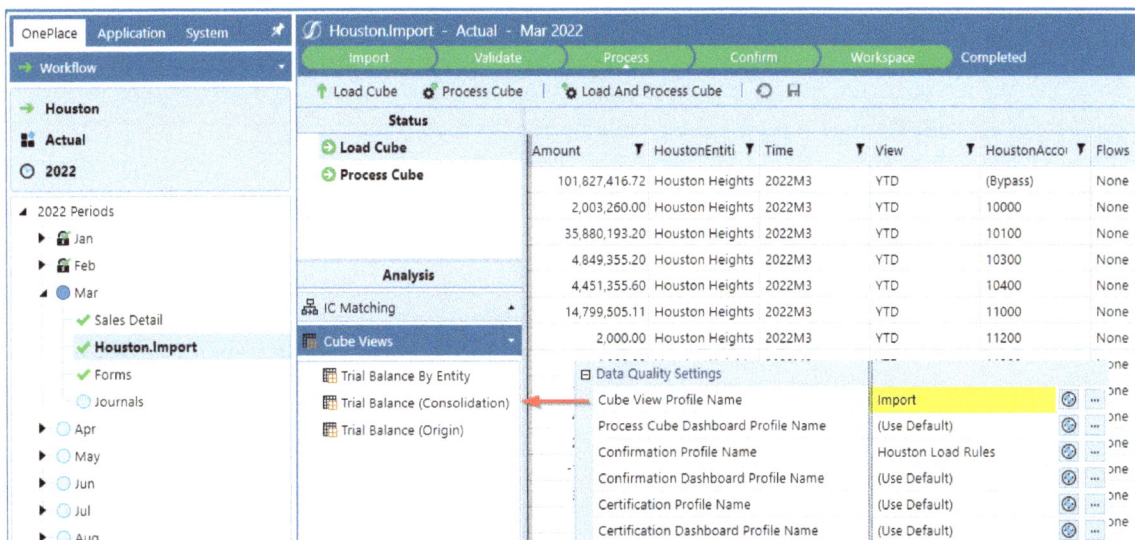

Figure 4.10

Once we've processed the information, we probably want to use Confirmation Rules to check that our data is right and has passed our validation checks. At that exact point in the Workflow, we can have a different group of Cube Views or Dashboards appear, most likely showing the data that we are validating and why it is passing (or failing) the checks.

Upon completion of the required Workflow tasks, the User needs to certify the data before submitting it for approval. "But how do I know my data is accurately stated? What do my financial statements look like after I have loaded data and made adjustments?" I often found myself asking these exact questions when preparing financial statements in my prior career. Well, in OneStream we can embed additional Reports and Dashboards again at the Certify step, if needed. This allows Users to be confident in signing off the numbers they are responsible for.

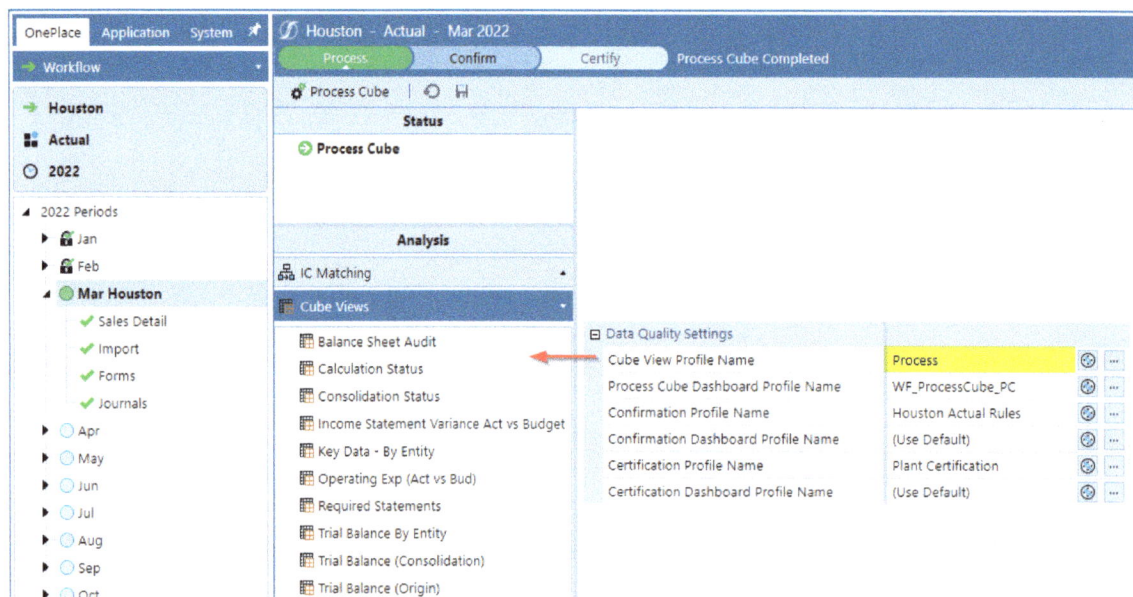

Figure 4.11

Dashboards

Dashboard Purpose

Dashboards are wildly popular since they can be fully configured both functionally and aesthetically. The sheer possibilities of dashboarding can be overwhelming – even to seasoned Consultants – so I like to think of them in these broad categories:

- Functional
- Call-to-action
- Informational

Functional Dashboards

Functional Dashboards collect data in some manner, whether from data entry Forms, Calculations, commentary, or file attachments. These Dashboards belong in a Workflow and *not* in OnePlace since they are Time- and Scenario-specific to a Workflow process. By restricting these Dashboards to Workflow-only visibility, the audit tables can inherently capture and streamline data activity.

Say you need a data entry Form in your Workflow process, but you want to give your Users something more visually appealing than the default Forms, or you simply want to add branding, instructions, you name it. How could I make Forms prettier, you ask? Use a Workspace!

Personally, I find it more enjoyable to do my work when I like what I am looking at, and even more when I can easily access training materials and supplemental data to help me be more efficient.

Keeping that in mind, I try to make Dashboards easy on the eyes so that Users are more likely to adopt and want to use them. Workspaces require configuration; however, the payoff to make the User Experience more interactive and personalized is worth it.

> **Tip**: When designing Cube Views that contain data entry cells, use the Cell Format WriteableBackgroundColor property to highlight which data cells the User can enter/update. This helps guide the User to the areas they are responsible for.

Figure 4.12 displays writable data cells with a yellow background. Notice that FICA % and FICA Limit are not writable in this example. The assumption in this example is that the FICA drivers have been entered by an Administrator or Power User and are displayed here for reference only.

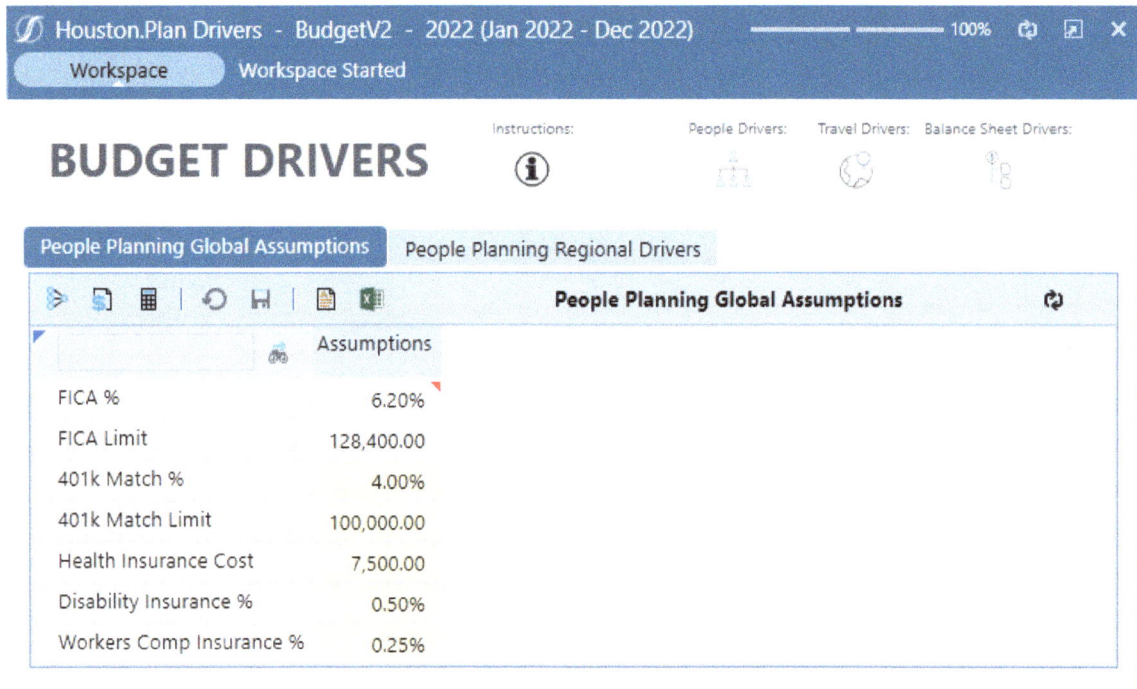

Figure 4.12

Call-to-Action Dashboards

Call-to-Action Dashboards are not functional in the sense that they impact Workflow directly; instead, they provide information tailored to the Users' responsibilities. They can, however, be functional (in a sense) if navigation buttons are added to take the User directly to an outstanding task or item to review.

Common uses for Call-to-Action Dashboards include:

- Workflow Status
- User Activity
- Application Audit

In the example below, an individual User can view Workflow-specific tasks they are responsible for, and quickly determine what is outstanding.

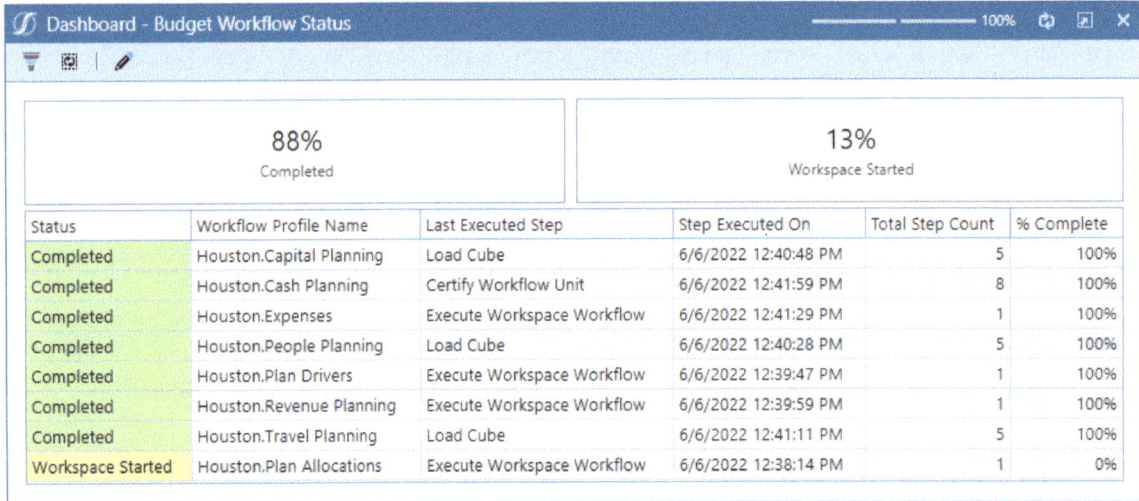

Chapter 4

| | 88% Completed | | | 13% Workspace Started | | |

Status	Workflow Profile Name	Last Executed Step	Step Executed On	Total Step Count	% Complete
Completed	Houston.Capital Planning	Load Cube	6/6/2022 12:40:48 PM	5	100%
Completed	Houston.Cash Planning	Certify Workflow Unit	6/6/2022 12:41:59 PM	8	100%
Completed	Houston.Expenses	Execute Workspace Workflow	6/6/2022 12:41:29 PM	1	100%
Completed	Houston.People Planning	Load Cube	6/6/2022 12:40:28 PM	5	100%
Completed	Houston.Plan Drivers	Execute Workspace Workflow	6/6/2022 12:39:47 PM	1	100%
Completed	Houston.Revenue Planning	Execute Workspace Workflow	6/6/2022 12:39:59 PM	1	100%
Completed	Houston.Travel Planning	Load Cube	6/6/2022 12:41:11 PM	5	100%
Workspace Started	Houston.Plan Allocations	Execute Workspace Workflow	6/6/2022 12:38:14 PM	1	0%

Figure 4.13

The following example shows all Workflows and their respective tasks with completion status. An Administrator or Power User would typically review this to identify Workflow tasks that are incomplete easily. Whether the Workflow is tracking Budget formulation, monthly financial close, or any other formal process, reviewing the *full* Workflow structure status makes it easy to keep Users on track to meet deadlines and eliminate bottlenecks.

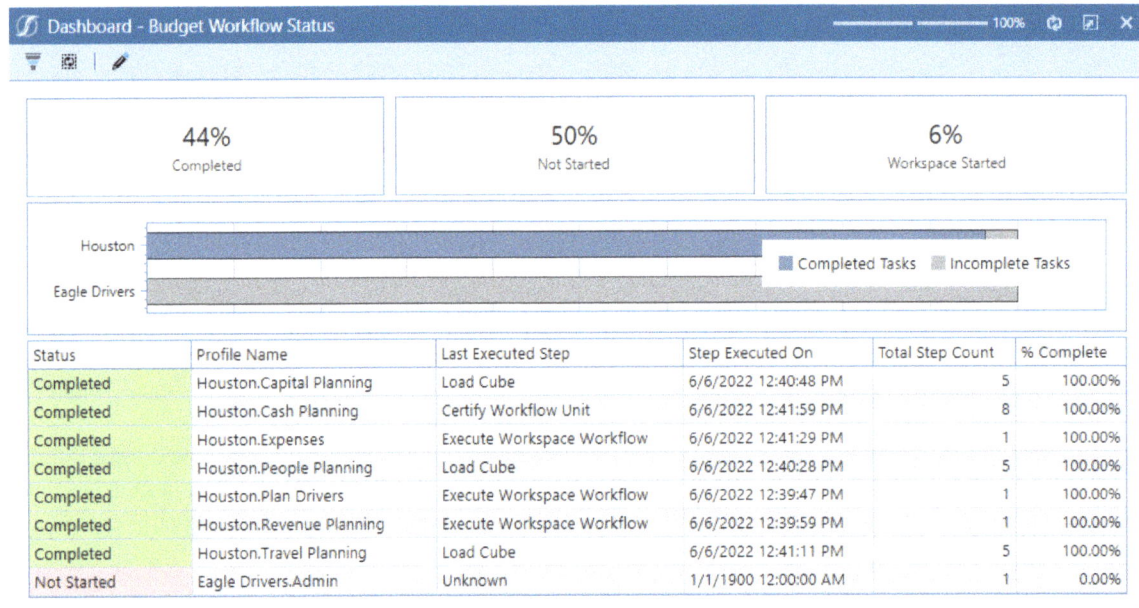

Status	Profile Name	Last Executed Step	Step Executed On	Total Step Count	% Complete
Completed	Houston.Capital Planning	Load Cube	6/6/2022 12:40:48 PM	5	100.00%
Completed	Houston.Cash Planning	Certify Workflow Unit	6/6/2022 12:41:59 PM	8	100.00%
Completed	Houston.Expenses	Execute Workspace Workflow	6/6/2022 12:41:29 PM	1	100.00%
Completed	Houston.People Planning	Load Cube	6/6/2022 12:40:28 PM	5	100.00%
Completed	Houston.Plan Drivers	Execute Workspace Workflow	6/6/2022 12:39:47 PM	1	100.00%
Completed	Houston.Revenue Planning	Execute Workspace Workflow	6/6/2022 12:39:59 PM	1	100.00%
Completed	Houston.Travel Planning	Load Cube	6/6/2022 12:41:11 PM	5	100.00%
Not Started	Eagle Drivers.Admin	Unknown	1/1/1900 12:00:00 AM	1	0.00%

Figure 4.14

Informational Dashboards

Informational Dashboards are intended to provide the User with on-demand measures and/or metrics. Administrators and Power Users are typically the consumers of these Dashboards as they relate to the entire User community's activity and application changes that should be monitored.

When designing an application, be sure to understand your Users' current process and what they like versus what their pain points are. Do they have strong process controls in place? How many Users are in the application? What types of Users are they?

Collecting this information early on will accelerate the requirements session and ensure that the end product is one that will make Users' lives easier.

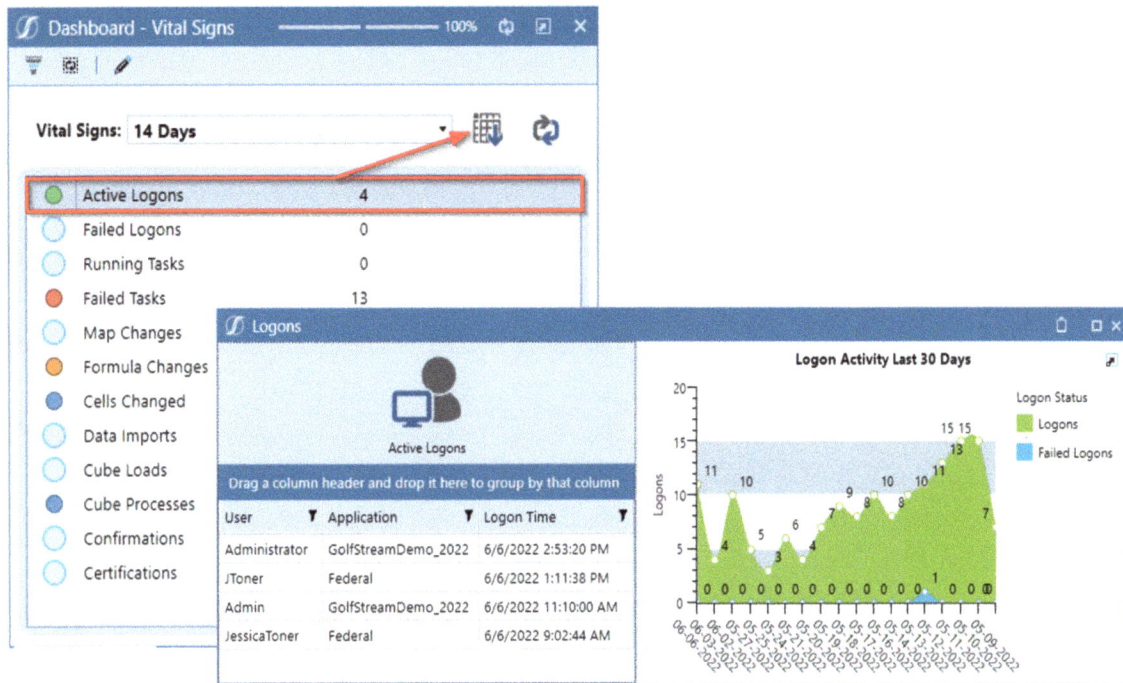

Figure 4.15

OnePlace

Dashboards are a collection of Components configured to streamline the Workflow process and provide an individualized User experience. The purpose of a Dashboard will determine where and when it should be surfaced, and for what Users.

Dashboard profiles can be made visible in the following locations:

- Workflow
- OnePlace
- Always
- Never

> **Tip:** *Always* indicates the profile will be made visible in both Workflow and OnePlace, while *Never* indicates that the profile will not be visible in Workflow or OnePlace.

Understanding your User is the first step in building meaningful Dashboards. What does the User *need* to do their job? Who is the User? How often does the User need to complete a task? By asking these questions, you will better understand:

1. *What* story does the Dashboard tell, and what information should it convey?
2. *Where* should the Dashboard be available?
3. *When* should the Dashboard be available?

The Dashboards we typically see in the OnePlace menu are self-service in nature, meaning the User can view reporting in a variety of ways, as well as interact with data unrelated to a Workflow process. Think of these as *read-only* Dashboards for on-demand reporting.

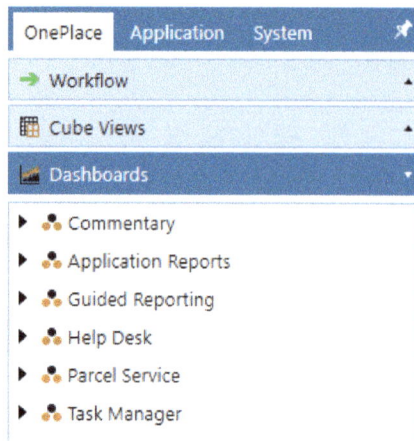

Figure 4.16

Dashboard Profiles

Dashboard profiles have visibility settings that can be tailored to display information according to the intended User experience. They can be visible in Workflows, in the OnePlace Dashboards pane, both, or never visible, depending on the content and use of a given **maintenance unit**. It is not uncommon for Dashboard profiles to be set to Visible=Always if the application has robust security to control who sees them and when.

Workspace

The purpose of a Workspace is to enhance Reports, functions, and interactivity to display visually tailored solutions for your User. Workspaces can be standalone Dashboards, or they can be layered onto existing Workflows to provide additional analysis and visual metrics.

You may recall that we mentioned – in the Workflow section – how Stage tables can be a powerful data querying source. My go-to Stage table is `vStageSourceAndTargetDataWithAttributes` because it contains the loaded data *and* the source data that is often forgotten.

Let us look at an example of a Workspace that has been added to the import Workflow. On the left, you see data that has been transformed and loaded into the Cube; on the right, you see the underlying source data.

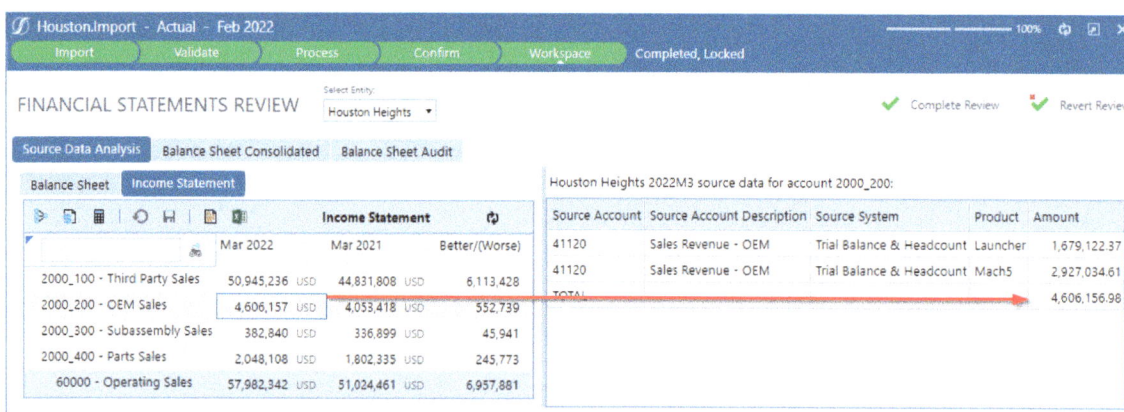

Figure 4.17

How are we able to display the source data when we only loaded target data?

1. Apply bound parameters to your Cube View to pass the parameters into the query.

2. Create a data adapter to query the Stage table to the Cube View-specific intersections.

3. Attach the data adapter to a Grid View Component.

4. Attach the Grid View Component to a Dashboard.

5. Create a Cube View Component and attach your Cube View.

6. Set the Cube View Component User Interface Action property to refresh the Dashboard where you have attached the Grid View.

That's it! Open the Dashboard and click a Cube View row to display source records dynamically.

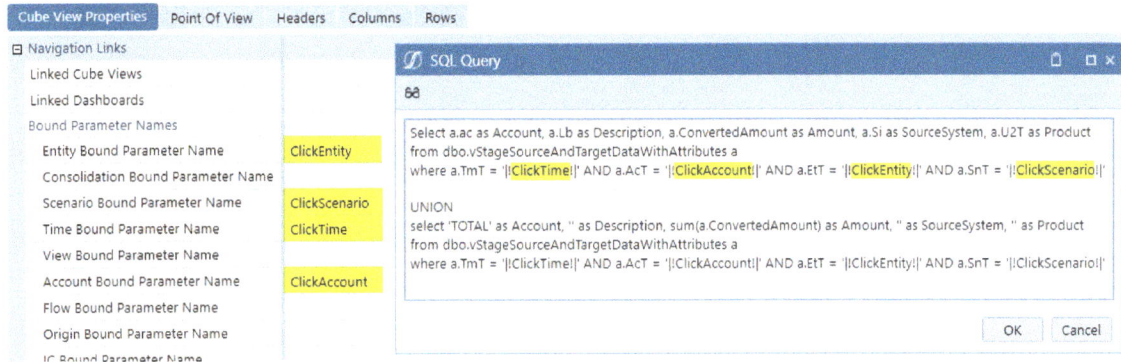

Figure 4.18

Documents

Do you ever find yourself scouring your inbox for files from colleagues? Or do you have documents on your desktop (or some other random location you cannot remember) that you need to access quickly?

The OnePlace Documents pane is where you can access shared files, as well as files you have stored for your individual use. Public and User folders come out-of-the-box with all applications; just like the folder names suggest, Users can utilize the tool to store files and other reference materials without cluttering the User community's storage system.

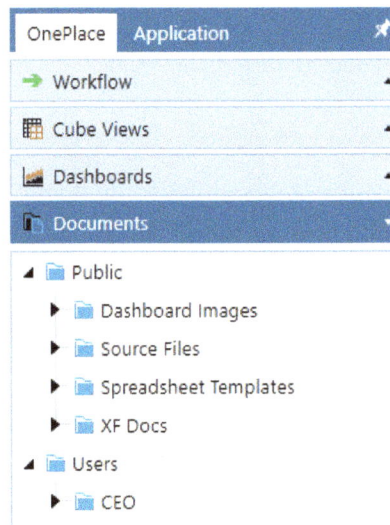

Figure 4.19

By now, you are likely familiar with OneStream's role-based security model. The same security concepts apply to document management to reduce maintenance and provide flexibility in granting or revoking file access within the File Explorer. Access and Maintenance Group assignments uniquely apply to all files, which means you have complete control over which Users can view files and which Users can modify files; the same concept applies to file folders.

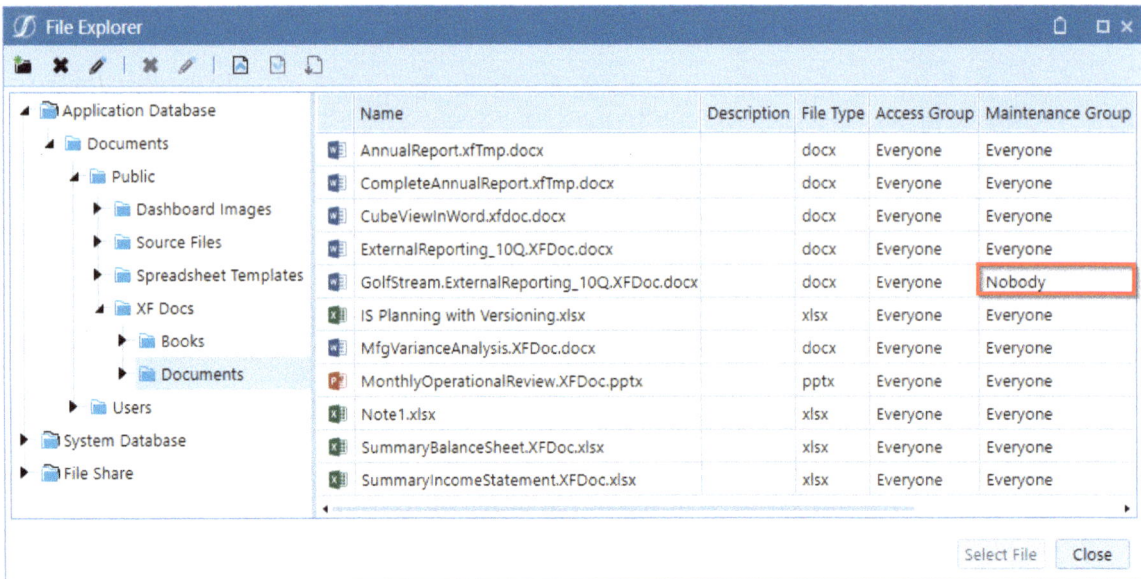

Figure 4.20

Conclusion

In this chapter, we covered OnePlace – the out-of-the-box landing page where Users perform their assigned tasks and access various Components within the application. We have also explained how role-based security lets you tailor the User Experience by read and write access assignments.

Here is the main takeaway: everything in the OneStream platform is fully configurable and should be designed methodically to give your Users the best experience possible.

5

Cube View Concepts

As we have learned, OneStream is full of different tools and techniques that are used to create an engaging User Experience. We have talked about reporting artifacts like Cube Views, Dashboards, Report Books, Extensible Documents, and Excel, and discussed how the OneStream UI itself can be tinkered with to create something that captures what Users need to do and when. Laying out your options and getting the hang of configuring each of them is how you can begin to answer any requirement that comes your way. So how do we get started?

This is the part of the book where we begin to dive into each of the artifacts we have discussed. We are going to pull them apart, stretch their boundaries, and get you discovering the art of the possible with each of them. So, get ready because Cube Views are up first!

Cube Views

Why start with Cube Views? Well, that question applies not only to this book but also to most people's careers in the software. If you are reading this book, you are probably looking to do some sort of maintenance, implementation, or design within OneStream Software, and Cube Views are commonly where most people start when they are ready to cut their teeth. This is usually because projects have a lot of Cube Views, and it is a great way for a new person to start plugging away and building.

Now I don't want to scare you, but Cube Views have A LOT of properties. Don't worry; this is a good thing! Each of these properties can be mixed and matched to get your Report or Form looking exactly how you want it. I can't help but think of the movie *Shrek*, a classic film for all ages. If you really want to get serious about OneStream… you should watch it. Although I digress (and am half-joking), there is a scene where Shrek is telling Donkey that ogres have layers as he peels back an onion. Cube Views are just like that! They have layer upon layer for you to explore. And these layers are what make Cube Views multifaceted. They can be stretched into their own beautiful Reports, configured to collect data as Forms, added to Dashboards as visual Components for feeding data, brought into Excel as a live connection, threaded together to make a polished Report Book, or added to Extensible Documents to provide a live grid from Microsoft tools into OneStream!

So, invest in your Cube View knowledge. Spend a little time, dig in there, explore as many properties as you can handle. I once had a Consultant ask me to tour every single property in a Cube View. No stone was left unturned, and it took about two hours. But by the end, we both learned a lot and started to really pop with ideas on how we were about to handle our reporting requirements. Now, I will go through every single property in a Cube View. Give me one moment to dramatically clear my throat and crack my knuckles for the typing frenzy that is about to begin…

Let's kick off our ode to Cube Views by discussing how Cube Views can be used: standalone Reports, data entry Forms, a starting point for Dashboards, within Report Books, within the Excel Add-in/Spreadsheet Tool, and within Extensible Documents. In this chapter, we will look at each of these pieces and discuss them at a high level. In the following chapters, we will look at how best to set up the design of our Cube Views.

Remember – when we write Reports – that we want to think about our audience and the purpose. So, let's go through how Cube Views can commonly be used, and examine the common audiences and purposes of each of these items. Along the way, I will give you some advice and setup instructions. One thing you will start to see early on is that Cube Views will automatically have three different outputs we have to consider: Excel, PDF, and the Data Explorer Grid. Don't feel overwhelmed! Consider this a good thing, as this will reduce the overall reporting maintenance going forward. We will dive into this more in the formatting chapter, but I want to lay out this concept so we start thinking about how versatile Cube Views are as we step through our common use cases. As we discuss each one, think, "How will be User likely interact with this?"

Cube Views as Reports

The most obvious way to use a Cube View is as a nicely formatted Report. Usually, OneStream customers require beautifully printed Reports for a few different reasons. In Chapter 3, we explained that these Reports are likely your Financial or Managerial Reports, but there could be many more use cases.

Let's isolate that first use case: Financial Reports. These are commonly added to reporting packages that are meant to communicate the health of the company. This means that our common User may be our End-Users, Executives, or even external Users. Then come Managerial Reports; they are obviously for our management team (it's in the name!), and they usually pull items that allow the managerial teams to make important business decisions. They are also nicely formatted, easy-to-digest Reports that typically pull high-level data and various KPIs or ratios.

It may sound like we basically just listed all our potential Users, but they all have one thing in common – they need to see their information quickly, concisely, and simply. This will not take a lot of effort because Cube Views are naturally easy to follow from a User's perspective. Really, the only mistake you can make is writing an *overcomplicated, slow-running Cube View*.

We have talked about our User when building Cube Views, but what about the person left maintaining the Reports after they have been built? Financial Statement Reports require a consistent and professional design that is repeatable and reusable to increase the longevity of any Cube View Reports. Businesses will continue to change – adding new people, branches, departments, you name it – so you want to make a Cube View Report as flexible as the business it represents!

Here are some great tips to follow when designing your Report for maintenance and flexibility:

1. Utilize the Application Properties Standard Reports tab as much as possible.

2. Set all common formatting as parameters.

3. Aim for consistency across Reports.

4. If you use Cube View Extender Rules, ensure your code is commented.

5. Make your Reports dynamic by prompting for Dimensions. This can often reduce the number of Reports you think you need.

6. Utilize row and column sharing where possible.

7. Utilize Member Expansions as much as possible. Resist the urge to pick individual Member names.

8. Explore creating dynamic Calculations in UD8 for common expressions, as opposed to rewriting the same formulas within your Cube Views.

In the upcoming chapters, we are going to explore how to create performant, legible, formatted, flexible Cube Views. We will establish how to build a simple Cube View and slowly start to incorporate more and more properties to allow it to take shape as a polished Report. Because of that, I will not provide you with too much configuration when it comes to Cube Views as Reports – because you are about to read a lot about that! – but I will take the time across the rest of this chapter to explain the configuration of adding Cube Views to Report Books, Extensible Documents, Dashboards, Forms, and Excel.

Cube Views as Report Books

Often, our polished Cube Views do not end their journeys as standalone Reports. Our Financial and Managerial Reports will typically be assembled into Report Books. This is where you are taking the most neatly formatted and legible Reports and tying them all together into a package for internal and external stakeholders to view.

We don't have a dedicated chapter for building Report Books in this book. However, it's worth taking some time to offer you a high-level view of creating Report Books, if you have never used them before.

Creating Report Books

So how do Cube Views become Report Books? If you have never been exposed to Report Books in OneStream, it might be daunting at first, but it is one of the easiest things you will ever need to build. You already put a lot of effort into creating your Cube View Reports; now we just sit back and start the assembly process.

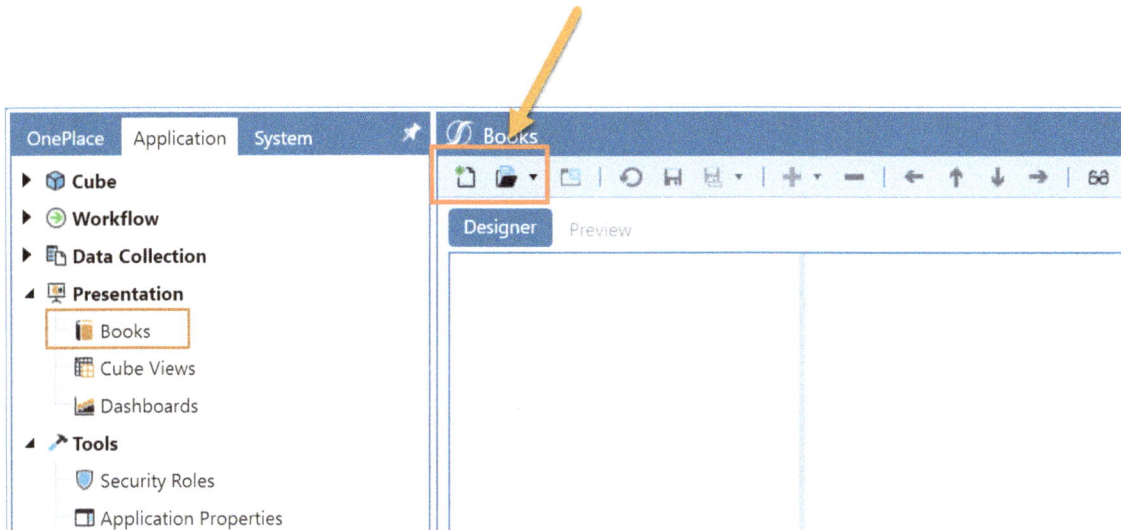

Figure 5.1

Let's look at the Books page within the Application tab to see where we start our assembly (Figure 5.1). Don't adjust your glasses or squint your eyes; that is what the page looks like at first. You have just entered the **Report Designer** and we have to bring it to life! Let's start by looking at the first two icons on the Books pane (Figure 5.1), where we create a new Book (left) or open an existing one (right).

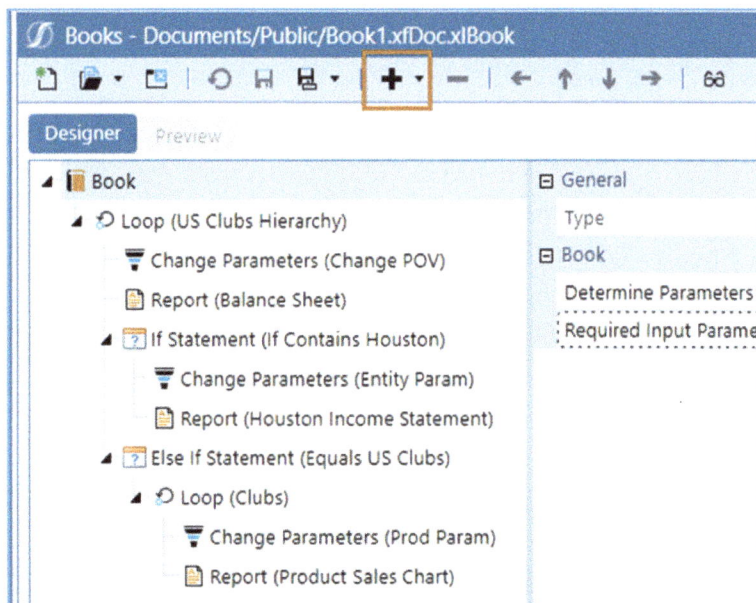

Figure 5.2

Figure 5.2 shows how the page looks when viewing an existing Report Book. Here, we see two Cube View Reports have been added to the Report Book: (Balance Sheet) and Report (Houston Income Statement), amongst a few other things. How did we add all these items to this Book? This was all done by clicking the + icon in the toolbar and choosing the item we wanted to add to our Report Book. You can choose to add a Report, file, Excel export item, Loop, If/Else If/Else statements, or Items to Change Parameters.

You may have guessed it, but our Cube View will be added to a Report through that + icon. We can see in Figure 5.3 that our Cube View is added by choosing the Report Type of Cube View and referencing an existing Cube View in the application.

But what if we need a Report that pulls data that is not stored in my Cube? Perhaps we need to provide information on Workflow Statuses or Intercompany mismatches. Maybe we incorporated MarketPlace solutions or Analytic Blend in our application design, and this data does not reside in the Cube and, therefore, cannot be queried by a Cube View. In these cases, you need a Dashboard Report to pull in this information and, as we can see from Figure 5.3, these are also options when adding a Report to a Report Book.

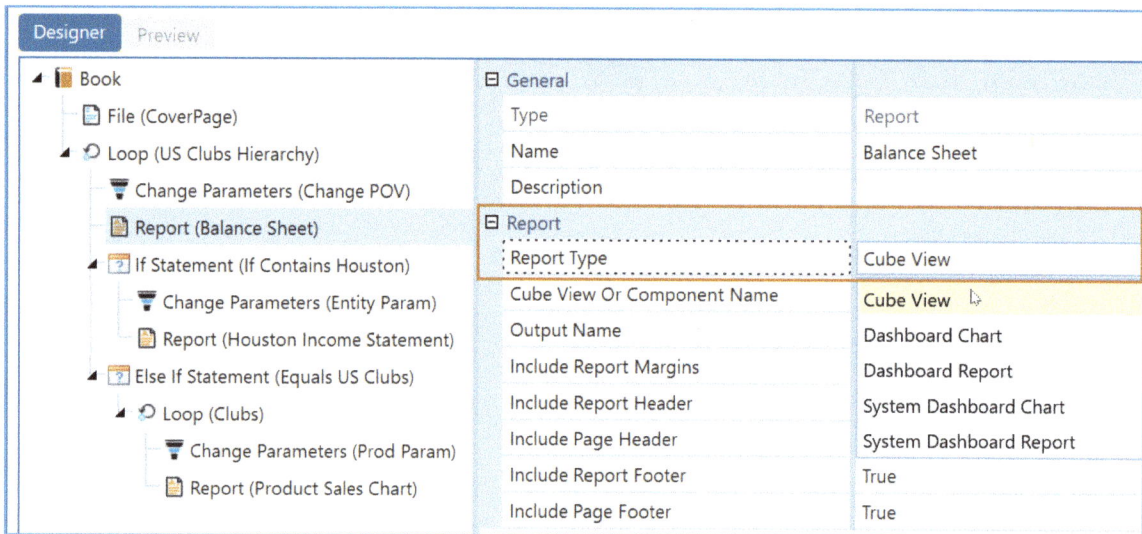

Figure 5.3

See how easy that was! Now for something fun. Let's say we need a cover page that pulls in real-time financial information, charts, and tables. This cover page is usually created as an Extensible Document and can be added to your Book as a file shown in Figure 5.4. We will discuss Extensible Documents a bit later in this chapter.

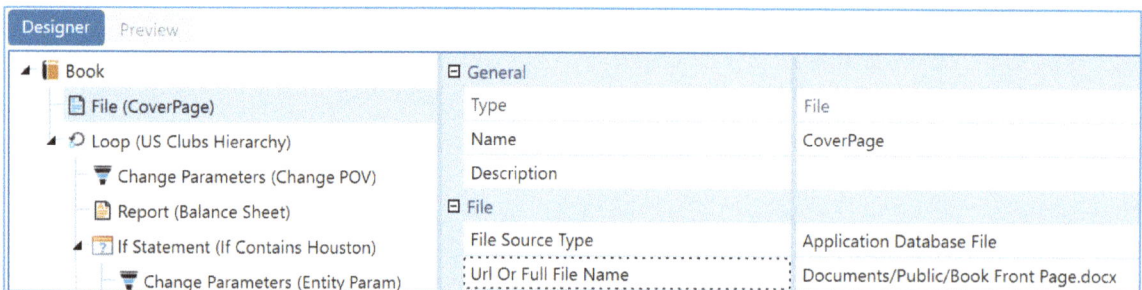

Figure 5.4

Great, so we know how to add content to the Report Book, but let's take things a step further and apply some logic to the Report Book. You can see that there are items called Loops, If statements, Else If statements, Else statements, and Change Parameters.

A **Loop** is a sequence of instructions that will continually run a process – multiple times – based on defined criteria. In one example, you may require a Report Book that pulls the Income Statement and Balance Sheet for all the Entities under a specific Entity Parent, or all the months of a year, or whatever. Any variability like this will require a Loop, and Figure 5.5 shows one example of a Loop and how it is configured. Here we are using a Loop to run multiple versions of the Report `Balance Sheet`. Each version of this Report will represent an Entity under the `US Clubs Hierarchy`.

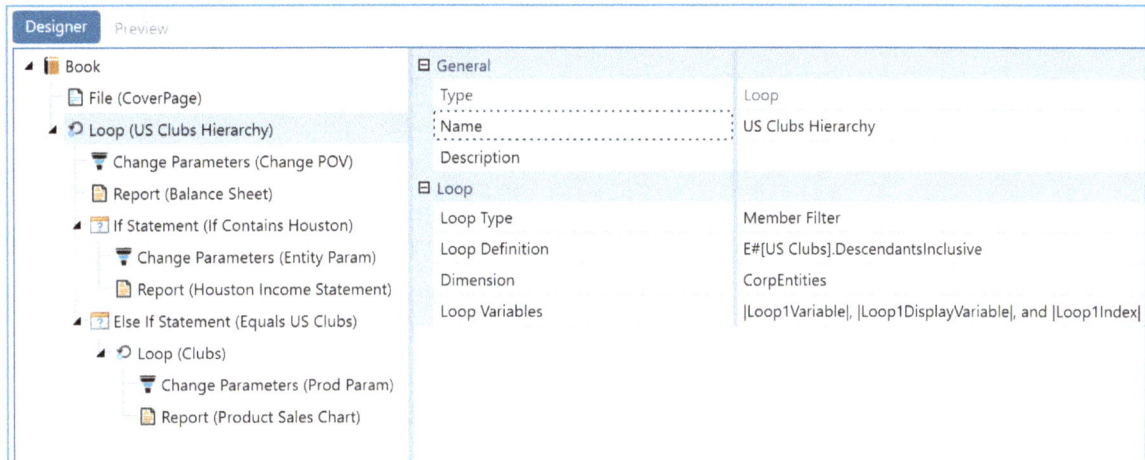

Figure 5.5

Figure 5.6 shows how this Loop can be created. In this image, the Loop will pull all the descendants under the `US Clubs` Member, meaning that we just expanded the number of Reports we are pulling quickly and dynamically. If you don't know what those Loop variables are at the bottom, this leads us to our next item: **Items to Change Parameters**. That is the first item under the `Loop`. This will allow you to turn off any parameters, variables, or adjust the Workflow or Cube POV.

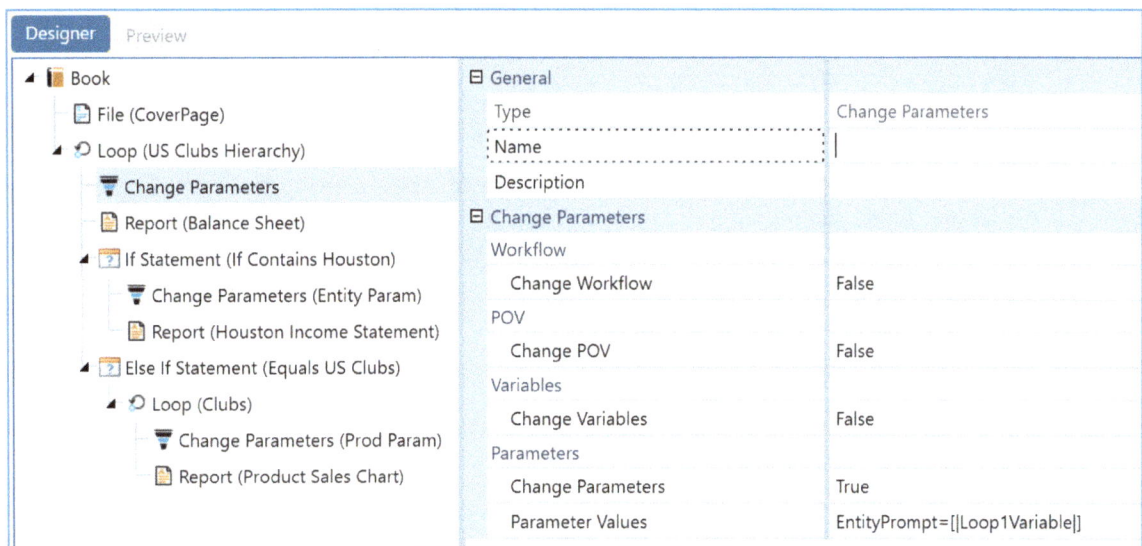

Figure 5.6

Figure 5.6 shows how we are using that **Change Parameter** to unwind an existing parameter found in the subsequent Report. Perhaps in that Balance Sheet Cube View Report, we were prompting for the Entity using a parameter called `EntityPrompt`. This Item to Change Parameter will tell the Report Book to ignore the parameter and not prompt the User for an Entity, but instead listen to whatever information is in the Loop.

Maybe we need a bit more logic applied to the Loop, though. This can be done through If, Else If, and If statements.

Alright, let's continue down our Report Book hierarchy and look at how these are set up, in Figure 5.7.

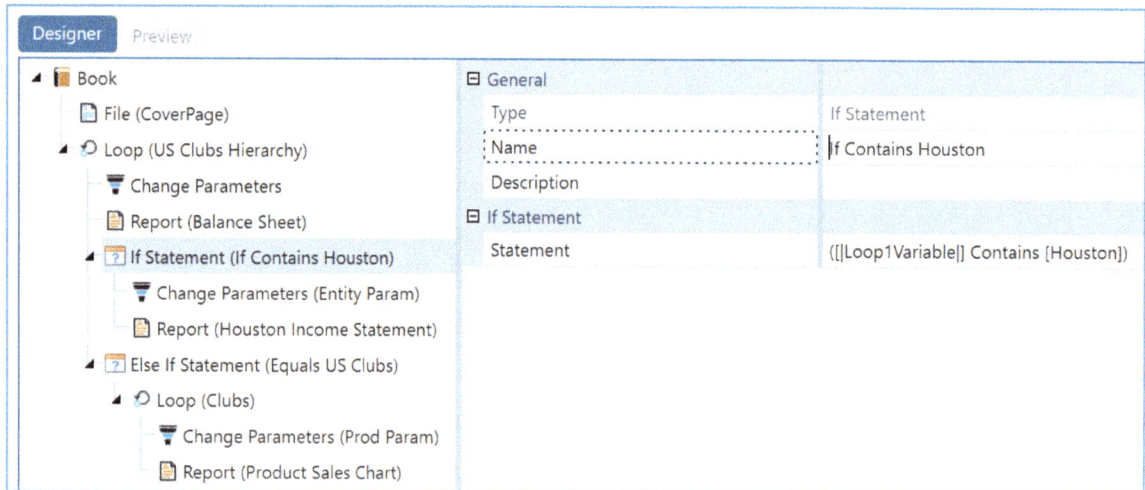

Figure 5.7

Here the `If` Statement is meant to add flexibility to the Loop we just explained. This syntax is saying that 'If' the Loop passes over an Entity Name that contains the text `Houston`, then pull an additional Cube View Report (Houston Income Statement). With Loops, Change Parameters, and If/Else If/Else statements, we can take a few ordinary Cube Views, incorporate files or Dashboard Reports, and flex them to generate a multifaceted Report Book.

Believe it or not, that is all it takes to get a Report Book up and running. Before we conclude, let's look at the three different types of Report Books we can create:

1. PDF Book
2. Zip Book
3. Excel Book

The Report Book we just broke down was a PDF Book, and this is configured when it comes time to save the Report Book and give it a file name. This is all done in the suffix of the file name. Really. So, for a PDF, key in the suffix `.xfDoc.PDFBook`; for Zip type `.xfDoc.ZipBook`; and for Excel, choose `.xfDoc.XLbook`. You DO need the `.xfDoc`, or else your Report Book won't work. You can see what I am talking about in Figure 5.8.

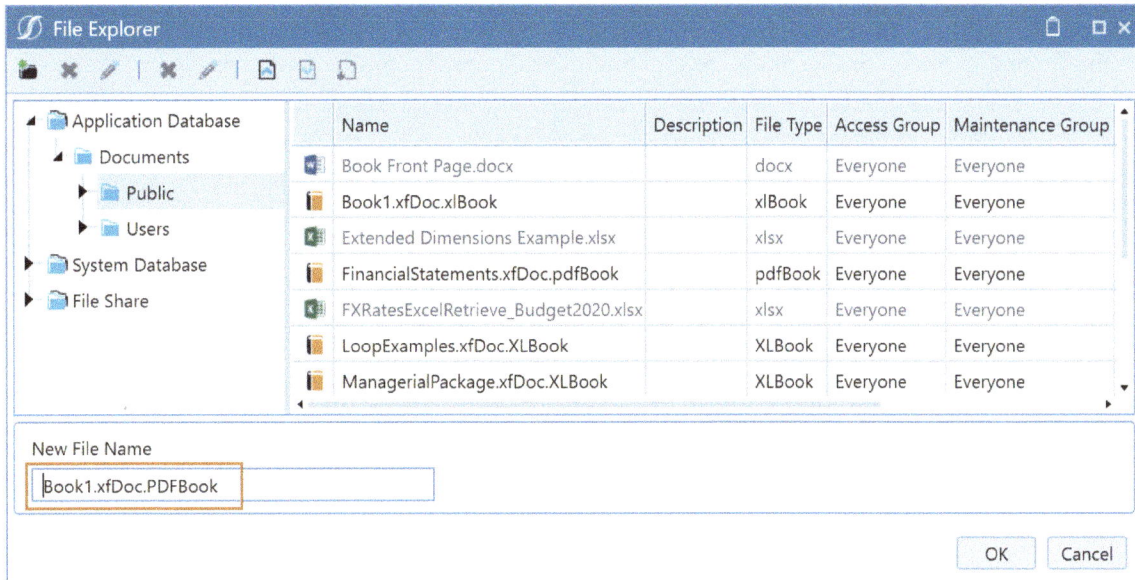

Figure 5.8

I do have one small caveat to point out. Each Report Book type can be created using the same steps outlined in this section. However, if you wish to create an Excel Book, there is one adjustment you need to make in the build. We must use **Excel Export Items** instead of Reports when adding content to the Book. These are created specifically for Excel Report Books, and they will pull the Excel-exported version of a Cube View. We can see the design of an Excel Report Book in Figure 5.9, so when we are formatting our Cube View Reports, we might not just want to think about how they look as a PDF but as an Excel file too. We will learn in Chapter 7 that both can be intricately formatted separately.

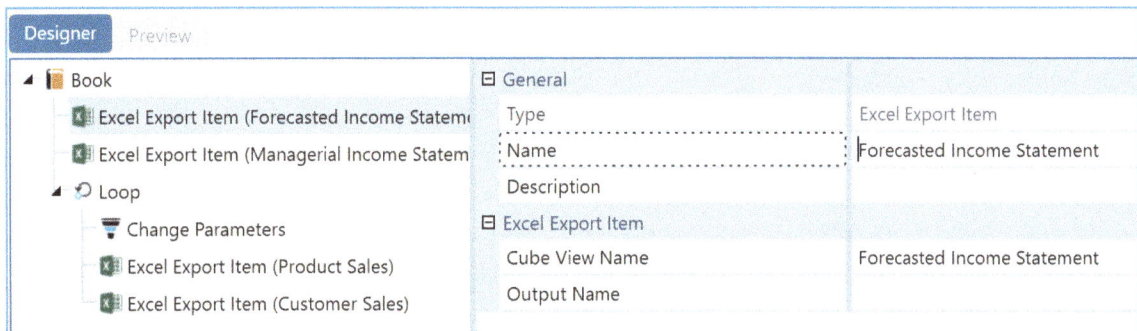

Figure 5.9

Once your Report Books are nicely assembled, you can keep them in the File Explorer, incorporate them into Dashboards, or run them through the **Parcel Service**. Parcel Service is a truly handy MarketPlace solution that emails Report Books (or other Extensible Documents), and where you don't even need a OneStream License to receive the reporting package. This is a great option if you are running very large Report Books that might take a little time to render. Instead of waiting, simply use the Parcel Service to email yourself. These can also be automated to send to an internal or external distribution list through the Task Scheduler.

Extensible Documents

You may not know this, but Report Books are a version of Extensible Documents. And that's the end of the section... thank you, tip your waiter on the way out. Just kidding. Extensible Documents, as we have said in prior chapters, are our way to incorporate a live connection of

OneStream data, Cube Views, Dashboard Reports, or Excel Add-in Reports into our various Microsoft tools.

In this section, we are going to go through how to add a Cube View into an Extensible Document. You may do this if you have a cover letter for a Report Book or a PowerPoint presentation that refers to a nicely formatted data grid. Perhaps we need this grid to be dynamic, based on selection (parameters), and update as data changes. This is an excellent way to use multiple reporting tools within OneStream to create an all-encompassing User Experience.

Adding Cube Views to Extensible Documents

So how do Cube Views find their way into Extensible Documents? It's an interesting trick that you can use, but Extensible Documents can take an ordinary picture and transform it into a Cube View, or a Dashboard Chart, or a Dashboard Report, or an Excel file.

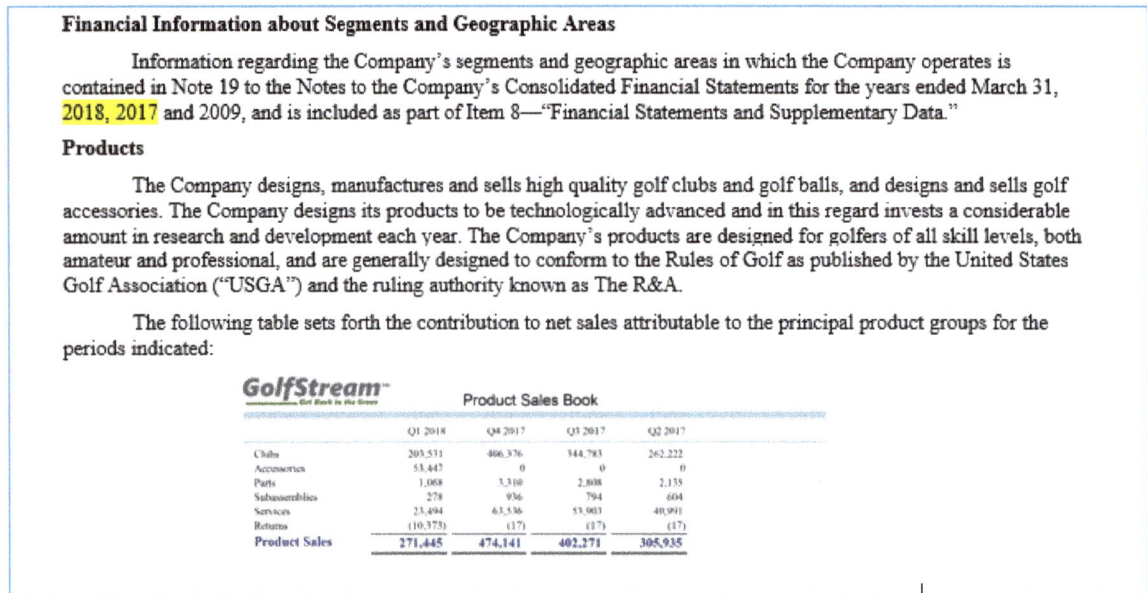

Figure 5.10

Figure 5.10 is not showing a mere picture of a Cube View. This is an Extensible Document pulling a live Cube View from a OneStream application. If this Cube View is adjusted in the application, it will be reflected in this image once the Extensible Document is re-run. If the data changes, same thing. And if any parameters are being referenced, you will be prompted to make any necessary selections.

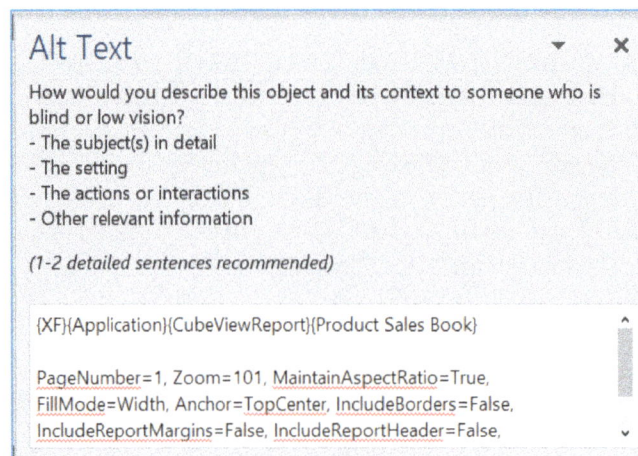

Figure 5.11

So how is this magic configured? It is all done through the **Alternate Text Properties** within the Microsoft artifact you are creating. Figure 5.11 shows an example of how this looks in Microsoft Word.

The first line of this syntax says to pull an existing Cube View Report called `Product Sales Book`. The rest of the syntax is for any necessary formatting you may have. For example, the `Page Number` could be for multi-paged Reports, and you can also trim margins off the Report as well. They can take a little tinkering to get things working, but it's a labor of love.

Don't worry, you don't have to type all of that in! You can use the **Object Lookup** icon back in the application to search for the syntax under the Extensible Document settings. The below image shows the required syntax for referencing a Cube View in an Extensible Document. The first line is what pulls in the Cube View. The second line is for any formatting. You don't need the second line if you are not applying any new formatting.

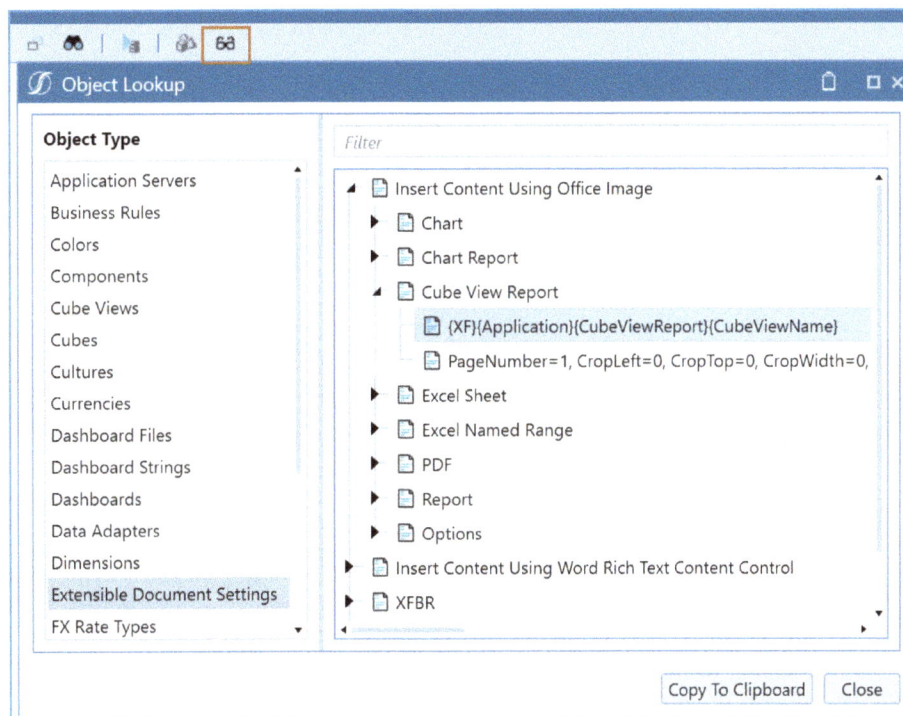

Figure 5.12

That's it. Simply copy, paste, and update.

Once again, don't forget to ensure that the Extensible Document is saved with the suffix `.xfdoc` in the file name and run through the File Explorer in OneStream. I have seen many people scratching their heads because they forgot this simple but crucial step.

> **Tip:** I like to pop a parameter in the Extensible Document, so when it is run through the File Explorer I will know if I have forgotten the suffix (or misspelled it) if I do not see a prompt. If you see the prompt, but the Cube View is not working, then you know you have something incorrect in your alternate text property.

Cube Views for Data Entry

After Reports, the second most common thing you will create with Cube Views is a mechanism for data entry.

When designing data entry within OneStream, you can choose if you want to collect data through Forms or Journals. Most of the time, we see people picking Forms and these can be built through

Chapter 5

Spreadsheets, Dashboards, or Cube Views. The interesting thing is that no matter which option you choose, I can almost guarantee that you will need to create a Cube View to get started.

In this section, we will focus on enabling an existing Cube View for data entry. We will not cover how to build a Form template, but we will give you a little advice on how to ensure your Cube View is dynamic, based on the Workflow. This is a MUST because our Users will need to interact with the Cube View through the Workflow to submit data, and we always want to prioritize creating dynamic Cube Views.

Enabling Cube Views for Data Entry

If you know how to make a Cube View as a Report, you can quickly pivot this into a Cube View for data entry. When a Cube View is not available for data entry, the cells will not be editable. In Figure 5.13, you can see that the white cells are editable, and the green cells are not editable.

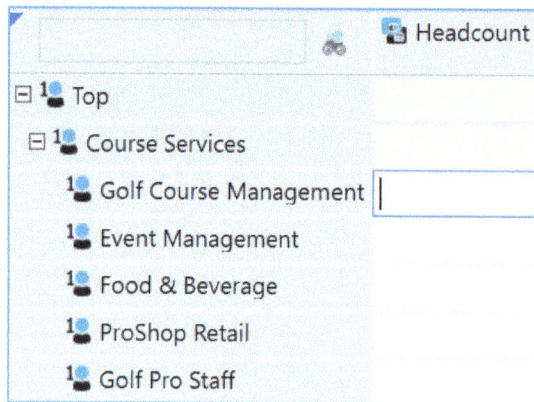

Figure 5.13

Moving slightly off-topic, you may already know that we can change the background color of your Cube View cells, but did you know the background color of the editable cells can be edited separately? This is done by changing the WriteableBackgroundColor, as depicted in Figure 5.14.

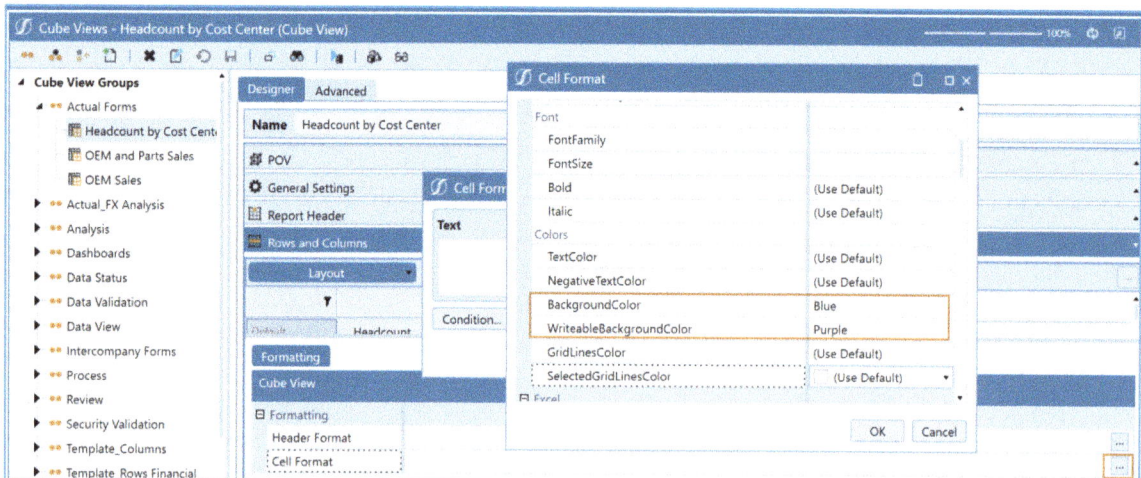

Figure 5.14

And now, if you turn your attention to Figure 5.15, we can see that our resulting Cube View looks a bit more... colorful. Okay, so you probably wouldn't see something that looks this wild in a live application (or maybe you will, I won't judge!), but it illustrates that you are not just stuck with green and white.

46

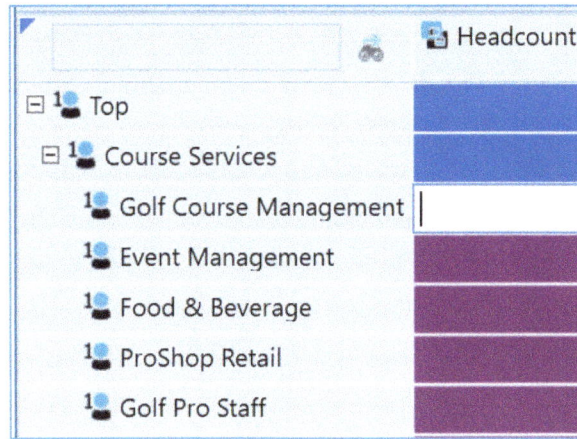

Figure 5.15

Let's get back on topic. How do we get to the point of making our Cube View editable for data entry? There are three things we need to adjust:

1. Set Cube View Can Modify Data.

2. Choose the appropriate Origin Member.

3. Ensure the Cube View is pulling all Base Members.

The first step is the easiest. All you need do is set the Can Modify Data property to True on the Common properties under the General Settings of the Cube View. You can see how to do this in Figure 5.16.

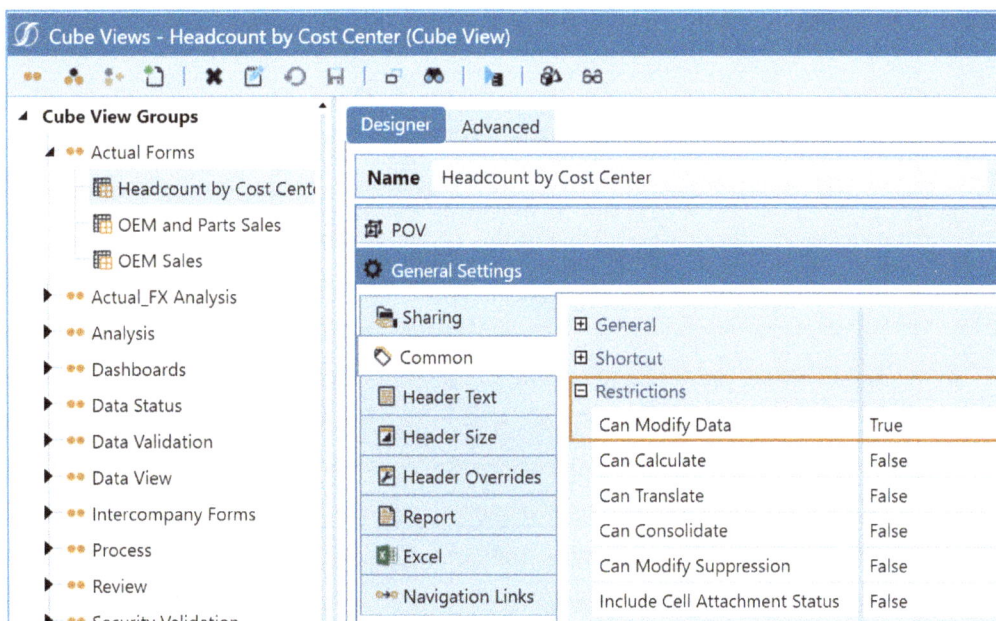

Figure 5.16

Step two is all about the Origin Dimension. The Origin Dimension is something unique to OneStream. This Dimension cannot be edited from anywhere in the application, meaning the Members you see are the Members you get. The purpose of this Dimension is to track how the data is brought into OneStream. The three ways that data can be brought into OneStream are by importing (requires data sources and Transformation Rules), Forms, and Journals. Let's look at the Origin Dimension shown in Figure 5.17.

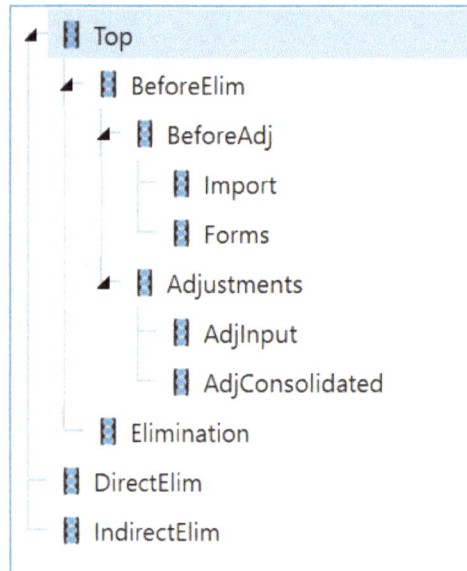

Figure 5.17

When configuring our Cube View for data entry, we want to ensure we are writing to either Forms or the BeforeAdj Member. Either of these options will open your cells up to receive data.

However, I may have just startled you if you jumped ahead to step 3 because BeforeAdj is a Parent Member! Well, this is an exception. The BeforeAdj Member aggregates the Import and Forms Member and is, in fact, available for data entry. This is a great option if you are loading some data and then potentially viewing and adjusting this data through Forms. This way, you can see what you are changing. One use case could be in a Planning situation. We often see data seeded into a Scenario Member and then Users perform data entry on top of this. This is a great way to see what came in versus what was adjusted using the Origin Dimension.

The below Cube View (Figure 5.18) shows you how this can work. We can see in the Mach5 line that 2,927,034.61 was imported. If you wanted to change that number to 3,000,000.61, you could key in the difference to the Forms Member, and OneStream will aggregate the two values into the BeforeAdj Member; or simply key in the final number into BeforeAdj and OneStream will calculate the difference and write it to Forms for you.

	Import	Forms	BeforeAdj
Clubs	4,606,156.98	72,966.00	4,679,122.98
Woods	4,606,156.98	72,966.00	4,679,122.98
Drivers	2,927,034.61	72,966.00	3,000,000.61
Mach5	2,927,034.61	72,966.00	3,000,000.61

Figure 5.18

The third and final step for enabling your Cube Views for Data Entry is to ensure that your Cube View is pulling all Base Members. We have learned that our exception to this rule is the BeforeAdj Origin Member. A great tip to check this quickly is to right-click on an individual cell and drill down. This can be done within the Data Explorer Grid of the Cube View and is your chance to quickly see the Members behind any cell. If any of the Members are green, they are a Parent Member, and you will want to make the necessary adjustments in your rows, columns, or Cube View POV.

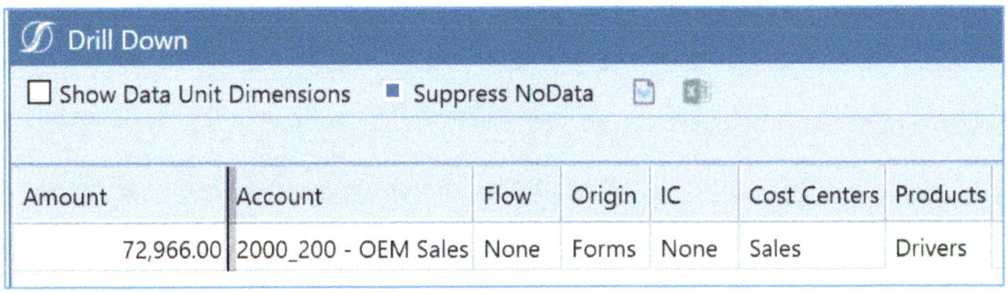

Figure 5.19

So, let's recap. There are three things you need to check to ensure your Cube View is available for Data Entry:

1. Set Cube View Can Modify Data.

2. Choose the appropriate Origin Member.

3. Ensure the Cube View is pulling all Base Dimensions.

But what if your cells are still editable, and you are positive you have checked all these things? You could be facing a few other problems:

1. Check to ensure you are not violating any constraints set in the **Dimension Library**.

2. The Workflow has been locked or completed. Data Entry Forms coincide with the Workflow. If the Workflow Profile has been locked or completed at this point, your cells will be barred from entry. This may not be the case if you are not assigning Entities to your Workflow Profiles.

3. Conditional Input Rules can prevent entry as well. This would be done through a Finance Business Rule on the Business Rules page.

Workflow and Data Entry

Simply enabling your Cube View for Data Entry is not enough to call it a Form! Our Cube View needs to be added to a **Form Template**, and then it can be added to the Workflow. To get started, we will want to ensure that our Cube View is dynamic, based on the Workflow POV. This is comprised of our Workflow Time, Workflow Scenario, and Workflow Profile.

Time and Scenario are easy to tackle, and we can begin here.

Typically, I will start by pulling the Member WF into the Scenario and Time section of the Cube View POV, rows, or columns. The variable WF comes with your application, so you don't need to add this to your Dimension Library; it is already there for you, I promise! If we reference this in our Scenario and Time, when this Cube View is run, it will not prompt me but update these Members in my Workflow POV. The setup of this can be seen in Figure 5.20.

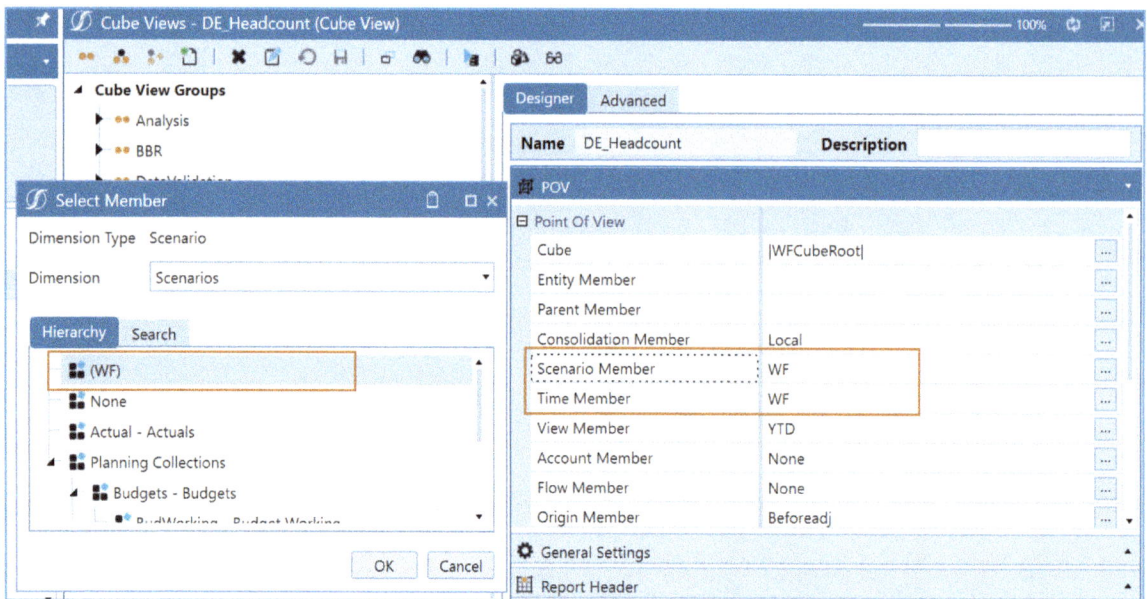

Figure 5.20

For the Scenario Dimension, this will likely be your best option, but for Time we often need a bit more flexibility, especially if our Form is being used for Planning purposes. Commonly, our Budget Scenario Members are configured in the Dimension Library with a **Yearly Workflow Tracking Frequency**. This means that WF for these Scenario Members would be pulling in the year, not a specific month. Even if this didn't happen – usually when entering Budget or Forecast data – we typically want to see the months in the year displayed in the rows or the columns. Figure 5.21 illustrates what you would likely want to see instead.

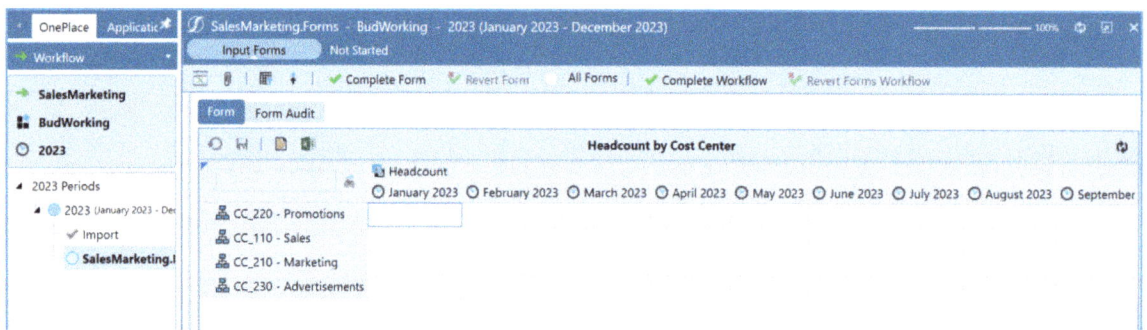

Figure 5.21

How did we get this to work? Well, there are many ways you could do this, but my trick is to construct a Time column that looks like Figure 5.22, below. That |WFYear| is what we call a **substitution variable**. Substitution variables resolve at runtime into a variety of things and can be referenced throughout the application. The best part is that they come with every OneStream application and require no additional setup. Whenever you see the little eyeglasses icon, this means you can access the object lookup, where you can copy and paste these variables (amongst other things) wherever you need. Figure 5.23 shows substitution variables in the object lookup icon. We will cover these thoroughly in Chapter 8 of this book.

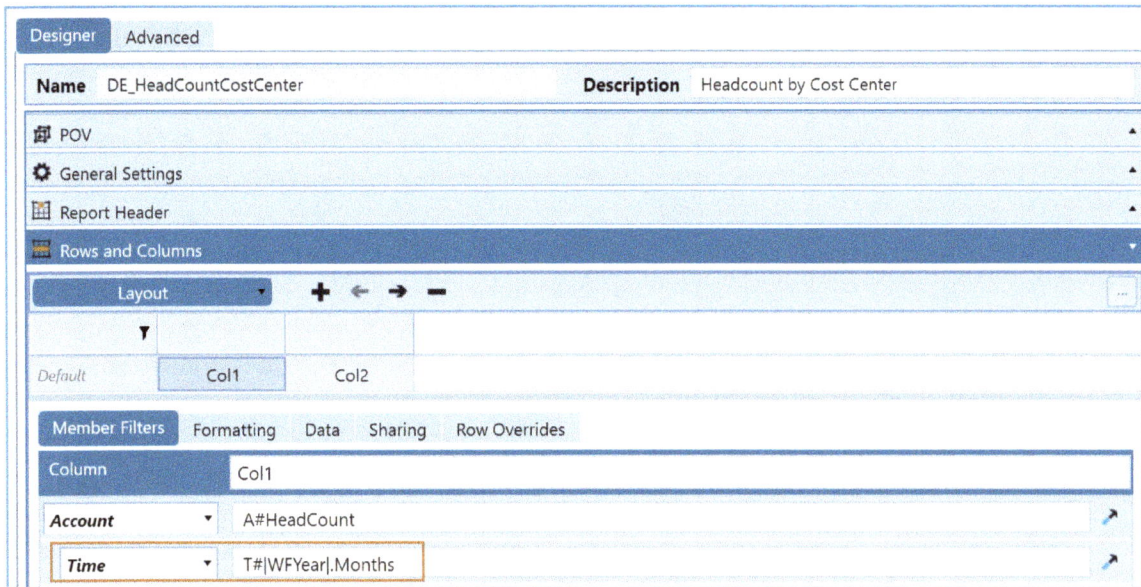

Figure 5.22

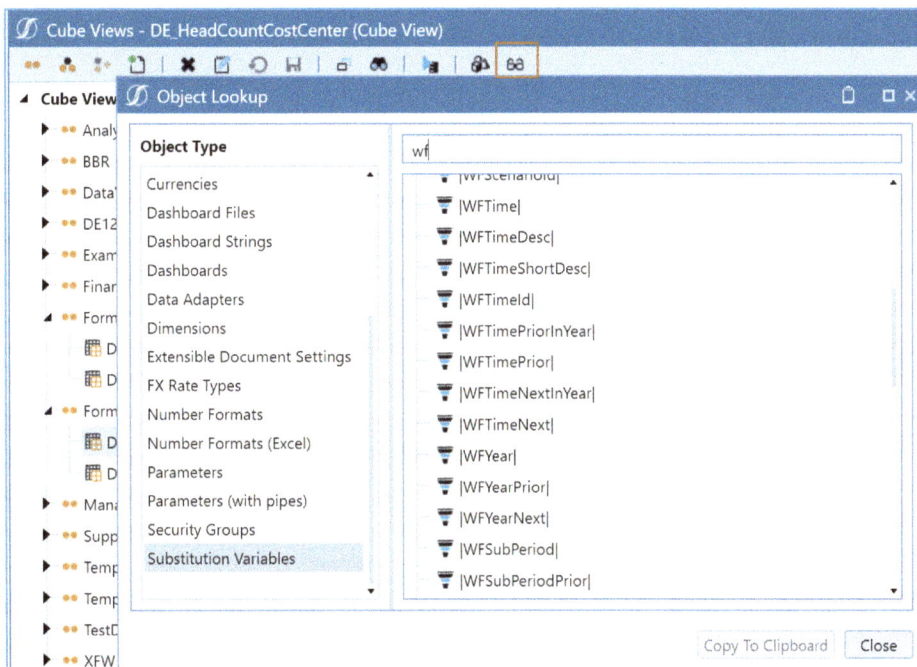

Figure 5.23

We now have our Workflow Scenario and Workflow Time accounted for, but what about the Workflow Profile? Also, why do we care about the Workflow Profile? That isn't a Dimension! Typically, we see many Workflow hierarchy designs have Entities assigned to the individual Workflow Profiles. This means that these Workflow Profiles likely only load and enter data for a specific batch of Entities. There is one handy expansion that will help you to ensure your Entity Dimension properly reflects what is assigned to the Workflow Profile: E#Root.WFProfilesEntities. This expansion will pull all the Entities assigned to the Workflow Profile, and we can see the syntax in the Member Filter Builder in Figure 5.24.

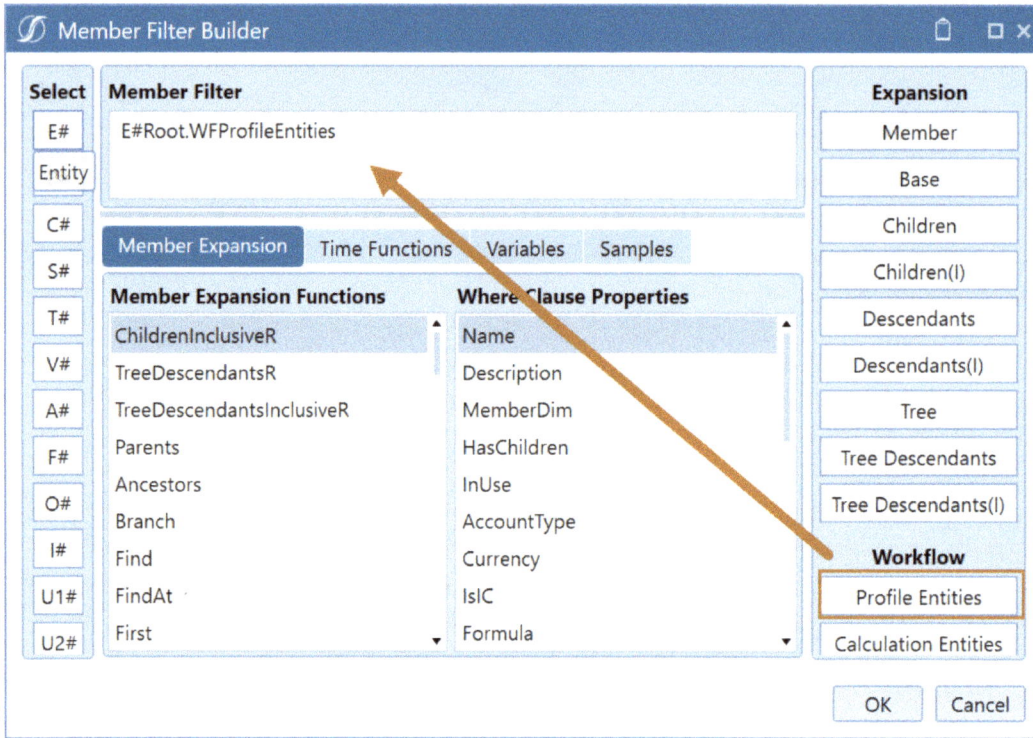

Figure 5.24

The other piece you will want to tie to your Workflow is the Cube. You may or may not know this, but your Workflow Profiles are very much tied to this, and behind every Workflow Profile is an assigned Cube. Setting this to be dynamic to the Workflow Profile is a great move when working with Data Entry Cube Views.

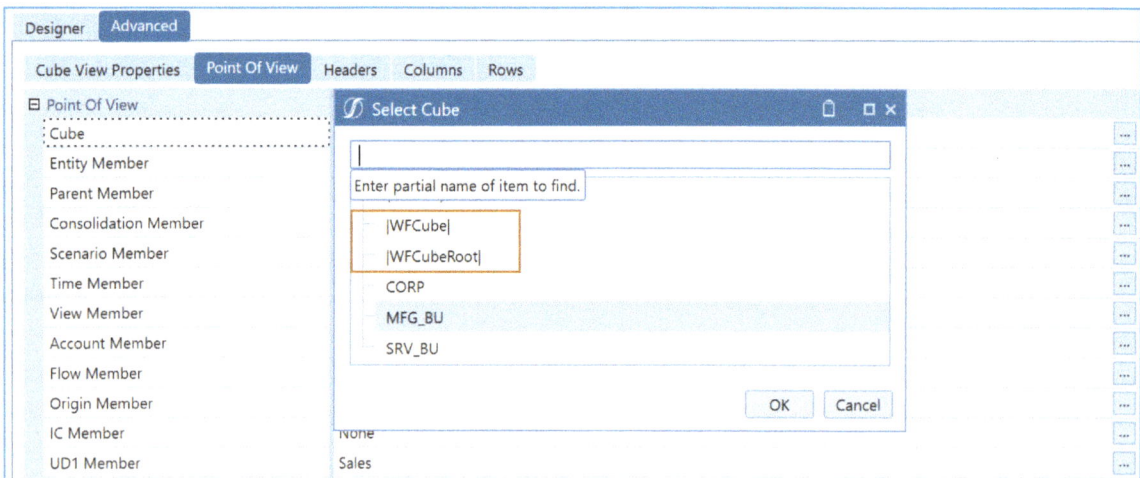

Figure 5.25

Figure 5.25 illustrates two potential options when dynamically referencing the Cube. You can choose the |WFCube| or the |WFCubeRoot| variable.

|WFCube| will pull whatever Cube is assigned to this specific Workflow Profile, while |WFCubeRoot| will pull the Workflow associated with the Cube Root Profile. If I just lost you, under most circumstances both should work for you, but |WFCube| will typically be more flexible. Think through your situation to see what is required.

There is a chance you may have another Dimension that you need to default off the Workflow in some shape or form. We may not have something out-of-the-box for this, but this is where you can utilize your Workflow text properties. These can be referenced using the |WFText1| through |WFText4| substitution variables. And the nice thing is… these can vary by Scenario Type!

Cube Views as Dashboards

In the last section, we talked about how Cube Views can be used to create Forms. We also mentioned that Dashboards and the Spreadsheet tool can be used for data entry as well. But did you know that a Cube View is required to make either of those things possible? In this section, we discuss how Cube Views can be added to Dashboards.

We are setting the stage with data entry in our minds, but there are a lot of reasons why Cube Views make their way into Dashboards. Typically, when it comes to data entry, we may be flexing the capability of our Forms by adding custom Calculations into the picture, or additional Dashboard Components.

Cube Views are a really simple way to bring data into our Dashboards, either as a Dashboard Component themselves or as a data adapter. I don't want to get too far into the setup of a Dashboard here because we have more chapters on this coming later. If you are totally new to Dashboards, keep this information in your back pocket, and we will go into the full setup of Dashboards later.

Cube View as Dashboard Components

I like to describe a Dashboard Component as the type of item that we visualize on the screen when we are running our Dashboards. These can be charts, logos, buttons, combo boxes, or (of course) Cube Views! Figure 5.26 continues where the prior section left off by showing a Cube View that is being incorporated into a data entry Dashboard. I feel like we could play a fun game here called "Can you spot the Cube View?" I will give you a hint; there are two…

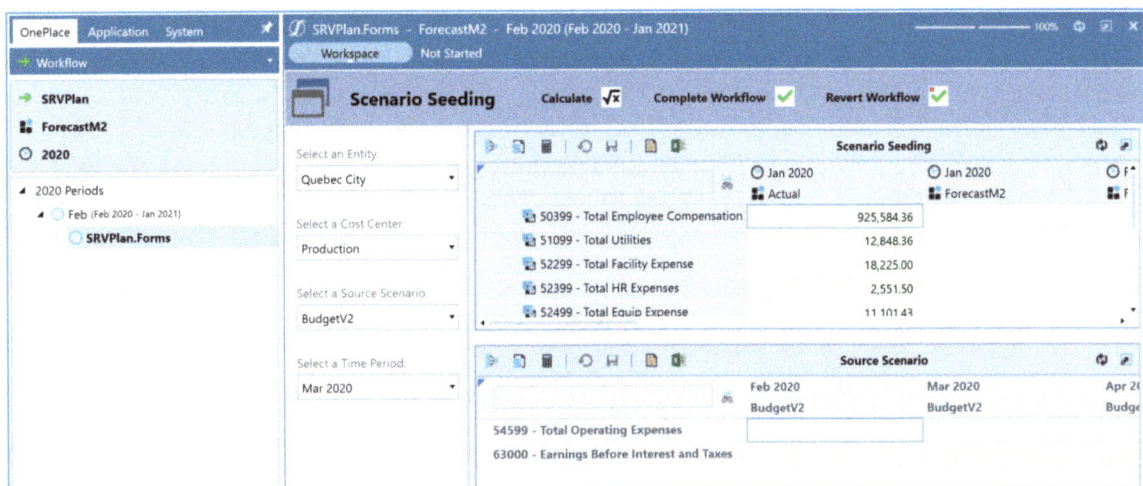

Figure 5.26

How did we sneak these two Cube Views into a Dashboard? Let's venture to the Dashboards page and see how this is set up in Figure 5.27. This image highlights the setup of what is called a **Cube View Dashboard Component**. The setup can be as simple as creating the Dashboard Component, and then adding your Cube View to the Component through the property entitled Cube View. How easy is that?!

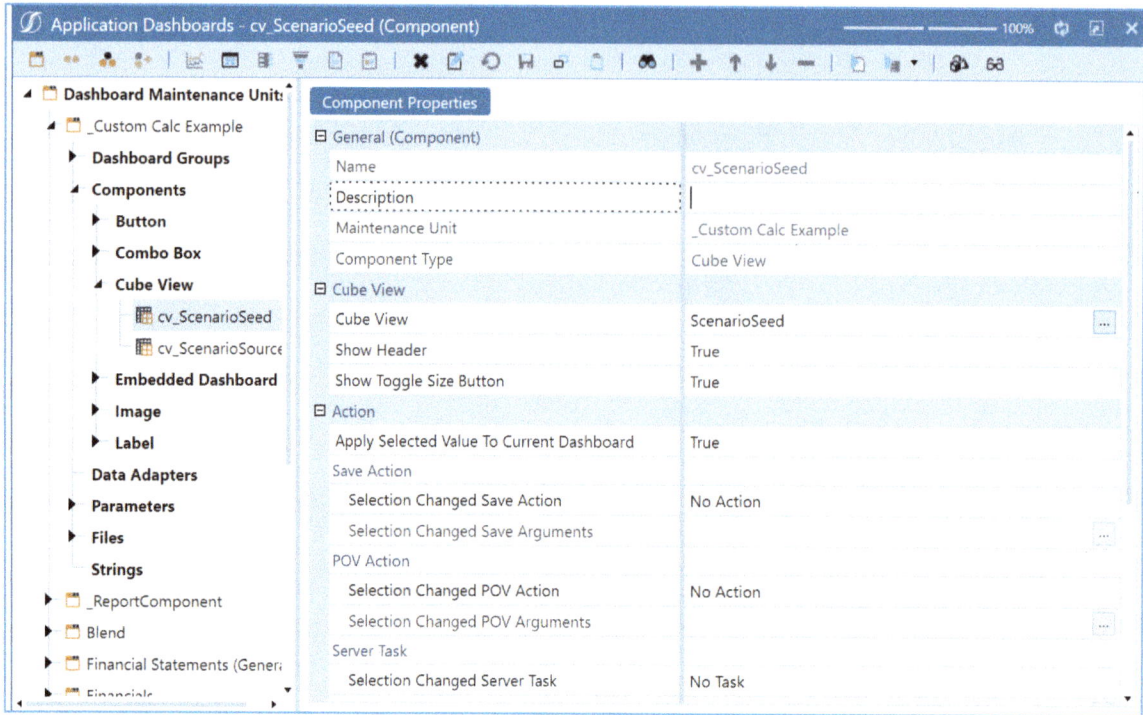

Figure 5.27

Cube View as a Data Adapter

The other way that we see Cube Views added to Dashboards is as a data adapter. A data adapter is what feeds your various Dashboard Components with data. So, while Dashboard Components are the visual aspects to our Dashboards, data adapters are a bit more behind the scenes.

Before launching into that explanation, I should clarify that not all Dashboard Components require a data adapter. Typically, our more robust Components, such as BI Viewer, Charts, Table Views, Grid Views, etc., will require one, while our simpler Components such as buttons, labels, combo boxes, or File Viewer will not. But how do I know if I need a data adapter? If you see a little tab like the one in Figure 5.28 on your chosen Dashboard Component, then you need to add a data adapter.

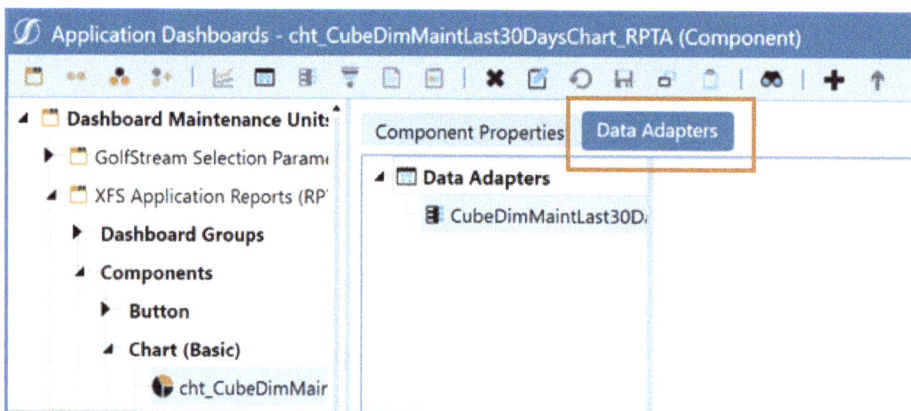

Figure 5.28

Where do Cube Views come into play? They can easily bring Cube data to our Dashboards. Simply choose Cube View MD or Cube View as the Command Type (this is a pull-down menu) and choose the Cube View you wish to reference. We can see the setup of the data adapter in Figure 5.29. Yes, I literally did name my Cube View as `Cube View MD`; I am not very creative. (I'll explain the meaning of `MD`, below.)

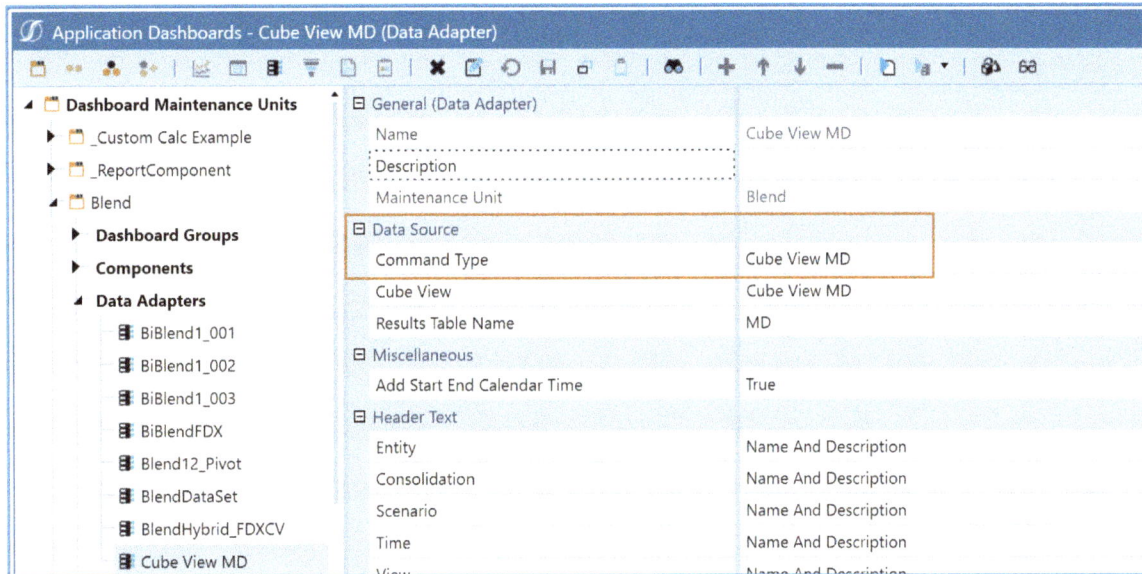

Figure 5.29

One of my favorite tips when building Dashboards is, "If you can get it into the data adapter, you can get it to look good on your Dashboard." It makes something that can often be very complex feel bite-sized and manageable. The act of using a Cube View as a data adapter is no more complicated than me highlighting a grid in Excel and then clicking on the create chart icon. It allows me to tinker with my Cube View as opposed to messing with other properties on the Dashboards side.

Let's look at an example.

I want to build a Dashboard that will show me a trend of 12 months of data for a chosen customer (let's say, a hotel chain). If this data resides in the Cube, the first thing I would do is build a Cube View with this information. Here is an example of the Cube View I might build.

Figure 5.30

Chapter 5

I don't need to do any wild formatting since this Cube View will not be seen, but I may want to give it a name that indicates why I have created this Cube View. I may also want to ensure that the Cube View POV is locked down as much as possible and anything dynamic is using substitution variables or parameters.

Then I am ready to venture off to my Dashboards page and build the data adapter. I have two options:

1. Cube View MD

2. Cube View

You may have guessed it – since I called the Cube View `Cube View MD` – but that is the Data Adapter Type I chose. I am personally quite fond of the Cube View MD data adapters because they do a wonderful job of displaying the information simply and have some interesting properties that increase their range of motion. Figure 5.31 shows the results of a Cube View MD data adapter that was built using the Cube View shown in Figure 5.30.

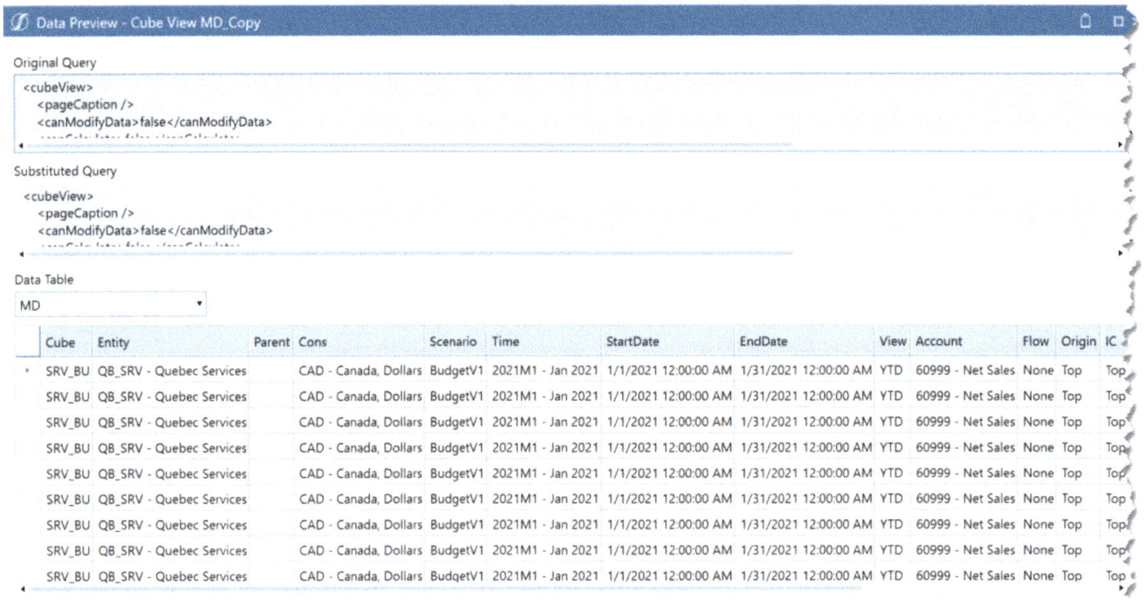

Figure 5.31

Look at that! How easy! This data adapter is pulling all my rows and displaying the Dimensions I am querying behind each row. The Figure cut off, but it will continue to show all my OneStream Dimensions and the Amounts. This is what puts the `MD` in `Cube View MD` (`MD` stands for Multi-Dimensional)! When bringing this information into a Dashboard, I can decide which of my Dimensions I would like to place where, making my Component configuration a breeze.

These data adapters also offer you some additional options. We can see the first batch of these in Figure 5.32.

Miscellaneous	
Add Start End Calendar Time	True
Header Text	
Entity	Name And Description
Consolidation	Name And Description
Scenario	Name And Description
Time	Name And Description
View	Name And Description
Account	Name And Description
Flow	Name And Description
Origin	Name And Description
IC	Name And Description
UD1	Name And Description
UD2	Name And Description
UD3	Name And Description
UD4	Name
UD5	Name And Description
UD6	Name And Description
UD7	Name And Description
UD8	Name And Description

Figure 5.32

The `Start End Calendar Time` will generate two additional columns in your data adapter. This is very handy when working with BI Viewer or the Report Component (formerly known as Studio) to display additional options for Time. Give it a try if you are curious.

Figure 5.32 also highlights that you can choose to display the Name, Description, or both of each Dimension Type. This is nice when formatting your Dashboards.

The other neat thing about the Cube View MD data adapter is the ability to loop through additional Members, as shown in Figure 5.33.

Loop Parameters	
Dimension Type 1	Entity
Member Filter 1	E#QB_SRV.ChildrenInclusive
Dimension Type 2	Account
Member Filter 2	A#61000.ChildrenInclusive
Dimension Level	
Dimension To Level	Outermost Row

Figure 5.33

Yes, just like our Report Books, we can add Loops here as well. Through the Loop Parameters, we can override what is in the Cube View, and loop through a given Member Expansion. This is handy if we need to use the same Cube View for many purposes.

The above screenshot shows that my Cube View MD data adapter will also render data for my Children under the Entity `QB_SRV` (including that Member) and my Children under Account `61000` (including that Member).

The last thing I will point out is the final property: `Dimension To Level`. This one really is a game-changer for those of you who are familiar with table structures.

If we look at the options, you will notice we can choose the outermost row, column, or both in the pull-down menu. In our Cube View, I was only pulling UD4 into the rows, so I could just choose outermost, but if the Cube View had multiple Dimensions to expand, we might tinker with our options.

Let me show the results of enabling this option (hint: It's the UD4_Level_0 and UD4_Level_1 columns that were added) in Figure 5.34.

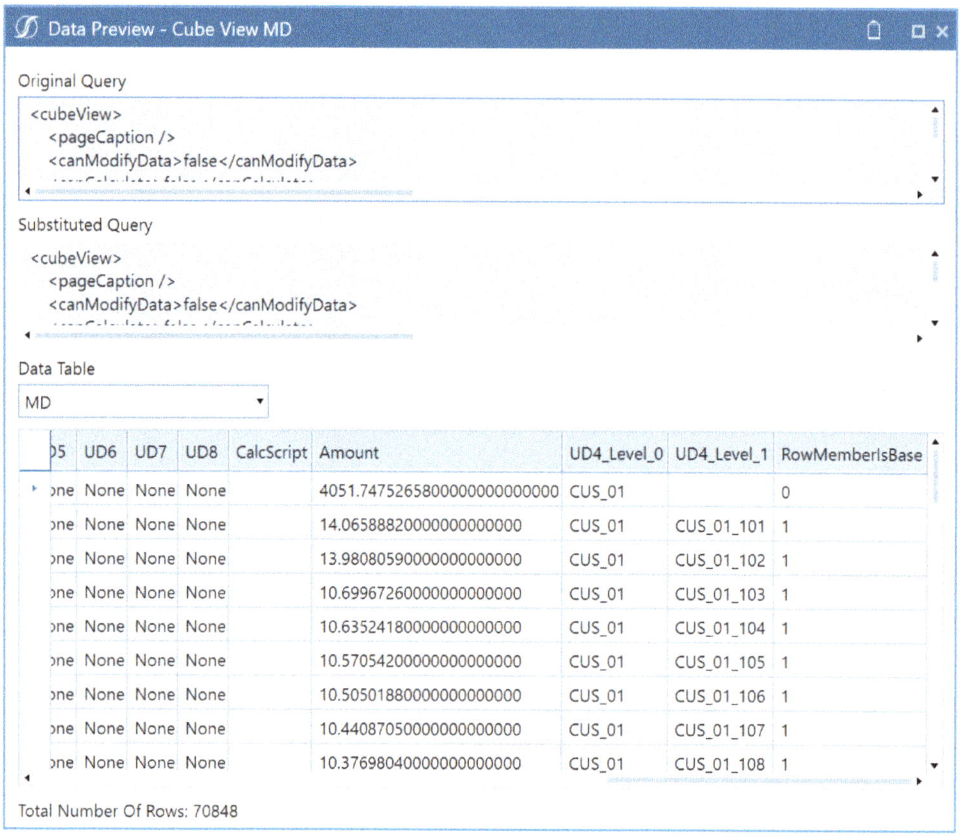

Figure 5.34

What this is doing is generating additional columns based on where the Members are in the hierarchy. So, my Parent is CUS_01 found in the UD4_Level_0 columns. Then all the Children are in UD4_Level_1. This will allow me to pull hierarchy Members based on my dimensionality in OneStream. This is huge because, in a table format, we typically cannot recreate the effect of a hierarchy; but with this property, you can use these additional fields to do just that if you are using Components such as BI Viewer or pivot grids.

We have covered Cube View MD data adapters, but what about Cube View data adapters? What is the difference? Configuration-wise, you still just reference a Cube View, but the output is a bit different, and we can see this in Figure 5.35.

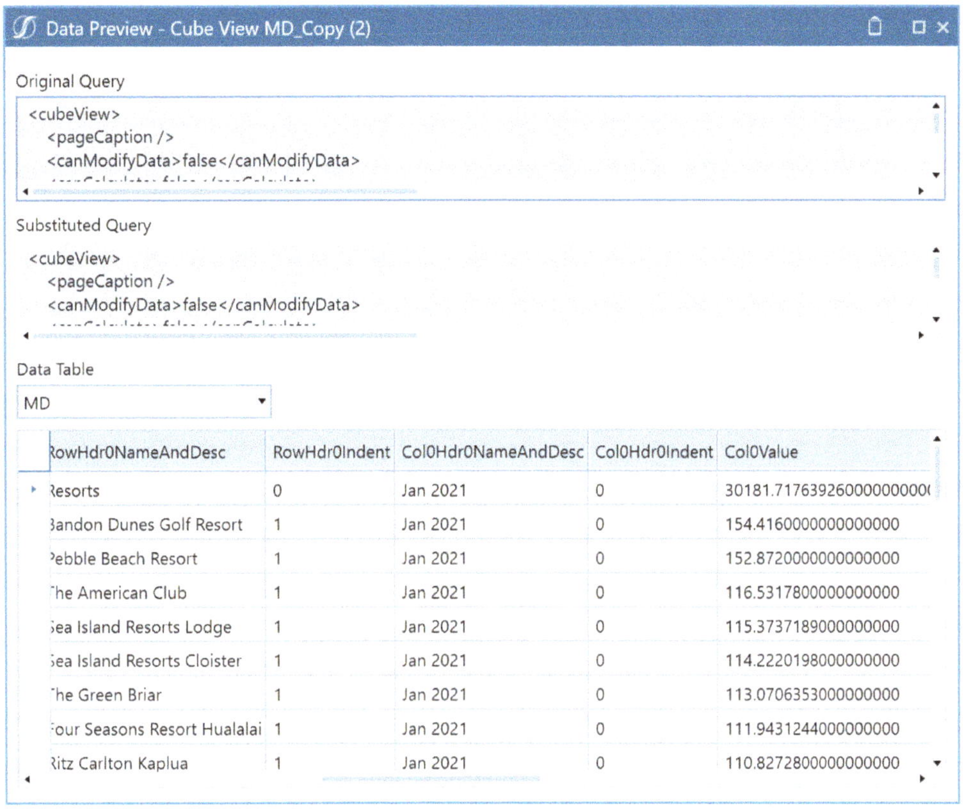

Figure 5.35

Can you see the difference? The fields across the columns are totally different! That is because they represent the items *within* the Cube View *not* the Dimensions.

This data adapter will work just fine, but I would recommend that if you are using Components such as BI Viewer, Report Component, pivot grids, and large data pivot grids, you may want to consider the Cube View MD Data Adapter. With that, you drop fields into the place you need them to be. This is much easier if your fields are Dimensions instead of Col0, RowHdr0Indent, or something like that.

Cube Views in Excel

Our final stop in all the places where Cube Views can be incorporated is our trusty Excel Add-in. Or, if you prefer, the Spreadsheet tool. Within these tools, you have three common options that people utilize to pull or submit data: Retrieve Formulas (XFGet or XFSetCells), Cube View connections, and Quick Views. Cube connections are what we will discuss in this chapter.

Cube View Connections

Creating a Cube View connection in Excel is much more powerful than simply exporting a Cube View. This provides a live connection into Excel and can be refreshed to ensure you are seeing the latest information, in case the data or the Cube View has changed.

Commonly, people will use Cube View connections for data entry. This is a great tool to use if you are going to make a Spreadsheet Form template or if you want to give Users the option to submit a Cube View Form in Excel (as opposed to through the application). Figure 5.36 shows the latter option, which is done by enabling the highlighted icon. You create your own file in the Excel Add-in or Spreadsheet function that uses a Cube View connection to reference the Cube View displayed on the Form template. This file is then added to the Form template.

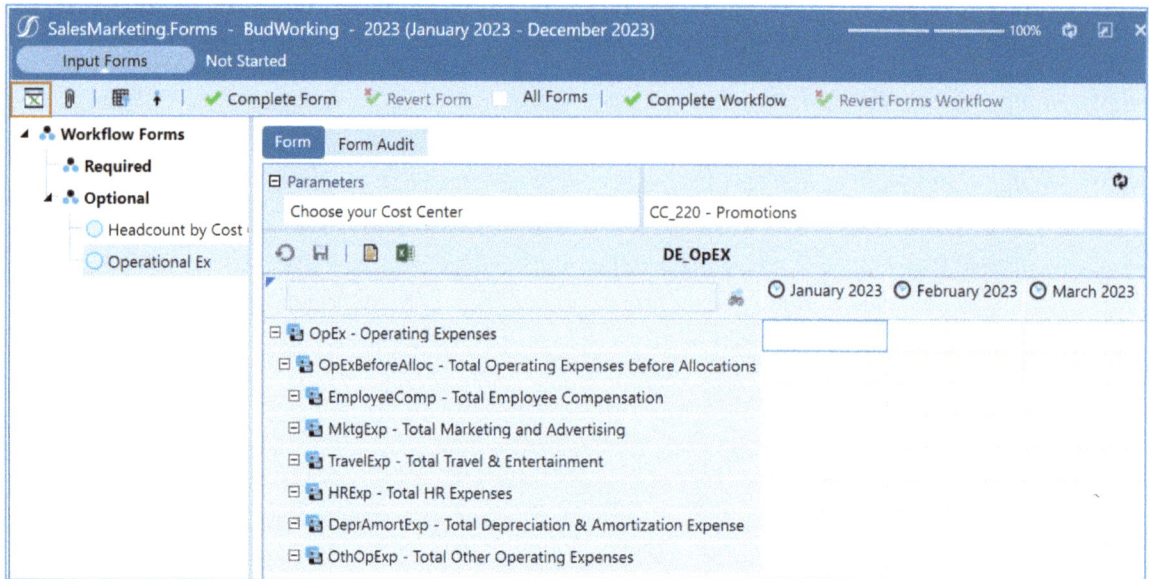

Figure 5.36

Whatever your use case is, Cube View connections are extremely simple to configure. Here, I will demonstrate this in the Spreadsheet tool by clicking the Cube Views icon at the top of the Spreadsheet. From this window, click the Add button to grab any Cube View in the application, as shown in Figure 5.37.

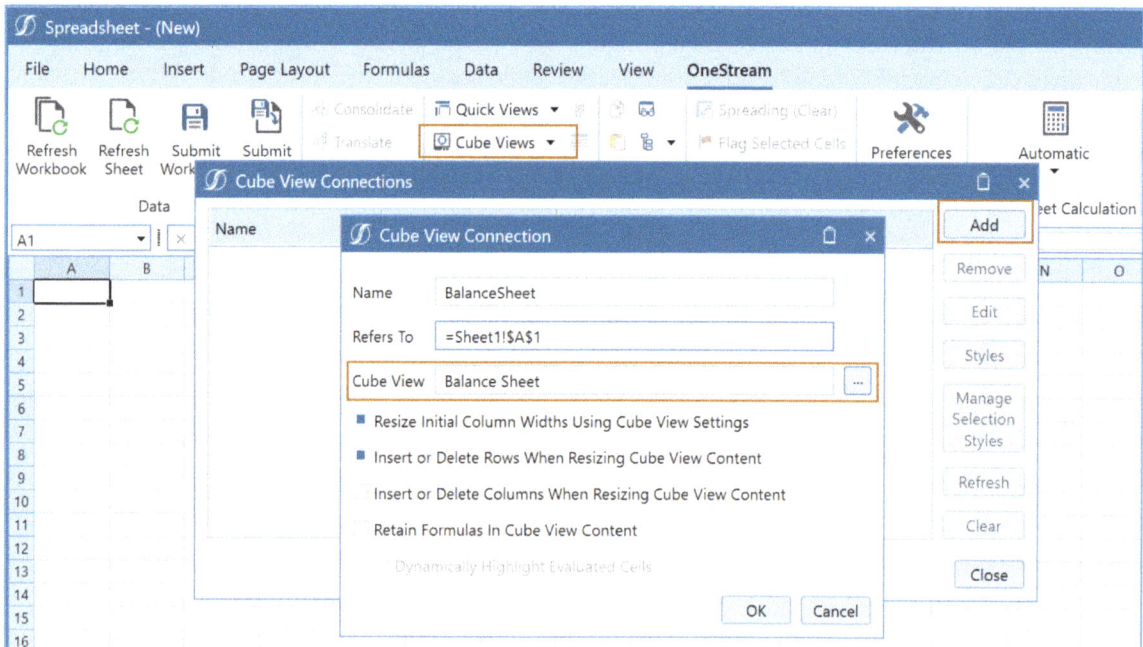

Figure 5.37

After that, you may be prompted for any parameters for the Cube View. Don't worry; whatever you choose at this stage is not permanent. Your Cube View should display within the grid and can now be refreshed to pull the latest data; or you can submit data you have entered through the Cube View if you have it properly configured.

With the Cube View connection made, you can now save this file to your desktop or to the File Explorer icon. Your file can now be added to a Form template to give Users the option to submit data through Excel, or you can incorporate this into its own Spreadsheet Form template.

These aren't the only reasons to use Cube View connections. Most commonly, they are used as an Excel reporting mechanism or perhaps to jumpstart an Excel Report that utilizes OneStream `XFGetCell` functions to retrieve data.

Conclusion

This chapter was a bit of a doozy, but you made it through! We discussed how Cube Views can be used as Reports, Excel Add-in/Spreadsheet, data entry, Dashboards (as Components and data adapters), Extensible Documents, and Report Books. These are all our Reporting Tools in OneStream. See how these simple little grids can be so much more useful than you ever imagined?

This chapter is just the first one in our Cube View journey. Next up, we are going to dive even deeper into the details of building and designing Cube Views. After that, we will spend an entire chapter discussing how Cube Views can be formatted. This is where we will want to take into consideration the three ways that our Cube View can be exported: Excel, PDF, and Data Explorer Grid. Finally, we will spend a little time looking at some more advanced concepts with Cube Views and how they lead to our other reporting options. And just when you think you have read all you can about Cube Views, we will have an interactive chapter where we will give you a step-by-step guide on how to build your very own Cube View!

6

Fundamentals of Cube View Design and Build

As we have discussed in previous chapters, Cube Views are an extremely valuable part of your reporting process. Whether or not you use Cube Views as your final reporting output, we learned (in the last chapter) that they are typically incorporated into Report building in some way

Remember, Reports are fundamentally the main output of our entire application. Therefore, in this section, we will discuss how our Cube Views need to be linked to our Dimension design.

Another massive portion of your application is based on the User Experience. Regardless of how your Cube Views are used, ensuring they are usable and performant will create a seamless End-User Experience. We will start addressing some of these areas in this chapter by diving into the setup of Cube Views.

Because our Cube Views are so versatile and ubiquitous, we may have to build a lot of them to meet our reporting, analysis, and data collection requirements! So, we will need to take extra care that they are easy to maintain and ensure that other Cube View builders can jump in at any point to share the load. You don't want to tackle this task lightly. Thinking ahead – by locking down a repeatable process – will make any implementation simple and future maintenance more palatable.

So, let's start to pull apart the Cube View build. If you are very new to Cube View creation, this is a great place to begin. We will start slow and tackle the initial setup, talk through some easy and challenging Member Expansions, and then discuss performance considerations and Calculations.

Getting Started with Cube Views

This section may (or may not) be a review for you, but we want to take a quick beat and teach you how to create a simple Cube View. We first start by explaining Groups and Profiles, then we build a Cube View before discussing the importance of Cube View templates. Finally, we shall illustrate how to share rows and columns effectively. Employing the advice in this section will help any beginner build Cube Views quickly and efficiently.

Groups and Profiles

Groups and Profiles are not unique to Cube Views. You may also see them in Transformation Rules, Form templates, Confirmation Rules, and certification questions. Typically, we think of Groups and Profiles as an organization metric, very similar to a folder structure.

Figure 6.1 shows an example of the Cube Views page with a few Cube View Profiles (denoted with the icon with three dots) created. Here, one Cube View Profile is expanded to show that it holds one Cube View Group called Analysis (denoted by the icon with two dots).

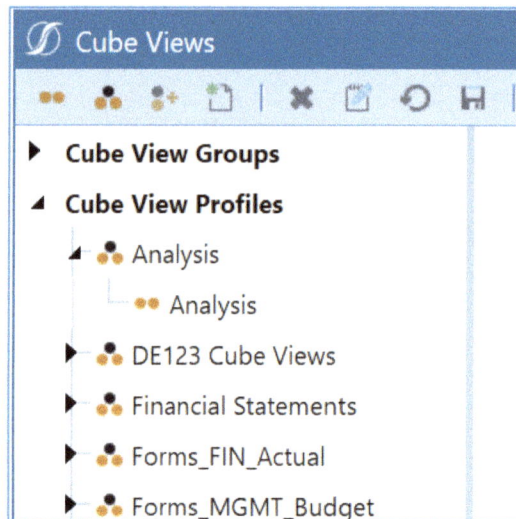

Figure 6.1

Okay, so you probably gathered that Cube View Groups are added to Cube View Profiles. And don't let that picture fool you – you can, of course, have multiple Groups within one Profile – but let's ask ourselves one important question: Why do we HAVE to do this?

The first reason is simple. You cannot start building a Cube View until a Cube View Group has been created. So, you are basically forced into it. In all seriousness, I cannot have any Cube Views floating out there on the page without being contained within a Cube View Group. So, my journey of creating Cube Views typically begins with me building a Cube View Group (first icon on the toolbar in Figure 6.2), after which I create a new Cube View underneath that Cube View Group (fourth icon on the toolbar in Figure 6.2).

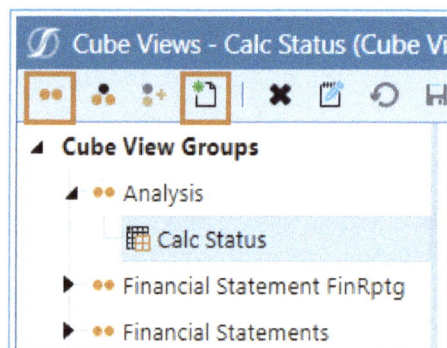

Figure 6.2

Okay, but why do we need Cube View Profiles? Cube View Profiles are what bring our Cube View Groups to Users. If a Cube View is not represented within a Cube View Profile, it cannot be run outside the Cube Views page. And most people will not have access to this page, meaning that you could have the most beautiful Cube Views out there, and no one would get to see them.

In general, Groups always need to be added to Profiles so that the artifacts you are building can be brought to the User. In training, I like to compare this to the little brother Randy from the movie *A Christmas Story*. There is a scene where Randy is all bundled up because his mom won't let him leave the house until he is properly equipped for the cold day. Think of your Cube View Groups as little Randy; his big hilarious coat is the Cube View Profile, and his mom is OneStream. Mom won't let him go outside until he is all packaged up. Hopefully, thinking of OneStream as your mom has warmed your soul a little bit.

At this point, the setup of your Cube View Groups and Profiles is almost complete except for one last item. Cube View Profiles (and Dashboard Profiles) have a special property called **Visibility** that controls *where* in the application the Cube Views can be incorporated. For example, this batch of Cube Views may be pulled into Excel to create a Cube View connection, added to a data adapter on the Dashboards page, incorporated into Form templates for data collection, or finally (gasps for air) added to the Cube Views pane in OnePlace to create an accessible Cube View Report repository. Requirements like these are controlled through the Visibility property. Choose any combination of Workflow, Excel, OnePlace, Forms, and Dashboards to meet your various needs.

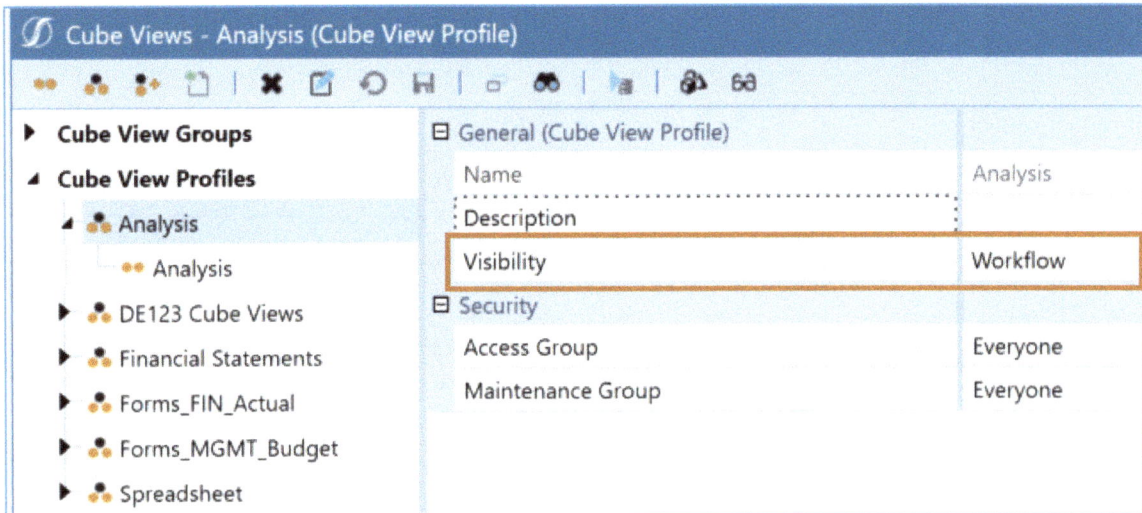

Figure 6.3

Now that we have explained the concept, how do we get organized with our Cube View Groups and Profiles? There is a section that goes into this quite heavily in the OneStream Foundation Handbook, so I will paraphrase it to ensure our messaging is consistent. One important quote I will pull from this section is, "The two main drivers of how you set these up are usage and security." What the author is trying to convey to you here is that you can use this Cube View Groups and Profiles structure to your advantage.

Let's look at Figure 6.4 to explain this.

Let's say I need to build Forms that will be used by Users in Group1, Group2, Group3, and Group4. There are some Forms that everyone will need, there are some that only Groups 2 and 3 will need, and there are some that only Groups 3 and 4 will need. Structuring my Cube View Groups and Profiles – as per Figure 6.4 – will allow me to create the most maintainable structure that still meets my requirements. Use these groups before you start duplicating Cube Views.

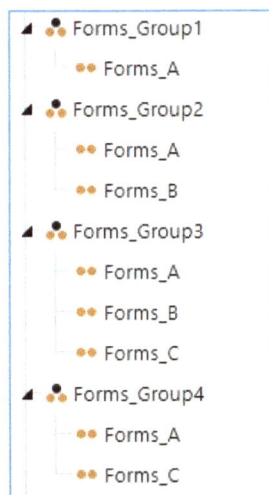

Figure 6.4

I have a few tips when creating Cube View Profiles that you can employ (or not, I can't chase you down). They have helped me stay organized over the years:

1. Have a consistent naming convention.

    a. A descriptive name that captures the purpose, process (Actuals/Budget), or business area of the Cube Views.

    b. A suffix or prefix that tells you if the Cube View Group is used for data entry or reporting.

    c. Apply a more informative Description than the long name.

2. Create a Cube View Group for row sharing.

3. Create a Cube View Group for column sharing.

4. Remember, your security settings are available on Cube View Groups and Cube View Profiles, if necessary.

    a. Access Group: Can the User see the Cube Views?

    b. Maintenance Group: Can the User edit the Cube Views?

    c. If the Access Group is secured, but the Maintenance Group is set to 'Everyone', that will undo your security. Ensure that both properties are secured!

Building your First Cube View

Now that we have explored Cube View Groups and Profiles, we shall look at how to build our first Cube View. So, what do we need to have a functioning Cube View?

1. A Cube View POV

2. Cube View rows

3. Cube View columns

To start our journey, let's first understand how data is queried within a Cube View. I should remind you there are two ways that you can edit a Cube View, through the Designer and the Advanced tab. Both tabs contain all of the same properties; it is up to you which one you prefer to work within. There is an order of operations when it comes to setting up your Cube View POV, rows, and columns, that you will want to remember:

1. Cube POV (this is controlled by the User)

2. Cube View POV

3. Cube View columns

4. Cube View rows

5. Cube View row overrides

6. Cube View column overrides

Now that we have our foundation, let's configure that Cube View POV, as shown in Figure 6.5. If you have not been exposed to this yet, these are all the Dimension Members we need to configure in the background of our Cube View. I will give you a bold recommendation: *set every Dimension Member*. We can talk about making them dynamic a little bit later. You want to do this to ensure that no data is pulled based on the User's Cube POV. Remember, we cannot control that!

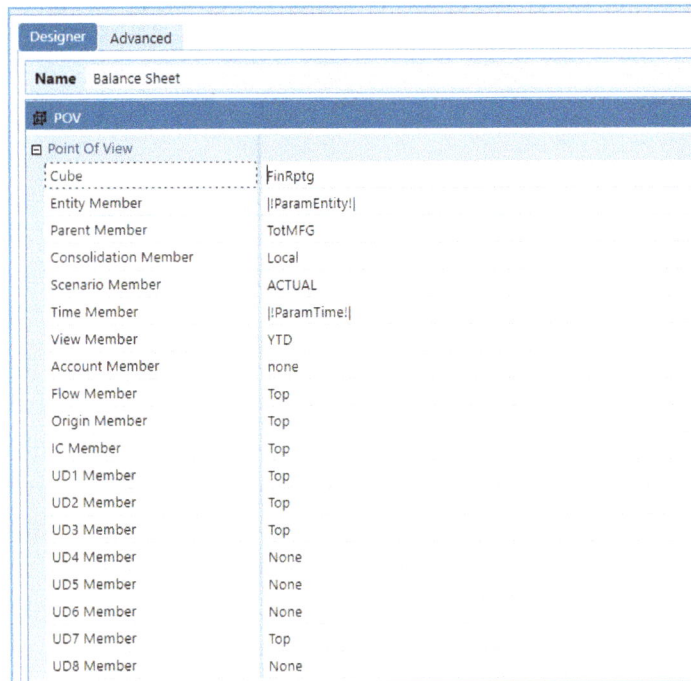

Figure 6.5

To get a functioning Cube View POV, you can do any of the following.

1. Set it manually by choosing a Dimension Member for every Dimension Type.

2. If you want to kick things up a notch, you can drag and drop your Cube POV into the Cube View POV.

3. Or… you can copy a Cube View POV from another Cube View, by right-clicking.

Next, we will build our rows and columns, which will override whatever is in our Cube View POV. Remember our order of operations; your rows will override your columns. These can be set up through the Rows and Columns pane shown in Figure 6.6. You can add rows or columns using the + and - sign icons and rearrange them using the arrows.

Next, we want to set the Dimension Type we wish to query. This is done using the highlighted pull-down menu. In this example, we chose Account. For rows, you can have up to four nested Dimension Types; for columns, you can have up to two.

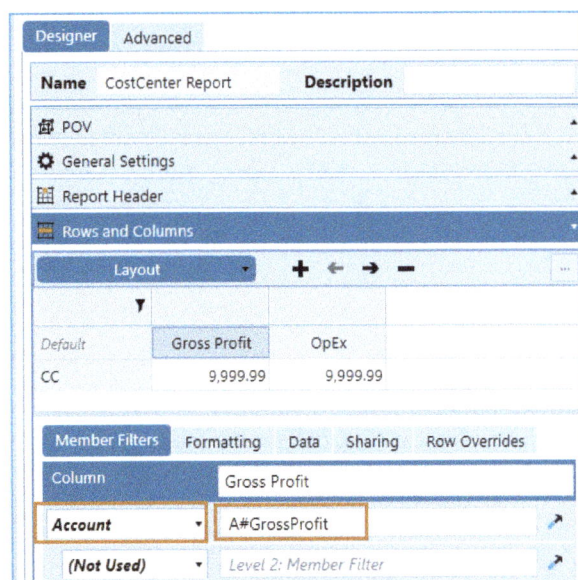

Figure 6.6

After this is set, we will want to create what is called a **Member Filter**. A Member Filter is used to query the Member or Members we need. The syntax of the Member Filter, at a minimum, must contain the combination of the **Dimension Token**, which denotes the Dimension Type and the Member name. Figure 6.7 shows an example of a simple Member Filter that would pull the Entity named TotSalesCC.

Figure 6.7

Figure 6.8 shows the Dimension Tokens for every Dimension Type in the OneStream application.

Dimension Tokens			
E#	Entity	I#	IC
P#	Parent	U1#	UD1
C#	Consolidation	U2#	UD2
S#	Scenario	U3#	UD3
T#	Time	U4#	UD4
V#	View	U5#	UD5
A#	Account	U6#	UD6
F#	Flow	U7#	UD7
O#	Origin	U8#	UD8

Figure 6.8

Now imagine this, you are a new Administrator or a User who was just given security access to the Cube View page. What is a Dimension Token? What does UD stand for? Is Flow a Dimension or a hot new dance move? Thankfully, the Member Filter Builder will make this syntax simple and digestible so that any newbie can craft their Cube View.

You can access the Member Filter Builder within any row or column through the hammer icon (you can see this in Figure 6.6, bottom right). You will learn that this tool is available across many places within the OneStream application. Figure 6.9 displays the Member Filter Builder.

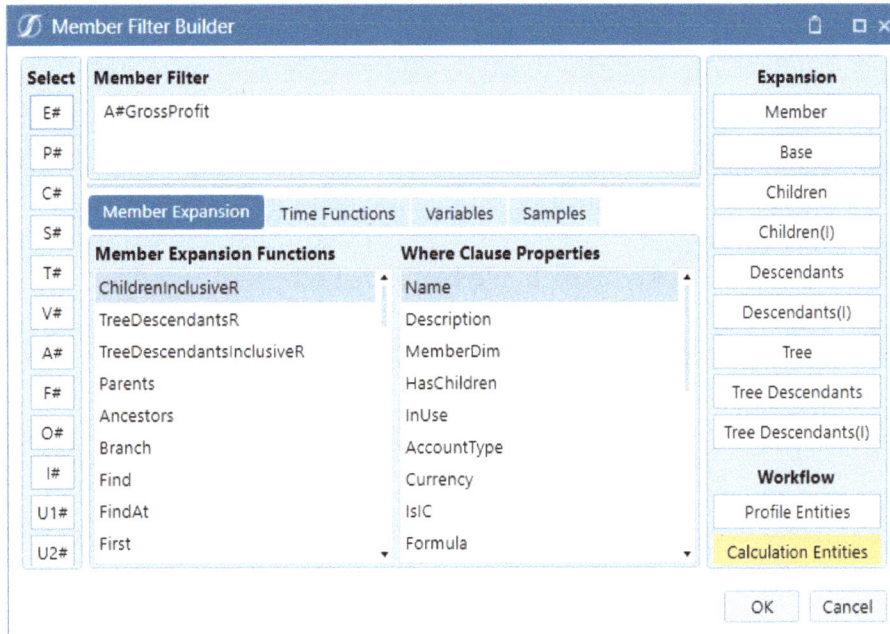

Figure 6.9

The Member Filter Builder is an extremely handy tool and a fan favorite. It is full of tool tips and samples that will make querying data in OneStream a breeze.

If we needed help writing the Member Filter A#GrossProfit (shown in Figure 6.9), we would start on the left-hand side of our Member Filter Builder and choose our Dimension Token A#. This would open a searchable pop-up window that shows the Account Dimensions created in the Dimension Library. This is great if I am new to OneStream, or if I am new to the application and have no idea what any of the Members are called.

We will end this section by just querying one Member at a time and kick things up a notch a little bit later. All these Components will get you a functioning Cube View.

Starting with a Cube View Template

We have created a simple Cube View, but as we go through our Cube View construction, we will have many more things to create:

1. Consistent Cube View POVs

2. Parameters and Substitution Variables

3. Fine-tuned formatting

4. Specific settings

5. Headers and Footers

However, before we dive in with any of those concepts, we will want to foster consistency through Cube View templates. A Cube View template is actually just one lone Cube View, but it should contain all the common configuration(s) across a larger population of Cube Views.

If you set up a Cube View template with common Cube View POV, settings, and formatting, then – when you are ready to create a new Cube View – you can make copies from this template instead of starting from scratch. If you are a Consultant, sit down with your client and agree on consistent formatting and construction so you can create a sustainable Cube View template.

Sharing Rows and Columns

Once we have an agreed upon our Cube View template (or templates), we can explore other ways to expedite our build. One common tactic is to share rows and columns. This is where creating a Report repository comes in handy. We typically see, in design sessions, that there is a laundry list of Reports that need to be created. If many of these are Cube Views, you are likely itching for options to kick off your build the right way. This is a great time to start identifying common rows and columns so they can be shared. Sharing rows and columns will reduce the amount of time you spend creating Cube Views as well as reduce future maintenance.

When you start your Cube View build, we typically recommend creating a Cube View Group that represents your rows, and one that represents your columns. You will also likely keep your Cube View template in one of these Groups. You may want to give the Cube Views themselves a naming convention that begins with a prefix and then provides an easy-to-decipher name. An example of what we usually see is shown in Figure 6.10.

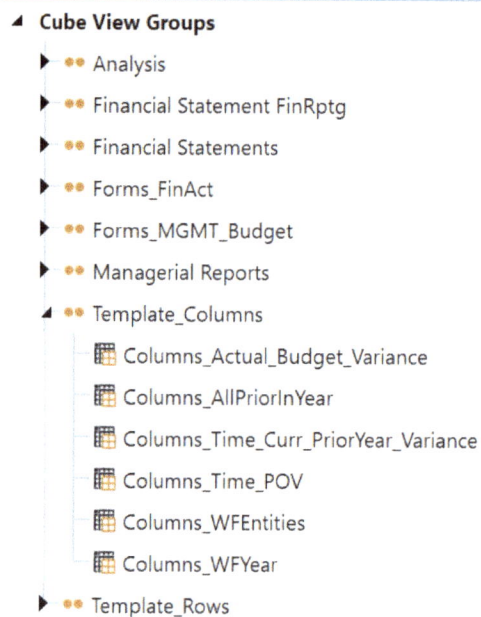

Figure 6.10

This way, you don't have to repeatedly recreate the same Cube View rows or columns. You can add up to two Cube Views to the row and column sharing section.

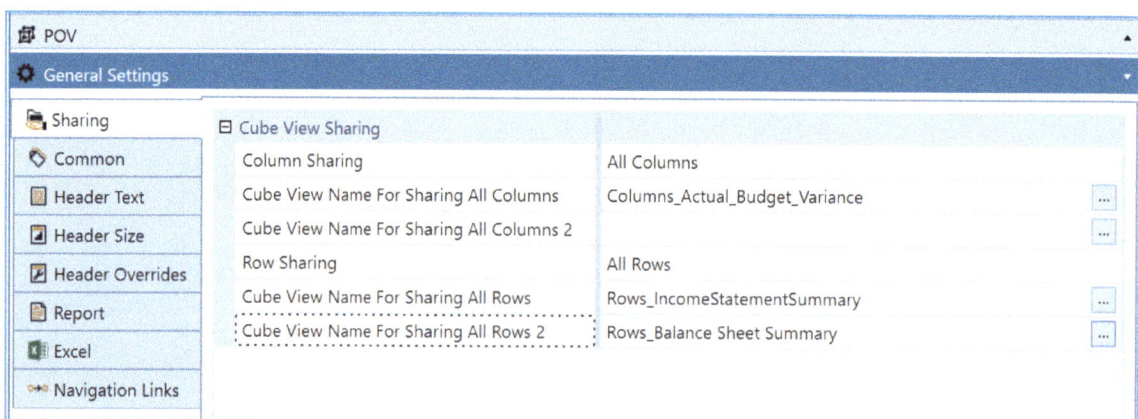

Figure 6.11

Moving on, how will maintenance work in the future? What if we need to update one of the rows/columns we are sharing? The update will affect the rows and/or columns for every Cube View referencing it. Typically, we want it to behave this way because that is what reduces our maintenance. However, what if we have a situation where that is not the case? How will we know (easily) what is impacted by our changes?

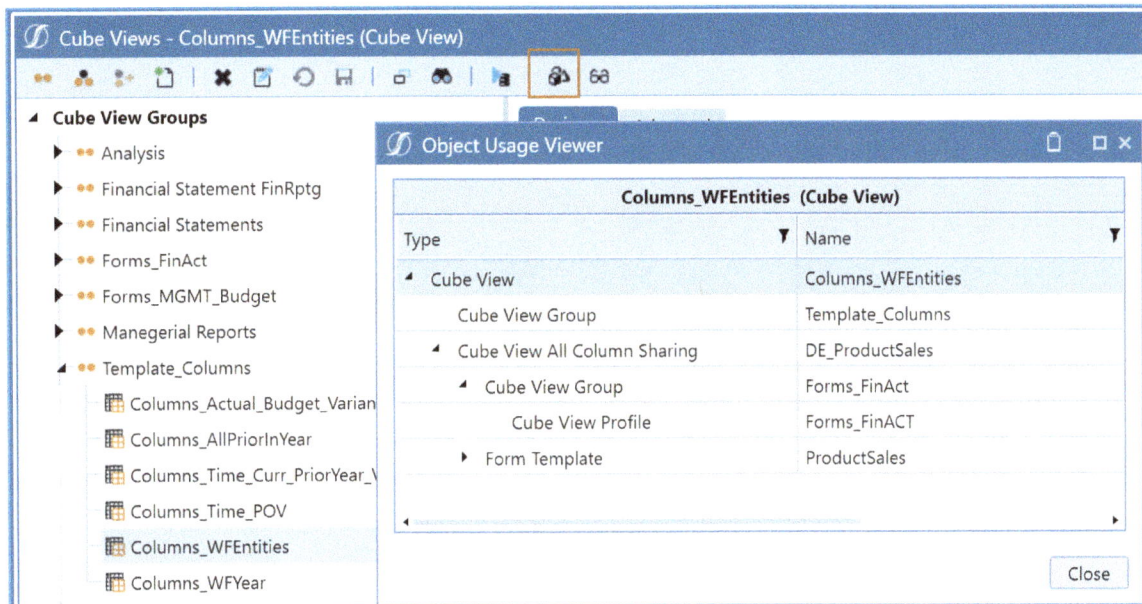

Figure 6.12

Figure 6.12 shows you a useful tool you can use to double-check if any artifacts are referencing the selected item. The highlighted icon is the **Object Usage Viewer**, and this is present on other pages in the application. In the image, we can see that this Cube View is being referenced for column sharing in `DE_ProductSales`, and that it has been added to the Form Template `ProductSales`.

In this section, we discussed how to start our Cube View build the right way. Let's summarize with some of the advice we learned along the way:

1. Make a Report repository of everything you need to create.

2. Establish a Cube View template.

3. Organize and effectively name your Cube View Groups and Profiles.

4. Share rows and columns effectively.

We are going to layer in more and more complexities as this chapter progresses. By the end of this, you should be able to create a versatile, functioning Cube View that you can doll up with formatting.

Member Expansions

If you are relatively new to Cube Views, the previous section hopefully got your feet wet with building something simple. If you are not new, maybe you got to hear a fresh take on something you have done a million times.

Now, we are ready to expand (pun intended) our Cube Views through Member Expansions. Member Expansions are something extremely important to our Cube View building experience because it gives us the opportunity to align with the hierarchy of our Dimensions. Expansions help expedite your Cube View build and reduce your future maintenance. If you spend a lot of time picking individual Members and manually adding many rows and columns, you are probably doing something wrong. Let's work smarter, not harder!

Using Simple Member Expansions

If you are new to Member Expansions, Figure 6.13 shows the required syntax. This expansion is taking the Member TotSalesCC from the Entity Dimension and providing you with the Children of this Member.

E#TotSalesCC.Children

Dimension Token · Member Name · Expansion

Figure 6.13

Let's bring up our Member Filter Builder once again and see how this can help us out. On the right side of Figure 6.14, you will notice that we have our common expansions. Check out the Design and Reference Guide for handy tool tips here. I would say the best way to learn them is to get in there and play around a little bit. I personally practice with the Time Dimension because it is (almost) always the same in every application.

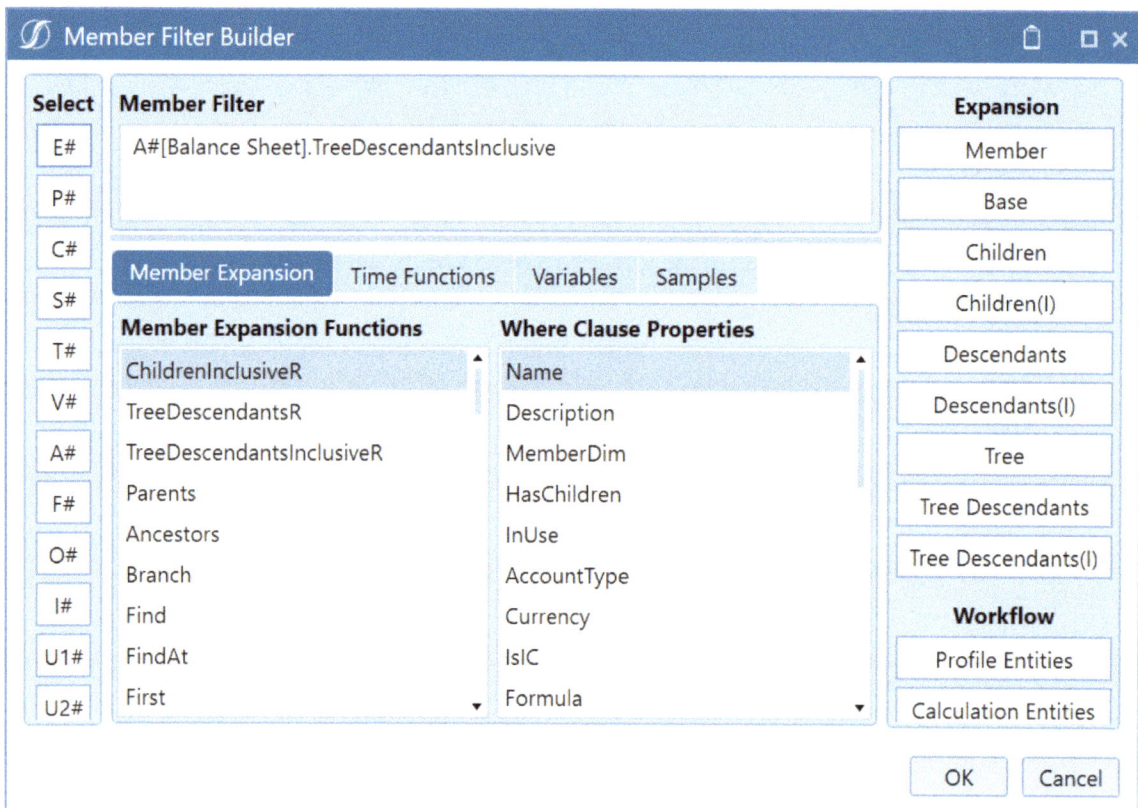

Figure 6.14

Simple Member Expansions are something that many people learn in their OneStream careers. They ensure that you are creating a Cube View that is tied to the Dimension Library. Let's say I work for a company that sells food, and this was built in my UD1 Dimension. If I wanted to pull sales per fruit, I wouldn't want to create a Member Filter that is U1#Apples, U1#Bananas, U1#Cherries, etc. I would want something dynamic like U1#Fruit.base. This way, if I expand my business to add Coconuts one day, it will be added to my Report without any Cube View intervention required.

As we continue, we are going to get into some heavier expansions. I am a proponent of creating the most dynamic Cube Views possible, but you may prefer to keep things simple. You may have other people join the Cube View building squad, and expansions like Base, Children, and Descendants, are common enough terms for people to follow.

Advanced Member Expansions

Sometimes a simple Member Expansion might not cut it. Do not give up and start cherry-picking individual Members, though. We may have to start getting creative and build something more robust. Don't worry; the Member Filter Builder is still by your side, with many options for you to try. Honestly, complex expansions are where things start to get a little fun in Cube View building; this is where the puzzle lovers shine!

So, let's start with an easier one to get the party started: **reverse expansions**. In the center of your Member Filter Builder (Figure 6.15), we can see that three expansions end with the letter R. These expansions are not for pirates; the R stands for 'Reverse' and behaves as you would expect. They reverse the order of the structure to display Parent-level Members *underneath* their Children. There are many OneStream clients who want to see their Reports displayed this way.

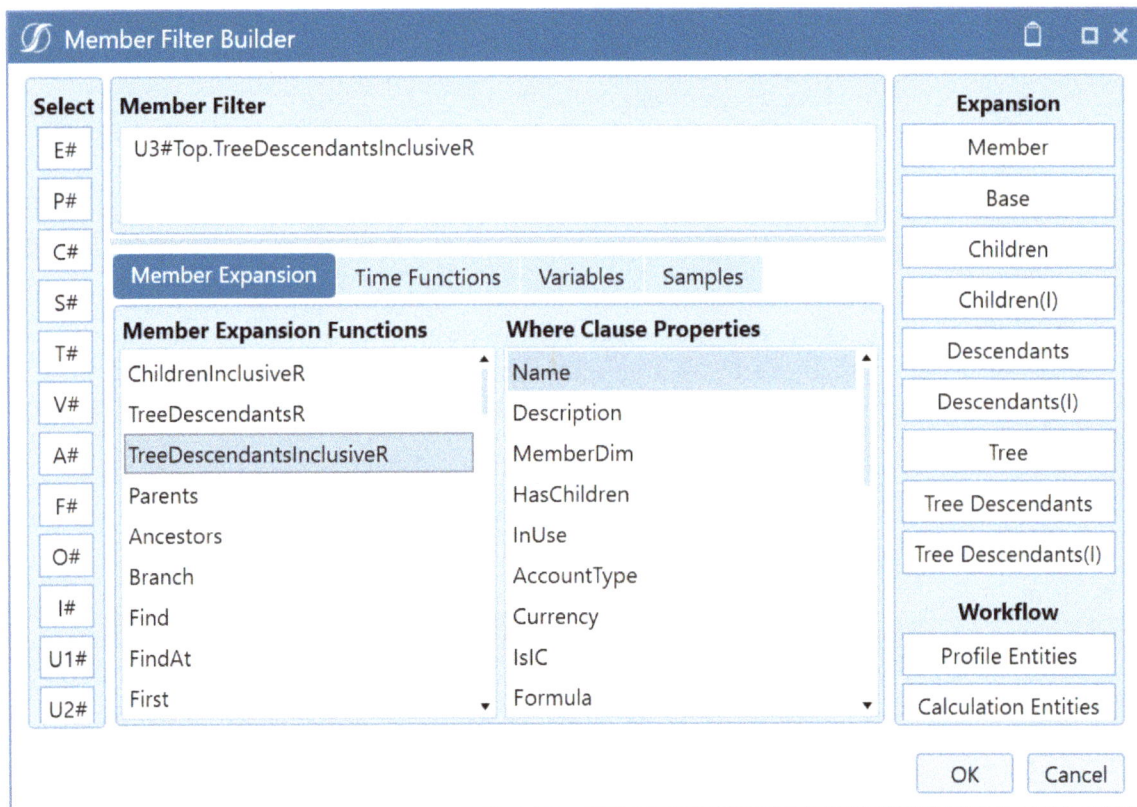

Figure 6.15

That one was easy! What else can we try? Let's move from the Member Expansions tab in the Member Filter Builder to broaden your horizons on what you can really do here. Figure 6.16 displays the Samples tab in the Member Filter Builder, and the screenshot shows you not only that there is a list of the same Member Expansions here, but the extremely handy tool tip that explains what each of them does. Simply double-click on the expression, and it will place the syntax in the tool tip into your Member Filter.

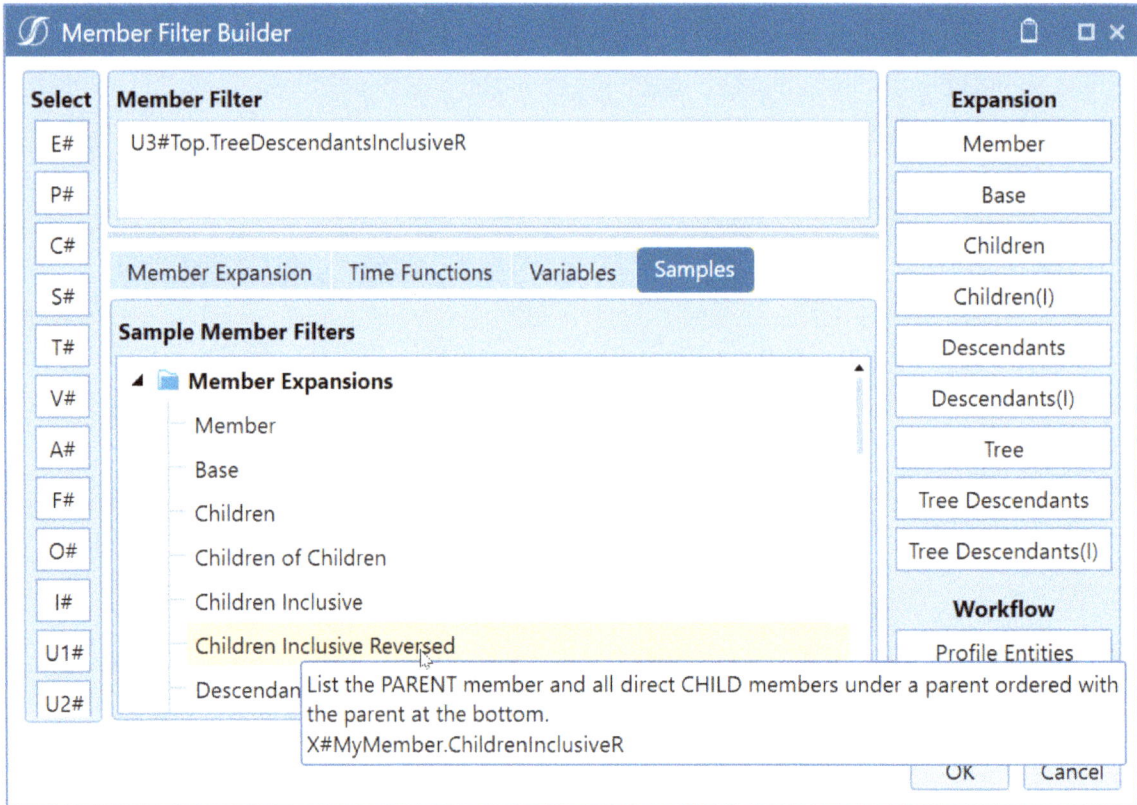

Figure 6.16

I won't go through each of them (and they can be found in the documentation), but I want you to open your mind to the possibility of trying something a little more advanced to ensure that you are thinking dynamically. Let's say we have a situation where we need to create a Report on Sales Region, and that is represented in our UD2 structure. Figure 6.17 illustrates the hierarchy we can refer to.

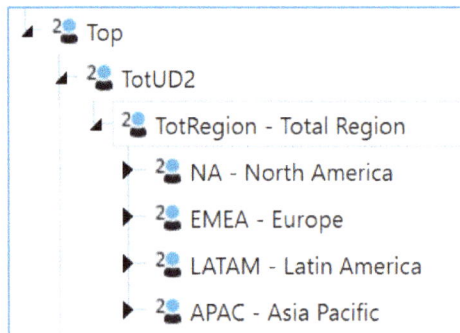

Figure 6.17

The reporting requirement is simple, we want to pull the Children under `TotRegion`, but we want to see Base Members under `NA` and the Children under `EMEA`. This is what I would do to meet this requirement:

```
U2#TotRegion.children.Branch(Find(NA).base, Find(EMEA).children)
```

The `Branch` expansion will allow us to do a combination of expansions and break out the levels in the hierarchy we need. So, it pulls the Children under `TotRegion` – which would be NA, EMEA, LATAM, and APAC – but when it locates the Member NA, it provides the Base Members, and when it finds the Member EMEA, it returns the Children.

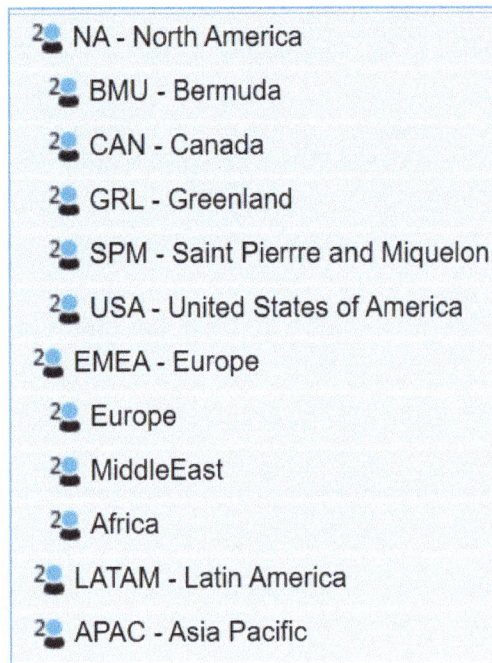

Figure 6.18

Moving on, Extensibility is an important Dimension design tactic that is featured in many OneStream applications. Typically, it incorporates multiple Cubes linked together (if you read the OneStream Design Handbook, our documentation, or have taken some of the Navigator course, you may know this concept as a **Super Cube**). Extensibility raises some questions when it comes to reporting, but it ends up being quite intuitive, and for the most part – through simple expansions and suppression – you can see the information you need. However, if this is ever *not* the case, the `.options` expansion may be able to help.

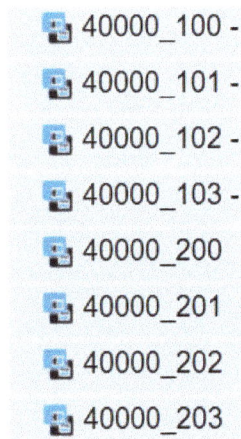

Figure 6.19

Let's say my Net Sales Account has the Base Members shown in Figure 6.19. This list would populate when I pull `A#NetSales.base` for my top-level Cube.

Now, the Members `40000_100` to `40000_103` belong to Child Cube 1, and the Members `40000_200` to `40000_203` belong to Child Cube 2. If you query an Entity from Child Cube 1, the cells for Members `40000_200` to `40000_203` will be invalid and you can, therefore, suppress them out (we cover suppression later in this chapter). If you query an Entity from Child Cube 2, the cells for Members `40000_100` to `40000_103` will be invalid and you can, therefore, suppress them out. This is usually how you want this to behave because Extensibility is very smart!

However, what if you didn't want things to work that way? Typically, I wouldn't recommend this, but every use case is different, so far be it from me to judge! We have had situations where someone says, "I only want to see the Base Accounts for Child Cube 2" regardless of the Entity chosen. What do we do? This is where the `.options` expansion comes in handy. I would write something like this:

```
A#40000.base.options(Cube = ChildCube2)
```

No matter what Entity I pull, I will only see the `40000_200` to `40000_203` Members, depending on any suppression settings I may have. Hopefully, looking at these examples opened your eyes to the possibilities of expansions. I would still recommend keeping things as simple as possible, but you have a lot of options, and choosing a laundry list of individual Members should be far out of your mind.

Where Clauses

We can't talk about flexibility without looking at `Where` clause Expressions. Where clauses can tack onto your Member Expansions to provide additional logic in a pinch. Your trusty Member Filter Builder is by your side with your Samples tab, as shown in Figure 6.20.

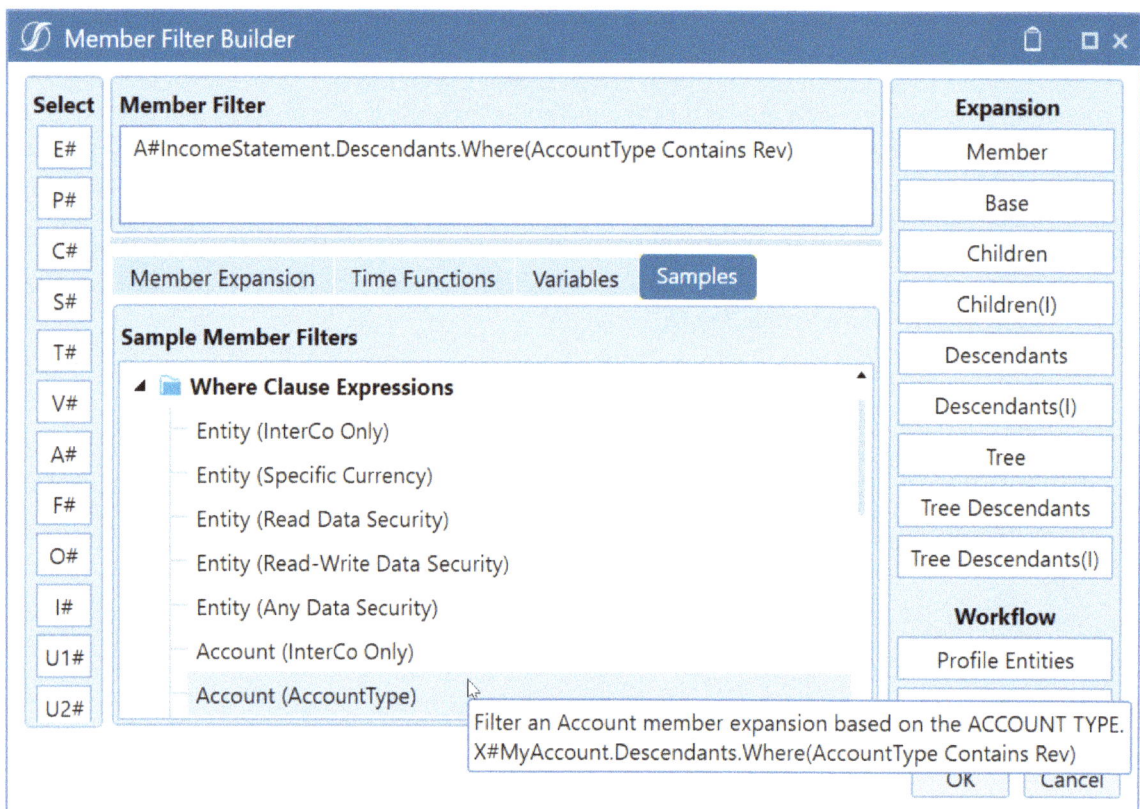

Figure 6.20

This is a common example I see, where we pull the entire Income Statement but only filter the Revenue Accounts. This looks towards the Account Type properties, set on the Dimension Library, but there are many more options. We can use specific expansions for Entity and Account properties as well as a whole slew of generic properties that can be applied to all Dimensions. We could use a `Where` clause to return only Entities with a local currency of USD, or Accounts that are marked as `IsIC` (Intercompany). More generic options, meanwhile, allow us to pull Members under any Dimension where the description contains the word "clubs" or something like that. My personal favorite is to filter based on Dimension Member text properties. Here, we have the luxury to span

Dimensions, grab specific properties, and employ logic like `contains` / `startswith` / `doesnotcontain`, or combine multiple Expressions using `and` / `or`.

Performance Considerations

We have looked at some of the basics for getting our Cube Views functioning. We learned that we should think of our dimensionality when building Cube Views, whether that means coming up with some creative expansions, parameterization, suppression options, or turning to dimensionality and adjusting hierarchies if necessary.

Before we move into the formatting chapter, we need to address one further thing… a great Cube View experience is not only something that is easy to read but also something that runs quickly. Typically, at OneStream, we use the benchmark of 10 seconds for a Cube View to render. Of course, there are always exceptions to the rule, but any long-running Cube Views may require a bit of investigation.

When it comes to performance considerations, people often chase the fastest Calculation, Consolidation, or Import, but slow reporting performance is something that can negatively impact your User Experience. So, are Reporting and Consolidation performance related? They can be, but there are other factors that impact reporting performance. Are there things we can do in our Cube View Design to improve this? You bet!

Recapping the Data Unit

I am going to step away from reporting for just a moment to give you a little back story on the Data Unit. I promise this all ties together and will hopefully help you to understand that your Dimensions, Data, and Calculations are all linked to your Reports.

If your experience of working with OneStream has been a bit more technical, you have probably heard of application design tactics like:

1. Watch the size of your Dimensions.

2. Use Extensibility.

3. Explore Analytic Blend.

4. Write Calculations thinking of the Data Unit Calculation Sequence (DUCS).

5. Consider Aggregation instead of Consolidation (if applicable).

6. Break up or automate your Consolidation/Calculation.

7. Partition when importing large amounts of data.

8. Explore Direct Load.

9. Explore Hybrid Scenarios.

All these items have evolved as we get smarter when working within OneStream and as the product evolves to cater for more use cases and audiences. These features and design tactics have formed over the years to address a common goal: to provide a variety of Users with the best application performance and experience possible. They do so by focusing on the Data Unit, which is core to OneStream's functionality and design.

If you are not familiar with the concept of the Data Unit, I would recommend diving into the Designing and Application Course on Navigator (our online learning portal) or the OneStream Foundation Handbook. There is a lot of great information on how it operates, and what we need to do to ensure it is protected to ensure a performant application.

If you are new to the OneStream community, this may sound a bit technical; don't worry, I will give you a brief synopsis.

There are three levels to the OneStream Data Unit: Level 1 is the Cube Data Unit, Level 2 is the Workflow Data Unit, and Level 3 is the Workflow Channel Data Unit. Most of the time, when people say "Data Unit" they are referring to the Level 1 Data Unit, but really all three levels make up one overarching concept.

The Level 1 Data Unit is the largest unit of work that is responsible for how data is cleared, loaded, copied, calculated, translated, and consolidated. So, the unit of work that I am referring to here is cultivated through your Level 1 Data Unit Dimensions: Cube, Entity, Parent, Consolidation, Scenario, and Time. When you define a Member from each of those Dimensions, you are querying a specific Data Unit.

So, what are the *other* Dimensions called? I have heard them referred to as the Account Type or Account-Level Dimensions: Flow, Account, Origin, UD1-8. The only Dimension you won't find in either is the View Dimension.

And if you were curious, the Level 2 Data Unit (aka the Workflow Data Unit) adds in the Account Dimension, and the Level 3 Workflow Data Unit (aka the Workflow Channel Data Unit) adds in a UD Dimension of your choosing. These two levels of the Data Unit are how data is cleared, loaded, and locked.

When we speak of the Level 1 Data Unit, we typically try to protect it as much as possible with our Dimension and Cube design. I think of the Account Type Dimensions as the amount of work that my Data Unit Dimensions must go through. Often, when we consolidate or calculate, we are trying to protect our Data Unit from running too many times for too many Account Type Dimensions.

What does this have to do with our innocent Cube Views? Well, just like when you run a Calculation, a cell query in a Cube View could lead to querying many more records than you initially think.

Let's say I am querying one Base-level Entity, for one month (in a monthly application), at local currency, for the Actual Scenario Member. There is an associated number for records behind this cell that is driving our final value. So, one cell at a low-level Data Unit can have many records behind it. Imagine what happens when we start pulling multiple Data Units or ones with Parent Entities! There is a lot more being queried than you think.

Building a larger Cube View, in general, may slow performance, and if this Report pulls a lot of records, this will make it even slower. In turn, it is possible to have a Cube View that isn't that large but still renders slowly. What could be causing this? As we explained, if this Cube View is pulling a lot of Parent Members, it could retrieve *more* records than you think, but there are a few other things that could also be happening. We will go into these in the next few sections.

Dynamically Calculated Data

If you are an avid Financial Calculation writer, you may have encountered the concept of Dynamic Calculations. These tend to be a fan favorite because they can be simple to write, and they run at no cost to your Consolidation times. A dynamically calculated Member is written within the Dimension Library within the Account, Flow, or any of the UD Dimensions. You can commonly see these representing various Ratio Accounts or any commonly calculated reporting variances (usually represented in UD8). But people come up with a variety of reasons to work these into their designs.

How do they work? As I mentioned, they do not run upon Calculation, meaning they will not impact your Consolidation times (although they will impact your Report rendering times). These Calculations run when they are queried; they are commonly built for Reports and center on a concept commonly referred to as 'calc-on-the-fly'.

Now, we mentioned dynamically calculated Members, but what about Calculations directly in your Cube View? If you don't know what I am referring to, there are plenty of examples available to you on how to write these in your Samples tab in the Member Filter Builder, shown in Figure 6.21. You can create your own calculated rows and columns using GetDataCell Expressions and Column/Row Expressions.

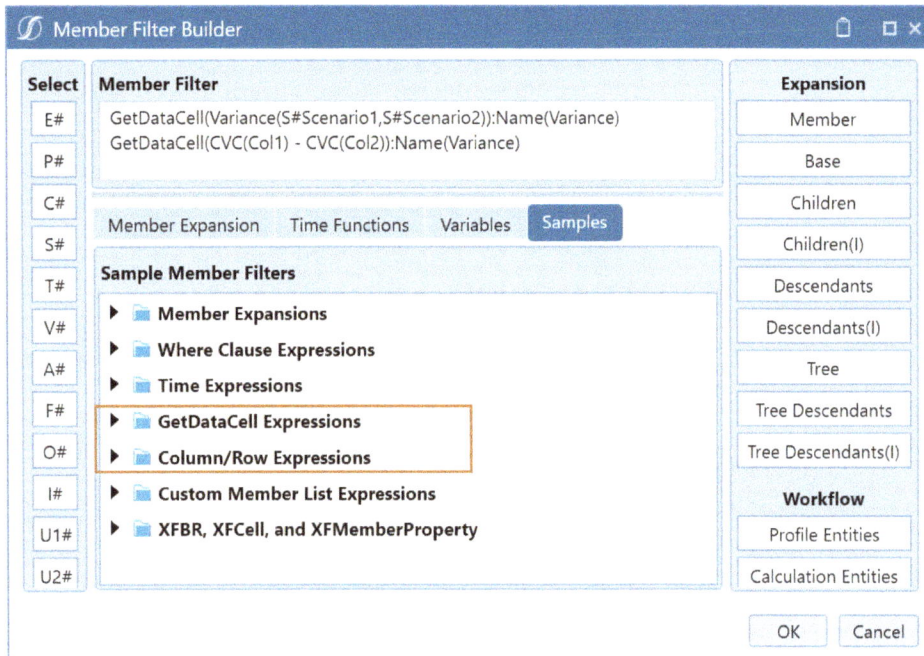

Figure 6.21

Dynamically Calculated Members, GetDataCell Expressions, and Column/Row Expressions function similarly. That is because they all use a `GetDataCell` to essentially query the results you need. Really, the choice between each of them comes down to your preference and what will facilitate the best maintenance experience going forward.

When it comes to maintenance, usually keeping your dynamic Calculations in Members is the most frugal. If you have similar Calculations across many Reports, they can be easily accessed and maintained in a repository. Therefore, many people opt to use UD8 as a Dimension entirely dedicated to reporting Calculations.

This will also allow you to drill down on any calculated data point through the **Calculation for Drill Down** property as well.

But you may choose to write your Calculations directly on the Cube View if you only have a few and they are unique. This may also be an option if you don't have access to build calculated Members in your Dimension Library, or if you are a fan of Column/Row Expressions. Column/Row Expressions allow you to write Calculations simply if you would like to just say *Column1 + Column2*, instead of hunting down the Member name. Many people like them because of their friendly syntax.

Back to performance. Does this mean we should avoid dynamically calculated data? Of course not! You likely won't see a significant impact on your reporting performance with just a calculated row or column here and there, and honestly, these are commonly required and a great alternative to storing every Calculation. Just be aware of how they work. I will say, though, that if you have an extremely large Cube View, pulling a lot of Data Units and records, and then you pop in a raft of dynamically calculated data, your performance will suffer.

Aggregated Data

You may not realize this, but even if you stripped your Cube View of all Dynamic Calculations, you will not eliminate all dynamically rendered data. One thing that tends to slow Cube View performance is the amount of aggregated data. (In this case, I am not referring to the aggregated Consolidation Dimension, that is a different concept.)

What other data gets queried dynamically? All Parent Members in any Dimension, besides Entity and Scenario, are dynamically rendered. Let's say we are looking at a Form, and we are querying `A#NetSales` and all the Members under it. If we key in data to a Base Member and save it, we will immediately notice my `NetSales` Member's data change. That's because this Member is dynamically aggregated. All Parent Members in Account, Flow, Intercompany, Origin, and UD1-8 operate this way.

Why is this a problem? Because this is a piece of work that our Data Unit must do. So, if I am querying a Report that pulls all top-level data across all these Dimensions, my poor Cube View is aggregating all that data at run-time. That is how a Cube View – which may not look too large – starts to run slowly. You could be aggregating a lot of high-level Members and spanning many Data Units, which means the amount of work and number of records is far greater than you think.

Other Members that naturally run dynamically are the majority of your View Dimension (only YTD is stored; if you key into Periodic, this is still true), and – depending on your application setup – some of the Members in your Consolidation Dimension (you can set up your Cube to store the Share Member).

Any of these items mean that any performance gains realized upon Calculation or Consolidation are passed to your Cube View. If a Cube View Report with this situation is starting to slow, you may explore chopping up the Report, utilizing the share data bindings within Hybrid Scenarios, or shipping your Cube View to Users via email through the Parcel Service, which – if you are unfamiliar – is a Report distribution tool that can be downloaded and deployed from the MarketPlace.

Suppression

Another concept that relates to our Data Unit, and which impacts Cube View building, is **sparsity**. We see sparsity when the Data Unit has sparsely populated data intersections across the Account Type Dimensions (Account, Intercompany, Flow, and User-Defined). This is an important issue we must watch out for when designing our Dimensions and Cube Views. Why are we so worried about this in reporting? The absence of data records can impact the legibility and User Experience of the Report.

This, of course, should be mitigated as much as possible using Extensibility, Cube Design, and Analytic Blend, but there may be pieces of it that are unavoidable. Suppression is applied to Cube Views to improve the overall User Experience. It will not only provide the obvious impact of pulling out unnecessary rows that have no data but can also greatly improve your Cube View performance.

Row and Column Suppression

Let's start with row and column suppression since this is typically the easiest to get our heads around. Think of it this way: suppression is the act of removing cells in a Cube View based on certain criteria. We may do this to remove any information that is irrelevant to the User and improve their experience when viewing/analyzing the Report. The criteria commonly revolve around whether the row or column is invalid, zero, contains no data, or is under a certain threshold.

I'll give you a quick run-through. Suppression is applied on the individual rows and columns of the Cube View. Commonly, people will suppress invalid rows or even columns and, usually, these are invalid intersections due to Members not being present in a queried Cube, or constraints being violated. Applying invalid suppression is a great tactic to improve the performance and readability of your Reports or even Forms, especially with a multi-faceted User population.

Typically, we see invalid intersections in Vertical Extensibility (extending per Entity Dimension). This happens when certain Members prove invalid for certain Entity Members. That's a good thing! This concept is addressed heavily in the OneStream Foundation Handbook, but what you need to retain here is simple: invalid Members are usually created due to your Dimension design and there is a reason why they are there.

We want to display information that is only relevant to certain Users and, therefore, may not be important to others and should be suppressed out. This is the beauty of Extensibility. For example, we can extend our Income Statement so certain Members are relevant with certain Entities and – when it comes time to create the Report – we can simply pull the entire Income Statement, allow our Users to choose their Entity (or perhaps security controls what they can choose), and the same Report will show each User only what they need to see if I have suppressed my invalid Members.

No data and zero suppression tend to be easily confused. No data means that no data record is present behind the cell; 0 is, in fact, a record. We typically recommend that people try to limit 0s as much as possible because they are data points and will impact Report and Consolidation performance. Zeros do happen, but you may want to investigate why you have them. It could be due to loading zeros, or perhaps a bad rule that is writing 0 or near-0 data into your Cube. If so, I would recommend tightening this up.

If any of this advice just scared you, there is a little trick you can do in your Cube Views. Let's say you have some heavy number formatting, and you are not sure if that 0 you are looking at is really a zero, or if it is no data, or you are scaling to the millions and it is a real number. You can right-click on any cell in your Cube View and View the Cell Status to see the Cell Amount and the Storage Type.

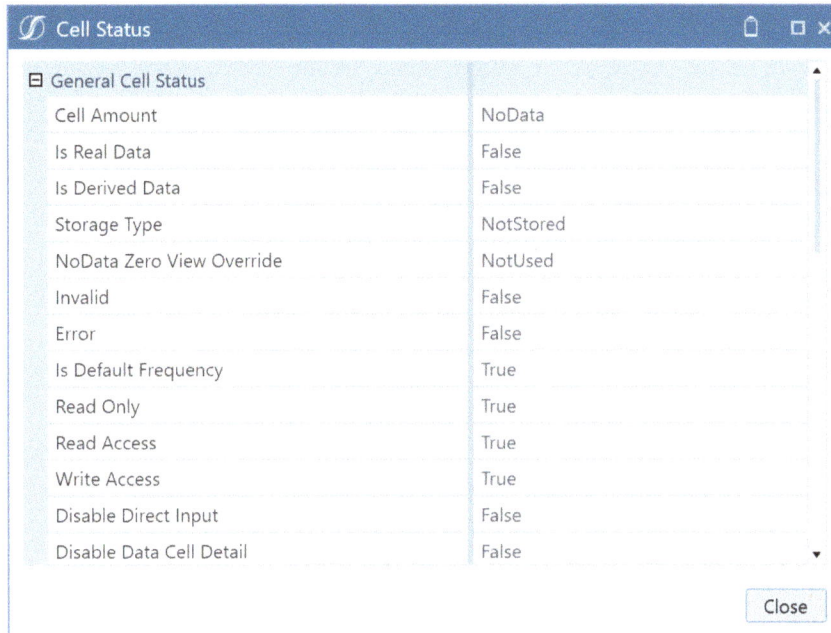

Cell Status	
General Cell Status	
Cell Amount	NoData
Is Real Data	False
Is Derived Data	False
Storage Type	NotStored
NoData Zero View Override	NotUsed
Invalid	False
Error	False
Is Default Frequency	True
Read Only	True
Read Access	True
Write Access	True
Disable Direct Input	False
Disable Data Cell Detail	False

Figure 6.22

The other thing that might have piqued your interest is my comment on having too many 0s. How can we easily see that within our Cube View? You are in luck, for if you right-click on a given cell once again, you can also pull the Data Unit Statistics.

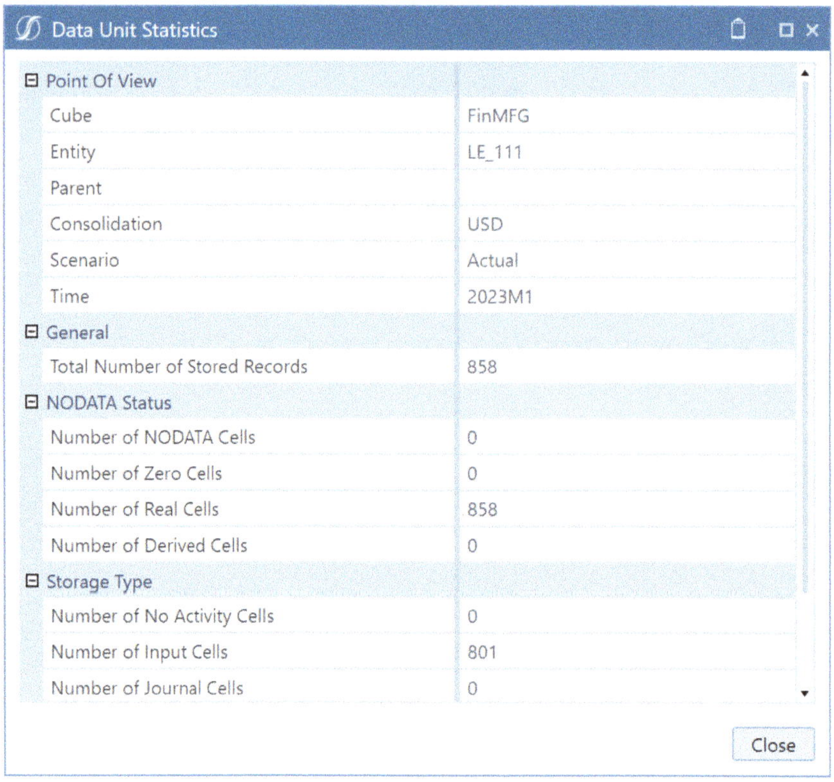

Figure 6.23

This window is giving us a lot of great information. Here I can see the Data Unit I am querying in this cell, plus the total number of records within this Data Unit. That means – when my Cube View is pulling this one cell of information – it is pulling all that information and applying any dynamic Calculations or Aggregations. That little cell is doing a lot of work!

If we keep looking at the properties, we can see the number of Zero Cells we have within this given Data Unit. Our typical recommendation is that fewer than 10% of your cells should be zero. This could be a signal to check some other areas in your application, but when we are speaking about Cube Views, this may be something we want to suppress out by applying zero and/or no data row/column suppression.

With our zero suppression, we also have the option to apply a **Zero Suppression Threshold**. This is commonly done when you are using scaling on a Cube View. To apply this, we can key in our desired threshold in the Zero Suppression Threshold property (this is an absolute value). We also need to set our Suppress Zero Rows/Column to True for this to take effect.

There are two more properties that are meant to provide flexibility with these suppression settings by Parent Members and columns. The **Use Suppression Settings** on a Parent row/column is a somewhat misunderstood property and causes some head-scratching in the Report building community. It's very easy and handy, though. This property relates to the zero, no data, and invalid settings and decides if these settings should be applied to the Parent Members in the Member Filter for this row or column.

I will give you an example. Let's say we are building an Income Statement Report pulling `A#NetSales.ChildrenInclusive` in the rows. Usually, if we have suppression turned on, we will want `NetSales` and all its Children to heed the settings applied. However, maybe we want the Parent Member to show up even if it had no data. It depends on the situation but, sometimes, this can really help with readability. Set this property to False, and the `NetSales` Parent Member would still show up.

The last property we will address is called **Use to Determine Row Suppression**. This one is only available on columns and allows you to better define how to apply row suppression. If you have a Cube View with multiple columns, you may not want the data in all these columns to be considered for suppression. You can 'turn off' certain columns – from being considered – by setting this property to False.

Allowing Users to Modify Suppression

Sometimes, we tick and tie every suppression setting, but this does not provide enough flexibility for our Users. Maybe we have a Cube View (usually added to a Dashboard) that is used for data entry for Planning and the Form is pre-seeded with data. Suppression is commonly applied to the Form to ensure better readability and usability. However, Users need to enter data for something that currently doesn't have any, and suppression is eliminating this row! What do we do? Turn suppression off? Inform your Users that they can search based on Member names and descriptions within the rows of any Cube View? That would work, but we have a few more options that may provide a better experience.

Our first option takes us back to the General Settings of the Cube View under the Common items. The Can Modify Suppression property can be set to True and allows Users to choose whether rows are suppressed from the Data Explorer Grid. This property is shown in Figure 6.24.

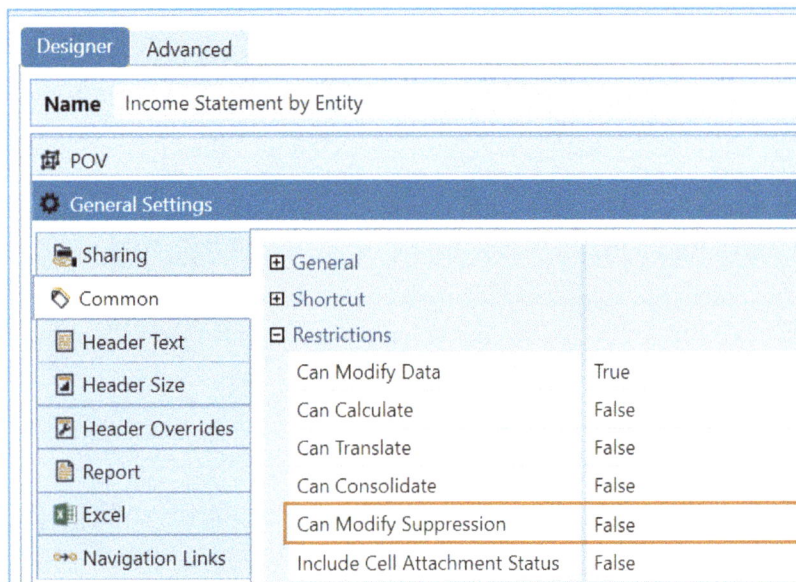

Figure 6.24

Users turn on and off their suppression settings in the Data Explorer Grid of the Cube View, through the icon displayed in Figure 6.25.

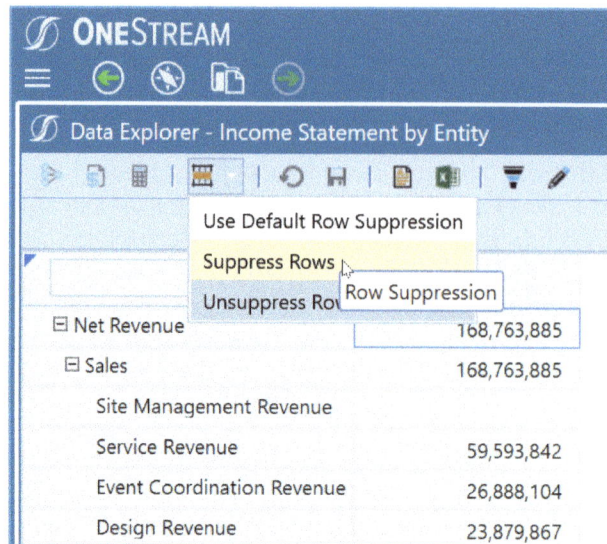

Figure 6.25

The next option is a bit more intricate, but great if we want to apply a bit more tact to our Cube View than simply turning all the suppression on or off. The **Allow Insert Suppressed Member** setting is available on the individual rows of the Cube View and allows Users to insert specific Dimension Members based on the settings defined. Choose this if you want to allow this property for all expansions of the row, just the first one (choose innermost for this one), or just the nested ones (expansions 2-4 on the rows).

This is particularly useful in Planning use cases, specifically with data entry. For example, we may build a Form where a User needs to enter sales data per product. If a product is in our rows, to improve the User Experience we may apply row suppression to a Calculation that pre-populated some data. But what if our User needs to access a product that was not populated with data? They would not see it due to the suppression. This is a situation where you may want to explore this feature and allow the User to take some control of what they can see.

An orange tick mark will be displayed at the bottom of the individual rows, as shown in Figure 6.26. Users can now right-click on this orange tick mark and choose Insert Suppressed Member. A pop-up window will then display the Members they are allowed to add. A User can only add Members with the expansion I have applied to the rows, so we don't have to worry about them venturing into other areas of the application. Security settings will still be applied here, as well.

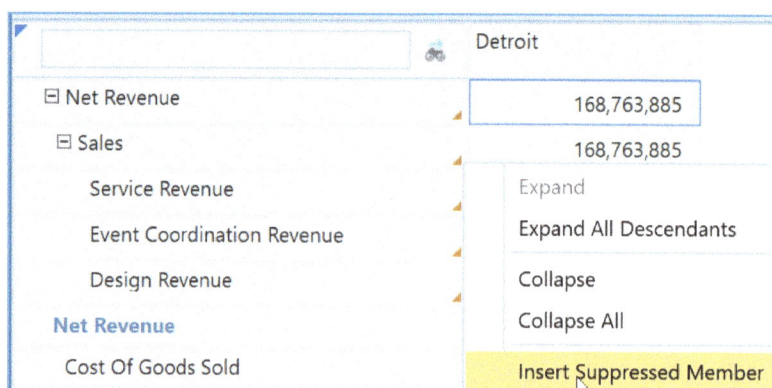

Figure 6.26

Sparse Suppression

We learned that sparsity is something that we can mitigate through our application design. However, even with an optimal design, sparsity can still occur if a large Report is required that pulls in a lot of Dimensions. Suppression settings can help improve reporting performance if this is the case.

If your row and column suppression settings are not cutting it, and you have some large Reports exhibiting poor performance, **Sparse Row Suppression** may be for you. Due to widespread sparsity, the Report could be returning many NoData records and taking a long time to run. This tends to surprise people, but – if this is the case – enable the Allow Sparse Row Suppression property (shown in Figure 6.27) and see if this helps your Cube View performance.

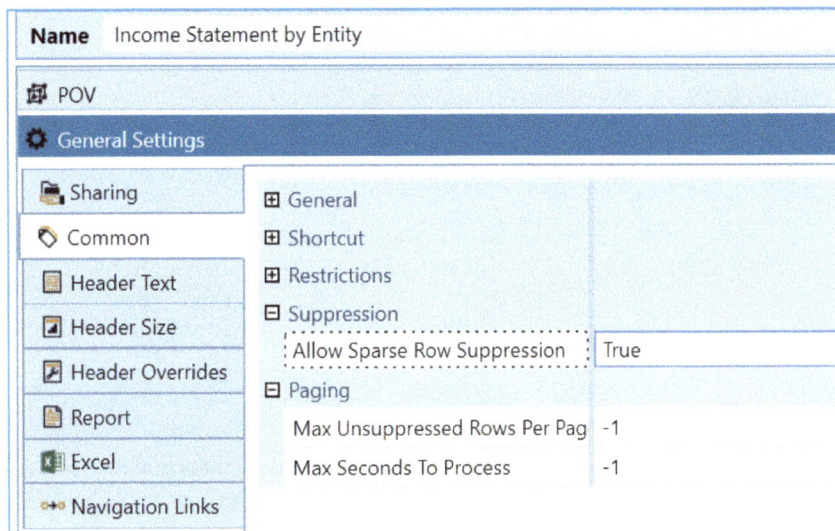

Name	Income Statement by Entity

🏛 POV
⚙ General Settings

🖼 Sharing	⊞ General
◇ Common	⊞ Shortcut
📄 Header Text	⊞ Restrictions
📑 Header Size	⊟ Suppression
📝 Header Overrides	Allow Sparse Row Suppression : True
📄 Report	⊟ Paging
📊 Excel	Max Unsuppressed Rows Per Pag -1
⟿ Navigation Links	Max Seconds To Process -1

Figure 6.27

So, what does this do differently from regular suppression? This property changes how our Cube View renders. It evaluates all the data records of the Cube View intersections at one time, and filters records with no data (not zeros). So, as opposed to reading the Cube View line by line, it consumes the entire data set and quickly eliminates any unneeded rows.

Many people immediately think they should always have Sparse Row Suppression on. Is this a good practice? Our typical recommendation would be to agree with you. However, there are some considerations you may want to watch out for. The biggest barrier to using Sparse Row Suppression is the use of dynamically calculated data through any `GetDataCells` Expressions (Dynamic Calculations). Technically, these are not stored data points and can cause errors to display.

Thankfully, this only applies to your columns and can be avoided by correctly utilizing the Allow Sparse Row Suppression settings. This requires venturing back to our Column Suppression settings and utilizing that last property; you may want to find your dynamically calculated columns and turn this property to False. Then your Cube View will run smoothly, and you will have the best of both worlds.

Cube View Paging

If you have a long-running Cube View, you may want to jump to immediately exporting it to Excel or PDF. But you must run it as a Data Explorer Grid first. Sometimes, people get a little impatient with this, so applying Cube View Paging can alleviate the time spent waiting for the Data Explorer Grid to return. We have observed these settings enhance the performance of Cube Views containing more than 10,000 unsuppressed rows. The purpose of paging is to protect the server from large Cube Views that could affect application performance.

By default, a Cube View will attempt to return up to 2,000 unsuppressed rows within a maximum processing time of 20 seconds. You can adjust these settings through the General Settings properties. The -1 denotes a default setting, but you can key in your own Max Unsuppressed Rows Per Page or seconds to process.

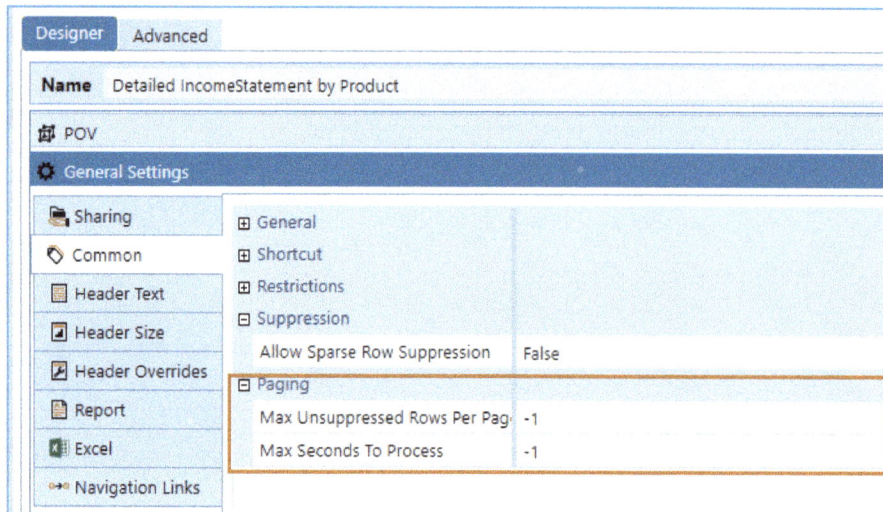

Figure 6.28

Conclusion

In this chapter, we learned that we have a variety of expansions to ensure that our Cube View maintenance is kept to a minimum. But if you are constantly bending over backwards, and twisting and turning with every expansion, you might need to look at your Dimension Library. Remember, you want to ensure your Dimension design considers the Reports you need to pull. It's a Cube View; don't pull a muscle!

What if you have bigger problems? What if Dimension structures are different, or there are total Members that you keep having to calculate? Then you are likely going to want to use an alternate hierarchy, and these can be neatly created within any of your Dimensions. Consider this approach, in particular, if you are constantly creating total Members; alternate hierarchies are typically much easier to create than Calculations and will be more dynamic.

What if we need to create Calculations in a Cube View, though? This can typically be done with a GetDataCell directly in a Cube View, but if you are constantly trying to recreate the same Calculation – well, you guessed it – turn to the Dimension Library! You can create Dynamic Calculations in your Dimension Members (usually Accounts and UD8) that can be referenced for Cube Views. The best part is that you can even add Calculations for drill down to enhance the End-User Experience.

Slow performance can be a bummer for Users, but a large, cumbersome Cube View is also not very legible. Is someone really peeling through all this information? If the answer is truly yes, we can get creative and utilize a few tools to help this along. Things like row/column suppression, sparse suppression, and paging within OneStream will help to make a large Report less cumbersome. And, if all else fails, a great option is to assemble these Reports into Report Books and use the OneStream Parcel Service found on the MarketPlace to 'ship' long-running Reports to an email address (or addresses) of your choosing.

As we continue through our book, we will learn a little bit more about Cube Views and other ways they can be configured. A little later, we will dive into further reporting options and start to understand how they can be used to meet common requirements or perhaps used to improve reporting performance.

7

Cube View Formatting

This is the chapter where we start to break the ice with Cube View formatting. Here, we will start things off simply and examine the lay of the land before continuing with more advanced options in Chapter 8.

Formatting a Cube View is something that can become a bit of an art form, and I must admit I do not know if anyone thinks they know how to handle every little thing. But that is not a goal you should be striving for when it comes to Cube View building.

When I first started with OneStream, I had a journey not unlike many other Consultants; I started building Cube Views. As a matter of fact – after my first six months with the company – I had built close to 300. They were not all for Financial Reports; some of them were for data entry, some for-data validation, some to eventually become Dashboards, and some for me to test my little rules.

But many of those Cube Views did become Financial Reports, and many of them were packaged up into Report Books and shipped through the Parcel Service. If you find yourself in the situation of building many Cube Views, your experience is probably not going to be too different from mine!

But this was back in 2015. Since then, the OneStream Community has grown, and the product has developed new enhancements to extend the capabilities of Cube Views and make them easier to build. The number of OneStream Administrators, Power Users, and Consultants building them has increased tenfold, and many of them are producing creative ways to stretch a Cube View. I must say, it has been incredible watching the new features pile in – some of them for my clients, some of them for things I never even thought to request. But I am proud to see these things come in and say crotchety things like, "Back in my day, you had to do that manually!" I cannot help but wonder what it would be like to learn Cube Views for the first time now.

You may be wondering why I am giving you this historical introduction when we have already talked about Cube Views quite a bit in this book. That is because this is where we start our first look at formatting. If you have had to build a lot of polished Reports, this is where you will spend most of your time. It did not take me that long to create my Cube Views; I started my first project with Consultants who had already created the Dimensions, built a few Dynamic Calcs, and even had some Forms going, so I could see how it was done. I plugged away at my shared rows and columns, copied Cube View POVs, skinned my knees on a few Time functions, and went cross-eyed, staring at Member Expansions like `.base` and `.tree`. But when the Cube View was built, the formatting was where I spent a lot of time.

I am not saying I was perfect; any Consultant who has been working with OneStream for a long time will shake their head at their mistakes, but I had the support and leadership of other great Consultants, the guidance of some whip-smart clients, and the patience and knowledge of everyone in the OneStream South Street (Rochester, MI) office to keep me going every day. Who would have thought that Cube View formatting would be so sentimental?!

Getting Started with Formatting

Formatting Order of Operations

In the last chapter, we learned that there is an order of operations when querying data. Let us review:

1. The Cube POV gets overridden by the…

2. Cube View POV gets overridden by the…

3. Columns get overridden by the…

4. Rows

And then you do the hokey pokey, and you turn yourself around… sorry, I couldn't resist. We could go into overrides as well, but we will get into that a little bit later in this chapter. Now we are ready to look at formatting, and there is a similar concept we must apply. Here we go:

1. Application Properties get overridden by the…

2. Cube View default formatting gets overridden by the…

3. Column formatting gets overridden by the…

4. Row formatting

Overrides can be applied here as well, but let's point out that we have one consistent message with our overrides: rows beat columns. Just like we kept our overrides in mind when building our Cube Views to query data, we do the same thing when formatting our Cube Views.

Application Standard Reports

Application settings are commonly forgotten about when implementing OneStream. But there are many important properties here that you should change when starting the application build or at least be aware of for later phases. I recommend reviewing each property and familiarizing yourself with what is available. Who knows, you might find some fun surprises that you didn't know could be altered.

When talking about the User Experience in general, if we look at the General tab, we may want to look at our Global Scenario and Global Time first. These can be referenced in Reports and Rules, but you need to have them set to load data into your application. If you are utilizing Global POV Substitution Variables (|GlobalTime| or |GlobalScenario|, for example), you will want to ensure these are set.

The other thing that we will want to look at is the Company Name and the Logo File. The Logo File will display on all your PDF printed Reports. You will want to ensure this is set because if one is not uploaded, it will display the OneStream logo! Upload your logo in a .png format and see the results on your PDF Cube Views. This can vary across the application using Cube View Extender Rules. These General properties are depicted in Figure 7.1 below.

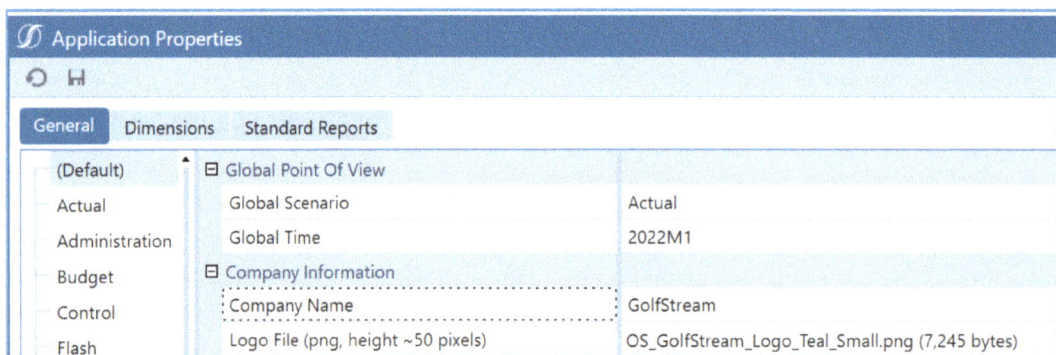

Figure 7.1

The Dimensions tab also has some important areas to look at. First, we have the Start Year and End Year. This defaults to 1996 and 2100. You may want to alter this so that whenever you have a selectable Time, your User does not have to scroll for too long and has more appropriate options based on what is in their application. You can always adjust these settings later.

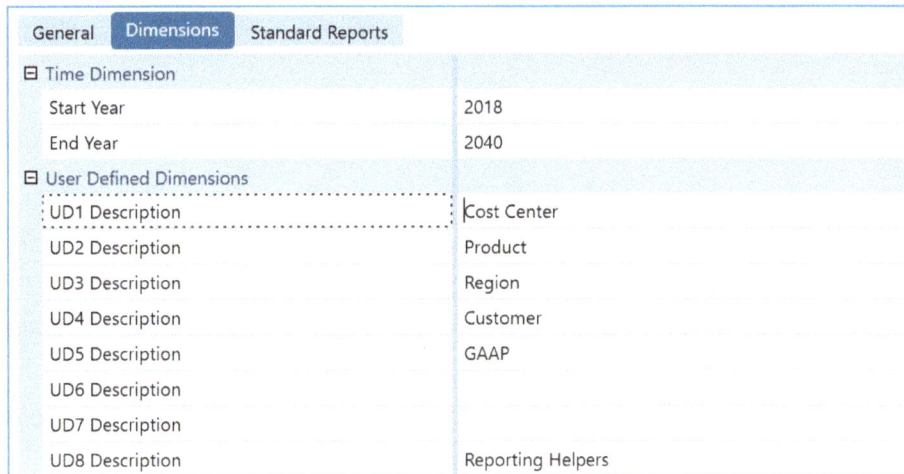

Figure 7.2

The above image also shows User Defined Description(s). These will populate the tool tips in the Cube POV, the drill down grid, and your Cube View rows and columns when building Cube Views (see Figure 7.3). They also play a major role in the End-User experience and should be updated for clarity. Remember, UD1 is likely a new concept for new Users, so having a friendlier name available to them will help them acclimate to their new OneStream application.

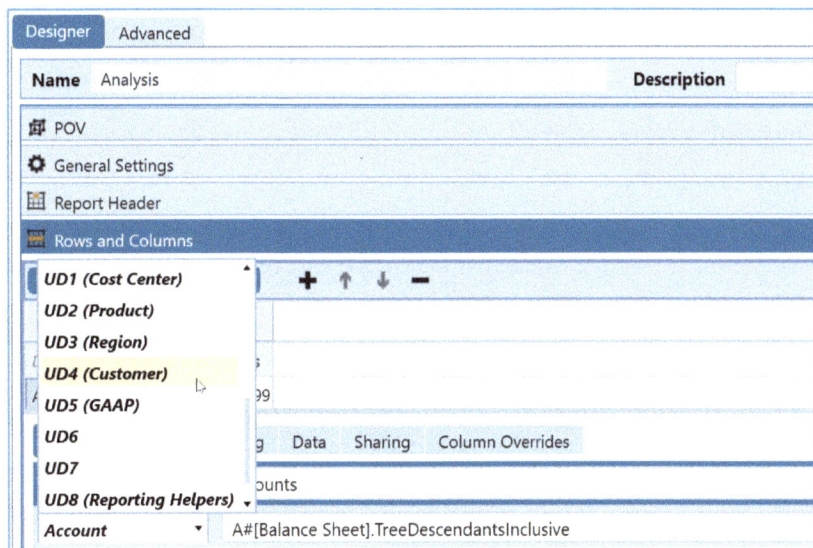

Figure 7.3

And finally – the real reason I brought you here – the Standard Reports tab. If you are a Consultant, I strongly encourage you to start every Phase 1 implementation by working through these properties and trying to match what you saw your clients display. Then, I would show them your work and get them to sign off on a general layout.

This tab is where you are going to set your general page formatting, but it is also where you alter the header bars and colors you see on the PDF versions of your Reports. So, if your Cube View is still showing blue lines and bars all over the place, this is editable. This is also an easy way to apply standard formatting (such as the font family) to the header, footer, and title of your Reports. We have highlighted these properties in Figure 7.4 and expanded it to show the Header Bar and Title settings, but they are very similar to the Header Labels and Footer formatting options. Any options here can also be overridden at the individual Cube View level using **Cube View Extender Rules**.

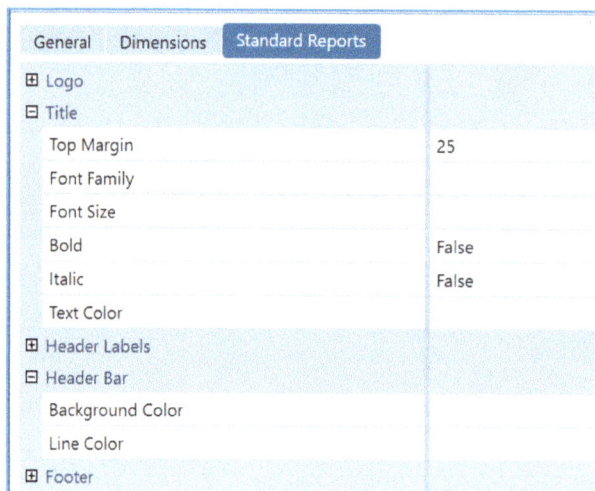

Figure 7.4

Versions of a Cube View

We have our application properties set; what's next? We may need to ask ourselves, what version of the Cube View are we trying to format? We know Cube Views are versatile and can be featured in many areas of the application; when it comes to digesting our Cube Views, we can see them in three different formats:

1. Data Explorer Grid

2. Excel exported version

3. Printed PDF Report

Figure 7.5 depicts the Data Explorer Grid. From here, you can drill down into individual cells or use the highlighted icons to export your Cube View to Excel or a PDF. And as we stated before, each of these options can be formatted separately.

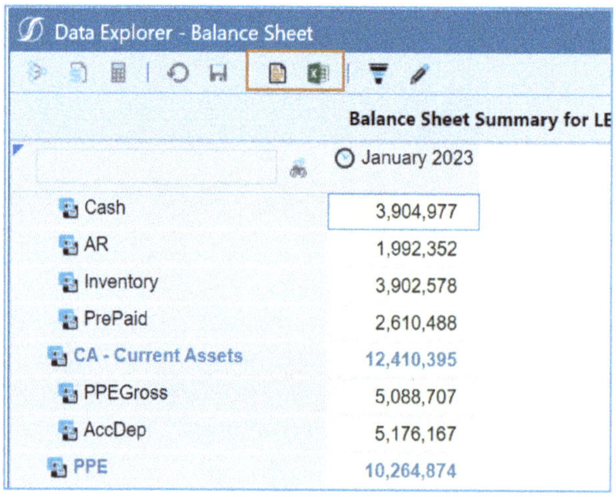

Figure 7.5

Typically, Data Explorer Grids are not as heavily formatted as the other two options. But you may consider throwing your weight into this version of the Cube View if your Cube View is being used within a Dashboard or even a Form. If the Cube View is eventually to be used as a Cube View Component in a Dashboard, people often employ tactics like making the grids white, turning off the grid lines, or altering the text in some way, shape, or form to make them sleeker. By the time you are done, people may not even think they are in a Cube View!

If you are looking at formatting a Cube View used for data collection, this may not require as much formatting. These Cube Views are more functional than stylish, and ensuring they create the best User Experience for data submission is key. However, if you are collecting information such as commentary, data attachments, or cell detail, providing some signal – such as a different background color in a cell – to the User may be wise as they are getting their feet wet with OneStream. Another thing to consider – when using Confirmation Rules – is how the use of conditional formatting can catch Users *before* they fail their rule (e.g., things like obvious traffic light coloring on the cells), thus expediting their End-User process. Sometimes functional is stylish!

What about the Excel exported version of the Cube View? Again, ask yourself the purpose of this Cube View and who will ultimately be using it. If you are a client or a Consultant, know your User population. Are they more likely to export their Cube Views to Excel and digest them there? If that is the case, you will want these formatted legibly (at least), so you can eliminate any need for a User having to reformat the Report or adjust any settings in Excel. You might also want to explore options like **Excel outline levels** when making a larger Cube View easier to digest. Usually, more robust formatting may also be required if the Excel exported version of your Cube View is used to create an Excel Report Book.

And finally, your PDF version of your Report. If you are creating Financial Statements, you likely have strict requirements to ensure these Cube Views look perfect. You may spend much of your time ensuring you have professional, legible, and consistent formatting. Because this tends to be the case for your Financial Reports, this may be more common on Consolidation projects or the first phase of a OneStream implementation. This is not always the case, but if you are sitting in a design session and seeing mostly printed Reports displayed, ensure ample time for review and formatting to be set up on the project.

Header versus Cell Format

Before we can get our hands dirty and start formatting our Cube Views, we have one more concept we need to address: are we formatting our headers or our cells? If this concept does not make sense to you, Figure 7.6 will help show what we are talking about.

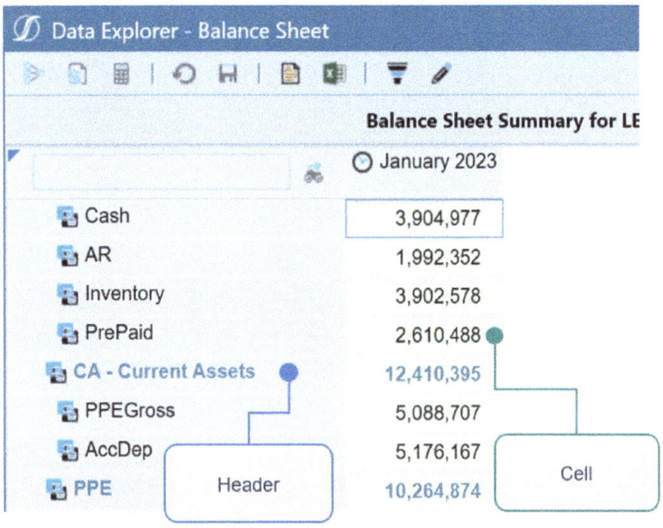

Figure 7.6

So not only do we have to think about Excel, PDF, or Grid, but we also have different formatting between the headers and cells of the Cube Views for each of these formats. Each of these is done separately, and we will have different properties between them. For example, cells will have number formatting, while headers are where we can apply Excel outline levels.

Where can this formatting be applied? If we remember our order of operations, this can be done within the default settings, the individual columns, and the individual rows, as well as the overrides. Figure 7.7 shows formatting applied to the default header and cell of the Cube View. This formatting can be set by choosing the various formatting options across the toolbar, or by clicking the ellipses icon next to the header/cell format properties.

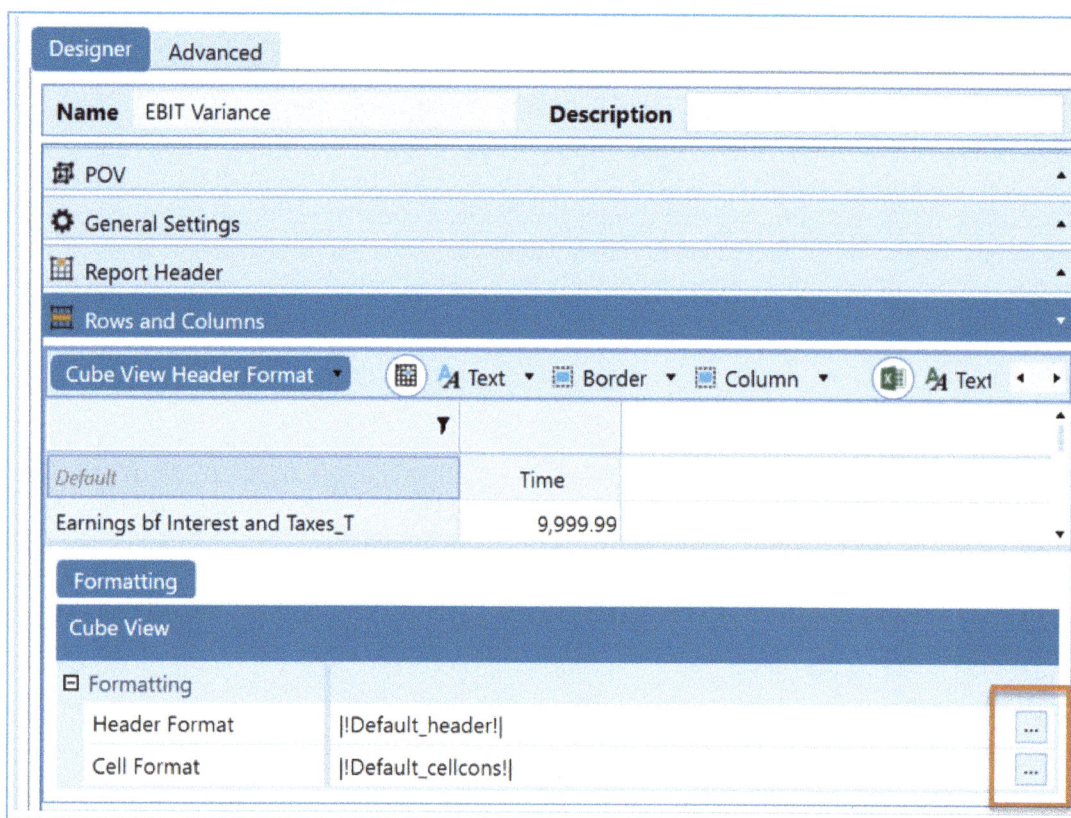

Figure 7.7

There will be slight differences between the column, row, and default formatting options, but for the most part, these options should be recognizable. If you are choosing to update via the toolbar, then you will know that if you are updating either the Data Explorer, Excel, or PDF by the color of the property, the Data Explorer is blue (and it is always first), Excel is green (second), and PDF is orange (always last). If you edit via the highlighted ellipses icons, see Figure 7.7, (which is how I like to do it), then you will just have the properties displayed to you in a list. Data Explorer is first, and referred to as general formatting, Excel is second, and PDF is last and referred to as Report. All your formatting gets applied in a comma-delimited list and can be keyed in if you start getting the hang of the syntax.

You may be wondering how intricate formatting can possibly get on the Data Explorer version of the Cube View. While we typically do see a little less activity here, there are two items you may want to take advantage of. The first is the ShowDimensionImages property, which you can set to False if you no longer want to see your Dimension icons in your Cube View. Figure 7.8 shows you the location of this property.

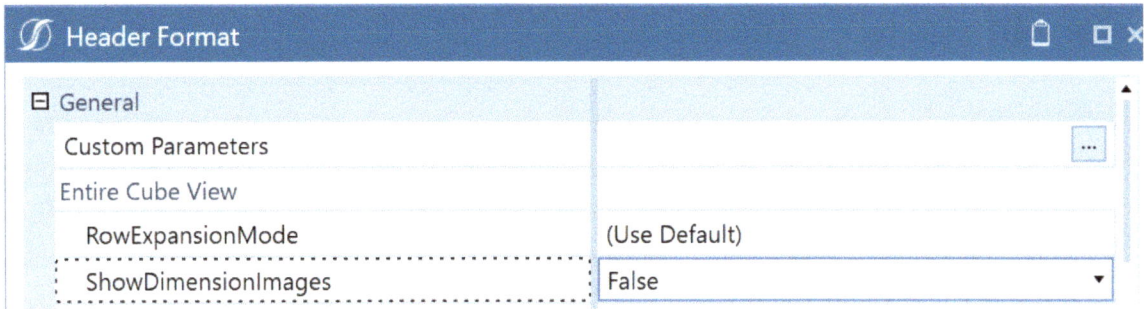

Figure 7.8

And Figure 7.9 shows you how a Cube View will look without the Dimension icons. This may be effective in reducing clutter on the page and creating a more professional look. Refer back to Figure 7.6 to see how a Cube View looks with the Dimension icons turned on by comparison.

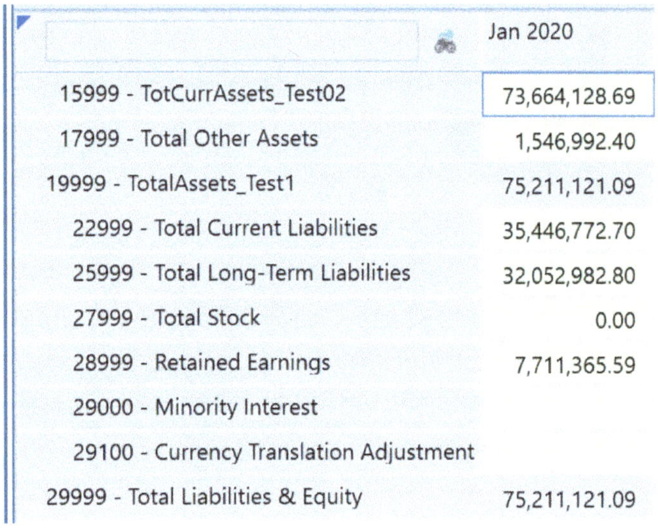

Figure 7.9

Another great option is to display the currency alongside the cells of the Data Explorer Grid. This is a top way to give the User some more information, especially if this Cube View is pulling multiple Entities. This setting is actually found in the default Cell Format of the Cube View. Figure 7.10 shows the property and the results.

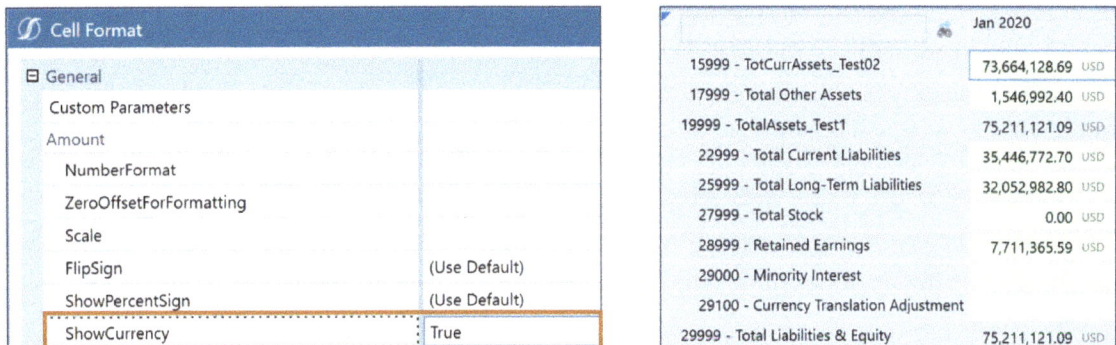

Figure 7.10

More Intricate Formatting

Overrides

One of the things we mentioned when listing the order of operations is that there is a final item that can be applied. These are your row and column overrides. This can be done for formatting or for Member Filters. How are they applied? If you are still on the screen we just showed, all you do is flip the last tab. If you are in the rows, you will have column overrides, and if you are in your columns, you will have a tab for row overrides. Overrides are entirely tied to the names that you provide on your rows and columns.

> **Note:** If you are using overrides, be careful when you change the names of rows and columns, or else you will undo them!

You can key in a range or a comma-delimited list to ensure that you save space with your overrides. This is shown in Figure 7.11.

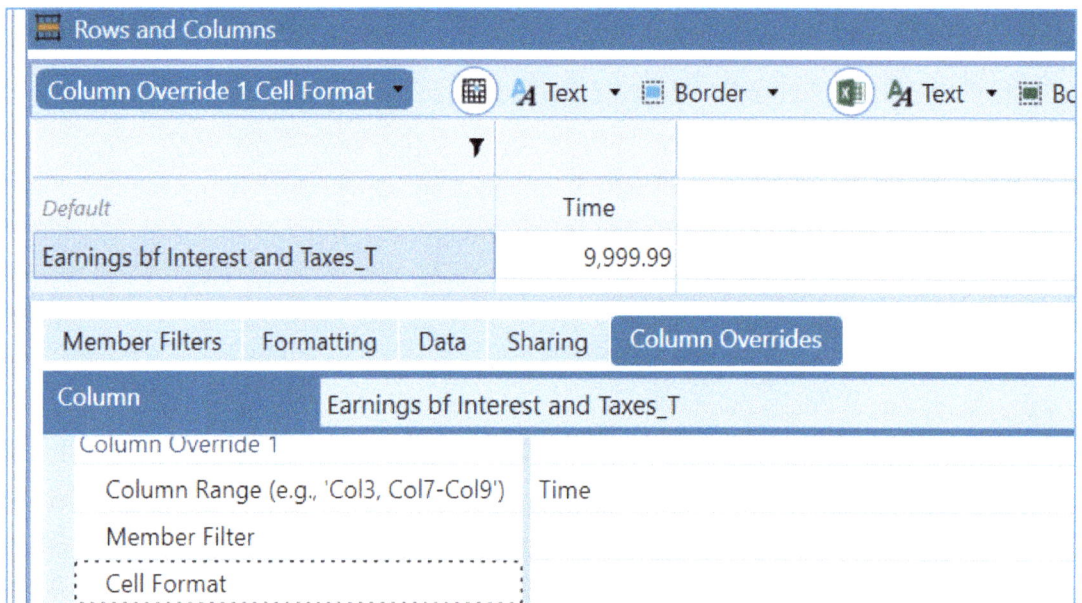

Figure 7.11

As you can see, you can choose a Member Filter or Cell Format. Why might I need an override? When it comes to overrides with formatting, you might choose this option if you have a variance column, and you need to have specific formatting on that variance column. Maybe you have a background color applied to your rows, and you want a different background color applied to the columns. This is common with cell formatting, as well.

In Figure 7.12, you will notice that there is a bright blue color applied to the rows, and a fun color called "blanched almond" is applied to the final column. The row overrides the column in this case (our default behavior). If you want this to be different, then you would need an override!

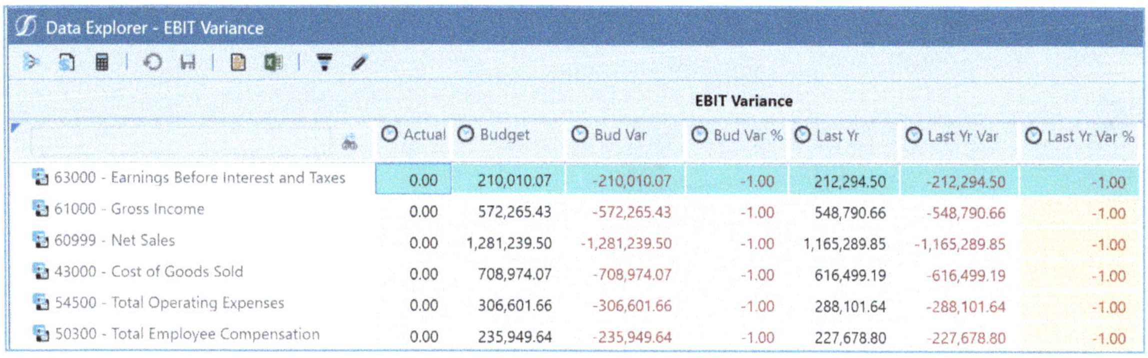

Figure 7.12

In this chapter, we are discussing formatting, but the most common reason for an override I see is more on the Member Filter side. This usually happens when we have a `GetDataCell` in the rows of the Cube View as well as in the columns. A calculated row and a variance column are not unheard-of when building Cube Views.

So, would I recommend overrides? My answer is if you need them, you need them, and it is awesome that OneStream gives you the option. They are great to keep in a pinch, but I would be careful if you rely on them too much. They are easy to miss when looking at the Cube View properties, and you only have four. If you can avoid them by being a little bit cleverer or more thoughtful in your design, the complexity and the maintenance of your Cube View will be reduced. For example, you can do things like placing as much formatting on the default formatting properties as possible. Furthermore, if there is consistent number formatting, instead of placing this in your rows or your formatting parameters, keep it on the default so you do not have collisions.

Okay, that makes the need for an override rare with formatting. However, what about the Calculation situation described above? That is a lot more common. One great way to combat this is to rely on creating calculated Members as opposed to `GetDataCell` columns for common formatting. This may not always be avoidable. Let's look at Figure 7.13, which illustrates a Cell POV that has a `GetDataCell` Calculation within the cell.

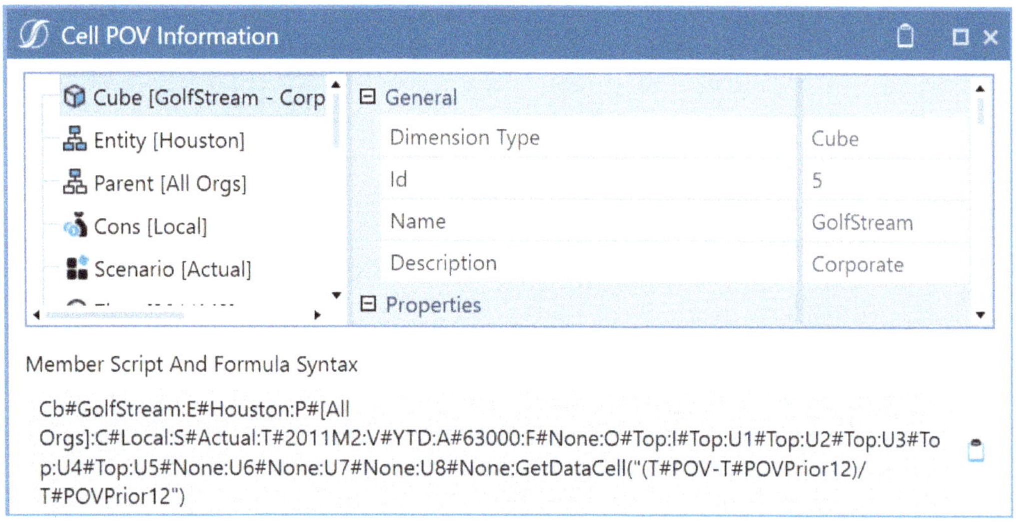

Figure 7.13

You can see that this cell queries a Member for each Dimension Type, but then there is a final portion tacked onto the end that represents the `GetDataCell`. So, if you had a calculated Member, then you would be able to have *both* Calculations working in tandem. You may have to tinker with things like which one is the Member, or how the Calculation is run, but this can set you up for a more simplified Cube View build that takes advantage of these calculated Members in the future. If not, you must write an override that encompasses both Calculations. And that can start to get a little messy!

Using Formatting Parameters

Before we start laying the groundwork for common properties, or anything fancy like that, there is one best practice we must lay out... creating parameters for formatting. This is honestly a MUST and should be a portion of your Cube View rows and columns for sharing or any Cube Views being used as templates. Parameters should be built and displayed in front of stakeholders early in the Report building process.

To help you understand how much parameters can help you, I will take a little time to explain things. Let's look at the setup in the GolfStream application in Figure 7.14.

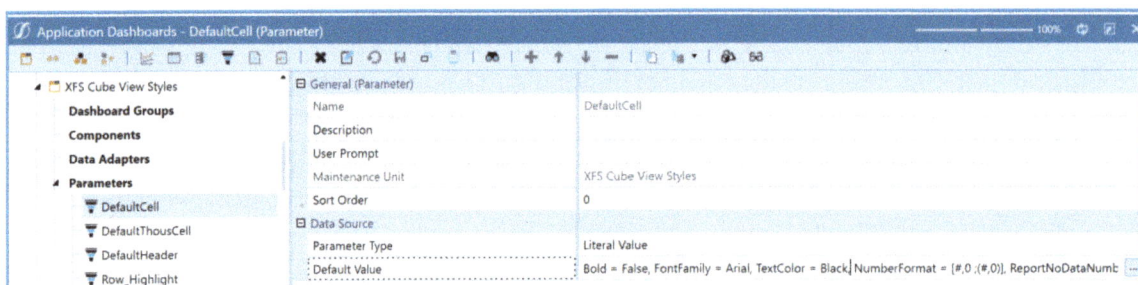

Figure 7.14

To create a parameter that can be used for formatting, we want to navigate to the Application Dashboards page, create a new parameter, and choose the Type of Literal Value. If you are new to parameters, you may have seen them in other areas of your application – as prompts – that display to ask you to key something in, choose a Member, or anything else. This Type of Parameter is different; it does not prompt; it simply holds a specific value. The most common use for this Type of Parameter is to hold your formatting for cells and headers. As you can see in the Default Value, we have the common delimited list of our Cube View formatting.

Why might you do this? Because it is much cleaner than seeing all that formatting displayed in your Cube View. Now, you just need to reference the parameter name in |!!| (||!ParameterName!|) and your formatting will be applied, plus you don't always have to format your Cube View manually. You can use parameters for things like:

1. Default header/cell formatting

2. Total header/cell formatting

3. Subtotal header/cell formatting

4. Variance columns or rows

You can always apply additional formatting *on top* of the parameter on the individual Cube View. Using these parameters not only expedites your Cube View build but will also reduce your maintenance. How? Let's say – down the line – that we no longer want our total cell formats to display a double line on the bottom of the cell. You only need to update the parameter now, and every Cube View that references this will be updated. No need to hunt and make a million changes! And, as a final tip, you can see the **Object Usage Viewer** icon on the Application Dashboards page to see what is referencing this parameter.

Typically, I would recommend building a Maintenance Unit to represent your Literal Value Parameters for Cube View formatting. This is a great way to host them all in one nice and neat place. You can bring in the Cube View styles Dashboard Maintenance Unit from GolfStream, but you may not require all those parameters, and you may have completely different formatting requirements. But it is nice to see the example to know how it is done.

Conditional Formatting

This is where things get suitably fun! Conditional formatting is something that gets a lot of people excited and can really bring some color to your Cube Views (sometimes literally). In its simplest form, it is applying formatting that says, "If the data is within this threshold, alter the formatting to signal this to the User." I see a lot of conditional formatting on Financial Reports, but they also make great tools when working with Cube Views that are incorporated into Dashboards for eye-catching analysis. I also use them in Forms quite a bit, especially for clients with more Confirmation Rules. This can signal to a User that they are about to have a problem before they fail a Confirmation Rule.

Conditional formatting within OneStream is an interesting topic because we have evolved how it is done over the years. Back in the day, conditional formatting was applied through OneStream Studio. This meant we would take a Cube View and bring it into OneStream Studio to apply formatting. Once this was done – to see your formatting – you were able to run it as a Dashboard Report.

Since then, much has changed. Dashboard Reports now have their own Designer tab where you can adjust your Reports directly and – as more releases pass – this interface gets easier to work with and has more and more capabilities.

Historically, we also saw one other change in conditional formatting: you were able to incorporate it into your Cube Views directly using **Cube View Extender Rules**. This Rule Type came with some coding required, but **Snippets** (the **Snippet Editor** Solution is found on the MarketPlace) made it a breeze to do things like change the logo, tweak headers and footers, and (of course) add conditional formatting. This could be done to PDF versions of Cube View Reports.

Then, conditional formatting underwent one more makeover and is now a part of regular Cube View formatting. This can be seen in Excel, PDF, and Data Explorer Views. This made conditional formatting much easier and is another example of how OneStream is always improving the product.

Now that I have whipped you up, let's take a quick look at how this is applied in OneStream.

When you open your header or cell formatting, you can write your conditional formatting directly in the text box, or you can click the Conditional Formatting icon to open the window seen in Figure 7.15 to help you get the syntax correct. If that is not enough, if you look in the left box – in Figure 7.15 – you can also hover over the question mark icon to see examples of conditional formatting syntax.

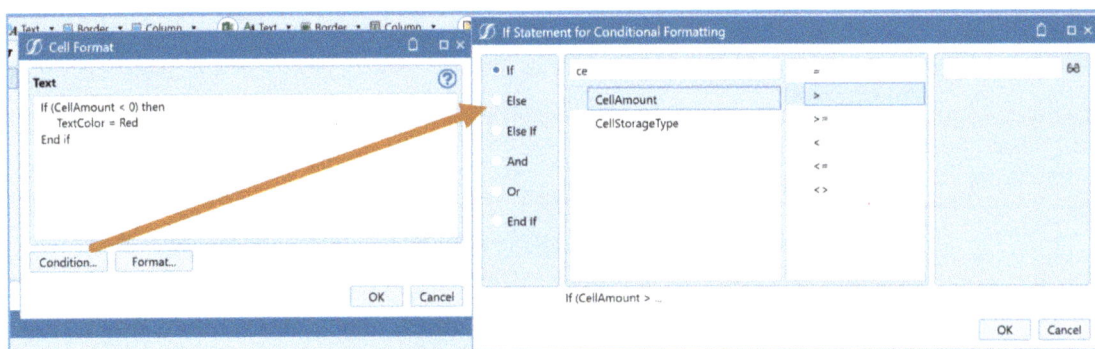

Figure 7.15

Using the question mark icon, conditional formatting dialogue box, the object lookup icon, and the formatting options available within the window, you should have no problem getting used to conditional formatting syntax.

I showed a simple and obvious example here, but as you peruse the various conditional formatting options, you can see that you can grab things like RowE1MemberName (Row Expansion 1 Member Name) or RowE2MemberDescription (Row Expansion 2 Member Description). You can also grab things like the expanded row numbers, even rows, cell Storage Type, indent level, the name of the row/column, and so much more.

Okay, the possibilities seem endless, but there is one very creative thing you can do to reduce your Cube View Maintenance using conditional formatting. The ability to grab the name of the row or column is what makes this possible. One of the most common Cube View design tips is to name your rows and column something descriptive, so someone can follow the logic of your Cube View build. People commonly call rows _T for total rows, _ST for subtotal rows, and _D for detail rows. If you establish a naming convention like this, you can use conditional formatting to make it so you no longer have to go into the individual rows and apply your formatting! If you really want to impress your friends, though, you can still have your parameters handy and drop them into your conditional formatting, making one cohesive, dynamic, easy-to-maintain formatting rule that anyone can follow. Figure 7.16 gives you an example of this.

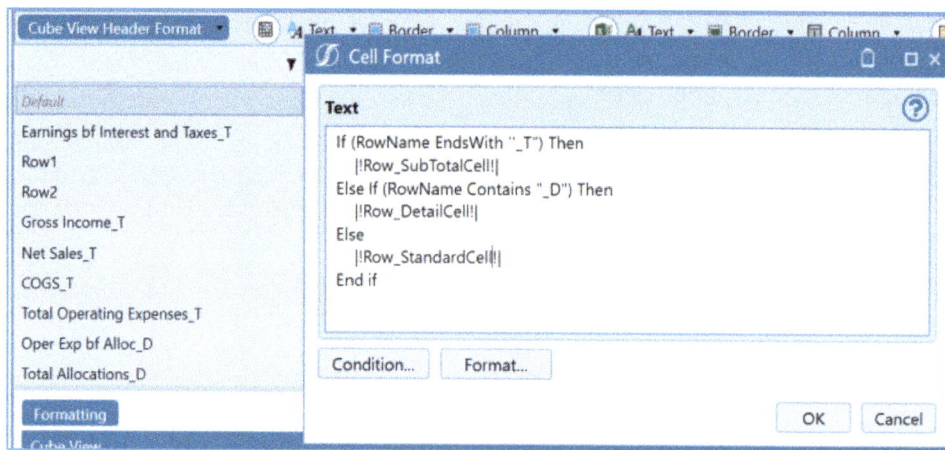

Figure 7.16

General Settings

Very few people take the time to go through the General Settings of the Cube View. There are some great tricks you can employ in your formatting with these properties.

I will start simply, with our header text properties. It is great to nail down – ahead of time – which Dimension Types should display the Member Name, Member Description, or both. If you set this one, you can place them in your Cube View template, and you never have to worry about them again. This is seen in Figure 7.17.

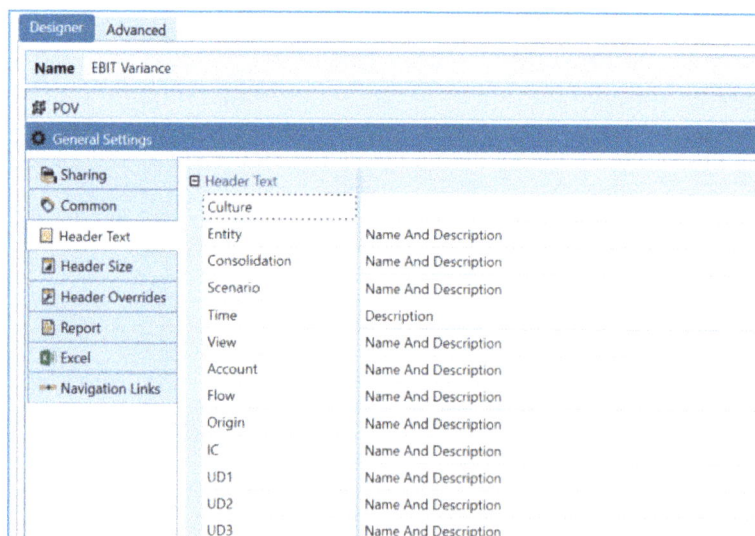

Figure 7.17

Next up is your header size. I am going to draw your attention to Row Header Widths because this has gotten me out of a few jams in my career. You may have a situation where you need to expand the widths of individual rows because the text is wrapping or – as I have used it – you may be trying to shrink your Report, which is just a few rows over one page, back down to a single page. This can be done by creatively tinkering with the width settings here. You can apply these to your Data Explorer (first), Excel (second), and PDF (third) options for each of your row expansions. Simply key in a pixel number and adjust as necessary. Pixels are small, so use increments of 100 to see a big impact. If you are fitting to one page, widthwise, and your Cube View is just a little too big, this can uniformly shrink the size of your font. Sometimes it does not work if you don't have many columns, but it has served me well over the years. Check out these settings in Figure 7.18.

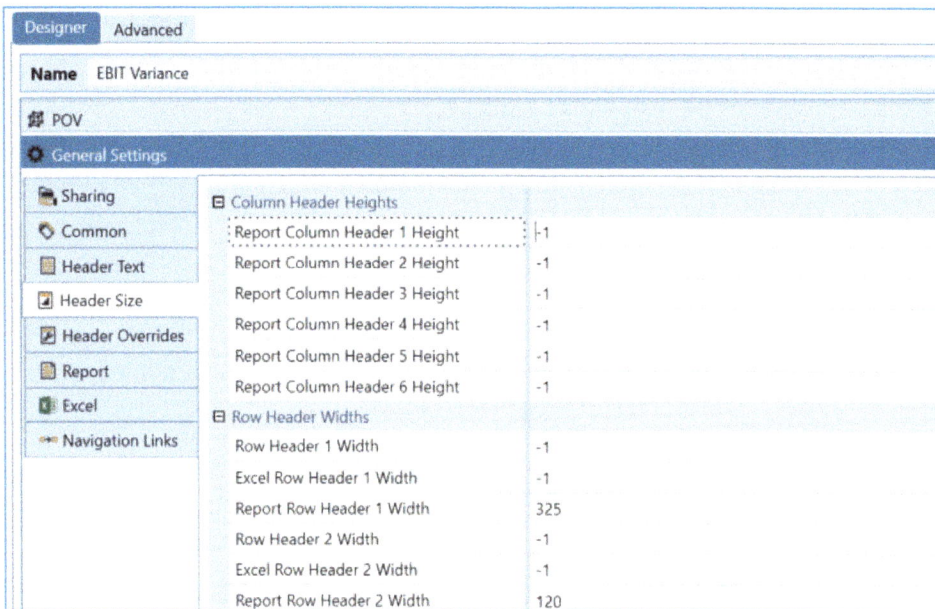

Figure 7.18

The next one is our Header Overrides, not to be confused with our row and column overrides. Header Overrides are a great option if you need to incorporate more Dimensions into your rows or columns than your expansions will allow. For example, let's say I have columns in my Cube View and am expanding upon Time and Entity, but I would also like to show my View Dimension across the columns. Our columns, though, only allow you to show two expansions, so you may feel out of luck. You could get creative with your column naming, or you could adjust your Column Headers in the Header Overrides to display View as well. This will allow you to show three Dimensions instead of just two. Figure 7.19 shows you the results.

	Actual Actual YTD	Budget Actual YTD	Bud Var Actual YTD	Bud Var % Actual YTD	Last Yr Actual YTD
63000 - Earnings Before Interest and Taxes	0.00	210,010.07	-210,010.07	-1.00	212,294.50
61000 - Gross Income	0.00	572,265.43	-572,265.43	-1.00	548,790.66
60999 - Net Sales	0.00	1,281,239.50	-1,281,239.50	-1.00	1,165,289.85
43000 - Cost of Goods Sold	0.00	708,974.07	-708,974.07	-1.00	616,499.19
54500 - Total Operating Expenses	0.00	306,601.66	-306,601.66	-1.00	288,101.64
50300 - Total Employee Compensation	0.00	235,949.64	-235,949.64	-1.00	227,678.80
51099 - Total Utilities	0.00	7,830.83	-7,830.83	-1.00	6,809.42
51199 - Total Professional Services	0.00	4,855.83	-4,855.83	-1.00	3,232.70

Figure 7.19

Check out these properties in the Header Overrides section to see how you can really flex your rows and columns. This is *also* a great trick if you would like to reorder the way your Dimensions display (maybe you want to flip-flop Expansion 1 and Expansion 2) without rebuilding your entire Cube View. Or perhaps you are sharing columns, and one Cube View needs to display an additional Dimension. No need to rebuild anything; use Header Overrides to flip your Cube View around!

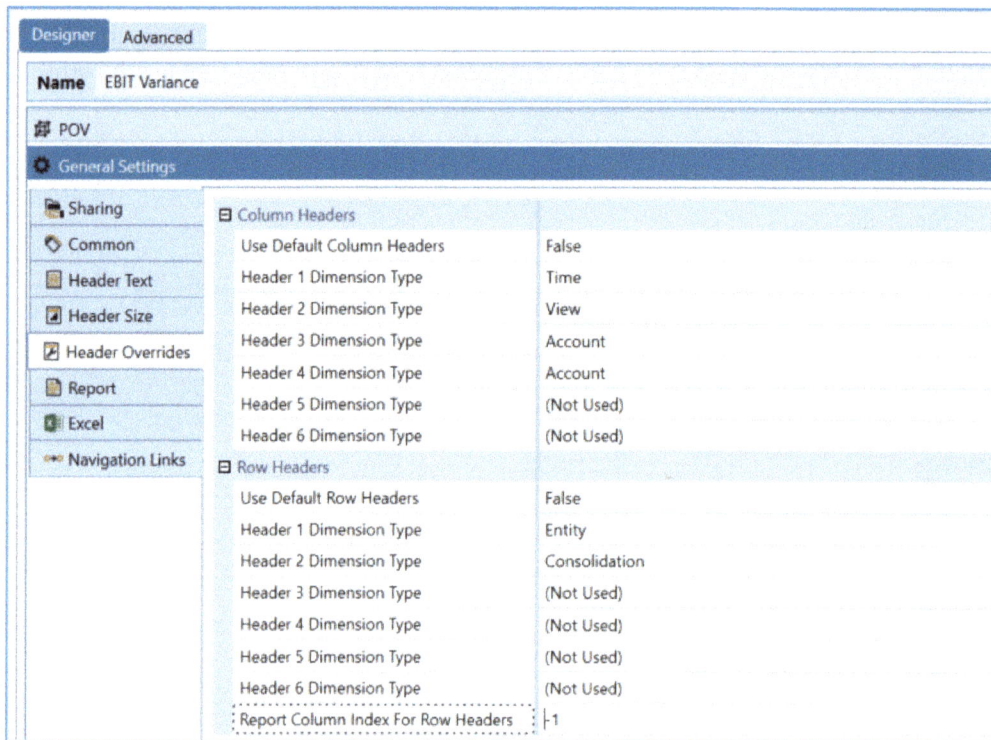

Figure 7.20

Before we leave these properties, I need to point out one final item, Report Column Index For Row Headers. Many people do not know this, but this is how you create a **Butterfly Report**. This is shown in Figure 7.21. Simply key in the number of columns you want your row headers to hop over. For example, in this image, I keyed in the number 2 instead of -1 (which means default) and looked at my majestic Report spread its wings! For reference, this is only visible in the PDF version of your Report.

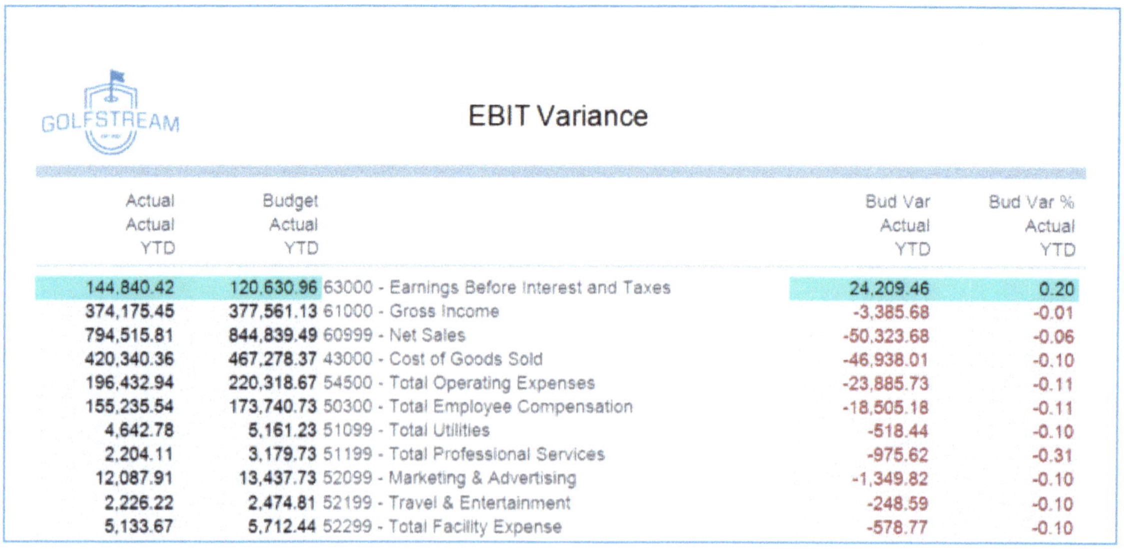

Figure 7.21

Conclusion

We still have a few more chapters to go with Cube Views, but at this point, we have laid a pretty good foundation. If you are new to them, I hope you have learned some important tips and even picked up a few tricks to get a handle on those final reporting requirements. I will leave you with a few final thoughts on the design of Cube Views, especially when it comes to formatting.

Try to nail down common formatting as soon as possible. Work with your application Standard Reports (if you are starting with a new application) to ensure your headers, logos, and colors are all set. Then start to pull together some common formatting and save them as parameters. This will make life a lot easier for any future Report builders that come into your application. In turn, use things like your general settings to your advantage and try your hand at some creative conditional formatting. Lastly, share rows and columns and create a Cube View template. All these things will expedite your build, reduce maintenance, and keep things organized!

8

Taking Cube Views to the Next Level

In this chapter, we will go a few steps further with our Cube Views. We will discuss using parameters to make Cube Views dynamic for the ultimate User Experience. We'll explore methods for using parameters for POV selections, rows and columns, and text. You will see examples of sharing Cube View rows and columns to help streamline reporting without sacrificing data quality.

Navigation links are a popular topic that will also be covered in this chapter with different ways to create and apply proper User navigation paths so that Users can access and consume data in a guided format. We will also explain the use of Cube View Extender Business Rules to fine-tune the look of formatted Reports and provide examples of how and when to apply this logic.

Cube View Sharing

When beginning an implementation, the first thing you'll do is requirements gathering – this is when your customer explains their business processes and defines expectations for the solution.

During this phase, your customer will provide detailed reporting requirements, including an Inventory of Financial Statements, supplemental reports, and visual presentations that must be produced from their solution upon going live. If you've been involved in this part of an implementation, you have likely received samples of Financial Statements from your customer; these samples often influence metadata design in terms of Account groupings and structure, Entity Aggregation, Currency Translation, and other variables that determine how your customer reports their data.

Requirements gathering is *the most critical* part of an implementation and serves as an outline of how the application should be configured. Think of this as a roadmap for your application build; requirements give you direct insight into what is important to your Users and provide guidance during the design phase.

It's not uncommon for Cube Views to take a backseat during an implementation; after all, you can't build Reports if you don't have metadata established. But I say Cube Views are the star of the show, and building them early allows you to evaluate metadata design and immensely improves data validation time.

There are three basic requirements when creating a Cube View:

1. Define your rows

2. Define your columns

3. Define your Point of View

This can be a daunting task if you have hundreds of Reports to build, but the good news is that there are tools available to help reduce the workload and let you focus on more value-add configuration work.

Row and Column Sharing

Row and column sharing are Cube View properties that allow you to leverage User-Defined row and column sets to quickly generate dynamic Cube Views that are consistent and which reduce maintenance.

The key benefits of Cube View sharing are that they can significantly accelerate your Cube View creation, reduce formatting maintenance, and maintain consistency and data quality when metadata changes result in altered Member Expansions. They are also a great way for companies to standardize the reporting landscape and provide 'one version of the truth' while still providing flexibility and assisting with 'self-service' reporting.

Say you have two business units that produce an Income Statement, and each business unit is responsible for a different region, but they use a common Account structure. Let's assume Cube View sharing is not being used, and you've created three separate Cube Views – the third being an aggregated business unit `Total Income Statement`. All the Cube Views have a POV, rows, and columns defined individually.

Figure 8.1

To add another layer of complexity, all business units must also produce Income Statements comparing Actual to Budget results, and Current Year to Prior Year. Keeping with the assumption that you have still not yet implemented Cube View sharing, you'll need to create six additional Cube Views to display the required Reports by Scenario and Time.

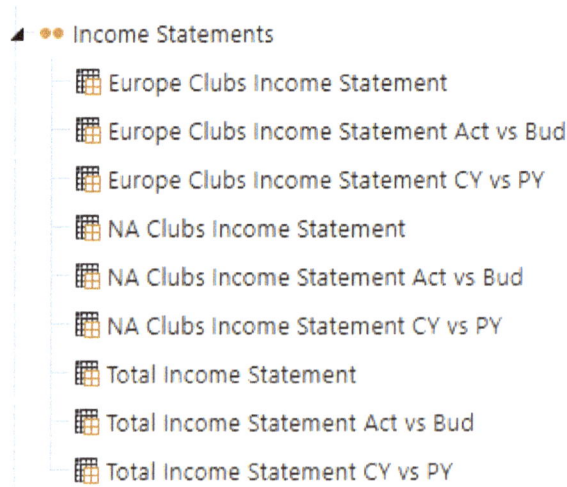

Figure 8.2

What happens when you add an Account Group to your Account Dimension, or even restructure your Accounts altogether? In this example, you would need to update the row sets on all nine Cube Views. Not only is this a time-consuming process, but its manual nature exposes risk since a User needs to remember to update all of the Cube Views. So how can you minimize risk and create Cube Views more efficiently? Use **templates** whenever possible to share rows or columns.

Templates

Templates are an easy way to establish solution standards for reporting and accelerate the future development of Cube Views. I highly recommend making a habit of establishing templates early on in an implementation, especially while building metadata, since the hierarchical structures will need to be validated when you begin loading and testing data.

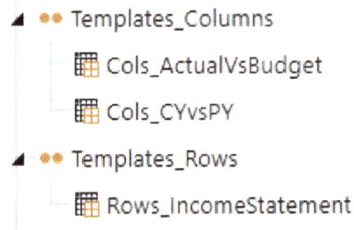

Figure 8.3

Notice above that we've created a row template for Income Statement Reports, and column templates for Scenario and Time comparisons according to our customer's requirements. Now we'll look at how to share the applicable rows and columns to our Total Income Statement Cube View. In practice, the Rows_IncomeStatement template would be shared with all Income Statement Cube Views.

Note: Row templates are typically associated with a specific Report or Cube View, while column templates are more universal in nature and can be shared with various Cube Views.

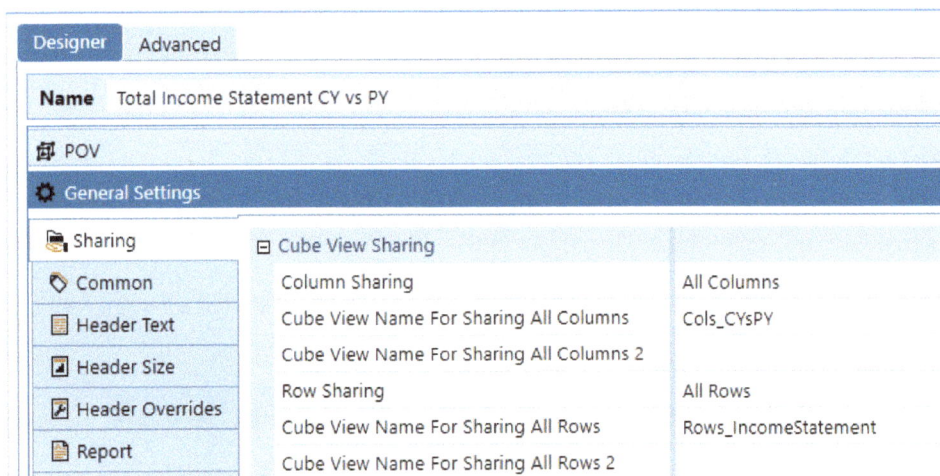

Figure 8.4

Thinking back to the example of Account structure changes, we have nine Cube Views, all using the same shared row template. This means that when we update the Rows_IncomeStatement template, all nine Cube Views will display the same row structure. This is much more manageable during implementation and sets your customer up for success.

Dynamic Cube Views

You likely know, by now, that Cube Views display data in an organized fashion, but what you may not know is just how dynamically these objects can be configured to support various reporting and analysis requirements. In theory, a single Cube View can produce multiple Financial Statements by varying reporting metrics that are completely filterable based on User selections.

With a few parameters and substitution variables, you'll be on your way to creating a User Experience that gives your Users more autonomy, but also guidance for finding the data that they care about. Financial analysis can sometimes be a daunting task – "Where do I look for data? How do I find where data came from? What am I even looking at?" – these are all questions I used to ask myself in my former career as an accountant. By the end of this chapter, you should have a basic understanding of how to make beautiful, consistent, manageable Cube Views that meet the needs of your Users.

Substitution Variables

Substitution variables are pre-defined parameters that come out-of-the-box with all applications and can be used in Business Rules, Cube Views, Dashboards, Books, and Extensible Documents.

General substitution variables are application-agnostic values that display fields such as User Name and text properties, Application Name, Point of View (POV) Members, and Date and Timestamp information in a variety of formats.

Substitution Variables are grouped into the following categories:

- Global – Time and Scenario

- Workflow

- Point of View

A complete inventory of substitution variables can be found from the Object Lookup button. This button is also available from Dashboard and Books.

Figure 8.5

From the Object Lookup dialog, scroll down and select Substitution Variables. Substitution variables are commonly used in Cube Views to display information in the page caption and the Report's header and footer. For example, if your organization uses multiple reporting currencies, you may want to use CVCurrency to display the reporting currency on Reports. Another common use is to display parameter selections; this helps the User understand what they are looking at.

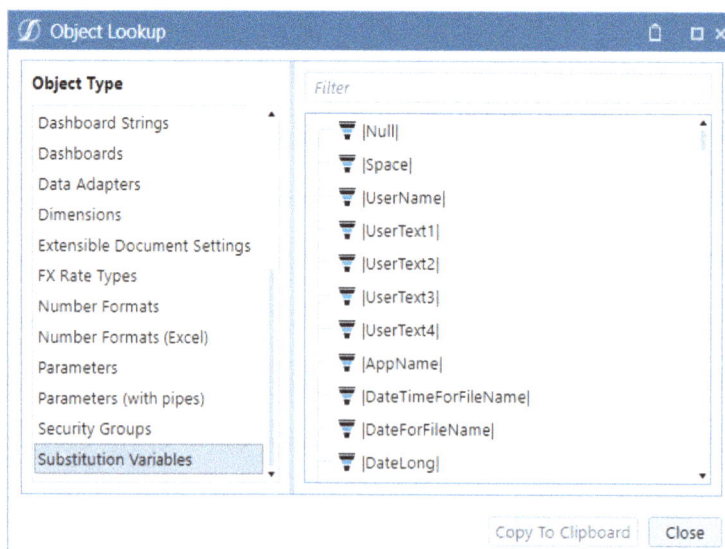

Figure 8.6

The next figure shows where substitution variables have been used to display Members on the Cube View's Page Caption.

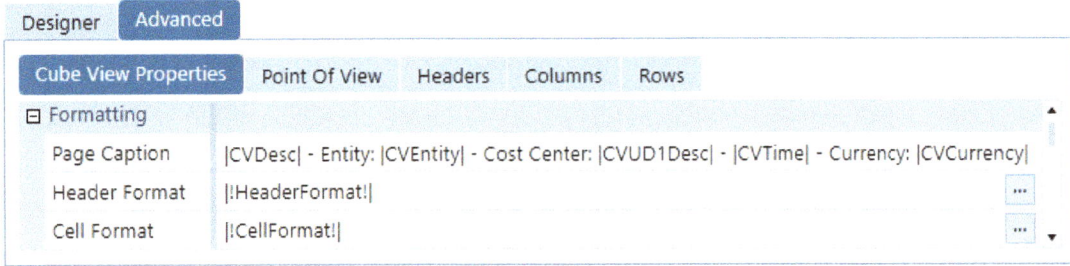

Figure 8.7

When viewing the Data Explorer, the page caption appears with the following information, based on the Cube View POV selections. Using substitution variables allows you to provide contextual information pertinent to the data being displayed.

Income Statement - Actual vs Budget - Entity: Paris - Cost Center: All Cost Centers - 2022M3 - Currency: EUR

	Actual	BudgetV2	Variance	Var %
Operating Sales	15,311,316	15,904,874	(593,558)	-3.7%
Returns & Allowances	387,032	851,471	464,439	54.5%
Net Sales	**14,924,284**	**15,053,403**	**(129,119)**	**-0.9%**
Operating Cost of Goods Sold	7,238,889	7,532,924	294,034	3.9%
Cost of Goods Sold	**7,238,889**	**7,532,924**	**294,034**	**3.9%**
Gross Income	**7,685,394**	**7,520,479**	**164,915**	**2.2%**

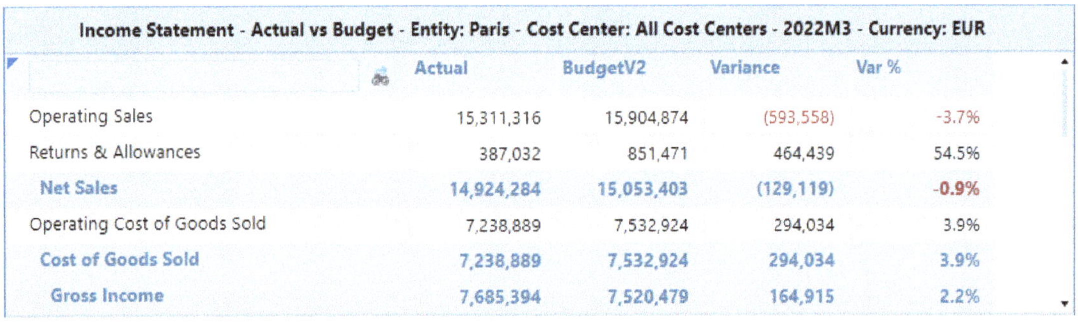

Figure 8.8

The same concept applies to substitution variables in the Report header and footer. See below, where we are using the same fields in the Report Header.

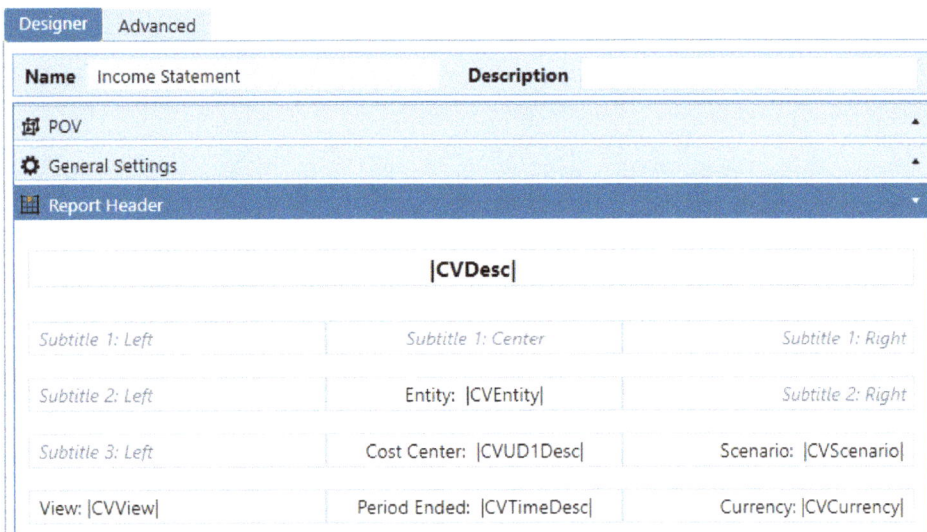

Figure 8.9

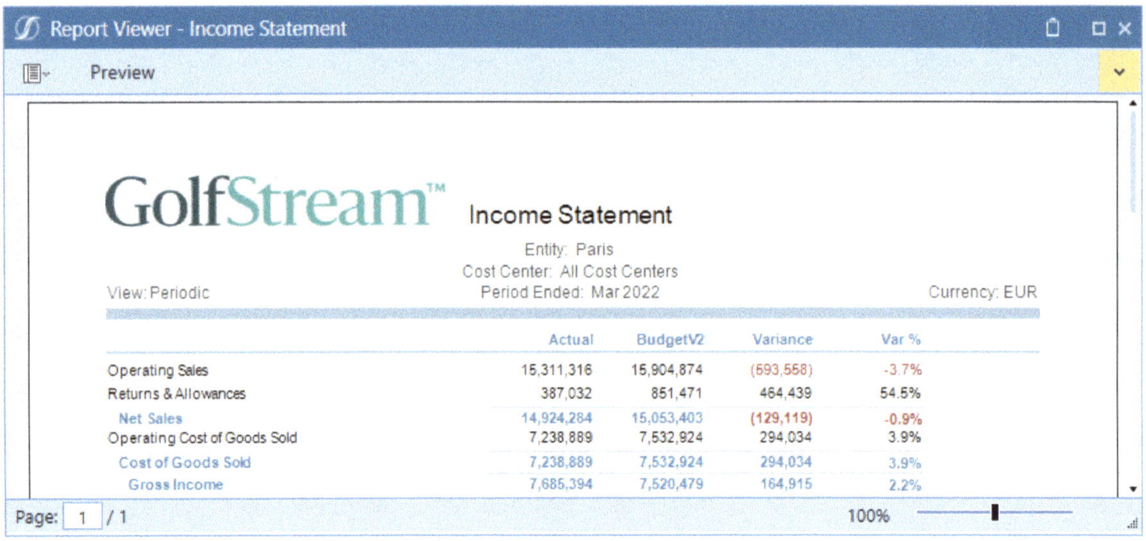

Figure 8.10

Parameters

Parameters can be used to drastically reduce the number of Cube Views required in your application by repurposing existing Cube Views, rows, and columns, and adding flexibility to Report properties. Parameters are located on the Application Dashboards menu and can be used throughout the application to provide lists and filters. Each Dashboard Maintenance Unit comes with a folder specifically for parameters; parameters, however, can be used across DMUs and in any Cube View.

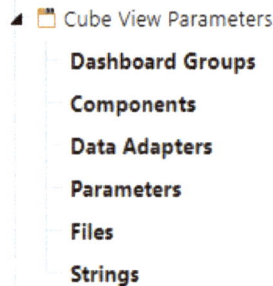

Figure 8.11

Parameter Types

The six standard Parameter Types are Literal Value, Input Value, Delimited List, Bound List, Member List, and Member Dialog.

- **Literal Value** parameters differ from the other Parameter Types in that they do not require the User to make a selection. They are set explicitly (or literally) and substitution variables can be used to query Global Settings like Time by setting the parameter to |GlobalTime|, for instance.

- **Input Value** parameters are the least commonly used Parameter Type from my experience; they require the User to key the Member Filter manually.

- **Delimited List** parameters are great for circumstances when you need to define certain elements or display selections in a more intuitive way; an example of this will be explained in the row and column sharing section to follow.

- **Bound List** parameters are the most advanced Parameter Type since they support commands for pre-defined Method Queries and SQL Queries.

- **Member Lists** are flat lists presented in a drop-down menu.

- **Member Dialogs** provide a tree structure of Members, which is often more intuitive for Users when picking a Report level.

Parameter Example

In this example, we have a Cube View using Bound List, Member List, Member Dialog, and Delimited List parameters to show how they work together.

Remember the example about sharing Income Statement rows to the nine Cube Views? Using parameter-driven columns now reduces the number of Cube Views back to three. To make your Cube Views even more dynamic, you can parameterize the Row Sharing setting to display different rows (i.e., Financial Statements), allowing the User to select the rows *and* columns.

Figure 8.12 shows a parameter named RowSet we've created to use for row sharing, and Figure 8.13 shows the ColumnSet parameter, where we've defined the column sets we want our Users to make a selection from. Notice that the parameters list the row and column templates we've defined as the Value Items, but the display values are different. Since Users may not know what the Value Items mean – based on the naming convention – we use the display value to create labels for these templates so the User will see logical names when making selections.

⊟ Data Source	
Parameter Type	Delimited List
Default Value	
Display Items (comma delimited)	Income Statement, Balance Sheet, Trial Balance
Value Items (comma delimited)	Rows_IncomeStatement, Rows_BalanceSheet, Rows_TrialBalance

Figure 8.12

⊟ Data Source	
Parameter Type	Delimited List
Default Value	
Display Items (comma delimited)	Current Year vs Prior Year, Actual vs Budget, Monthly Trend, Current Period vs Prior Period, Entity Aggregation
Value Items (comma delimited)	Cols_CYvsPY, Cols_ActualVsBudget, Cols_MonthlyTrend,Cols_CurPeriodVsPriorPeriod, Cols_EntityAggregation

Figure 8.13

Once you've created delimited list parameters for |!ColumnSet!| and |!RowSet!|, you can apply the parameters to the Cube View's sharing settings. This prompts the User to select which Financial Statement they need to view, as well as the columns they want to see when the Cube View is launched. This is incredibly useful when Reports need to be run by varying Scenarios, Time, Entity, and any other variables that query your data set.

⊟ Cube View Sharing	
Column Sharing	All Columns
Cube View Name For Sharing All Columns	|!ColumnSet!|
Cube View Name For Sharing All Columns 2	
Row Sharing	All Rows
Cube View Name For Sharing All Rows	|!RowSet!|
Cube View Name For Sharing All Rows 2	

Figure 8.14

Now that our row and column filters have been created and applied to the Cube View, we'll also want to enable Users to filter the Cube View's overall POV settings. Instead of creating additional

Cube Views for our Entities, Cost Centers, and Time periods, we can parameterize these Dimensions so that Users can query data at any level without ever leaving this Cube View.

Below, we see where the new parameters have been applied to our Cube View in this example. We're only parameterizing a few Dimensions, but if we wanted to make a fully filter-enabled Cube View, we could create parameters for every Dimension and apply them accordingly. Keep in mind that there's a trade-off with parameterizing the entire POV; the User would need to make a selection for each item when launching a Cube View.

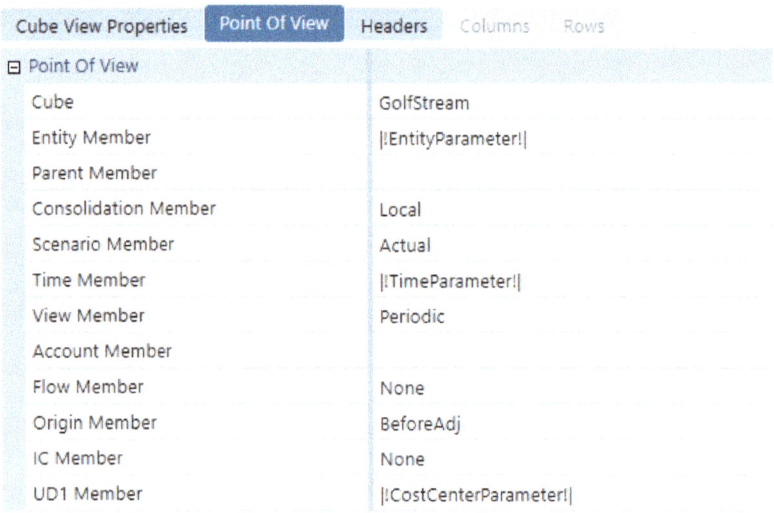

Cube View Properties	Point Of View	Headers	Columns	Rows

Point Of View	
Cube	GolfStream
Entity Member	|!EntityParameter!|
Parent Member	
Consolidation Member	Local
Scenario Member	Actual
Time Member	|!TimeParameter!|
View Member	Periodic
Account Member	
Flow Member	None
Origin Member	BeforeAdj
IC Member	None
UD1 Member	|!CostCenterParameter!|

Figure 8.15

When the Cube View is launched, the User will be prompted to make the following selections. This seems simple, right? If we had parameterized *all* Dimensions, the User would see many more options to select, and that could prove overwhelming.

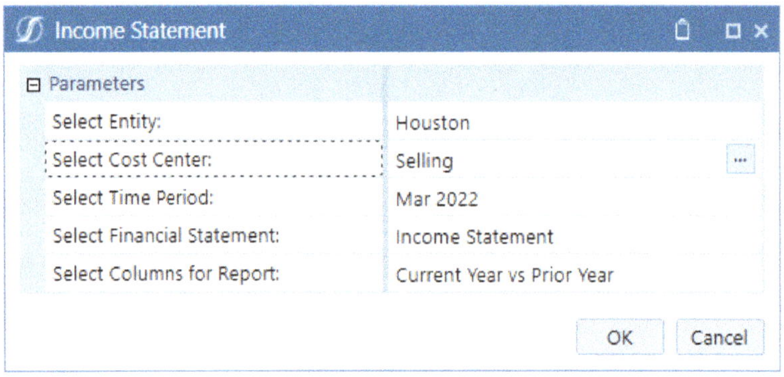

Income Statement		

Parameters		
Select Entity:	Houston	
Select Cost Center:	Selling	...
Select Time Period:	Mar 2022	
Select Financial Statement:	Income Statement	
Select Columns for Report:	Current Year vs Prior Year	

OK   Cancel

Figure 8.16

The Cube View is displayed below. In order to hide the Accounts with no data, we can apply row suppression and give our Users the ability to expose them.

Income Statement - Actual vs Budget - Entity: Houston - Cost Center: Selling - 2022M3 - Currency: USD				
	Actual	BudgetV2	Variance	Var %
Operating Sales				
IC Sales				
Returns & Allowances				
Other Outside Sales				
Net Sales				
Operating Cost of Goods Sold	465,388	349,041	(116,347)	-33.3%
IC Cost of Goods Sold				
Cost of Goods Sold	**465,388**	**349,041**	**(116,347)**	**-33.3%**
Gross Income	**(465,388)**	**(349,041)**	**(116,347)**	**-33.3%**
Total Employee Compensation	2,127,599	705,536	(1,422,063)	-201.6%
Total Utilities				
Total Professional Services				
Marketing & Advertising	774,700	581,025	(193,675)	-33.3%
Travel & Entertainment	103,739	77,804	(25,935)	-33.3%
Total Facility Expense				
Total HR Expenses				
Total Equip Expense	12,673	9,505	(3,168)	-33.3%
Total Telecom	10,532	7,899	(2,633)	-33.3%
Total R&D Expenses				
Depreciation & Amortization Expense				
Total Other Operating Expenses	3,296	2,472	(824)	-33.3%
Total Operating Expenses	**3,032,539**	**1,384,241**	**(1,648,298)**	**-119.1%**
Total Operating Income	**(3,497,927)**	**(1,733,282)**	**(1,764,645)**	**-101.8%**

Figure 8.17

To allow Users to view suppressed rows, we need to change the Can Modify Suppression setting to True. This setting will be made on the Income Statement Cube View.

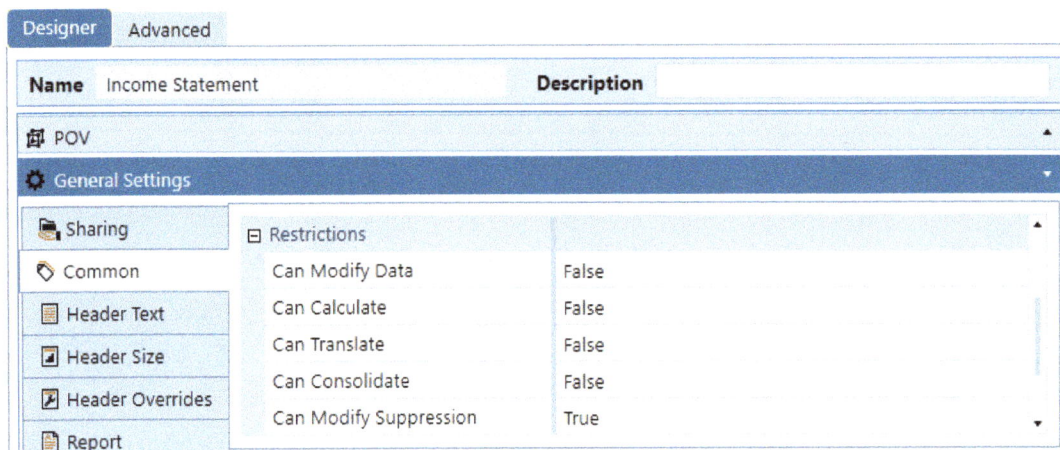

Figure 8.18

Chapter 8

To apply row suppression, we need to return to the row template. We set all suppression settings for each of our rows to True, except for the last row, OperatingIncome_GT. We leave this row in case the Report truly has no data; then our Users will see a row with no data rather than a blank screen.

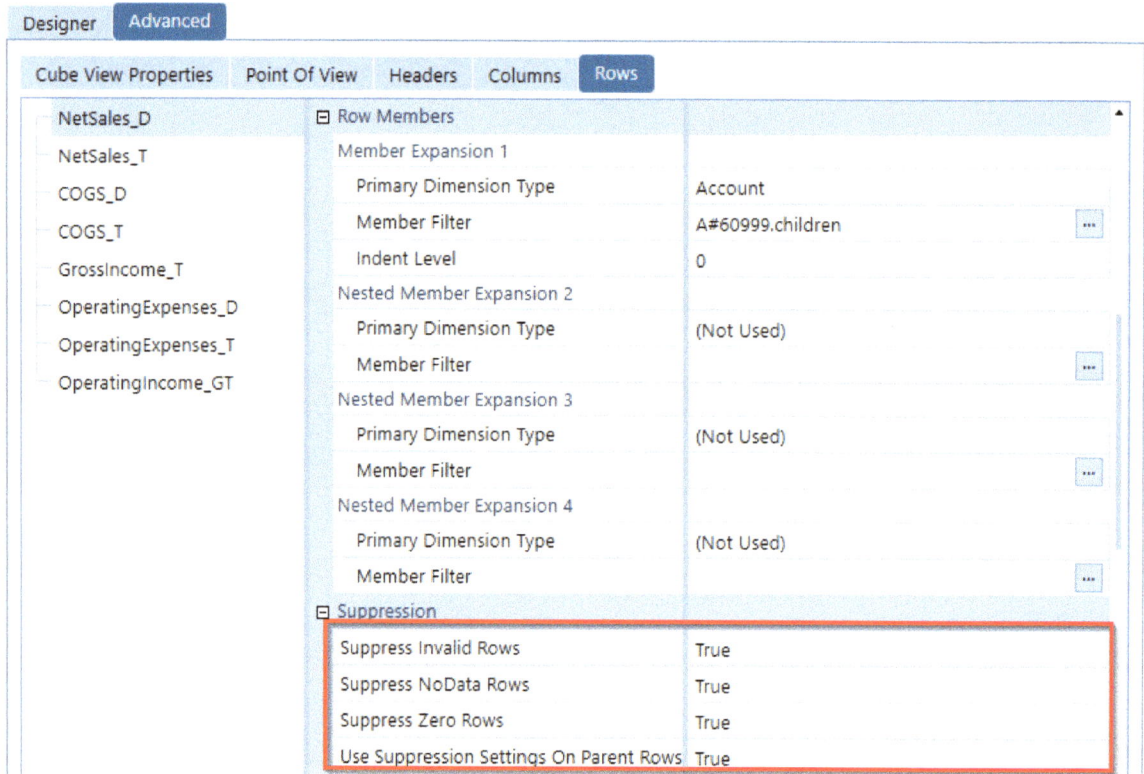

Figure 8.19

When we view the Data Explorer after applying suppression, we no longer see the blank rows, and there's a visible button on the header bar that allows us to view the suppressed rows.

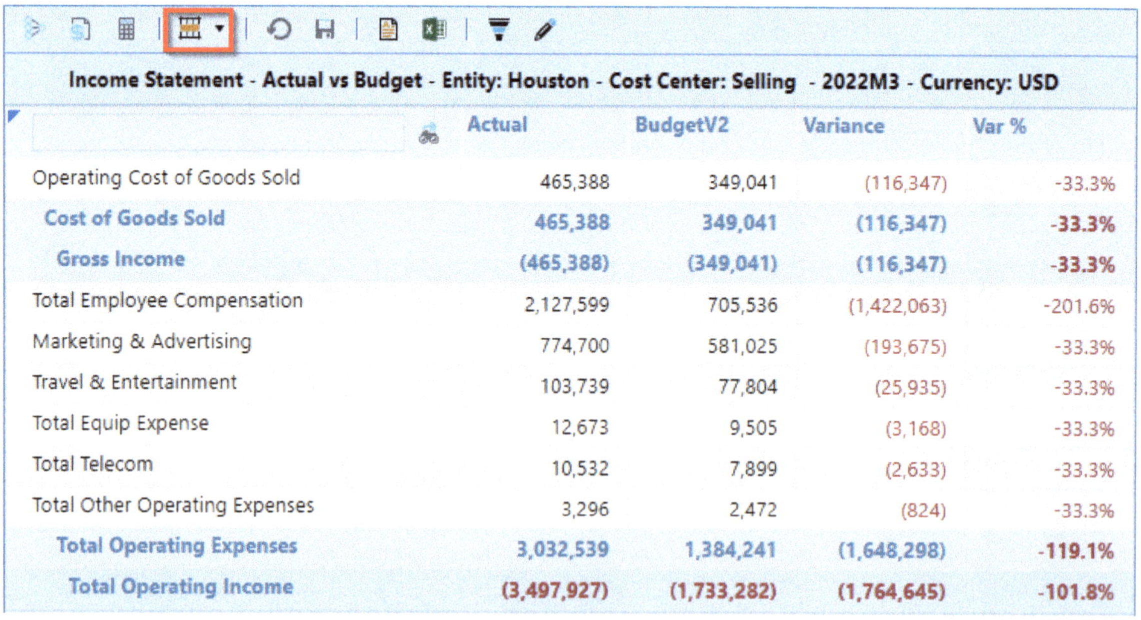

Figure 8.20

Parameterized Scaling

Organizations often scale their Financial Reports and show amounts in millions, billions, sometimes trillions. This can be a lengthy process and prone to error if you manually divide your data by different factors. OneStream has a simple solution for this, the **Scale** format, which is a numeric field indicating the number of characters to move the decimal, left or right. We created a parameter called **ScaleParameter** to prompt User selection. Scaling will be applied according to the selection made.

General (Parameter)	
Name	ScaleParameter
Workspace	Default
Maintenance Unit	UX Parameters
Description	Scale
User Prompt	Select Numeric Scaling:
Sort Order	10
Data Source	
Parameter Type	Delimited List
Default Value	0
Display Items (comma delimited)	Ones, Millions, Billions
Value Items (comma delimited)	0,3,6

Figure 8.21

The scale format property is found on the Cube View's general settings, but we only apply this to our numeric columns since the percentage column will not change.

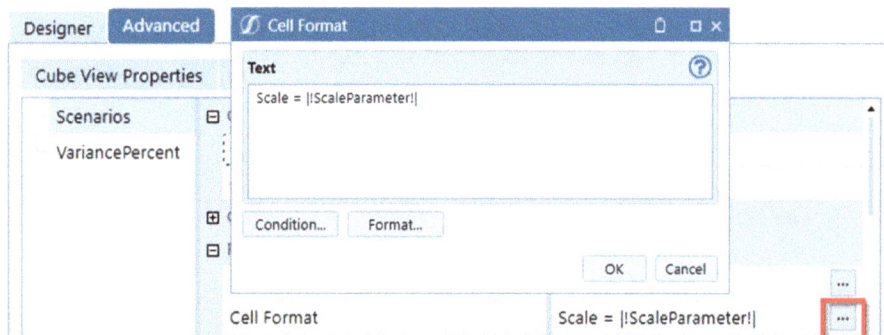

Figure 8.22

When we run the Report after applying the parameter to the scale format, we see an additional combo box with a prompt for Numeric Scaling.

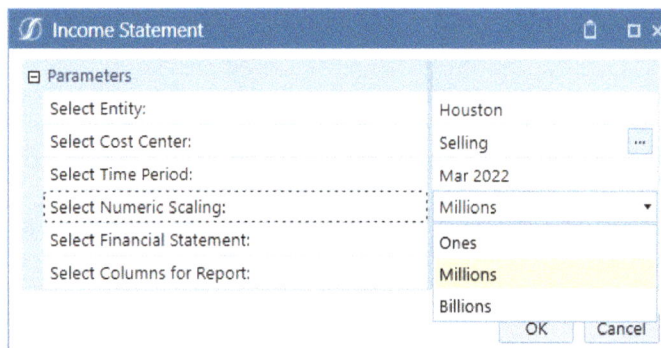

Figure 8.23

Here is the same Report again, but with the scaling format turned on.

Income Statement: Actual vs Budget - Entity: Houston - Cost Center: Selling - 2022M3 - Currency: USD				
	Actual	BudgetV2	Variance	Var %
Operating Cost of Goods Sold	465	349	(116)	-33.3%
Cost of Goods Sold	**465**	**349**	**(116)**	**-33.3%**
Gross Income	**(465)**	**(349)**	**(116)**	**-33.3%**
Total Employee Compensation	2,128	706	(1,422)	-201.6%
Marketing & Advertising	775	581	(194)	-33.3%
Travel & Entertainment	104	78	(26)	-33.3%
Total Equipment Expense	13	10	(3)	-33.3%
Total Telecom	11	8	(3)	-33.3%
Total Other Operating Expenses	3	2	(1)	-33.3%
Total Operating Expenses	**3,033**	**1,384**	**(1,648)**	**-119.1%**
Total Operating Income	**(3,498)**	**(1,733)**	**(1,765)**	**-101.8%**

Figure 8.24

Security-based Parameters

Parameters are useful in guiding Users to the data they are looking for, while providing security. The parameter below shows how to use the Security Access Group field within a parameter. This parameter checks Entity Security Groups to determine what Entities to include in the list.

General (Parameter)	
Name	EntityParameter
Workspace	Default
Maintenance Unit	UX Parameters
Description	Entity
User Prompt	Select Entity:
Sort Order	0
Data Source	
Parameter Type	Member List
Default Value	Houston
Display Member	
Cube	GolfStream
Dimension Type	Entity
Dimension	CorpEntities
Member Filter	E#[Total GolfStream].base.where(UserInReadDataGroup = True)

Figure 8.25

Culture Parameter

International organizations have added complexity when it comes to translating Financial Statements, with Users all over the world needing to consume and/or act on reporting metrics. But how do you act if your Reports are not in your native language? We parameterize a Report by applying the parameter below.

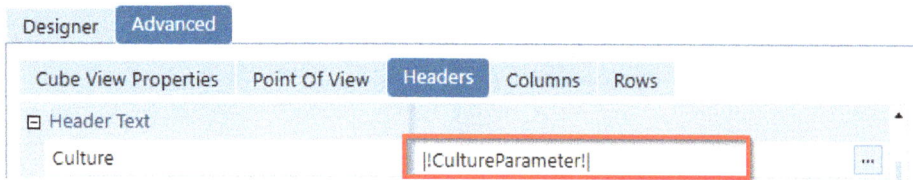

Figure 8.26

When the Report is launched, we see a prompt to select the language.

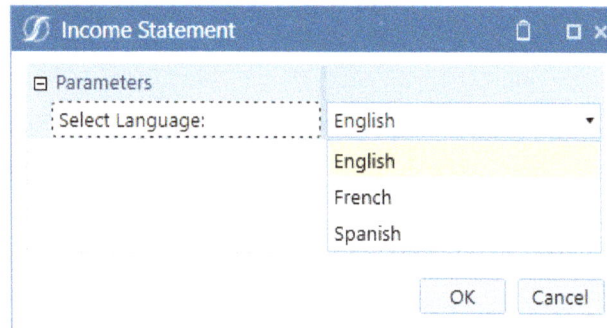

Figure 8.27

The Report shows the same data, but the text is in French.

	Actual	BudgetV2	Variance	Var %
Ventes d'exploitation	54,512,866	40,497,026	14,015,841	34.6%
Retours et indemnités	1,551,122	1,163,341	(387,780)	-33.3%
Ventes nettes	**52,961,745**	**39,333,684**	**13,628,060**	**34.6%**
Coût d'exploitation des marchandises vendues	28,016,691	21,012,518	(7,004,173)	-33.3%
IC Cost of Goods Sold	6,000	4,500	(1,500)	-33.3%
Coût des marchandises vendues	**28,022,691**	**21,017,018**	**(7,005,673)**	**-33.3%**
Revenu brut	**24,939,054**	**18,316,666**	**6,622,388**	**36.2%**

Figure 8.28

Navigation Links

Navigation links provide additional methods for displaying details, drilling into data, and exposing visuals without needing to navigate away from a specific Report or Cube View. The purpose of this functionality is to facilitate guided analysis and provide an intuitive click path for Users to access relevant data on the fly. This is an invaluable feature when Users tend to continuously drill on specific Dimensions from their Reports; for example, drilling on a Sales Account then into Product, Region, or Customer Dimensions; or drilling from an Expense Account down into Cost Centers.

Instead of just using the standard drill down screen, why not also give them the data they are looking for in another Cube View, which they can access from their right-click menu?

When configuring the source Cube View, consider when and where your Users will access the data. Navigation Links can be surfaced from 1. PDF Reports with hover and click behavior, or 2. enabled from a data grid similar to native drill down functionality.

Dashboard to Open in Dialog

Navigation links can be used on fully formatted Reports where, instead of a Grid View being exposed, the source Cube View is displayed in a PDF Report. The Cube View row defines the navigation path so that (as you can see in Figure 8.29) you could create links with alternate Dashboards to show depending on the row; or – in our example – by Account row.

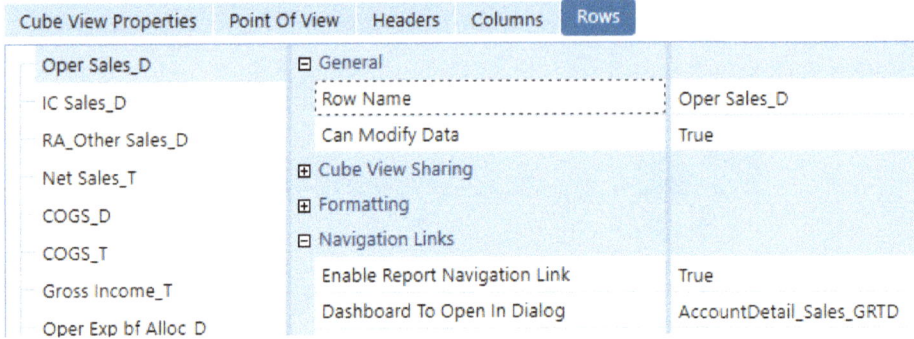

Figure 8.29

In the example below, the Operating Sales row is configured with a navigation link to show the Account detail that makes up the Operating Sales total. This is super helpful when you want to show Account detail for Operating Sales, Account trends for IC Sales, and chart visuals for Returns & Allowances. Of course, navigation links are completely configurable and should be built according to your Users' requirements.

	Actual	BudgetV2	Variance	Var %
Operating Sales	57,982,342	52,305,570	5,676,772	10.9%
IC Sales	15,000	13,200	1,800	13.6%
Returns & Allowances	1,841,894	1,620,867	-221,027	-13.6%
Net Sales	56,155,448	50,697,903	5,457,545	10.8%

Figure 8.30

	Actual	BudgetV2	Variance	Var %
Third Party Sales	50,945,236	45,891,770	5,053,466	11.0%
OEM Sales	4,606,157	4,274,565	331,592	7.8%
Subassembly Sales	382,840	336,899	45,941	13.6%
Parts Sales	2,048,108	1,802,335	245,773	13.6%
Operating Sales	57,982,342	52,305,570	5,676,772	10.9%

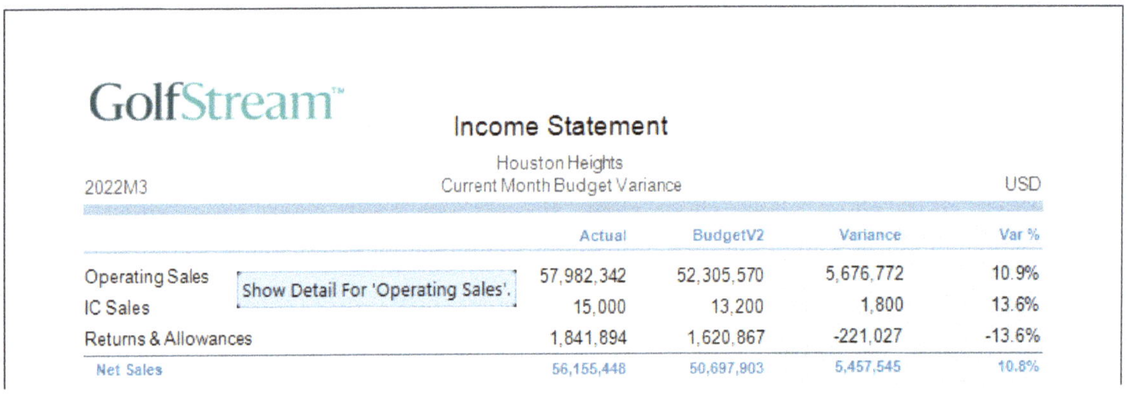

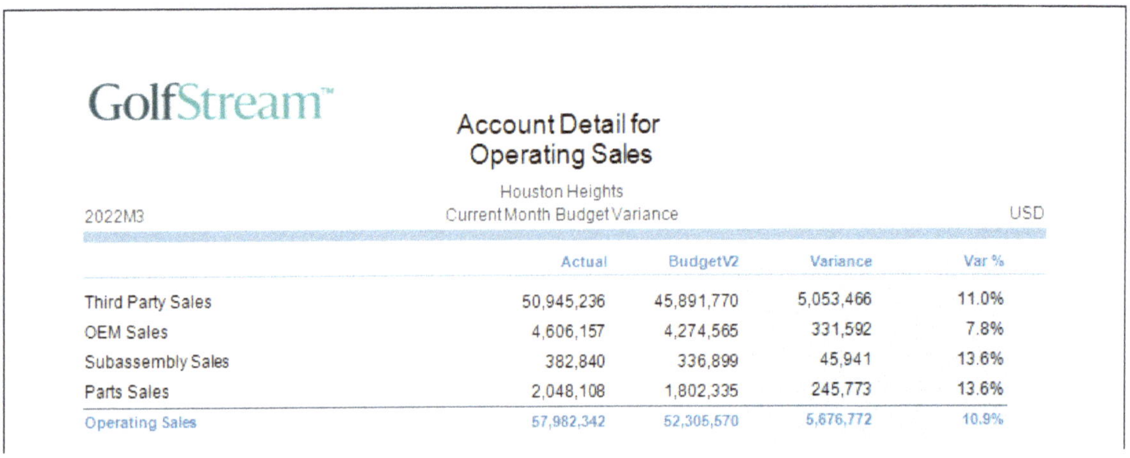

Figure 8.31

Linked Cube Views and Linked Dashboards

Linked Cube Views and Dashboards are intended to be exposed from a data grid. These are drill methods that Users navigate to by right-clicking on a data grid's cell and viewing optional navigation paths, and can include multiple navigation links, but separated with a comma.

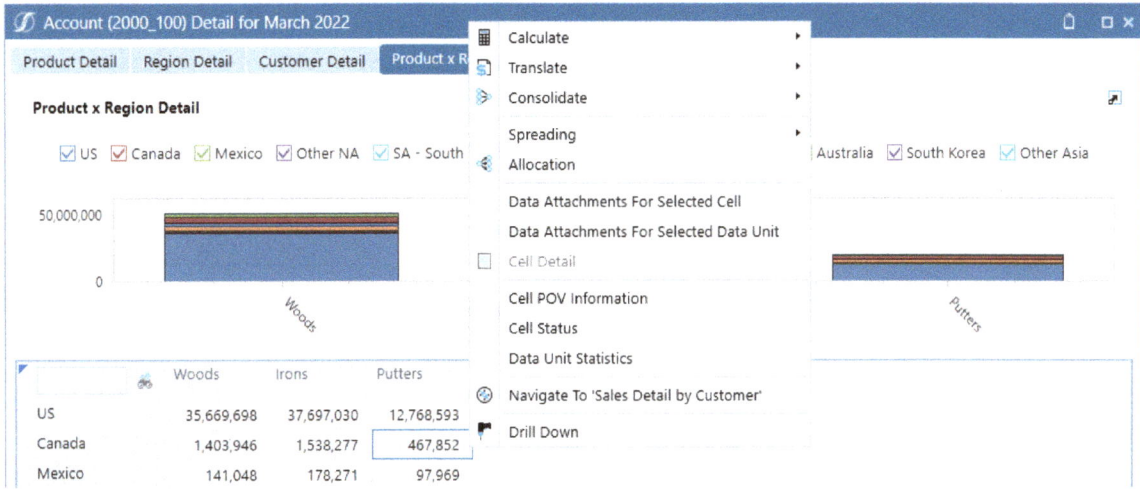

Figure 8.32

Bound Parameters

Dashboard parameters are commonly used to prompt User selection of reporting variables that determine the data queried when a Cube View is opened; these are stored parameters in a Dashboard Maintenance Unit. Bound Parameters are the parameter selections from a specific intersection held in memory when a Cube View is opened.

I regularly get asked the question, "Where do I find the Bound Parameters?" The short answer is that they don't exist. So, what does this mean, and how do you use them? Let's look at an example.

Assigning Bound Parameters

In Figure 8.33, we see the Budget Review Cube View; this is the source Cube View that will initially be displayed to the User. Under the Cube View Properties menu, you will notice a section labeled Navigation Links where the Linked Cube Views, Dashboards, and Bound Parameter Names have been assigned.

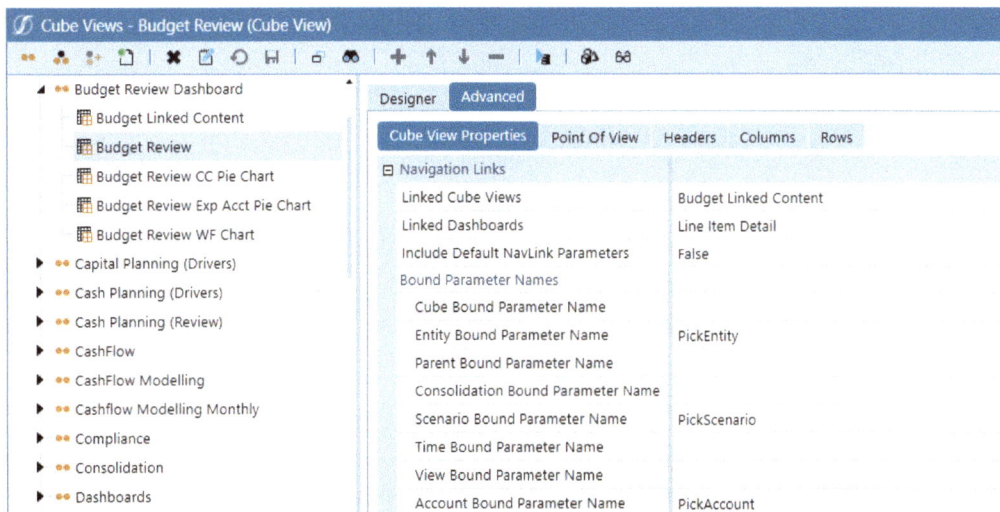

Figure 8.33

Applying Bound Parameters

In Figure 8.34, we see the `Budget Linked Content` Cube View; this is the target Cube View that we want to navigate to – from the source Cube View – in order to display trend detail. Under the Cube View Point of View menu, you'll notice the Entity Member, Scenario Member, and Account Member selections are the same Bound Parameter names that we assigned to the source Cube View's Navigation Links.

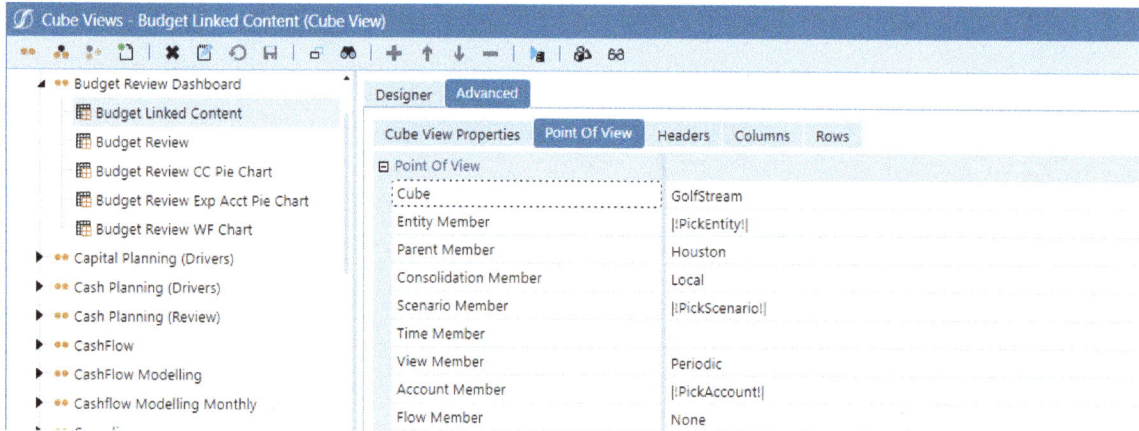

Figure 8.34

Cube View Extender

Cube View Extender Business Rules are used when creating highly customized and formatted Cube View PDF Reports. These rules allow you to configure properties that are not available from the standard Cube View settings and apply only to the Cube View PDF output.

There are two methods for applying Cube View Extenders to a Cube View:

- Inline Formula
- Business Rule

Inline Formula

To apply an Inline Formula to a Cube View, navigate to the Report and select Cube View Properties. Then, set the Custom Report Task property to Execute Cube View Extender Inline Formula, and click the ellipse button to access the Formula Editor.

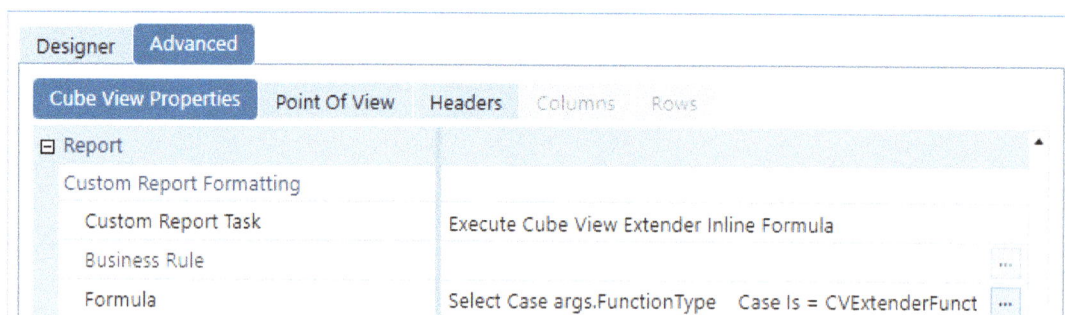

Figure 8.35

Figure 8.36 shows an example of an Inline Formula where we change the page header settings. Notice that the window exposes the code that runs when you launch a Cube View PDF; this functionality essentially provides the Business Rule framework for you.

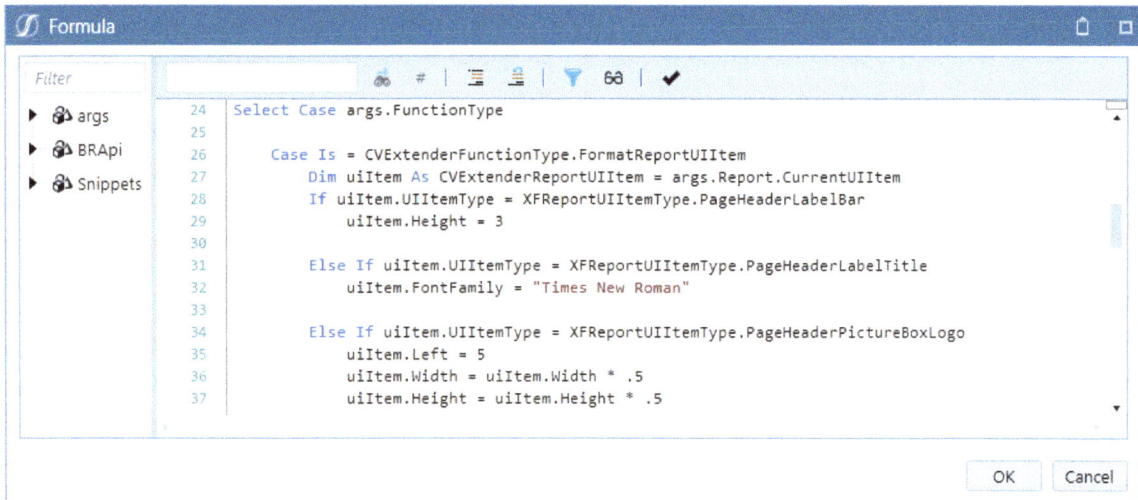

Figure 8.36

Inline Formula use of Cube View Extenders is recommended when you need to customize a single Cube View or when the customization differs by Cube View. For instance, if you want to display the Balance Sheet Report title font size as 12, the Income Statement Report font size as 14, and the Cash Flow Report title font as bold, you can quickly apply an inline formula directly to your Cube Views as needed.

Business Rule

To apply Business Rule logic to a Cube View, navigate to the Report and select Cube View Properties. Set the Custom Report Task property to Execute Cube View Extender Business Rule, and select the appropriate Business Rule.

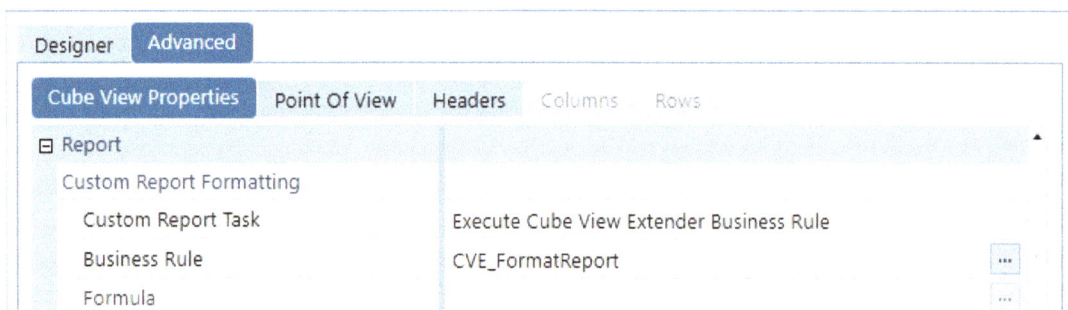

Figure 8.37

Cube View Extender Business Rules are located under the Cube View Extender folder from the Business Rules menu, as shown in Figure 8.38.

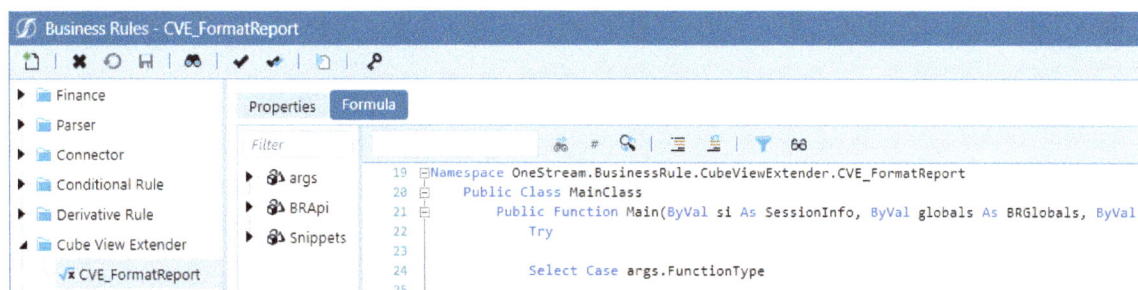

Figure 8.38

119

Business Rules are recommended when you want to apply formatting to multiple Cube Views without manually inserting the Inline Formula into each Report. Something to consider – when using Business Rules – is *who* will be creating Cube Views that require custom formatting, and this may prompt you to proactively create a variety of Business Rules that apply to specific groups of Reports. For example, if you require specific formatting for external reporting, and another User – who is unfamiliar with Inline Formulas – is creating the Reports, you may benefit from creating Business Rules for said User to choose from.

Over the years, I have found myself recreating custom formatting for three main Report groups: Financial Statements, footnotes, and supplemental Reports. After realizing how much time I was spending on formatting and tracking down all of the Reports that I needed to update, a lightbulb went off! I can create the three rules and never have to touch the individual Reports again!

Common Uses

Cube View Extenders are intended to allow the formatting of objects that are not configurable from standard Cube View settings (such as page headers, footer headers, page layout, and Report headers). They can also be used to supplement conditional formatting that applies to the data cells for multiple Cube Views, without manually configuring your entire Cube View Inventory.

Figure 8.39 shows a Cube View PDF with standard Cube View formatting. While there is nothing wrong with this Report, we want to make some cosmetic changes, including shrinking the logo, changing the title font to Times New Roman, and drawing the User's eye to certain variances.

GolfStream™ Income Statement

2022M3	Houston Heights Current Month Budget Variance			USD
	Actual	BudgetV2	Variance	Var %
Operating Sales	115,964,707	104,662,281	11,302,426	10.8%
IC Sales	1,846,263	1,757,235	89,028	5.1%
Returns & Allowances	3,683,789	3,440,990	-242,799	-7.1%
Other Outside Sales	466,157	474,565	-8,408	-1.8%
Net Sales	114,593,338	103,453,091	11,140,247	10.8%

Figure 8.39

See Figure 8.40 for the PDF Report display after we've applied the Cube View Extender. Our logo is proportionately sized, our Statement title is in Times New Roman font, and conditional formatting has been applied to display cells that exceed 10% highlighted in yellow, and cells less than -5% are shown as bold, italic, and in red font.

GolfStream™

Income Statement

2022M3	Houston Heights Current Month Budget Variance			USD
	Actual	BudgetV2	Variance	Var %
Operating Sales	115,964,707	104,662,281	11,302,426	10.8%
IC Sales	1,846,263	1,757,235	89,028	5.1%
Returns & Allowances	3,683,789	3,440,990	-242,799	-7.1%
Other Outside Sales	466,157	474,565	-8,408	-1.8%
Net Sales	114,593,338	103,453,091	11,140,247	10.8%

Figure 8.40

Below is the syntax used to apply conditional formatting to the Variance % cells. To modify the data grid section of the Report, the code is calling `XFReportUIItem.DataCellLabel`, but in order to limit formatting to the variance % column for detail rows, we need to apply filters.

Line 42 refers to the column name I've used in my Cube View to display the Variance %, and line 43 refers to the row name I've used in my Cube View to display the subtotals; the `If Not` syntax indicates that the formatting will not be applied to subtotals.

```
39      Else If uiItem.UIItemType = XFReportUIItemType.DataCellLabel Then
40          Dim cvCol As CubeViewCol = uiItem.GetCubeViewColumn()
41          Dim cvrow As CubeViewRow = uiItem.GetCubeViewRow()
42              If cvCol.Name.XFEqualsIgnoreCase("VariancePercent") Then
43                  If Not cvRow.Name.XFContainsIgnoreCase("_T") Then
44                      If uiItem.XFHasData Then
45                          If uiItem.XFAmount < -5 Then
46                              uiItem.TextColor = XFColors.Firebrick
47                              uiItem.Italic = True
48                              uiItem.Bold = True
49                          Else If uiItem.XFAmount > 10.0 Then
50                              uiitem.BackgroundColor = XFColors.Yellow
51                          Else
52                              uiItem.Italic = False
53                              uiItem.Bold = False
54                          End If
55                      End If
56                  End If
57              End If
```

Figure 8.41

Another common use of Cube View Extenders is when you need to display Cube View PDFs that appear similar to Grid Views with borders on data cells as well as headers. Below is the syntax that would produce the output shown in Figure 8.43.

```
97
98      If uiItem.UIItemType = XFReportUIItemType.DataCellLabel Then
99          uiItem.BorderSides = XFSides.All
100         uiItem.BorderColor = XFColors.XFDarkGray
101         uiItem.BorderThickness = 1
102     End If
103
```

Figure 8.42

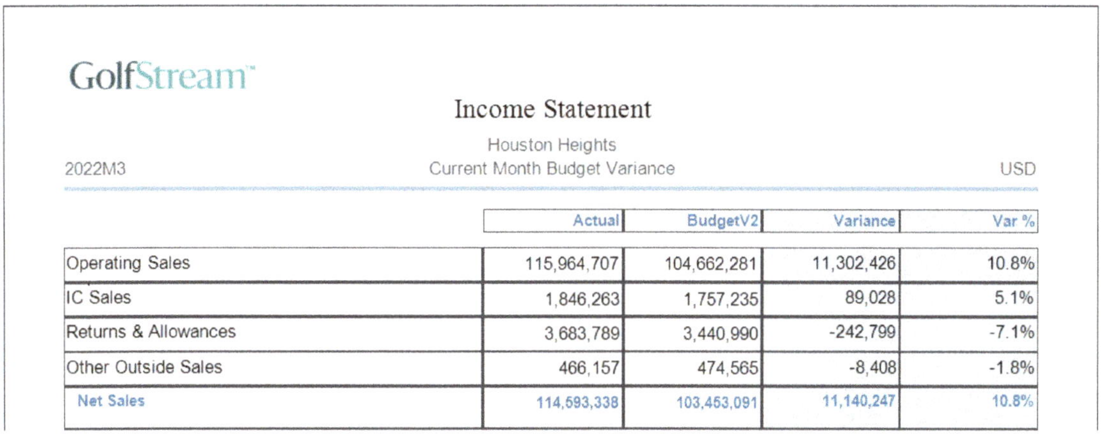

GolfStream
Income Statement
Houston Heights
2022M3 — Current Month Budget Variance — USD

	Actual	BudgetV2	Variance	Var %
Operating Sales	115,964,707	104,662,281	11,302,426	10.8%
IC Sales	1,846,263	1,757,235	89,028	5.1%
Returns & Allowances	3,683,789	3,440,990	-242,799	-7.1%
Other Outside Sales	466,157	474,565	-8,408	-1.8%
Net Sales	114,593,338	103,453,091	11,140,247	10.8%

Figure 8.43

Fields and Properties

Available fields from the `XFReportUIItem` Inventory are listed below; these are the Report fields that can be modified within a Cube View Extender. OneStream's built-in Intellisense feature guides you as you insert syntax into the code lines; once you've started querying the items and type `uiItem.UIItemType = XFReportUIItemType.` a drop-down menu will appear with the following options.

PageHeaderLabelBar	PageHeaderLabelLeft3	PageFooterPageNumber
PageHeaderLabelTitle	PageHeaderLabelLeft4	PageFooterLabelLeft1
PageHeaderPictureBoxLogo	PageHeaderLabelCenter1	PageFooterLabelLeft2
DataCellLabel	PageHeaderLabelCenter2	PageFooterLabelLeft3
ColHeaderLabel	PageHeaderLabelCenter3	PageFooterLabelLeft4
RowHeaderLabel	PageHeaderLabelCenter4	PageFooterLabelCenter1
UpperLeftLabel	PageHeaderLabelRight1	PageFooterLabelCenter2
LabelBottomLine1	PageHeaderLabelRight2	PageFooterLabelCenter3
LabelBottomLine2	PageHeaderLabelRight3	PageFooterLabelCenter4
LabelTopLine1	PageHeaderLabelRight4	PageFooterLabelRight1
LabelTopLine2	PageFooterLine	PageFooterLabelRight2
PageHeaderLine	PageFooterDate	PageFooterLabelRight3
PageHeaderLabelLeft1	PageFooterLabelTitle	PageFooterLabelRight4
PageHeaderLabelLeft2		

Figure 8.44

The **OneStream API Details & Database Documentation** utility is extremely helpful for searching database components, objects, and Members. Below is a view that contains the objects available to format, displayed in the right pane. This utility provides a view into the database framework and guides you through the solution's built-in Intellisense feature.

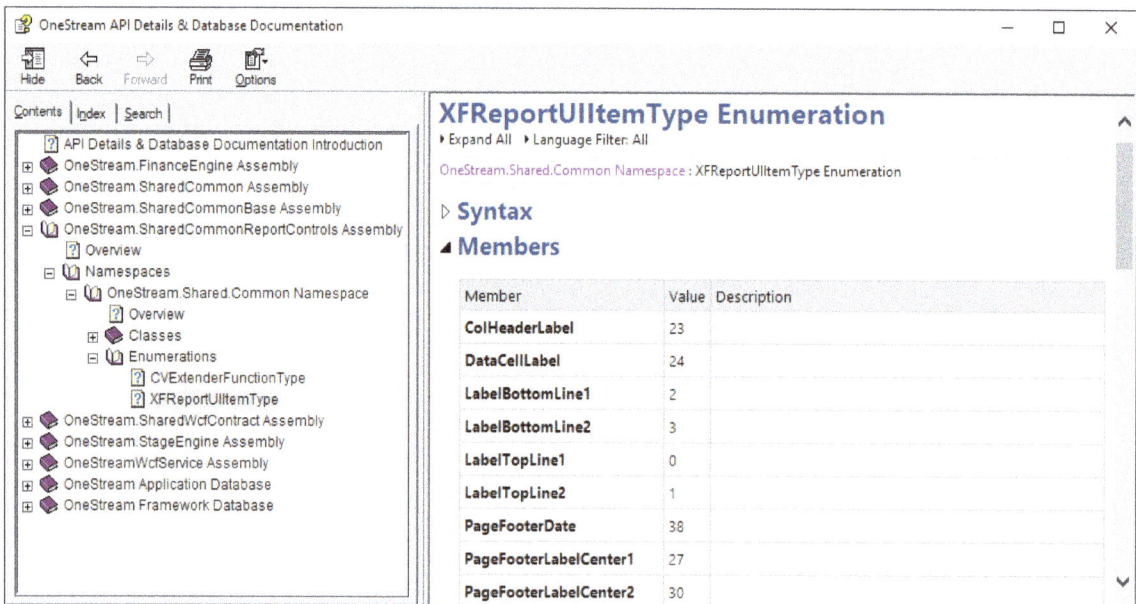

Figure 8.45

Conclusion

In this chapter, we covered a few advanced Cube View design techniques to minimize maintenance of your application, streamline consistency in formatting and, most importantly, provide your Users with seamless navigation to meaningful information.

Row and column sharing between and across Cube Views mean fewer redundancies in Cube Views and increased accuracy in reporting when you're viewing consistent data.

Parameters are perhaps the most useful tool at your disposal; they greatly reduce the number of Cube Views you'll need to build during an implementation, provide your Users with the flexibility to query data when (and how) they want on-demand, and truly make the most robust Cube structures dynamic.

Navigation links make data analysis and viewing much more intuitive by guiding your Users to the underlying data that can be displayed in a plethora of ways.

Cube View Extender Rules are your friends! They can seem a little scary when you think of them like coding, but with some solid examples to reference, the formatting possibilities are endless.

9

Build Your Own Cube View

In this chapter, we will go through the creation of several related Cube Views using a step-by-step approach. Creating Cube Views can be complex and may seem daunting, so we will look at tips and tricks along the way to help make the process as straightforward and User-friendly as possible.

The goal is not only to help you create these Cube Views, but also to make them flexible and adaptable for your Users. We understand that everyone has different needs and preferences when it comes to data visualization, so our Cube Views will be designed to be modifiable and able to suit different Users' needs.

By the end of this chapter, you will have a comprehensive understanding of how to create effective and flexible Cube Views, with the knowledge and skills to apply these techniques to your own work. Whether you are new to Cube Views or are looking to improve your existing skills, this chapter should give you the resources you need to succeed!

Cube View Recap

Cube Views are a display mechanism that allow you to present data from a 'Cube' in a 'View' that is easily understood by consumers of the data. In other words, a Cube View is a multi-dimensional representation of data that enables Users to analyze and interact with large volumes of data from multiple perspectives.

There are hundreds of tools that can help you collect data, but if you can't tell a story with the data, then what's the point? Imagine you have a spreadsheet with critical information about your organization's financial data – but no way to sort, filter, organize, or pivot your data. Cube Views are OneStream's foundational reporting tool and allow you to define information in a digestible way simply by querying the Cube and displaying the information that is relevant to you.

Cube Views display data as a set of Cubes or Dimensions that can be rotated and manipulated to view the data from different angles. Each Dimension represents a different aspect of the data, such as Time, Product, Geography (or any Attribute that your organization defines as a reporting requirement or need). Thoughtful selection and combinations of different data Dimensions can help answer specific business questions and solve financial challenges.

Cube Views can be used to perform a wide range of analyses, such as trend analysis, variance analysis, and forecasting. They can also be used to create templates for data entry Forms to collect valuable financial and non-financial data that your organization needs in Financial Planning. They are particularly useful for analyzing large datasets, as they enable Users to drill down into the data to uncover insights and identify trends.

Okay, let's get into the nitty-gritty.

A Step-by-Step Example

In this example, we'll build an Income Statement Variance Cube View with dynamic filters and navigation links – to linked Cube Views and linked Dashboards – to enable your Users to access more granular data via an intuitive click method. We'll leverage parameters to accelerate formatting with consistency that can be used across the application, and a Cube View Extender Rule to apply Report formatting for objects that are not editable from the UI. The end result will be a fully formatted Cube View for viewing in Data Explorer, Excel, and Reports.

The key components of our Cube View include:

- Point of View
- Rows and Columns
- Formatting
- Navigation Links

Step 1: Creating a Cube View

Navigate to the Presentation menu from the Application tab, and click Cube Views to access your Cube View library. The Cube View library is an Inventory of your Cube Views. Cube View Groups allow you to organize Reports and data entry Forms in a way that makes sense to your organization.

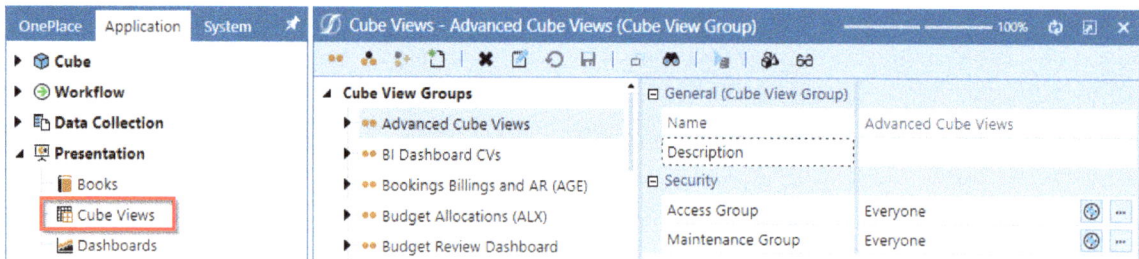

Figure 9.1

To create a new Cube View, select the Cube View Group where you want to store the Cube View and then click the Create Cube View button from the header toolbar.

Figure 9.2

Enter Income Statement Variance in the name field, leave the description blank, then save. If your application uses specific naming conventions to sort Cube Views, consider entering User-friendly descriptions. For example, you can name the Cube View IncomeStatementVariance, but if you want users to see Income Statement Variance, then you would enter Income Statement Variance as the description. It's important to remember that substitution variables are available to display these properties using |CVName| or |CVDesc|.

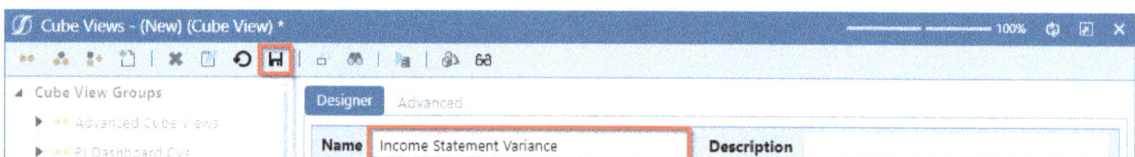

Figure 9.3

Step 2: Point of View

The POV is ultimately what you define as your default filters for a given Report. There are many different approaches to designing Cube Views depending on different variables – including the nature of the Report, your organization's preferences, and the purpose of the Report, to name but a few. There are certainly use cases for not setting POV filters in a Cube View. For instance, if you want a Cube View to be driven off your Users' Cube POV selections rather than controlling the filters, then leaving Member Filters blank in the Cube View POV would default to a given User's Cube POV.

In my experience, relying on User Cube POVs can be tricky since they are User-sensitive, which means different Users may not see the same data, and that can cause confusion. A personal best practice of mine is to define each Member Filter to adhere to consistency in the data that Users see.

The figure below is how we've set the Cube View POV. Notice that we've parameterized the `EntityMember`, `TimeMember`, and `ViewMember` to allow the User to select these filters upon displaying the Cube View. The `ScenarioMember` and `AccountMember` are not defined intentionally; the `ScenarioMember` will be set in our columns and the `AccountMember` will be set in our rows. The remaining filters are explicitly defined to restrict the data from differing between Users.

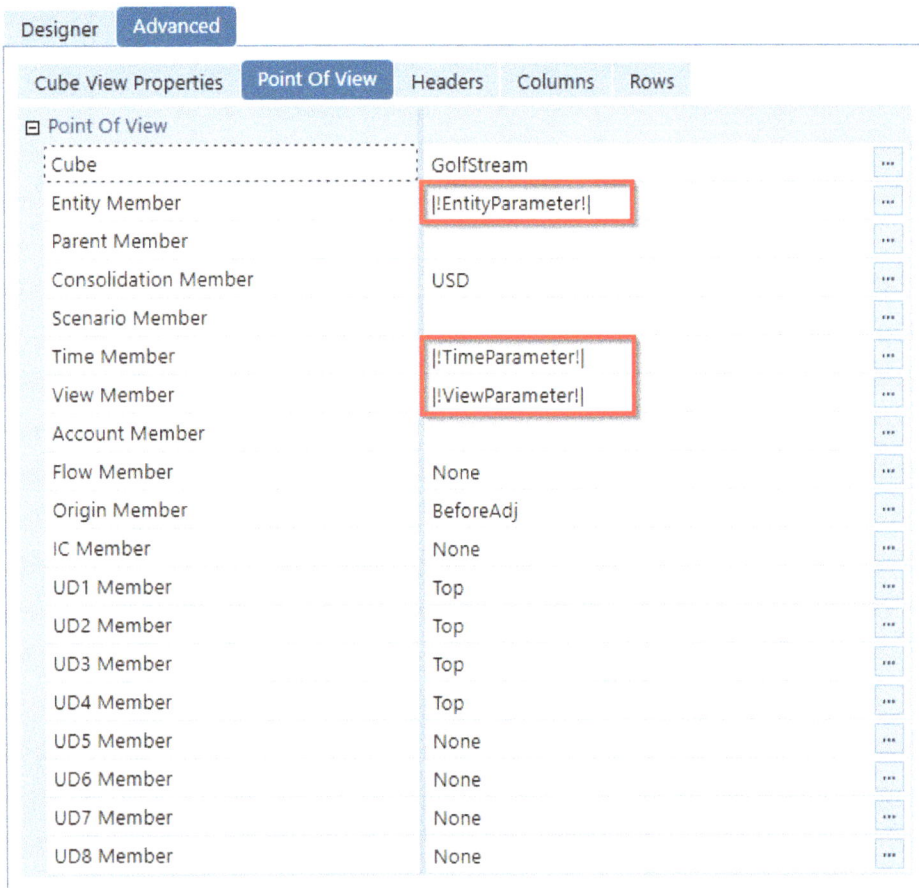

Figure 9.4

The parameters used in the Cube View's POV are shown here. Notice the Default Value and Display Member settings for each parameter; the Default Value(s) are what we want to see initially selected when the prompt dialog appears, and the Display Member will show the Member descriptions for the selections.

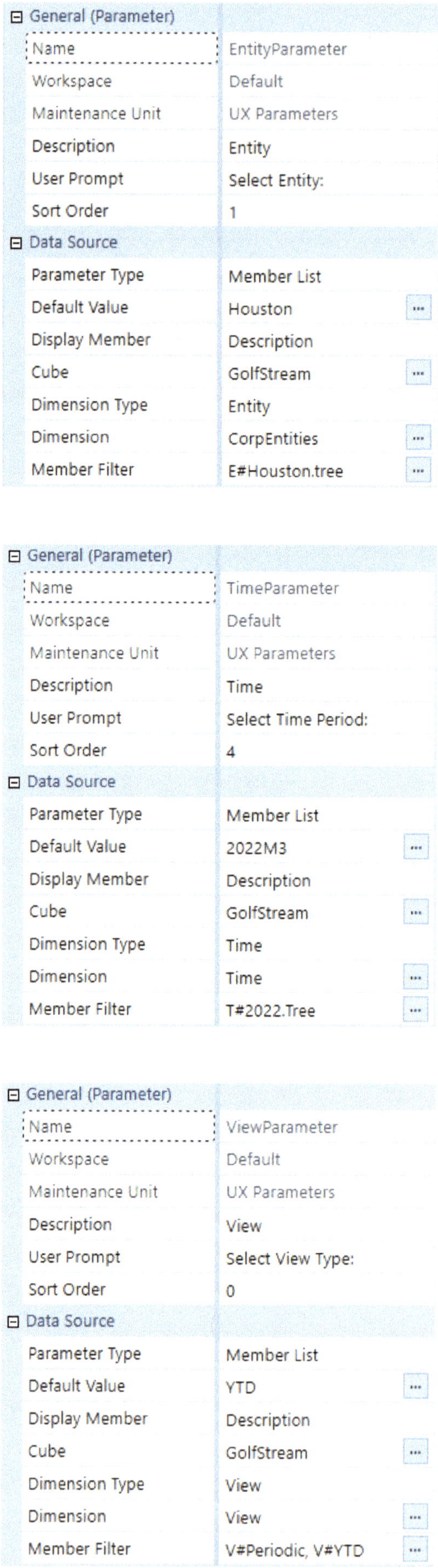

General (Parameter)	
Name	EntityParameter
Workspace	Default
Maintenance Unit	UX Parameters
Description	Entity
User Prompt	Select Entity:
Sort Order	1
Data Source	
Parameter Type	Member List
Default Value	Houston
Display Member	Description
Cube	GolfStream
Dimension Type	Entity
Dimension	CorpEntities
Member Filter	E#Houston.tree

General (Parameter)	
Name	TimeParameter
Workspace	Default
Maintenance Unit	UX Parameters
Description	Time
User Prompt	Select Time Period:
Sort Order	4
Data Source	
Parameter Type	Member List
Default Value	2022M3
Display Member	Description
Cube	GolfStream
Dimension Type	Time
Dimension	Time
Member Filter	T#2022.Tree

General (Parameter)	
Name	ViewParameter
Workspace	Default
Maintenance Unit	UX Parameters
Description	View
User Prompt	Select View Type:
Sort Order	0
Data Source	
Parameter Type	Member List
Default Value	YTD
Display Member	Description
Cube	GolfStream
Dimension Type	View
Dimension	View
Member Filter	V#Periodic, V#YTD

Figure 9.5

Note: The Member List Parameter Type will show a flat list within a combo box.

While we're defining the Report's content, we should also consider the Report's header and footer fields to provide clarity into the data we're presenting. From the Report settings, we have the opportunity to surface pertinent information about the Report so our Users know *what* relevant data points are being presented; this is the perfect time to leverage **substitution variables**.

Since we're parameterizing the Report's Time, Entity, and View Members, we'll want to present the selected filters on the Report so our Users can easily identify the data set they are viewing. Setting the subtitle fields to display our chosen substitution variables will greatly help Users validate what they've selected from the filters.

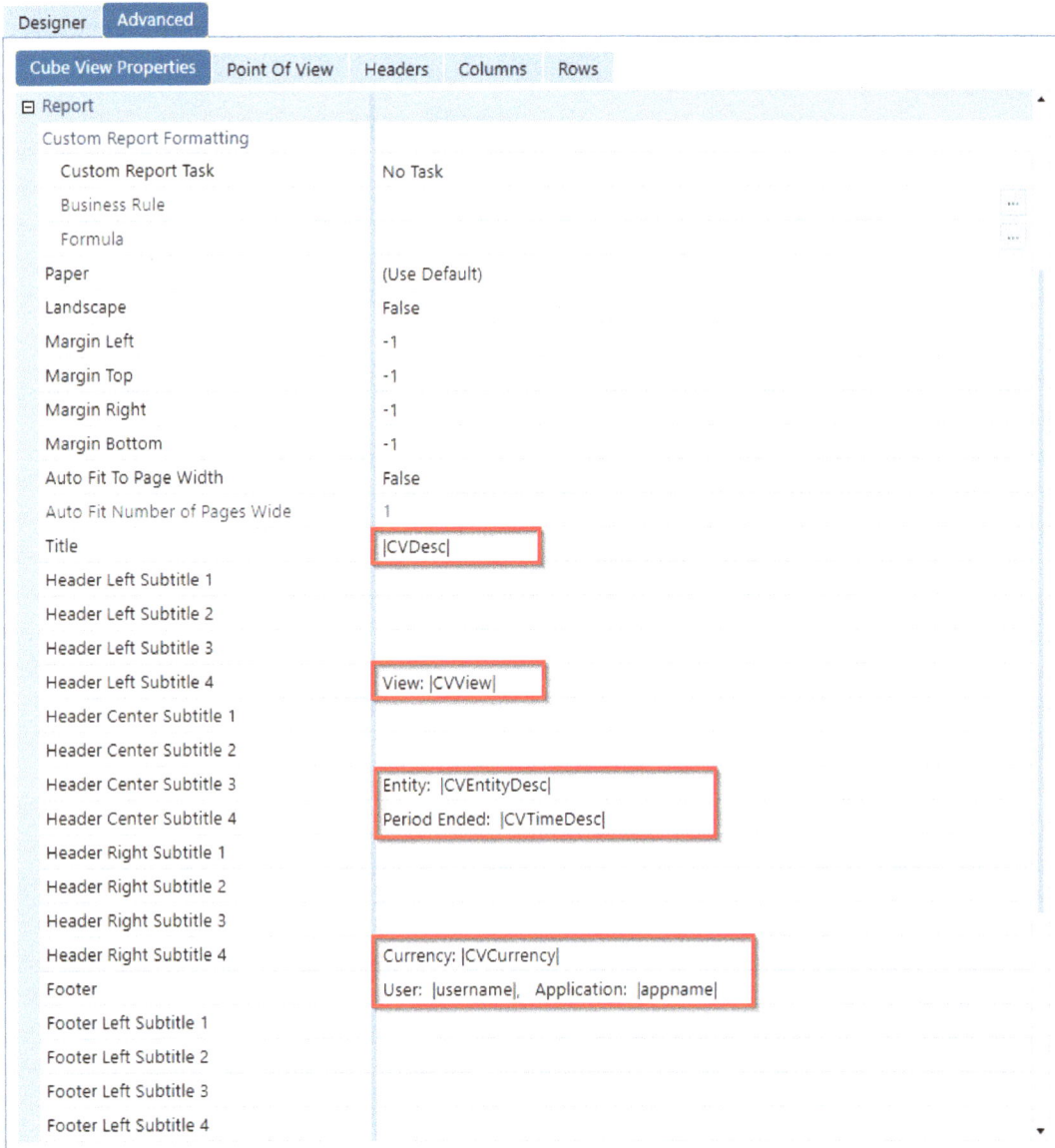

Figure 9.6

Here's what the Report header looks like when we add context to the Report settings. It makes the Report content a little more clear, right? When building Cube Views, I highly suggest incorporating these settings to give your Reports transparency into what is being presented.

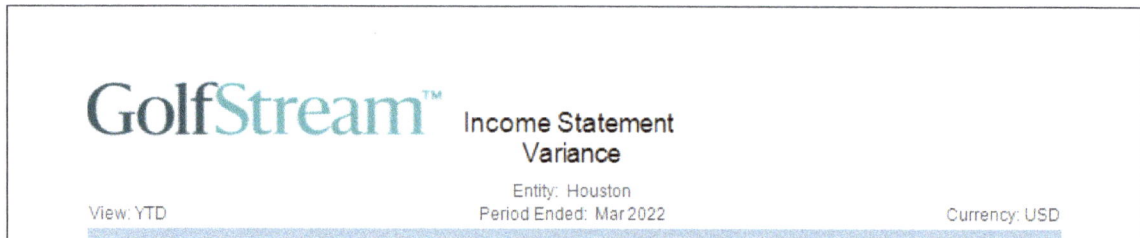

Figure 9.7

Another important factor to consider when building Cube Views is how you want to display the Member Names. Do you want to include the Account name, description, or both? This is where you can use the selectors to dictate how the Member Filters are displayed in your Cube View.

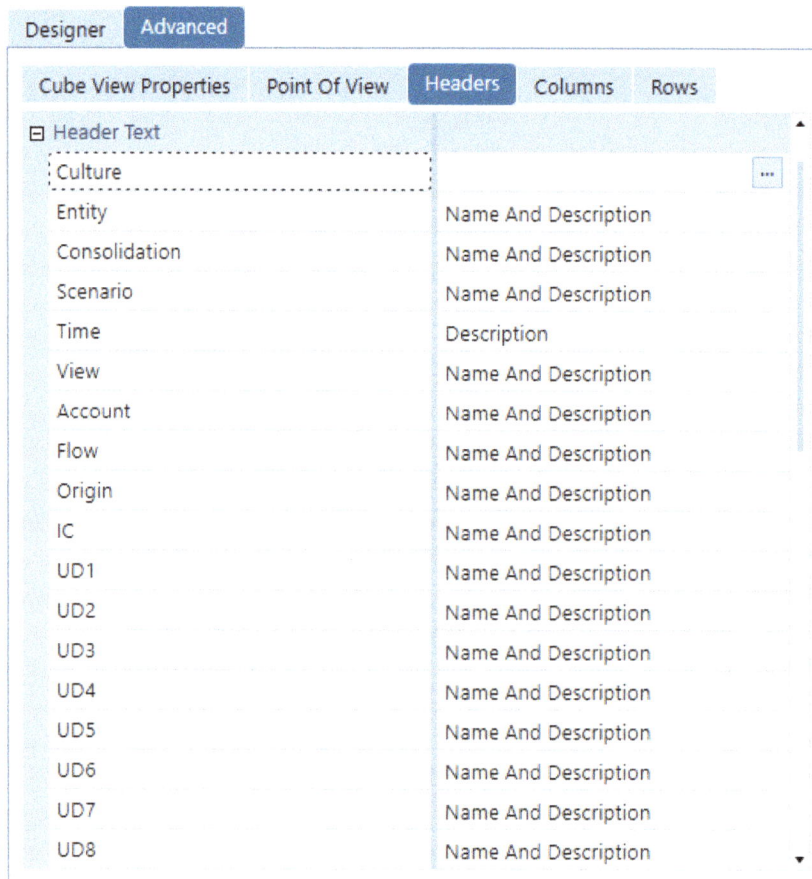

Figure 9.8

Step 3: Rows and Columns

The arrangement of information in a Report is determined by its rows and columns. Rows represent the horizontal organization of data, while columns represent the vertical arrangement of data. Together, rows and columns form a grid that provides a clear and structured layout for the Report's content. This layout helps readers to quickly locate and understand the information they need.

Rows

The Income Statement requires the inclusion of several key financial metrics to accurately represent the financial performance of a business. These metrics typically include Net Sales, Cost of Goods Sold, Gross Income, Operating Expenses, and Operating Income; these are the Accounts we'll include in our Cube View.

The table below is how we'll set up our rows. The **Row Names** include suffixes to indicate Detail, Subtotals, and the Grand Total, which will be used in formatting the rows using conditional formatting later in this chapter.

It's important to note that building Cube Views requires some knowledge of your metadata structure to ensure accurate reporting; we've selected the Accounts below based on our Account hierarchy shown in Figure 9.10. Notice that the indent levels relate to the leveling in our Account hierarchy.

Row Name	Primary Dimension Type	Member Filter	Indent Level
NetSales_D	Account	A#60999.Children	0
NetSales_T	Account	A#60999	1
COGS_D	Account	A#43000.Children	0
COGS_T	Account	A#43000	1
GrossIncome_T	Account	A#61000	2
OperatingExpenses_D	Account	A#54500.Children	0
OperatingExpenses_T	Account	A#54500	2
OperatingIncome_GT	Account	A#62000	3

Figure 9.9

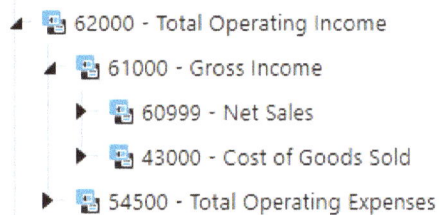

Figure 9.10

We'll add these rows to our Cube View by navigating to the Rows tab from the Advanced view, and then clicking the Add Row or Column button in the header toolbar.

If you prefer to use the Designer view, navigate to the Rows and Columns slider and complete the following: rename Row1 as NetSales_D, select the Account as the Member selection, and enter A#60999.Children in the Member Filter. Click the Add Row button and repeat this process for the remaining rows. See Figure 9.11 for how this completed row should appear.

> **Note**: To access the Row Indent Level from the Design view, select the Rows and Columns slider, select the row name, and click on the Formatting tab.

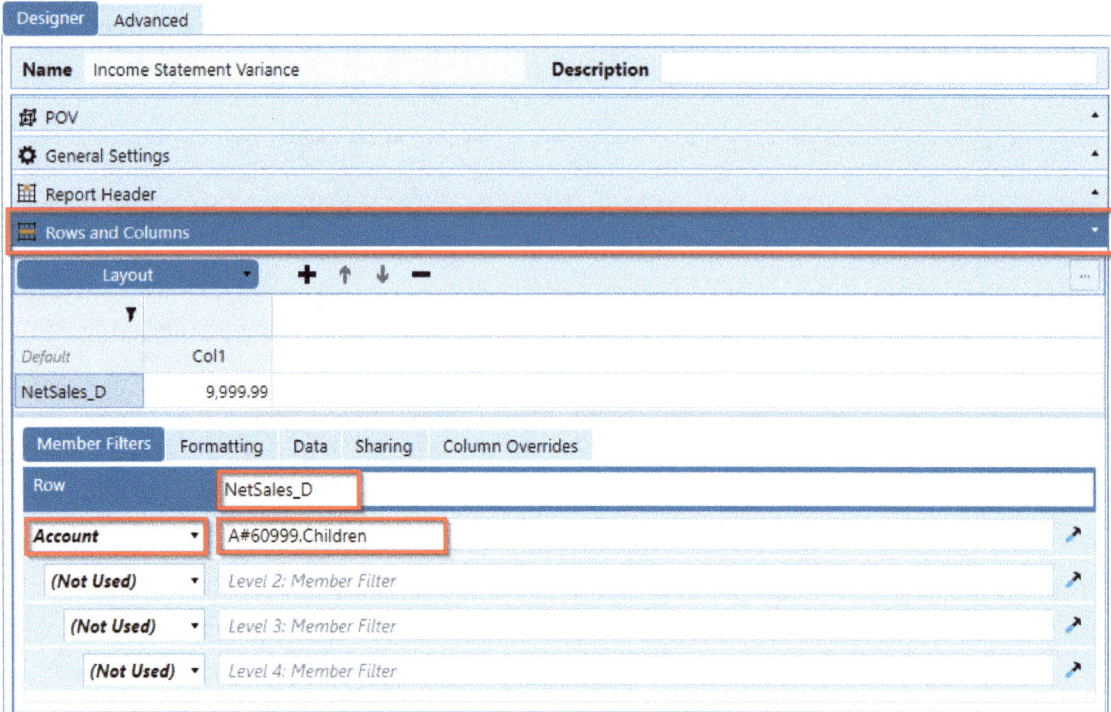

Figure 9.11

The figure below displays the rows we've added to our Cube View from the Advanced view.

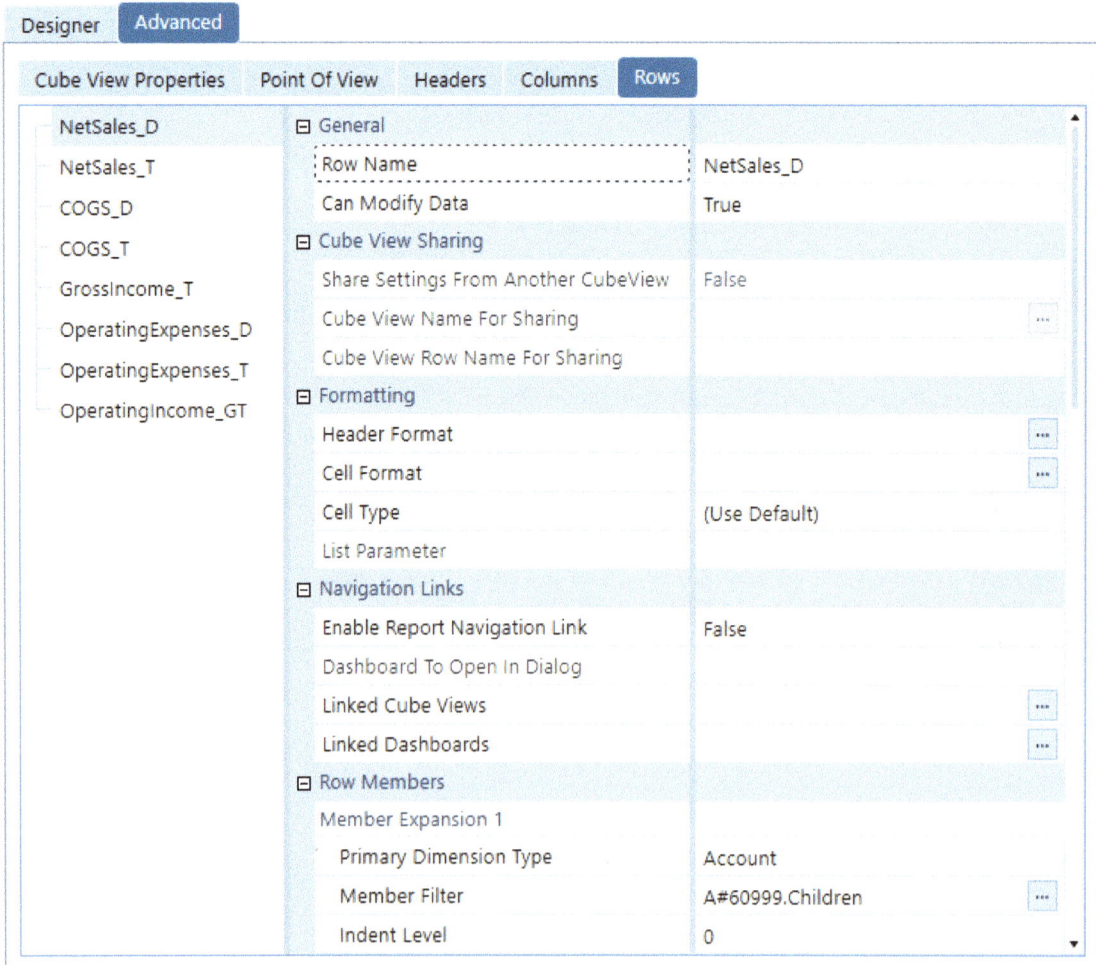

Figure 9.12

Columns

For our columns, we'll display Actual and Budget Scenarios, as well as variance in dollars, variance %, and an explanation field to collect information about the organization's performance. Variance reporting typically refers to Planned versus Actual data comparison, with Scenario being the most common Dimension to use in columns. Trend or year-over-year reporting, on the other hand, usually uses the Time Dimension in the columns.

The Actual column displays the actual performance of the metric for the given period, while the Budget column displays the expected performance based on the budgeted figures. The Variance in dollars column represents the absolute difference between the Actual and budgeted performance in monetary terms, while the Variance % column represents the percentage difference between the two. Finally, the Explanation field provides a space for you to collect commentary from your Users to explain volatility, unique occurrences that caused the variance, and overall explanations to help the organization make future business decisions.

Column Name	Primary Dimension Type	Member Filter
Actual	Scenario	S#Actual
Budget	Scenario	S#BudgetV2
Variance	Scenario	GetDataCell(BWDiff(S#Actual,S#BudgetV2)):Name("Variance")
VariancePercent	Scenario	GetDataCell(BWPercent(S#Actual, S#BudgetV2)):Name("Var %")
Explanation	Scenario	S#Actual:V#Annotation:Name("Explanation")

Figure 9.13

The figure below displays the columns we've added to our Cube View from the Advanced view.

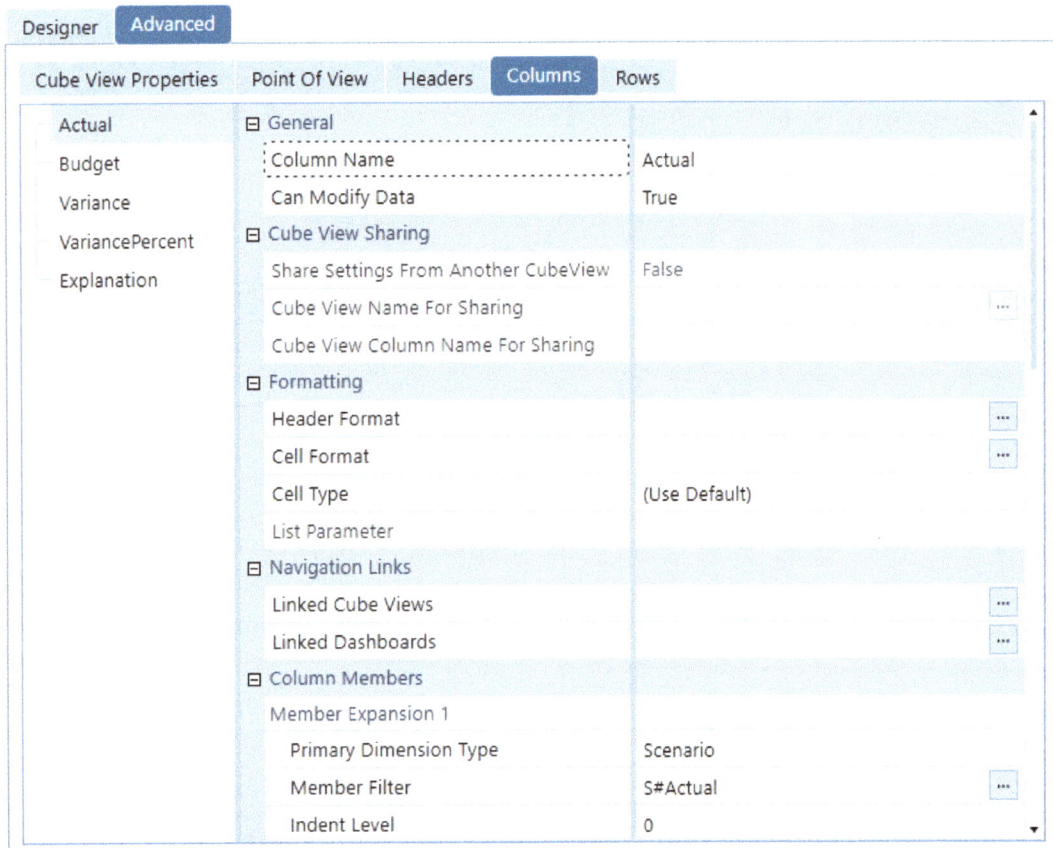

Figure 9.14

Step 4: Formatting

At this point, we have the layout configured for our Cube View, so you may think we're done – but are we? Let's look at the current state of the Report.

GolfStream™ Income Statement Variance

Entity: Houston

View: YTD | Period Ended: Mar 2022 | Currency: USD

	Actual	BudgetV2	Variance	Var %	Explanation
60000 - Operating Sales	136,282,129.80	120,086,264.67	16,195,865.13	13.49	
60200 - Returns & Allowances	3,877,804.12	3,412,467.63	-465,336.49	-13.64	
60999 - Net Sales	132,404,325.68	116,673,797.04	15,730,528.64	13.48	
41000 - Operating Cost of Goods Sold	70,041,726.67	61,636,719.47	-8,405,007.20	-13.64	
42000 - IC Cost of Goods Sold	15,000.00	13,200.00	-1,800.00	-13.64	
43000 - Cost of Goods Sold	70,056,726.67	61,649,919.47	-8,406,807.20	-13.64	
61000 - Gross Income	62,347,599.01	55,023,877.57	7,323,721.44	13.31	

Figure 9.15

At a glance, the Report serves its purpose and displays the data we're expecting, but you probably wouldn't present this to your Users; aside from the indentation, the data isn't super clear in differentiating detail from totals. Let's dive into formatting as our next step.

UI Formatting Options

Formatting options are tools that allow you to customize the way that data is presented. In the context of General Cube Views, Excel, and Reports output, there may be variations in the available formatting options. For example, General Cube Views offer a specific set of formatting options that allow you to adjust the appearance of data in a tabular format within OneStream's interface. Excel formatting options include controls that are valid specifically in a spreadsheet tool. Reporting offers yet another set of formatting options that allow you to produce polished, professional Reports.

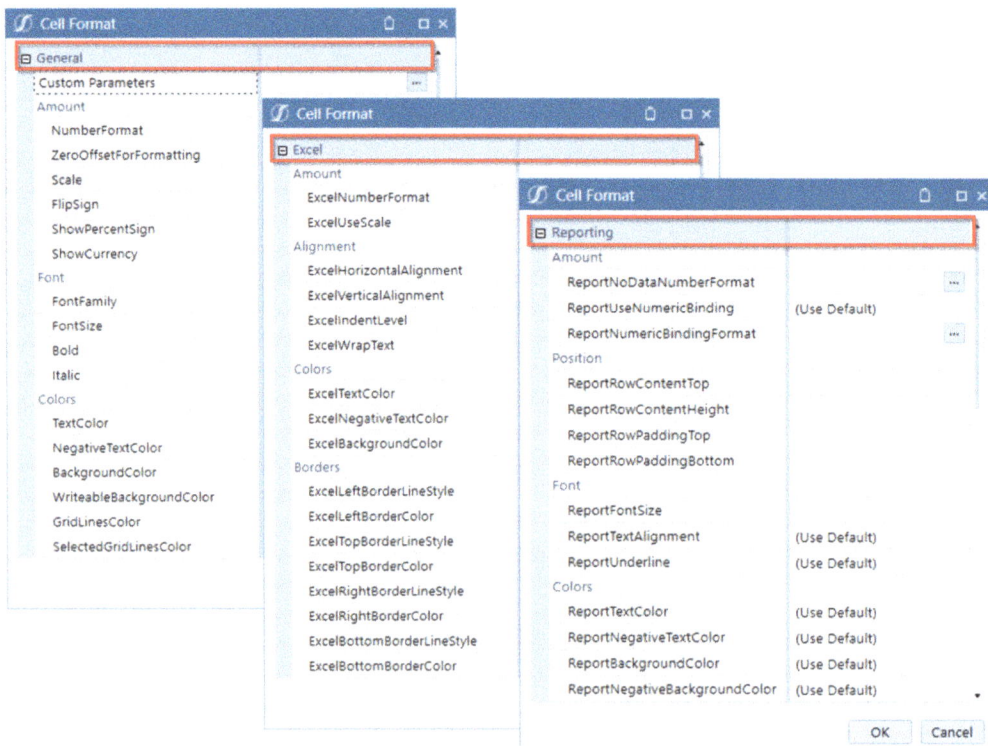

Figure 9.16

Remember, in the rows section, how we used suffixes on the row names to indicate the level of data being presented? That naming convention allows us to use conditional formatting on the Overall Cube View's header and cell format, rather than manually having to format each row and column set. This is incredibly powerful when you have many rows or columns and need to update specific formatting (whether it be font size, number format, etc.); you only need to update the parameter and the formatting will be applied globally.

Figure 9.17 shows how to access the Cube View's global formatting settings from the Design view; while figure 9.18 shows the same fields from the Advanced view.

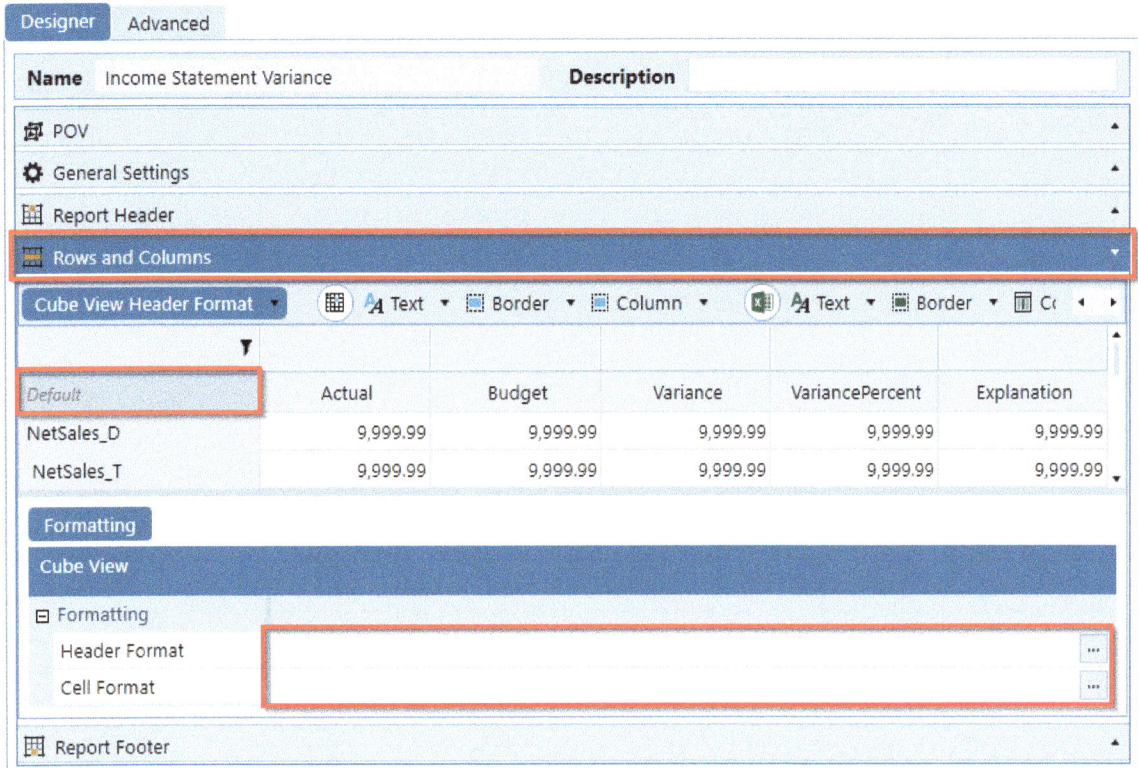

Figure 9.17

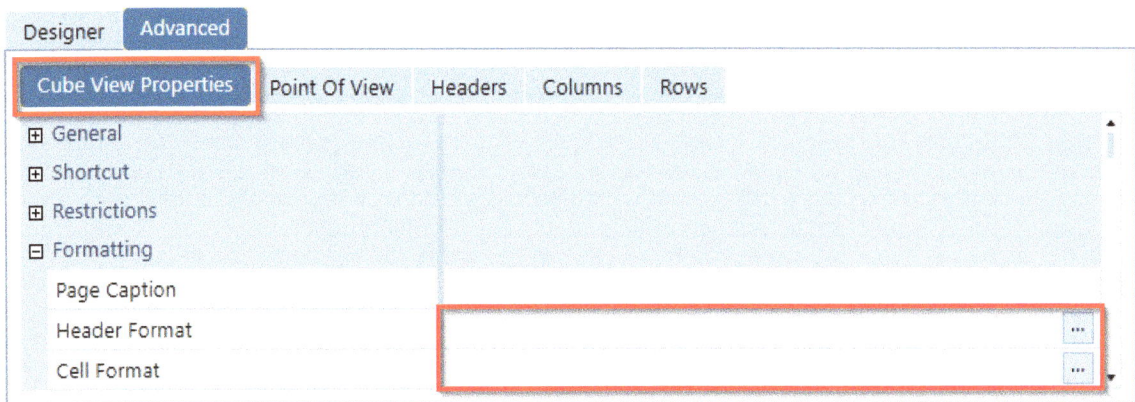

Figure 9.18

Note: Global Cube View header formatting will apply to both row and column headers. You can set default formatting in this section, and any formatting set on explicit row or column headers will override the global header formatting.

For this example, we've created the following formatting parameters for different cell types to accelerate this step, as defined below.

Parameter Name	Literal Value
DetailCell	IF (IsRowNumberEven = True) THEN BackgroundColor = White, ELSE BackgroundColor = #FFF5F7FB, END IF, ReportFontSize = 8, SelectedGridLinesColor = XFDarkBlueBackground, NegativeTextColor = Firebrick, ReportNoDataNumberFormat = ["-"], ExcelNumberFormat = [#,##0_);[Red](#,##0)], ReportBackgroundColor = White, ReportTextColor = black, ExcelTextColor = Black, ExcelBackgroundColor = White, NumberFormat = [#,###,0;(#,###,0);0], ReportRowContentHeight = 17,SelectedGridLinesColor = Transparent
SubTotalCell	ReportBackgroundColor = White, BackgroundColor = XFLightBlue2, ExcelNumberFormat = [#,##0_);[Red](#,##0)], ReportTopLine1Color = XFMediumBlueBorder, ReportFontSize = 8, ReportRowContentBottom = 10,ReportUseTopLine1 = True, ReportTextColor = SteelBlue,ReportNegativeTextColor = Firebrick,Bold = True, TextColor = SteelBlue, NumberFormat = [#,###,0;(#,###,0);0], GridLinesColor = Transparent
GrandTotalCell	ReportBackgroundColor = White, BackgroundColor = XFLightBlue, GridLinesColor = Transparent, Bold = True, ReportTextAlignment = MiddleRight, ReportFontSize = 8, ExcelNumberFormat = [#,##0_);[Red](#,##0)], NegativeTextColor = Firebrick, ReportTopLine1Color = XFMediumBlueBorder, ReportTopLine2Color = XFMediumBlueBorder, ReportUseTopLine1 = True, ReportUseTopLine2 = True, ReportTextColor = SteelBlue, TextColor = SteelBlue, ExcelBackgroundColor = XFMediumBlueBackground, NumberFormat = [#,###,0;(#,###,0);0]
ColumnHeader	Bold = True, ReportFontSize = 8, ReportTextAlignment = MiddleRight, ReportTextColor = SteelBlue, TextColor = SteelBlue, ShowDimensionImages = False,ReportColumnWidth = 85, ColumnWidth = 110
VariancePctCell	BackgroundColor = AliceBlue, NegativeTextColor = Firebrick, NumberFormat = = [#,###,0.0\%], ExcelNumberFormat = 0.00\%, ExcelNegativeTextColor = Red, ReportFontSize = 8, ReportBackgroundColor = White, If (RowName Contains '_D') AND (CellAmount < -15) Then BackgroundColor = Yellow, ExcelBackgroundColor = Yellow End If
VariancePctCellSubTotal	ReportBackgroundColor = White, BackgroundColor = XFLightBlue2, GridLinesColor = Transparent, Bold = True, ReportTextAlignment = MiddleRight, ReportFontSize = 8, ExcelNumberFormat = 0.00\%, ExcelNegativeTextColor = Red, NegativeTextColor = Firebrick, ReportTopLine1Color = XFMediumBlueBorder, ReportUseTopLine1 = True, ReportTextColor = SteelBlue, TextColor = SteelBlue, ExcelBackgroundColor = XFLightBlue2, NumberFormat = = [#,###,0.0\%]
VariancePctCellGrandTotal	ReportBackgroundColor = White, BackgroundColor = XFLightBlue, GridLinesColor = Transparent, Bold = True, ReportTextAlignment = MiddleRight, ReportFontSize = 8, ExcelNumberFormat = 0.00\%, ExcelNegativeTextColor = Red, NegativeTextColor = Firebrick, ReportTopLine1Color = XFMediumBlueBorder, ReportTopLine2Color = XFMediumBlueBorder, ReportUseTopLine1 = True, ReportUseTopLine2 = True, ReportTextColor = SteelBlue, TextColor = SteelBlue, ExcelBackgroundColor = XFMediumBlueBackground, NumberFormat = = [#,###,0.0\%]
DetailHeader	IF (IsRowNumberEven = True) THEN BackgroundColor = White, ExcelBackgroundColor = White ELSE BackgroundColor = #FFF5F7FB, ExcelBackgroundColor = White END IF, ReportFontSize = 8, ReportBackgroundColor = White, ReportTextColor = black, ExcelTextColor = Black, ShowDimensionImages = False, ExcelVerticalAlignment = Top, ReportRowContentHeight = 17
SubTotalHeader	Bold = True, ReportRowContentBottom = 10, GridLinesColor = Transparent, TextColor = SteelBlue, BackgroundColor = XFLightBlue2, ReportBackgroundColor = White, ShowDimensionImages = False, ReportFontSize = 8, ReportTopLine1Color = Transparent, ReportUseTopLine1 = True
GrandTotalHeader	ReportBackgroundColor = White, BackgroundColor = XFLightBlue, GridLinesColor = Transparent, Bold = True, ReportFontSize = 8, ReportTopLine1Color = Transparent, ReportTopLine2Color = Transparent, ReportUseTopLine1 = True, ReportUseTopLine2 = True, ReportTextColor = SteelBlue, TextColor = SteelBlue, ExcelBackgroundColor = XFMediumBlueBackground, ShowDimensionImages = False

Figure 9.19

From either the Design or Advanced view, click on the Header Format ellipse to edit the headers and enter the syntax below to apply the format parameters to the headers. Conditions available for header formatting and cell formatting differ in that cell conditions include options for cell status, Storage Type, amount, etc.

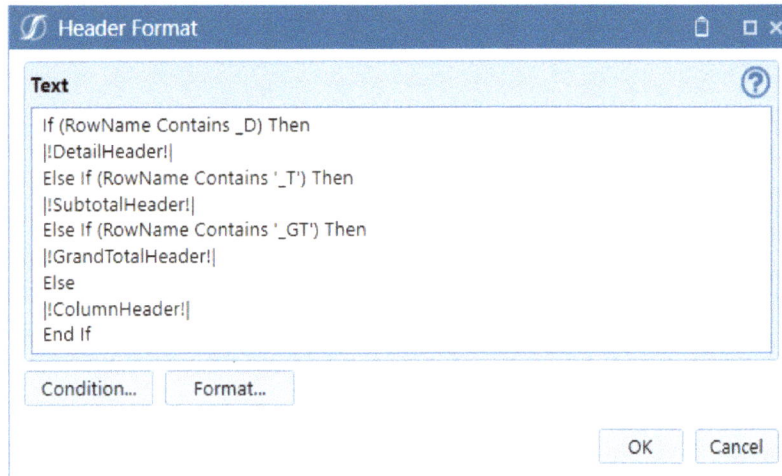

Figure 9.20

Now, let's apply cell formatting using the same logic. Notice that we use different parameters for data cells where additional formatting is necessary, since we're working with numeric fields.

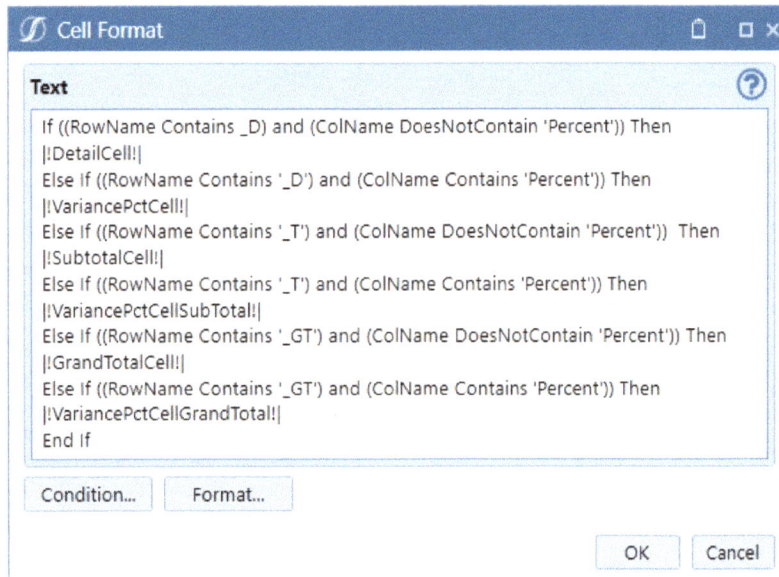

Figure 9.21

Cube View Extender

Cube View Extenders offer additional flexibility to modify Report objects that may not be directly accessible from the UI. These Report objects include elements such as labels, Calculations, or formatting options which are not easily adjustable through the standard Cube View options.

While the use of Cube View Extenders may require some additional knowledge or training, they can be a powerful tool for creating more effective and engaging Reports. By allowing you to fine-tune Report objects that may not be accessible through the standard Cube View UI, Cube View Extenders give you the ability to create Reports that are truly tailored to your specific needs and objectives.

Let's view the Cube View Report and see if we need to make any adjustments to the format.

Figure 9.22

The Report looks great, but the logo draws too much attention away from the actual content of the Report, and the Report title would look better on one line instead of being wrapped. To address this, the use of a Cube View Extender can be implemented.

To apply a Cube View Extender, navigate to the Report and select Cube View Properties. Then, set the Custom Report Task property to Execute Cube View Extender Inline Formula, and click the ellipse button to access the Formula Editor.

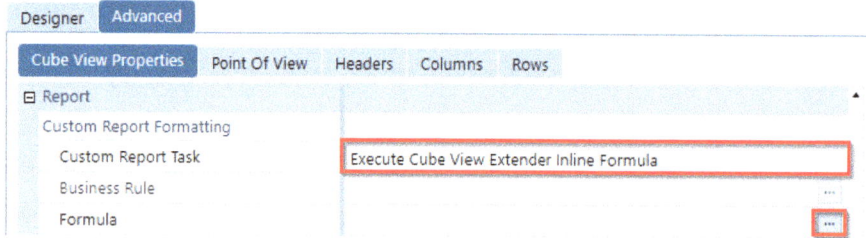

Figure 9.23

When you first enable the **Inline Formula** feature, the Formula Editor window provides you with sample syntax. This is helpful because it can be overwhelming to try to figure out how to write the correct code from scratch.

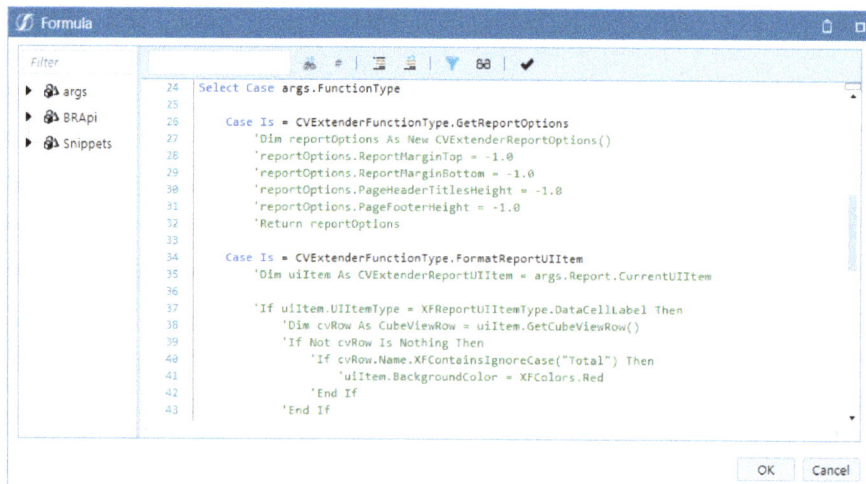

Figure 9.24

We will be using the following syntax to resize the logo, as noted above.

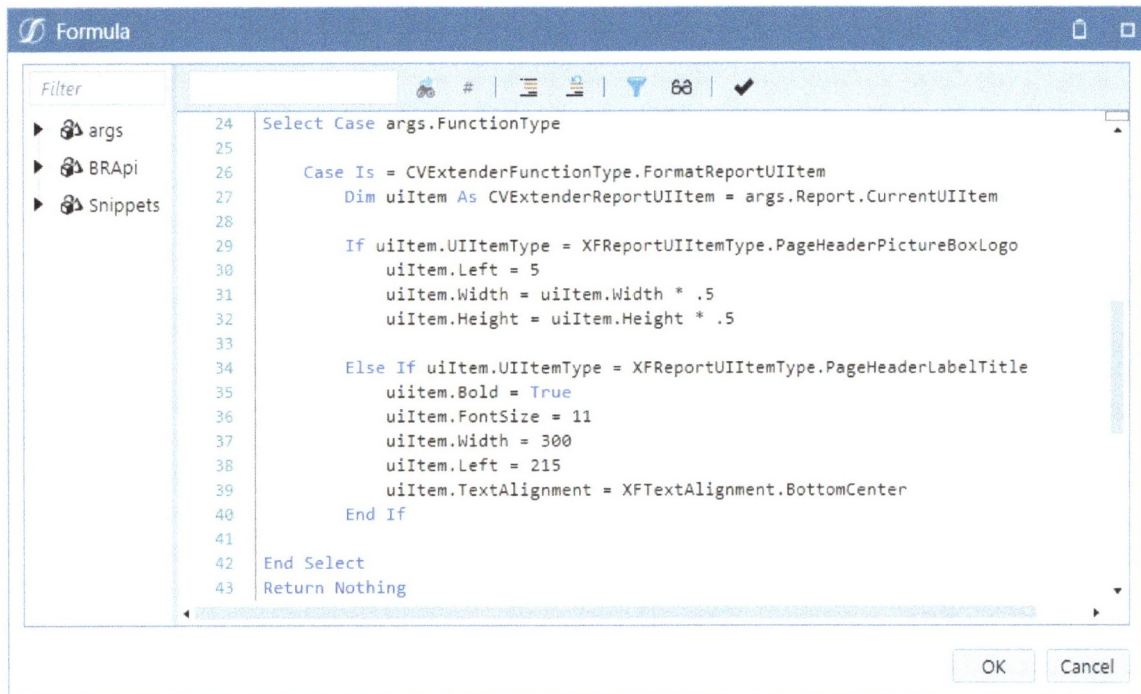

```
24   Select Case args.FunctionType
25
26      Case Is = CVExtenderFunctionType.FormatReportUIItem
27          Dim uiItem As CVExtenderReportUIItem = args.Report.CurrentUIItem
28
29          If uiItem.UIItemType = XFReportUIItemType.PageHeaderPictureBoxLogo
30              uiItem.Left = 5
31              uiItem.Width = uiItem.Width * .5
32              uiItem.Height = uiItem.Height * .5
33
34          Else If uiItem.UIItemType = XFReportUIItemType.PageHeaderLabelTitle
35              uiitem.Bold = True
36              uiItem.FontSize = 11
37              uiItem.Width = 300
38              uiItem.Left = 215
39              uiItem.TextAlignment = XFTextAlignment.BottomCenter
40          End If
41
42   End Select
43   Return Nothing
```

Figure 9.25

After implementing the Cube View Extender, we can see a significant improvement in the appearance of our Report. The changes we made to the Report – including resizing the logo and adjusting the title to fit on one row – have helped to create a more polished and professional look.

One major improvement we can see is that the Report now looks much cleaner and easier to read. The large logo that was once a distraction has been resized, allowing readers to focus on the important data presented in the Report. The adjustments made to the Report title also contribute to this improvement, as the title is now clear and easy to read on a single line.

GolfStream

Income Statement Variance

Entity: Houston

View: YTD   Period Ended: Mar 2022   Currency: USD

	Actual	BudgetV2	Variance	Var %	Explanation
60000 - Operating Sales	136,228,130	120,086,265	16,141,865	13.44%	
60200 - Returns & Allowances	3,877,804	3,412,468	(465,336)	-13.64%	
60999 - Net Sales	132,350,326	116,673,797	15,676,529	13.4%	
41000 - Operating Cost of Goods Sold	70,041,727	61,636,719	(8,405,007)	-13.64%	
42000 - IC Cost of Goods Sold	15,000	13,200	(1,800)	-13.64%	
43000 - Cost of Goods Sold	70,056,727	61,649,919	(8,406,807)	-13.6%	
61000 - Gross Income	62,293,599	55,023,878	7,269,722	13.2%	
62000 - Total Operating Income	62,293,599	55,023,878	7,269,722	13.2%	

Figure 9.26

Step 5: Navigation Links

Navigation links are a powerful tool for creating drill paths that enable Users to navigate through subsets of data and visualizations easily. We strongly recommend including navigation links in every application; it is a feature that gives Users a truly seamless experience when they need to dig into the details or quickly navigate to related data. If you're familiar with linked Forms, you'll love this feature! Not only can you link data Forms, no, we go a step further and also link Reports together. By incorporating navigation links into your Cube Views, you can enhance the User Experience and create a more intuitive and User-friendly interface.

One of the key benefits of navigation links is that they allow Users to *drill down* into subsets of data with ease. This means that Users can quickly and easily access more detailed information about specific data points without having to sift through large amounts of data. This not only saves time but also helps to improve the accuracy and reliability of data analysis, as Users can more easily identify trends and patterns in the data.

Navigation links also make it easy to create drill paths that guide Users through various visualizations. This means that Users can move seamlessly from one visualization to another without having to navigate through multiple screens or menus. This creates a more fluid and intuitive User Experience that encourages exploration and discovery.

> **Note**: Setting the Include Default NavLink Parameters property to True generates bound parameters that will be passed into linked Cube Views and linked Dashboards.

Below are the Dimensions and related bound parameters that can be used in linked content. How and where to apply them to detailed content will be addressed in this section.

Dimension Name	Bound Parameter
Cube	|!CubeNavLink!|
Entity Member	|!EntityNavLink!|
Parent Member	|!ParentNavLink!|
Consolidation Member	|!ConsolidationNavLink!|
Scenario Member	|!ScenarioNavLink!|
Time Member	|!TimeNavLink!|
View Member	|!ViewNavLink!|
Account Member	|!AccountNavLink!|
Flow Member	|!FlowNavLink!|
Origin Member	|!OriginNavLink!|
IC Member	|!ICNavLink!|
UD1 Member	|!UD1NavLink!|
UD2 Member	|!UD2NavLink!|
UD3 Member	|!UD3NavLink!|
UD4 Member	|!UD4NavLink!|
UD5 Member	|!UD5NavLink!|
UD6 Member	|!UD6NavLink!|
UD7 Member	|!UD7NavLink!|
UD8 Member	|!UD8NavLink!|

Figure 9.27

Linked Cube View navigation should only be applied where relevant. In the figure below, we are enabling Sales Accounts to be drilled into for further detail related to Product Detail, Region

Detail, and Customer Detail. Conversely, Operating Expense Accounts wouldn't be tied to these details; for those Accounts, we would instead use a Cost Center Detail-linked Cube View.

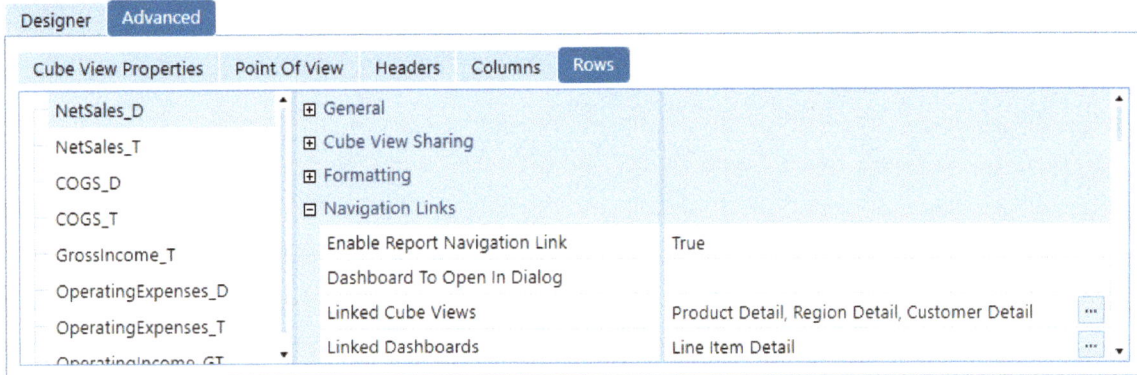

Figure 9.28

By enabling navigation links with linked content, Users can right-click on a cell and see navigation options (as shown below).

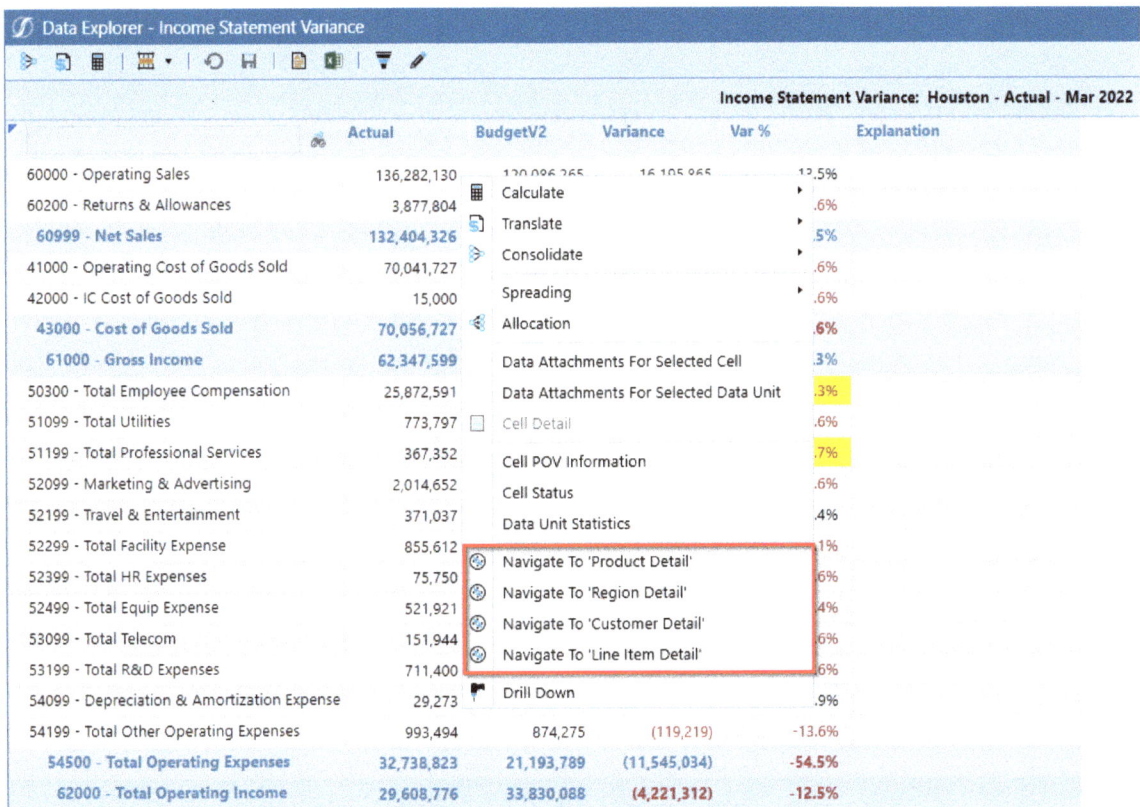

Figure 9.29

Depending on the navigation selected, the corresponding linked Cube View will be displayed in a new window.

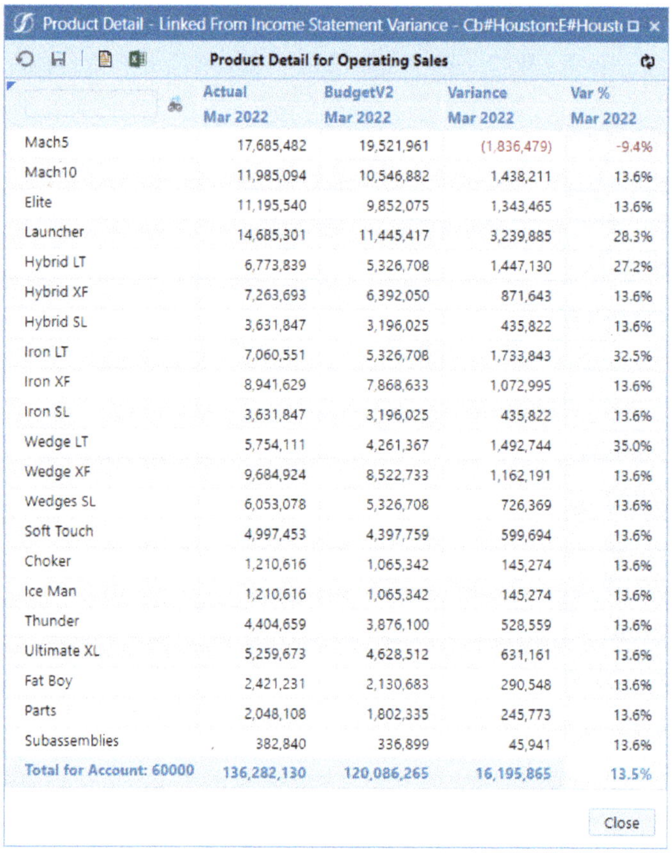

Product Detail - Linked From Income Statement Variance - Cb#Houston:E#Housti

Product Detail for Operating Sales

	Actual Mar 2022	BudgetV2 Mar 2022	Variance Mar 2022	Var % Mar 2022
Mach5	17,685,482	19,521,961	(1,836,479)	-9.4%
Mach10	11,985,094	10,546,882	1,438,211	13.6%
Elite	11,195,540	9,852,075	1,343,465	13.6%
Launcher	14,685,301	11,445,417	3,239,885	28.3%
Hybrid LT	6,773,839	5,326,708	1,447,130	27.2%
Hybrid XF	7,263,693	6,392,050	871,643	13.6%
Hybrid SL	3,631,847	3,196,025	435,822	13.6%
Iron LT	7,060,551	5,326,708	1,733,843	32.5%
Iron XF	8,941,629	7,868,633	1,072,995	13.6%
Iron SL	3,631,847	3,196,025	435,822	13.6%
Wedge LT	5,754,111	4,261,367	1,492,744	35.0%
Wedge XF	9,684,924	8,522,733	1,162,191	13.6%
Wedges SL	6,053,078	5,326,708	726,369	13.6%
Soft Touch	4,997,453	4,397,759	599,694	13.6%
Choker	1,210,616	1,065,342	145,274	13.6%
Ice Man	1,210,616	1,065,342	145,274	13.6%
Thunder	4,404,659	3,876,100	528,559	13.6%
Ultimate XL	5,259,673	4,628,512	631,161	13.6%
Fat Boy	2,421,231	2,130,683	290,548	13.6%
Parts	2,048,108	1,802,335	245,773	13.6%
Subassemblies	382,840	336,899	45,941	13.6%
Total for Account: 60000	136,282,130	120,086,265	16,195,865	13.5%

Close

Figure 9.30

Linked Cube Views

Following the previous example, here is how our Product Detail Cube View POV will be configured. The rows displayed in the Product Detail Cube View are restricted to our product Dimension's hierarchy.

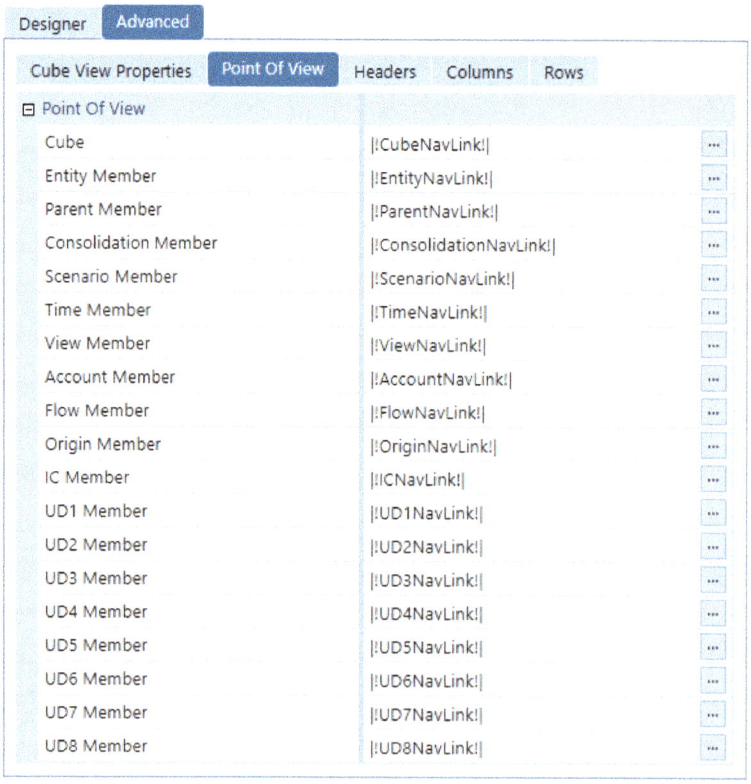

Figure 9.31

Linked Dashboards

Similarly, linked Dashboards will be configured with the Bound Parameters and displayed with a visual object to give the User even more context to trend data.

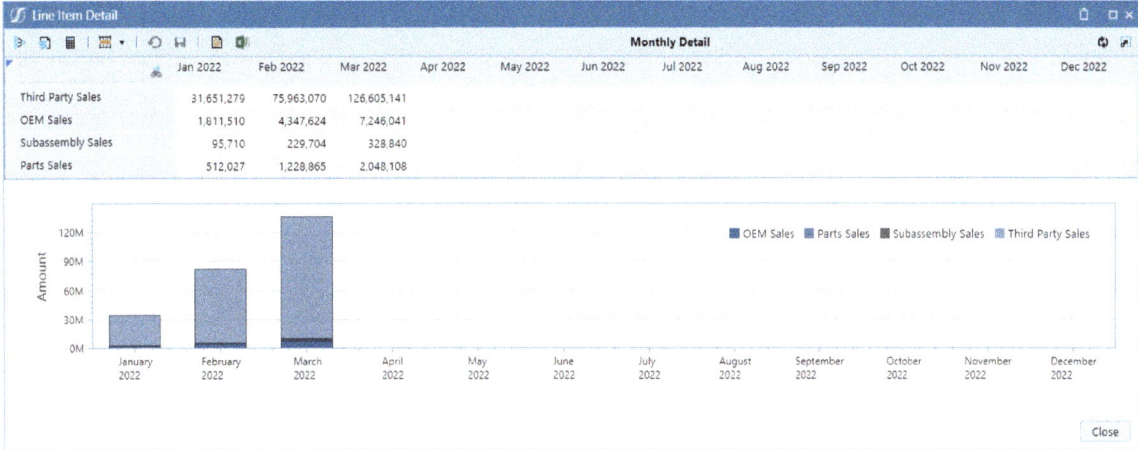

Figure 9.32

Completed Cube View

Data Explorer Result

Income Statement Variance: Houston - Actual - Mar 2022

	Actual	BudgetV2	Variance	Var %	Explanation
60000 - Operating Sales	136,282,130	120,086,265	16,195,865	13.5%	
60200 - Returns & Allowances	3,877,804	3,412,468	(465,336)	-13.6%	
60999 - Net Sales	132,404,326	116,673,797	15,730,529	13.5%	
41000 - Operating Cost of Goods Sold	70,041,727	61,636,719	(8,405,007)	-13.6%	
42000 - IC Cost of Goods Sold	15,000	13,200	(1,800)	-13.6%	
43000 - Cost of Goods Sold	70,056,727	61,649,919	(8,406,807)	-13.6%	
61000 - Gross Income	62,347,599	55,023,878	7,323,721	13.3%	
50300 - Total Employee Compensation	25,872,591	15,193,411	(10,679,180)	-70.3%	
51099 - Total Utilities	773,797	680,942	(92,856)	-13.6%	
51199 - Total Professional Services	367,352	193,634	(173,718)	-89.7%	
52099 - Marketing & Advertising	2,014,652	1,772,894	(241,758)	-13.6%	
52199 - Travel & Entertainment	371,037	400,801	29,765	7.4%	
52299 - Total Facility Expense	855,612	756,598	(99,015)	-13.1%	
52399 - Total HR Expenses	75,750	66,660	(9,090)	-13.6%	
52499 - Total Equip Expense	521,921	460,416	(61,505)	-13.4%	
53099 - Total Telecom	151,944	133,710	(18,233)	-13.6%	
53199 - Total R&D Expenses	711,400	626,032	(85,368)	-13.6%	
54099 - Depreciation & Amortization Expense	29,273	34,417	5,143	14.9%	
54199 - Total Other Operating Expenses	993,494	874,275	(119,219)	-13.6%	
54500 - Total Operating Expenses	32,738,823	21,193,789	(11,545,034)	-54.5%	
62000 - Total Operating Income	29,608,776	33,830,088	(4,221,312)	-12.5%	

Figure 9.33

Chapter 9

Excel Result

	A	B	C	D	E	F
1			Income Statement Variance			
2						
3			Entity: Houston			
4	View: YTD		Period Ended: Mar 2022			Currency: USD
5						
6		Actual	BudgetV2	Variance	Var %	Explanation
7	60000 - Operating Sales	136,282,130	120,086,265	16,195,865	13.49%	
8	60200 - Returns & Allowances	3,877,804	3,412,468	(465,336)	-13.64%	
9	60999 - Net Sales	132,404,326	116,673,797	15,730,529	13.48%	
10	41000 - Operating Cost of Goods Sold	70,041,727	61,636,719	(8,405,007)	-13.64%	
11	42000 - IC Cost of Goods Sold	15,000	13,200	(1,800)	-13.64%	
12	43000 - Cost of Goods Sold	70,056,727	61,649,919	(8,406,807)	-13.64%	
13	61000 - Gross Income	62,347,599	55,023,878	7,323,721	13.31%	
14	50300 - Total Employee Compensation	25,872,591	15,193,411	(10,679,180)	-70.29%	
15	51099 - Total Utilities	773,797	680,942	(92,856)	-13.64%	
16	51199 - Total Professional Services	367,352	193,634	(173,718)	-89.71%	
17	52099 - Marketing & Advertising	2,014,652	1,772,894	(241,758)	-13.64%	
18	52199 - Travel & Entertainment	371,037	400,801	29,765	7.43%	
19	52299 - Total Facility Expense	855,612	756,598	(99,015)	-13.09%	
20	52399 - Total HR Expenses	75,750	66,660	(9,090)	-13.64%	
21	52499 - Total Equip Expense	521,921	460,416	(61,505)	-13.36%	
22	53099 - Total Telecom	151,944	133,710	(18,233)	-13.64%	
23	53199 - Total R&D Expenses	711,400	626,032	(85,368)	-13.64%	
24	54099 - Depreciation & Amortization Expense	29,273	34,417	5,143	14.94%	
25	54199 - Total Other Operating Expenses	993,494	874,275	(119,219)	-13.64%	
26	54500 - Total Operating Expenses	32,738,823	21,193,789	(11,545,034)	-54.47%	
27	62000 - Total Operating Income	29,608,776	33,830,088	(4,221,312)	-12.48%	

Figure 9.34

Report Result

Figure 9.35

144

Conclusion

Building Cube Views may seem like a formidable task, but this chapter has explained use cases for incorporating filters, format parameters, Cube View Extenders, and navigation links to give you the tools to create robust and intuitive interactions for your Users.

Determining what you want to display in your rows and columns defines the actual Report, while the POV dictates the Report's restrictions in order to display relevant data. Using templates for your Reports provides standardization and consistency; you can create as many as needed, and the best part is you can quickly swap them out if/when needed to instantly update your Report Inventory. Also, Administrators and Power Users can build their own templates for other more specific User requirements, which opens up even more possibilities. We can't forget about Guided Reporting, a OneStream MarketPlace solution that's available to you; the solution is based on templates, which gives your Users the self-serve experience they want and need.

The takeaway is that once you build these complex components into your Cube Views, the options for drilling and formatting are endless!

10
Dashboards

Introduction

We have spent a good amount of time looking at Cube Views, and this is a common place for many people to start their reporting journey. But we have also learned that this book is about so much more than simply creating Reports; it's about crafting a User Experience in OneStream. In a way, these things have one big thing in common, they both have the goal of bringing those working with OneStream the information that they need. And while we know there is a prescribed, substantial side to reporting, User Experience challenges us to broaden our goals and add elements of style and interactivity into our design.

Cube Views might have felt more like our cold, hard Reports. Our faithful tool is there to display our (typically financial) information in a professional grid-like format. But we started to see how our Cube Views can be so much more than that, and how they play into our User's journey. We learned that our Cube Views can play a large role in our data entry, we saw how we can make them more dynamic through parameters, we looked at flexing some formatting muscles, craft interesting Calculations and incorporate them into the Workflow, and we talked about how they can be used to calculate/translate/and consolidate. There are so many other things we can look at when it comes to Cube Views, so don't let this end your learning journey! If you want to learn more, there is a lot of self-paced training being updated on the **Navigator** (the OneStream Learning Management System) and the OneStream Documentation.

Let's not forget what Cube Views are most famous for: their connection to the other areas of the application. If you find any OneStream literature on Cube Views, you will likely have seen them referred to as a "building block". They adorn this title like a crown because of their ability to elevate elements such as Dashboards, Form Templates, and Spreadsheets. But like any art form, developing certain foundational skills prepares your body and mind to bend certain rules, play on different tactics, and use your creativity to create an experience.

So how can we take our User Experience to the next level? For this, many people turn to Dashboards. This iconic tool can be used to bridge the gap between many items in OneStream. Dashboards are widely regarded as one of the most powerful features within OneStream and for good reason. Their flexibility and plethora of options are what allow you to mix and match Components to create a variety of pages.

Now, I do have to begin this chapter with a bit of a disclaimer. As I am writing this sentence, we are about one month away from releasing 7.4 into the software. With the release of 7.3, we have witnessed a large change to the Dashboards page… the introduction of **Workspaces**. With the release of 7.4, we are seeing even more features making their way into this area. I will try to keep this as current as possible, but we are undergoing a lot of changes in this realm, so rely on the release notes of each software release to stay current.

Working for a software company, I am always chasing changes. We have a wide variety of clients that all use the software differently, and with the launch of **IdeaStream** we can see a constant influx of requests that are being incorporated into the software. I think we would all be pretty disappointed if the software wasn't constantly changing and improving, but let's deal with the here and now. Hopefully, if you see something else change in the future, you will be excited to snap up the knowledge and apply the things you learned here. You may be asking yourself, "Why should I learn how to build a Dashboard?", "Who builds Dashboards?", "How can I get started with

Dashboards?" I hope to answer some of these questions for you, next. So, buckle up! You are on the cusp of really getting your hands dirty in the software!

Getting Started

Many people don't need much convincing when it comes to the value of Dashboards. For a lot of clients, Dashboards were something they first saw during their pre-sales journey and they thought "Yes! I need that at my fingertips!" Or maybe a customer who knew they were going to be an Administrator saw how they could report on data that lived in the Cube (or outside the Cube). This happens with our clients using OneStream Financial Close, Task Manager, People Planning, or other solutions (even BI Blend). Or maybe people were just excited they could create a bespoke landing page for the End-User, or a sophisticated control panel of tasks to kick off or statuses to monitor. Dashboards are great because:

1. They create excitement, and people want to see them in their applications.

2. They solve certain reporting requirements.

3. They cultivate the best User Experience possible.

Because They are Exciting!

Clients… this reason applies to you too! Maybe you no longer have an implementation team at your disposal, and someone in your organization really wants a Dashboard. Or maybe you want one for yourself; I won't judge.

Meanwhile, if you are an Implementor (Consultant), maybe this first reason got you energized. You can't wait to dramatically crack your knuckles and start weaving together SQL statements and Dashboard Components. It's in your SOW (Statement of Work) and you want to be the one to do it and proudly show the final design to your client!

A lot of times, the Dashboards we build don't come to fruition simply because someone asked for them. Many times, they work their way into the build as a creative solution to a requirement. This is the art of the OneStream Application Design, and many times answers are not always obvious; we have to be a little creative. After all, we did say earlier in the book that one of the best ways to be proficient in OneStream is to learn a little bit about each of the tools at your disposal!

To Solve Certain Reporting Requirements

The better you get at working with Dashboards (and just operating in OneStream in general), the more comfortable you will be in diagnosing how to solve certain requirements. Here are a few things that should start screaming "You need a Dashboard!"

1. **If non-Cube Data needs to be queried/submitted.** I will get into this one a little bit later – because there are other options besides Dashboards – but this really is your best bet.

2. **If an interactive element is required.** If you want to create a guided experience for the User that has pop-ups, clickable elements, movable charts, buttons, etc. This will typically involve a Dashboard.

3. **If your existing reporting tools aren't getting you there.** I hate to say anything to knock any other reporting tool, because the beauty of their existence gives you options, but Dashboards give you the most flexibility and allow you to fine-tune every element.

Non-Cube Data

I want to dive into one thing just a bit further: Dashboards can report on non-Cube data. This might be an unfamiliar concept to you, but it is important. Whenever we are looking to report on a mixture of data that lives in the Cube, with data that does not live in the Cube, this is called **Analytic Blend**. You typically employ this design tactic when some aspect of your reporting causes large sparse data to exist in your Cube (potentially hurting the performance of your application), or you have highly transient metadata that should not be built in the Dimension Library. We won't go far into the architectural elements of this. If you are curious to learn about the why and how of Analytic Blend, check out the OneStream Foundation Handbook or the Designing and Application course on Navigator.

So, how can we report on data that does not live in the Cube? First, you must know how to find it! I like to break this down by asking, 'Where else can this data live besides the Cube?' Commonly, we think of Stage, application solution tables, and tables residing in an external database. Whenever you want to query these elements, the easiest way is within Dashboards. The most common examples of this could be the batch of Reports you see coming with your various solutions like OneStream Financial Close (OFC) or People Planning (PLP).

Now, there are a few exceptions to the rule of 'You NEED a Dashboard to report on data living outside of the Cube'. There is a dynamic Calculation that you can write that will pull some Stage data into a Cube View. If you didn't know about this, the functions listed in Figure 10.1 will help you write them. This is a quick way to grab some data, but if you need more flexibility and fanfare, you will find yourself turning to Dashboards.

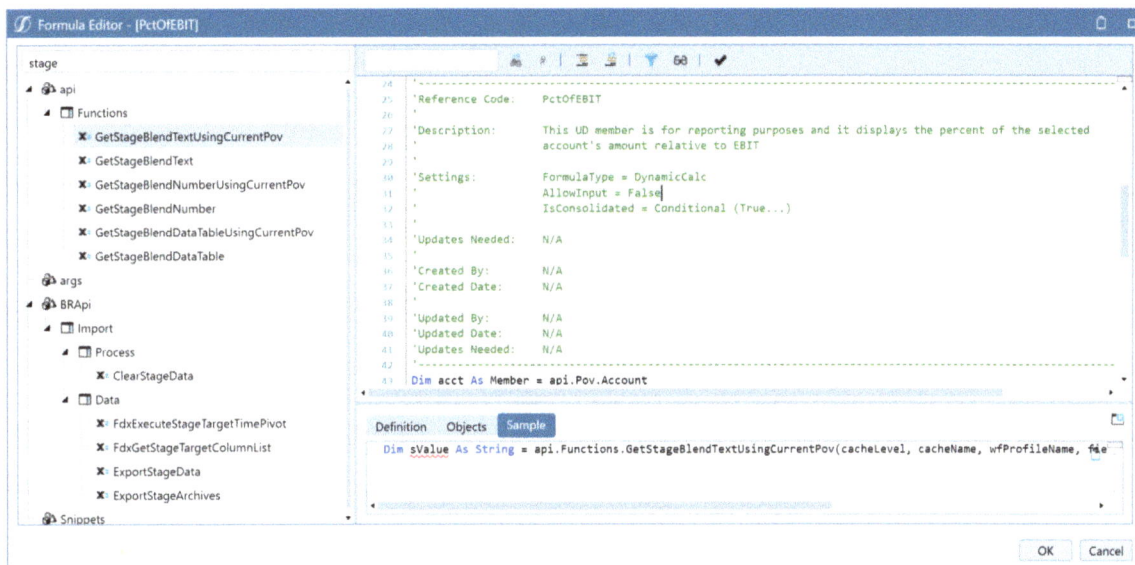

Figure 10.1

The Excel Add-in and Spreadsheet tools can also report on non-Cube Data through **Table Views**.

Table Views are created using a Spreadsheet Business Rule and will allow you to pull an editable grid of non-Cube data into the Excel Add-in or Spreadsheet tool. I like to think of these as the non-Cube data version of a Quick View; however, the use of the Business Rule makes it feel more like a Dashboard Component.

So, if you have the requirement of pulling non-Cube Data into Reports, Dashboards should be your go-to. While it's not your only option, the ability to fine-tune every aspect makes Dashboards an easy choice for many designers.

To Cultivate the Best User Experience Possible

This book is about User Experience, and we have talked a lot about reporting. Dashboards can form a beautiful partnership with the OneStream Workflow to really add some pizzazz to their Close or Planning process.

1. **Data Entry.** I always turn to a Dashboard if I would like to incorporate some sort of User-controlled Calculation in the data entry process. This is common with Planning Calculations, for example. Of course, there are other options, like using a pre-process Workflow task or an Extender Business Rule, but people love to push buttons. If you need to submit non-Cube data, you will need a Dashboard to do this (this is how the MarketPlace solutions are created!).

2. **Analysis.** Many times, people incorporate Dashboards into the analysis sections of their Workflow. This is a great tool to help your User along the way. You could show them thresholds they are about to break, quick ratios, or even a video on how to complete their Close process through a Dashboard.

This isn't a recommendation or a warning, but I have known people to rely more on Dashboards than the Workflow itself. You should not be persuaded for or against it; it's simply an option on how any Workflow and Dashboard partnership can be formed. We would typically see this on a Planning project, but Consolidation projects may turn to another MarketPlace solution called **Task Manager** to accomplish a similar effect. This allows your Users to see their required tasks in a fancy Dashboard that is clickable and which will navigate them to the appropriate location in OneStream for task completion. Many people like this solution for its flexibility and stylish appearance, as well as its ability to provide additional process orchestration and visibility.

What really drives the User Experience that Dashboards can create, though, is the *flexibility*. Dashboards are essentially a blank canvas with which you can tailor OneStream specifically to any customer. Basically, you can show your Users exactly what they need to see. On top of this, if you create your Dashboards wisely, they can be created and maintained by your Finance Administrators or Power Users.

Who Should Be Building Dashboards?

This is an interesting question because I think most people have the capacity to build a halfway decent Dashboard; no one should be afraid to jump in and be uncomfortable for a little time.

Some Dashboards can be extremely simple. They do not have to have a hundred Components, complex rules, or various items interacting with one another. We turn to this tool to solve a specific use case for our Users. Starting with a plan and a well-thought-out design is something that everyone can do, and you may be surprised by a simple solution.

> **Tip**: Remember to always think of the User and how *they* want to interact with what you have created.

Okay, but what if we can't come up with a simple solution without sacrificing the User Experience? Throughout my career, I have encountered many people who have better technical backgrounds than myself and who create some really impressive Dashboards. They truly shine in this category and go on to develop beautiful solutions that you may see offered on the Solution Exchange! We often refer to these people as "Solution Developers". Many of these people work within OneStream, but many of them are our clients and partners.

In this book, we are not planning to deep dive on how to build solutions, but rather how to get your feet wet and start to see the art of the possible. So, what skills does it take to build Dashboards? If you are new to Dashboards, here are four areas you should consider being able to accomplish:

1. Breaking down the anatomy of a Workspace.

2. Creating at least five Dashboard Components.

3. Building each of the Data Adapter Types.

4. Working with Embedded Dashboards.

Breaking Down Workspaces

First and foremost, where do we build Dashboards? You may notice there are two types of Dashboards: **Application** and **System Dashboards**. We will be talking about Application Dashboards as these are the most common, but the pages are very similar and if you can build one type, you can build the other. Application Dashboards are built in the Dashboards page on the Application tab, while System Dashboards are built in the Dashboards page on the System tab. If you are curious why there are two pages, System Dashboards are for reporting on more general system information such as security or User activity.

Let's get to the Application Dashboards page, and then we can start to break down Workspaces.

Workspaces

As I write, we are on the precipice of changing how Dashboards are created and structured. The way that we used to explain the breakdown of Dashboards was to start with the Dashboard Maintenance Unit, but the release of 7.3 marks the end of this era, with Dashboard Maintenance Units being the top node. Now, there is a new proverbial sheriff in town, Workspaces.

As we move into 7.4, the Dashboard page looks something like Figure 10.2.

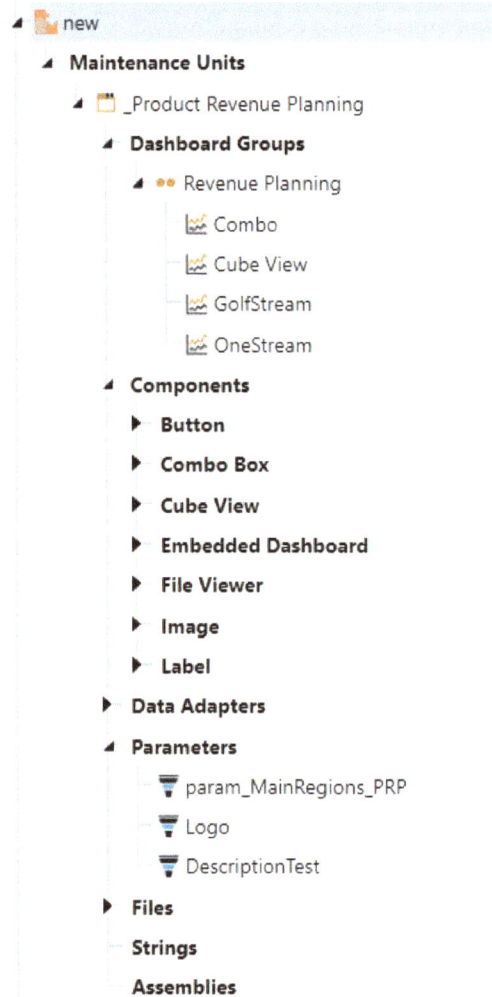

```
▲ 🔶 new
   ▲   Maintenance Units
      ▲ 🗂 _Product Revenue Planning
         ▲   Dashboard Groups
            ▲ •• Revenue Planning
                  📈 Combo
                  📈 Cube View
                  📈 GolfStream
                  📈 OneStream
         ▲   Components
            ▶   Button
            ▶   Combo Box
            ▶   Cube View
            ▶   Embedded Dashboard
            ▶   File Viewer
            ▶   Image
            ▶   Label
         ▶   Data Adapters
         ▲   Parameters
                  🔽 param_MainRegions_PRP
                  🔽 Logo
                  🔽 DescriptionTest
         ▶   Files
             Strings
             Assemblies
```

Figure 10.2

Looking at Figure 10.2, Workspaces sit at the top of your structure and hold your Dashboard Maintenance Units, Dashboard Groups, Components, data adapters, parameters, files, strings, and assemblies. Workspaces facilitate community development by providing an isolated environment for developers to segregate and organize Dashboard objects. They are the new foundation for Dashboards and will continue to evolve into the framework that encapsulates the artifacts needed to develop business solutions.

Workspaces were created to provide the following benefits:

- **Isolation between Dashboards.** This allows developers to work on the same Dashboard in a sandbox environment.

- **Greater flexibility for developers.** Better control amongst team members for changes, testing, and overall design.

- **They allow same-name items to exist in separate Workspaces.** This reduces the likelihood of naming conflicts, especially when importing/exporting them from other applications or sources.

- **You can share Workspace objects with other Workspaces.** This provides the opportunity to re-use objects rather than having to copy them.

You may have noticed that there is a Default Workspace. This is where all existing Dashboards – prior to 7.3 – were created if you were using an older version of OneStream and recently upgraded. This is a system-controlled Workspace, and if there is no need for multiple Workspaces, you can use this for all Dashboard storage and creation. Don't worry; you can easily move items out of this Workspace using copy/paste functionality. We do have one early recommendation, though, and that is to hold any universal parameters in the Default Workspace.

To create a new Workspace, locate the highlighted icon in the toolbar.

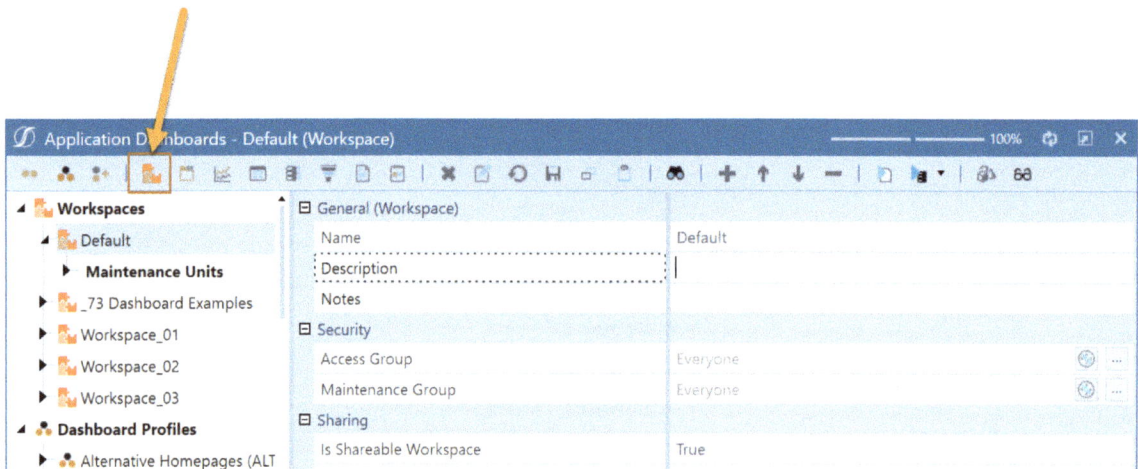

Figure 10.3

Really, the only property worth debating is whether this is a shareable Workspace or not. If you select True, other Workspaces can reference the objects in this Workspace. This property is basically acting as the security guard at the front door of all the items in the Workspace. The default Workspace always has this property set to True.

The second property, Shared Workspace Names, is where you can key in a comma-delimited list of Workspaces that this Workspace can take objects from. This means that each of these Workspaces would need to have the is Shareable Workspace property set to True.

Workspaces will continue to have evolving benefits as we see more releases of the software. Currently, they relieve the maintenance of requiring uniquely-named items across other Workspaces. You can also share items with other Workspaces. This may come in handy for more complex solutions, but anyone can take advantage of these new features.

Dashboard Groups and Profiles

Let's zoom in, first, on Dashboard Groups in Figure 10.4.

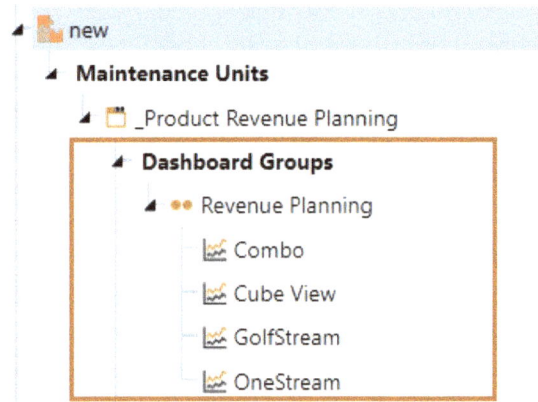

Figure 10.4

Dashboards themselves are always housed in Dashboard Groups. If you are experiencing a bit of *déjà vu*, you are not crazy; Dashboards – like Transformation Rules, Cube Views, Form Templates, and Journal Templates – have the same concept of groups and profiles. Dashboard Groups reside with the Dashboard Maintenance Unit, and then the respective Dashboard Groups are added to the Dashboard profiles outside the maintenance unit. Like everything else, the profile itself is what gets brought to the User through OnePlace.

This is an important concept because you use the various pieces within the Dashboard Maintenance Unit to create the Dashboards, which live in the groups, but they must be added to a profile to leave this page. If you are building one simple Dashboard, this may seem redundant, but as we increase in complexity and even start adding Dashboards to Dashboards, this will help you stay organized.

Maybe I can clarify this with another food-related metaphor (And it's not just because I have no real hobbies besides eating). Let's say you are making a delicious Chicken Parmigiana (I am American, so I say "Chicken Parm" with a strong midwestern accent). Think of the final dish as your Dashboard, the plate you serve it on as your Dashboard Group (because you can't huck loose pieces of chicken at your guests), your Dashboard profile is the table you serve it on. Your kitchen counter – with all your ingredients and tools nicely laid out – is Workspace.

Components

Let's zoom in once again, but this time on Dashboard Components.

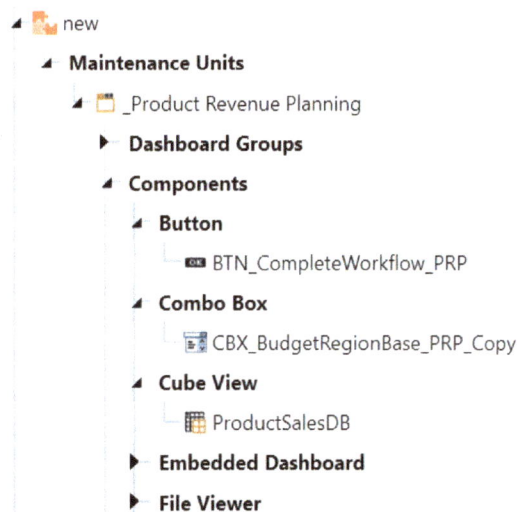

Figure 10.5

Figure 10.5 shows a few Components under our Workspace. They are any item that you can visually see on your final Dashboard. They are your charts, pivot grids, buttons, combo boxes, video players, Reports, and the list goes on and on.

In the context of our Chicken Parm, these would be the main ingredients that you can see on the plate: your chicken, your cheese, and your sauce. Some of these Components are as substantial as your chicken and might be something front and center like a Cube View, chart, or pivot grid, while your cheese is a supporting character and might be a combo box where you choose a Time Member or a button that runs a Calculation. Some people would throw a fit if you served them chicken parm without cheese; yes, I am one of those people.

Data Adapters, Parameters, and Files

Your data adapters, parameters, files, and strings are the unsung heroes of Dashboards. You may not be able to see them, but they bring your various Components to life.

If we go back to our cooking metaphor, these are the ingredients that you don't immediately see on the plate, but which you need! Maybe your chicken is breaded, so these are the breadcrumbs, egg, and flour. If you make your own sauce, this could be your garlic, olive oil, tomatoes, garlic, etc. Heck, you can even think of these items like your salt and pepper.

Data Adapter

Let's start with a data adapter. These are used to flood your Components with data, either from the Cube or application/external tables. Components like pivot grids, Reports, charts, BI Viewers, grids, and Data Explorers – just to name a few – will all require a data adapter to function. You rarely escape a Dashboard build without having to build a data adapter. I personally like to advise people to put a lot of work into their data adapter(s) to ease the amount of configuration on the Component. If you buy good quality ingredients, your food will taste better!

Parameters

We have already talked about parameters extensively, but they can be used throughout the entire OneStream application. Commonly, they are created to be added to combo box Components, but they often get incorporated into data adapters to create selectable elements in the Dashboard.

Files

Files may not be used as commonly, but if you are using a Book Viewer (for OneStream Report Books), Spreadsheet, or File Viewer Component, you will likely need some files! Even if this is not the case, you will likely have a nice logo or icon on a button to jazz up the appearance of your Dashboard. Files can be functional or more decorative items.

Strings

I won't get into strings too much because we usually see them being referenced in Cube Views. I like to think of strings as something to be prompted – based on User culture properties. This creates the effect of having multiple languages in your application.

For example, if you have multiple cultures enabled in your application for different languages, you will be able to provide a different Member description for each of them in the Dimension Library. But where else could we apply this? That is where your strings come in handy (they are found on the Dashboards page). The common example we see is to allow a different page caption to be visible, based on the User's culture. To see how to do this, refer to the Design and Reference guide under the section "Reference Alias Via XFString".

Assemblies

Another item I will just touch on is assemblies. Assemblies were released in 7.4, and they grant you the ability to write rules directly in the Dashboards page. You no longer need to travel to the Business Rules page if your Dashboard requires rules. You can choose to write a Dashboard data set, XFBRstring, Spreadsheet, or Dashboard Extender Rule. These can be written in C# or Visual Basic.

Tip: The Assemblies node relies on right-clicking to get things going. Once you have added an assembly to your Workspace, right-click and add a file to start writing your rule.

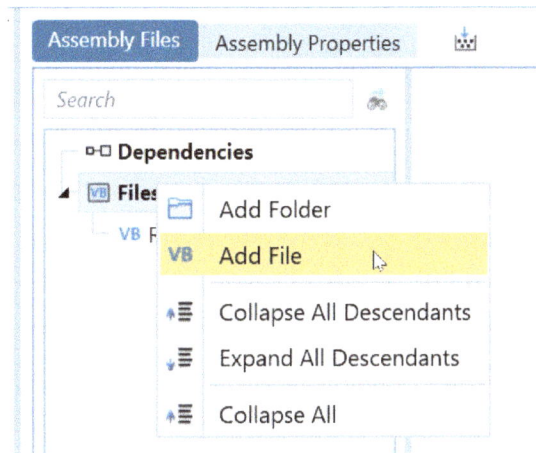

Figure 10.6

Be Able to Build at least Five (or Ten) Components

One of the things I said everyone should know is how to build around ten Dashboard Components proficiently. There are more than that, but this will be a great way to get yourself well-rounded. I will give you my top ten based on what I have found to be the most helpful in my career; the top five are the most important.

1. Buttons
2. Combo Boxes
3. Grid View
4. Charts (advanced)
5. Cube View

If you are up for the challenge, here are the next five Components I recommend trying:

6. Labels: Show a nice title on your Dashboard. Labels can offer so much; you can display dynamic items like parameters, substitution variables, and even query data.

7. Book Viewer: Unpopular opinion, maybe, but everyone should know this. A Book Viewer will display any of the items created in the Books page in OneStream. They can be stored in the File Explorer, emailed out through the Parcel Service, or presented in Dashboards using this Component.

8. BI Viewer: Our most dynamic Dashboard Component. This Component embodies the common Dashboard experience with interactions and drag and drop. You can use charts, pivot grids, data grids, and much more… all within this one Component.

9. Report: A great way to show non-Cube data in a polished format. The Report Designer makes this Component easy to use and you can incorporate them into Books. I really think everyone should be able to be able to build one of these Components; there is a great short lesson in The Navigator on how.

10. Pivot Grid: An interactive way to query data for your Users. They can choose rows, columns, filters, and even some formatting. Plus, they are very easy to set up. Large data pivot grids are similar and are great for… you guessed it… large amounts of data. They do have less formatting functionality, though.

Getting Started

Creating a Dashboard Component will typically take a little love because you have so many options. Figure 10.7 shows you the icon that you need to click to create a Component. From here, you will get a pop-up window for all the Components you can create. You can search for your Component or scroll through the list.

Once you create the Component, notice the running list of the types of Components you have. For example, in 10.7, I have at least one BI Viewer, Embedded Dashboard, and Pivot Grid Component. This is an excellent way to stay organized within your maintenance units and quickly see what you have created.

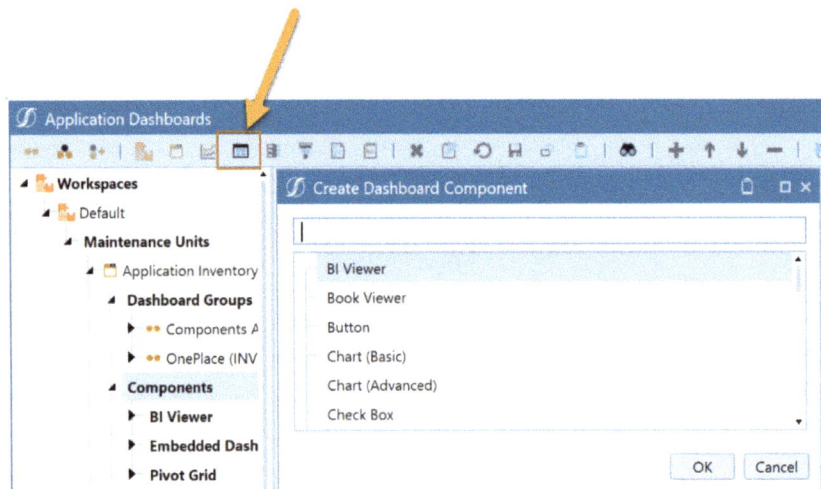

Figure 10.7

There are a wide number of Component properties that you can configure. You will notice that many of these properties overlap based on how similar some of them are. We are going to talk about some common favorites.

If you ever want to try making a Component, follow the steps illustrated, and set up the necessary properties. Then, I would recommend adding your Component(s) – one at a time – to a Dashboard to see how you did. This will help you get comfortable building Components and simplify any troubleshooting you need to perform.

To do this, you will need:

1. A Workspace created.

2. At least one Dashboard Maintenance Unit added.

3. A Dashboard Group under the Dashboard Maintenance Unit.

4. One Dashboard under the Dashboard Group.

Figure 10.8 shows an example of a Workspace I created to test a button. This would be great if I had never created a button before and wanted some practice. If you didn't know this, you can add Components to your Dashboard by clicking the highlighted + sign.

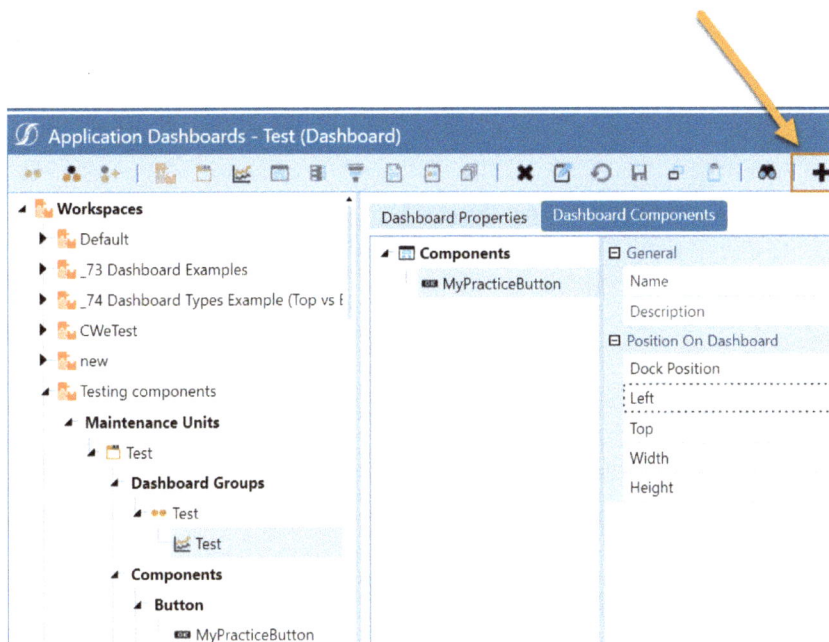

Figure 10.8

Buttons

Buttons are great for kicking off data management jobs, navigating to another page (or URL), or launching other Dashboards as a dialog box. My most common use case for them is running Custom Calculate Business Rules within Planning Forms. I often incorporate a button that can run a Data Management Sequence into many Planning implementations, as it is a great way to create an interactive Form that allows my Users to run rules on only the slice of data they need... when they need it. This reduces any reliance on automation or an Administrator when it comes to running rules, and gives my User what they need at their fingertips.

Figure 10.9 shows an example of a Dashboard I might be talking about. The button in question is the Calculate Revenue button at the top-right of the screen.

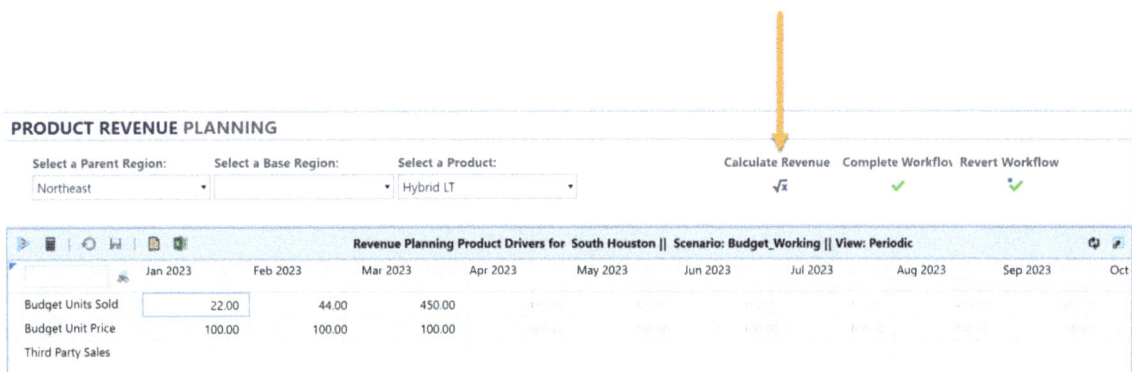

Figure 10.9

Let's peel back the curtain. Buttons are not that hard to set up, and I will point out the key properties you need here. I have collapsed the ones that are not as commonly used, in Figure 10.10.

Component Properties	
⊞ General (Component)	
⊟ Formatting	
Text	Calculate Revenue
Tool Tip	Calculate Revenue Plan
Display Format	|!lv_btnformat_PRP!|
⊟ Image	
Image File Source Type	Dashboard File
Image Url Or Full File Name	BUX_CalcRevPlan.png

Figure 10.10

1. Text: This property is what I use to display – directly to the User – what the button will do. You can see in Figure 10.10 the text Calculate Revenue is displayed.

2. Tool Tip: Users can hover over tool tips for clues or more information. I have a tool tip here, but you may not always need this (unless, of course, it actually helps the User). You cannot see this in Figure 10.10.

3. Display Format: I am using a Literal Value Parameter. You can open this window to provide any necessary formatting for your button.

4. Image File Source Type: You can see in Figure 10.10 that there is an image displayed for my button. This property tells me where this image is stored in OneStream. I like to store images in the Dashboard files section, so I can stay organized in my Workspace. But you can store them elsewhere.

5. Image URL or Full File Name: The name of the image file I am referencing in this button. This .png was uploaded to the Dashboard Files section.

Okay, now your button will look nice on the page. But will it work? Well… no. There is one other important section we need to configure: actions. Action settings are available with many Dashboard Components. Conveniently, if you learn how to set them up for a button, you can apply the same logic to combo boxes, charts, Cube Views, or any other Component that has them.

In this case, I want my button to be able to run a Custom Calculate Business Rule. I will run this rule through a Data Management Sequence. Figure 10.11 shows how my actions are configured.

Component Properties		
⊞ General (Component)		
⊞ Formatting		
⊞ Image		
⊞ Button		
⊟ Action		
Bound Parameter		...
Parameter Value For Button Click		
Apply Selected Value To Current Dashboard	True	
Save Action		
Selection Changed Save Action	No Action	
Selection Changed Save Arguments		...
POV Action		
Selection Changed POV Action	No Action	
Selection Changed POV Arguments		...
Server Task		
Selection Changed Server Task	Execute Data Management Sequence	
Selection Changed Server Task Arguments	{Revenue_CustomCalc}{param_Products_PRP=[|!param_Products_PRP!|]}	...

Figure 10.11

The first thing I needed to do was set the Selection Changed Server Task to Execute Data Management Sequence. For any Custom Calculate Finance Business Rules, this will be what you need to choose.

The next thing is to configure the Selection Changed Server Task Arguments. You may want to click the highlighted ellipses icon to help you out. This will give you the syntax that this property is expecting. The first item in the curly braces is the name of my data management sequence Revenue_CustomCalc and the second item is any parameters that I need to resolve. You may not have these, but in this case I am prompting my Users to choose a product. This may look strange, but since I would still like this prompt to occur, I am setting my parameter name equal to itself. I could hardcode the value here if I didn't want my User to choose this, but I am going to have them choose it through a combo box.

That is all you need. I would test this out by running my button on a Dashboard alone to see if it works. If I get an error, I like to test this by running the data management sequence from the Data Management page, since you can isolate where something is wrong with your rule or if you just configured the button incorrectly.

Combo Boxes

Combo boxes are the simplest way to make your Dashboard dynamic. Instead of parameter prompts, resolve parameters through an attractive combo box. Let's look at the same example Dashboard, once more, in Figure 10.12. This time, we are looking at the combo boxes across the top left of the screen (asking us to select a Parent Region, Base Region, and a Product).

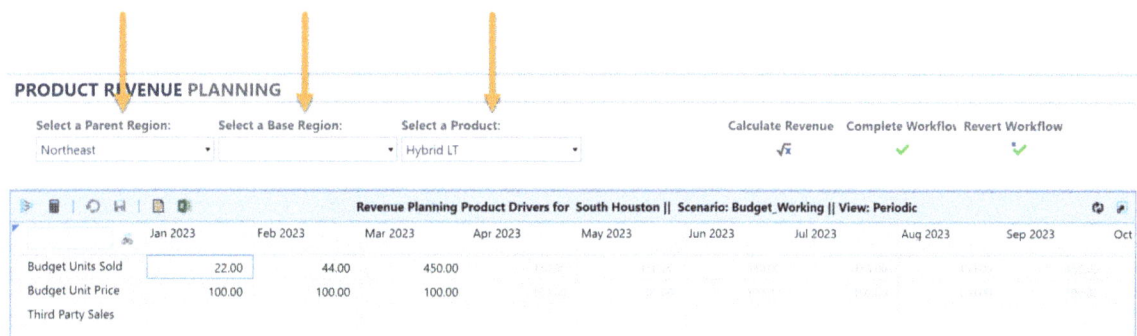

Figure 10.12

Now let's look at some of the properties we want to set up in our combo box. Notice that we have the same first three – Text, Tool Tip, and Display Format – as we had with buttons.

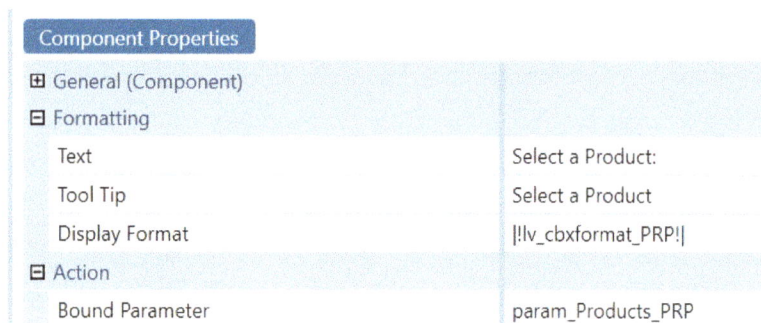

Figure 10.13

I won't go into these again, but the main property you will want to configure is the Bound Parameter property. Here I place the name (notice it is not in pipes and exclamation points) of the parameter that I need to fill my combo box with; in other words, the selections for my User to pick from. This means I will need to have a parameter already made for this Component to work. Luckily, we discussed how to do this in previous chapters. **Member List** and **Delimited List** parameters work best here.

Once again, we have some actions that we need to fill out. This might be surprising since, unlike our buttons, we don't need to run a rule or show a page. However, we will want to refresh any items on our Dashboard that may need to change, based on our User's selection. This way, our User doesn't have to refresh their own page intuitively.

Component Properties	
⊞ General (Component)	
⊞ Formatting	
⊟ Action	
Bound Parameter	param_Products_PRP
Apply Selected Value To Current Dashboard	True
Save Action	
Selection Changed Save Action	No Action
Selection Changed Save Arguments	
POV Action	
Selection Changed POV Action	No Action
Selection Changed POV Arguments	
Server Task	
Selection Changed Server Task	No Task
Selection Changed Server Task Arguments	
User Interface Action	
Selection Changed User Interface Action	Refresh
Dashboards To Redraw	2_MainBudgetContent_PRP

Figure 10.14

Figure 10.14 illustrates how I have this set up. I have chosen my User Interface Action to be Refresh, and the Dashboards To Redraw is the name of the Dashboard I have created. You can choose to refresh the entire Dashboard, or if you were clever enough to nest Dashboards within Dashboards, you may select one of them. You DO NOT choose a Component here; it is the actual Dashboard you choose.

Grid View

I don't see a lot of people using these Components, but they are a really easy way to query non-Cube data. We use them extensively in the Analytic Blend course because it allows people to see their results in something interactive and simple to create. Users can even filter and sort the data, making this an intuitive User Experience.

In the spirit of how I am doing these other Components, I am only going to explain what you need to get started. The truth is your grid Component has a lot of formatting properties that you may want to tinker with, and you can even apply some actions. For the sake of simply displaying data, you can leave many of these properties to their default settings. Indeed, the only thing you really NEED to get your Grid View working is a data adapter. Figure 10.15 will show you how to do this in three easy steps:

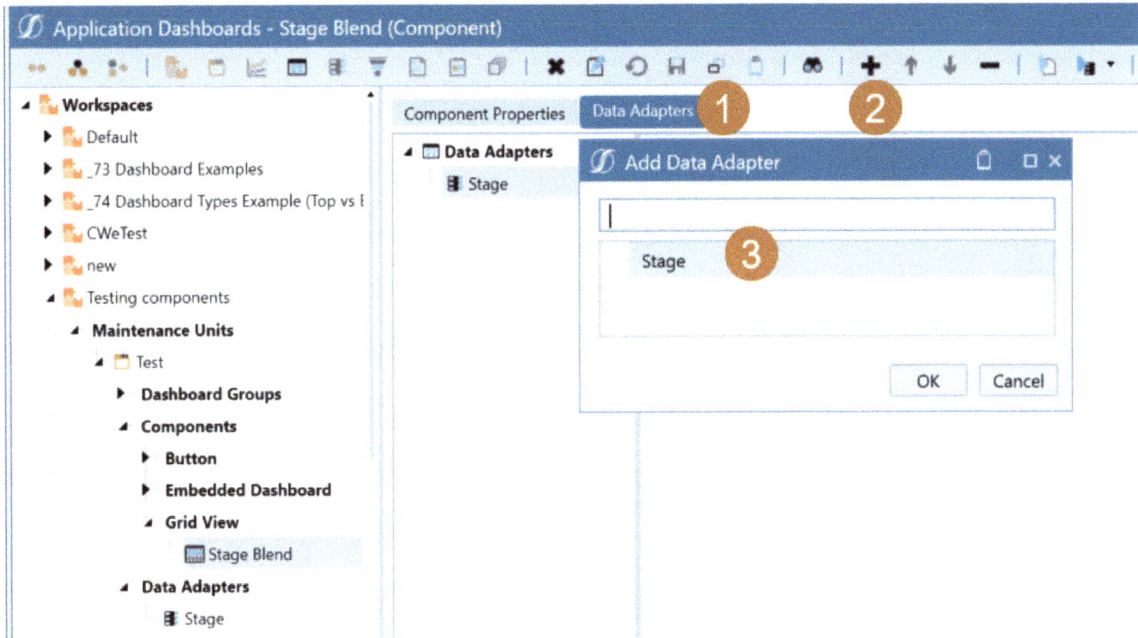

Figure 10.15

Choose the Data Adapters tab, then click the + sign and add the data adapter you would like to bring your Component to life. This is the first Component we have seen that requires a data adapter, but if you see that tab in your Component's properties, that is a good indicator that you might want to get one ready.

And if you are curious about what one of these looks like, here is Figure 10.16 to help you.

	Ac	TmT	U3	U3T	A1	ConvertedAmount
▸	PipelineRev	2022M4	Southwest	Southwest	Clubhouse Golf	2527.777777778
	PipelineRev	2022M6	Northeast	Northeast	Lindas Loop Resort	6525.000000000
	PipelineRev	2022M6	Southwest	Southwest	Clubhouse Golf	2527.777777778
	PipelineRev	2022M6	Southeast	Southeast	Dog Leg Golf Club	2738.888888889
	PipelineRev	2022M8	West	West	Antelop Canyon	7534.722222222
	PipelineRev	2022M8	Southeast	Southeast	Great Lakes Golf	11962.500000000
	PipelineRev	2022M8	Southeast	Southeast	East Side Family Golf	14137.500000000
	PipelineRev	2022M8	Midwest	Midwest	Wild Boar Golf	775.000000000
	PipelineRev	2022M9	Midwest	Midwest	Easy Par 3 Course	12012.500000000
	PipelineRev	2022M9	Southeast	Southeast	East Side Family Golf	14137.500000000
	PipelineRev	2022M9	Northeast	Northeast	West Side Fairways	12787.500000000

Figure 10.16

This is what happens if you do no formatting whatsoever to it. Notice that the filtering properties are still intact, and I am displaying selected columns for my Stage and Attribute tables.

I am querying a view that many people do not know about in OneStream called vStageSourceAndTargetDataWithAttributes. If you are a fan of SQL queries and need to grab Stage data, this is a great view, and it comes with every OneStream implementation.

In this figure, I am displaying my Source Account (column Ac), my Target Time (column TmT), my Source UD3 (column U3), my Target UD3 (column U3T), my First Attribute (column A1), and my Amount (column ConvertedAmount).

Chart (Advanced)

Everyone should know how to make one pretty chart. They are in all your sales demos! Don't let the number of properties fool you; they are much easier to craft than you think. Figure 10.17 shows an advanced chart that I have built.

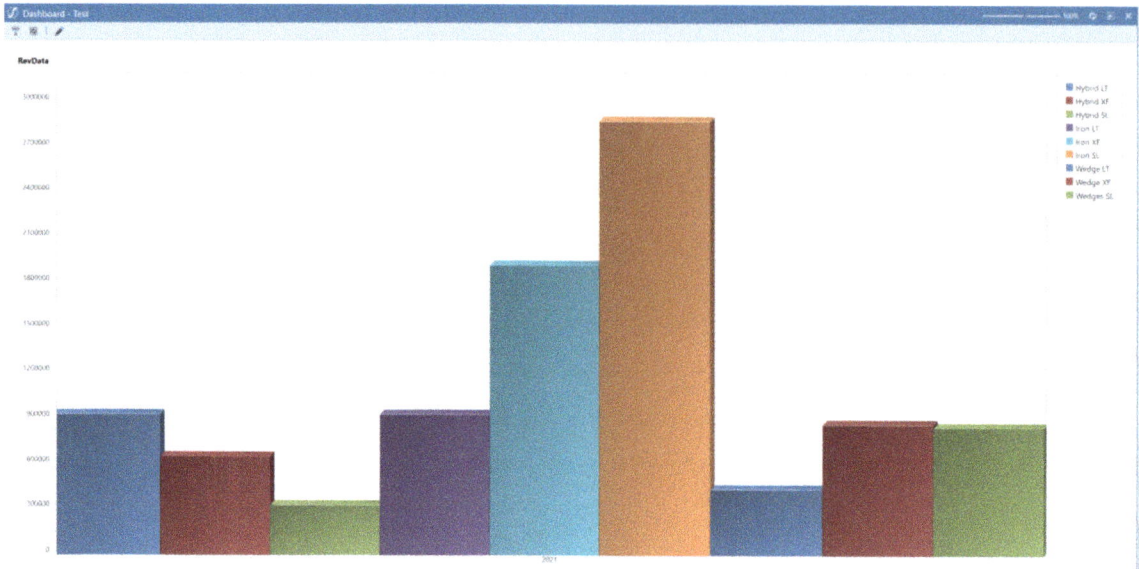

Figure 10.17

It's not too fancy, and really takes next to nothing to set up. My chart simply shows me revenue by product for one year.

I wanted to keep this chart as simple as possible because the number of properties on this Component can intimidate a lot of people. My advice is to try one thing at a time. Figure 10.18 shows you the only two things that I changed from their default settings. I chose my type of chart (which is a bar chart) and I added a simple Cube View data adapter, which we already learned how to do with the prior Component.

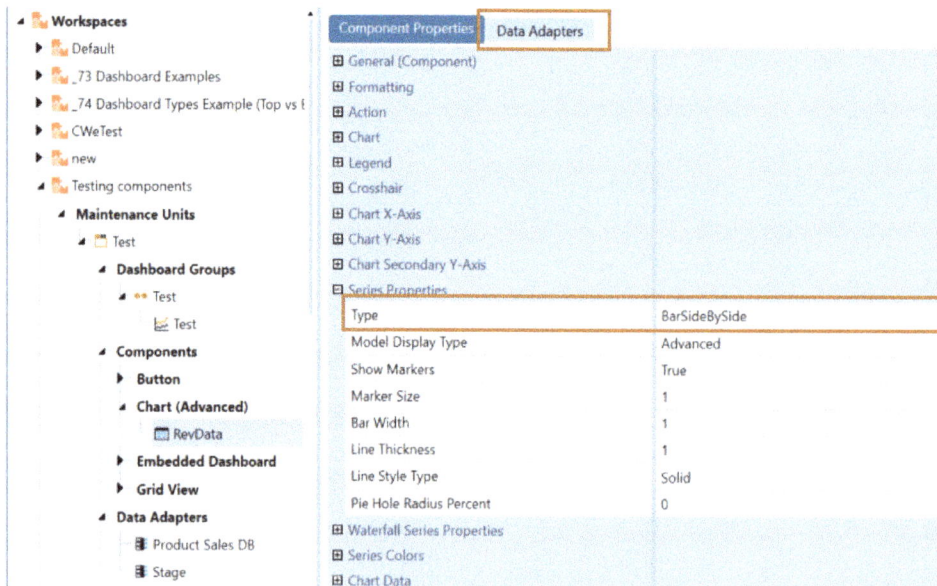

Figure 10.18

I kept all the other properties collapsed (but in view) on purpose, so you could see exactly how much you can toggle for more advanced charts. My tip, however, is to start small; just get it working. Many people miss this on advanced charts, but this particular Component can also be incorporated into Report Books and Extensible Documents. You can incorporate them just as easily as you would a Cube View!

Cube View

Cube View Components could not be easier to make, and they are a staple in many people's Dashboards. They are extremely helpful if you are creating a Dashboard for data collection, but really, they are just a simple way to display data. The great thing about them is that they are performant, and you keep all your great Cube View functionality – like drill-down – when referencing this Component. Also, you can format the Data Explorer of your Cube View heavily, to the point where you might not even know that a Cube View is on your page.

I'll bring back our familiar Dashboard in Figure 10.19. My Cube View is the large blue grid.

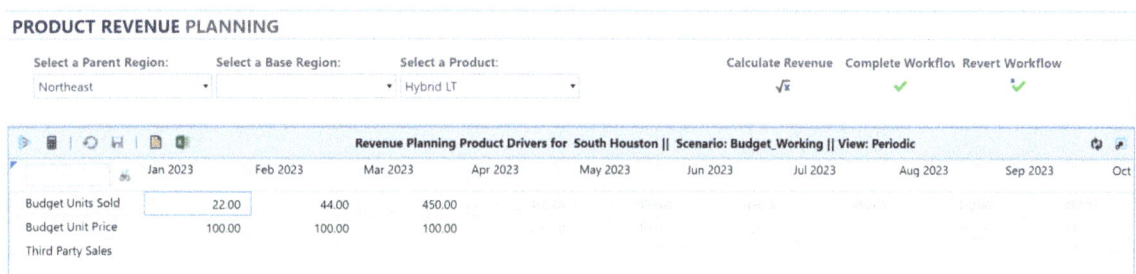

Figure 10.19

Now, this Component is easy to configure; you don't need a data adapter or anything to get it working. Check out Figure 10.20 to see what I am talking about:

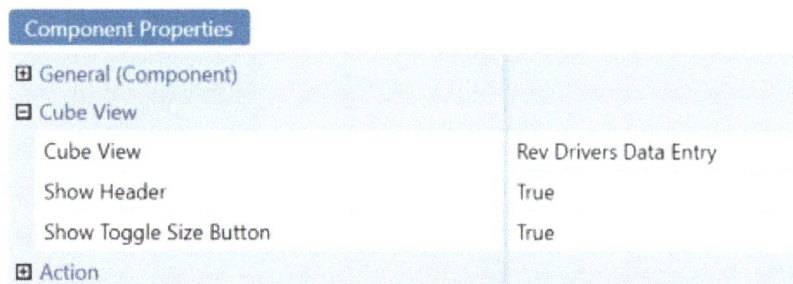

Figure 10.20

See? It could not be any easier! You just need to add a Cube View to get this working.

Note: For a Cube View to be visible on the Dashboards page, it needs to be added to a Cube View Profile with the appropriate visibility settings defined.

You will also notice that our actions are available here as well. That means our Cube Views can be more interactive than we originally thought. A common use case I see for this is if I want to have a Cube View and a Grid View Component displayed side by side in a Dashboard. If the User selects a cell in the Cube View, the Grid View Component will update to display the Stage data behind that cell. We create that exact Dashboard in the Level 3 Dashboards course.

Building Different Types of Data Adapters

In the prior section, we saw two Components that required a data adapter for them to work properly. There are certainly more Components out there that require a data adapter, so being armed with the ability to create each type is pivotal to your Dashboard career. There are five types of data adapters:

1. Cube View

2. Cube View MD

3. Method

4. SQL

5. BI Blend

It would be nice if you were able to build all five, but really I would settle for Cube View, Cube View MD, and SQL. BI Blend is most helpful only if you have BI Blend in your application. Realistically, you could also recreate this same query with a SQL data adapter.

On top of that, Method data adapters can also be done with a SQL data adapter. However, one caveat I will make is that Business Rule Method data adapters are extremely important if you are incorporating rules into your Dashboard. I will show you how to set these up because this is often required to take your Dashboard to the next level.

The different Data Adapter Types are used to bring different styles of data to your Dashboard. Remember, one of the key reasons why we use Dashboards is to query Cube and non-Cube data. So being well-versed in data adapters is fundamental to your success as a Dashboard builder.

Cube View

Your Cube View data adapter is very easy to set up and will typically be used with Components such as charts (advanced), charts (basic), or Data Explorer Reports. You can use them for much more, but I will give you an additional option that might prove valuable. Your Cube View Component does not require a data adapter at all. If you are simply adding a Cube View to a Dashboard, you can move straight to the Component.

How can we get started with creating a Cube View data adapter? Well, easily enough, Figure 10.21 shows you the only two properties you really need to update. The Command Type is where you decide your Data Adapter Type, so we have chosen Cube View. Notice that – when you choose your Command Type – this will update the subsequent properties you need. The only other crucial property is the Cube View we need to assign, and you can see that my Cube View Name is Product Sales DB.

⊞ General (Data Adapter)	
⊟ Data Source	
Command Type	Cube View
Cube View	Product Sales DB

Figure 10.21

I would recommend pausing here to run this data adapter and view your results before evaluating the other properties. It is important to preview data adapters before moving on. Figure 10.22 shows my results.

Data Table

Table ▼

	RowId	RowName	PovCubeNameAndDesc	Pov00EntityNameAndDesc	Pov02ScenarioNameAndDesc	Pov03TimeNameAr
▸	0	Products	Houston - Houston Clubs	South Houston	Actual	2018M3 - Mar 2018
	1	Products	Houston - Houston Clubs	South Houston	Actual	2018M3 - Mar 2018
	2	Products	Houston - Houston Clubs	South Houston	Actual	2018M3 - Mar 2018
	3	Products	Houston - Houston Clubs	South Houston	Actual	2018M3 - Mar 2018
	4	Products	Houston - Houston Clubs	South Houston	Actual	2018M3 - Mar 2018
	5	Products	Houston - Houston Clubs	South Houston	Actual	2018M3 - Mar 2018
	6	Products	Houston - Houston Clubs	South Houston	Actual	2018M3 - Mar 2018
	7	Products	Houston - Houston Clubs	South Houston	Actual	2018M3 - Mar 2018
	8	Products	Houston - Houston Clubs	South Houston	Actual	2018M3 - Mar 2018

Total Number Of Rows: 9

Figure 10.22

This is hard to depict, but even though I only have nine rows of data, there are many columns present. When you use a Cube View data adapter, the fields are essentially the items within the Cube View. You can see the columns are pulling in my row name and the elements of the POV and – if I kept scrolling to the right – you would see the Components in the row as well as the data points for every single column.

This is what makes the Cube View data adapter great with the Components I listed before, but (maybe) not so much for other ones. I usually try to recommend the Cube View MD data adapter for Components like BI Viewer, large data pivot grids, and pivot grids if you require data that resides in the Cube. This is because these Components rely heavily on you, or even your End-User, at times, placing their appropriate fields into the spaces within these Components. Pov00EntityNameAndDesc will not typically mean a lot to anyone.

I won't leave you hanging on the other properties. You likely won't need to alter them, but you may want to understand them. This series of True/False properties is here to allow you to activate certain aspects of the Cube View. We saw PovCubeNameAndDesc in Figure 10.22; notice that the property Include Cube POV is set to True in Figure 10.23. We could turn off the POV Members that we don't want to see from the Cube View POV. We can also turn on the Cube View subtitles in the headers or footers of the Cube View here. Essentially, you can choose to simplify or add more items to your resulting table.

Include Header Left Label 3	False
Include Header Left Label 4	False
Include Header Center Label 1	False
Include Header Center Label 2	False
Include Header Center Label 3	False
Include Header Center Label 4	False
Include Header Right Label 1	False
Include Header Right Label 2	False
Include Header Right Label 3	False
Include Header Right Label 4	False
Include Cube POV	True
Include Entity POV	True
Include Parent POV	False
Include Cons POV	False

Figure 10.23

You likely won't need the headers. I had one situation – back in my consulting career – where I enabled these properties because I was fine-tuning one of my Cube Views with the Report Designer. I needed to enable the headers in my data adapter because I was using substitution variables to make them dynamic. Therefore, I needed my data adapter to flood my Report with the appropriate header, as opposed to me hardcoding in things like the Time period, Entity, or Product used to pull the data in the Report. Since then, many updates have come into the Cube Views page, and those use cases are thinning out, but they still do happen.

Cube View MD

I loved it when this data adapter came out. It has been a lifesaver when building Reports for Analytic Blend use cases, where I need to grab existing Cube data effortlessly. Let's break down the name of this data adapter. Cube View suggests you are going to start the build of this data adapter like the one we just discussed (and you would be correct), but MD stands for Multi-Dimensional. We can see this reflected in the output of this data adapter in Figure 10.24.

Data Table

Table

Cube	Entity	Parent	Cons	Scenario	Time	View	Account
Houston	South Houston		USD - United States of America, Dollars	Actual	2021M1 - Jan 2021	Periodic	2000_100 -
Houston	South Houston		USD - United States of America, Dollars	Actual	2021M1 - Jan 2021	Periodic	2000_100 -
Houston	South Houston		USD - United States of America, Dollars	Actual	2021M1 - Jan 2021	Periodic	2000_100 -
Houston	South Houston		USD - United States of America, Dollars	Actual	2021M1 - Jan 2021	Periodic	2000_100 -
Houston	South Houston		USD - United States of America, Dollars	Actual	2021M1 - Jan 2021	Periodic	2000_100 -
Houston	South Houston		USD - United States of America, Dollars	Actual	2021M1 - Jan 2021	Periodic	2000_100 -
Houston	South Houston		USD - United States of America, Dollars	Actual	2021M1 - Jan 2021	Periodic	2000_100 -
Houston	South Houston		USD - United States of America, Dollars	Actual	2021M1 - Jan 2021	Periodic	2000_100 -
Houston	South Houston		USD - United States of America, Dollars	Actual	2021M1 - Jan 2021	Periodic	2000_100 -

Total Number Of Rows: 117

Figure 10.24

If we check out the columns, we see some familiar faces. Each of our Dimensions is visible for each data point. If you scrolled to the right, despite this Cube View having multiple columns, there will be only one Amount. Figure 10.25 is going to show you why this data adapter works so well with certain Components.

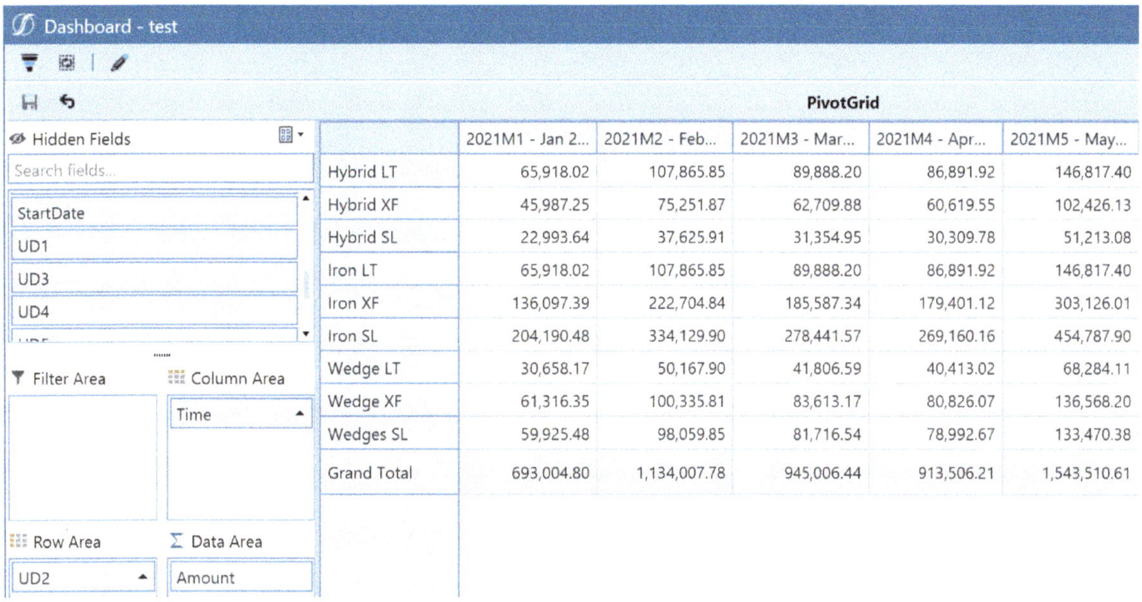

Figure 10.25

Above is an example of our Cube View MD data adapter and a pivot grid. This pivot grid has had nothing special done to its properties besides adding the data adapter. You can see that I get all my Dimensions displayed. So as a User, I was able to drag my Time to the columns area, my UD2 to my rows, and my Amount to the data area. This was all done easily and in a matter of seconds, thanks to my easy-to-interpret Cube View MD data adapter.

There are some cool things that you can add to your Cube View MD data adapter as well. I will point out two neat property sections: **Loop Parameters** and **Dimensions To Level**.

Loop Parameters allow me to use the Member Filter Builder to add additional Members to my data adapter that may not be present in my Cube View. In Figure 10.26, you can see that I have added `V#YTD` and `V#Periodic` into my Cube View.

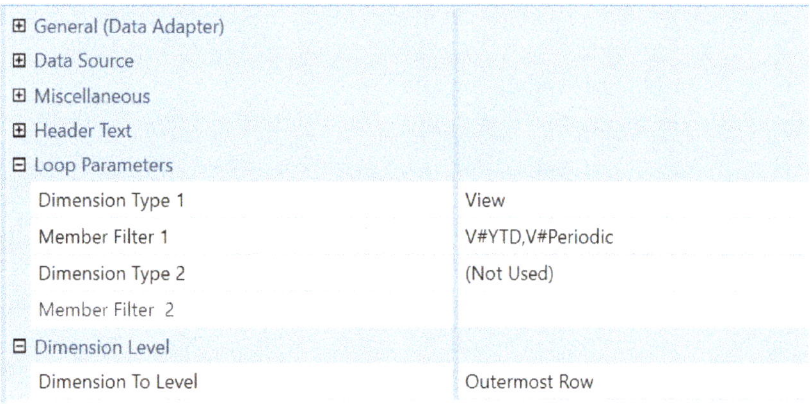

Figure 10.26

Dimension To Level is something exciting. You can pick the outermost row, outermost column, or both. This is handy if your Cube View is pulling an expansion with multiple levels. If this is enabled, you can add fields to your data adapter to denote which level is in the hierarchy being pulled. This is a little hard to explain, so let's look at the results in our pivot grid in Figure 10.27.

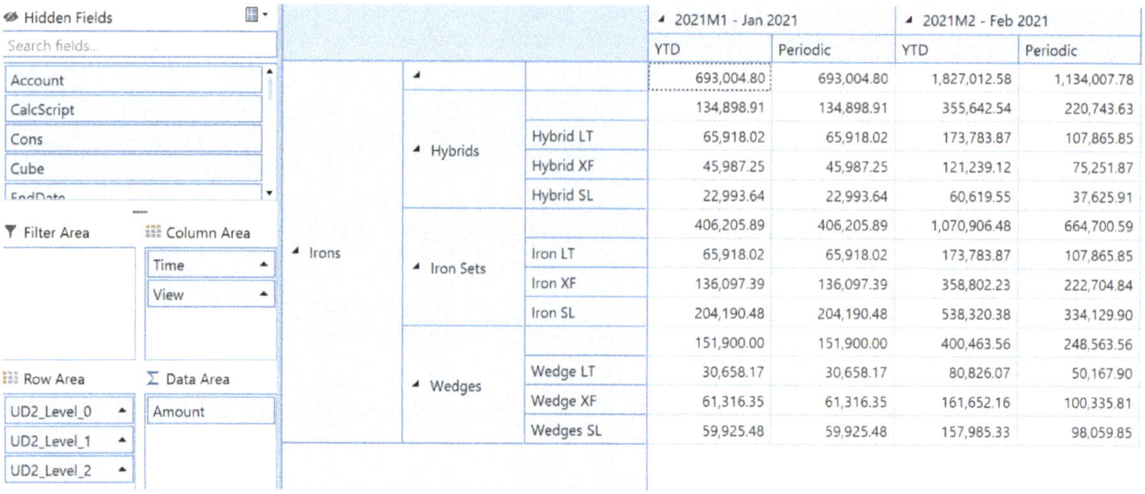

Figure 10.27

Notice in the Row Area, instead of just placing UD2 here, I now can place UD2_Level_0, UD2_Level_1, and UD2_Level_2.

If we look to the grid:

- level 0 is displaying the top level UD2 Dimension displayed in my hierarchy
- level 1 is the Child under that
- and level 2 is the Children under that

The Cube View MD data adapter will decipher how many levels are present and split out the fields appropriately. This gives me the ability to create a tree-like view in my Dashboards and, therefore, enhance my User Experience. It may take a moment to get used to the new column names, but you can't argue with those results.

SQL

Next, I am going to hop to the SQL data adapter. This is a staple in our data adapters and the most flexible way to query data that does not reside in the Cube. This is where we may lose a few people as not everyone has a background in SQL, but there is a lot of great documentation out there that can help you out, including the Microsoft website.

But let's stick with our theme and continue to break down our necessary properties in Figure 10.28. As you can see, besides the SQL Query itself, there is not much to it. You just decide SQL as your Command Type and the location of your database. Application will be great for querying all your application tables. You may also choose Framework, although it is a little less common. If you have incorporated BI Blend into your application, you must choose External as your Database location.

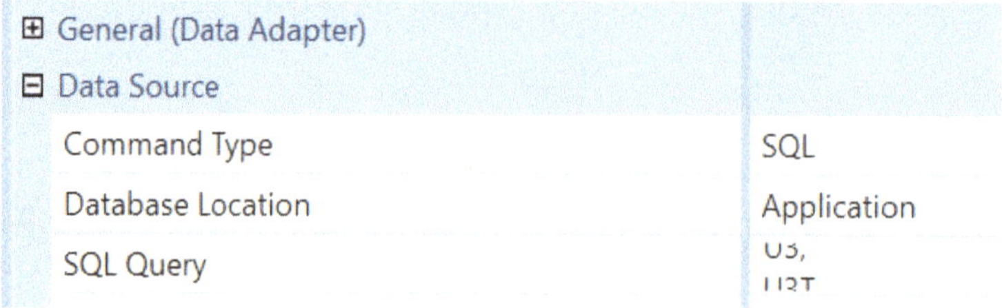

Figure 10.28

After that, you are ready to write your query. If you are in a Dev environment and you are struggling with learning SQL, you can start with a simple SELECT * FROM *YourTableName*. This will give you all the records in each table. You probably don't want to make a habit of doing this, as this can be a lengthy query. Homing in as much as possible will ensure better performance. Calling out specific column names (or fields) and fine-tuning with `where` clauses will help. Figure 10.29 shows the simple SQL Query I wrote to pull Stage data.

```
Select
Ac,
TmT,
U3,
U3T,
A1,
ConvertedAmount
From vStageSourceAndTargetDataWithAttributes
Where TmT like '2022%'
```

Figure 10.29

This code selects a list of my required fields from my view with Source, Target, and Attribute Dimensions where the Target Time Member starts with 2022. You can, of course, add parameters. There are many ways to write a sophisticated SQL query, but if you know your table name, you can figure it out.

Speaking of which, if you have no idea what any of the OneStream table names are, I recommend going to the Database page found on the System tab. The list of Application and System database tables can be found here; if you click on them, you can preview the fields available.

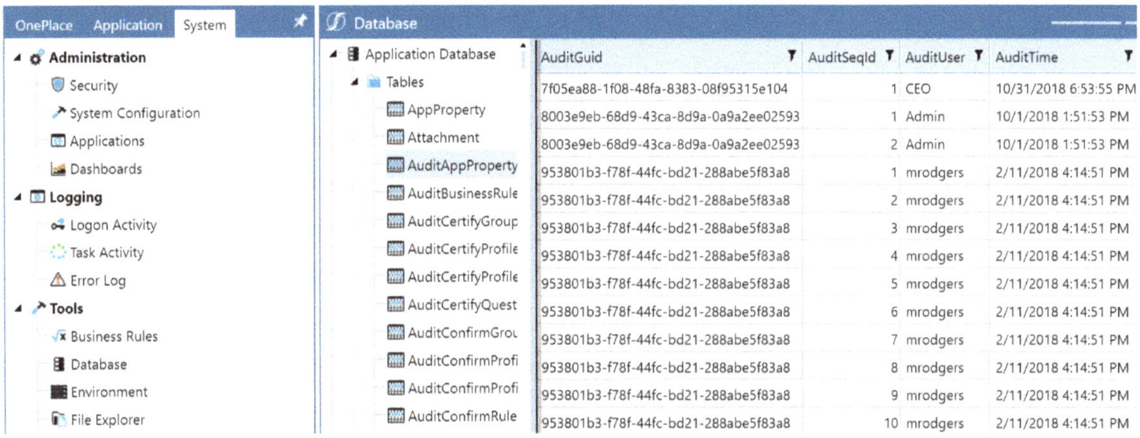

Figure 10.30

The only thing you will not find here are the views that come with OneStream, which is why I wanted to include the one I find the most helpful for pulling Stage data in Figure 10.29. In turn, you will not find anything in your external databases, so that means no BI Blend. However, you can easily pull the list of BI Blend Table names from the OneStream Workflow or through the `StageBiBlendInformation` table. This table is shown in Figure 10.31.

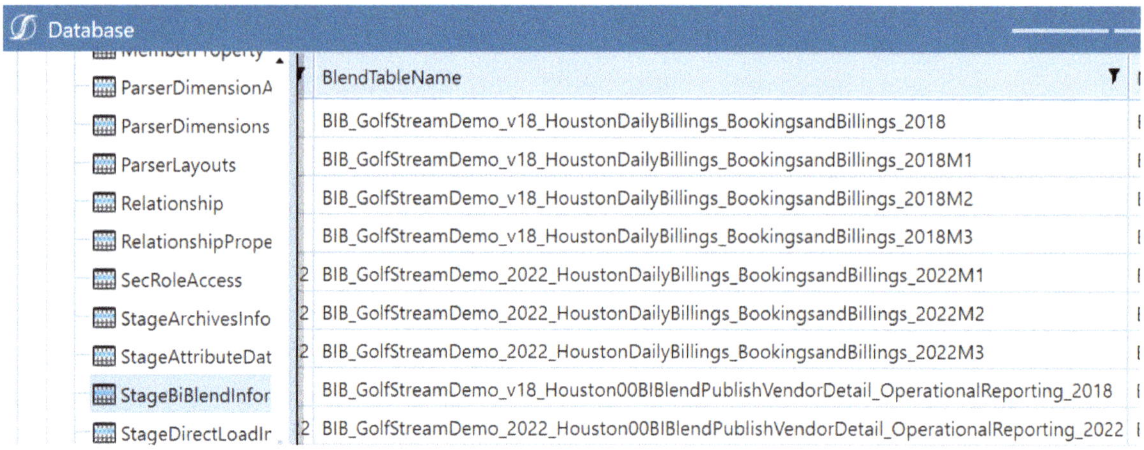

Figure 10.31

BI Blend

I am partial to using a SQL data adapter whenever I query BI Blend data, mostly because I like the flexibility that this can provide. However, the BI Blend data adapter was created to facilitate the ability to pull data from BI Blend if you are uncomfortable writing SQL queries. Instead of a scary query, you just fill out the necessary properties.

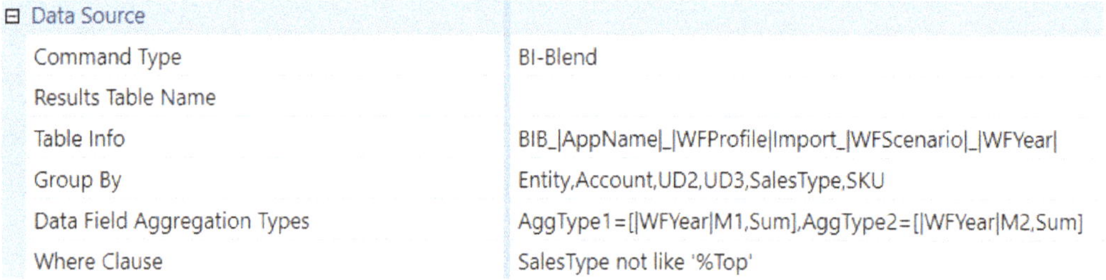

Figure 10.32

Figure 10.32 shows the properties that you may want to fill out. I took it a step forward and parameterized this query to make it more dynamic.

First, you need your Table Info. There is an ellipsis here that will pull the list of potential tables to help you out. I just placed some substitution variables to make this more dynamic. Your Group By property should be filled out with the fields you wish to include. Then, Data Field Aggregation Types will be the amounts that you need.

> **Note**: There is a specific syntax expected here, and you can hover over the property to get the tool tip if you are worried you will not remember it.

I also added substitution variables to my amounts to make them dynamic. And finally, you can add a `Where` clause to filter your data down and improve performance. That last one is optional.

Method

We covered this one in the parameters section, so I won't go back into it. Method data adapters are another option if you are uncomfortable writing a SQL query. They will help you with common queries for your Application and System database tables.

However, there is one very specific use case where you will require a Method data adapter. That is if you are using a Business Rule – usually a Dashboard data set – to populate your data. We can see an example of this Method query in Figure 10.33.

General (Data Adapter)	
Name	BlendHybrid_FDXCV
Description	
Maintenance Unit	Blend
Data Source	
Command Type	Method
Method Type	BusinessRule
Method Query	{FDX_CubeView}{ExtractCubeViewTimePivot}{cvNameToExtract=FDXParent}
Results Table Name	

Figure 10.33

The syntax for this Method query is

`{BusinessRuleName}{DataSetName}{Parameter1=Value, Parameter2=Value}`. You may not have any parameters. Remember, if you do not know the syntax of the Method Type you have selected, do not just fill the item out and run the data adapter. It will return an error with the expected syntax for MOST Method types. If not, the syntax is also available in the OneStream Design and Reference Guide. Currently, this can be found on the Data Adapters page (you might have to scroll).

Embedding Dashboards

We have learned a lot of pieces about Dashboards, but the trick of setting one up that works nicely lies in running the Dashboard in design mode. This is a great way to learn how to troubleshoot Dashboards that maybe you did not build. As we move into embedding Dashboards into other Dashboards, things might start to get more complicated, so we want to think of this tactic as not something that should scare us, but something that enables us to break down a complicated solution into small pieces. Then (food metaphor alert!), we just eat them one bite at a time.

Running a Dashboard in Design Mode

If you ever meet someone who claims to know a little of a language, and ask them how much exactly, they might reply, "It's hard for me to speak it, but I can understand it." Once you learn enough pieces and recognize certain words, you can start to understand others. The more you listen, the more you can pick up, but the hardest part is speaking. You find yourself stalling and searching for the right grammatical structure or conjugation. But the only way to get good is to keep trying.

I think of unwinding complex Dashboards through the Dashboard design mode as being able to understand a language. You might not jump in and build a full, complex page from scratch just yet, but you can pull out the parts that you need and tinker with them. If you know how to make parameters, data adapters, and a few Components in their simplest form, that is – in a way – equivalent to learning basic vocab terms and sentence structures. It will help you to start troubleshooting because you have a foundation. The more examples you are exposed to, and the more Dashboards you see, the closer you will get to becoming fluent.

Let's keep this in mind and learn how to run our Dashboard in design mode (if you don't already). If you are in your Dashboards page, notice that there are two icons at the top of your screen that allow you to preview a given Dashboard. You will want to click the icon I have highlighted in Figure 10.34 to run this Dashboard in design mode.

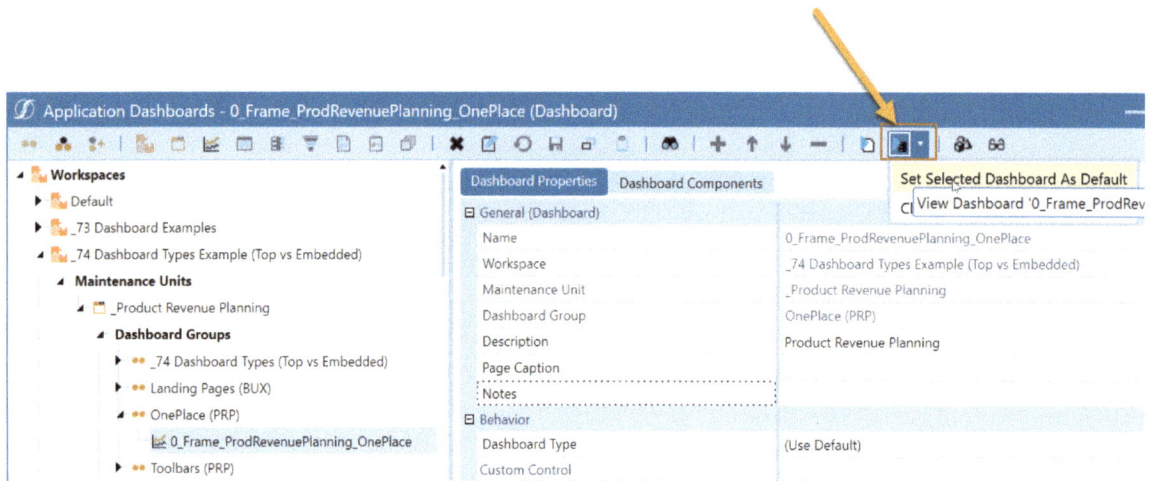

Figure 10.34

You will also notice that there is a small arrow that gives you the option to Set Selected Dashboard As Default. Click this item first to save the selected Dashboard as the one you would like to run in design mode. Why? We have learned that you may be jumping around quite a bit in the Dashboards page, so isn't it handy that you could simply click this icon while you make changes in various Components and just see your Dashboard in preview mode?

Let's check out the simple Dashboard we have been running throughout this chapter in the design mode. In Figure 10.35, on the left side of your screen, is your Dashboard displayed in a hierarchical format. You'll notice that we have many Dashboards within Dashboards in this example. That is a concept called **Embedding Components**, and we will cover that in the next section.

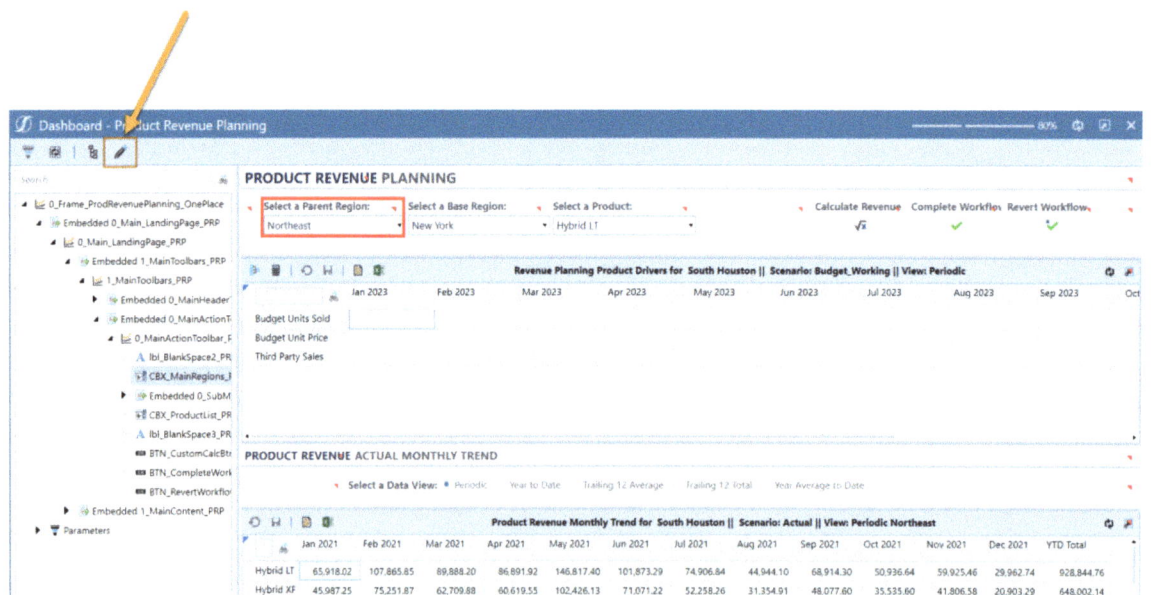

Figure 10.35

If I am on a particular item in the Dashboard hierarchy, the item will be selected with a red box (I didn't draw that in, above), and it allows me to see which item links to which Dashboard or Component. You can also click on one of the little red tick marks above each of the objects, and it will take you to the item in the hierarchy. Basically, you now can point at something and say, "What is that? I want to change it."

One last thing, there is a little pencil icon (highlighted in yellow and with an arrow pointing at it, in Figure 10.35). If you click this, it will take you to whichever item you selected in edit mode.

The design mode is great if you would like to update something that you or someone else has created. You don't have to search through the Dashboards page to find a specific item; just point and click.

Breaking Down Embedded Dashboard Components

When we say "Embedding Dashboards" or "Dashboards within a Dashboard", we are using Embedded Dashboard Components. Embedded Dashboard Components nest one Dashboard inside another. Figure 10.36 has an example of this in practice.

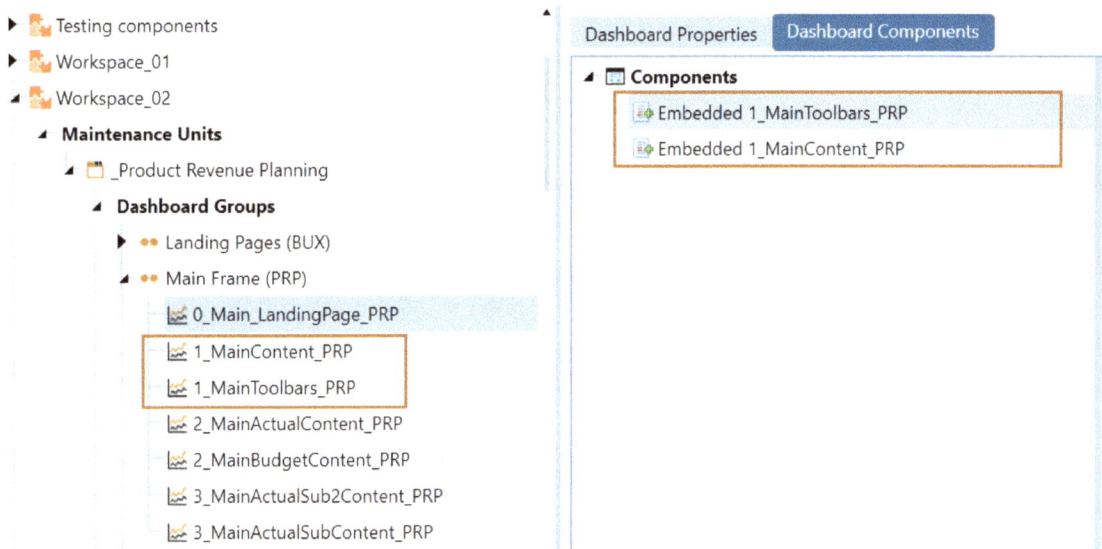

Figure 10.36

This figure shows one Dashboard made up of two other Dashboards. This is done with two Embedded Dashboard Components: 1_MainContent_PRP and 1_MainToolbars_PRP. In the design mode (Figure 10.37), we can see that these two Embedded Components make up the top and bottom.

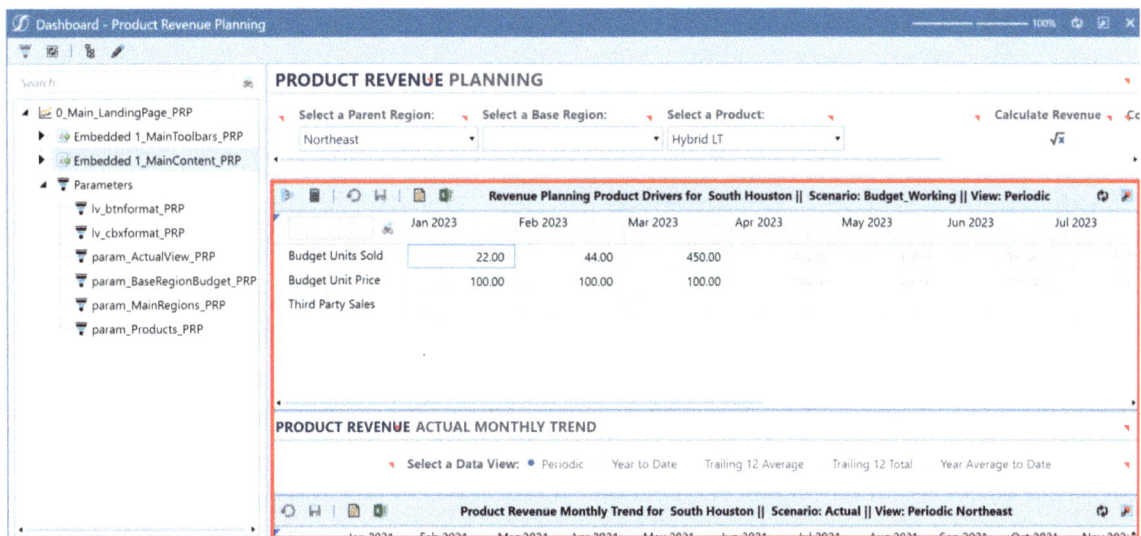

Figure 10.37

Why would you want to do this? Two key reasons could force you into this:

1. You are trying to create actions.
2. You are trying to build a complex layout with many Components.

We learned from our other Components that we sometimes have actions. These actions allow us to refresh, show, hide, or open a dialog of other Dashboards. Remember, these actions cannot be applied to our Components, only to Dashboards. One reason why you may create multiple Dashboards referencing other Dashboards is because you are trying to isolate a particular area with an action.

Another reason for Embedded Dashboard Components is to accommodate complex layouts. It's a lot easier to get that top toolbar laid out perfectly by itself before encapsulating other items. This allows you to think of your Dashboard in digestible pieces, as opposed to one giant Dashboard juggling a lot of Components.

How are Embedded Dashboard Components Created?

Embedded Dashboard Components are automatically created every time a Dashboard is generated. You can take advantage of them without having to do anything!

Let's look at the properties of our Embedded Dashboard Components in Figure 10.38. The only property you really need is called Embedded Dashboard, and it will be automatically populated for you. Notice that this property is editable.

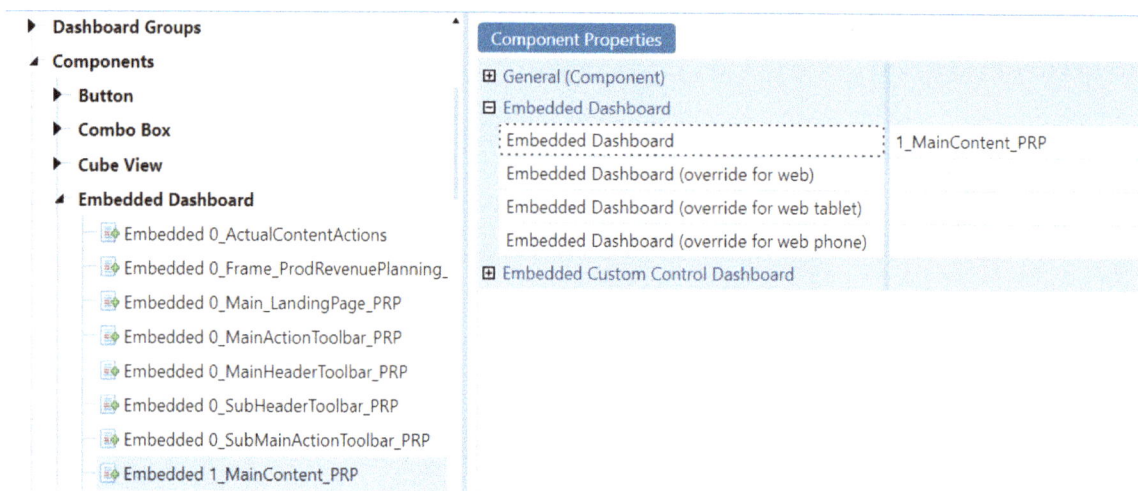

Figure 10.38

Dashboard Naming Conventions

One of the best tips we can give you is to stay organized with the naming conventions of your Dashboards. As you may have guessed, sometimes nesting multiple Dashboards within each other can get tricky. A clear naming convention can keep your Dashboard (or, more likely, Dashboards) easy to follow.

A good naming convention pattern to stick to is one we teach in training. Figure 10.39 illustrates a simple pattern that we follow. It contains prefixes highlighting the Dashboard hierarchy, a solution code to keep this group of Dashboards organized together, and a good description that describes how each Dashboard is being used.

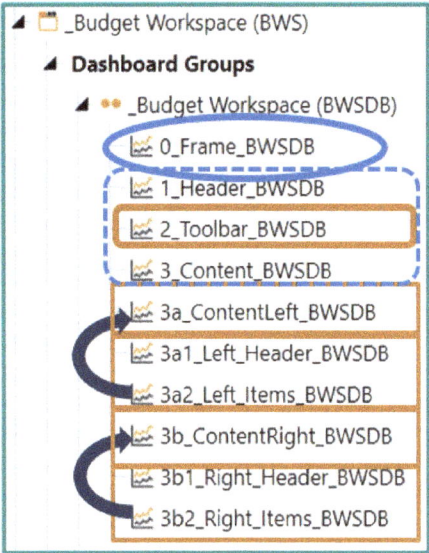

Figure 10.39

Let's start with the prefixes. From the bottom, I can see that:

- 3b1_ and 3b2_ embed into 3b_

- 3a1_ and 3a2_ embed into 3a_

- After that, 3a_ and 3b_ embed into 3_ and so on and so forth

The prefixes are to highlight which Dashboards have nested into other Dashboards.

Notice there is also a solution code BWSDB included as a suffix. This is something our engineers employ, but I have known other Dashboard builders to adopt a similar strategy to facilitate the structure and searching of the Dashboard pieces.

The center of the naming convention tells you the placement/purpose of the Dashboard. The frame holds the final Dashboard, while the header sits across the top; the toolbar sits below that (and would likely contain my icons and combo boxes). Finally, my content resides in 3_.

Let's look at something more complicated and highlight another key item in Figure 10.40. This shows how our solution Guided Reporting (GDR) looks behind the scenes. One of the first things that you notice is that there are multiple Dashboard Groups that contain multiple Dashboards. The final Dashboard Group is named OnePlace (GDR). The Dashboard itself has the name 0_Frame_GDR_Main_OnePlace, so there are some slight variations, but let's see if we can break down this logic.

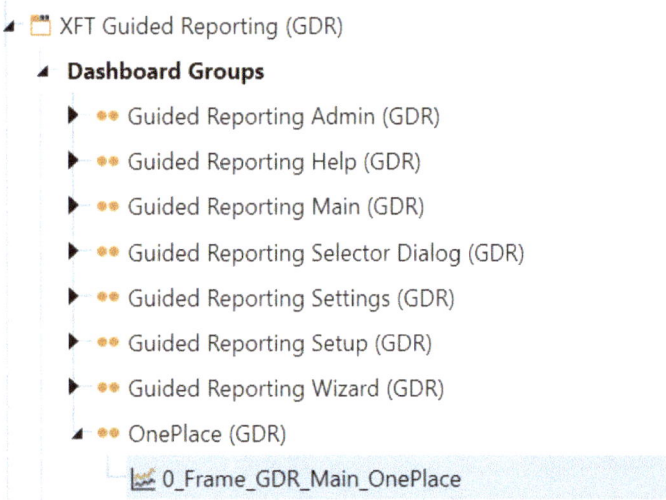

Figure 10.40

First, one of the things that the Group and the Dashboard name have in common is GDR. This is called a **solution code** and it indicates that these items are for Guided Reporting.

Next, notice that both the Group and the Dashboard have OnePlace in their name. This is commonly done to denote the Dashboard that is our final Dashboard and that it will reside in OnePlace. Then, this Group is the only one that gets added to the Dashboard profile and is therefore brought to the End-User. This prevents your Users from seeing all the pieces of the Dashboard that you have built.

You may adopt a similar strategy depending on how large your Dashboard has grown. However, with the release of 7.4, a new property will be making its way into Dashboards which may cause us to rethink our common practice. This is the **Dashboard Type** property. With this property, you can designate specific Dashboards as 'embedded'. This will eliminate the Dashboard from OnePlace even if it resides in a Dashboard Group that was added to a Dashboard profile. Figure 10.41 shows you this new property if you want to try it out.

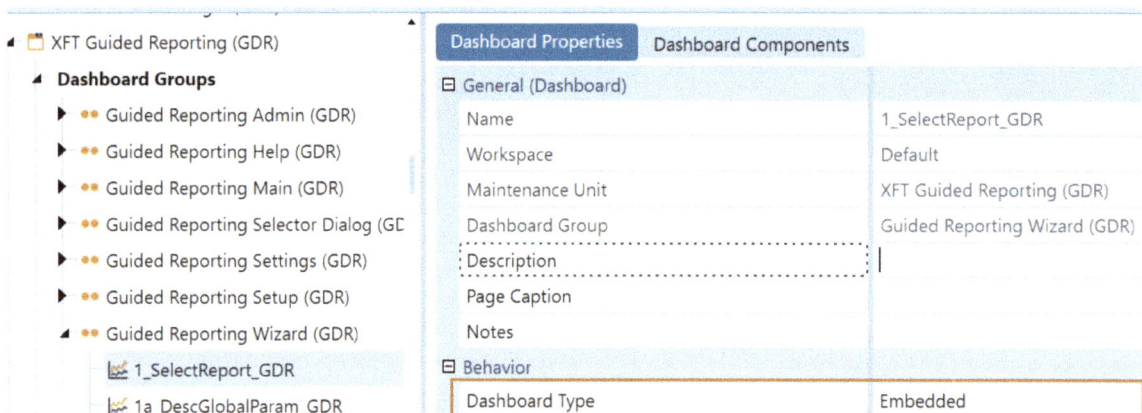

Figure 10.41

If you really want to take things to the next level, the Components that are added to the Dashboards and their parameters can also contain the codes as well as their alphanumerical prefixes. The important thing is to stay consistent so you and others can follow the Dashboard taxonomy. You will see other recommendations for naming conventions discussed in the later chapters.

Conclusion

This chapter is the first place where we started to dive into Dashboards. We have learned that Dashboards are a portion of OneStream that is always on the move and flexing with the latest requests from our community. We are about to undergo many fresh updates to the Dashboards page in 2023 and beyond, so be prepared for some of these items to continue to change. Rest assured, this is done to extend the capabilities of this sought-after feature in OneStream.

In this book, we are trying to give you the tools to craft the best User Experience as an Implementor or Admin in OneStream. Dashboards are often a place that people struggle to break into. In the following chapters, you are going to get a breakdown into some of the different Dashboards that you may have seen in OneStream demonstrations. If you are new to Dashboards, this chapter hopefully gave you an easy introduction and pointed out some key areas where anyone can begin their Dashboard journey.

No matter how much you learn, or how complicated a solution you are tasked with, remember that we are trying to benefit our End-Users' lives. I am not a UI designer, so all my advice is from the perspective of someone who has had to explain items within OneStream to people who are learning. If you can't explain it to someone, it is too complicated.

My final advice is to design a Dashboard that looks like anyone could build it. Whether it be a Report, a home page, a solution, or a Form. They can get complicated if you let them, but if you place your End-User first, you cannot go wrong. Also, think about the person who will administer and maintain the Dashboard after you are gone, even if you think that day will never come. Cryptic!

11

Splash Screens and Home Pages

In the previous chapter, we learned about the fundamental concepts of OneStream Dashboards, the Components that we use to build them, and how we can include our Dashboards in the End-User Experience through Workflows.

In this chapter, we will take an in-depth look at how we can use these concepts and Components to design and build an actual Dashboard that will serve as the landing page our Users see when they first sign on to the application.

By setting this Dashboard as the User's home page, it will provide a welcoming and attractive splash screen as well as provide 'big button' one-click navigation to our Users' most frequently used Workflows and reporting assets.

In the pages that follow, we will start with an initial idea – sketched on a piece of scrap paper – and work through all the steps needed to create a fully functioning Dashboard, ready to be deployed.

Designing our Splash Screen

As we discussed in the opening chapters, a well-designed User Experience must 1. provide the functionality that the User requires and 2. provide that functionality in as clear and efficient a way as possible. With that in mind, we often build a splash screen to serve as the home page for our Users.

The purpose of a splash screen (also known as a landing page) is to give our Users a jumping-off point to guide them to the more detailed and complex application content they need with as few mouse clicks as possible, and provide that guidance in a way that is as clear and easy to understand as we can. Ideally, the User's splash screen will be virtually 'training-free' – that is, we want to make the operation of this screen so obvious and intuitive that our Users will understand it at a glance.

With this in mind, we can start sketching out a design for our splash screen. Often, the design of a Dashboard starts in a very low-tech way: a blank sheet of paper, a pen, and an idea. For our hypothetical landing page, we might want to present our Users with:

- A few buttons to lead them directly to their most important Workflows or Reports.

- A few of our most important KPI values with positive/negative variance indicators.

- A nice big picture of our new headquarters building.

Thinking through how we can assemble the landing page in a logical way, we might sketch out something like this:

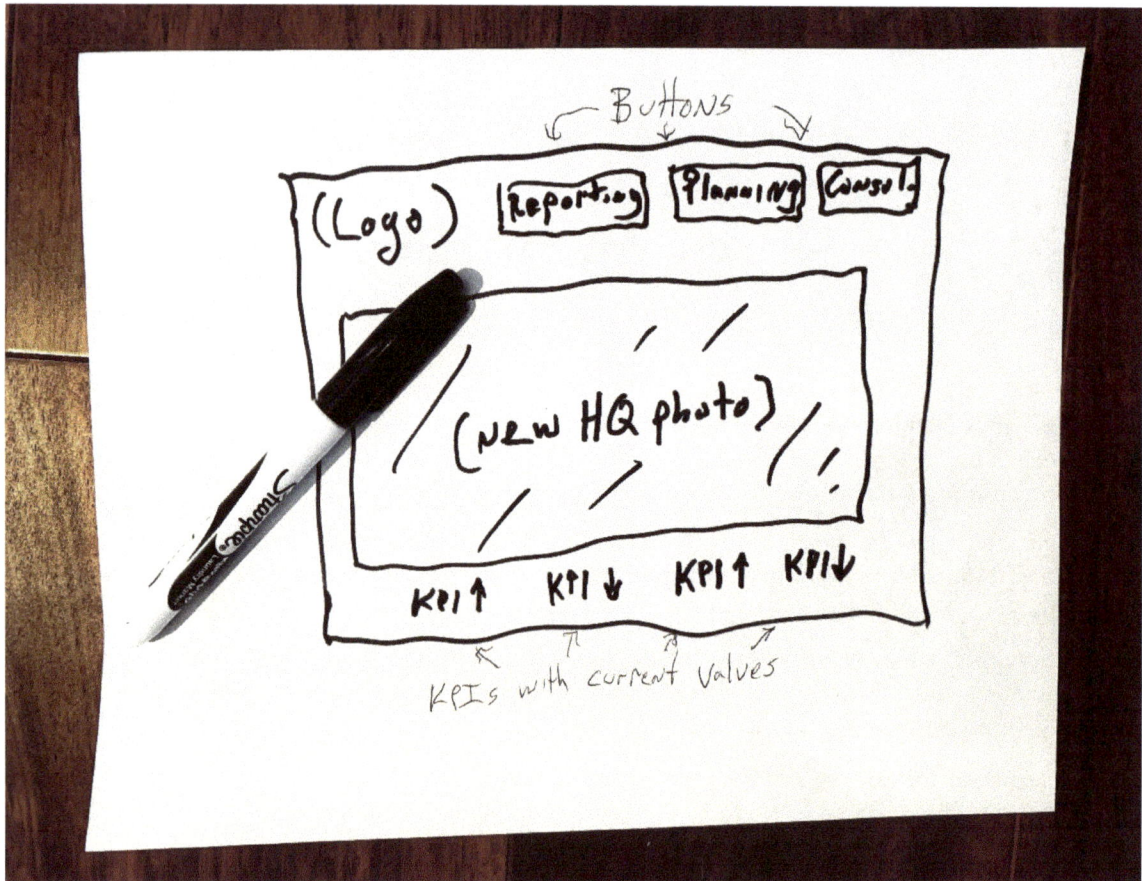

Figure 11.1

We will undoubtedly revise and refine this as we build the actual Dashboard, but this is a great place to start.

From this small beginning, we can already start to think about the various Components we will need to bring our Dashboard to life, and how we will organize them in their proper positions on the screen.

Starting from the top-left corner of the screen, we can see three logical 'sections' of our splash screen.

1. The top portion of the screen will have our company's logo, then several big buttons to take the User directly to the main application content they will need to access (e.g., "Reporting", "Planning", and "Consolidation").

2. The center of the screen will have a large and attractive graphic, perhaps a photo of our new headquarters building, or the graphical imagery used on the cover of our most recent Annual Report.

3. And, at the bottom of the screen, we would like to include the primary key performance indicators that our organization uses to measure our success. Although in our sketch we show four generic KPIs as placeholders, we will determine what the actual metrics will be, and how many we can fit on the screen, as our design and build process continues.

These three sections can be thought of as a three-row grid, with the top row used for navigation, the center row used for a graphic, and the third row used for KPIs. As our design starts to take shape, we can start putting together a more formal blueprint (sometimes called a **Wireframe** design). Here is the beginning of our design, sketched out in a spreadsheet.

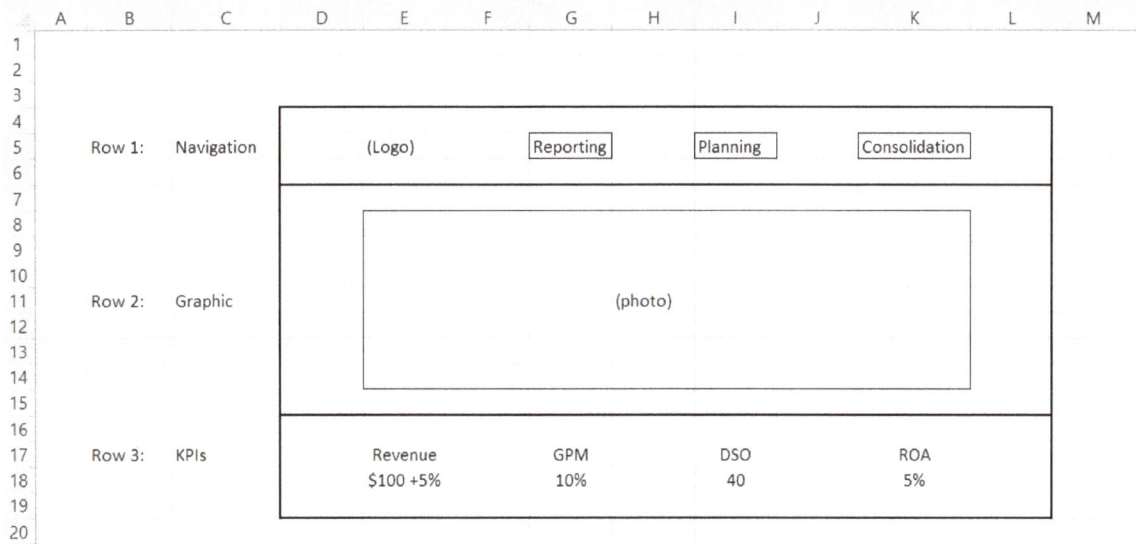

Figure 11.2

With this simple design, we can already begin to identify the Components we will need to configure our Dashboard. On the top portion of our Dashboard (Row 1), we will need four Components: a logo and three buttons. For the center portion (Row 2), we will need an image. And for the bottom portion (Row 3), we will need a handful of tiles for our KPIs, with each tile displaying the name of the KPI as well as its value.

To organize these objects, we will use a Dashboard of Type Grid as the 'main' Dashboard with three rows and one column.

One of the most powerful and useful concepts in the design of OneStream Dashboards is the ability to nest Dashboards within other Dashboards – or embed them. For our splash screen Dashboard, we can take advantage of this concept to further organize the Components on rows one and three. For both rows, we will use Dashboards of Type **Horizontal Stack Panel**, and embed these two Component Dashboards in our main three-row grid.

Creating a Dashboard Maintenance Unit

We are now ready to start building our Dashboard. All OneStream Dashboards are created within a Dashboard Maintenance Unit (DMU), which stores and organizes one or more related Dashboards and their Component parts. The first step in creating a brand-new Dashboard is to create a new DMU to work in.

Although there is no technical requirement to use any particular naming convention, we consider it best practice to give the DMU a short, meaningful name, and include a brief 3-5 character alphanumeric identifier that will be consistently included in the names of all the Components and Dashboards within this DMU, as well as any related Business Rules that may be created.

This naming convention is used by OneStream's MarketPlace solutions team – for example, if you download and install the People Planning MarketPlace solution, a DMU named `XFW People Planning (PLP)` will be created, and all the Dashboards, Components, Business Rules, and tables that make up this solution will have `_PLP` appended to the end of their names. Again, you aren't required to follow this convention, but it is highly recommended – you will find it makes managing and maintaining an application with multiple large and complex Dashboards a much simpler process.

For our example, we will create a DMU called `A Splash Screen (SPL)`, and we will use the code `_SPL` as the suffix of the name of all Dashboard Components. To create this DMU, we have signed on to our application with a User ID that is a member of the Security Group assigned to the `DashboardAdminPage` security role. Using the navigation pane on the left side of the screen, select the Application tab, and in the Presentation group, select Dashboards (Figure 11.3).

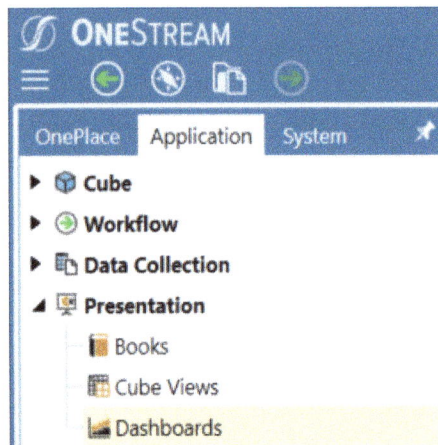

Figure 11.3

Existing DMUs will now be visible in the main portion of the screen, and the Dashboard Maintenance toolbar will be visible at the top of the screen (Figure 11.4).

Figure 11.4

Clicking the first button on the toolbar will create a new DMU, with fields to enter the name of the DMU, an optional description, a True/False combo box to indicate if this Dashboard will be visible on mobile devices, and security settings to identify User groups that will have access to this DMU (as well as the ability to maintain it).

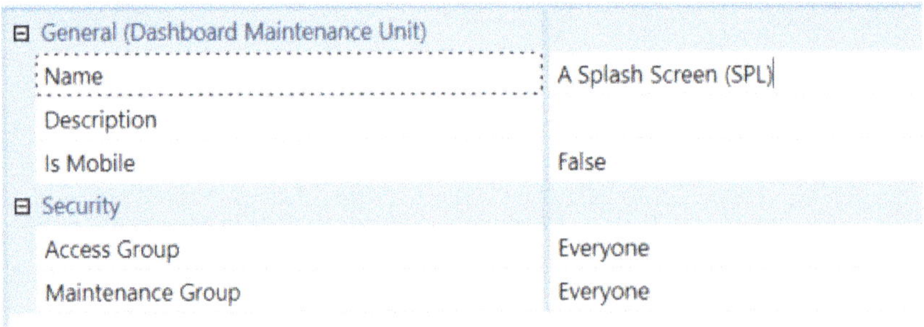

Figure 11.5

We now have a DMU, and under that DMU we have a list of the six Types of objects that are used when creating Dashboards. The first item on that list is Dashboard Groups, and that is where we will go next.

Creating Dashboard Groups

Now that we have created our DMU, we will create two Dashboard Groups that will hold and organize our Dashboards. A single Dashboard Group can be used to hold all of the Dashboards that you create in a DMU, but you will find it much easier to work with and maintain your Dashboards if you create at least two: 1. to hold the top-level Dashboards that will be presented to your End-

Users, and 2. a second one to hold any lower-level Dashboards that we will embed in the top-level Dashboard. For example, in the splash screen we are building, we will have a top-level Dashboard that looks like the design sketch we have made, and we will have lower-level Dashboards for the navigation panel at the top of the screen, plus the KPI panel at the bottom of the screen.

With the Dashboard Group item selected, clicking the second button on the toolbar will create a new Dashboard Group, which we will name `Splash Screen Dashboard (SPL)`. Then, we will repeat this process to create a second Dashboard Group, which we will name `Splash Screen Panels (SPL)`.

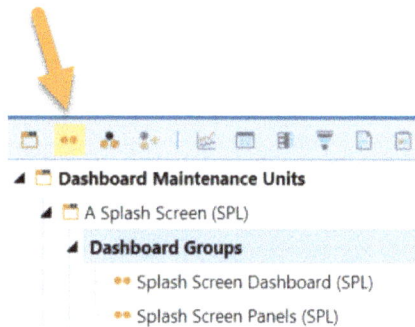

Figure 11.6

Creating Dashboard Components

All the individual objects that the User will see on the Dashboard are called Components. For the splash screen we are creating, we have already identified several Types of Component we will need: a logo, several buttons, an image, and some labels. Each of these will be created under the Components item in our DMU.

We will start with our logo. One of the application properties that is available in every OneStream application is the **Logo File**, which can then be used on any Dashboard or Report without the need to have duplicate copies. Every logo Dashboard Component displays this image file. If and when this file is updated (e.g., if the company logo is revised), uploading a new image file in Application Properties will instantly update every Dashboard and Report, with no further maintenance required.

To create the logo Component for our Dashboard, select the Components item in our DMU, then click the sixth button on the toolbar. This will display a dialog box with a list of every Component Type available. Select Logo, then click OK to create a logo Component for our Dashboard.

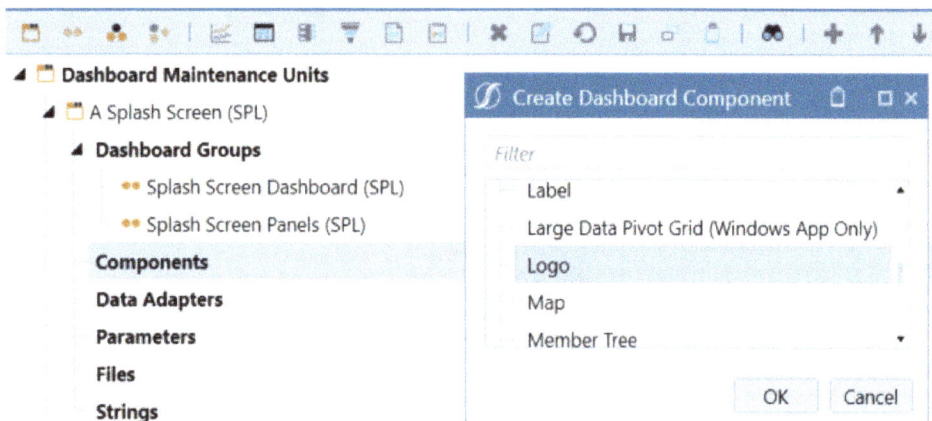

Figure 11.7

We will now configure the initial properties of this Component. All we really need right now is a name. As we have discussed, we will use the suffix `_PLP` for this and all other Components.

Chapter 11

Another best practice for naming Components is to use a simple prefix to identify the Type of Component. For example, for logos, we often use `lgo_` as the prefix. So, we will name this new Component `lgo_Logo_SPL`. There are several other properties that we will configure later, but for now this is all we need.

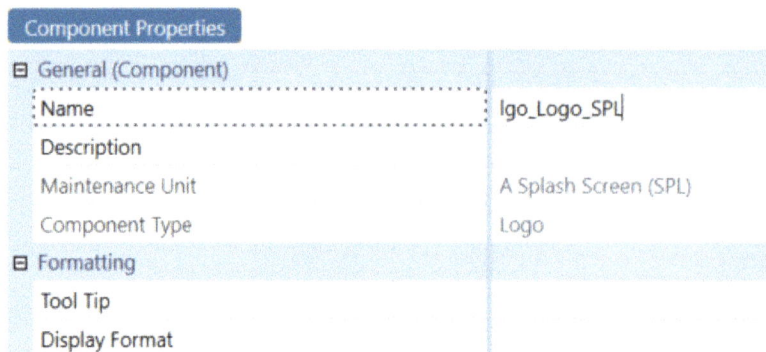

Figure 11.8

In the center of the Dashboard we are creating, we will display a large photograph of our headquarters. This Component is made up of two parts – the photograph itself (e.g., a .jpg, .gif, or .png file), and a Dashboard Component that allows us to fine-tune the way the photograph is presented.

First, we will import our photograph. With the Files category of our Maintenance Unit selected, we can click on the Create File button in the toolbar.

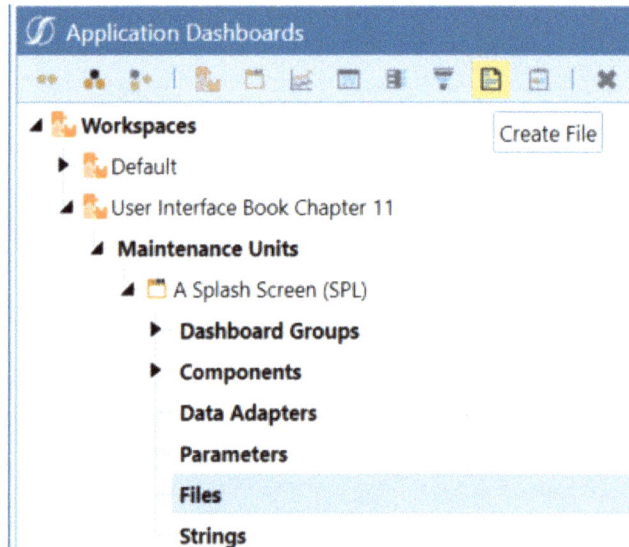

Figure 11.9

On the Content File property of our new file, clicking on the Upload File button on the right side of the screen will allow us to select a file from our local machine.

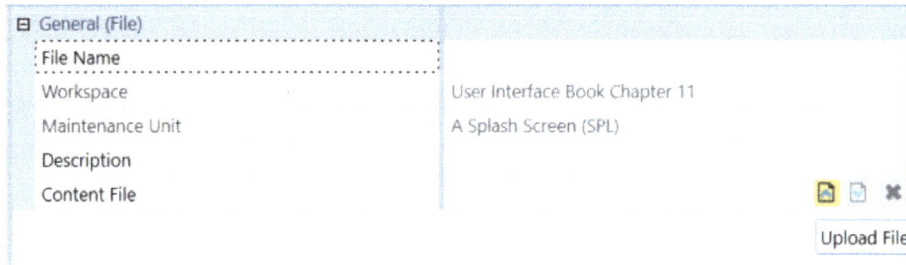

Figure 11.10

When we select a file to upload, the File Name property will automatically default to the actual name of the file we have uploaded. Since the file we have chosen has a clear, meaningful name, we will keep that name as our Dashboard file name.

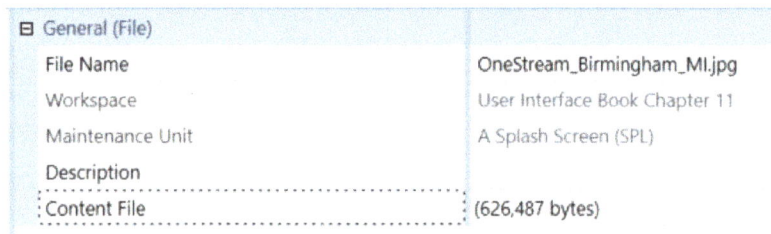

Figure 11.11

Now that we have the photograph uploaded to our application, we can create the **Image Component** that we will use to display this photo on our Dashboard. With the Component category of our Maintenance Unit selected, we will click the Create Component button on the toolbar and select Image as the Component Type on the dialog box. Using our naming convention, we will enter `img_Office_SPL` as the name of this Component and set the File Source Type to Dashboard File. On the Url or Full File Name property, we can click the [...] button on the right side of the screen and select the .jpg file we just uploaded.

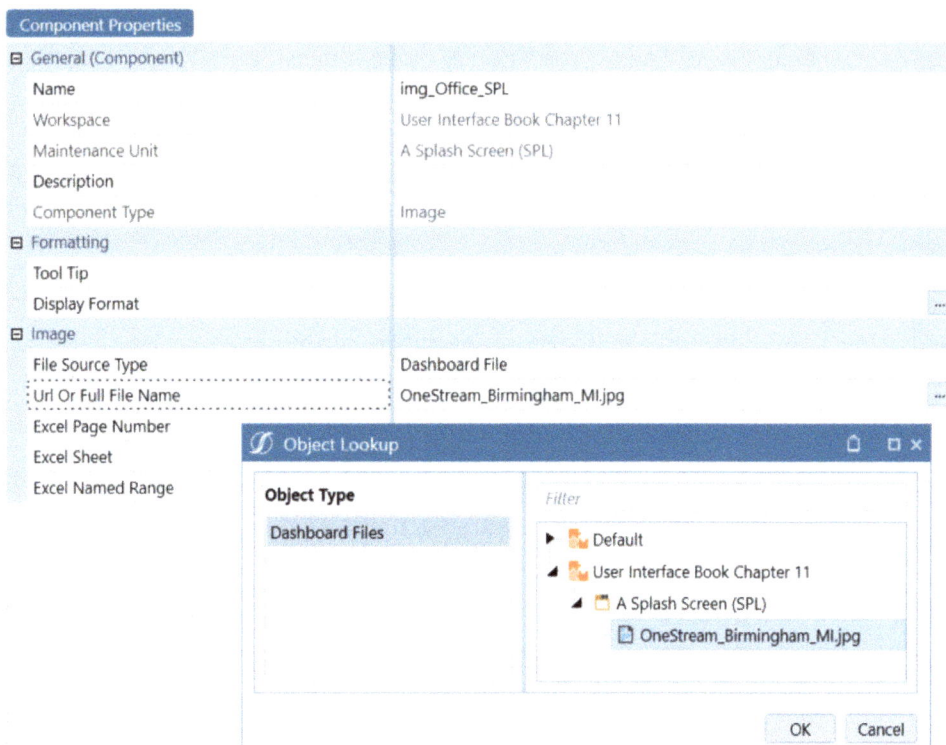

Figure 11.12

Now that we have a preliminary design for our Dashboard, and we have Components to work with (our standard logo and our custom photograph), we can start to build the actual Dashboard.

Creating the Dashboard

If we refer to our wireframe diagram (Figure 11.2), we can see that the main frame of the Dashboard will be a grid with three rows (the header, the central image, and the KPIs at the bottom). Each of these three rows will use an embedded Dashboard to organize the Components in those sections.

First, we will create the main frame Dashboard. Since this will be our primary Dashboard, we will create this in the Dashboard Group Splash Screen Dashboard (SPL). With that Dashboard Group selected, clicking the Create Dashboard button will open the Dashboard Properties screen for our new Dashboard.

Figure 11.13

We will name our main Dashboard 0_Frame_SPL. Again, although it is not required, this name follows a best practice naming convention that includes a number as the prefix, a meaningful name, and then the consistent Dashboard code we have chosen (SPL) as the suffix.

Since we are building the main Dashboard as a three-row grid, we will select the layout Type as Grid. This will then display the properties for a Grid Dashboard, and we can select the number of rows as 3 and the number of columns as 1 (see Figure 11.14).

For several of the following settings, we need to specify the height or width of a particular Component. Rather than inches or centimeters, the unit of measure we use for these dimensions is called a 'pixel' (which means 'picture element'). If you look at your computer monitor through a magnifying glass, you will see that everything displayed is made up of tiny dots – these are the pixels. When we specify the resolution setting of our monitor (say, 1920 x 1080), we are really describing the width and height of our screen in pixels. So, if we define an object as 960 pixels wide by 540 pixels high, this will take up about 25% of the screen on our 1920 x 1080 monitor. If our monitor is 20 inches wide, there are about 96 pixels per inch, and this object will appear to be about 10 inches tall by 5 ½ inches wide.

Following our design, we want the first row to be relatively narrow to display our logo and a few buttons. Setting the row height for this row to be 100 pixels high – a little over an inch on our 20-inch monitor - should be a reasonable first guess. We can always change this setting as we fine-tune the look of the Dashboard. We will make row three – at the bottom of the screen – 100 pixels too, and let the middle row fill whatever screen space is left (that's what the default * in row 2's height, and column 1's width, will do. There are several other ways to define row height and column width, but we will discuss those later.).

Dashboard Properties	Dashboard Components	
⊟ General (Dashboard)		
Name	0_Frame_SPL	
Workspace	User Interface Book Chapter 11	
Maintenance Unit	A Splash Screen (SPL)	
Dashboard Group	Splash Screen Dashboard (SPL)	
Description		
Page Caption		
⊟ Formatting		
Layout Type	Grid	
Is Initially Visible If Embedded	Canvas	
Display Format	Dock	
Show Title	Grid	
⊟ Literal Parameter Values	Horizontal Stack Panel	
Name Value Pairs (e.g., Param1=Value1, ...)	Tabs	
⊟ Action (Primary Dashboard Only)	Uniform	
Server Task	Vertical Stack Panel	
Load Dashboard Server Task	Wrap	
Load Dashboard Server Task Arguments		
⊟ Grid Layout Type		
Number Of Rows	3	
Number Of Columns	1	
Row 1		
Row 1 Type	Component	
Row 1 Height (e.g., 150, *, 2*, Auto)	100	
Row 2		
Row 2 Type	Component	
Row 2 Height	*	
Row 3		
Row 3 Type	Component	
Row 3 Height	100	
Column 1		
Column 1 Type	Component	
Column 1 Width (e.g., 150, *, 2*, Auto)	*	

Figure 11.14

Again, referring to our wireframe diagram (Figure 11.2), we will also create two additional Dashboards that will be embedded in our main Dashboard. These embedded Dashboards will contain and organize the logo and other Components at the top of the screen, and the key performance indicators at the bottom of the screen. We will create these as simple **Horizontal Stack Panels** – effectively, one-row grids that simply line up the Components we assign to them, from left to right, in the order we specify.

With our `Splash Screen Panels (SPL)` Dashboard Group selected, we will add these two Dashboards, naming them `1_Header_SPL`, and `2_Footer_SPL`, selecting layout Type Horizontal Stack Panel for each (Figure 11.15). These stack panel Dashboards are very simple to configure; no other properties need to be specified.

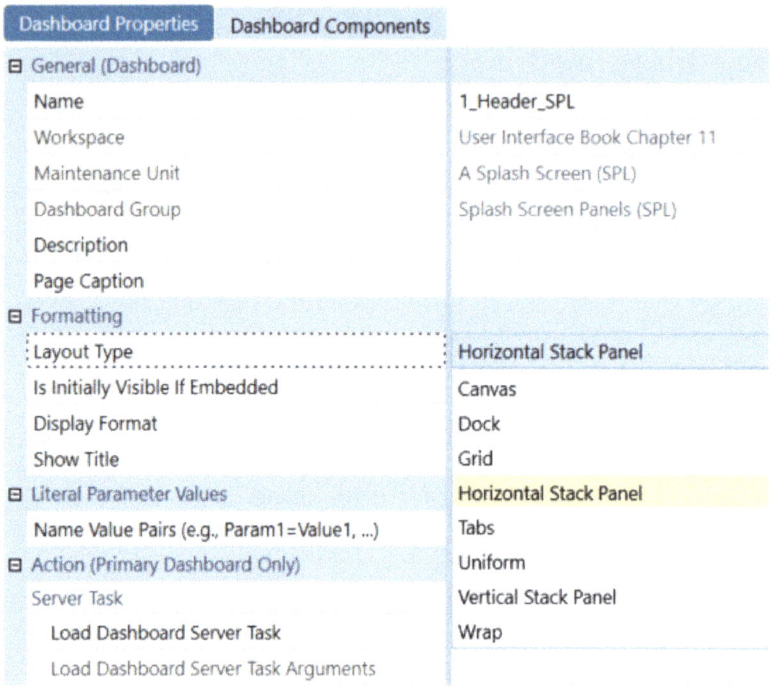

Figure 11.15

Assembling our Dashboard

Now, we can add our Components to our Dashboard.

Our first Component – the logo – belongs at the top of the screen, so we will add it to the 1_Header_SPL Dashboard we created in the Splash Screen Panels (SPL) Dashboard Group. With that Dashboard selected, clicking on the Dashboard Components tab will activate the Add Dashboard Component [+] button in the toolbar. When we click this button, we will see a dialog box listing all the Dashboard Components available to us in this Maintenance Unit (Figure 11.16).

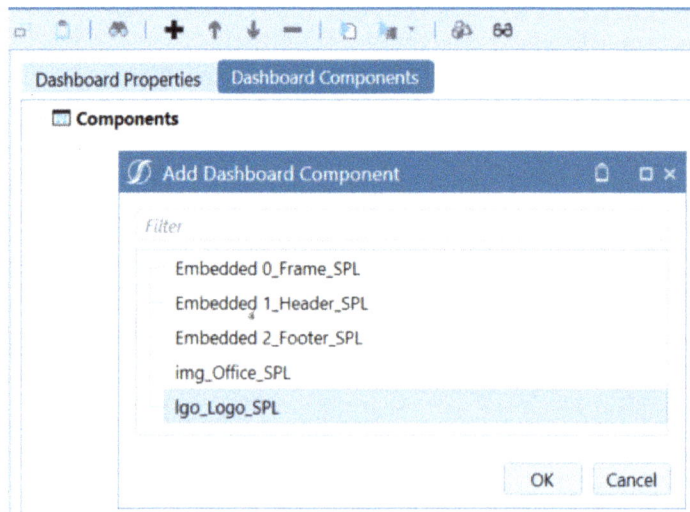

Figure 11.16

When we select our logo Component and click OK, that Component is added to the list of Components that will be displayed on this Dashboard. Later, we will add other Components here to complete the header section of our Dashboard.

This header Dashboard will be used as the first row of our main Dashboard. Using the same process, we will add this Dashboard as the first Component of our main Dashboard by selecting the Dashboard 0_Frame_SPL from our Splash Screen Dashboard (SPL) Dashboard Group, selecting the Dashboard Components tab, and using the Add Dashboard Component [+] button. This time, instead of selecting the logo, we will select the header Dashboard itself, which will be listed in the Add Dashboard Component dialog box as Embedded 1_Header_SPL (Figure 11.17).

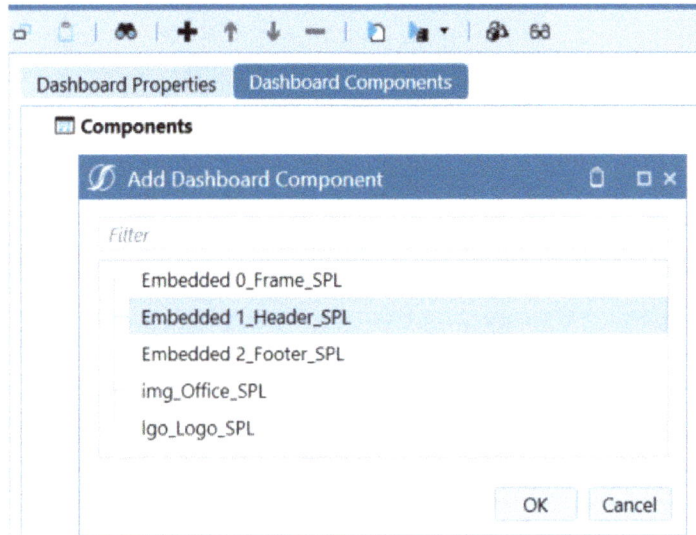

Figure 11.17

Embedded Dashboards are a special Type of Component that OneStream creates every time you create a Dashboard. This is how we include 'subsidiary' Dashboards, such as our header and footer Dashboards, as rows or columns in our main Dashboard. Later, we will learn how we can also create our own embedded Dashboard Components that we can use to embed content from other Dashboard Maintenance Units, dynamically change the content displayed in one of our main Dashboard panels, and more.

To finish assembling the first draft of our main Dashboard, we will add the content for the second row (the image) and the third row (the footer). It is important that the Components are listed in the correct order – for example, we don't want our header to appear in the middle of the screen. If we have selected these Components in the wrong order, we can simply use the Move Up and/or Move Down arrow buttons in the header to rearrange them.

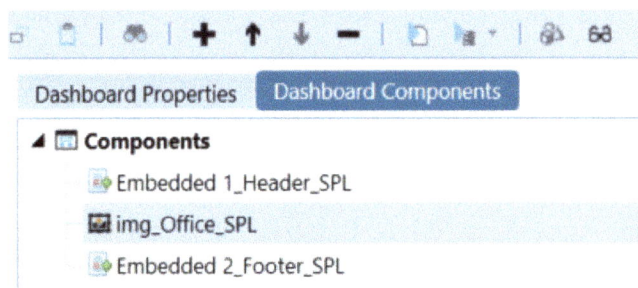

Figure 11.18

With our Dashboard now assembled, we can have our first look at it in **User mode**. With the main Dashboard selected, clicking the View Dashboard button in the toolbar will open the Dashboard live in a new tab (Figure 11.19).

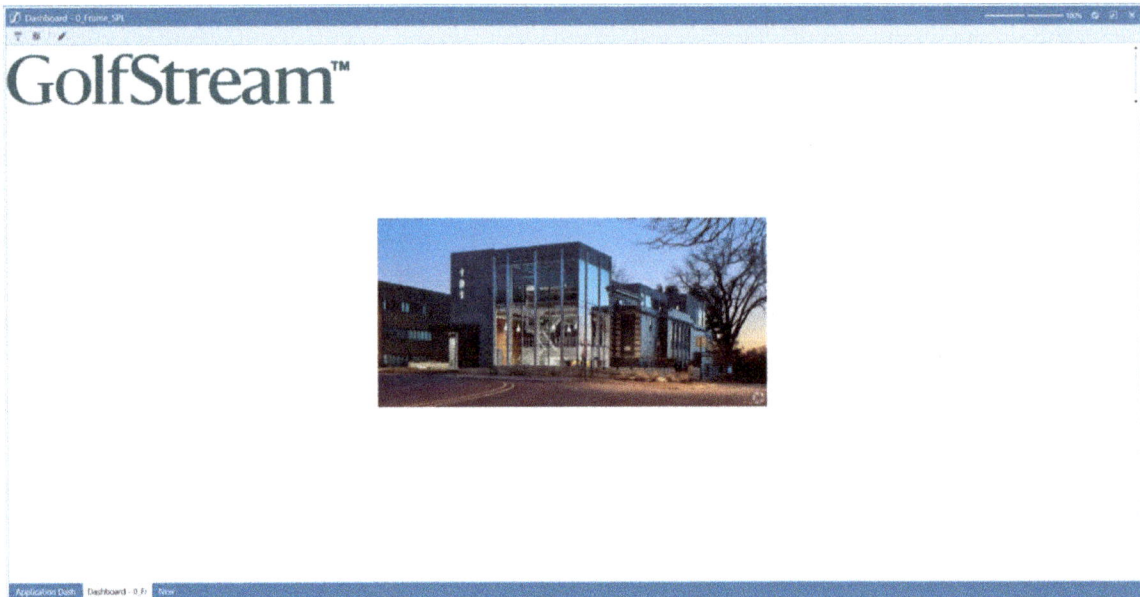

Figure 11.19

Adjusting Component Display Formatting

It's not a masterpiece (yet), but it's a start!

Before we continue fleshing out our Dashboard, let's make a few revisions. First, the GolfStream logo seems a little too large, and it would probably look nicer if it weren't pressed right up against the left edge of the frame. Also, the photograph is way too small – we want the picture on our splash page to have a little more…well, splash.

We will start with the logo. Back on our Application Dashboard Maintenance tab, we can expand the Components hierarchy until we can select the lgo_Logo_SPL Component. On the Display Format property, clicking the [...] button – on the right side of the screen – will open a dialog box that allows us to make various decisions about how the logo will appear. To make our logo a little smaller, we will specify a Height of 60 pixels. To put a little white space between the edge of the logo and the left frame of the Dashboard, we will specify a MarginLeft value of 30 pixels. We will also set the MarginRight value to 30 pixels, so there will be some white space to the right of the logo too.

Next, we will make our image object more prominent. Again, when we select the img_Office_SPL Component and click the [...] button on the Display Format parameter, we will see various settings to control the size and position of this Component.

The ImageStretch setting lets us automatically resize the image to fill the available space – the UniformToFill option will keep the proportions of the image consistent to avoid distorting it but allow the image to expand in every direction to fill the space available (even if that means some of the image is cropped out if there isn't enough room). As with the logo, we don't want the image to press all the way up to the frame of the Dashboard, so we will set both the MarginLeft and MarginRight parameters to 30 pixels.

After saving these changes and re-running the Dashboard, it now looks like this – not too bad!

Figure 11.20

Adding Navigation Buttons

Now we are ready to add some navigation buttons to our Dashboard. In our wireframe design, we included buttons in the header section of the Dashboard to take us directly to three major functions: Reporting, Planning, and Consolidation.

Of the many Types of OneStream Dashboard Components, buttons are among the most useful and versatile. They can be configured to look almost any way you like – e.g., a button can appear as a simple rectangle with some text on, another might display a custom-designed image icon, and a third might even display different images or text, depending on specific User, data, or Workflow conditions.

Buttons can also perform many different functions, or even multiple functions at the same time. These functions fall under several broad categories:

1. Selecting a Member from one of our application's Dimensions.

2. Setting the value of a parameter.

3. Saving data the User has entered through another Component on the Dashboard.

4. Changing the User's current POV and/or Workflow selections.

5. Running a server process such as a Consolidation, Business Rule, or data management sequence.

6. Refreshing the Dashboard or opening another Dashboard in a dialog box.

7. Navigating to another Dashboard, Workflow, external file, or website.

Our First Button

The first button we will add to our Dashboard will be very simple: we will provide our Users with a one-click path to our application's **Guided Reporting** home page (Guided Reporting, like many of OneStream's MarketPlace solutions, uses a well-designed OneStream Dashboard as its User interface.)

Let's start with the basics, and just add the button without using any specific formatting or even making it 'do' anything just yet.

To create this first button, we will select the Components category of our Dashboard Maintenance Unit, click the Create Dashboard Component button, and select Button from the dialog box.

191

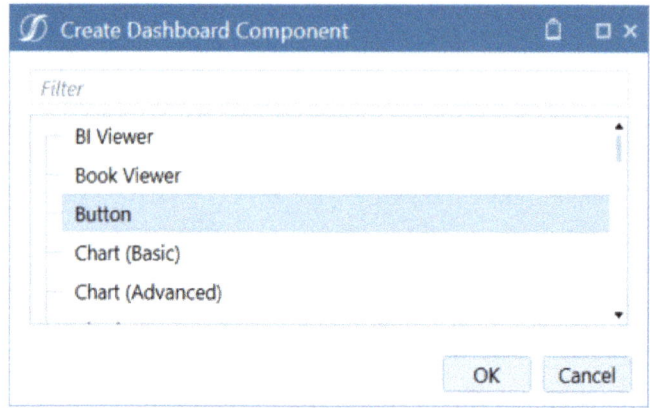

Figure 11.21

As with our other Components, we will give this new button a name following our consistent naming convention – in this case, we will call it btn_Reporting_SPL. We will also add some Text – for this button, we will show the word Reporting. For the rest of the button's properties, for now, we will just leave them blank or accept the default values (see Figure 11.22).

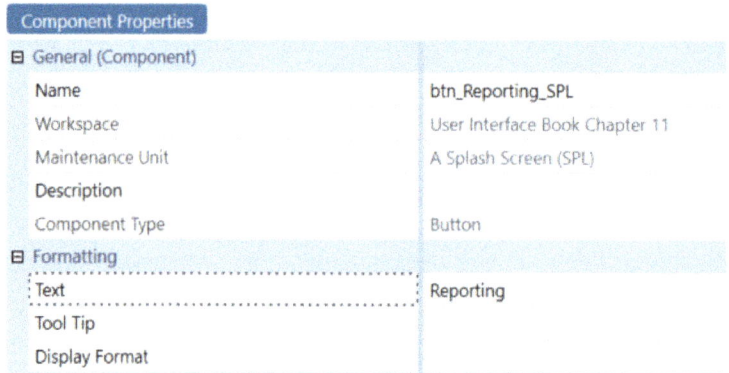

Figure 11.22

This button will be just to the right of our logo on the Dashboard's header, so we will select that Dashboard in our Splash Screen Panels (SPL) Dashboard Group, click the Dashboard Components tab, and use the Add Dashboard Component [+] button on the toolbar to place our button directly after the logo.

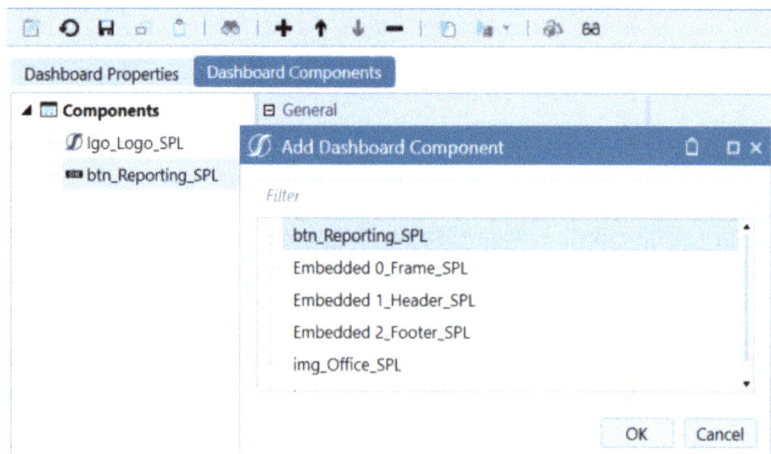

Figure 11.23

Running our main Dashboard (0_Frame_SPL) now shows this new button in its proper place. It doesn't do anything when we click on it yet, and it doesn't look particularly appealing, but it's there (see Figure 11.24).

Figure 11.24

Let's address the cosmetic issues first, then we will make the button do its intended job.

To make our splash page both attractive and easy to use, we will make the navigation buttons very clean to the eye, and very obvious to the User. Two things that we can immediately do to accomplish those goals are to make the font larger on the Reporting text and remove the gray box that surrounds the button.

Clicking on the [...] button on the Display Format property for our button brings up a dialog box with the various formatting options we can work with. The display properties are organized into three groups – the second group has options that apply to buttons with images on them, and the third group has options that apply to buttons that show each button's text as a label next to the button.

For our button, only the first group of properties – the General properties – will be relevant. The first thing we will do is make the FontSize larger – 30 pixels should be about right.

There are also several color-related properties in the General section. The default appearance for a button includes a gray line around its border. Since we don't need or want this line for our button, we can change the color of this border to Transparent. This is a very useful option that is included with every color-related property throughout the OneStream platform.

We will also change the HoverColor property from Use Default to the color option XFLightBlue (Figure 11.25). This is the color that is used in many places in OneStream's standard User Interface, including toolbars, section dividers, and as the background color for selected Components within Dashboard administration. Choosing this color as the hover color for our button will make it show this background when the User moves their mouse over the button and will look very consistent with the rest of the standard OneStream User Experience.

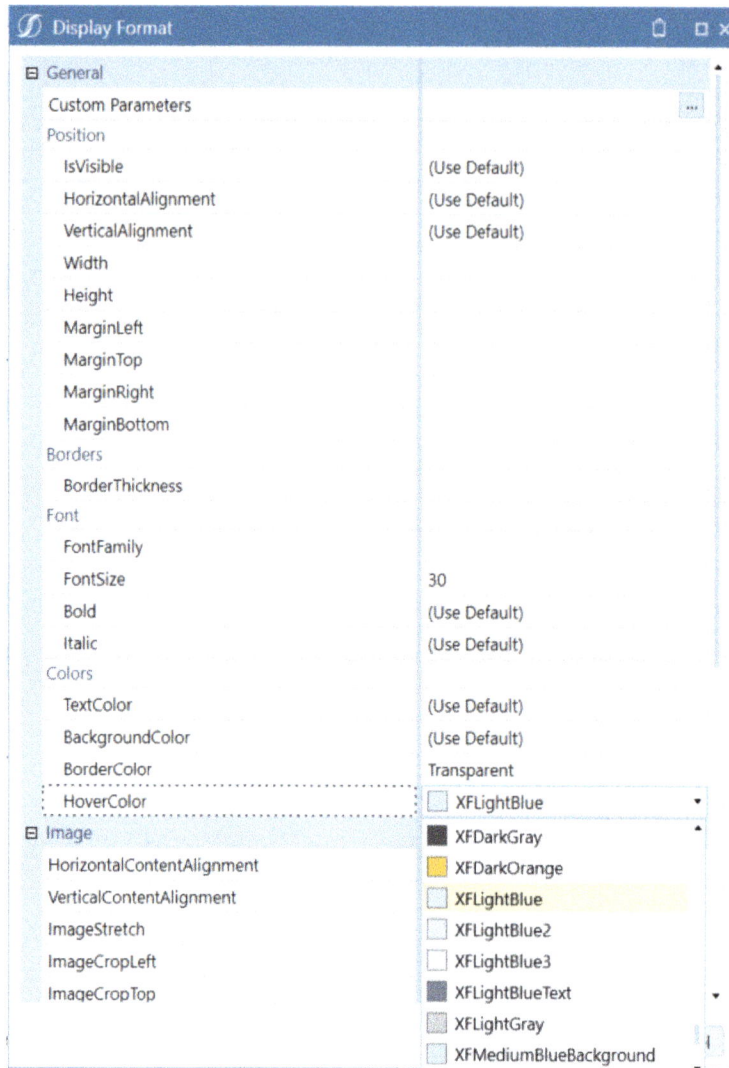

Figure 11.25

Making Copies of Our Button

Before we make this button functional, let's add the other two buttons we have planned for our header. The easiest way to do this is to right-click on our existing button, select copy, and then right-click again and select paste (Figure 11.26). If we do this twice, we will have two more identical buttons, each with _Copy added as an extension.

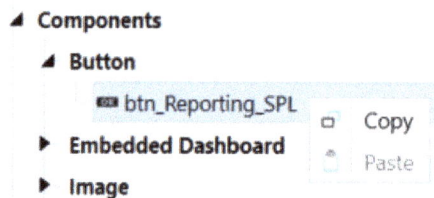

Figure 11.26

Using the Rename Selected Item button in the toolbar, we will rename the first copy of our button btn_Planning_SPL, and the second copy btn_Consolidation_SPL.

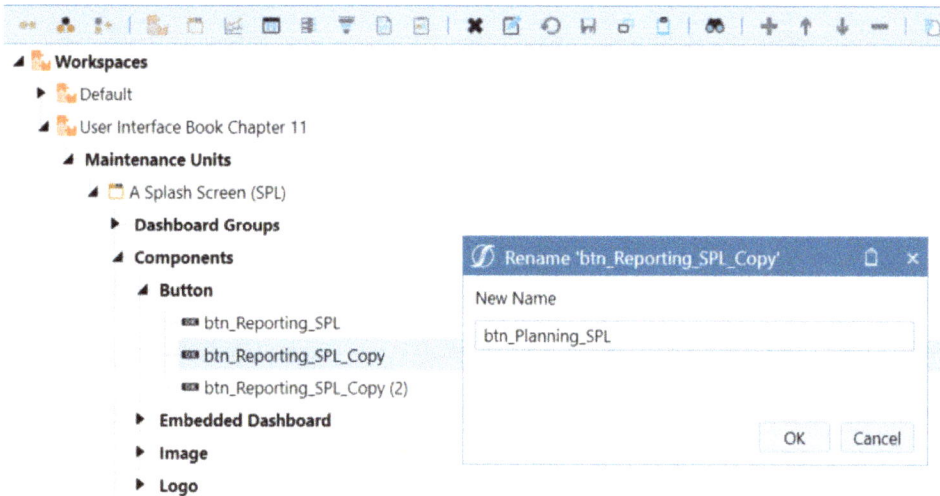

Figure 11.27

We now have three identical buttons. As far as the appearance of these buttons goes, the only thing we want to be different between them is the text they display; so, for the two new buttons, we will change the Text properties to Planning and Consolidation as appropriate.

Just as we did with our Reporting button, we can now add these two additional buttons to our header Dashboard (1_Header_SPL) using the Dashboard Components tab and the Add Dashboard Component [+] toolbar button.

When we test our Dashboard now, and hover our mouse over one of the buttons, we can see the results of our formatting changes, and the addition of the new buttons (Figure 11.28).

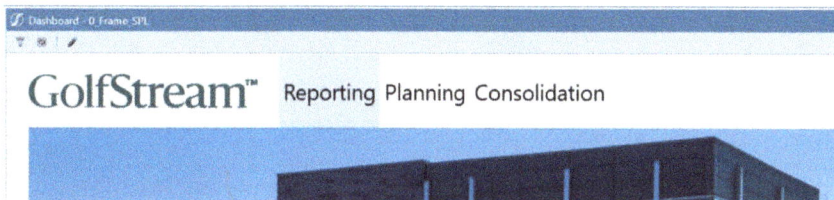

Figure 11.28

The font size looks good, and the hover color – highlighting the button – is what we wanted, but there are still some cosmetic improvements we can make.

First, the buttons are too close together, with each button wide enough to fit its text, but no wider – this is the default behavior for the width property. Similarly, the grey mouse-hover color looks good, but it might look better if it didn't stretch all the way from the top to the bottom of our embedded header Dashboard. Like the buttons' widths, this is also the result of using the default height for our buttons; unless we specify a height, the buttons will expand vertically to use all the space available. With a little trial and error, we find that a width of 400 and a height of 50 looks pretty good.

Formatting Components with Parameters

We can, of course, update all three buttons to have these consistent display settings. But there is an easier way – especially if we are working on a Dashboard that has multiple similar Components that we want to keep consistent both now and following any future modifications.

OneStream's **Dashboard parameters** are another extremely powerful and versatile tool at your disposal and can be leveraged to perform a multitude of functions. Parameters are often used to provide lists of valid Dimension Members to choose from when running a Report, or to store information provided by a User, or to hold application-wide values that change infrequently – but shouldn't be hard-coded – such as the name of the current active Forecast Scenario.

Parameters can also be used to hold just about any text that you want to use in multiple places, but only update in one place. As you have probably noticed, even though we use convenient dialog boxes with complete lists of formatting properties and valid values when configuring a Component, the actual formatting information is stored in the Display Format property as a line of plain text. For example, to configure all three of our buttons the same, using the properties we have settled on, we could configure just one of them, and then copy and paste the text from that one button's display format to the other two. But if we use a parameter to hold that formatting string, any future changes can simply be made to the parameter, and all Components using that parameter will be updated simultaneously.

To do this with our buttons, first we will create a parameter to store our formatting string. When we click on the Parameters category in our Maintenance Unit, the Create Parameter button will be activated on the toolbar (Figure 11.29). Clicking this button will allow us to create a new parameter, which we will name `prm_ButtonFormat_SPL` to maintain consistency with our naming convention.

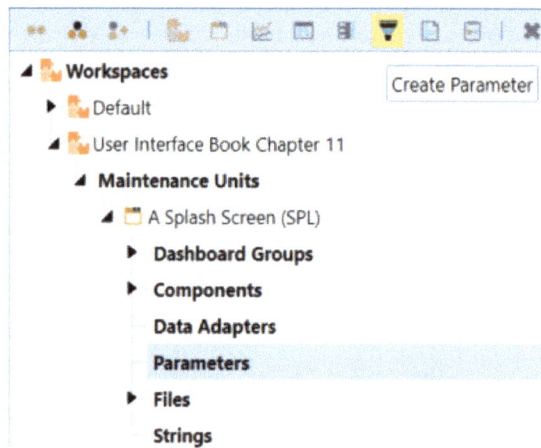

Figure 11.29

As we have discussed, there are many use cases for parameters within the OneStream platform, and multiple different Types of parameters. We will be using this parameter to store a single string of text, so we will use the default Parameter Type of Literal Value. For now, we will leave the other properties blank.

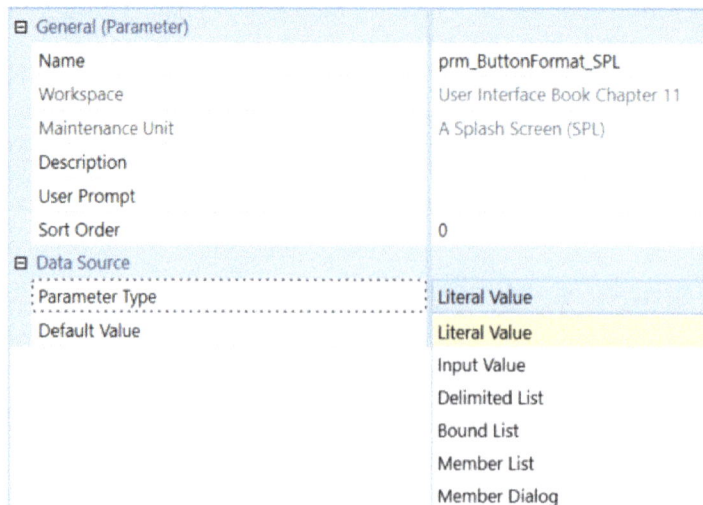

Figure 11.30

When we have configured one of our buttons 'just right' we can highlight the full text of the Display Format for that button, copy that text into our clipboard, and then paste that text as the Default Value property of our parameter (Figures 11.31 & 11.32).

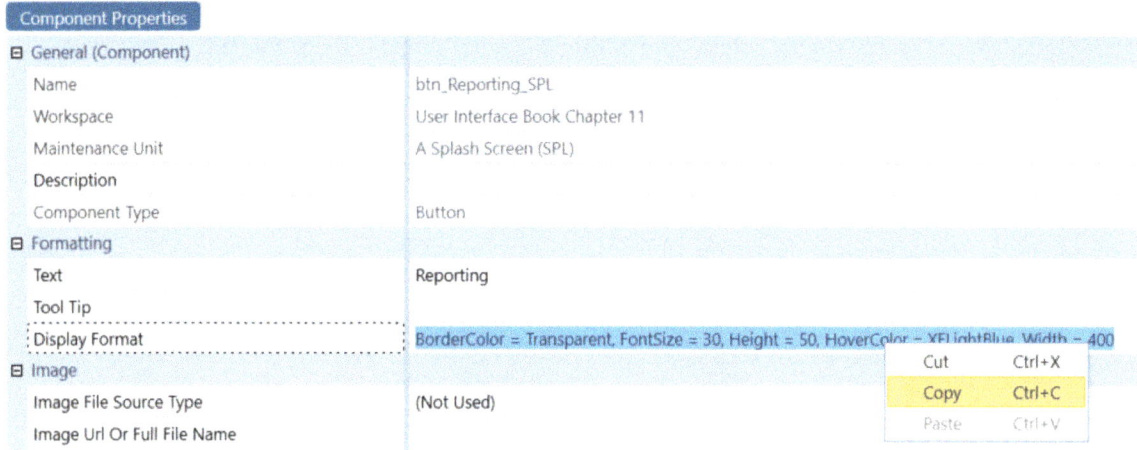

Figure 11.31

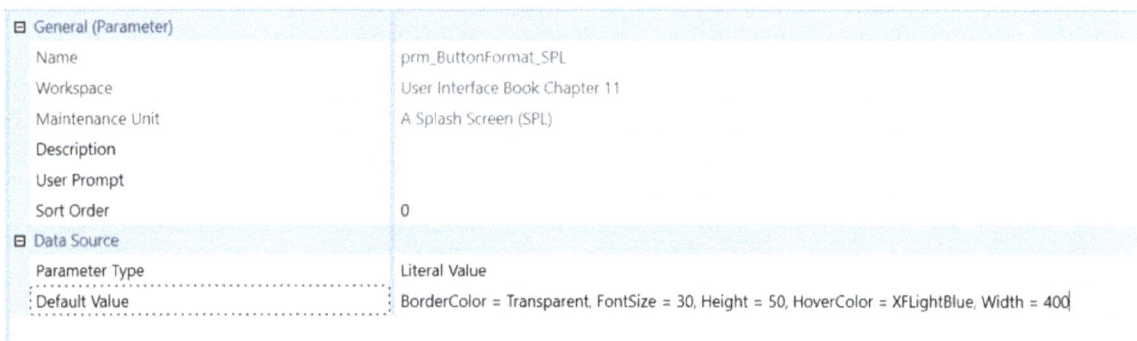

Figure 11.32

Now, for each of our buttons, we can delete the text in the Display Format property, use the [...] open button to open the formatting dialog box, and use the [...] button on the Custom Parameters button to select the parameter we just created.

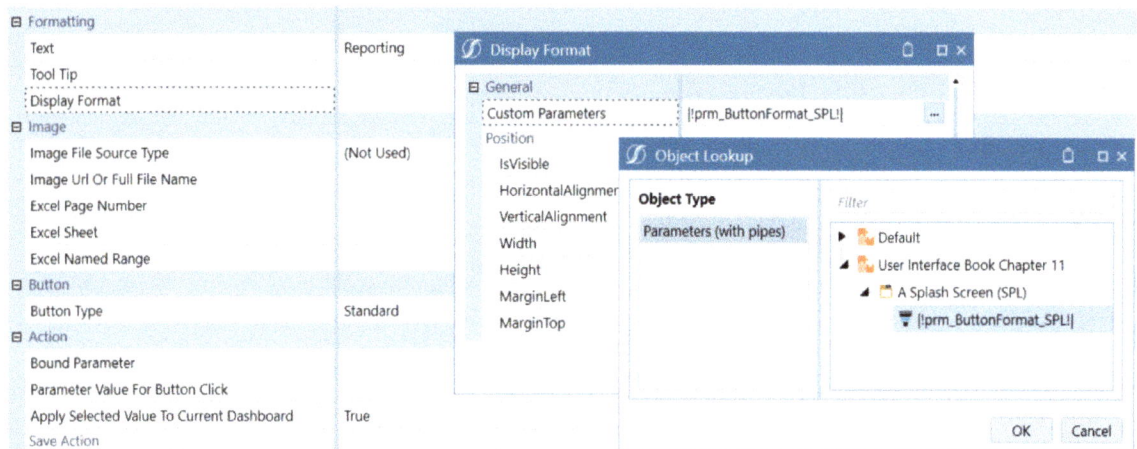

Figure 11.33

When we close these dialog boxes, the Display Format will simply show `|!prm_ButtonFormat_SPL!|`. This is, of course, the name of our parameter, and it includes the opening and closing punctuation that lets OneStream know that this is a parameter (`|!` and `!|`).

We can now copy and paste this parameter from this button to the other two, replacing the specific display formatting for each (Figure 11.34). Any future changes we wish to make to our buttons (or any buttons we may add in the future) can simply be made to the parameter value.

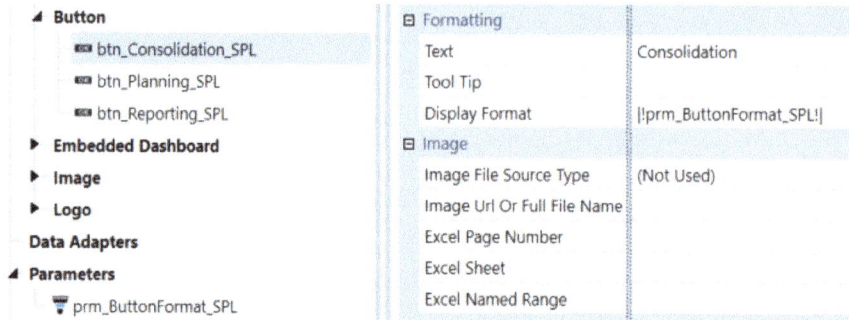

Figure 11.34

The Reporting Button

Now that we have the three navigation buttons added to our Dashboard, and they are looking fantastic, it's time to make them actually DO something. We will start with our Reporting button.

In our sample application, we have installed and configured the OneStream MarketPlace solution called Guided Reporting (GDR). The main Dashboard for this solution is named 0_Frame_GDR_Main_OnePlace. If you have this solution installed in your environment, you will see this Dashboard in the XFT Guided Reporting (GDR) Maintenance Unit, under the OnePlace (GDR) Dashboard Group (Figure 11.35). Although we will use this Dashboard in our example, the same process will work for any other Dashboard in your application, including your own custom Dashboards.

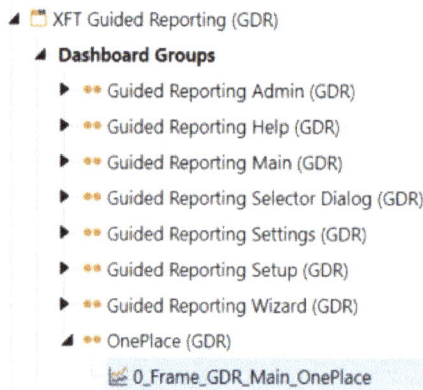

Figure 11.35

With our Dashboard Component btn_Reporting_SPL selected, the lower half of the properties list includes a section called Action. These are the properties that control what happens when a User clicks the button. For this button, we want the User to be directed to the Guided Reporting home page. To make this happen, we will select the Navigation Action called Open Page.

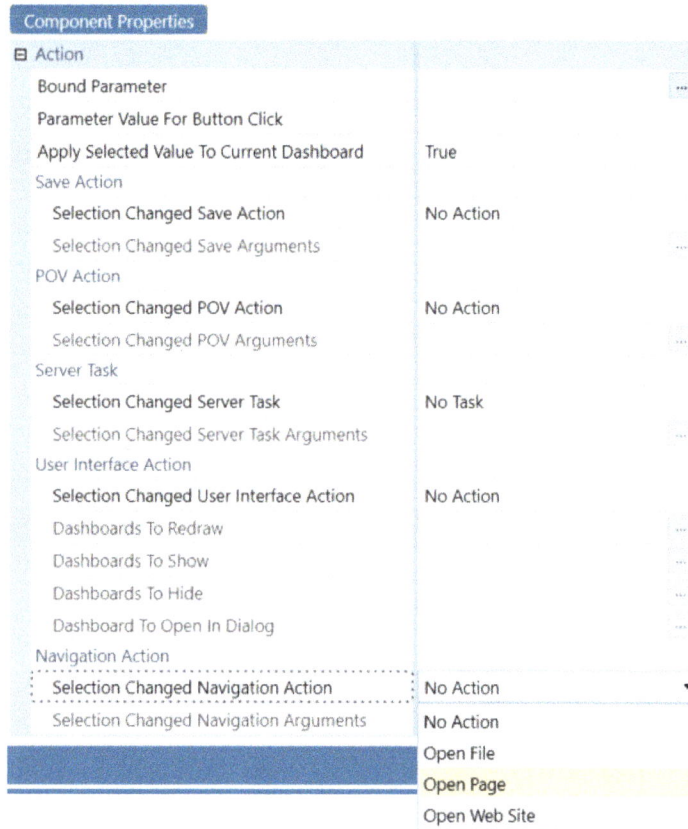

Figure 11.36

With the Navigation Action set to Open Page, the Selection Changed Navigation Arguments property immediately below this will become active. Clicking the [...] button for this property will open a dialog box with a long list of syntax examples that are valid for this property (Figure 11.37).

For our Reporting button, the relevant syntax for this property is the second one on the list, which opens a specified Dashboard in the same tab the current Dashboard is displayed in. There is also an example showing how to open a Dashboard in a new tab by adding `OpenInNewXFPage=True` to the string, which would leave our Splash Dashboard open in its current tab.

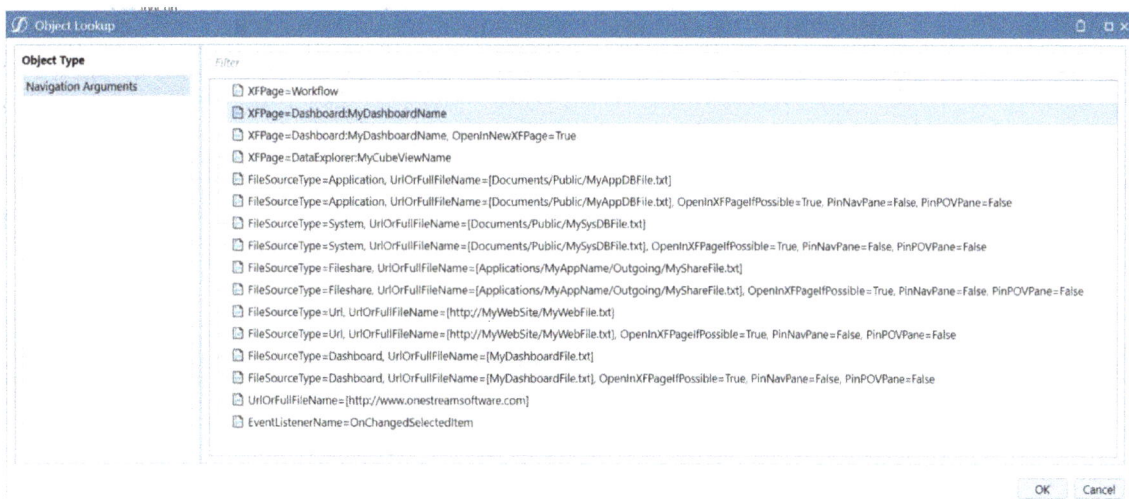

Figure 11.37

Note that although this list has many useful examples, it is not exhaustive. There are many combinations of options that are not shown but which are valid – for example, the option to set

Chapter 11

`PinNavePane=True` is shown for several examples, but not every possible case where it can be used if desired.

Selecting the example closest to the use case we want (in this example, `XFPage=Dashboard:MyDashboardName`) and clicking OK places that text into the Navigation Arguments property.

To complete the configuration of this button, we simply replace the example Dashboard name (MyDashboardName) with the actual name of the Dashboard we want this button to direct us to (in this case, `0_Frame_GDR_Main_OnePlace`).

Figure 11.38

Now, if we run our Dashboard and click on the Reporting button, we are taken directly to the Guided Reporting home page (Figure 11.39).

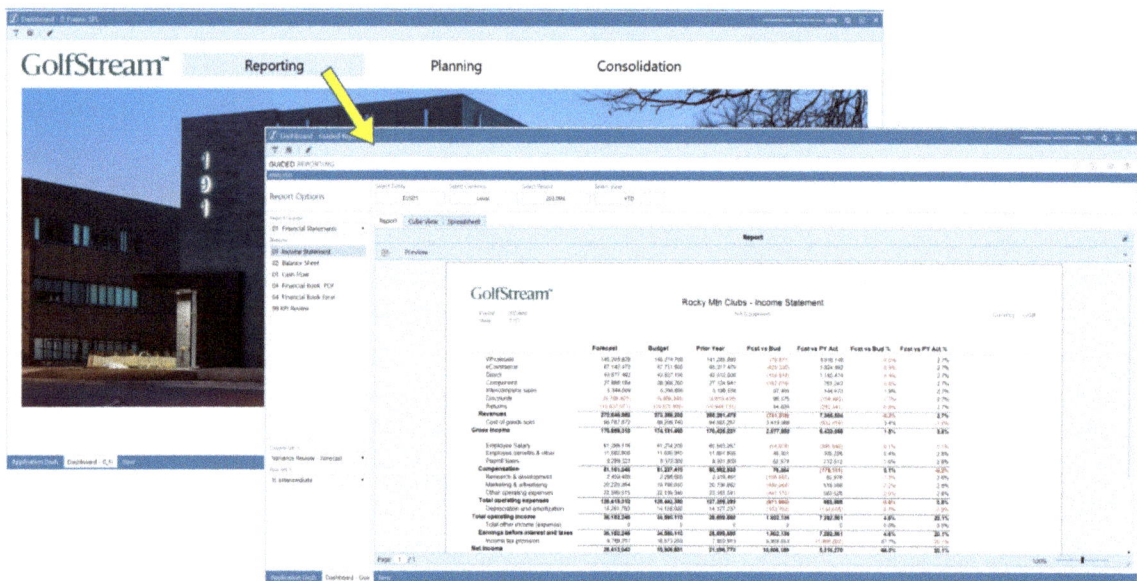

Figure 11.39

To navigate back to our Splash Dashboard, we can simply click the Back button at the top-left corner of the screen.

The Consolidation Button

Next, we will configure the action for our Consolidation button. When the User clicks this button, we want them to be directed to the Workflow appropriate for this User, the Actual Scenario, and the current global Time period for our application. To accomplish this, we will configure two actions for this button – we will use the POV Action to change the active Workflow selections, plus the Navigation Action to direct the User to the Workflow navigation page itself.

For the POV Action, we will select Change Workflow as the Selection Changed POV Action (the options that include Change POV would allow you to update the User's Member selections on the POV Pane, which is not necessary for this example). With this Action selected, the Selection Changed POV Arguments property is now active. Clicking the […] button for that property will provide examples of the syntax required by this property; we will select the example that includes the `WFProfile`, `WFScenario`, and `WFTime` settings (Figure 11.40).

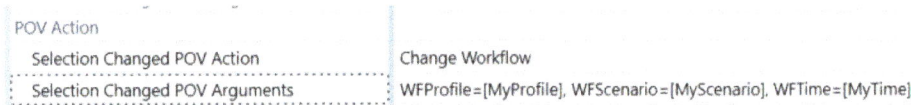

POV Action	
Selection Changed POV Action	Change Workflow
Selection Changed POV Arguments	WFProfile=[MyProfile], WFScenario=[MyScenario], WFTime=[MyTime]

Figure 11.40

To update the arguments with our required settings for this example, we will use a few different techniques, including hard-coded text, a global substitution variable, and a setting specific to the User currently signed on.

First, and simplest, for the `WFScenario` we will simply replace `MyScenario` with the name of the Scenario Member that we want the User's Workflow set to when this button is clicked – in this case, Actual, as seen in Figure 11.41 below.

For the `WFTime` setting, we will use a global substitution variable called `GlobalTime`. Much like the logo file, in the Application Properties for every OneStream application, there is an Administrator-set default Time period (Figure 11.41).

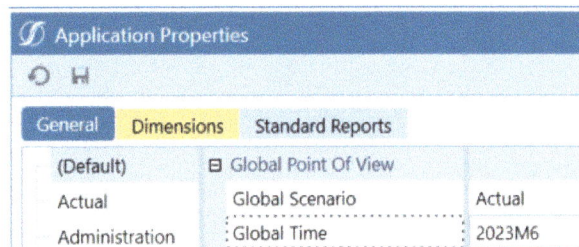

Figure 11.41

This setting can be easily retrieved throughout the OneStream platform using the syntax `|GlobalTime|`. This can be manually typed in to replace the `MyTime` text. However, if you can't quite remember the name of that variable, there is a very convenient way to look it up. The toolbars for many administrative screens (including Dashboards) include an **Object Lookup** button (Figure 11.42).

Figure 11.42

This button will open a dialog box that allows you to find and copy the names or syntax for many Types of objects, including substitution variables. Clicking this button, selecting Substitution Variables, then filtering for global will provide you with a short list of useful examples, including `|GlobalTime|`. You can select this item and click Copy to Clipboard.

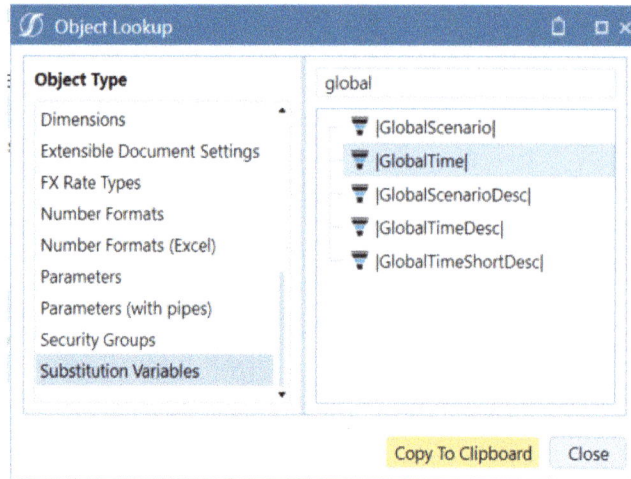

Figure 11.43

Then, you can simply paste that variable into the WFTime setting to replace the sample MyTime text (Figure 11.44).

Figure 11.44

For the WFProfile setting, we will use a simple technique often employed in OneStream implementations. Each OneStream User profile includes four free-form text fields, that can be used for anything your application design requires. In this sample application, we have decided to use the Text 1 property for each User to identify which (if any) Workflow Profile is appropriate for this User when working on the Consolidation process (Figure 11.45).

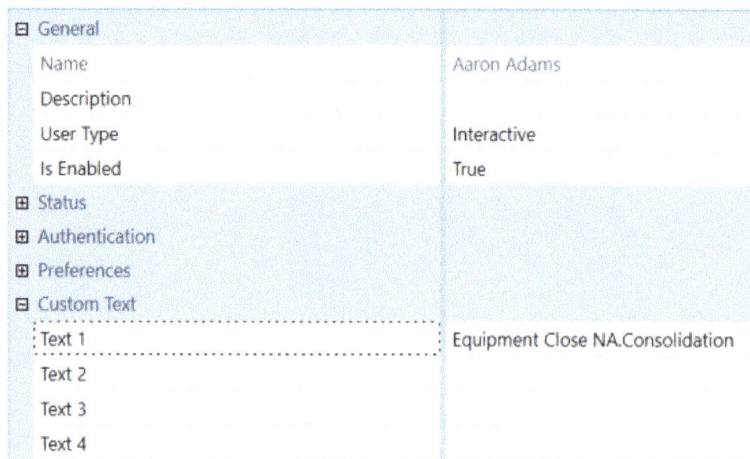

Figure 11.45

Then, just as we did for the global Time period, we can use the Object Lookup tool to find the appropriate substitution variable for this User property.

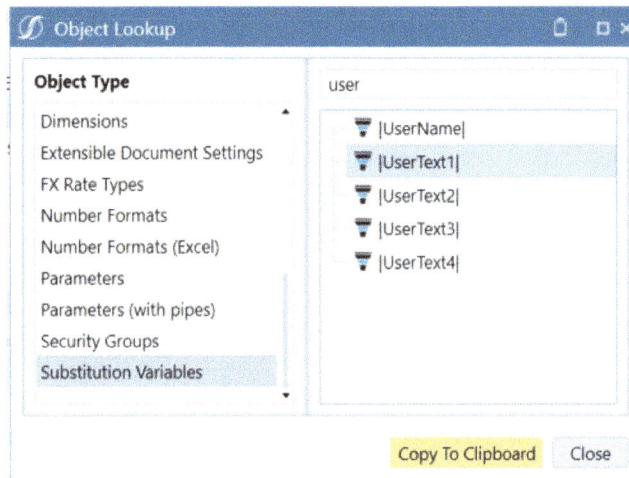

Figure 11.46

Again, we can copy and paste the substitution variable (this time, for the current User's Text 1 property) directly to the Change POV Arguments property for our button (this time, for the WFProfile setting).

Figure 11.47

Now that we have configured the Consolidation Button to change the User's selected Workflow settings, we need to do one last thing: set the Navigation Action so that clicking the button also opens that Workflow page.

Much like we did with the Reporting button, for this Consolidation button we will set the Selection Changed Navigation Action to Open Page and use the […] button to find an example of the syntax we want for the Navigation Arguments. For the Consolidation button, the Navigation Arguments setting is very simple – the first example in the list has the exact syntax we need, and there is no 'example' text that needs to be updated (Figure 11.48) – since the button has already changed the Workflow to the required selections, all we need to do is open OneStream's Workflow page.

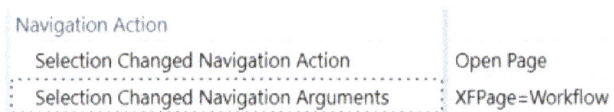

Figure 11.48

To fine-tune the navigation action, we can also include PinNavPane=True in our Navigation Arguments (Figure 11.49). When the button is clicked, this will open the Workflow Navigation pane on the left side of the screen and pin it open so it doesn't close until the User unpins it. Although this isn't included in the XFPage=Workflow example provided by the Navigation Arguments dialog box, it is used in several other examples, and will work with any configuration.

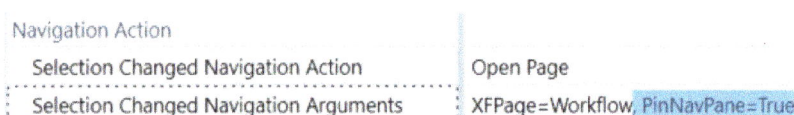

Figure 11.49

There is one final thing we can do to make our Consolidation button even more User-friendly. Many Dashboard Components include a property called **Tool Tip**. Any text you enter in the Tool Tip will be displayed to the User when they hover their mouse over the Component. This text can be a simple hard-coded explanation of the Component's function (e.g., Open the Consolidation Workflow), but it can also include Dashboard parameters and substitution variables to make the text very dynamic and context-specific.

For our Consolidation button, we will use the same parameters and variables we used in the Changed POV Parameter, but this time we will embed them in a User-facing explanation of the button's function. With this added, the full configuration of our Consolidation button looks like this (Figure 11.50):

Component Properties	
General (Component)	
Name	btn_Consolidation_SPL
Workspace	User Interface Book Chapter 11
Maintenance Unit	A Splash Screen (SPL)
Description	
Component Type	Button
Formatting	
Text	Consolidation
Tool Tip	Change Workflow selections to WF Profile=|UserText1|, Scenario=Actual, Time=|GlobalTime|, and navigate to the Workflow page.
Display Format	[!prm_ButtonFormat_SPL!]
Image	
Button	
Action	
Bound Parameter	
Parameter Value For Button Click	
Apply Selected Value To Current Dashboard	True
Save Action	
Selection Changed Save Action	No Action
Selection Changed Save Arguments	
POV Action	
Selection Changed POV Action	Change Workflow
Selection Changed POV Arguments	WFProfile=[|UserText1|], WFScenario=[Actual], WFTime=[|GlobalTime|]
Server Task	
Selection Changed Server Task	No Task
Selection Changed Server Task Arguments	
User Interface Action	
Selection Changed User Interface Action	No Action
Dashboards To Redraw	
Dashboards To Show	
Dashboards To Hide	
Dashboard To Open In Dialog	
Navigation Action	
Selection Changed Navigation Action	Open Page
Selection Changed Navigation Arguments	XFPage=Workflow, PinNavPane=True

Figure 11.50

Now, if we run our Dashboard and hover our mouse over the Consolidation button, we will see text explaining the button's function; if we click the button, we are taken directly to our appropriate Consolidation Workflow step (Figure 11.51).

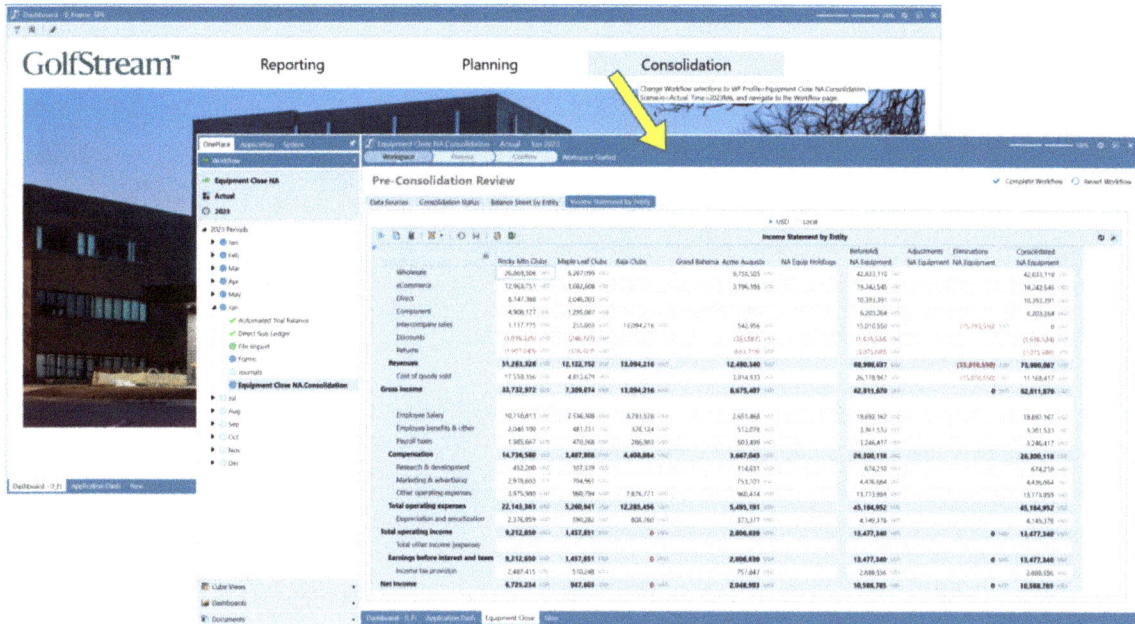

Figure 11.51

The Planning Button

Our final button will take the User directly to their Planning Workflow. The techniques we will use for this button are very similar to those of the Consolidation button.

As with the Consolidation button, we will use the POV Action properties to change the current Workflow selections, but this time we will determine the appropriate Workflow from the User's Text 2 parameter, which in our application is used to specify each User's Planning Workflow. We will determine the appropriate Scenario to select by using the contents of a Dashboard parameter that has been established in our application just for this purpose; in our application, the `prm_CurrentForecastScenario_STDOBJ` will always be set to the Forecast Scenario currently in use.

We will also use the Navigation Action properties to open the Workflow page, but for this process, Dashboards have been configured for each Workflow step to simplify navigation and maximize screen real estate – there is no need to pin the navigation pane open.

Finally, we will add a tool tip giving a clear explanation of the function of this button. When fully configured, our Planning button looks like this:

Component Properties	
⊟ General (Component)	
Name	btn_Planning_SPL
Workspace	User Interface Book Chapter 11
Maintenance Unit	A Splash Screen (SPL)
Description	
Component Type	Button
⊟ Formatting	
Text	Planning
Tool Tip	Change Workflow selections to WF Profile=[UserText2], Scenario=[!prm_CurrentForecastScenario_STDOBJ!], Time=[GlobalTime], and navigate to the Workflow page.
Display Format	[!prm_ButtonFormat_SPL!]
⊞ Image	
⊞ Button	
⊟ Action	
Bound Parameter	
Parameter Value For Button Click	
Apply Selected Value To Current Dashboard	True
Save Action	
Selection Changed Save Action	No Action
Selection Changed Save Arguments	
POV Action	
Selection Changed POV Action	Change Workflow
Selection Changed POV Arguments	WFProfile=[[UserText2]], WFScenario=[[!prm_CurrentForecastScenario_STDOBJ!]]
Server Task	
Selection Changed Server Task	No Task
Selection Changed Server Task Arguments	
User Interface Action	
Selection Changed User Interface Action	No Action
Dashboards To Redraw	
Dashboards To Show	
Dashboards To Hide	
Dashboard To Open In Dialog	
Navigation Action	
Selection Changed Navigation Action	Open Page
Selection Changed Navigation Arguments	XFPage=Workflow

Figure 11.52

When our User clicks this button, they are taken directly to the Dashboard that has been set as the Workspace for the assigned Forecast Workflow and Scenario (Figure 11.53).

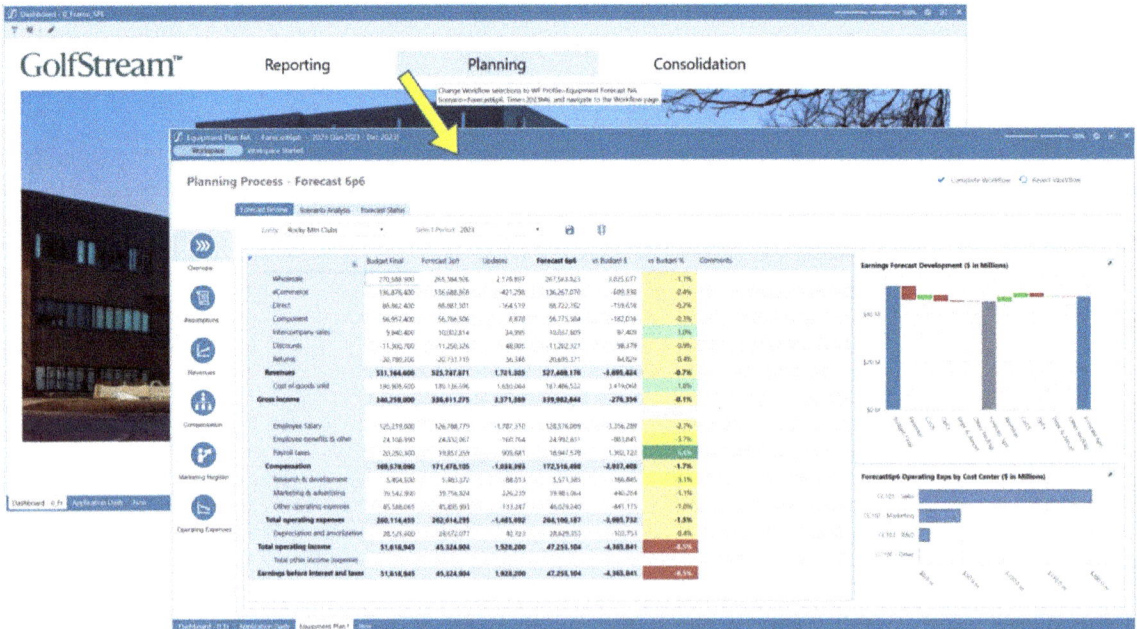

Figure 11.53

Adding Our KPIs

Our Dashboard is almost done! If we compare what we now have with our original sketch, all we are missing is the row of Key Performance Indicators (KPIs) at the bottom of the screen. We have already embedded our footer Dashboard (`2_Footer_SPL`) as the third row of our main Dashboard (`0_Frame_SPL`) – now we need to add some content to that section of the Dashboard.

To display our KPIs, we will use a Component called **BI Viewer**. This Component allows you to configure and arrange a large variety of data presentation and visualization options, such as pivot grids, charts, gauges, and maps, all with an intuitive drag-and-drop interface. We will use the BI Viewer Component's **Cards** object to display our KPIs.

OneStream's BI Viewer Components exist to display data, and the data they display can come from almost anywhere. In this simple example, we will source our KPI data from a Cube View, but we could also incorporate data from SQL databases, Business Rules, Workflow status information, and more. We will go into greater depth on BI Viewer Components in the next chapter.

Creating our Dashboard Data Adapter

To retrieve our KPI values, we will create a simple Cube View, with the KPI Accounts in the rows, and columns for our Actual, Prior Year, Budget, and Forecast values. Needless to say, every OneStream application will have different dimensionality, Member names, and business requirements. For this example, we will show data and metadata from OneStream's standard demonstration, but the concepts will be the same for any application; to recreate this, simply create a similar Cube View, with your application's metadata.

In our example, we have configured the Cube View's POV to use the top-level Members for most of our Dimensions – e.g., Flow, Origin, Intercompany, and all the User-Defined Dimensions are set to their top-level Members. For our Entity Dimension, we will use the current Member selected in the Point of View pane – on the right side of the screen – by setting the Cube View's Entity POV Member to the substitution variable `|PovEntity|`. This will ensure that each User will see KPI values for the Entity they are interested in.

As with many OneStream applications, our demonstration application uses the UD8 Dimension to provide convenient dynamically calculated 'reporting helpers', such as frequently used variances, 'percent of' Calculations (such as 'percent of net sales'), and many more. For the columns of our Cube View, we have leveraged these UD8 Members to provide easy access to our Current Year, Prior Year, Final Budget, and Current Forecast values. When we run our Cube View, it looks like this:

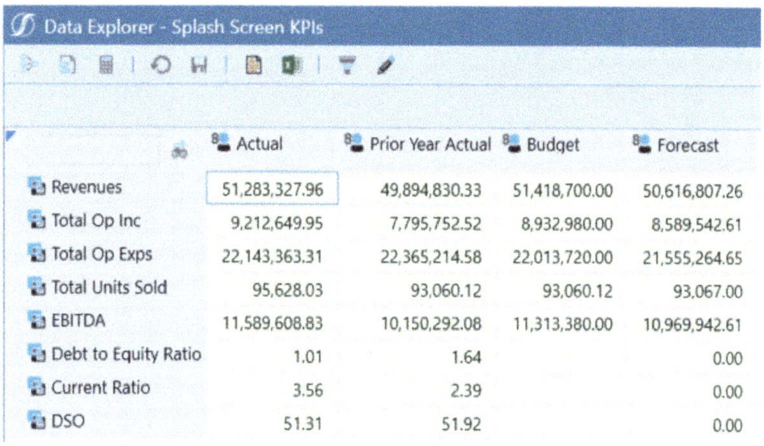

	Actual	Prior Year Actual	Budget	Forecast
Revenues	51,283,327.96	49,894,830.33	51,418,700.00	50,616,807.26
Total Op Inc	9,212,649.95	7,795,752.52	8,932,980.00	8,589,542.61
Total Op Exps	22,143,363.31	22,365,214.58	22,013,720.00	21,555,264.65
Total Units Sold	95,628.03	93,060.12	93,060.12	93,067.00
EBITDA	11,589,608.83	10,150,292.08	11,313,380.00	10,969,942.61
Debt to Equity Ratio	1.01	1.64		0.00
Current Ratio	3.56	2.39		0.00
DSO	51.31	51.92		0.00

Figure 11.54

Using this Cube View, we will provide the data that our BI Viewer Dashboard Component will need to display our KPIs.

Chapter 11

The first step in creating our BI Viewer Component is to create a **Dashboard Data Adapter**. From our Dashboard Maintenance Unit, select the Data Adapters category, then click the Create Data Adapter button in the toolbar. Following our usual naming convention, we will name this dat_KPIs_SPL.

As discussed above, Dashboard data can be sourced from almost anywhere – the first properties we need to configure for our data adapter are grouped together in the Data Source section. The Command Type property has a drop-down list that lets us specify the kind of data we will be working with – including two ways of working with data from Cube Views. For the Data Source Command Type we will choose Cube View MD – this means that the data adapter will understand how to work with the data in a multi-dimensional context, rather than just as rows and columns in a table (Figure 11.55).

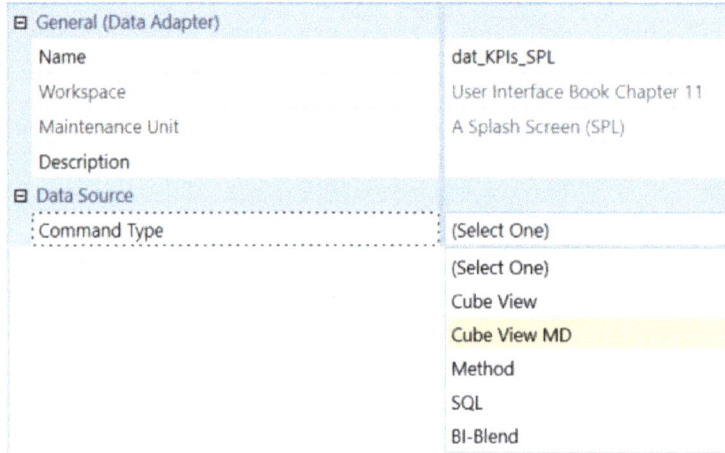

Figure 11.55

Once we have selected the Data Source Command Type, the relevant properties for this Type of data are displayed.

The next property we will set is the name of the Cube View that we have created to provide this data. Using the […] button on the Cube View property, we can navigate to – and select – this Cube View.

Finally, for the Data Source section, we will specify a **Results Table Name** – this should simply be a meaningful name that will clearly describe this data. For this example, we will type in KPIs.

In the Header Text group of properties, we can see each Dimension in our model, with the default setting of Name And Description. The first Dimension we are concerned with (for our KPIs) is the Accounts Dimension, which will look best if we just display the Description; so, we will change that setting using the drop-down. We will also be working with the reporting helper Members in our UD8 Dimension – for these Members, the Member names will be most useful for us, so we will change the UD8 header text to Name (Figure 11.56). The rest of the properties can be left to their default values.

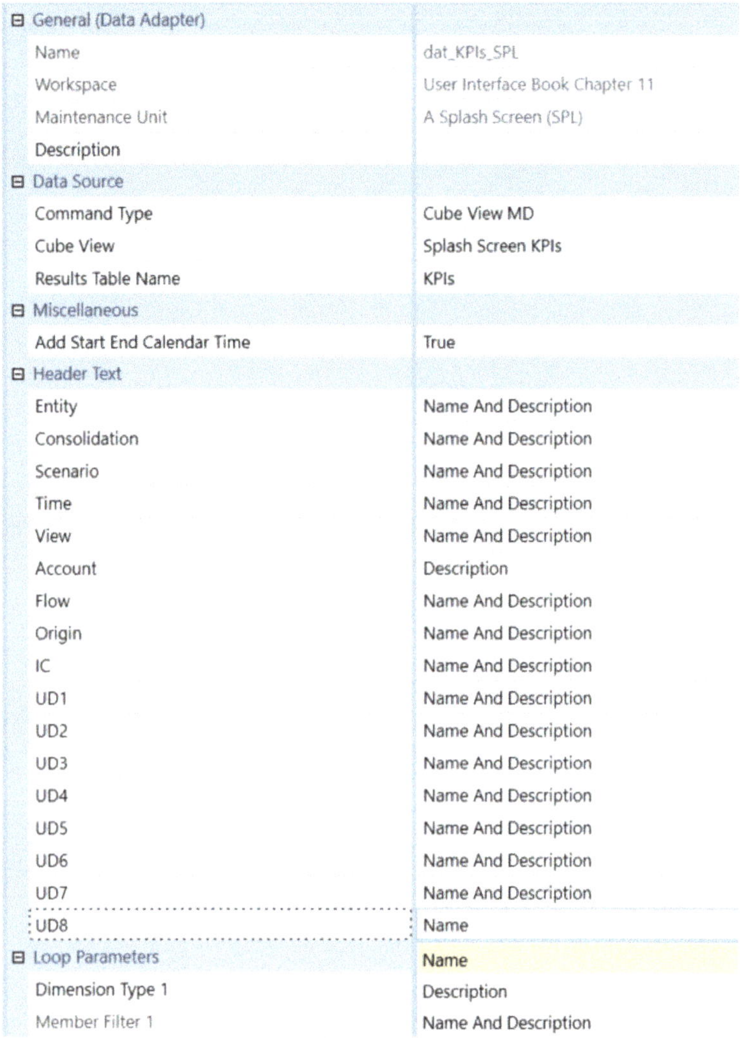

⊟ General (Data Adapter)	
Name	dat_KPIs_SPL
Workspace	User Interface Book Chapter 11
Maintenance Unit	A Splash Screen (SPL)
Description	
⊟ Data Source	
Command Type	Cube View MD
Cube View	Splash Screen KPIs
Results Table Name	KPIs
⊟ Miscellaneous	
Add Start End Calendar Time	True
⊟ Header Text	
Entity	Name And Description
Consolidation	Name And Description
Scenario	Name And Description
Time	Name And Description
View	Name And Description
Account	Description
Flow	Name And Description
Origin	Name And Description
IC	Name And Description
UD1	Name And Description
UD2	Name And Description
UD3	Name And Description
UD4	Name And Description
UD5	Name And Description
UD6	Name And Description
UD7	Name And Description
UD8	Name
⊟ Loop Parameters	Name
Dimension Type 1	Description
Member Filter 1	Name And Description

Figure 11.56

We can now test our data adapter to make sure it's getting us the data we want, and in the format we prefer. With our data adapter selected, clicking the Test Data Adapter button in the toolbar will display our data as it will be provided to the Dashboard. The table consists of columns for each Dimension in the model, and each row contains a data point for each cell in our Cube View, with each Dimension column containing either the Member name, description, or both, depending on the selection we made for that Dimension. Notice that using the selections we made in our data adapter, the Account Dimension column shows just the description, and the UD8 Dimension is showing just the Member name (Figure 11.57).

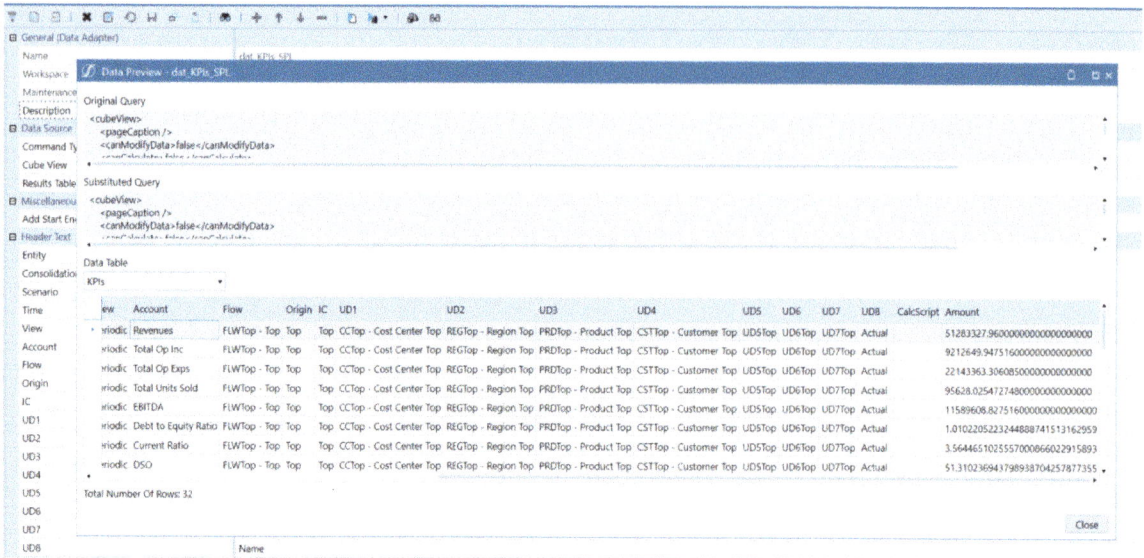

Figure 11.57

Creating our BI Viewer Component

Now that we have our Cube View to collect the data we need, and our data adapter to organize that data in a table that will be easy for our Dashboard to work with, we are ready to configure our BI Viewer Component.

As with our other Components, we start by selecting the Component category in our Dashboard Maintenance Unit, clicking the Create Dashboard Component button in the toolbar, and selecting BI Viewer from the list of Component Types.

The BI Viewer has three tabs: Component Properties, Data Adapters, and BI Designer. On the first tab, using our naming convention, we will call this Component biv_KPIs_SPL. The first tab also has properties to show or hide a Toggle Size button and Borders outlining the Component. To keep the clean, uncluttered look of our Dashboard, we will set these to False. All other properties can be left to their default values (Figure 11.58).

Figure 11.58

On the second tab, we add our Data Adapter to the BI Viewer. This adapter (or adapters) will provide the data we will display via the charts, graphs, and other objects on the BI Viewer. Clicking the [+] button in the toolbar displays the data adapters available to us – in our case, there is only one, but more complex Dashboards might include data from multiple sources. We will select our data adapter and click the Save button in the toolbar. With the data adapter added, and the BI Viewer Component saved, the BI Designer tab is now selectable.

Clicking the BI Designer tab presents us with a 'blank canvas', a toolbar at the top of the screen showing the various Types of objects we can include, and a panel on the left side of the screen showing the data fields that have been provided by the data adapter.

Just as a quick experiment to get a feel for working with the BI Viewer and the data we have at hand, let's add a simple grid to the Dashboard. Clicking the Grid button places an empty white box on the screen – this is the beginning of a data grid (Figure 11.59). We now need to tell the grid what data we want to see.

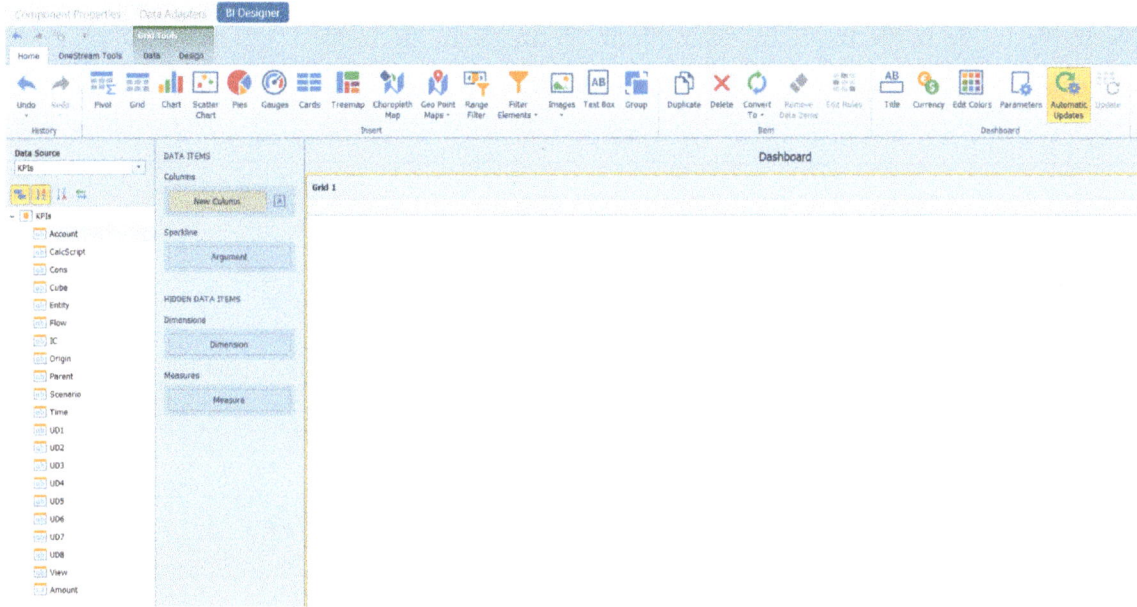

Figure 11.59

From the list of Data Source fields on the left side of the screen, drag the Account field onto the Columns section of the grid's Data Items panel (Figure 11.60).

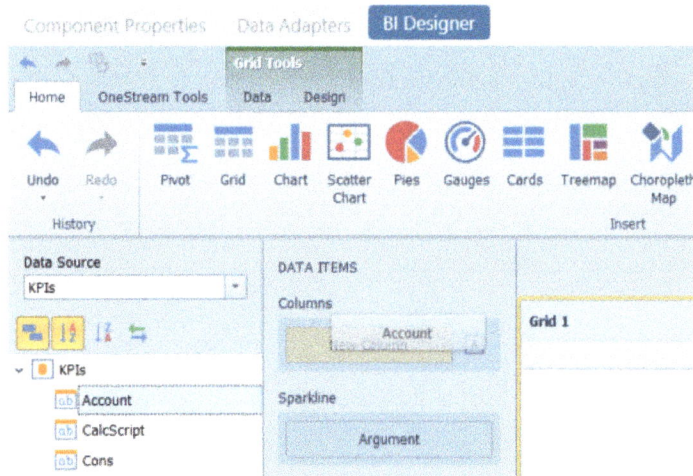

Figure 11.60

We now see a list of the Accounts that are included on our Cube View. Notice that, based on how we configured our Data Source, we are seeing the Account Member descriptions, not the Member names (Figure 11.61).

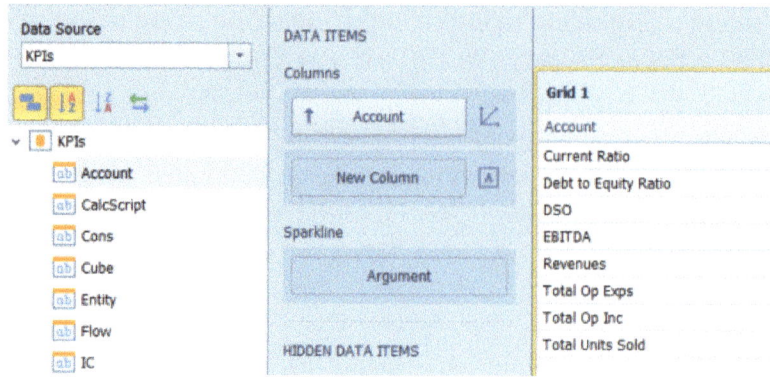

Figure 11.61

If we drag the Amount field into the Columns section, we will see the totals for each of the Accounts in our Data Source (Figure 11.62).

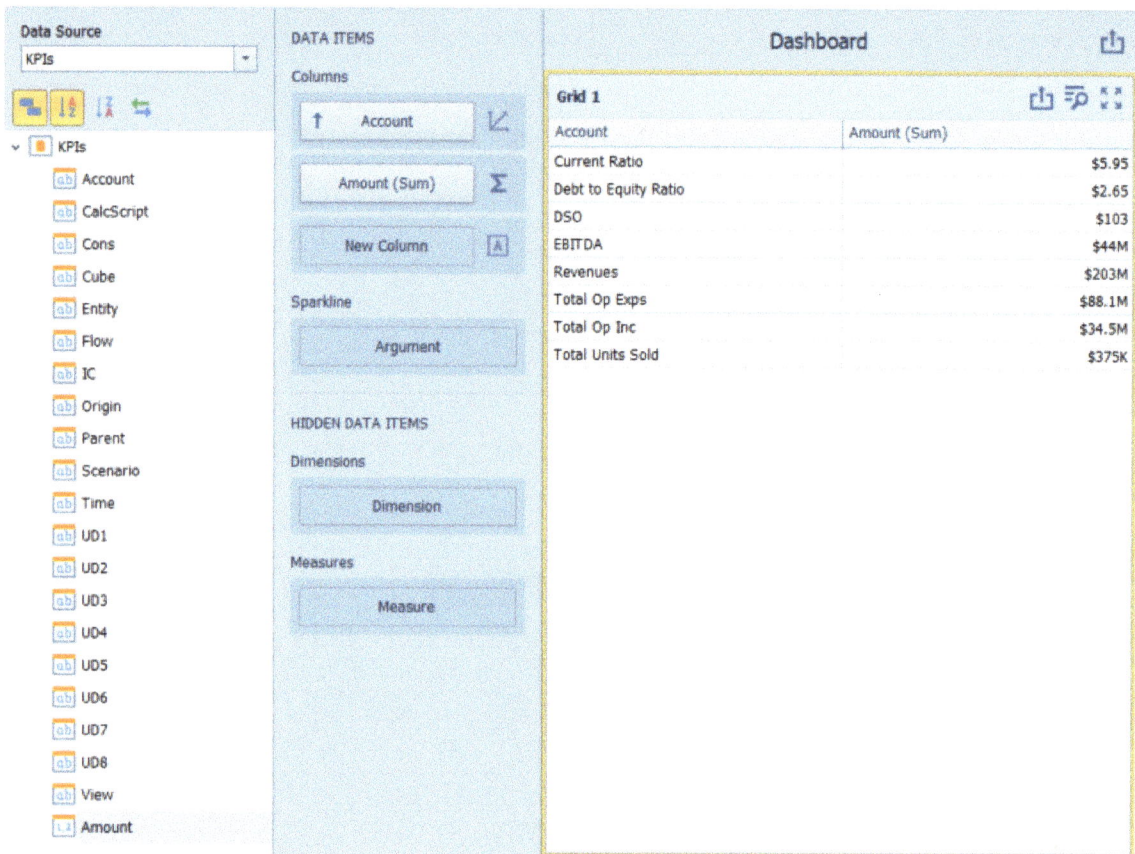

Figure 11.62

Our Cube View is using the reporting helper Members from our UD8 Dimension to dynamically retrieve the various Scenarios that we are interested in. If we pull the UD8 Dimension into the Columns section between Account and Amount, we will now see all the data for each Scenario (Figure 11.63).

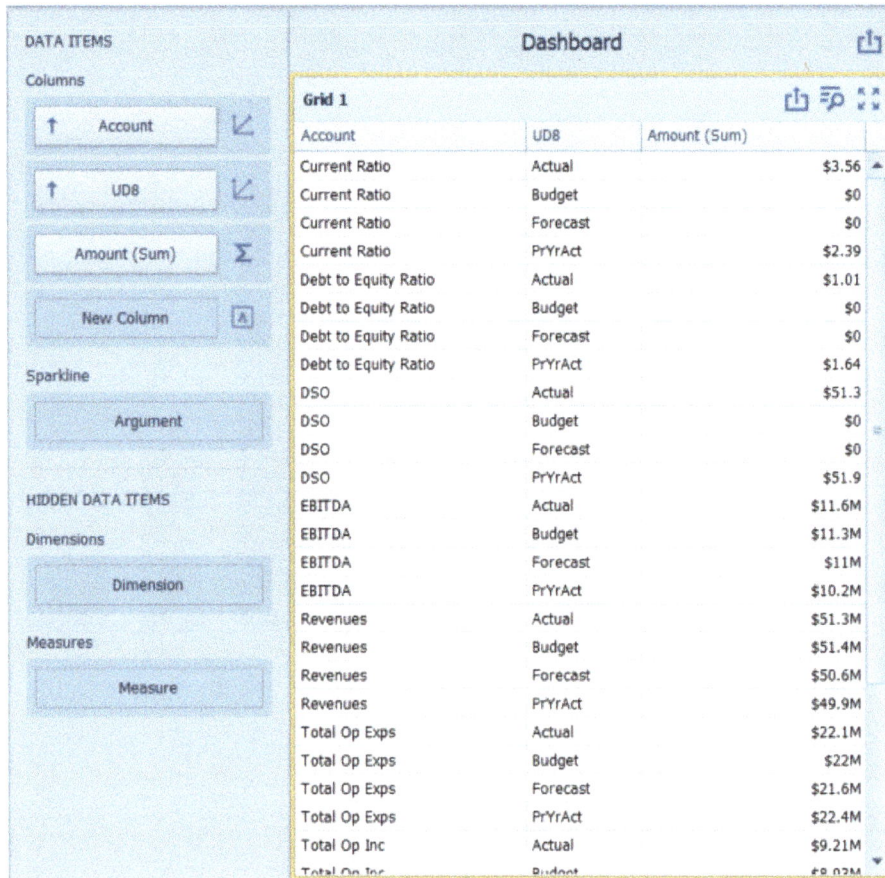

Figure 11.63

If we right-click on the Grid object, a menu will appear that will allow us to convert the Grid to other object Types – if we select Convert To > Chart, the currently selected data will be included in a bar chart like this:

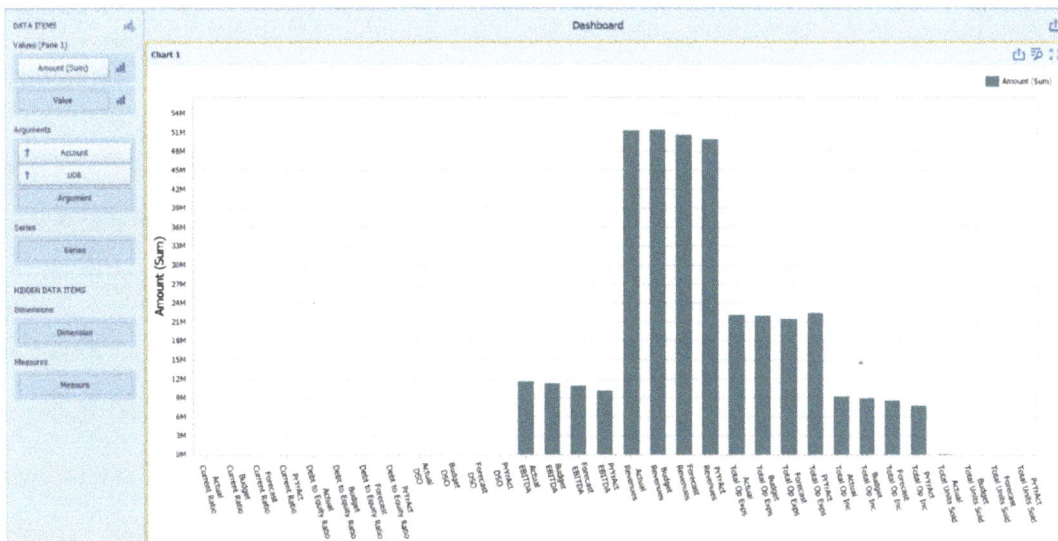

Figure 11.64

If we drag our UD8 Dimension from the Arguments section to the Series section, the graph will change accordingly (Figure 11.65).

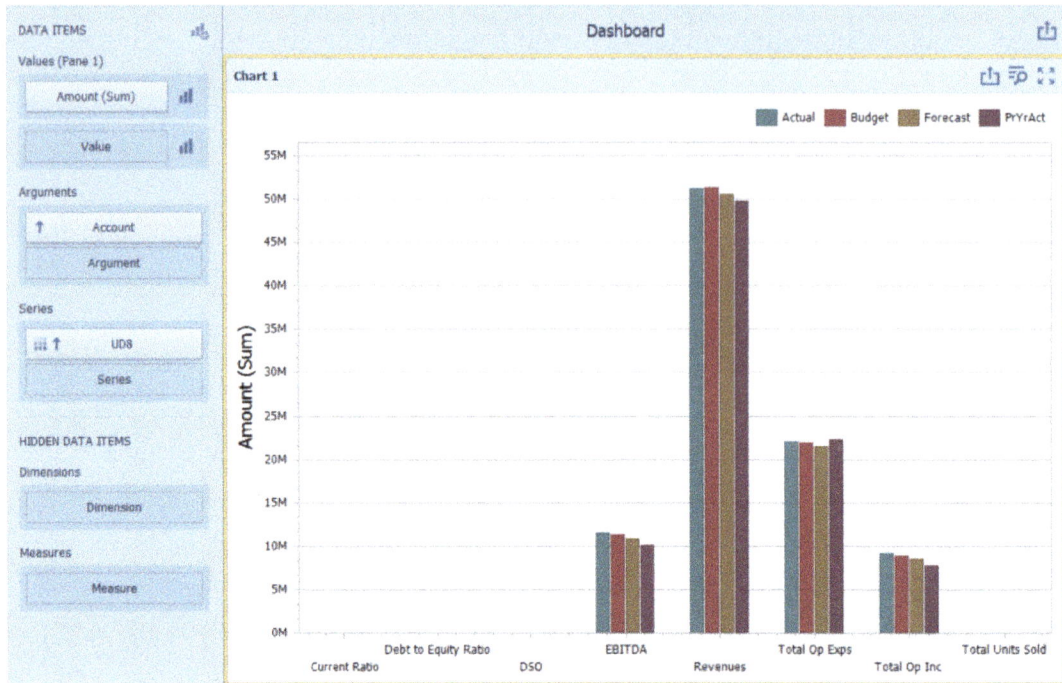

Figure 11.65

Now that we have a feel for working with the BI Viewer Component, let's start configuring the KPIs for our Dashboard. To delete our practice chart, click the red [X] delete button. We are now back to our blank canvas.

We will be using BI Viewer Cards to display our KPIs. But before we configure this object, we will do some simple Dashboard-based manipulation of our data.

You may have noticed that although our Data Source is giving us all the information in our Cube View, it is formatted with a table that has just one 'value' field – Amount. All the other columns are the metadata that define the meaning of each Amount. For our KPI columns, it would be convenient to have specific value fields for two of our UD8 Members – Actual and Prior Year. We can include those fields by adding 'calculated fields'.

If we right-click on the list of existing fields and select Create Calculated Field, the Expression Editor dialog will open (Figure 11.66). This is where we explain to the BI Viewer what information we want to include in our calculated fields.

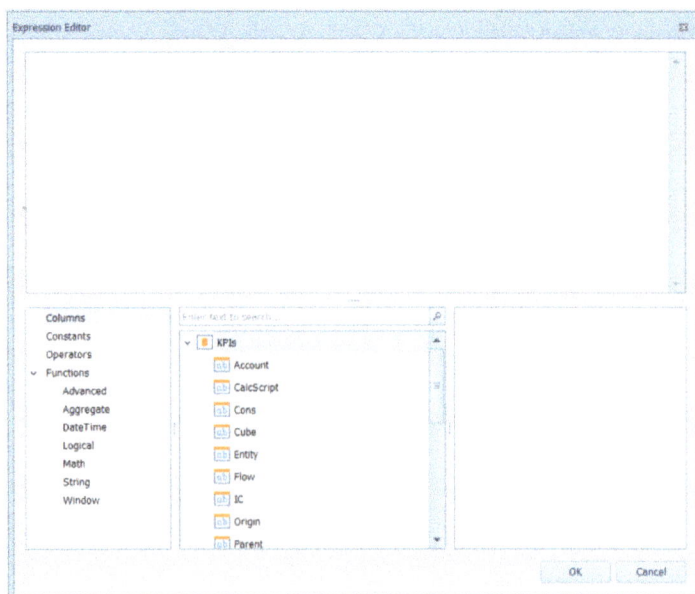

Figure 11.66

Since we want amount fields specific to the Current Period Actual and Prior Year Actual UD8 Members, we will use this dialog to filter for those values in our new fields. First, we will create a field called `Actual` that selects data from the UD8 Member called Actual using the Logical `Iif` function. Selecting `Logical` in the first panel, and `Iif` in the second panel, we see an explanation of the syntax for this function in the third panel. If we double-click on `Iif` in the second panel, the top of the screen displays the beginning of our expression (Figure 11.67).

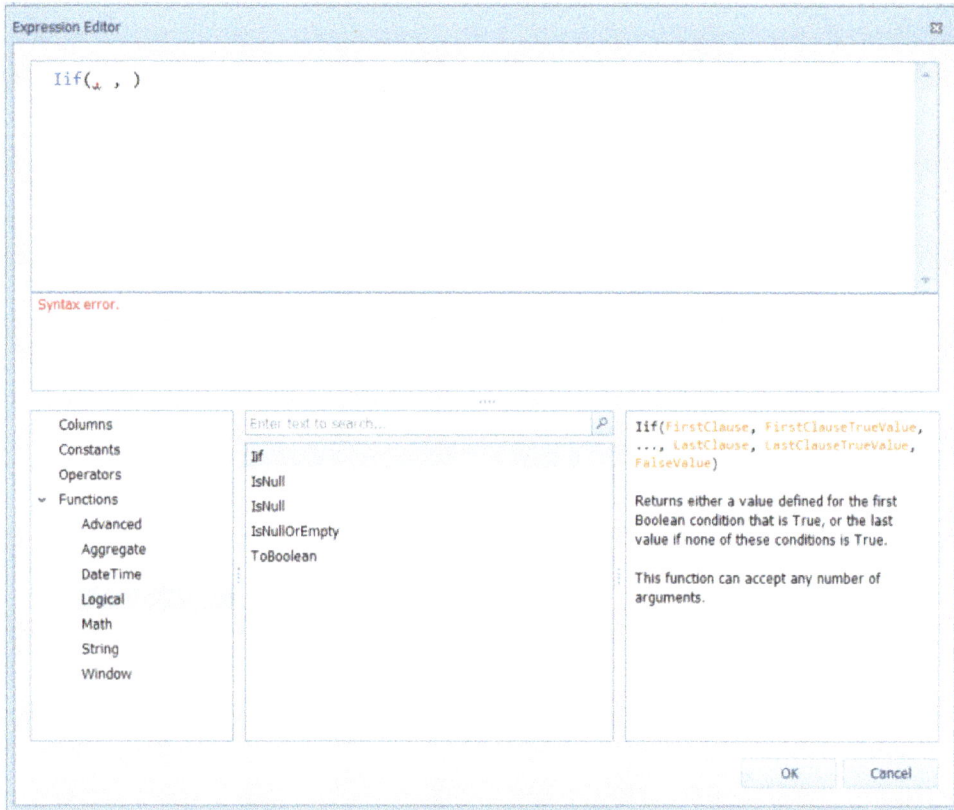

Figure 11.67

To have this new field display the value from the UD8 Actual Member, we can position our cursor before the first comma of the `Iif` expression, then use the Columns selector to choose the UD8 Dimension by double-clicking on it (or we can simply type this in). To check the UD8 Dimension for the Member called `Actual`, we manually type an equal sign and the name of the Member surrounded by single quotes.

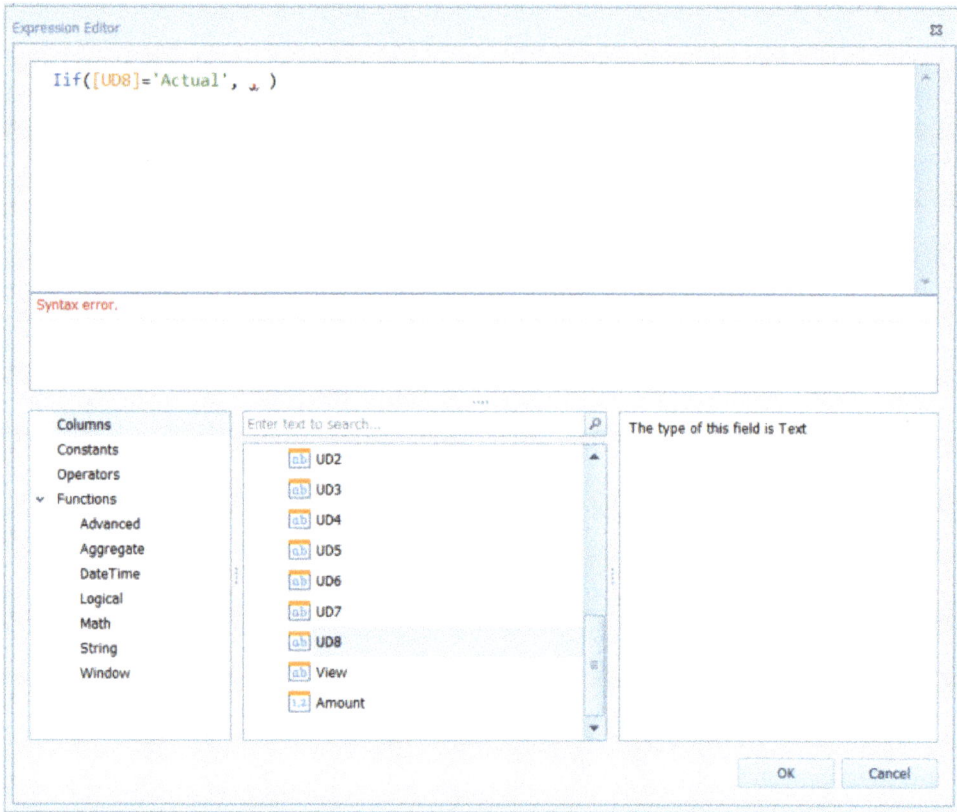

Figure 11.68

The second parameter of this `Iif` expression tells the field what to show if this condition is true. If the UD8 Member is Actual, we want this new field to show the Amount, so we can position our cursor after the first comma and double-click the Amount field. The third parameter defines what the new field should display if the UD8 Member is NOT Actual – for this third parameter, we just enter the number 0 (Figure 11.69).

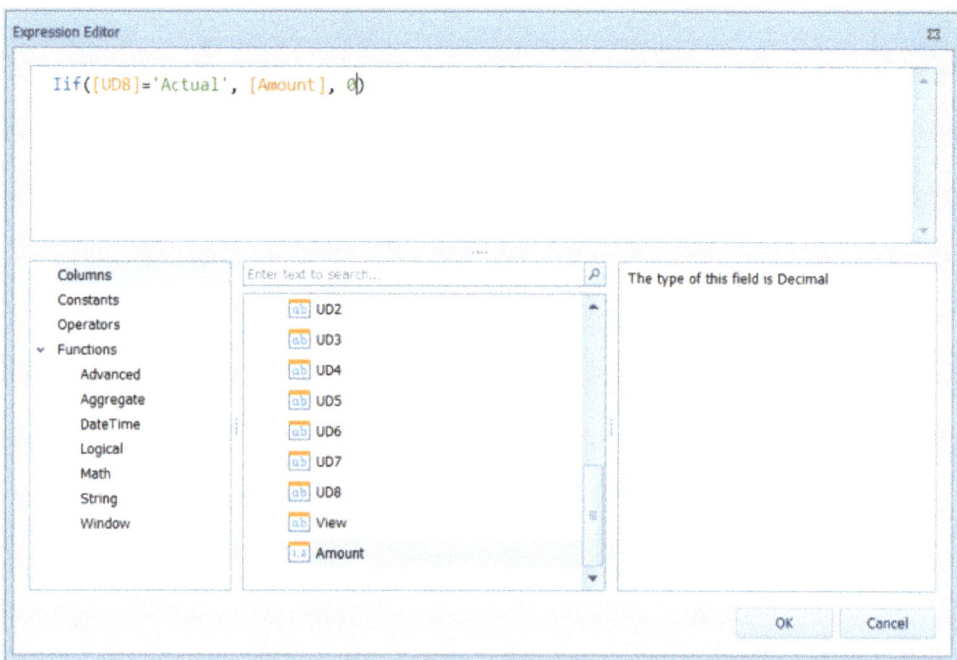

Figure 11.69

When we click OK, the field list on the left panel now shows a new calculated field with the default name `Calculated Field 1`. We will right-click on this field and rename it to `Actual`.

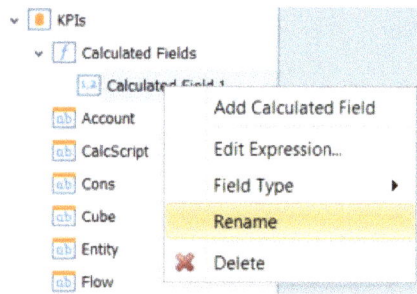

Figure 11.70

For our KPIs, our Dashboard will highlight the variance between this year and last year; it will also be helpful to have a field specific to the `PrYrAct` Member of the UD8 Dimension. Repeating this process, we will create another calculated Member like this:

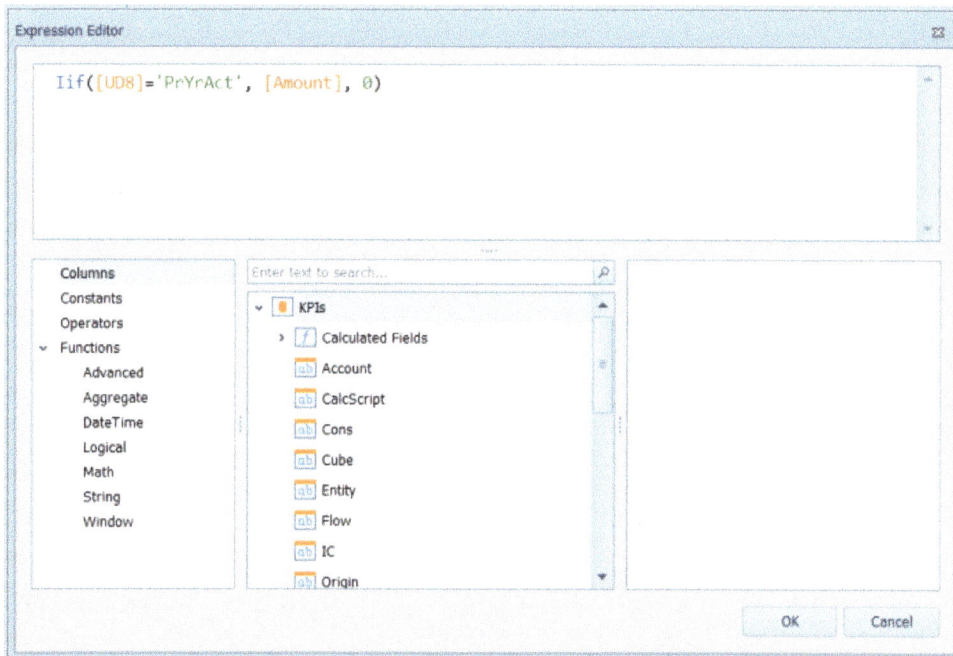

Figure 11.71

With this second calculated field renamed `PriorYear`, we are ready to configure our KPIs (Figure 11.72).

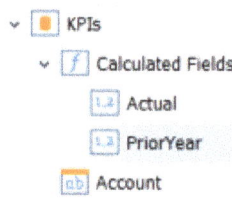

Figure 11.72

As mentioned, the BI Viewer object we will use for our KPIs is called Cards. Clicking this button on the toolbar gets a blank object to work with, and dragging the calculated Actual and PriorYear fields onto the respective Actual and Target positions in the Cards section of the Data Items panel gets us started. Dragging the Account field to the Series section creates a card for each of the rows of our Cube View (Figure 11.73).

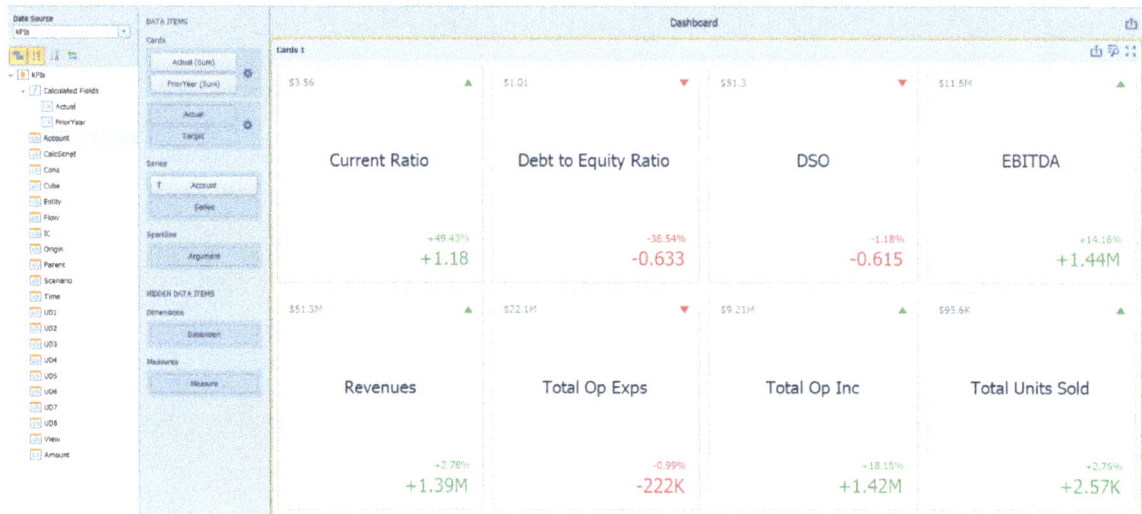

Figure 11.73

We will be displaying these cards in the narrow footer section at the bottom of our Dashboard, so screen real estate will be at a premium. Although we drew four KPI placeholders in our initial design sketch, we would really like to include as many as we can fit in the space available without the screen looking cluttered. The first thing we can do to conserve some space is remove the grey Cards 1 bar at the top of the screen by right-clicking on that bar and toggling off the Show Caption menu item (Figure 11.74).

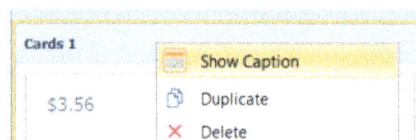

Figure 11.74

Next, we can click on the Gear button in the Cards section of the Data Items pane and adjust the way the cards are formatted. Selecting the Compact template makes the tiles much more efficient in their use of space (Figure 11.75).

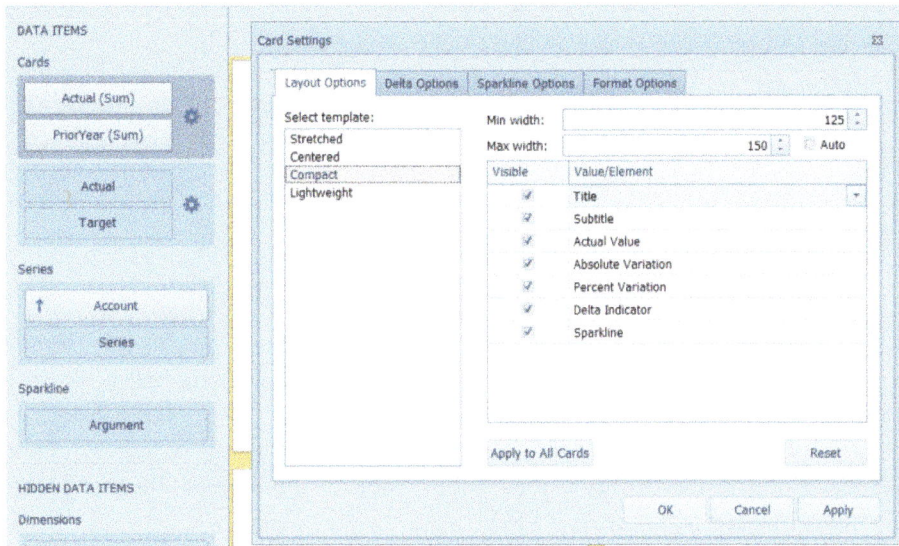

Figure 11.75

Finally, we will want our KPI cards arranged in a single horizontal row along the bottom of our Dashboard. Thus, we select Design in the menu bar, click the Arrange in Rows button, and set the Count to 1 (Figure 11.76).

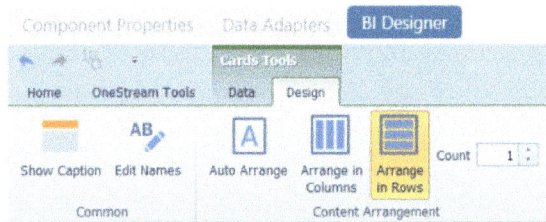

Figure 11.76

We can now save our BI Viewer object and see how it looks on our Dashboard.

To add our BI Viewer to the Dashboard's footer section, we simply select the `Dashboard 2_Footer_SPL`, click the Dashboard Components tab, click the [+] Add Dashboard Component button, and select our BI Viewer Component.

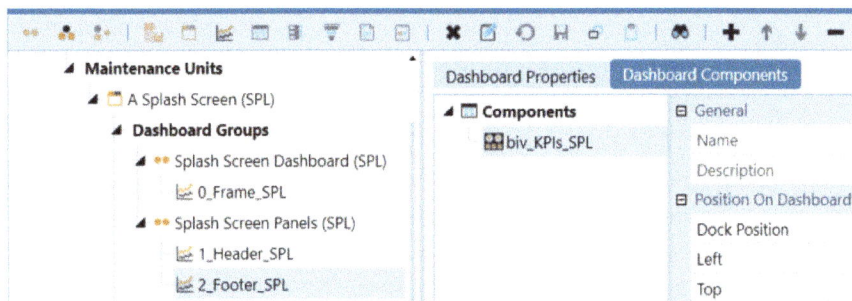

Figure 11.77

Now we can run our main Dashboard and see… well, where are our KPIs? If you look very closely, you will notice that the only thing that seems to have changed on our Dashboard is that there are now a pair of thin scroll bars at the bottom and right side of our footer section. If we drag the bottom scroll bar to the right, we will find that our KPIs have been hiding far off the right side of the screen (Figure 11.78).

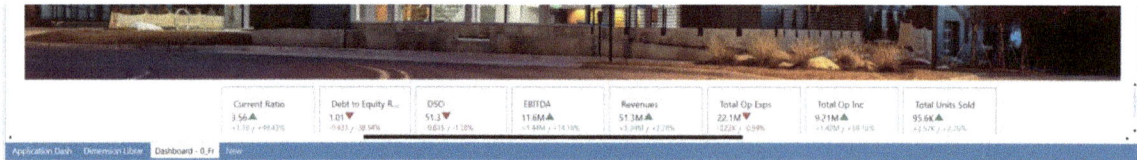

Figure 11.78

When we first created our footer Dashboard, we tentatively configured it as a horizontal stack panel, but now that we are further along with our build, we will want to reconsider that. Our BI Viewer KPI cards look great, but since the BI Viewer Component doesn't have a 'width' property, it has a habit of taking more space than it really needs. To easily solve this, we can change the footer Dashboard from Horizontal Stack Panel (which doesn't enforce any limits on how far Components can stretch) to a Grid (which does).

After changing the 2_Footer_SPL Dashboard to Grid with 1 row and 1 column, and re-running the Dashboard, the footer section looks like this:

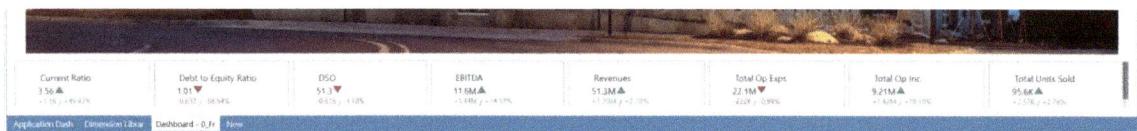

Figure 11.79

Closer! But we still will need to make a couple of adjustments. First, the BI Viewer is still a little too tall to fit in the 100-pixel space we have allocated for the footer. Also, we should probably include a label to clarify the context for these KPIs – e.g., what Entity are we using, and what are we comparing these values to? And a minor cosmetic tweak: the right edge of the final KPI card should line up with the right edge of the picture.

The first issue is very simple to fix. Changing the height of row 3 on the main Dashboard (0_Frame_SPL) changes the bottom of the screen to look like this – no more scroll bars, and the KPI cards fit nicely.

Figure 11.80

Next, to add an explanatory label to our KPI panel and adjust the alignment, we will change the number of columns on the footer Dashboard from one to three. This way, we can have a column to display some text to the left of the KPIs, and another narrow column after the KPIs to add some white space to align the KPIs with the right edge of the picture.

For our explanatory text, we will add a **Label** Component. With the Components category selected in our Dashboard Maintenance Unit, we can click the Create Dashboard Component button in the toolbar and select the Component Type Label. Again, we will follow our naming convention and call this Component lbl_KPIs_SPL.

For the text property, we could simply type in a few words explaining the context of the KPIs, but we can also make this label much more dynamic and informative. The Cube View that is providing the KPI data is using substitution variables to set the POV for the Entity and Time Dimensions – we can do the same with our label. Using the |PovEntityDesc| and |GlobalTimeDesc|

substitution variables, we can show the User-friendly descriptions of both the Entity and Time period Members currently in use, and embed them in a meaningful label, like this:

|PovEntityDesc| |GlobalTimeDesc| Actual vs Prior Year:

For our label's display formatting, we can use the […] button to open the formatting dialog, and set MarginLeft to 30 (to align with the white space we have used before our logo and image Components), set MarginRight to 10 (to provide a little white space between this label and the KPIs), and UseTextWrapping to True (to use line breaks to adjust the text to fit in the available space).

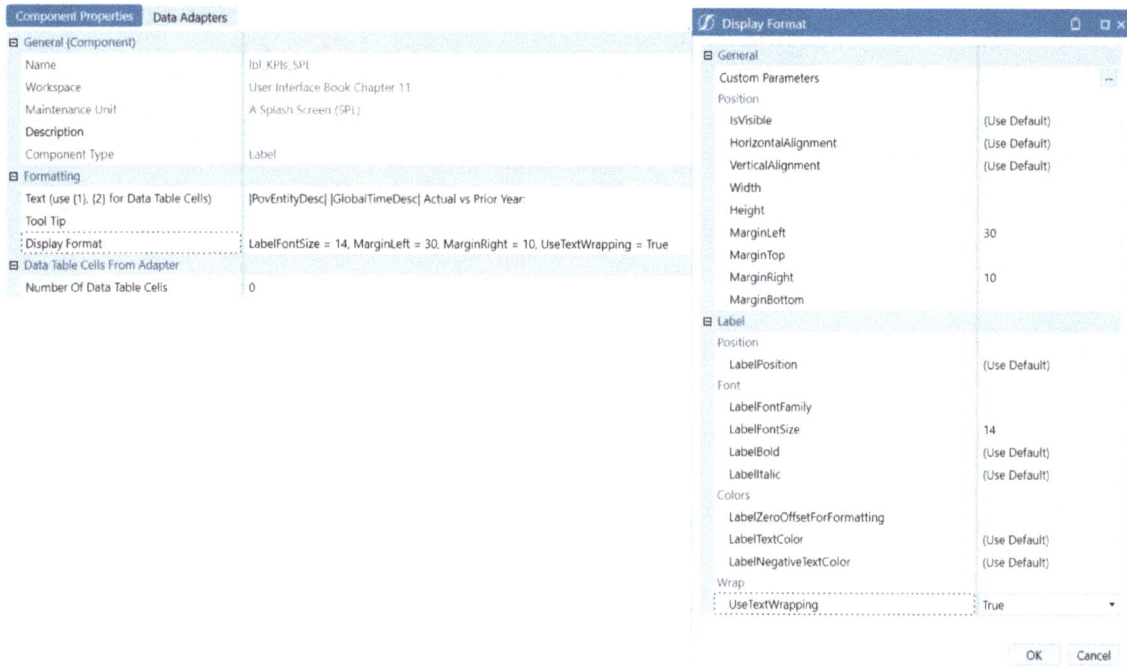

Figure 11.81

On our footer Dashboard's Dashboard Properties tab, we will change the number of columns to 3 to accommodate our new label on the left, the BI Viewer, and some white space to provide visual alignment on the right side of the screen. We will set the Column 1 Width to 150, and the Column 3 width to about 20.

On the Components tab, we will use the [+] Add Dashboard Component on the toolbar to add the label Component and use the Move Up / Move Down arrow buttons to ensure the label comes before the BI Viewer (Figure 11.82).

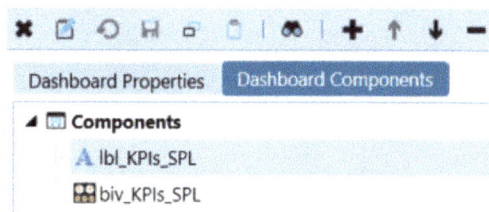

Figure 11.82

With these last adjustments, we should have our Dashboard just the way we pictured it when we drew our first sketch on a piece of scrap paper – or maybe even a little better!

Just a reminder – here's where we started:

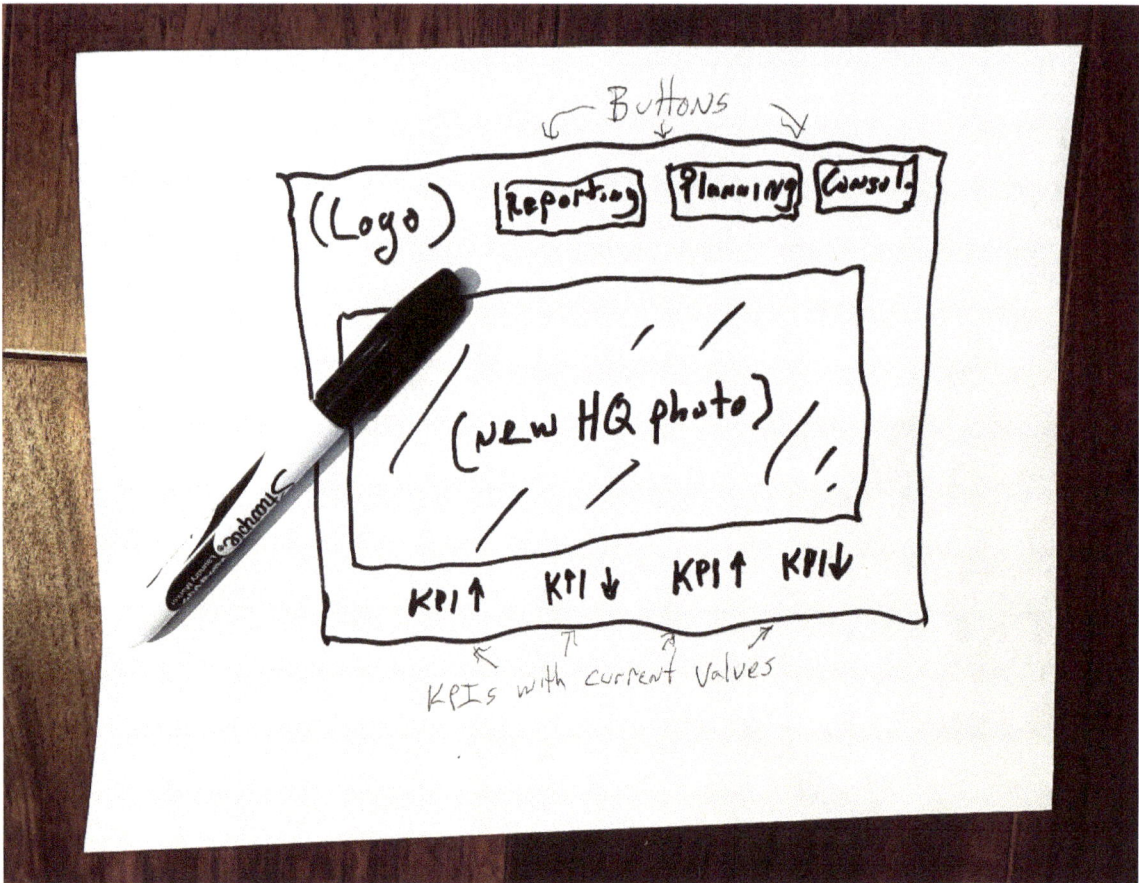

Figure 11.83

And here's where we are now:

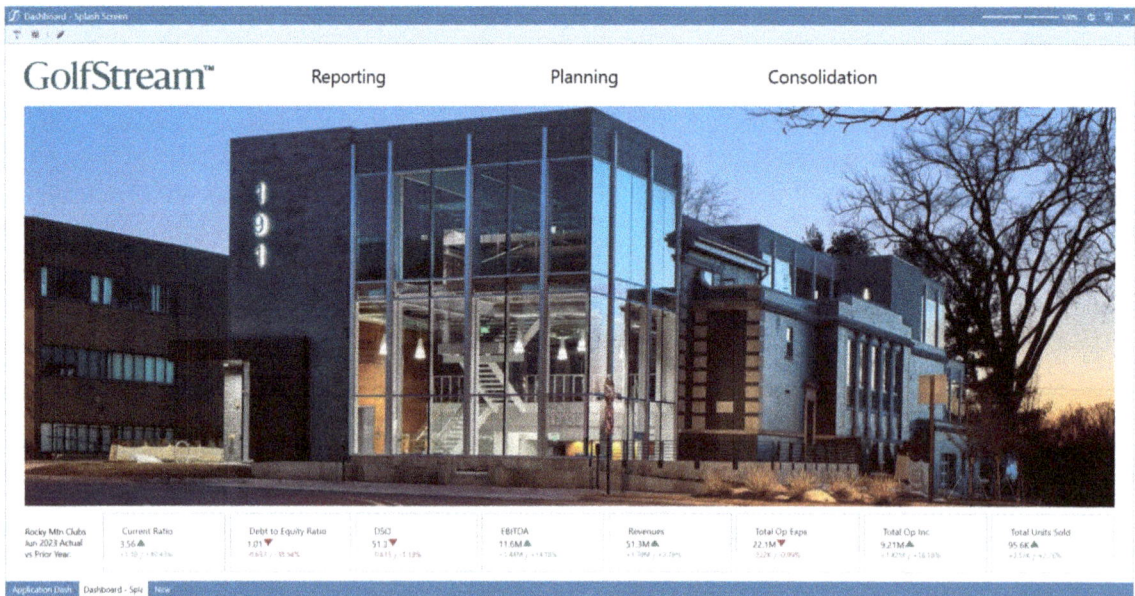

Figure 11.84

Not too bad!

But one last thing. Our reason for building this Dashboard was to give our Users a simple, intuitive, and attractive point of entry when signing on to our OneStream application. The last thing we need to do is to set this Dashboard as our Users' home page.

There are a few ways to accomplish this. Any individual User, when signed on to the application, can navigate to this Dashboard (or any other page) and click the OneStream logo in the title bar of the current screen (that's the lower of the two logos visible in the upper-right corner of the screen).

Clicking this logo opens a menu that includes the option to Set Current Page As Home Page. For Administrators, there is also an option to Save Home Page Setting As Default for New Users (Figure 11.85).

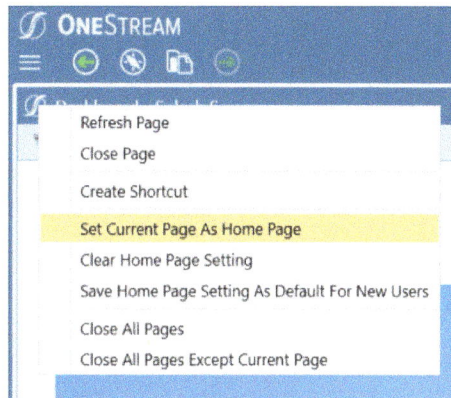

Figure 11.85

And, within the **Administrative Solution Tools** MarketPlace solution, there is a **Home Page Manager** that uses a OneStream Dashboard to provide application Administrators with a simple, intuitive, and attractive way to manage the home pages of the rest of the User community (Figure 11.86).

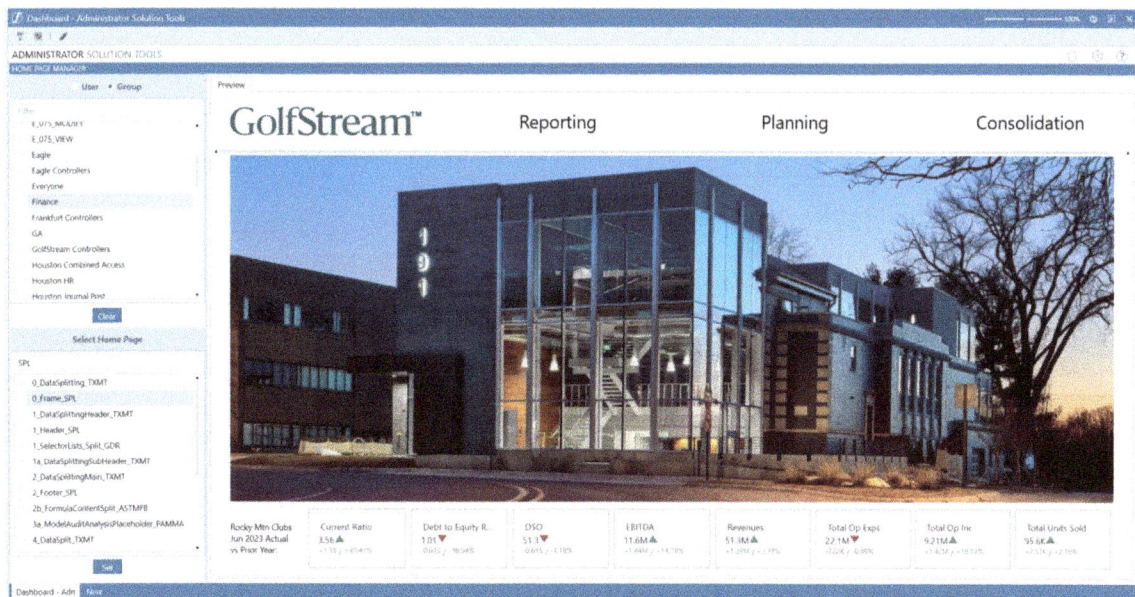

Figure 11.86

Conclusion

Let's step back for a moment and think about what we have just created.

Before we started this chapter, when signing on to the application, our End-Users would have been greeted by a blank screen. If they had some training and a good understanding of the design of our application's underlying model, dimensionality, etc., they would certainly have been able to navigate to any content they were interested in, but the clicks involved wouldn't necessarily have been obvious.

Now, after completing this exercise, our End-Users have a completely different experience. The first thing they see is a clear, clean, inviting, and intuitive home page, with one-click navigation to the reporting content and Workflows they are most concerned with. In turn, they also have up-to-date values for their most critical key performance indicators right on the very first screen.

And(!) we created this without a single line of code. Now that we have mastered the fundamental concepts of Dashboard configuration, we will build on these techniques in the chapters that follow and learn how to create even more sophisticated User Experiences for Executive Dashboards, Financial Planning processes, and more.

12

Executive Dashboards

In this chapter, we will focus on how Dashboards can provide Executives and Managers with quick and easy access to relevant information regarding their organization's performance. This will involve exploring the various Components that make up a Dashboard, such as charts and tables, and how they can be customized to display the necessary information. Additionally, we will touch on the importance of parameterizing Dashboard Components to allow for easy filtering and data navigation. Finally, the chapter will discuss how existing Cube Views can be leveraged as data sources for these Dashboard Components to ensure consistency and accuracy in the information presented.

In the upcoming step-by-step exercise, you will learn how to create an Executive Dashboard similar to the one shown in a standard demo. This Dashboard will display a variety of charts, KPIs, and other relevant content. You will also learn how to add combo boxes and radio buttons to allow for easy filtering and data selection, as well as tabs to facilitate intuitive User navigation. By following the steps in this exercise, you will be able to create a functional and visually appealing Executive Dashboard that can be used to quickly and easily monitor the performance of your organization!

When, Why, and How to use them

Executive Dashboards are designed to provide timely and accurate information about KPI metrics and other business-specific data to streamline financial operations. OneStream provides you with the tools to deliver this efficiency within your organization. With some guidance on how to set up a simple Dashboard, you are sure to walk away with ideas for how your organization can best leverage your application.

Financial signaling is critical in today's volatile economic environment, and Executives require precise and up-to-date information to make informed decisions. By understanding the needs of the User group, the Dashboard design can be customized to provide the most relevant and useful information. This can increase productivity, streamline Workflows, and improve decision-making.

Design Considerations

Effective Dashboard design involves more than just creating an aesthetically pleasing layout. It requires a deep understanding of the intended User group and their needs to ensure that the Dashboard provides actionable and relevant insights.

When creating Dashboards, it is crucial to consider the message you want to convey. It is also essential to understand who your Users are and what information they need to see. Consider whether there are specific actions that need to be taken based on the results displayed or if the Dashboards are for informational purposes only.

Before building Executive Dashboards, it is recommended to collaborate with Executive Users to create an outline of the Dashboard's look and feel. This collaboration will greatly reduce the possibility of rebuilding the Dashboard later on.

Build Your Own

In this exercise, we will construct a tabbed Executive Dashboard comprising four KPIs and three charts. The following are the Components that we will create:

- Labels with conditional formatting and tool tips
- Dialog buttons
- Combo box
- Radio buttons
- Cube Views
- Line Chart
- Waterfall Chart
- Bar Chart
- Data Explorer Report

Layout and Testing Preparation

When building Dashboards, I like to test certain Dashboard Components throughout the build process to see how the individual Components render. Not only does this help me focus on each part of the Dashboard – without the distraction of other parts – but it also helps me determine the size of the Components and how much Dashboard space I need to earmark for the respective Components.

The first step is to create the Dashboard Maintenance Unit (DMU) and a Dashboard called TestingDashboard_Exec as a placeholder for testing the Dashboard Components we will build. Navigate to Dashboards from the Application tab.

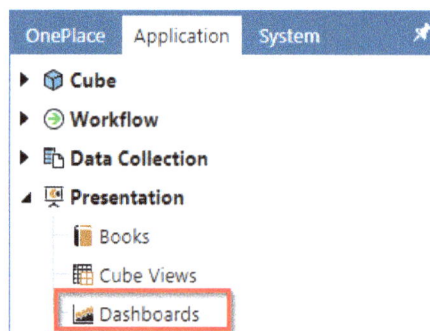

Figure 12.1

Select Maintenance Units and then click Create Maintenance Unit. Give the DMU a name and save.

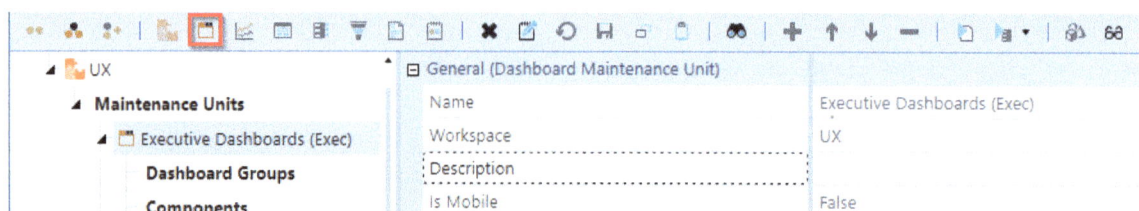

Figure 12.2

Now, select the DMU we created in the previous step and then click Create Group. Give the Dashboard Group a name and save.

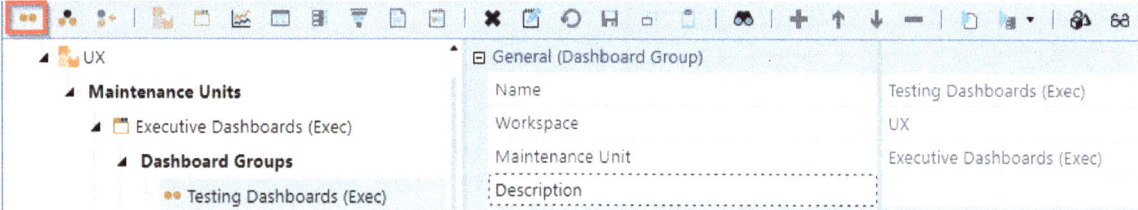

Figure 12.3

Select the Group we created in the previous step and then click Create Dashboard. Give the Dashboard a name and save.

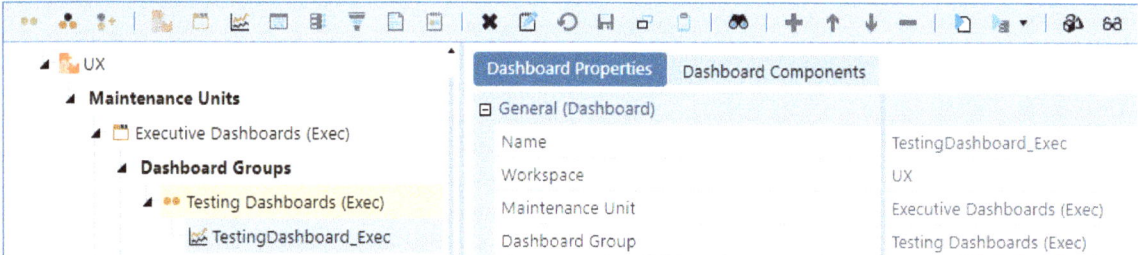

Figure 12.4

Note: This Dashboard will be used in the following steps but will be deleted afterward.

Select the DMU again, then click Create Group. Name the Group Executive Dashboards (Exec).

Figure 12.5

Select the Group we created in the previous step and click Create Dashboard. Name the Dashboard 1_Main_Exec and enter Executive Home as the Description.

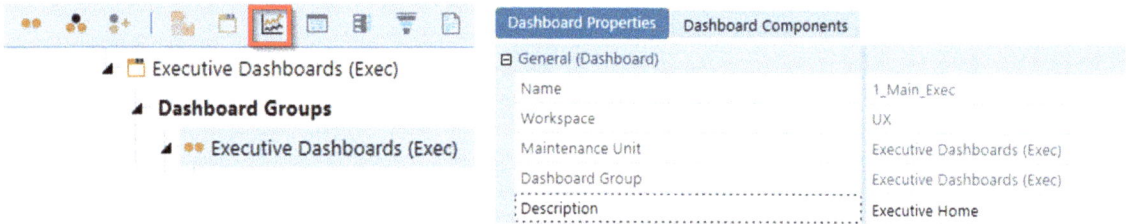

Figure 12.6

Data Adapter

In order to effectively monitor the overall performance of our business, it is important to keep a close eye on Key Performance Indicators (KPIs). To achieve this, we will leverage the Cube View below, which is currently accessible from the Cube Views menu in OnePlace. The Cube View POV will typically be reflective of the Executive's reporting view; however, it can also be parameterized for the Dashboard User if we want them to be able to control the selections.

Figure 12.7

Under the DMU we just created, select Data Adapters and click Create Data Adapter.

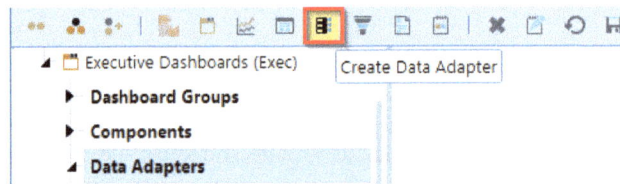

Figure 12.8

Name the data adapter, then select Cube View as the Command Type. Click the Edit button to open the object lookup dialog. Start typing the name of the Cube View KPIs_Exec and you will see the Cube View in the list. Click OK to then save the data adapter.

Figure 12.9

Click the Test Data Adapter button from the menu bar to see what the adapter results display.

Figure 12.10

228

The data adapter displays the following table; we will reference it when creating the labels.

Figure 12.11

Cube View

In future steps, we will create buttons for our KPIs that will open dialog boxes for the KPI Cube View; this step configures the dialog boxes. Select Components and click Create Dashboard Component.

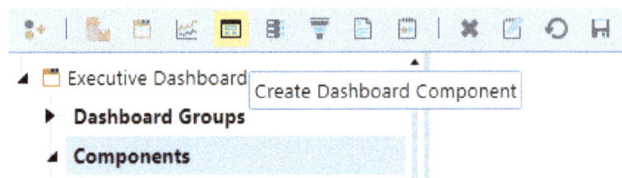

Figure 12.12

Select Cube View from the dialog box and click OK.

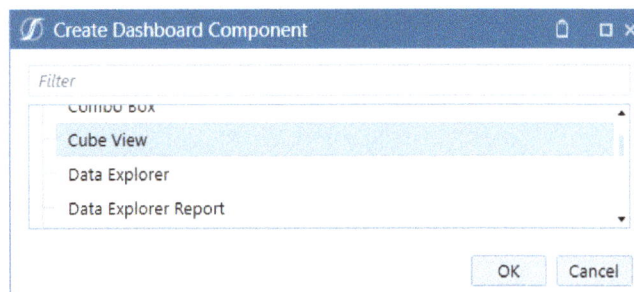

Figure 12.13

Chapter 12

Name the Cube View Component and type KPIs_Exec into the Cube View field.

Figure 12.14

Select Dashboard Groups and click Create Group.

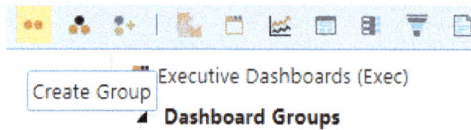

Figure 12.15

Name the Group Dialogs (Exec) and then save.

Figure 12.16

Select the new Dashboard Group and click Create Dashboard, then name the Dashboard KPIs_Exec.

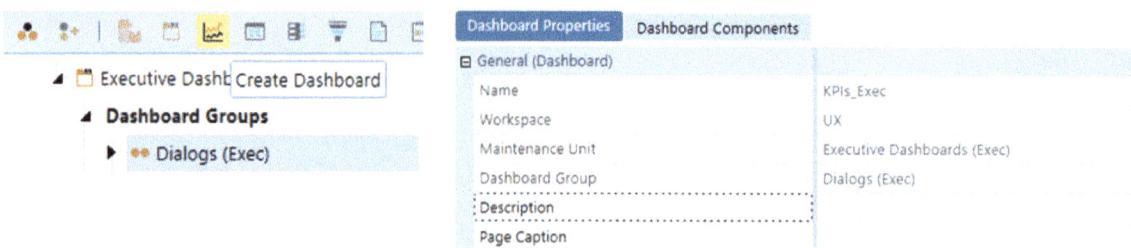

Figure 12.17

Navigate to the Dashboard Components tab and click Add Dashboard Component. Select the Cube View Component we previously created.

Figure 12.18

Labels

To start creating the KPI labels, Select Components and click Create Dashboard Component. Select Label from the dialog box and click OK.

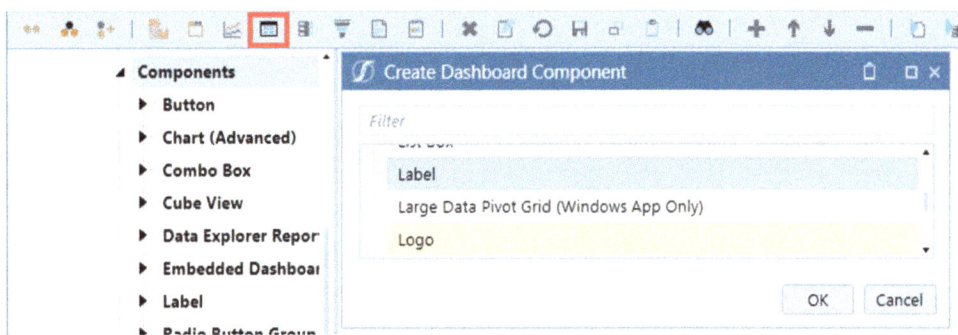

Figure 12.19

Select the Data Adapters tab, then click Add Data Adapter and select the item we created in the previous step.

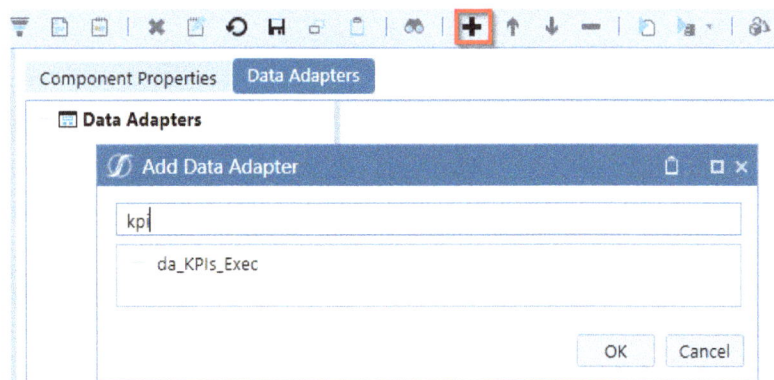

Figure 12.20

Return to the Component Properties tab and enter the properties as shown in Figure 12.21. Notice in the Key Column Value or Row Index field we entered 1; the value entered in this property corresponds to the data table displayed in Figure 12.11. By entering 1, we are querying the data table to display attributes of the Sales Per Employee data record. The Results Column Name property was also selected based on Figure 12.11. The Number Format property allows us to control how the amount is displayed.

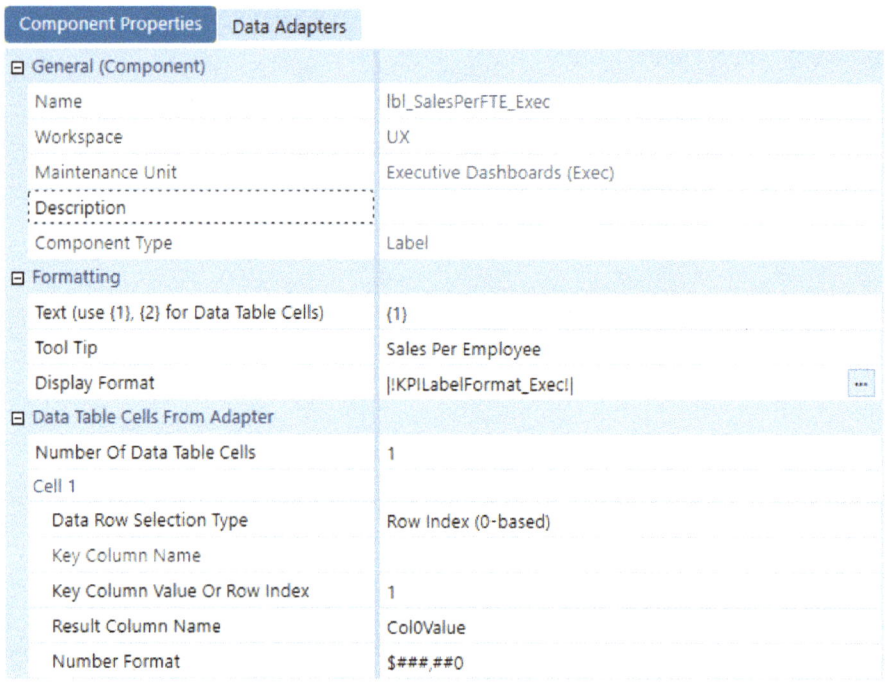

Figure 12.21

We have created our first label. We need three more, so select the label we created and click Copy, then click Paste to create a cloned label.

Figure 12.22

Select the copied label and click Rename Selected Item.

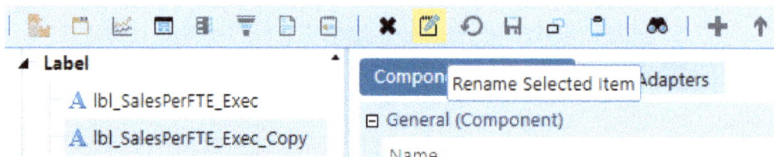

Figure 12.23

Name the new label `lbl_OpMgnPct_Exec` and click OK.

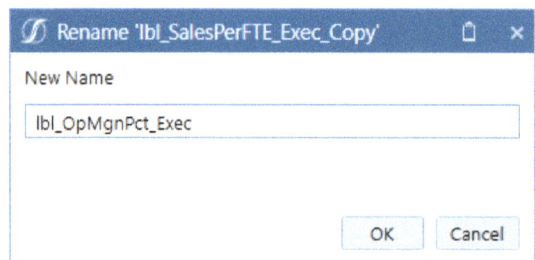

Figure 12.24

Update the Key Column Value or Row Index and Number Format properties, then save.

Figure 12.25

Repeat this process for the two remaining labels; make sure to update the Key Column Value or Row Index and Number Format properties!

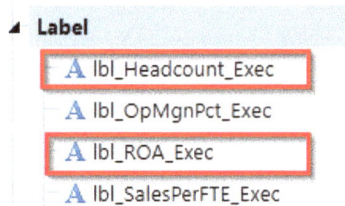

Figure 12.26

> **Note:** The KPILabelformat_Exec parameter uses a Literal Value:
>
> HorizontalAlignment = Center, LabelBold = True, LabelFontSize = 38,
> LabelNegativeTextColor = XFDarkOrange, LabelTextColor = XFMediumBlueText,
> VerticalAlignment = Bottom.

Buttons

Next, we need to create buttons for the four KPIs; these buttons will open the dialog box we created in the Cube Views section previously. Select Components and click Create Dashboard Component. Select Button from the dialog box and click OK.

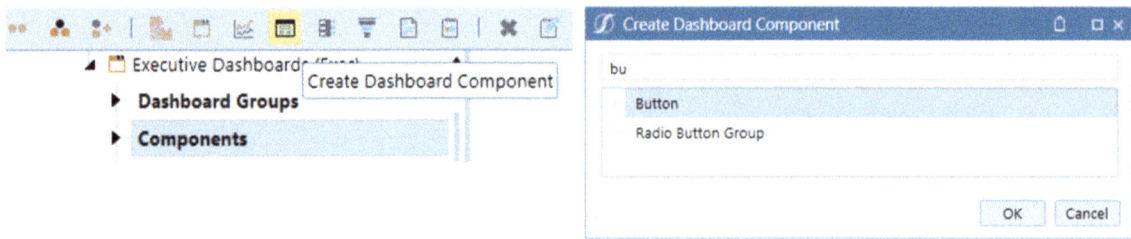

Figure 12.27

Name the button `btn_SalesPerFTE_Exec` and then save.

Figure 12.28

Enter the Text and Tool Tip as shown below. We can also configure the Selection Changed User Interface Action to Refresh and enter `KPIs_Exec` in the Dashboard to Open in Dialog field. This will allow us to open the KPI's Cube View with a button click.

Figure 12.29

Select the button and click Copy, then click Paste to clone the Component.

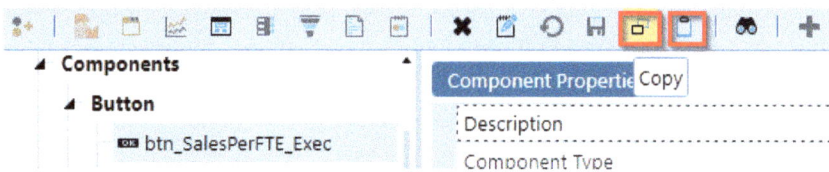

Figure 12.30

Select the copied button and click Rename Selected Item.

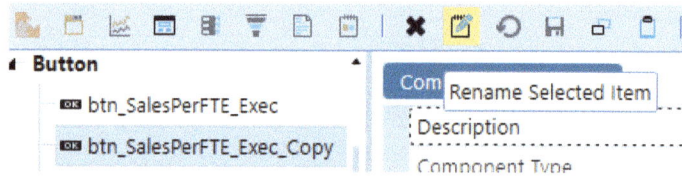

Figure 12.31

Enter `btn_OpMgnPct_Exec` as the new name and click OK.

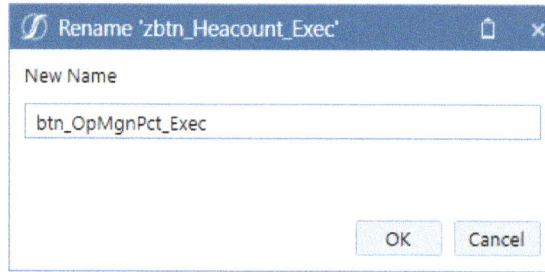

Figure 12.32

Note: The `KPIButtonformat_Exec` parameter uses a Literal Value:

```
BackgroundColor = Transparent, BorderColor = Transparent, FontSize = 12,
HorizontalAlignment = Center, HoverColor = XFLightBlue3, Italic = True,
LabelItalic = True, MarginBottom = 5, TextColor = XFMediumGray,
VerticalAlignment = Top.
```

Repeat this process for the two remaining buttons.

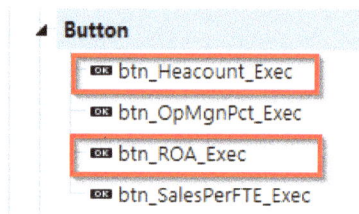

Figure 12.33

We now have four buttons that not only usefully display our KPI information but which also allow our User to click them and be taken to another Dashboard that will show a nice drillable Cube View, where an inquisitive User can query the KPIs and underlying source data should they desire!

Line Chart

Our first chart will be a line chart based on the `GrossMargin_Exec` Cube View. This chart will display a 12-month trend of revenue and expenses, with each line represented by a different color.

This approach will allow us to easily identify the correlation between revenue and expenses and gain a better understanding of the overall financial performance of our business. We will use the data points displayed in the Cube View below as the data source for our chart.

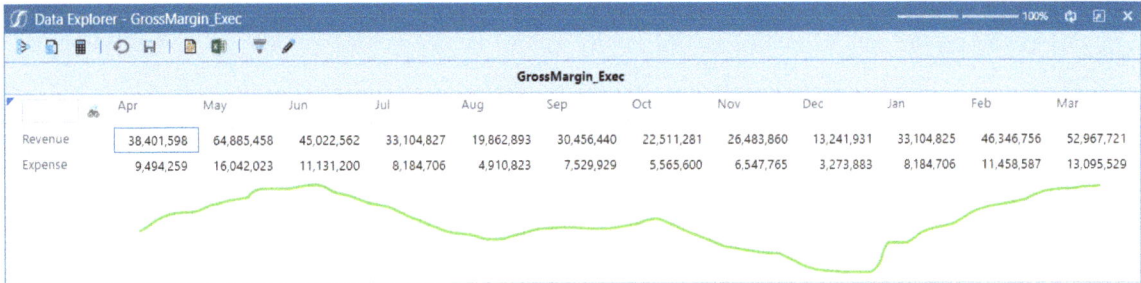

Figure 12.34

First, we need to create a Data Adapter. Select Data Adapters and click Create Data Adapter. Give the data adapter a name, pick the Command Type Cube View and select the Cube View.

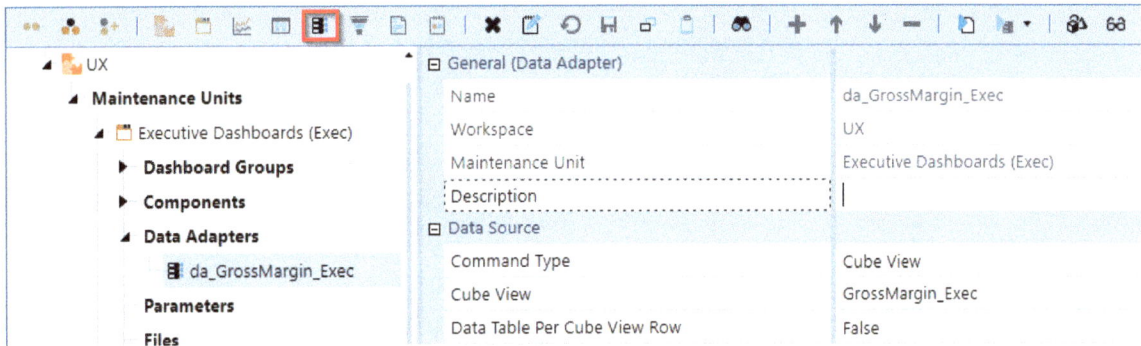

Figure 12.35

Select Components and click Create Dashboard Component. Select Chart (Advanced), then click OK.

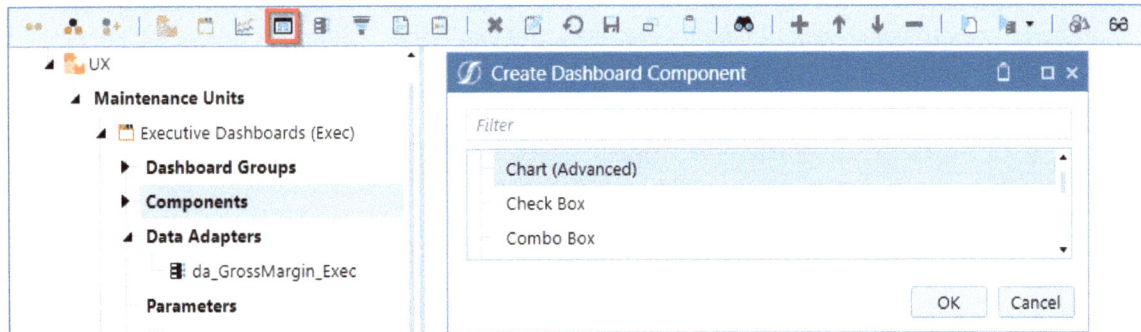

Figure 12.36

Give the chart a name and then select the Data Adapters tab.

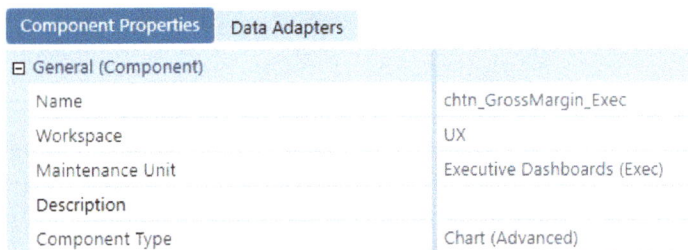

Figure 12.37

Chapter 12

Click Add Dashboard Component, then select the data adapter created in the previous step and save.

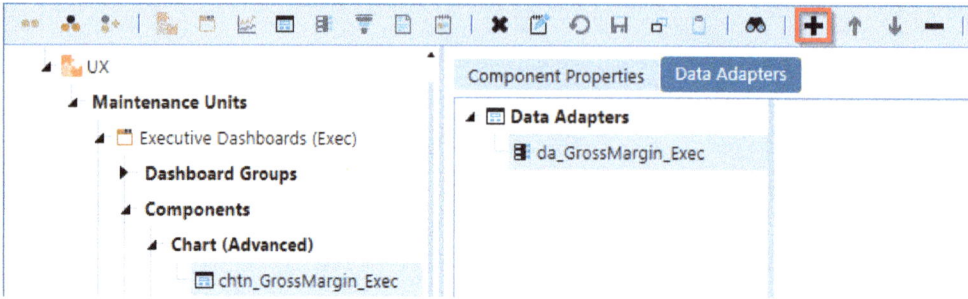

Figure 12.38

This is a great opportunity to stop and review the chart. Navigate to the Dashboard named TestingDashboard_Exec and select the Dashboard Components tab. Click Add Dashboard Component and select the Component chtn_GrossMargin_Exec, then click View Dashboard.

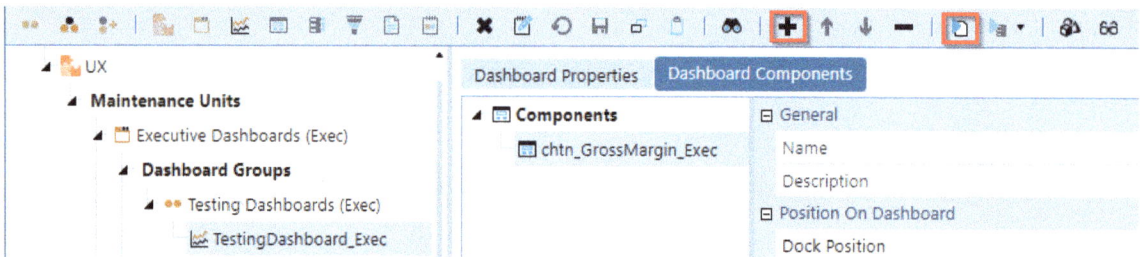

Figure 12.39

Now it's time to get really fancy. Although the initial display of the chart appears satisfactory, we can enhance its visual appeal and optimize its functionality by implementing certain formatting measures available from the UI. Specifically, we may consider relocating the legend above the chart, utilizing varying shades of blue for the lines, and exploring additional line options that are available.

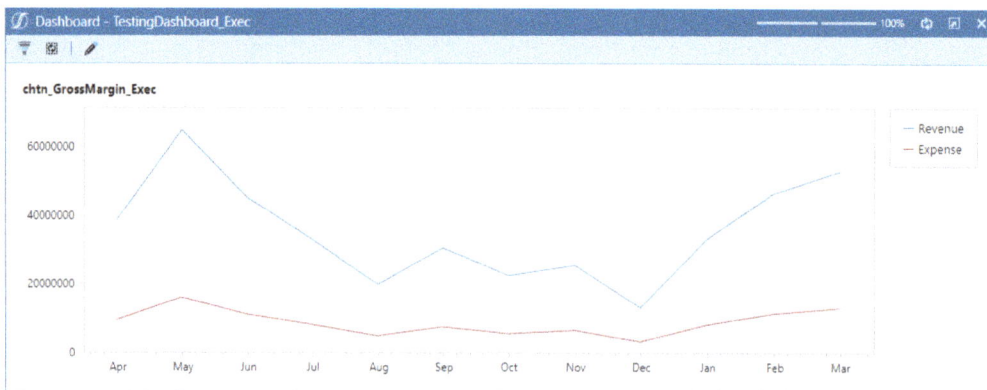

Figure 12.40

The following figure highlights the chart Component properties that we have modified for our line chart. We made the intentional choice to select a spline-type chart under Series Properties to highlight trends and create a more visually appealing Dashboard. These modifications will help us better interpret the data and make informed business decisions. Navigate back to Component Properties and make the following changes.

238

Chart	
Show Toggle Size Button	False
Diagram Type	XY2D
Swap Axes	False
Domain Color	...
Show Point Labels	False
Point Label Text Format	{V:N0}
Enable Animations	False
Show Border	False
Use Clockwise Rotation	True
Legend	
Show Legend	True
Title	
Vertical Position	Top
Horizontal Position	Center
Orientation	Horizontal
Show Check Boxes	False
Show Border	False
Crosshair	
Crosshair Enabled	True
Show Crosshair Lines	False
Show Crosshair Labels	True
Crosshair Label Mode	Show Common For All Series
Crosshair Label Text Format	{S}: ${V:N0}
Series Properties	
Type	Spline
Model Display Type	Basic
Show Markers	True
Marker Size	10
Bar Width	1
Line Thickness	3
Line Style Type	Solid
Pie Hole Radius Percent	0
Series Colors	
Series 1 Color	XFDarkBlueBackground ...
Series 1 Point Colors	XFDarkBlueBackground ...
Series 2 Color	XFDarkGray ...
Series 2 Point Colors	XFDarkGray ...
Chart Data	
Data Series Source Type	Cube View
Suppress Zeros	True
Row List Type	All Rows
Row Index List	
Cube View Data Point Legend Type	Default
Chart Y-Axis	
Show Y-Axis	True
Title	
Text Format	{V:N0}
Label Rotation Angle	0

Figure 12.41

Let's also give our chart a label that describes the data model (so we know what we are looking at). In the chart Component's Description field, type Revenue & Expense Trend, then save the Component.

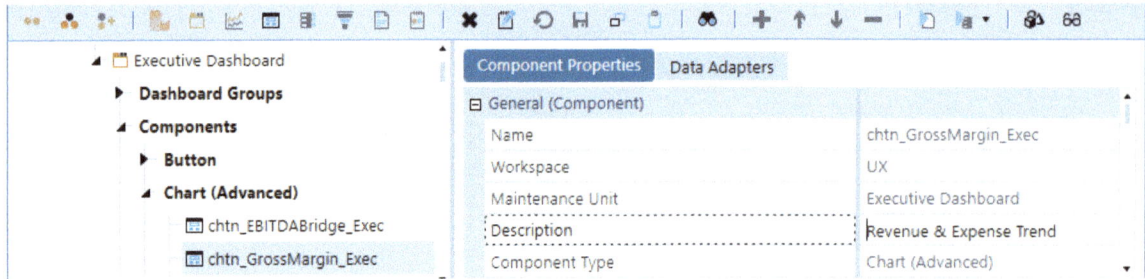

Figure 12.42

After applying our modifications to the chart Component, we can navigate back to the Dashboard and click the View Dashboard button to preview the updates.

The formatted chart now appears more visually cohesive and polished, presenting a significant improvement over its previous iteration. The label tells us what we are looking at, the legend placement gives us more real estate for the actual chart, and the larger markers help identify the data points for easy navigation. The overall look of the chart is more modern and easier to read.

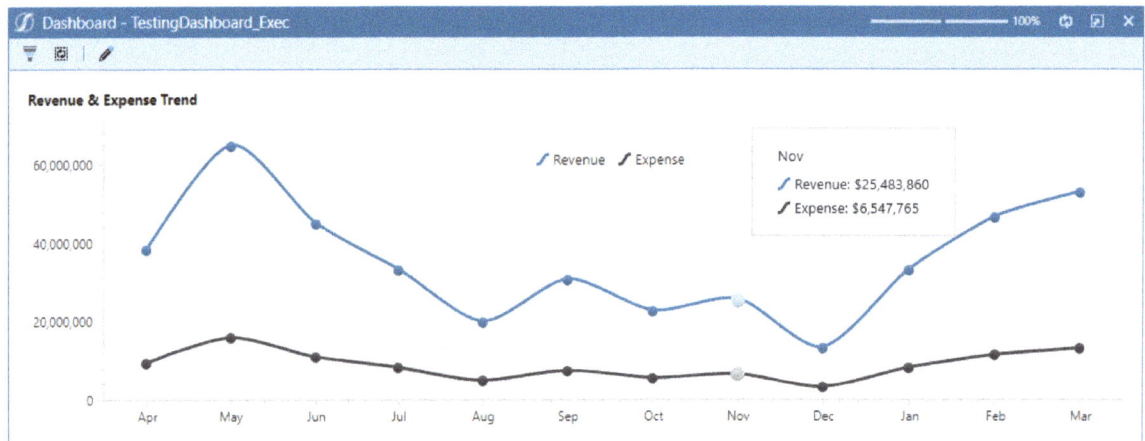

Figure 12.43

Waterfall Chart

Our next Component to build is a waterfall chart demonstrating the prior year's EBITDA walk to the current period EBITDA. The waterfall chart allows us to present this information in a visually impactful manner, which will facilitate decision-making. To do this, we will utilize a Cube View named EBITDABridge_Exec as the data source.

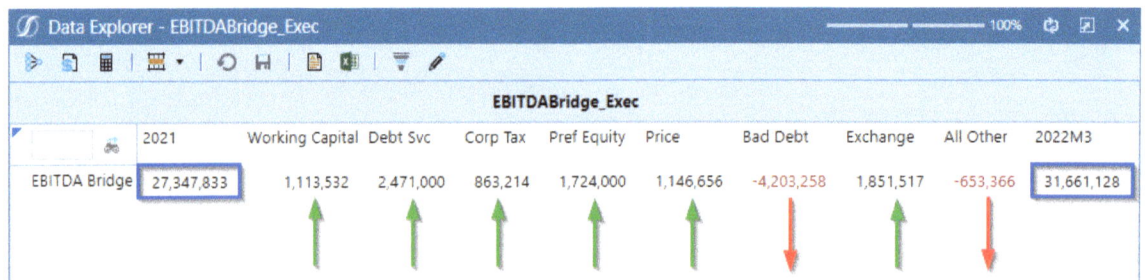

Figure 12.44

As we did for the previous chart, we need to create a Data Adapter for the Cube View. Navigate to Data Adapters and click Create Data Adapter. Give the data adapter a name and save.

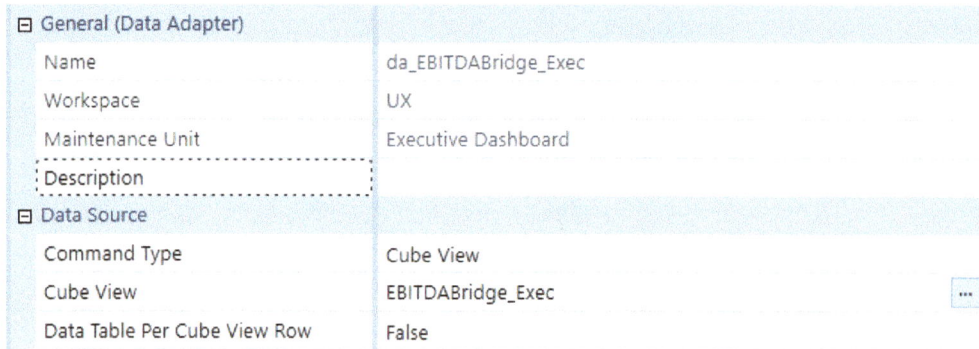

General (Data Adapter)	
Name	da_EBITDABridge_Exec
Workspace	UX
Maintenance Unit	Executive Dashboard
Description	
Data Source	
Command Type	Cube View
Cube View	EBITDABridge_Exec
Data Table Per Cube View Row	False

Figure 12.45

Next, select Components and click Create Dashboard Component for the new chart, just like we did for the previous chart and name the new chart Component (chtn_EBITDABridge_Exec). Select Waterfall as Type under the Series Properties.

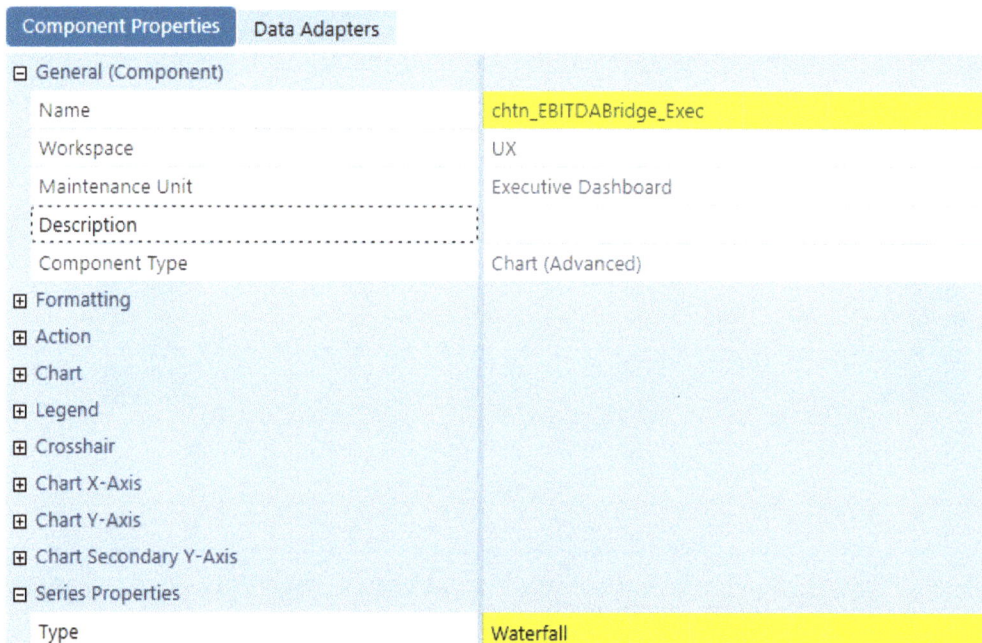

Component Properties	Data Adapters
General (Component)	
Name	chtn_EBITDABridge_Exec
Workspace	UX
Maintenance Unit	Executive Dashboard
Description	
Component Type	Chart (Advanced)
Formatting	
Action	
Chart	
Legend	
Crosshair	
Chart X-Axis	
Chart Y-Axis	
Chart Secondary Y-Axis	
Series Properties	
Type	Waterfall

Figure 12.46

Select the Data Adapters tab and click Add Dashboard Component. Then, select the data adapter that we created in the previous step.

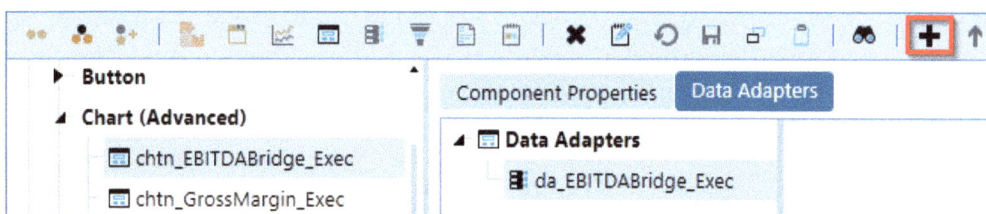

Figure 12.47

241

This is another great opportunity to stop and review the new chart using our handy-dandy testing Dashboard. Navigate to the Dashboard named `TestingDashboard_Exec` and select the Dashboard Components tab. Select the existing Component and click Remove Selected Dashboard Component, then click Add Dashboard Component and select the new chart Component, then click View Dashboard.

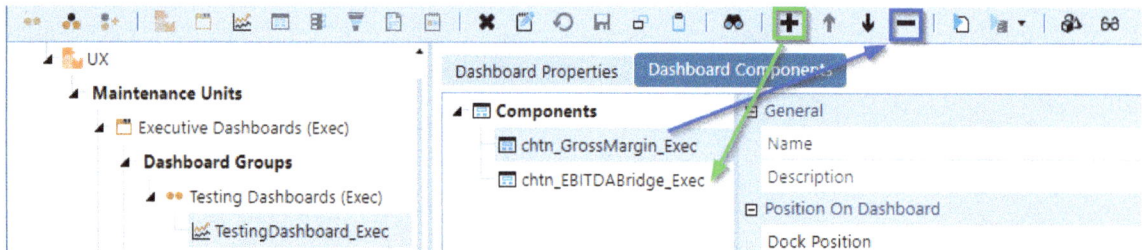

Figure 12.48

The chart looks good, but it could use some adjustments to really polish it. We can give it a title, fix the number format on the Y-axis, remove the legend that is irrelevant to this chart, and change the bar colors to soften the chart up.

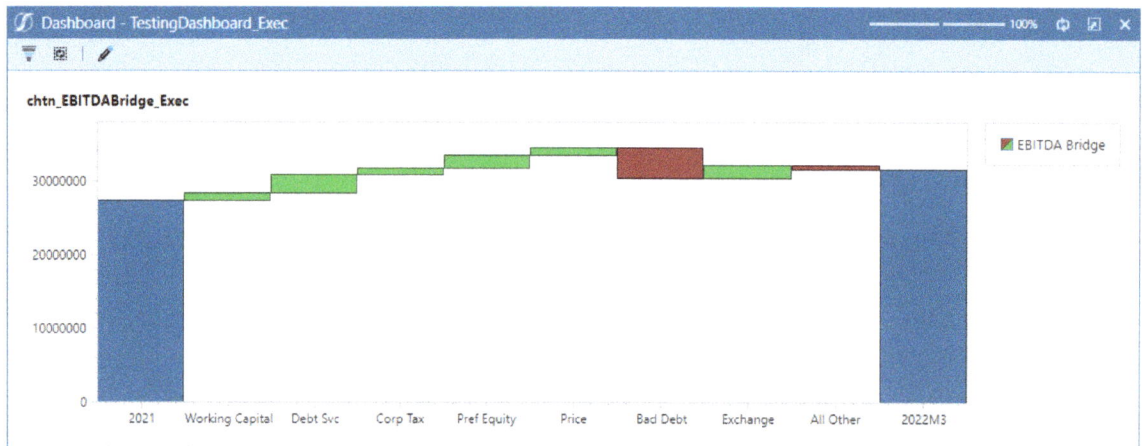

Figure 12.49

The following figure highlights the changes made to the chart Component. Navigate back to Component Properties and make the following changes to the chart Component.

Figure 12.50

After making these changes, navigate back to the Dashboard named `TestingDashboard_Exec` and click View Dashboard.

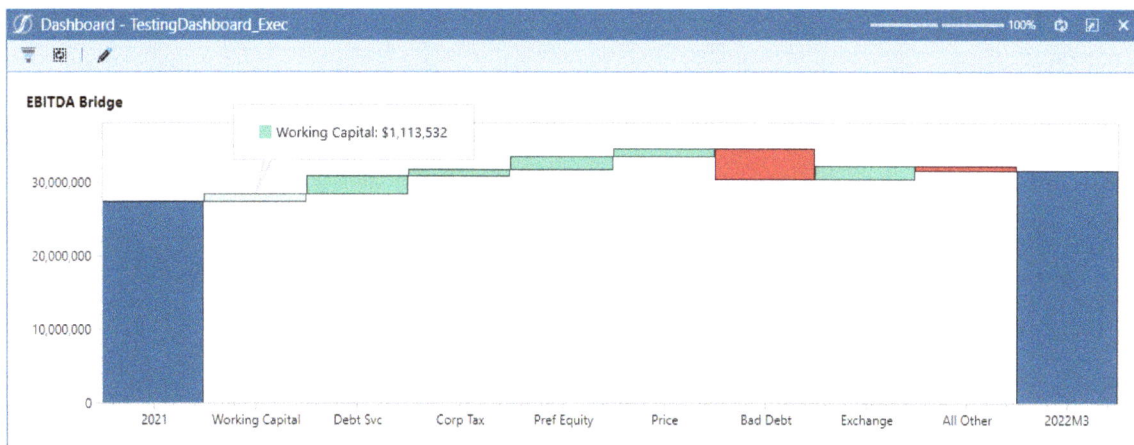

Figure 12.51

Chapter 12

Bar Chart

The final chart we need to build is a bar chart that displays Actual Sales compared to Budget. We want to make this chart dynamic with radio buttons to show sales by region and sales by product; this will allow us to use less real estate on the Dashboard without sacrificing either chart. The Cube View below shows the Sales by Region Cube View that will serve as the data source for the first data set.

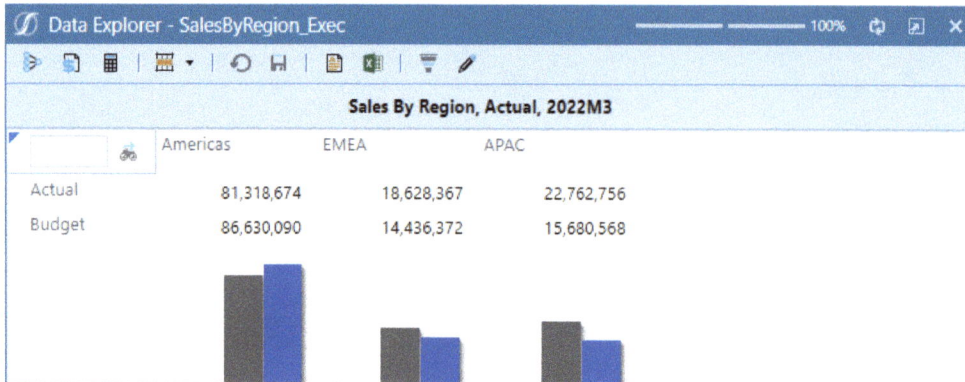

Figure 12.52

Navigate to Data Adapters and click Create Data Adapter. Give the data adapter a name and then save. The naming of the data adapter is crucial to allow parameterization, so consistency is key.

General (Data Adapter)	
Name	da_SalesByRegion_Exec
Workspace	UX
Maintenance Unit	Executive Dashboards (Exec)
Description	
Data Source	
Command Type	Cube View
Cube View	SalesByRegion_Exec
Data Table Per Cube View Row	False

Figure 12.53

The next Cube View shows the Sales by Product Cube View that will serve as the data source for the second data set.

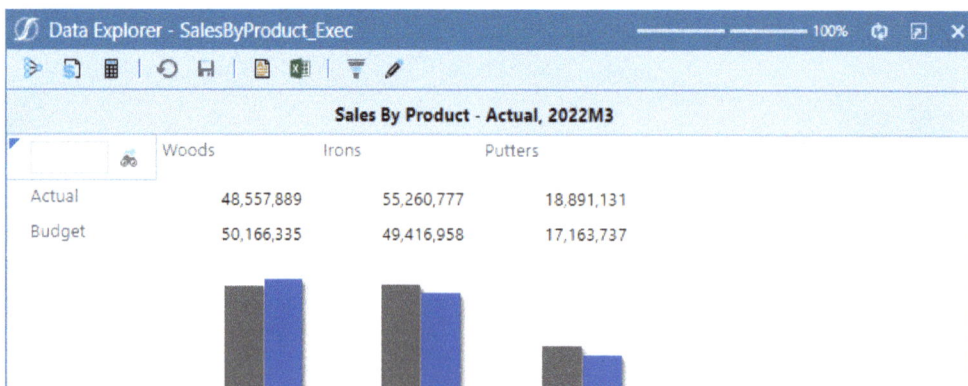

Figure 12.54

Again, select Data Adapters and click Create Data Adapter to create the second data source data adapter. Give the data adapter a name and save.

General (Data Adapter)	
Name	da_SalesByProduct_Exec
Workspace	UX
Maintenance Unit	Executive Dashboards (Exec)
Description	
Data Source	
Command Type	Cube View
Cube View	SalesByProduct_Exec
Data Table Per Cube View Row	False

Figure 12.55

Normally the next step would be to create a chart Component, but in order to make this chart dynamic, we need to use a data adapter that will query the data source based on a radio button selection.

The next step is to create a parameter for our two data adapters that will be passed into the final data adapter. Navigate to Parameters and click Create Parameter, then create the parameter as shown below. Notice that we set the Default Value to Region; this means that when a Dashboard Component uses this parameter, it will initially display Region as the selection.

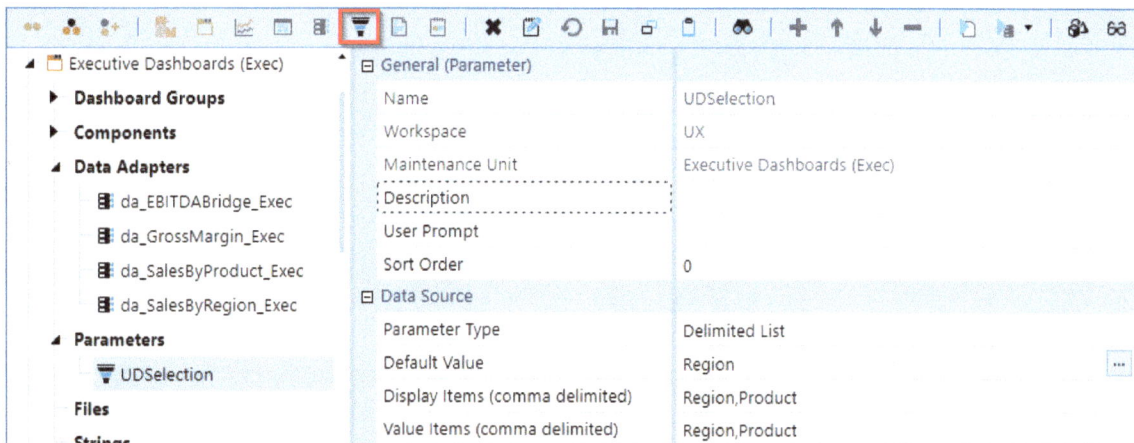

Figure 12.56

Before we can create the final data adapter, we need to create a Business Rule that will pass in the parameterized data adapters. You're probably asking, "Do I really *need* to use a Business Rule to create a chart?" Nope! You can create beautiful, dynamic, interactive charts by configuring chart Components with absolutely no coding. For this example, we're simply showing another method for configuring how a chart is displayed to give you the tools to get even more creative.

The benefit of using this method is that we only need to create one chart Component with a parameterized data adapter that will call the selected data adapter at run-time. An alternative approach would be to create two separate chart Components and attach the respective Product and Region data adapters to them. But, for the sake of maintenance, we've decided to leverage a single chart Component which also keeps our DMU decluttered. Business Rules are not for everyone, and the best part is that you don't need them – keep that in mind as we go through this next example.

From the Application tab, select Business Rules under Tools, and click Create Business Rule.

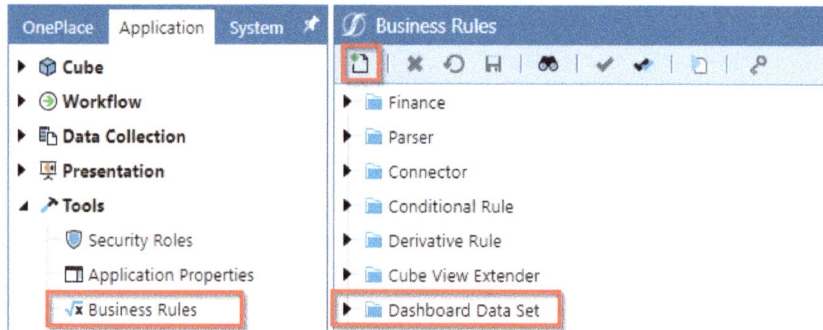

Figure 12.57

Select Dashboard Data Set under Type and name the Business Rule, then click OK. This is the name of the Business Rule that our data adapter will use to render the chart Component.

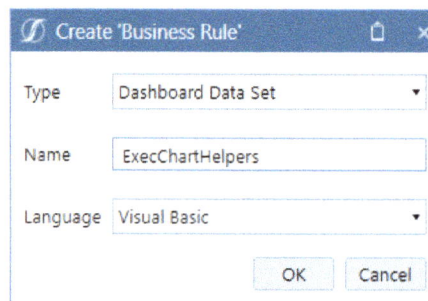

Figure 12.58

Below is the syntax used to control the chart Component; these properties will be used in the next data adapter we will create.

```vb
Namespace OneStream.BusinessRule.DashboardDataSet.ExecChartHelpers

    Public Class MainClass
        Public Function Main(ByVal si As SessionInfo, ByVal globals As BRGlobals,
ByVal api As Object, ByVal args As DashboardDataSetArgs) As Object
        Try
            Select Case args.FunctionType
                Case Is = DashboardDataSetFunctionType.GetDataSet
                    If args.DataSetName.XFEqualsIgnoreCase("BarFormat") Then

    Dim oSeriesCollection As New XFSeriesCollection()
    Dim DataAdapter As String = args.NameValuePairs.XFGetValue("DataAdapter")

    oSeriesCollection.FillUsingCubeViewDataAdapter(si, False, "UX", DataAdapter,
    xfdataRowlistType.AllRows,String.Empty,xfChartCubeViewDataPointLegendType.Defa
    ult,False,XFChart2seriesType.BarSideBySide, args.CustomSubstVars)

    Dim sequence As Integer = 0
        For Each oSeries As XFSeries In oSeriesCollection.Series
            oSeries.BarWidth   = 0.7
            oSeries.ModelType  = XFChart2ModelType.BarRange2DSimple
            oseries.Color       = Me.chartColors(si,sequence)
            sequence            = sequence + 1
        Next
    Return oSeriesCollection.CreateDataSet(si)

                    End If
                End Select
            Return Nothing
        Catch ex As Exception
            Throw ErrorHandler.LogWrite(si, New XFException(si, ex))
        End Try
End Function
```

```
#Region "Helpers"
Private Function chartColors(ByVal si As SessionInfo, ByVal sequence As Integer)
    Try
        Dim colorArray(34) As String
            colorArray(0)  = "#FF787778"   'grey
            colorArray(1)  = "#FF3172AF"   'blue
        Return colorArray(sequence)
        Catch ex As Exception
            Throw ErrorHandler.LogWrite(si, New XFException(si, ex))
        End Try
End Function
#End Region

End Class
End Namespace
```

Next, we need to create the data adapter to query our parameterized data set. Unlike the previous data adapters we created, this data adapter will use a **Method Command Type** and **Business Rule Method Type**. The reason for this is that we cannot parameterize the Cube View data adapter; they must be explicitly selected from the Cube View Inventory.

In order to use the Business Rule Method Type, we need to populate the Method Query field with a Business Rule, Data Set Name, and Optional Name-Value pairs. Notice the third section in the string includes the parameter we created to query Region or Product; this will control the data adapter that is passed into our Business Rule.

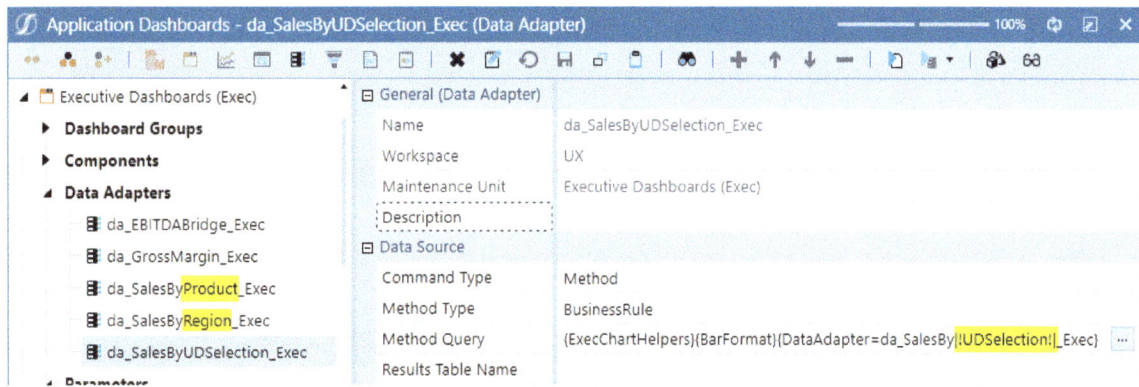

Figure 12.59

We can test our data adapter by clicking Test Data Adapter. You should see a dialog box appear with the parameter options we listed in the parameter `!!UDSelection!!`. Click OK.

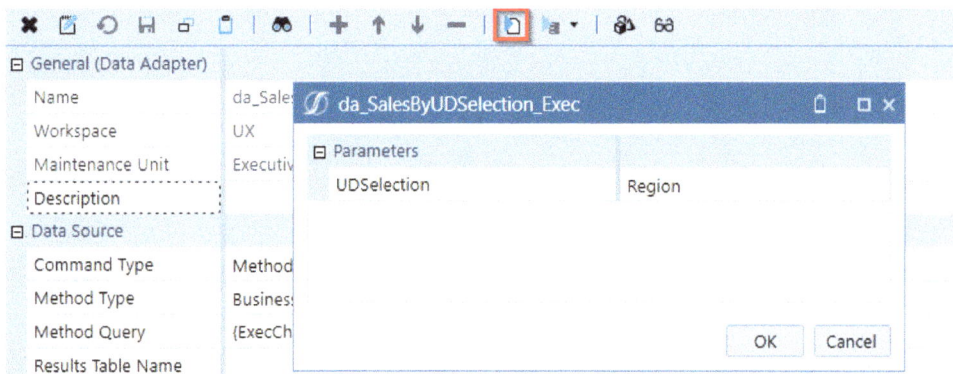

Figure 12.60

Chapter 12

The result will show the Original Query and Substituted Query. Notice the Substituted Query shows the name of the `da_SalesByRegion_Exec` data adapter; this tells us our parameter is working as expected, and the Series being populated tells us that the query is returning data.

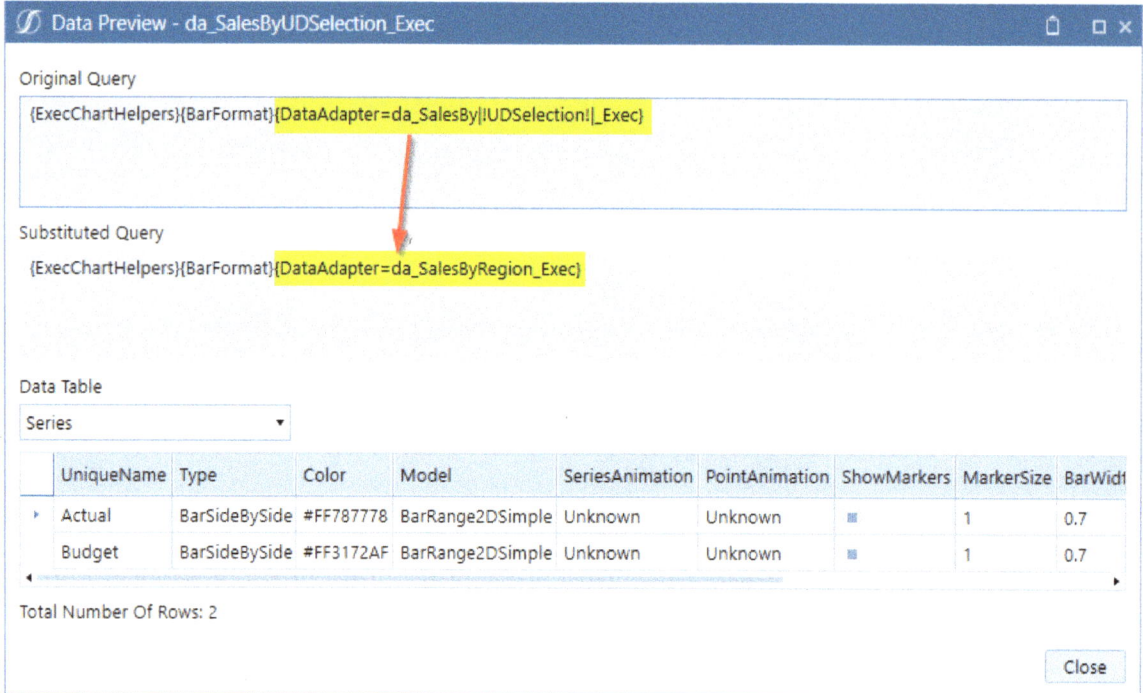

Figure 12.61

To create the chart, navigate to Components and click Create Dashboard Component. Select Chart (Advanced) and name the chart Component. Finally, select the Data Adapters tab, click Add Dashboard Component, and select the newly created data adapter.

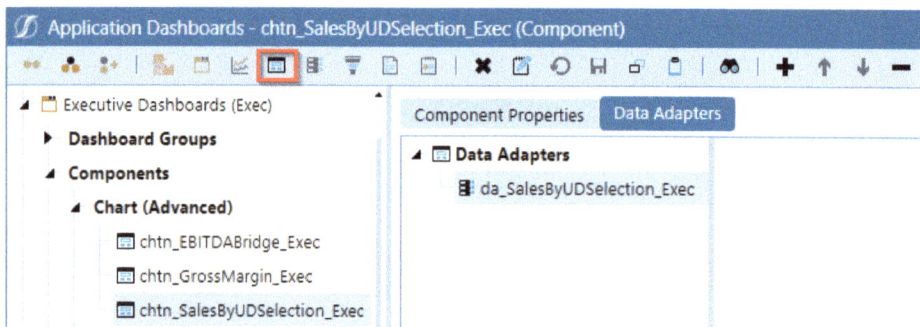

Figure 12.62

Navigate back to the Component Properties and make the following changes to the chart Component.

Component Properties	Data Adapters	
General (Component)		
Name	chtn_SalesByUDSelection_Execold	
Workspace	UX	
Maintenance Unit	Executive Dashboards (Exec)	
Description	Sales By |!UDSelection!|	
Component Type	Chart (Advanced)	
Formatting		
Action		
Chart		
Show Toggle Size Button	False	
Diagram Type	XY2D	
Swap Axes	True	
Domain Color		...
Show Point Labels	False	
Point Label Text Format	{V}	
Enable Animations	False	
Show Border	False	
Use Clockwise Rotation	True	
Legend		
Show Legend	True	
Title		
Vertical Position	Center	
Horizontal Position	Right	
Orientation	Vertical	
Show Check Boxes	True	
Show Border	False	
Chart Y-Axis		
Show Y-Axis	True	
Title		
Text Format	{V:N0}	
Label Rotation Angle	0	
Logarithmic	False	
Logarithmic Base	10	
Use Automatic Range	True	
Minimum Value	0	
Maximum Value	100	
Use Automatic Step	True	
Step	10	
Reverse Order	False	
Interlaced	False	
Interlaced Color		...
Show Grid Lines	False	
Show Minor Grid Lines	False	
Scale Break Style Type	(Not Used)	
Maximum Number of Scale Breaks	0	
Chart Secondary Y-Axis		
Series Properties		
Waterfall Series Properties		
Series Colors		
Chart Data		
Data Series Source Type	Business Rule	
Suppress Zeros	False	
Row List Type	All Rows	
Row Index List		
Cube View Data Point Legend Type	Default	

Figure 12.63

249

Next, we will create the radio button group to surface the parameter for use on a Dashboard. Navigate to Components and click Create Dashboard Component. Enter the parameter we created (see Figure 12.56) in the Bound Parameter field, and set the Selection Changed User Interface Action to Refresh.

Component Properties	
⊟ General (Component)	
Name	rbg_UDSelection_Exec
Workspace	UX
Maintenance Unit	Executive Dashboards (Exec)
Description	
Component Type	Radio Button Group
⊟ Formatting	
Text	Sales By:
Tool Tip	
Display Format	HorizontalAlignment = Center, IsHorizontalOrientation = True, LabelBold = True, LabelPosition = Left ···
⊟ Action	
Bound Parameter	UDSelection ···
Apply Selected Value To Current Dashboard	True
Save Action	
Selection Changed Save Action	No Action
Selection Changed Save Arguments	···
POV Action	
Selection Changed POV Action	No Action
Selection Changed POV Arguments	···
Server Task	
Selection Changed Server Task	No Task
Selection Changed Server Task Arguments	···
User Interface Action	
Selection Changed User Interface Action	Refresh

Figure 12.64

Data Explorer Report

The last thing we need to build is the Financial Statement for the second tab. Click Create Data Adapter, name the data adapter and select Cube View for the Command Type, then select the Cube View below.

⊟ General (Data Adapter)	
Name	da_IncomeStatement_Exec
Workspace	Default
Maintenance Unit	A_XFT Actor Workspaces (AWSe1)
Description	
⊟ Data Source	
Command Type	Cube View
Cube View	IncomeStatement_Exec

Figure 12.65

Select Components, click Create Dashboard Component, select Data Explorer Report, then click OK. Name the Component and enter Income Statement as the description.

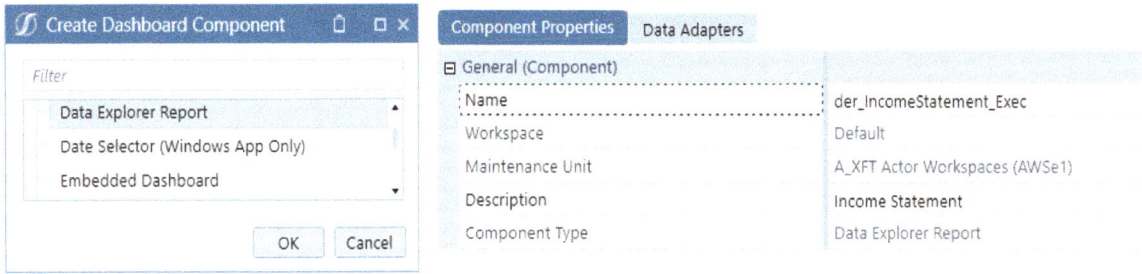

Figure 12.66

Click on the Data Adapters tab of the Component and click the Add Dashboard Component button. Select the data adapter we created in the previous step, da_IncomeStatement_Exec, and then save the Component.

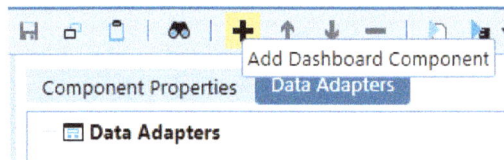

Figure 12.67

Navigate to the Dashboard Group and click the Create Dashboard button from the menu bar. Name the Dashboard 2b_FinancialStatements_Exec and save.

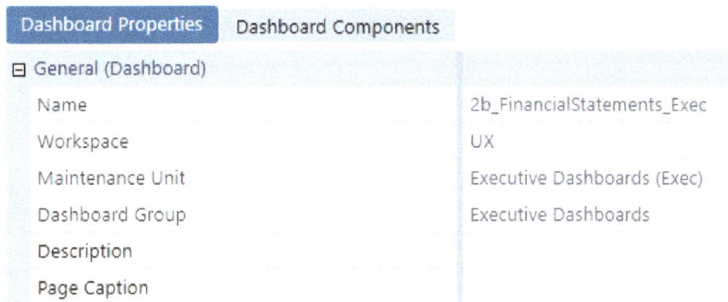

Figure 12.68

Select the Dashboard Components tab and click Add Dashboard Component, then select der_IncomeStatement_Exec to attach the Data Explorer Report.

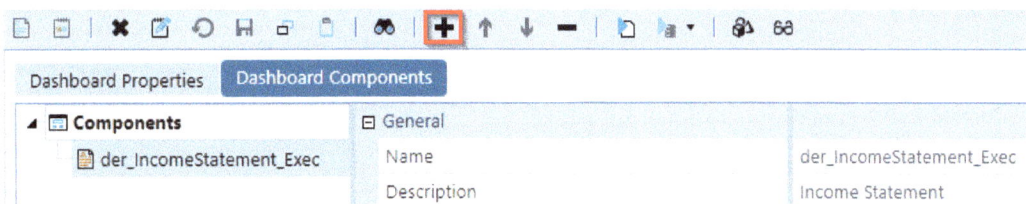

Figure 12.69

To provide additional flexibility, we will create a parameter and combo box to filter the Dashboard's data by Entity. Navigate to Parameters and click Create Parameter.

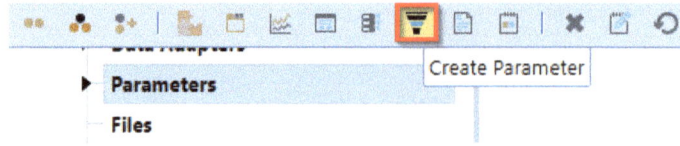

Figure 12.70

Enter `EntitySelection` as the parameter name and make the following selections to create the parameter that will be used to filter the data based on the combo box selection.

General (Parameter)	
Name	EntitySelection
Workspace	UX
Maintenance Unit	Executive Dashboards (Exec)
Description	
User Prompt	
Sort Order	0
Data Source	
Parameter Type	Member List
Default Value	Houston
Display Member	
Cube	GolfStream
Dimension Type	Entity
Dimension	CorpEntities
Member Filter	E#[Houston].Tree

Figure 12.71

Navigate to Components and click Create Dashboard Component. Select Combo Box from the dialog window, then set the following Component properties.

Figure 12.72

In order to apply the parameter to our Dashboard, we need to update the Cube Views we are using in the data adapters. Navigate to Cube Views from the Application Menu.

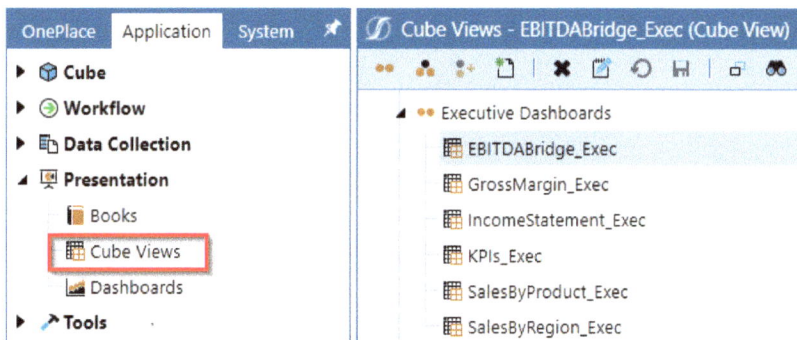

Figure 12.73

On each of the Cube Views, open the Point of View and type in ||!EntitySelection!|| for the Entity Filter.

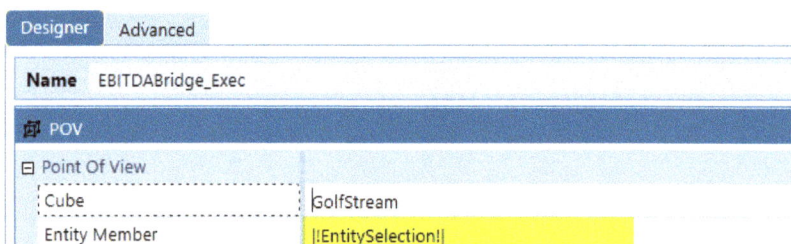

Figure 12.74

Chapter 12

Dashboard Layout

Now we are ready to bring the Components together and create the layout for our Dashboard. Navigate to the `Executive Dashboards (Exec)` Dashboard Group and click Create Dashboard.

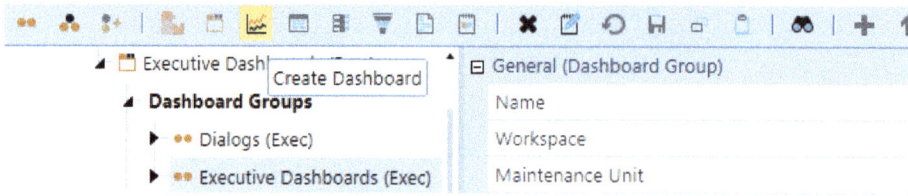

Figure 12.75

Name the Dashboard `2a_Header_Exec` and pick Layout Type as Grid with 1 row and 2 columns.

Dashboard Properties	Dashboard Components
General (Dashboard)	
Name	2a_Header_Exec
Workspace	UX
Maintenance Unit	Executive Dashboards (Exec)
Dashboard Group	Executive Dashboards (Exec)
Description	
Page Caption	
Formatting	
Layout Type	Grid
Is Initially Visible If Embedded	True
Display Format	
Show Title	True
Literal Parameter Values	
Name Value Pairs (e.g., Param1=Value1, ...)	
Action (Primary Dashboard Only)	
Server Task	
Load Dashboard Server Task	No Task
Load Dashboard Server Task Arguments	
Grid Layout Type	
Number Of Rows	1
Number Of Columns	2
Row 1	
Row 1 Type	Component
Row 1 Height (e.g., 150, *, 2*, Auto)	*
Column 1	
Column 1 Type	Component
Column 1 Width (e.g., 150, *, 2*, Auto)	*
Column 2	
Column 2 Type	Component
Column 2 Width	*

Figure 12.76

254

Click on the Dashboard Components tab and click Add Dashboard Component, then add the two items shown below.

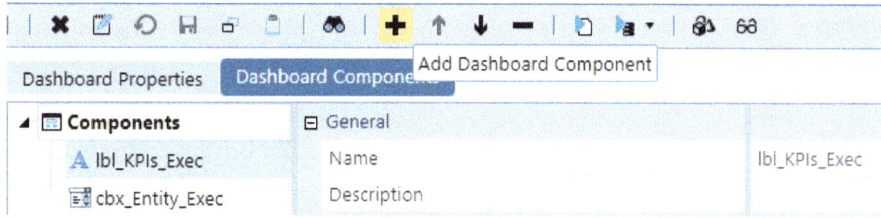

Figure 12.77

Use the copy and paste function to clone the 2a_Header_Exec Dashboard, then rename the copied Dashboard 2a1_KPIs_Exec and change the Number of Rows and Number of Columns.

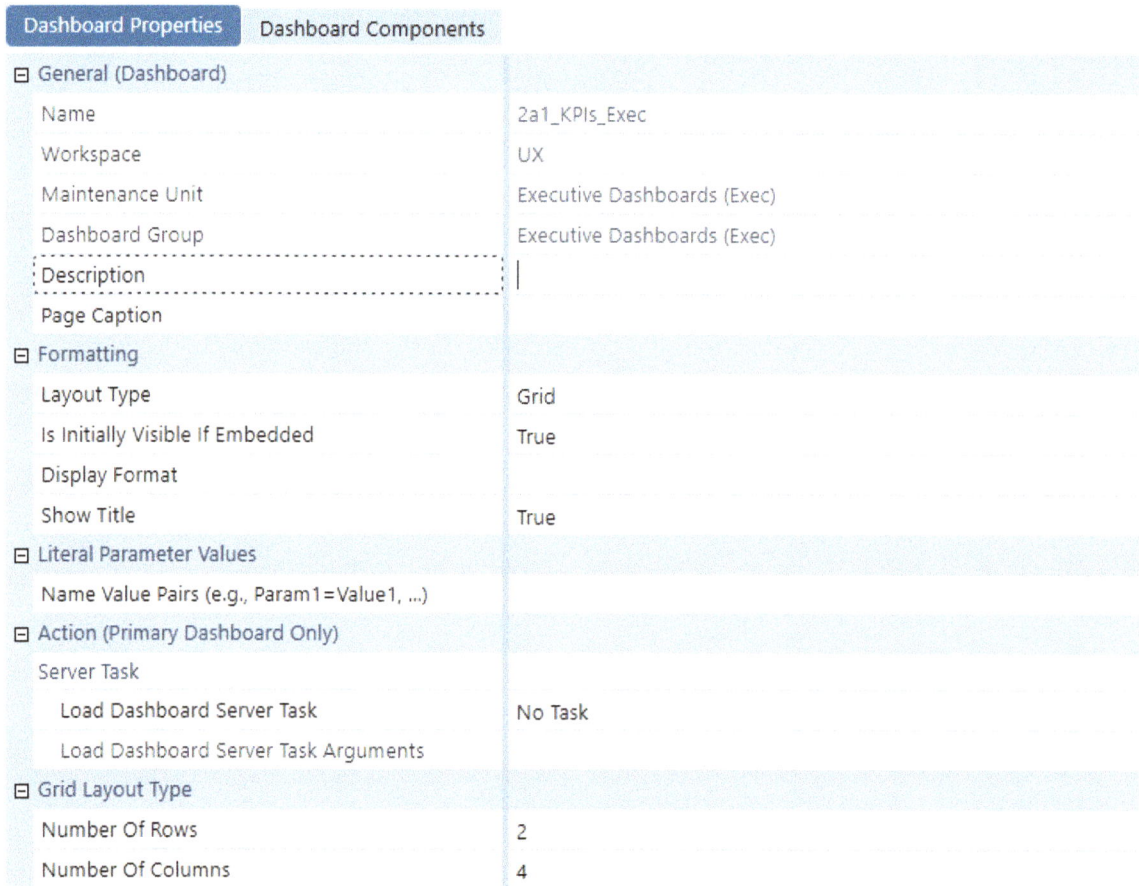

Figure 12.78

Click on the Dashboard Components tab and click Remove Selected Dashboard Component twice to remove the copied Components from the new Dashboard.

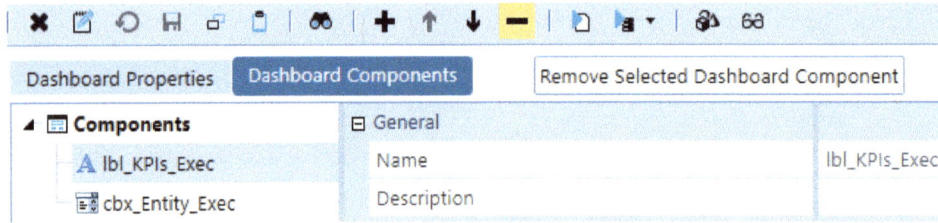

Figure 12.79

Click Add Dashboard Component, then select the four labels and four buttons we created for the KPIs.

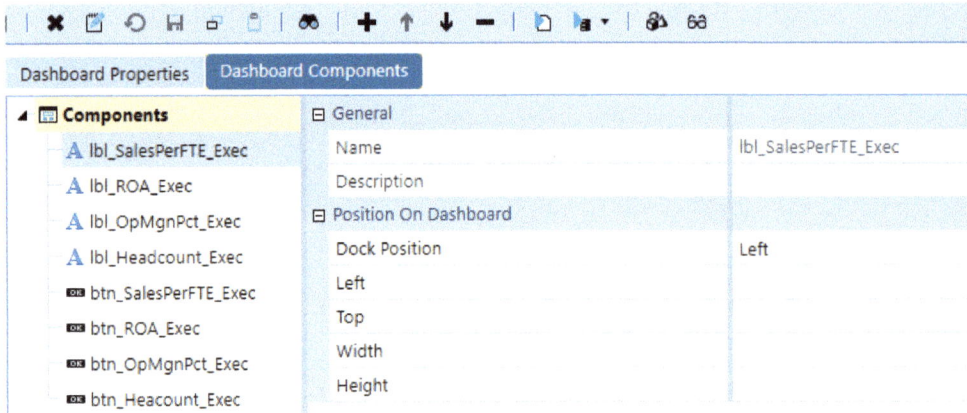

Figure 12.80

Use the copy and paste function to clone the 2a1_KPIs_Exec Dashboard, then rename the copied Dashboard 2a2a_ChartsLeft_Exec and change the Number of Rows and Number of Columns.

Dashboard Properties	Dashboard Components	
⊟ General (Dashboard)		
Name	2a2a_ChartsLeft_Exec	
Workspace	UX	
Maintenance Unit	Executive Dashboards (Exec)	
Dashboard Group	Executive Dashboards (Exec)	
Description		
Page Caption		
⊟ Formatting		
Layout Type	Grid	
Is Initially Visible If Embedded	True	
Display Format		
Show Title	True	
⊟ Literal Parameter Values		
Name Value Pairs (e.g., Param1=Value1, ...)		
⊟ Action (Primary Dashboard Only)		
Server Task		
Load Dashboard Server Task	No Task	
Load Dashboard Server Task Arguments		
⊟ Grid Layout Type		
Number Of Rows	2	
Number Of Columns	1	
Row 1		
Row 1 Type	Component	
Row 1 Height (e.g., 150, *, 2*, Auto)	*	
Row 2		
Row 2 Type	Component	
Row 2 Height	*	
Column 1		
Column 1 Type	Component	
Column 1 Width (e.g., 150, *, 2*, Auto)	*	

Figure 12.81

Click on the Dashboard Components tab and click Remove Selected Dashboard Component eight times to remove the copied Components from the new Dashboard. Click Add Dashboard Component, then select the chart Components shown below.

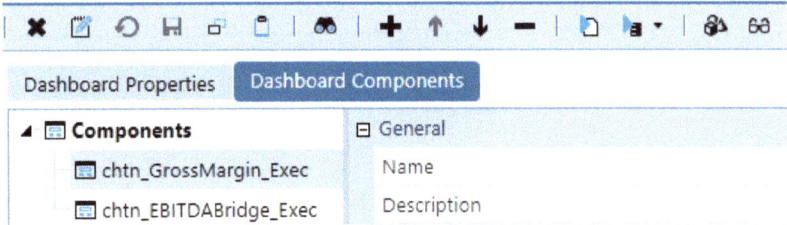

Figure 12.82

Use the copy and paste function to clone 2a2a_ChartsLeft_Exec to a new Dashboard, then rename the new Dashboard 2a2b_ChartsRight_Exec and change the Row 1 Height setting to Auto, as shown below.

Dashboard Properties	Dashboard Components

General (Dashboard)

Name	2a2b_ChartsRight_Exec
Workspace	UX
Maintenance Unit	Executive Dashboards (Exec)
Dashboard Group	Executive Dashboards (Exec)
Description	Sales
Page Caption	Sales

Formatting

Layout Type	Grid
Is Initially Visible If Embedded	True
Display Format	
Show Title	True

Literal Parameter Values

Name Value Pairs (e.g., Param1=Value1, ...)	

Action (Primary Dashboard Only)

Server Task

Load Dashboard Server Task	No Task
Load Dashboard Server Task Arguments	

Grid Layout Type

Number Of Rows	2
Number Of Columns	1
Row 1	
Row 1 Type	Component
Row 1 Height (e.g., 150, *, 2*, Auto)	Auto
Row 2	
Row 2 Type	Component
Row 2 Height	*
Column 1	
Column 1 Type	Component
Column 1 Width (e.g., 150, *, 2*, Auto)	*

Figure 12.83

Click on the Dashboard Components tab and click Remove Selected Dashboard Component twice to remove the copied Components from the new Dashboard. Click Add Dashboard Component, then select the radio button Component and chart Component shown below.

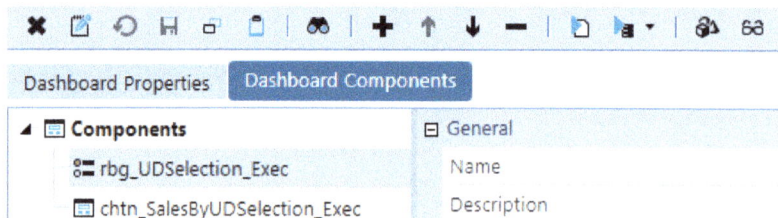

Figure 12.84

Use the copy and paste function to clone 2a2b_ChartsRight_Exec to a new Dashboard, then rename the copied Dashboard 2a2_Charts_Exec and change the Number of Rows and Number of Columns, as well as the Row 1 Height and Column 1 Width. The result is shown below.

Dashboard Properties	Dashboard Components	
⊟ General (Dashboard)		
Name	2a2_Charts_Exec	
Workspace	UX	
Maintenance Unit	Executive Dashboards (Exec)	
Dashboard Group	Executive Dashboards (Exec)	
Description		
Page Caption		
⊟ Formatting		
Layout Type	Grid	
Is Initially Visible If Embedded	True	
Display Format		
Show Title	True	
⊟ Literal Parameter Values		
Name Value Pairs (e.g., Param1=Value1, ...)		
⊟ Action (Primary Dashboard Only)		
Server Task		
Load Dashboard Server Task	No Task	
Load Dashboard Server Task Arguments		
⊟ Grid Layout Type		
Number Of Rows	1	
Number Of Columns	2	
Row 1		
Row 1 Type	Component	
Row 1 Height (e.g., 150, *, 2*, Auto)	*	
Column 1		
Column 1 Type	Component	
Column 1 Width (e.g., 150, *, 2*, Auto)	1200	
Column 2		
Column 2 Type	Component	
Column 2 Width	*	

Figure 12.85

Click on the Dashboard Components tab and click Remove Selected Dashboard Component twice to remove the copied Components from the new Dashboard. Click Add Dashboard Component, then select the radio button Component and chart Component shown below.

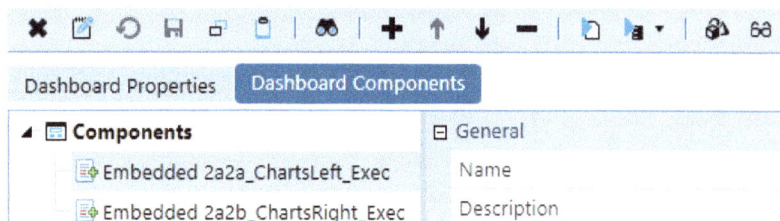

Figure 12.86

Use the copy and paste function to clone 2a2_Charts_Exec to the Dashboard, then rename the copied Dashboard 2a_Content_Exec and change the Number of Rows and Number of Columns. Also, be sure to set the Row 3 Type to Line and set Row 1 and Row 2 Heights to Auto.

Dashboard Properties	Dashboard Components	
□ General (Dashboard)		
Name	2a_Content_Exec	
Workspace	UX	
Maintenance Unit	Executive Dashboards (Exec)	
Dashboard Group	Executive Dashboards (Exec)	
Description		
Page Caption		
□ Formatting		
Layout Type	Grid	
Is Initially Visible If Embedded	True	
Display Format		
Show Title	True	
□ Literal Parameter Values		
Name Value Pairs (e.g., Param1=Value1, ...)		
□ Action (Primary Dashboard Only)		
Server Task		
Load Dashboard Server Task	No Task	
Load Dashboard Server Task Arguments		
□ Grid Layout Type		
Number Of Rows	4	
Number Of Columns	1	
Row 1		
Row 1 Type	Component	
Row 1 Height (e.g., 150, *, 2*, Auto)	Auto	
Row 2		
Row 2 Type	Component	
Row 2 Height	Auto	
Row 3		
Row 3 Type	Line	
Row 3 Height	*	
Row 4		
Row 4 Type	Component	
Row 4 Height	*	

Figure 12.87

Click on the Dashboard Components tab and click Remove Selected Dashboard Component twice to remove the copied Components from the new Dashboard. Click Add Dashboard Component, then select the following embedded Dashboards.

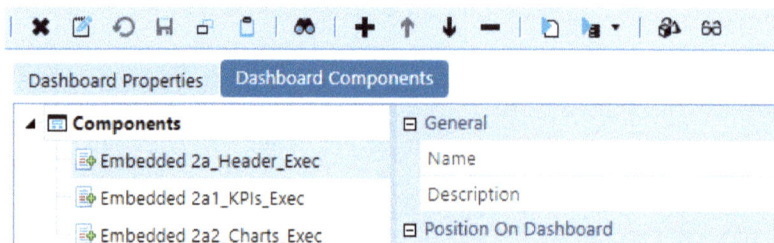

Figure 12.88

Create a new Dashboard and name it `2_Body_Exec`. Select Layout Type Tabs and select the Rounded Corners style from the Edit dialog button.

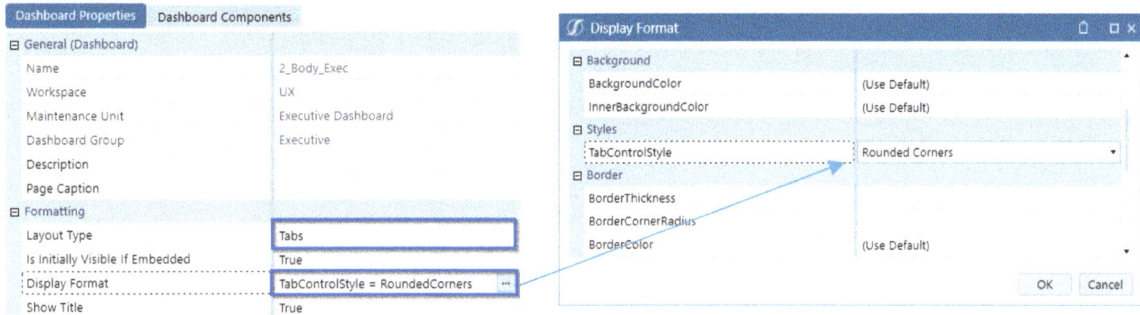

Figure 12.89

Click Add Dashboard Component, then select the following embedded Dashboards.

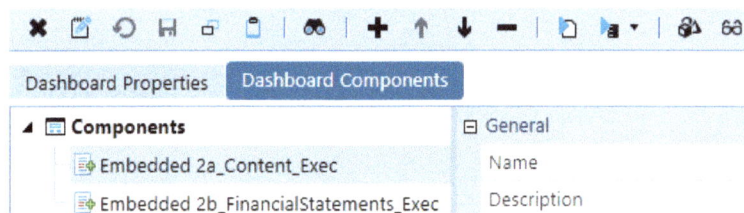

Figure 12.90

Completed Dashboards

Phew! We made it. This is what our Dashboard structure should look like. Notice that we have methodically named the Dashboards to follow a stacked sequence; this is intended to help with organization.

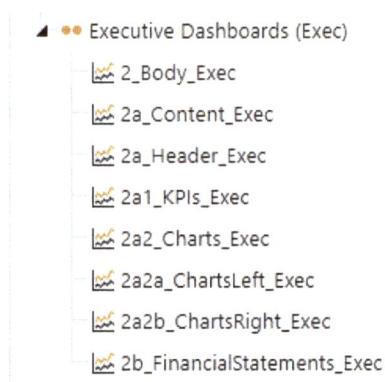

Figure 12.91

We can review the Dashboard by selecting `2_Body_Exec` and clicking View Dashboard.

Chapter 12

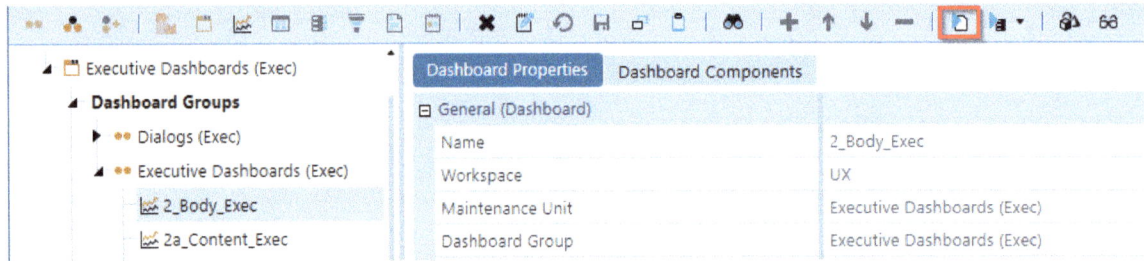

Figure 12.92

Notice the combo box in the upper right-hand corner. It allows the User to change the Point of View on the Dashboard to display Entity-specific data.

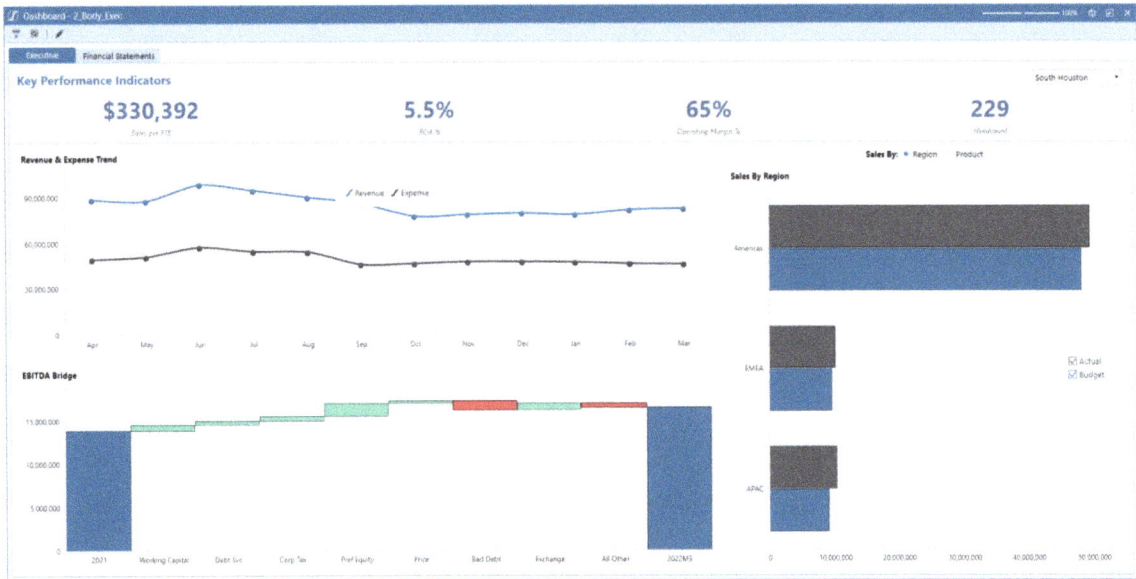

Figure 12.93

If we change the combo box selection, we see the data change for all Dashboard Components.

Figure 12.94

Another Component to review is the radio button we created to parameterize the Sales By Region Chart. If we select the Product radio button, we can see a different data model. This is just one example of how to get the most out of OneStream. We could have additional tabs for pivot grids or Spreadsheet reporting and ad hoc analysis, we could have our Annual Report and monthly PowerPoint packs embedded, we could have our ESG Reports and Dashboards (increasingly important for the Executive!), our stock price, the local weather forecast... the list goes on and on!

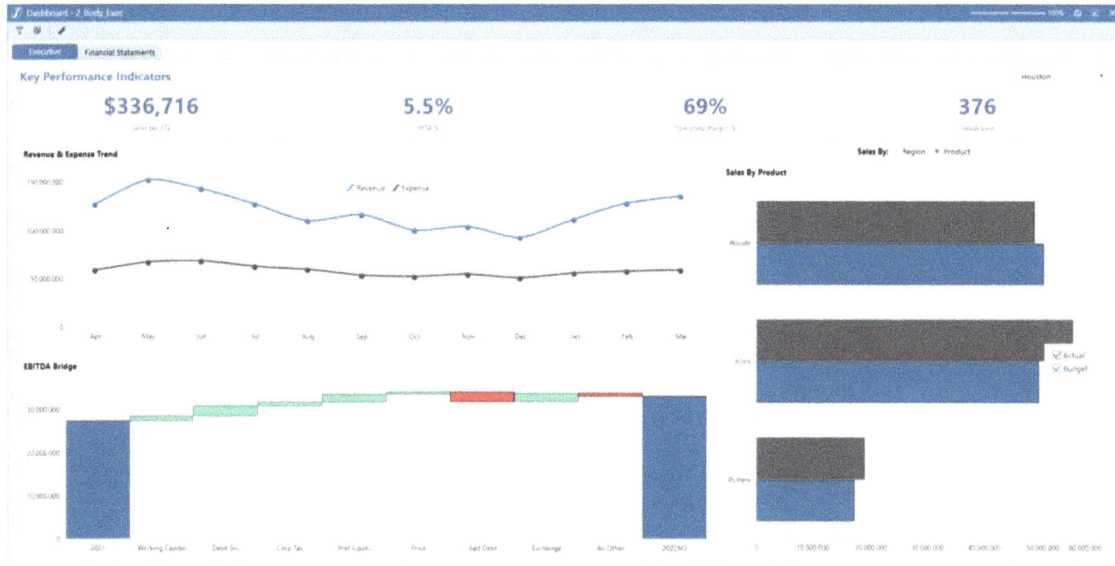

Figure 12.95

Lastly, we can review the Financial Statements tab to view our formatted Income Statement for the current period and prior year comparison.

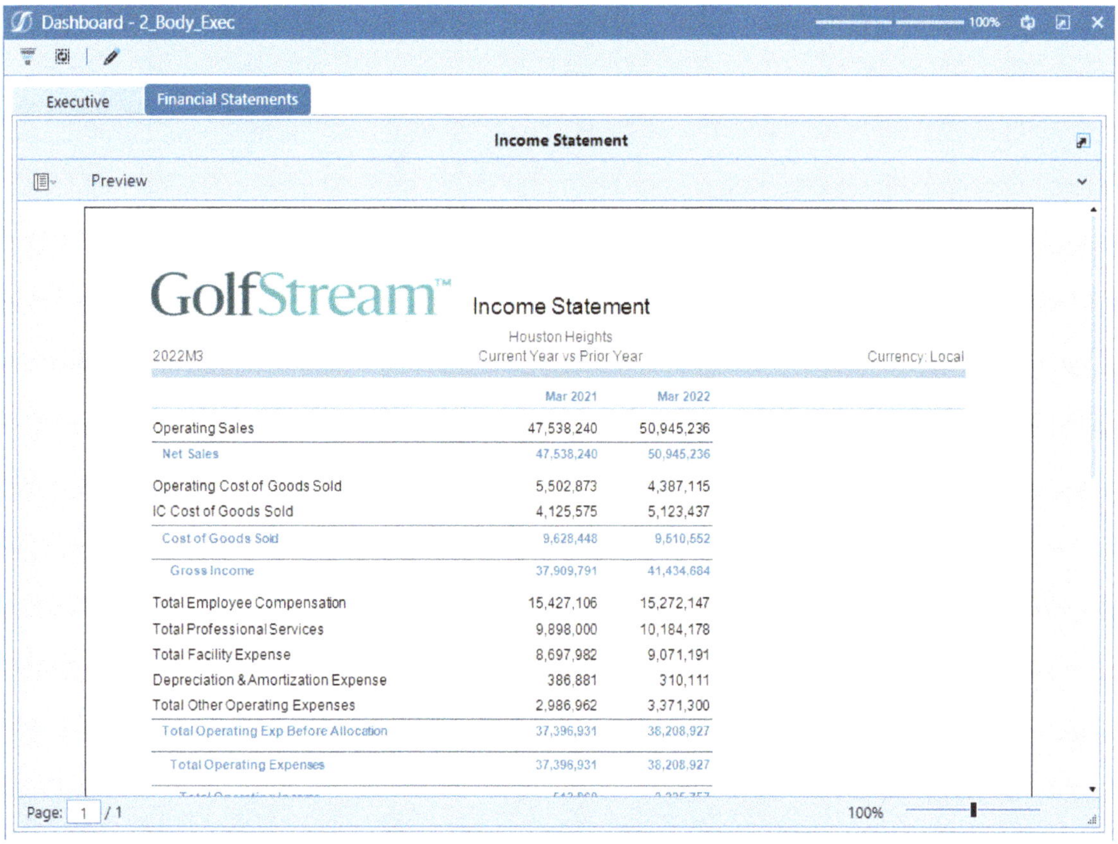

Figure 12.96

Conclusion

In this chapter, we created a simple Executive Dashboard with a variety of charts and methods for creating new data sources. We also created dynamic labels to query the Cube data, which are now available to our Executives to access at their leisure. Finally, we parameterized the Dashboard data and created filters using combo boxes and radio buttons to show the flexibility of how you can tailor Dashboards to meet your needs.

Keep in mind that we've only scratched the surface in terms of what is possible when creating Dashboards, but this should give you a bit of an idea how you might want to build your own. Dashboarding in OneStream is one of those things where – once you get the hang of it – it's actually really exciting to see what you can build, and how you can truly make the application meet your needs and guide your Users. Creating Dashboards in OneStream can seem overwhelming, but once you get the hang of it, you will be building them in minutes. The possibilities are endless, do not be afraid to get creative!

13
Administrator Dashboards

In this chapter, we will discuss the benefits of providing Administrators and Power Users with their own special-purpose home pages to provide a finger on the pulse of any application, including at-a-glance Workflow status information. One of the great things about OneStream is its built-in ability to report on just about anything – not just financial data but also non-financial information, such as headcount data, task activity, commentary, security activity, your favorite sports team's stats... you name it! This capability is particularly useful for OneStream Administrators as it provides them with a powerful means of tracking things like Workflow status and End-User activity.

In the following step-by-step exercise, we will build a simple administrative Dashboard with graphs and tables displaying relevant Workflow status information, as well as a simple Business Rule and table to show several vital signs such as active logins, running tasks, and more.

When, Why, and How to Use Them

Administrator Dashboards are intended to serve as a one-stop shop for Administrators to access application vitals, metadata changes, data errors, and other functionality that they will need to administer the application efficiently.

Design Considerations

What are the roles and responsibilities of your Administrator? Are they tasked with monthly data activities, such as seeding new forecasts, setting targets, etc.? Or are they solely focused on application performance and User maintenance? You will want to gather as much information on the role of the Administrator before building your Administrator Dashboard so you can be sure you are capturing relevant information and functionality.

Standard Application Reports

The OneStream MarketPlace has numerous solutions and tools that are designed to help and assist our beloved OneStream Administrators. These include Task Manager, Application Control Manager, System Diagnostics, and others – more about these later. The MarketPlace also contains some very handy pre-built Report packages, namely Security Audit Reports, which are useful when the Auditors are in town, and Standard Application Reports – a suite of 70+ application-ready Dashboards and Reports that detail things like Workflow status, Application Dimension counts, formulas, commentary, and more. If you don't already have these in your OneStream application, please install them today!

Figure 13.1

After installation, you are good to go and get all of these (and more) right out of the gate.

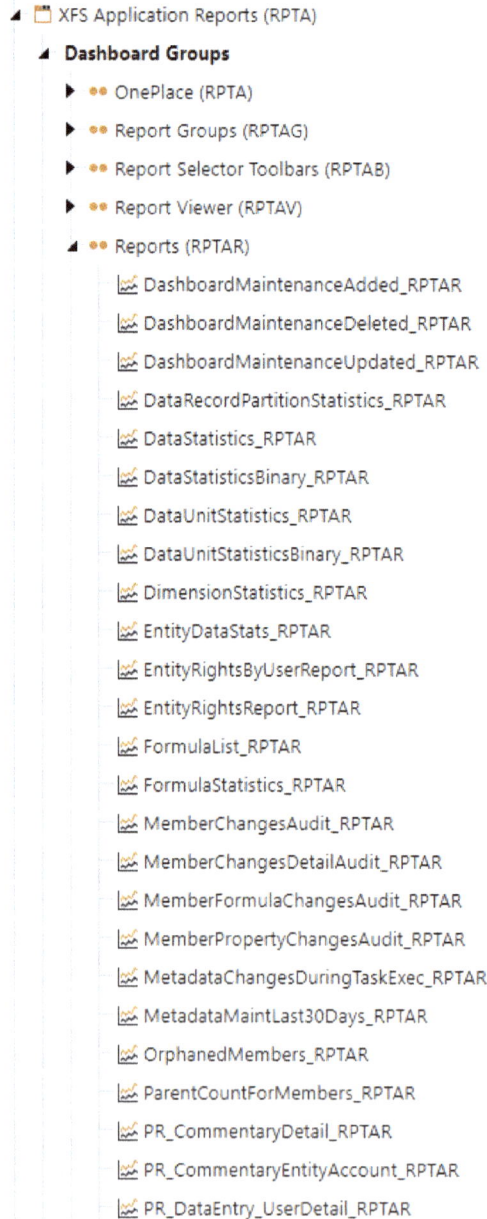

Figure 13.2

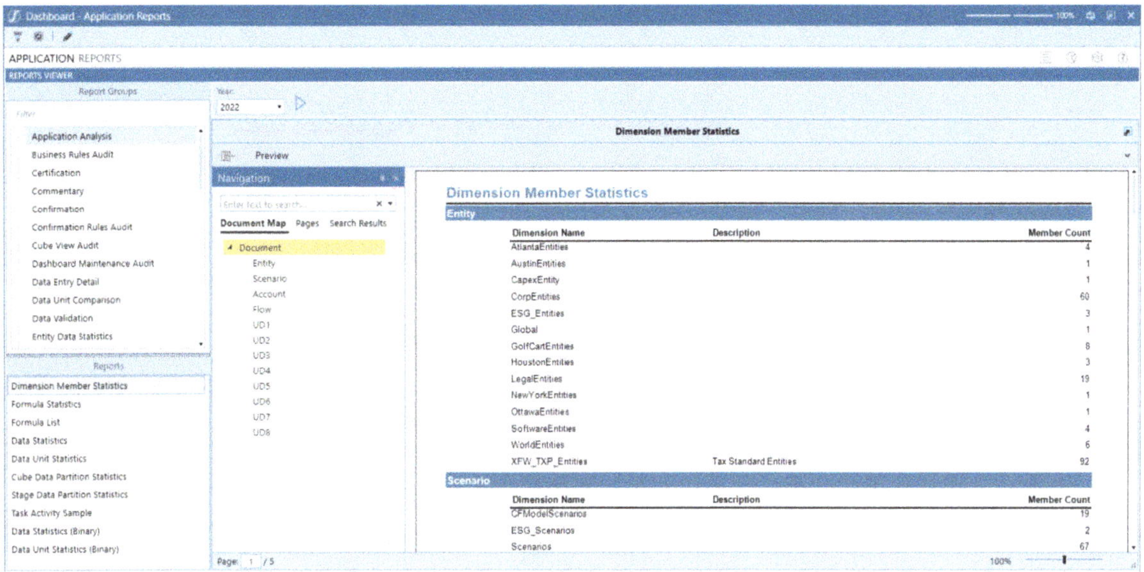

Figure 13.3

Build Your Own

The first step in building an Administrator Dashboard is to create the Dashboard Maintenance Unit (DMU) by navigating to Application Dashboards from the Application tab.

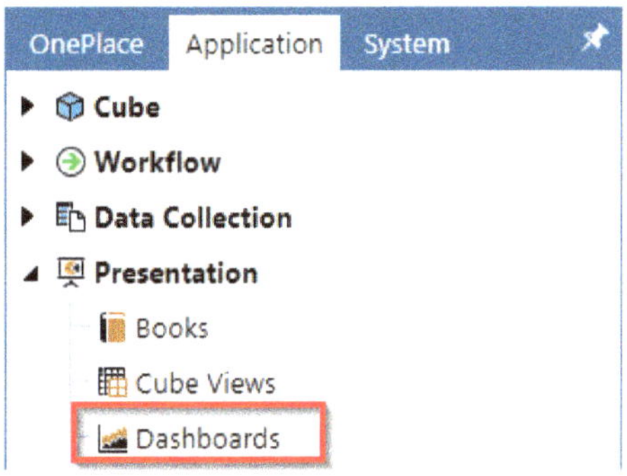

Figure 13.4

Select Maintenance Units and then click Create Maintenance Unit.

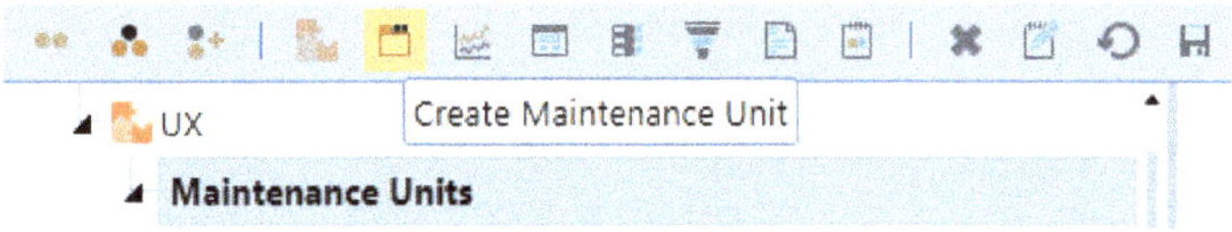

Figure 13.5

Name the Dashboard Maintenance Unit Administrator Dashboards and click save.

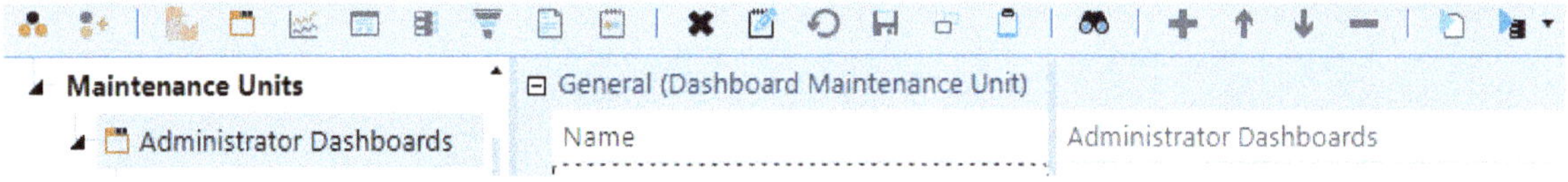

Figure 13.6

Select Dashboard Groups and click Create Group.

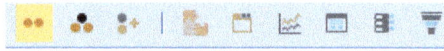

Figure 13.7

Name the Dashboard Group `Administrator Dashboards (Admin)` and click save.

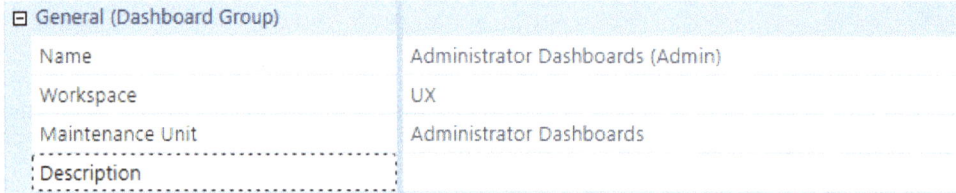

General (Dashboard Group)
Name
Administrator Dashboards (Admin)
Workspace
UX
Maintenance Unit
Administrator Dashboards
Description

Figure 13.8

Select Components and click on the Create Dashboard Component icon.

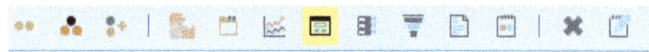

Figure 13.9

Select Label from the dialog and click OK.

Create Dashboard Component
label
Label
OK
Cancel

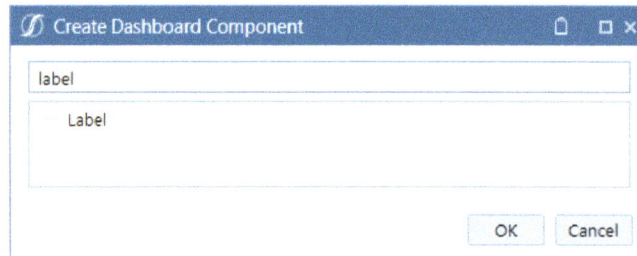

Figure 13.10

Name the label `lbl_Title_Admin`, type ADMINISTRATOR into the Text field, apply the Display Format settings, then save.

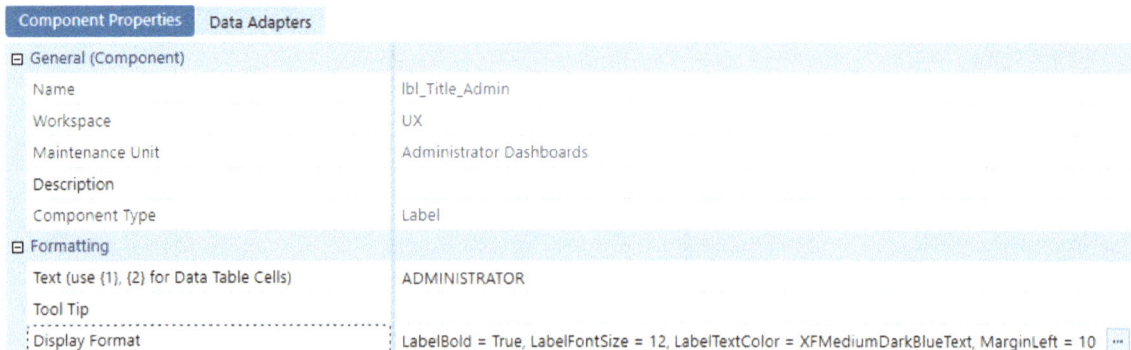

Component Properties
Data Adapters
General (Component)
Name
lbl_Title_Admin
Workspace
UX
Maintenance Unit
Administrator Dashboards
Description
Component Type
Label
Formatting
Text (use {1}, {2} for Data Table Cells)
ADMINISTRATOR
Tool Tip
Display Format
LabelBold = True, LabelFontSize = 12, LabelTextColor = XFMediumDarkBlueText, MarginLeft = 10

Figure 13.11

Select the Group Administrator Dashboards (Admin) and click Create Dashboard.

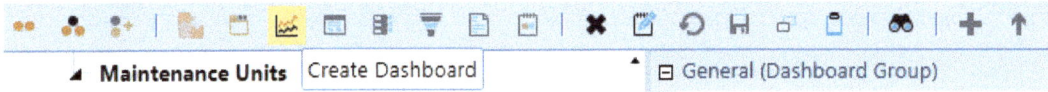

Figure 13.12

Apply the following: Name of Dashboard: 1_Header_Admin.

Type BackgroundColor = WhiteSmoke into the Display Format field and save the Dashboard.

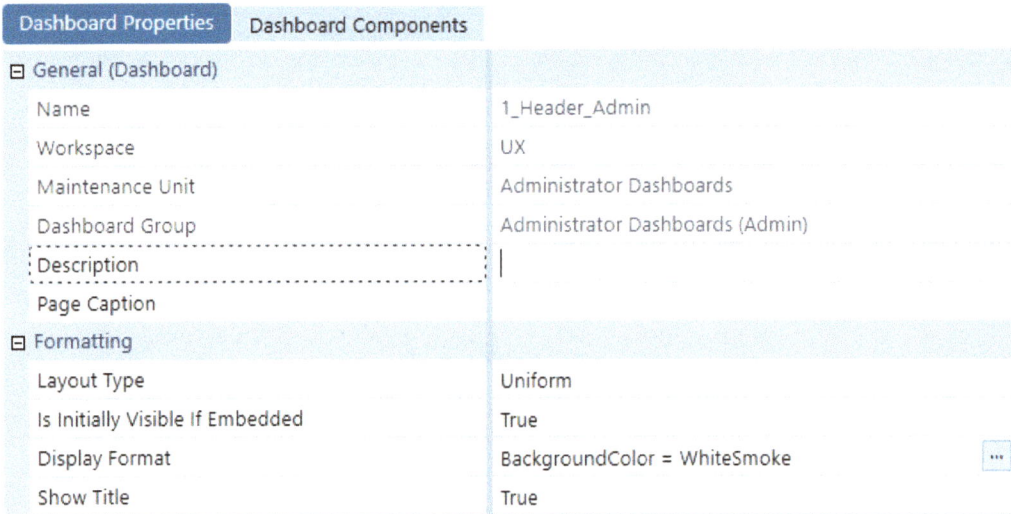

Figure 13.13

Select the Dashboard Components tab and click Add Dashboard Component.

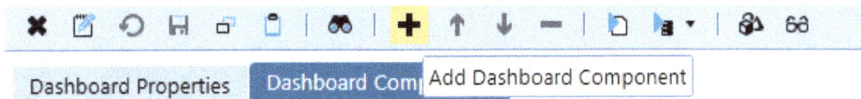

Figure 13.14

Select the label we created previously and click OK.

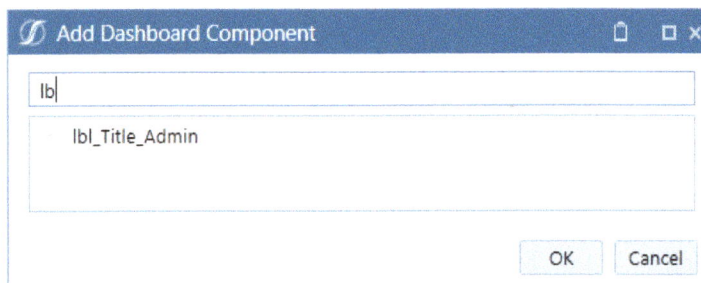

Figure 13.15

Select the Group Administrator Dashboards (Admin) and click Create Dashboard.

Figure 13.16

Create the following Dashboards; we will attach Dashboard Components to them later in the exercise.

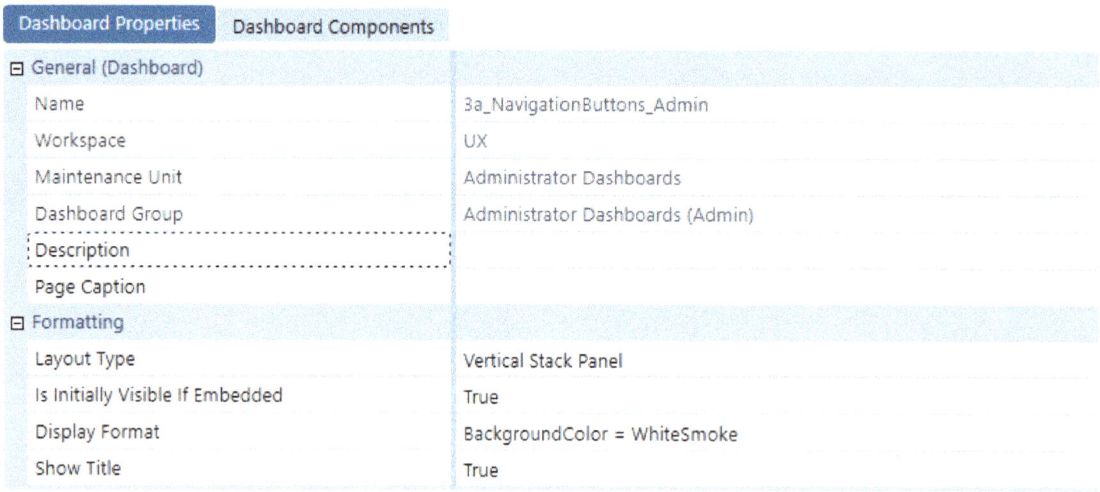

Figure 13.17

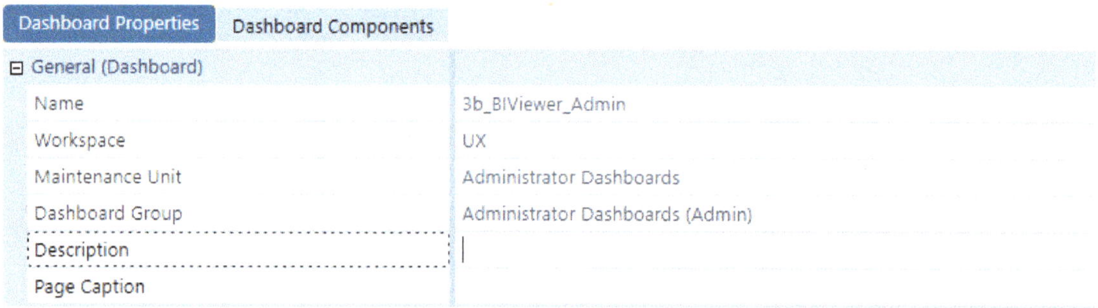

Figure 13.18

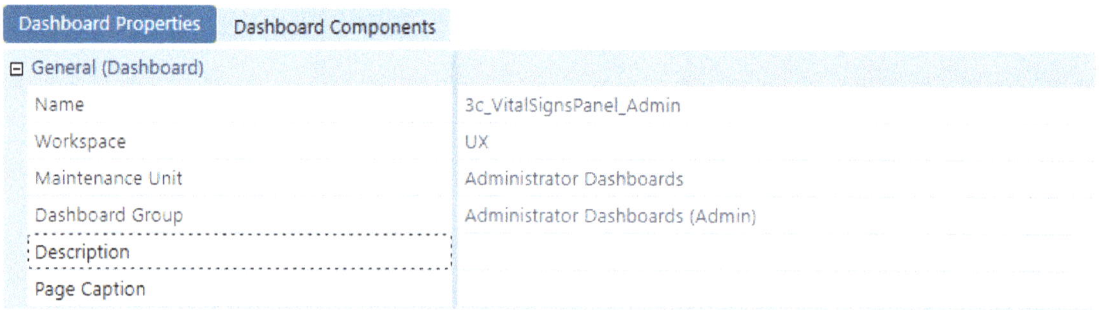

Figure 13.19

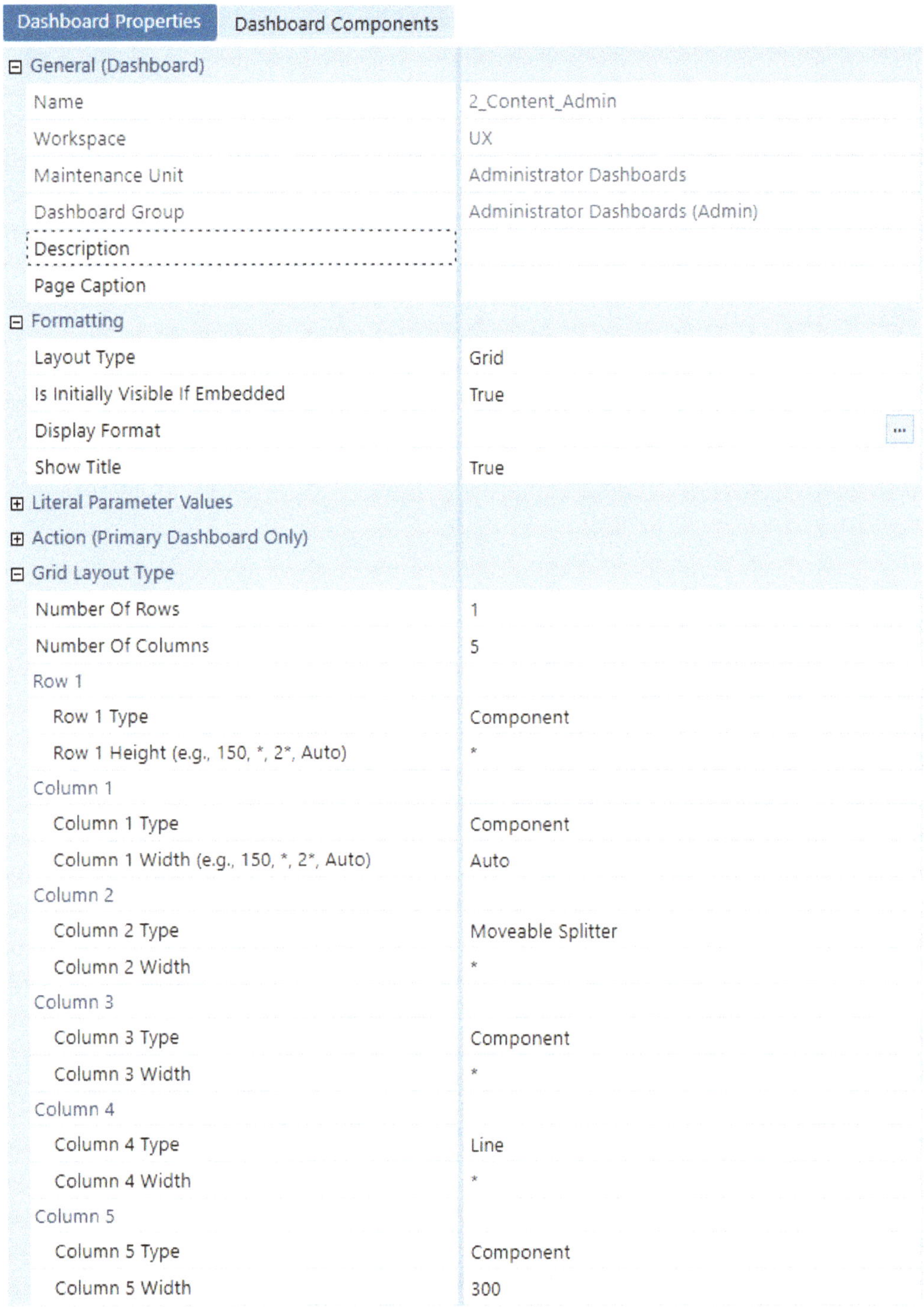

Dashboard Properties	Dashboard Components

General (Dashboard)

Name	2_Content_Admin
Workspace	UX
Maintenance Unit	Administrator Dashboards
Dashboard Group	Administrator Dashboards (Admin)
Description	
Page Caption	

Formatting

Layout Type	Grid
Is Initially Visible If Embedded	True
Display Format	...
Show Title	True

Literal Parameter Values

Action (Primary Dashboard Only)

Grid Layout Type

Number Of Rows	1
Number Of Columns	5
Row 1	
Row 1 Type	Component
Row 1 Height (e.g., 150, *, 2*, Auto)	*
Column 1	
Column 1 Type	Component
Column 1 Width (e.g., 150, *, 2*, Auto)	Auto
Column 2	
Column 2 Type	Moveable Splitter
Column 2 Width	*
Column 3	
Column 3 Type	Component
Column 3 Width	*
Column 4	
Column 4 Type	Line
Column 4 Width	*
Column 5	
Column 5 Type	Component
Column 5 Width	300

Figure 13.20

Select the Dashboard Components tab and add the Components shown below.

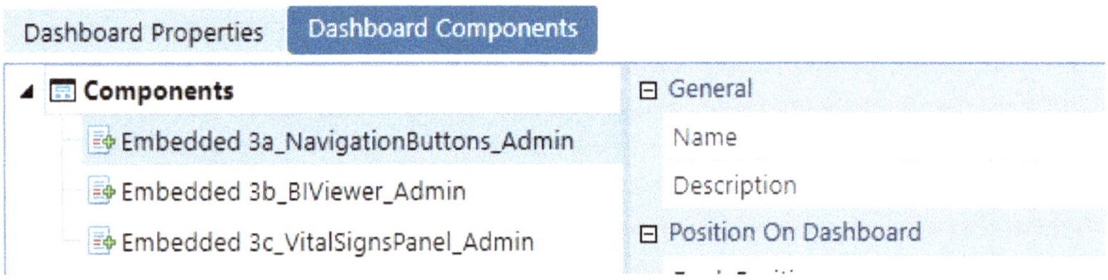

Dashboard Properties	Dashboard Components

Components
- Embedded 3a_NavigationButtons_Admin
- Embedded 3b_BIViewer_Admin
- Embedded 3c_VitalSignsPanel_Admin

General
Name
Description
Position On Dashboard

Figure 13.21

Chapter 13

Name the Dashboard 0_Frame_Admin and enter Administrator as the Description. The Dashboard will consist of a header and content section separated by a line, so we will use a grid layout to control the section size. Change the layout Type to Grid and select 3 rows and 1 column, then set the Row 1 Height to 20 and change the Row 2 Type to Line.

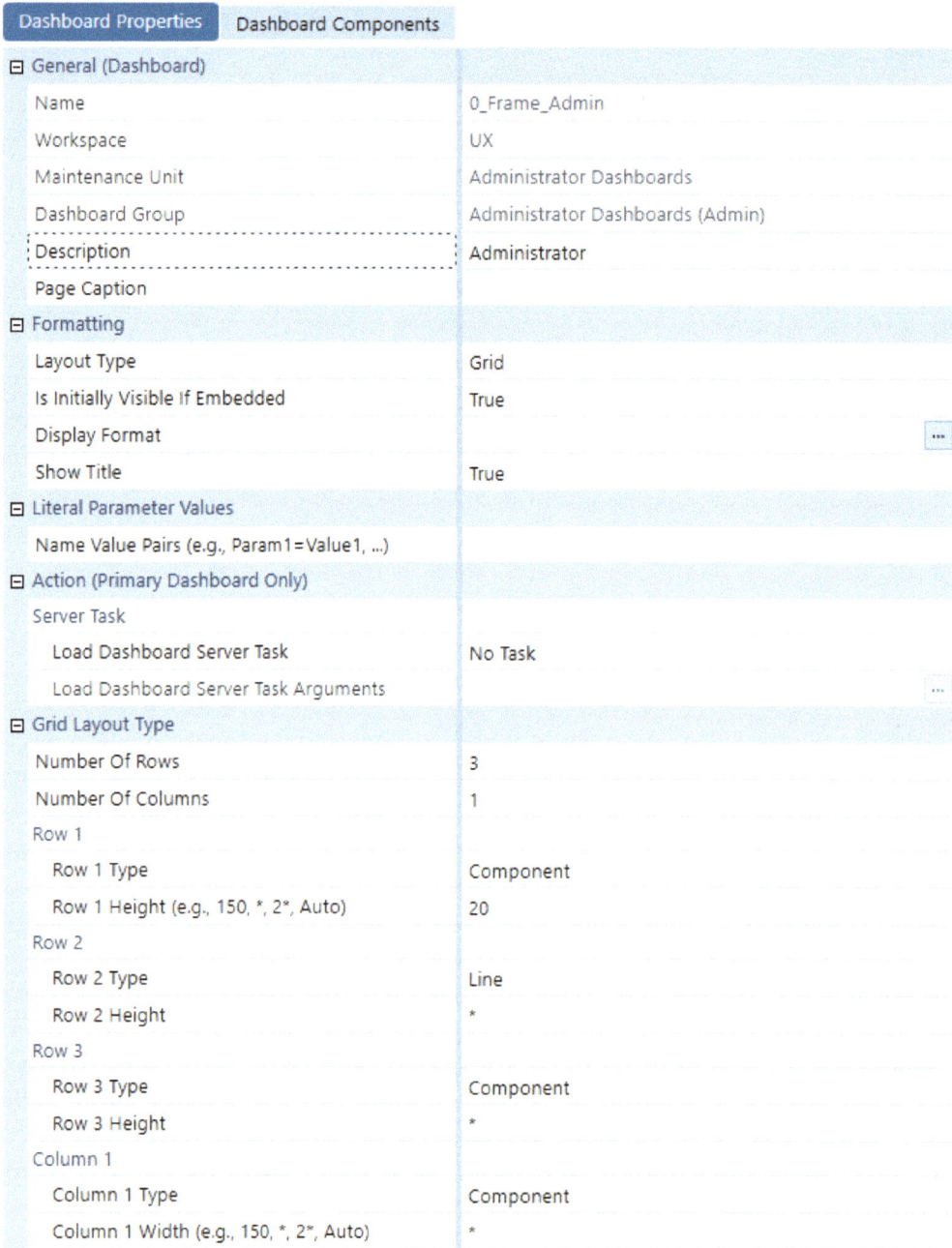

Dashboard Properties	Dashboard Components
General (Dashboard)	
Name	0_Frame_Admin
Workspace	UX
Maintenance Unit	Administrator Dashboards
Dashboard Group	Administrator Dashboards (Admin)
Description	Administrator
Page Caption	
Formatting	
Layout Type	Grid
Is Initially Visible If Embedded	True
Display Format	...
Show Title	True
Literal Parameter Values	
Name Value Pairs (e.g., Param1=Value1, ...)	
Action (Primary Dashboard Only)	
Server Task	
Load Dashboard Server Task	No Task
Load Dashboard Server Task Arguments	...
Grid Layout Type	
Number Of Rows	3
Number Of Columns	1
Row 1	
Row 1 Type	Component
Row 1 Height (e.g., 150, *, 2*, Auto)	20
Row 2	
Row 2 Type	Line
Row 2 Height	*
Row 3	
Row 3 Type	Component
Row 3 Height	*
Column 1	
Column 1 Type	Component
Column 1 Width (e.g., 150, *, 2*, Auto)	*

Figure 13.22

Select the Dashboard Components tab and add the Components shown below.

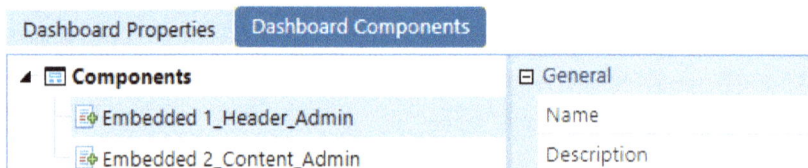

Dashboard Properties	Dashboard Components	
▲ Components		General
Embedded 1_Header_Admin		Name
Embedded 2_Content_Admin		Description

Figure 13.23

272

Workflow Status

For this exercise, we will create a Workflow Status Dashboard using a data adapter and BI Viewer Component to display statuses using colors, descriptions, and progress completion bar charts to enhance the appearance.

Data Adapter

Navigate to Application Dashboards and select Data Adapters, then click Create Data Adapter.

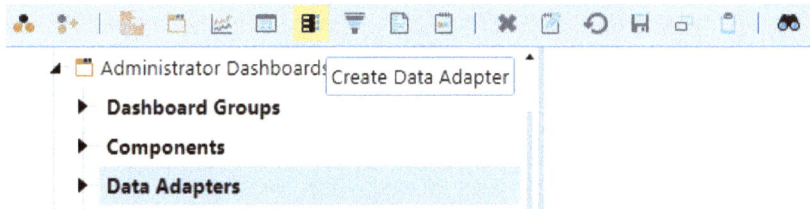

Figure 13.24

Type da_WorkflowStatus_Admin in the Name field and select Method from the Command Type combo box.

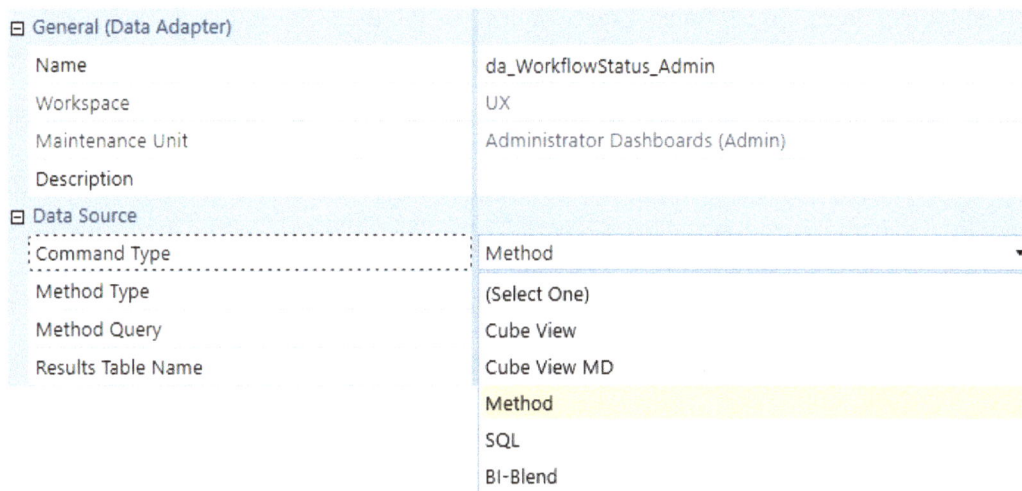

Figure 13.25

Once you have selected Method, the Method Type combo box will appear with a variety of available queries. Select WorkflowAndEntityStatus, then save the data adapter.

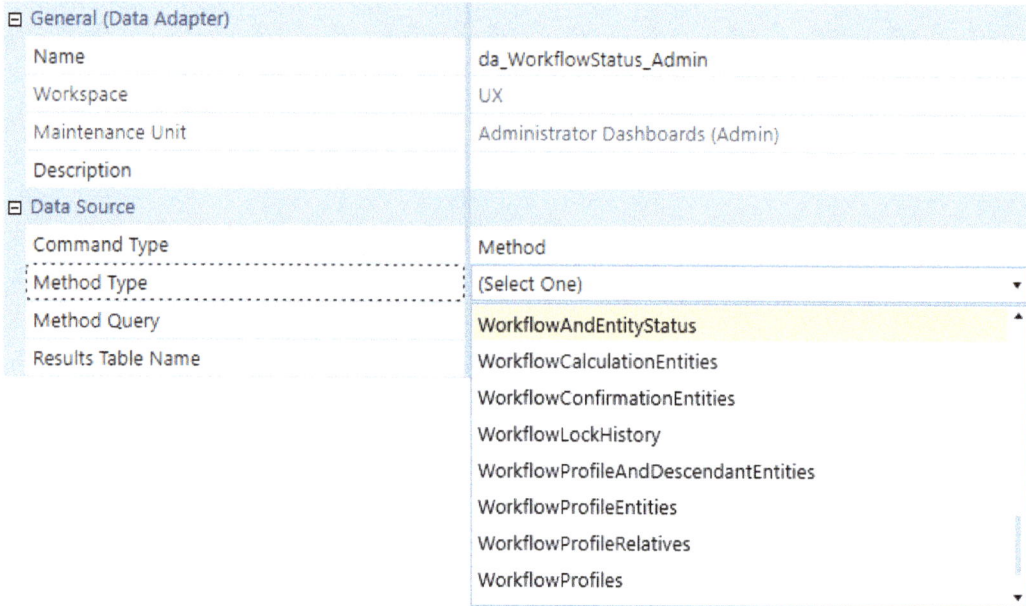

Figure 13.26

If you have never used this Type of query before, you are in for a real treat! Method queries are available as out-of-the-box helpers, which means you do not have to know how to code to use them. The logging feature is extremely powerful because it tells you exactly what you need to supply for a given query. Click Test Data Adapter to prompt the query definition.

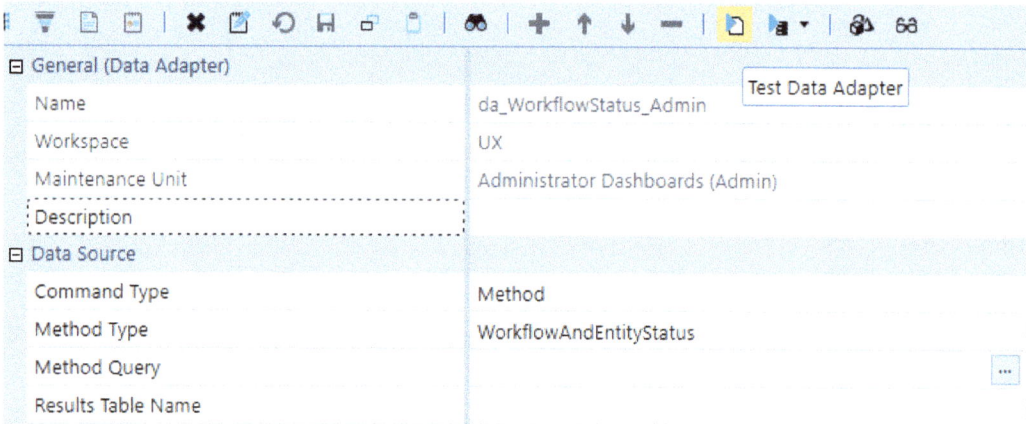

Figure 13.27

A dialog box appears with the following message and example syntax. Click OK to close the dialog, then double-click the Method Query field to open the query editor.

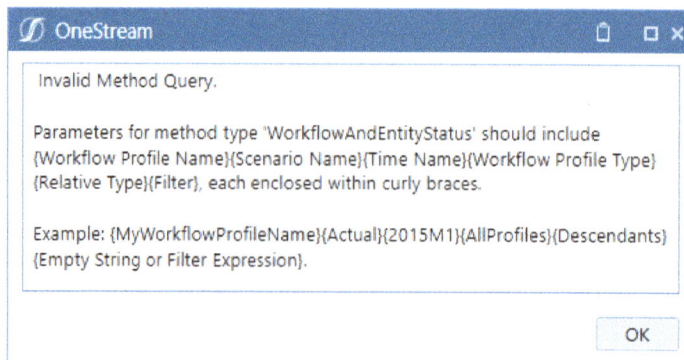

Figure 13.28

For our query, we need to use the Workflow Profile named `Total Golfstream`, and then we will use the `Global Scenario` and `Time` parameters to ensure the status is reflected for the current period.

Enter the query below and click OK, then save the data adapter. We have included a **filter expression** to only return valid input Workflows, but your query may differ based on the Workflow design.

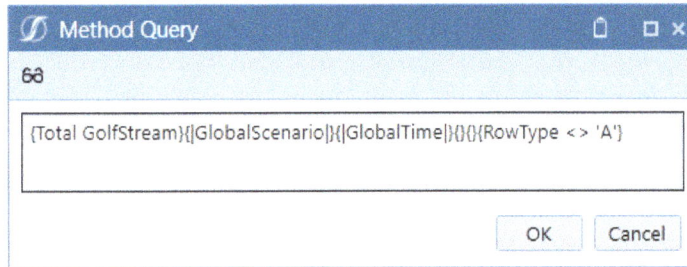

Figure 13.29

Click Test Data Adapter again to view the table data the query returns. If you see what appears to be duplicate rows for a ProfileName, scroll to the right in the data table and you will notice that the Workflow status is broken out by Entity.

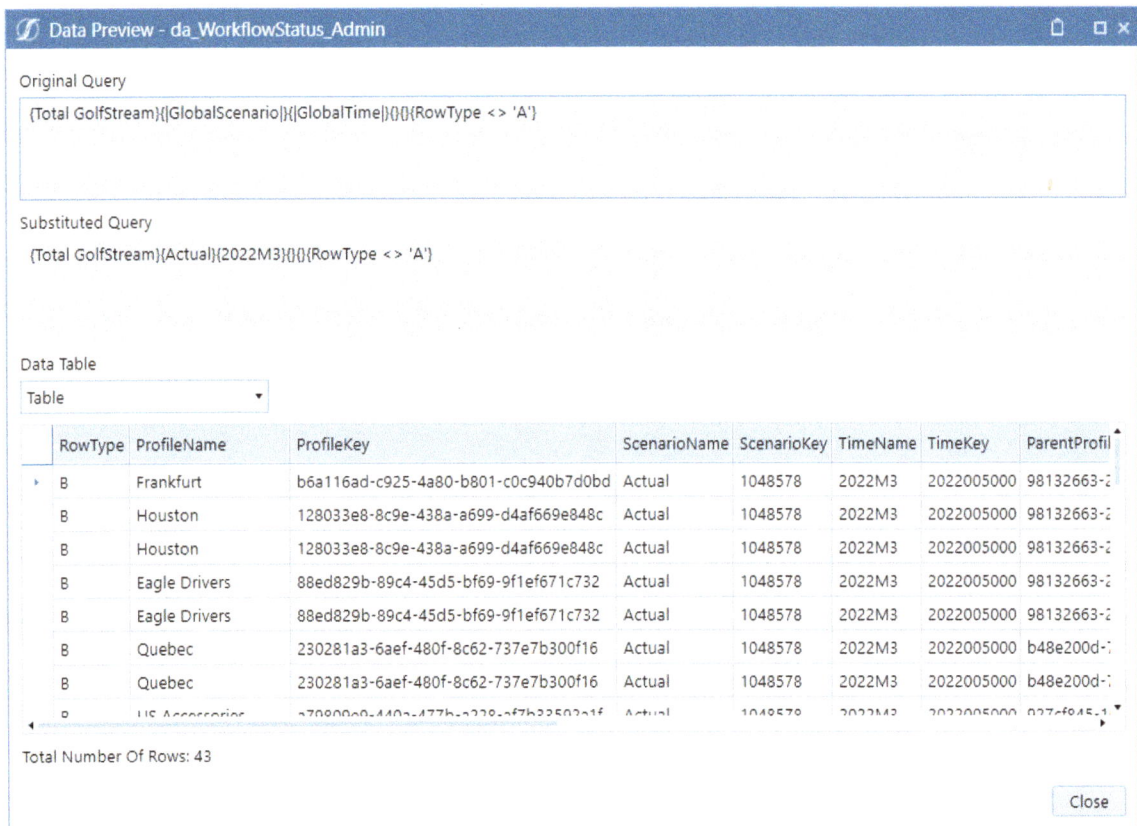

Figure 13.30

BI Viewer

Our BI Viewer Component will consist of filters, cards to display contextual completion percentages, a bar chart to help visualize the Workflow progress, and grids to provide Workflow-specific tracking information. Navigate to Components and click Create Dashboard Component.

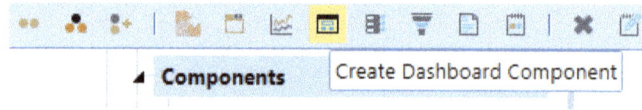

Figure 13.31

Select BI Viewer from the dialog and click OK.

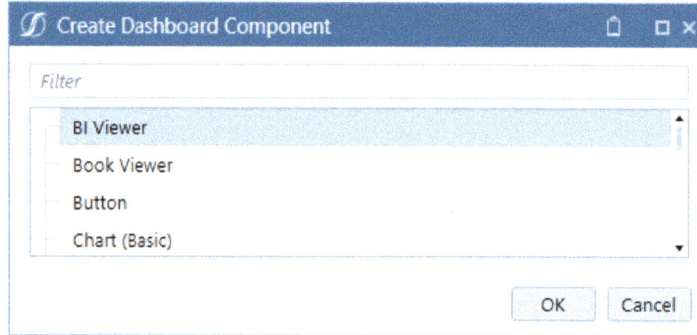

Figure 13.32

Type `biv_WorkflowStatus_Admin` in the Name field and then save.

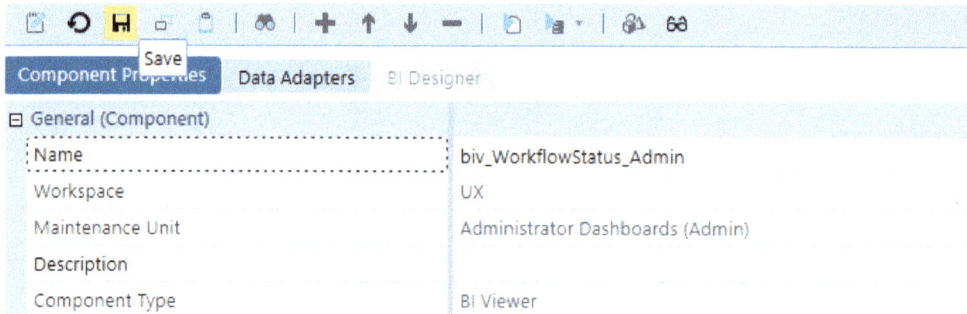

Figure 13.33

Select the Data Adapters tab and click Add Data Adapter. Select the data adapter we created, click OK to close the dialog, then save the Component.

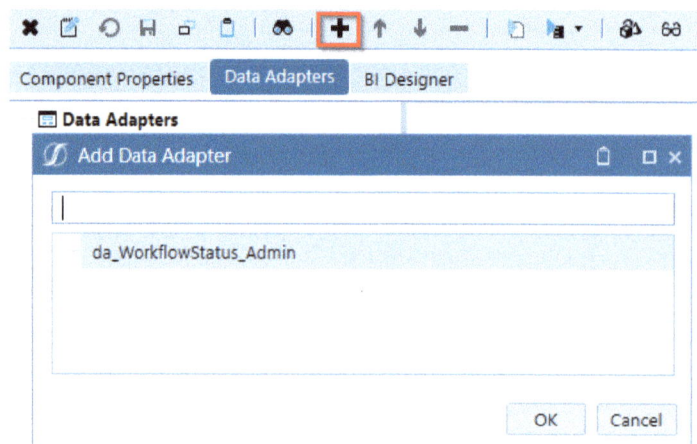

Figure 13.34

Select the BI Designer tab to open the Dashboard Designer.

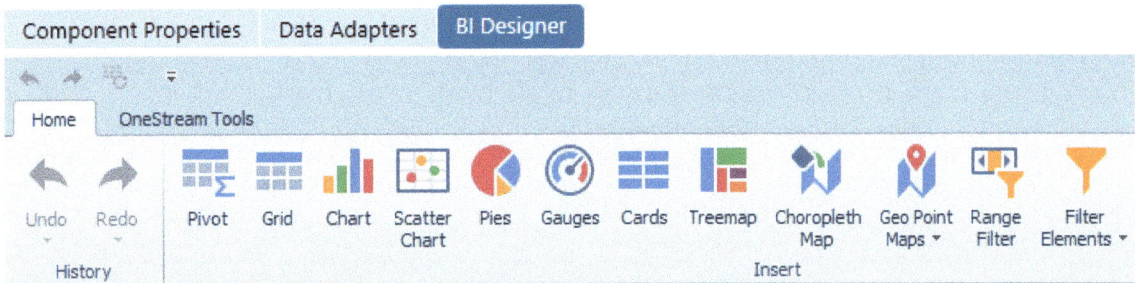

Figure 13.35

Right-click anywhere in the Data Source field list and select Add Calculated Field.

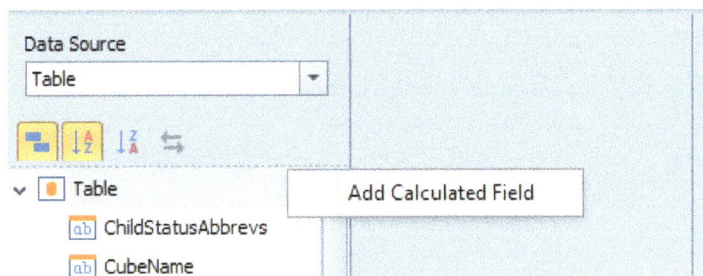

Figure 13.36

Insert the following string in the Expression Editor, then click OK. This expression strips off the characters to the right of the period (.) of the ProfileName. For example, Houston.Import will return Houston; this will be used for grouping and filtering later in this exercise.

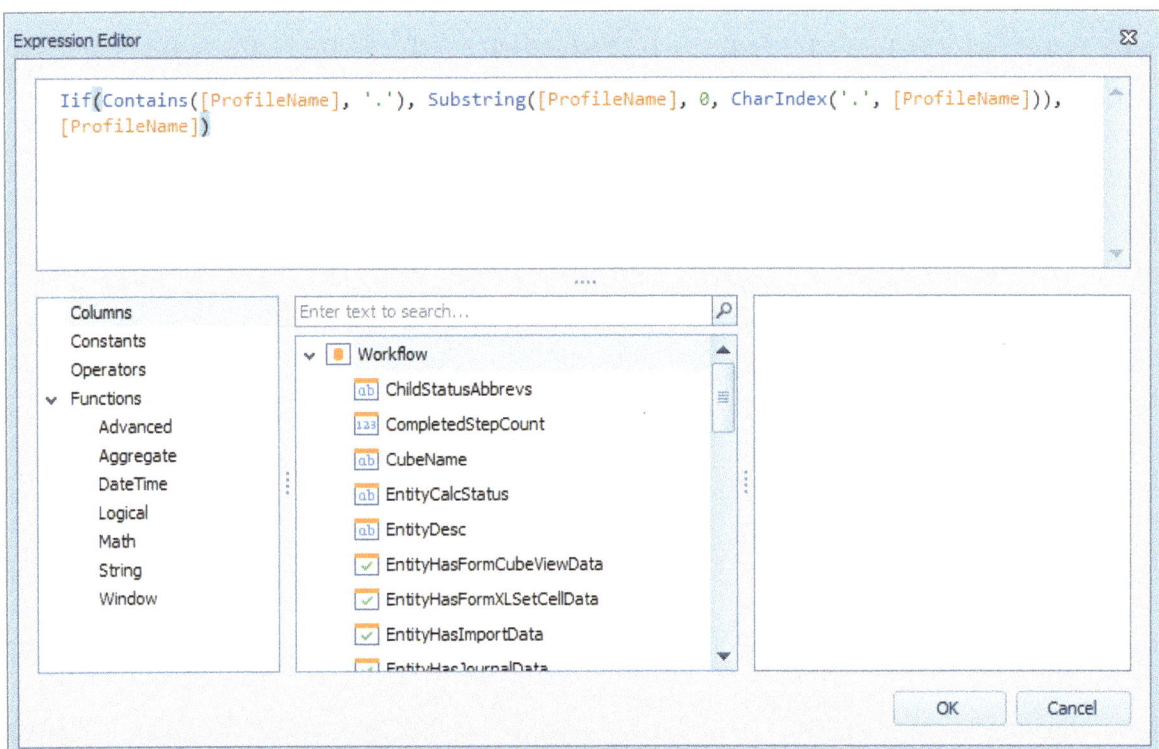

Figure 13.37

Right-click on Calculated Field 1 and click Rename. Backspace the name and type Workflow, then hit tab on the keyboard to update the name.

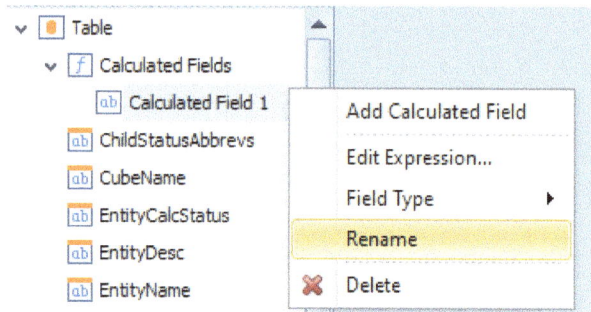

Figure 13.38

Repeat the steps completed in Figures 13.36-13.38 to create two additional calculated fields named Workflow Task and Incomplete Steps.

Workflow Task strips off the characters to the left of the period (.) of the ProfileName; for example, Houston.Import will return Import.

Incomplete Steps will be used in the bar chart to show the outstanding steps count as a percentage of the total steps.

Calculated Field	Expression
Workflow	Iif(Contains([ProfileName], '.'), Substring([ProfileName], 0, CharIndex('.', [ProfileName])), [ProfileName])
Workflow Task	Iif(Contains([ProfileName], '.'), Substring([ProfileName], CharIndex('.', [ProfileName])+1), 'Review')
Incomplete Steps	[TotalStepCount] - [CompletedStepCount]

Figure 13.39

Workflow Filter

The first Dashboard item we will create is a filter element showing our Workflow hierarchy structure in a visual format to enable multi-selection filtering. From the Home menu, click Filter Elements and select Tree View.

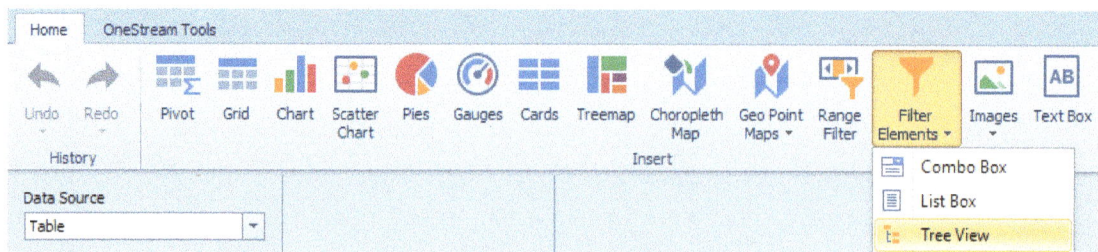

Figure 13.40

Click and drag Workflow to the Dimensions field on the Data Items pane, then click and drag Workflow Task beneath it. Navigate to the Design tab and click Show Caption to turn off the header, and click Auto Expand to show the full hierarchy.

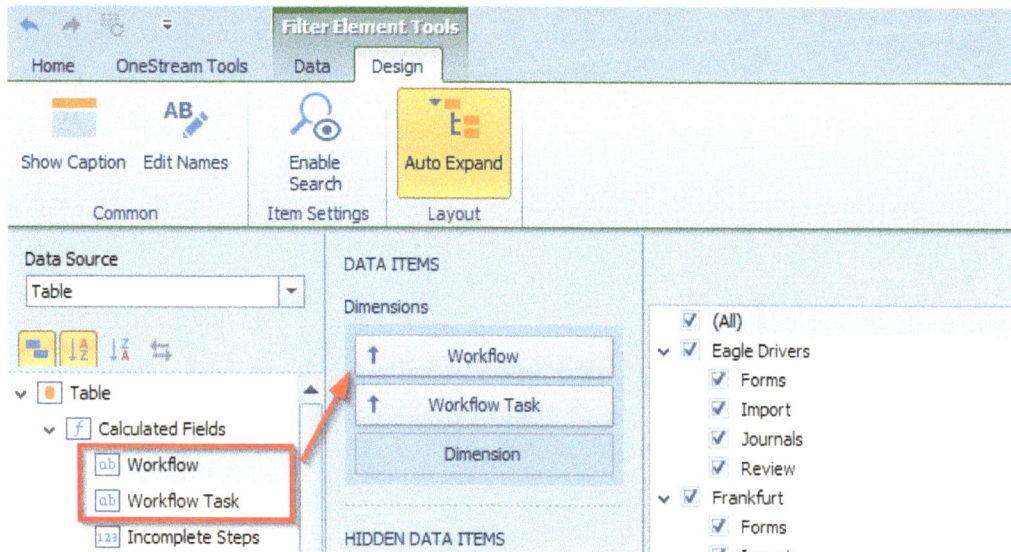

Figure 13.41

> **Note:** Save the BI Viewer Component to see the Tree View auto-expand in the Designer.

Workflow Task Grid

Next, we will add a grid to list Workflow tasks and respective statuses. This will allow us to provide detailed task information that can be filtered using the tree view we created, or from the cards that we will add later in this section. From the Home menu, click Grid.

Figure 13.42

Drag Workflow, Workflow Task, WorkflowName, and StatusText to the Columns field.

Navigate to the Design tab and click Show Caption, Horizontal Lines, and Vertical Lines to turn them off.

Chapter 13

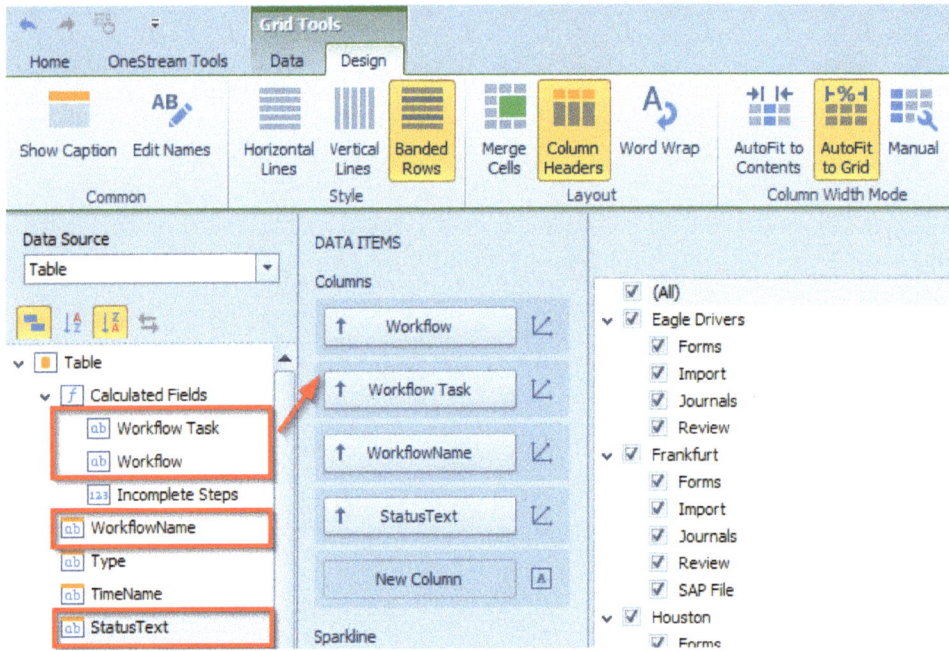

Figure 13.43

Let's apply colors to the status field using green for Completed, red for Not Started, and yellow for anything that is in process. Right-click in the grid and select Edit Rules.

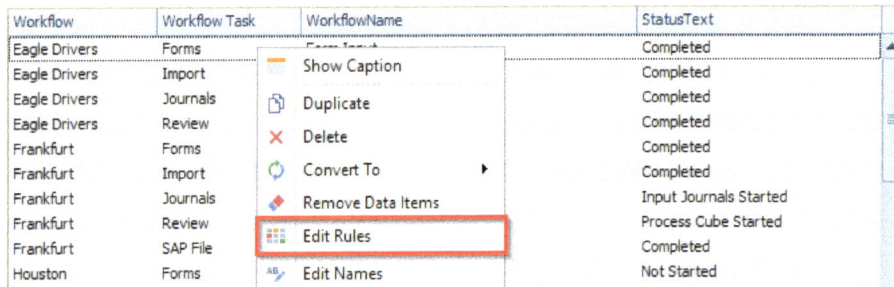

Figure 13.44

The Edit Rules dialog appears. Select StatusText from the calculated by drop-down menu and then click Add and select your expression.

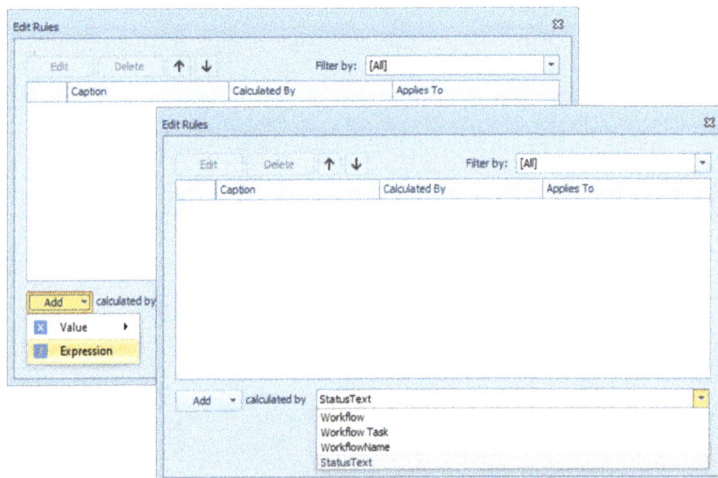

Figure 13.45

The Expression Editor dialog opens. Hover over the word And to view the expression actions, click + to add a condition, then pick StatusText = Completed from the selectors as shown below. Select pale green as the appearance and change the Apply to selection to StatusText before clicking OK.

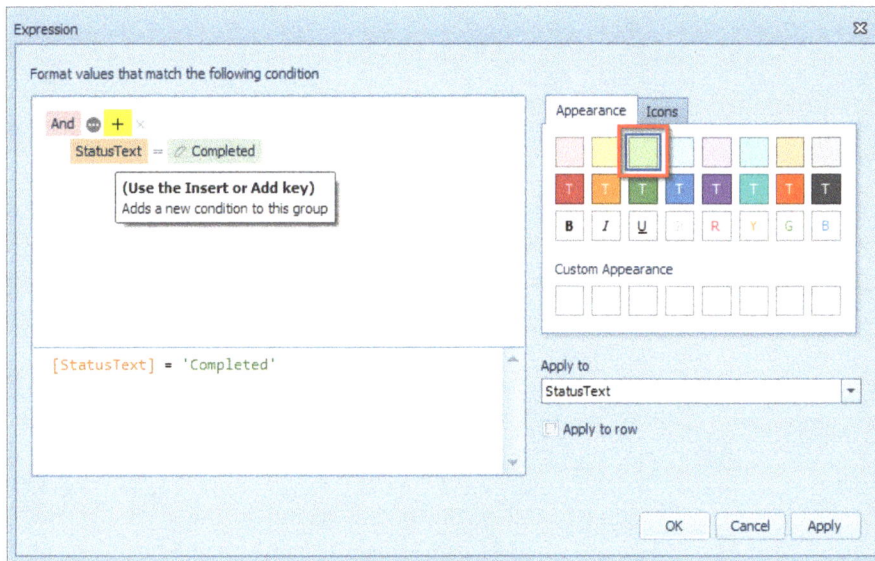

Figure 13.46

Repeat the steps in Figures 13.45-13.46 to apply pale red to StatusText = Not Started, and pale yellow to StatusText <> Completed and StatusText <> Not Started. Figure 13.47 shows the end result.

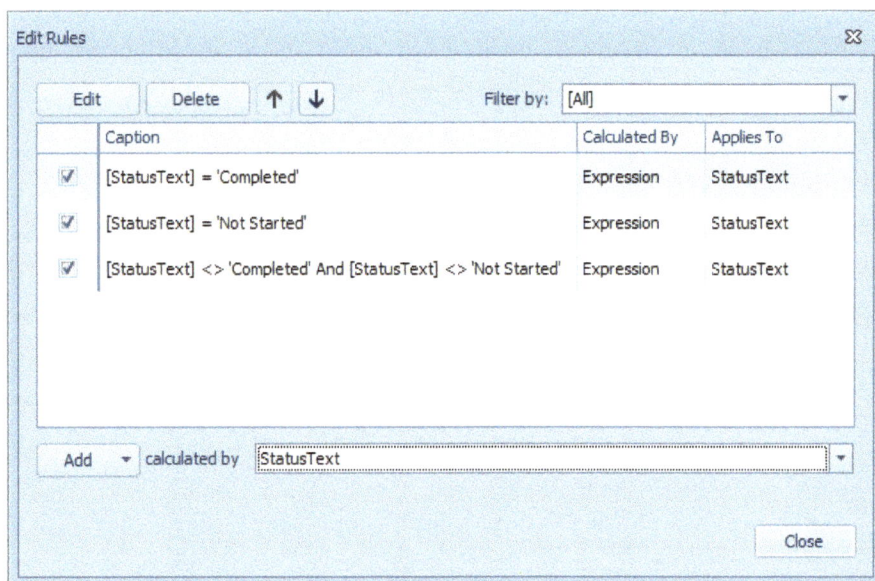

Figure 13.47

Bar Chart

Next, we shall add a bar chart to show Workflow completed versus incomplete Workflow step count with percentages; this will be the focal point of our Dashboard. From the Home menu, click Chart.

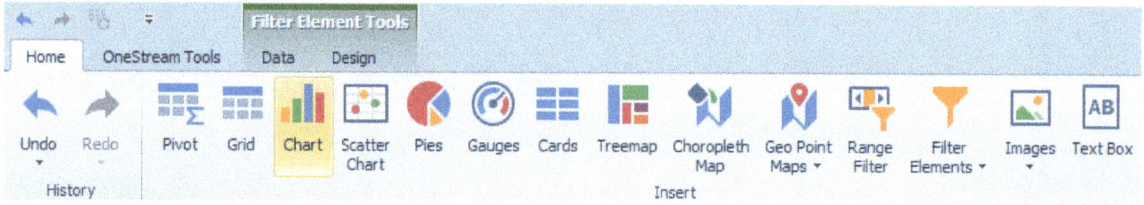

Figure 13.48

Drag CompletedStepCount to the Value field, drag Incomplete Steps beneath it, then drag Workflow and Workflow Task to the Arguments field.

Navigate to the Design tab and click Rotate, Center Legend Horizontally, and Full-Stacked Bar to apply these settings. Click Show Caption to turn this off; I think the cards look cleaner without the caption, but you can certainly leave this setting on if you prefer. Your settings should look like the figure below.

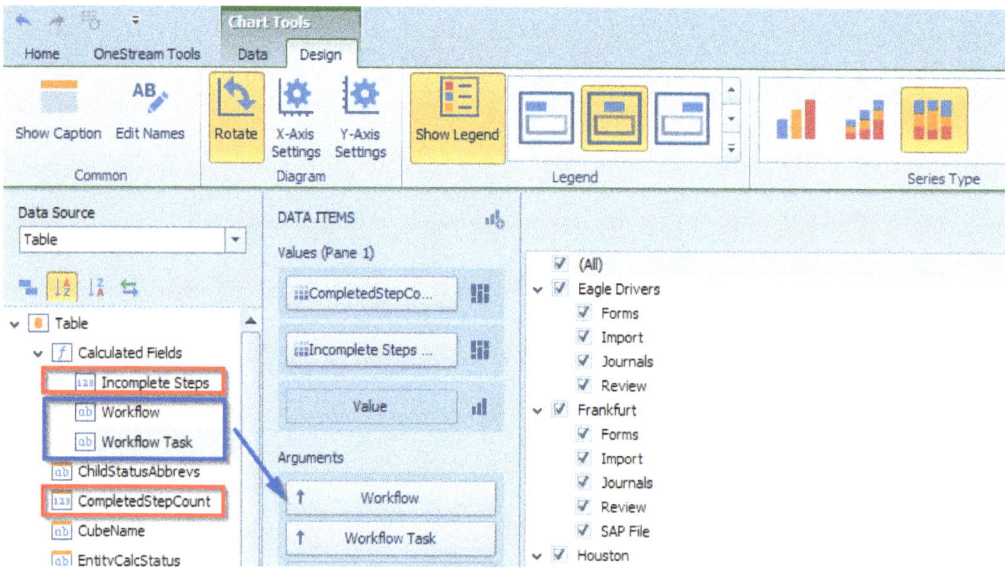

Figure 13.49

Click Y-Axis Settings, uncheck the boxes for Show grid lines and Show title, then click OK.

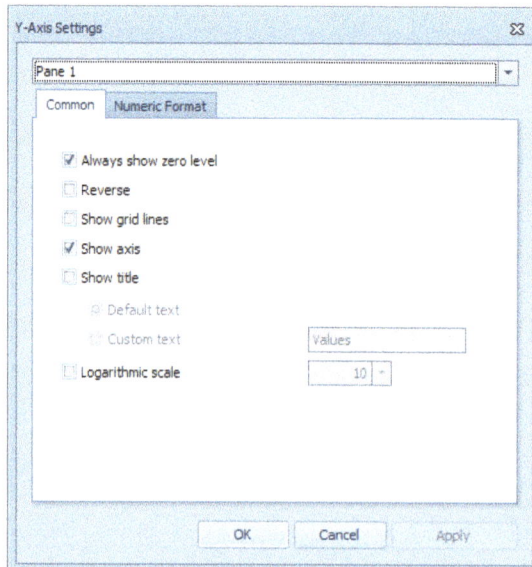

Figure 13.50

Navigate to the Data tab and click Drill Down and Arguments. Applying these settings will suppress the Workflow tasks associated with a Workflow while making the Workflows drillable.

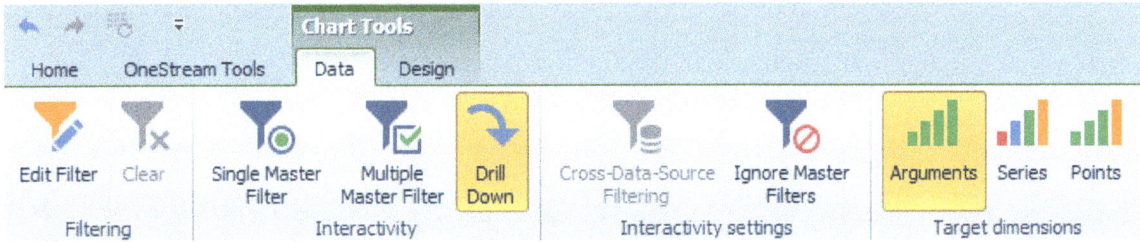

Figure 13.51

Right-click on the chart and click Edit Names.

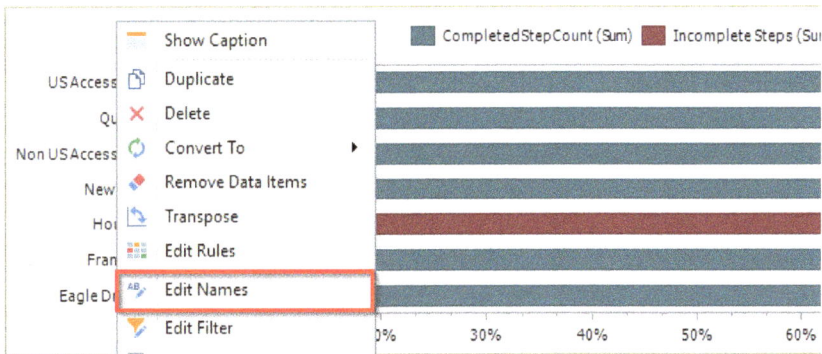

Figure 13.52

Update the names to Completed Steps and Incomplete Steps, then click OK.

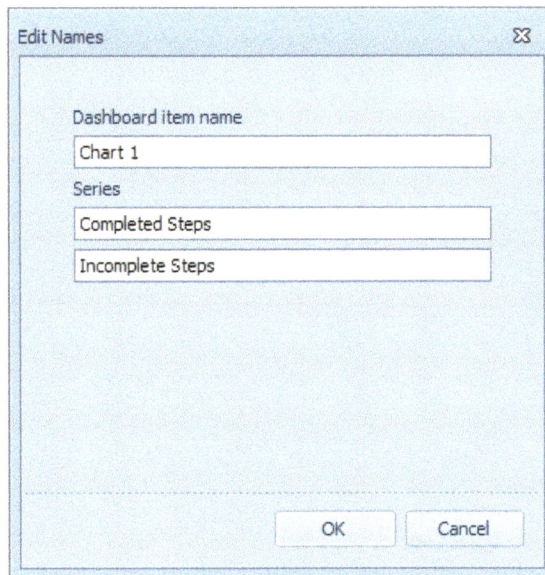

Figure 13.53

Note: Names can also be updated by right-clicking on the data field and selecting Rename.

Chapter 13

Cards

Next, we will add cards to display Workflow status percentages with multi-select enabled to show additional filtering capability. From the Home menu, click Cards.

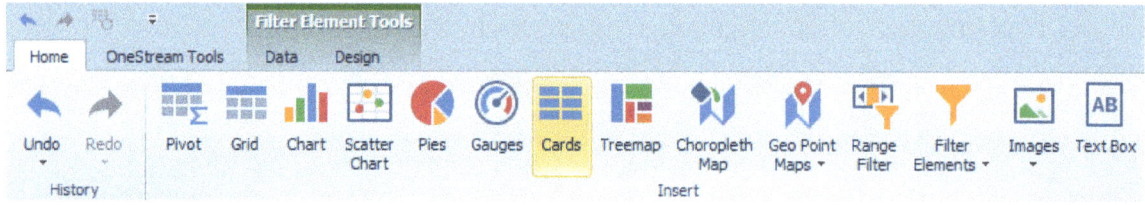

Figure 13.54

Drag StatusText to the Actual field, then drag StatusText to the Series field. This will populate a card for each status and the percentage of the total number of steps. Navigate to the Design tab and click Show Captions.

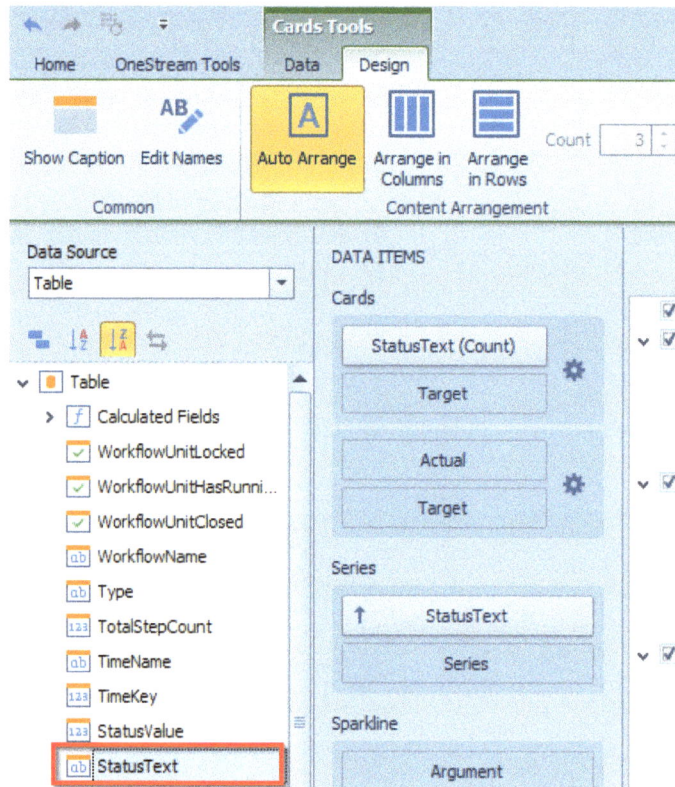

Figure 13.55

Hover over the StatusText data field and click the arrow to open the data item menu. Click Percent of Total from the Calculation options. Navigate to the Data tab and click Multiple Master Filter.

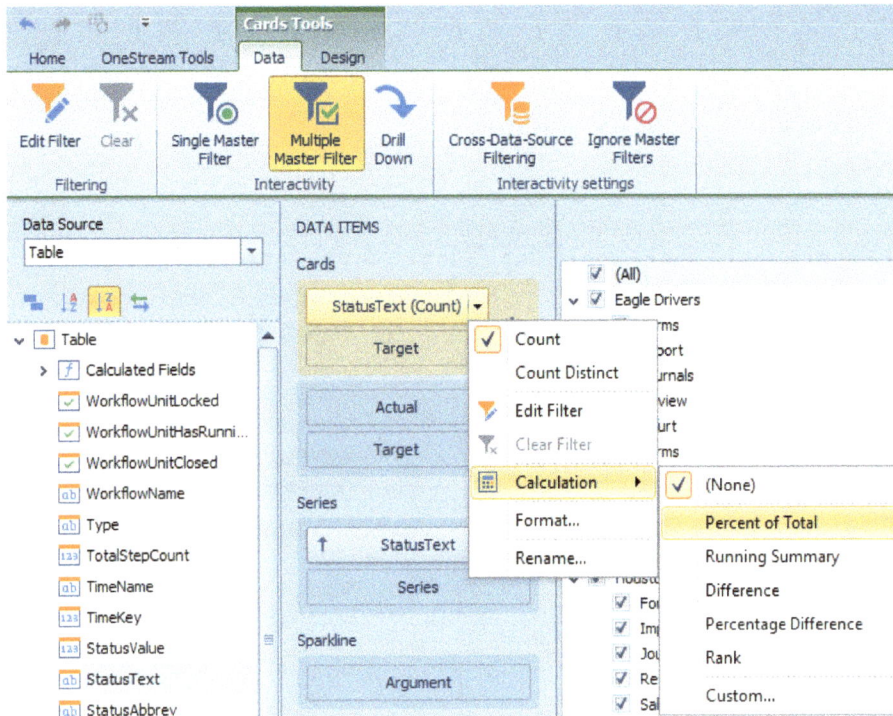

Figure 13.56

From the Data Items pane, click the gear icon.

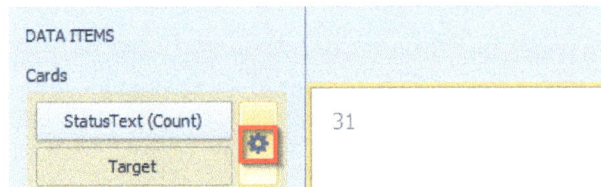

Figure 13.57

Select the Lightweight template, then navigate to the Format Options tab and change the Actual value format to Percent with a Precision of 2. Click Apply, then click OK to close the dialog.

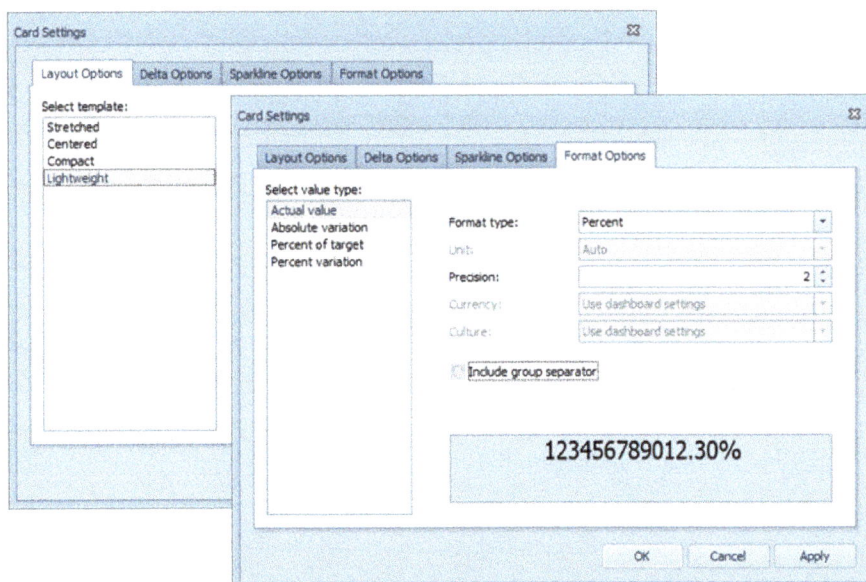

Figure 13.58

Once we have completed adding our Dashboard items, we need to organize the Dashboard in a way that is intuitive and easy to navigate. In the figure below, we have mocked up where we want to move the items. The cards will be placed horizontally across the top, the chart will nest below it to the right of the tree view, and the grid will sit below the chart.

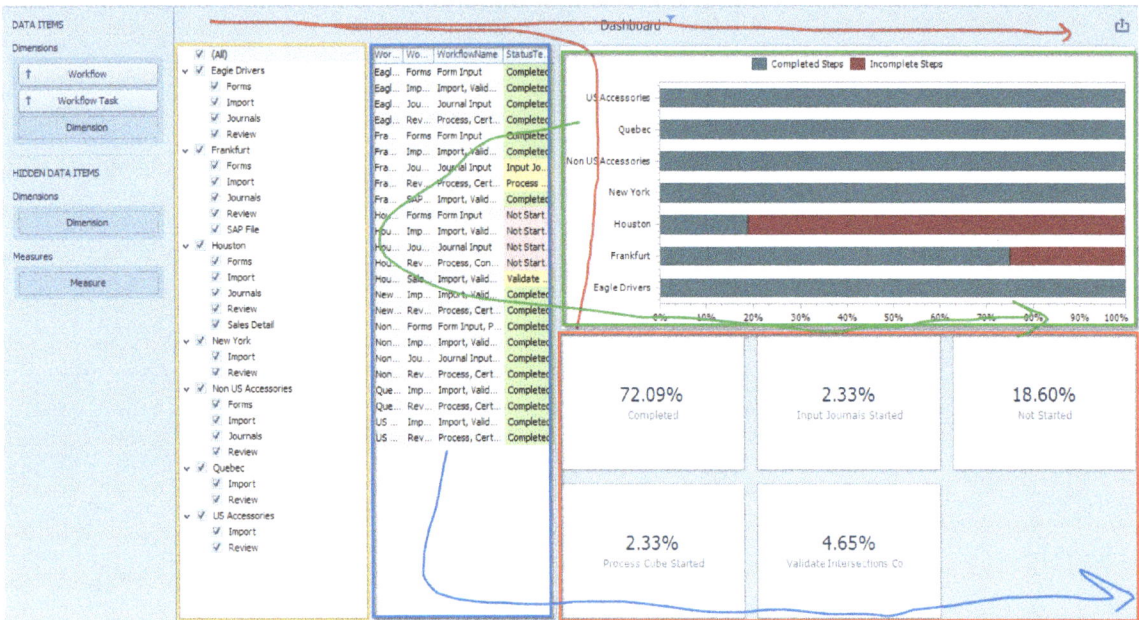

Figure 13.59

Move each item using drag and drop functionality. Drag the cards to the top until a thick blue block appears, then release the mouse button to position it in the desired location. Move the other items until you are satisfied with the layout.

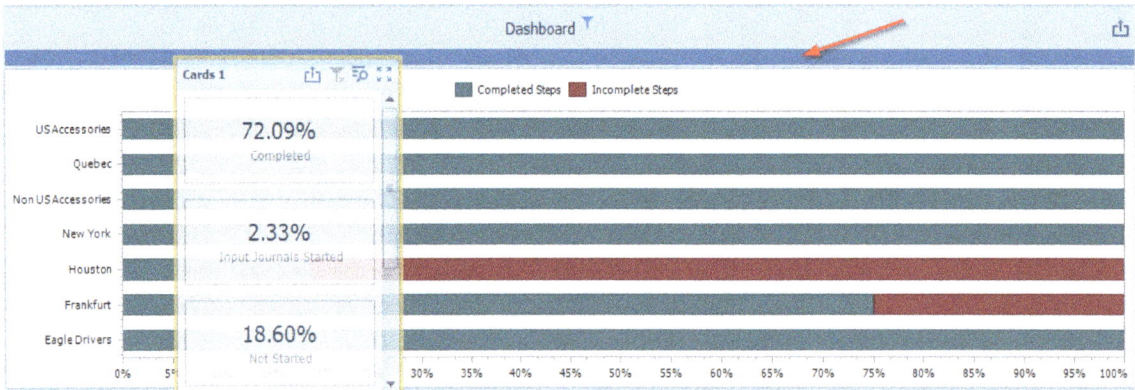

Figure 13.60

Note: Right-click on the Component and click Show Captions to identify the object easily.

After we have positioned the Dashboard items, we can make additional modifications to the title and bar chart colors to improve the appearance.

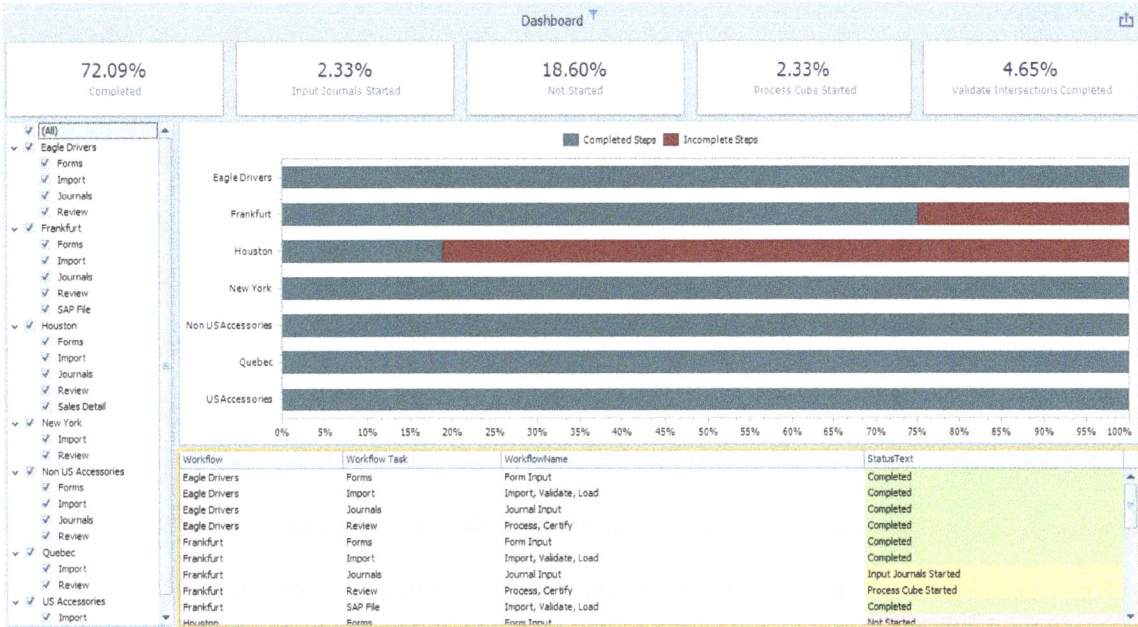

Figure 13.61

From the Home tab, click Title.

Figure 13.62

Uncheck the Show Master Filter state box and change the Text to Workflow Status, then click OK.

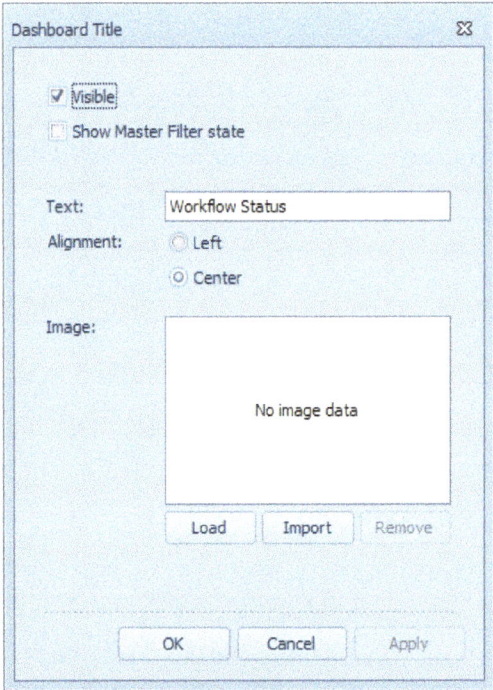

Figure 13.63

Chapter 13

From the Home tab, click Edit Colors.

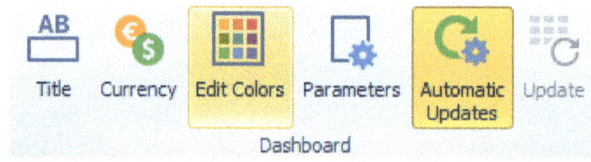

Figure 13.64

Change the colors for each of the values to update the bar chart, then click OK.

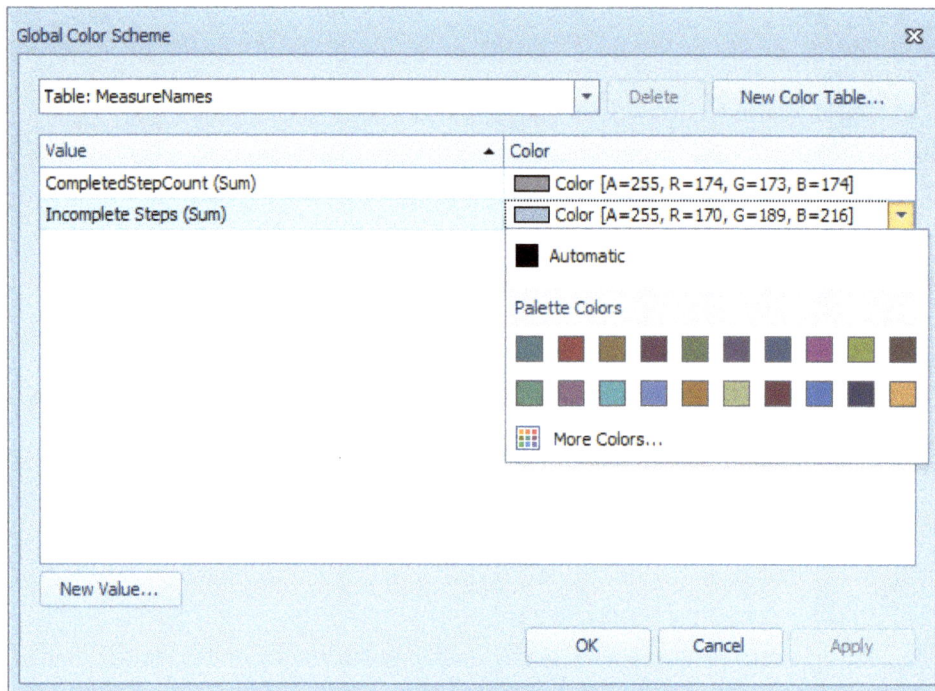

Figure 13.65

Here is what the end result looks like; we are now ready to add this to our main Dashboard.

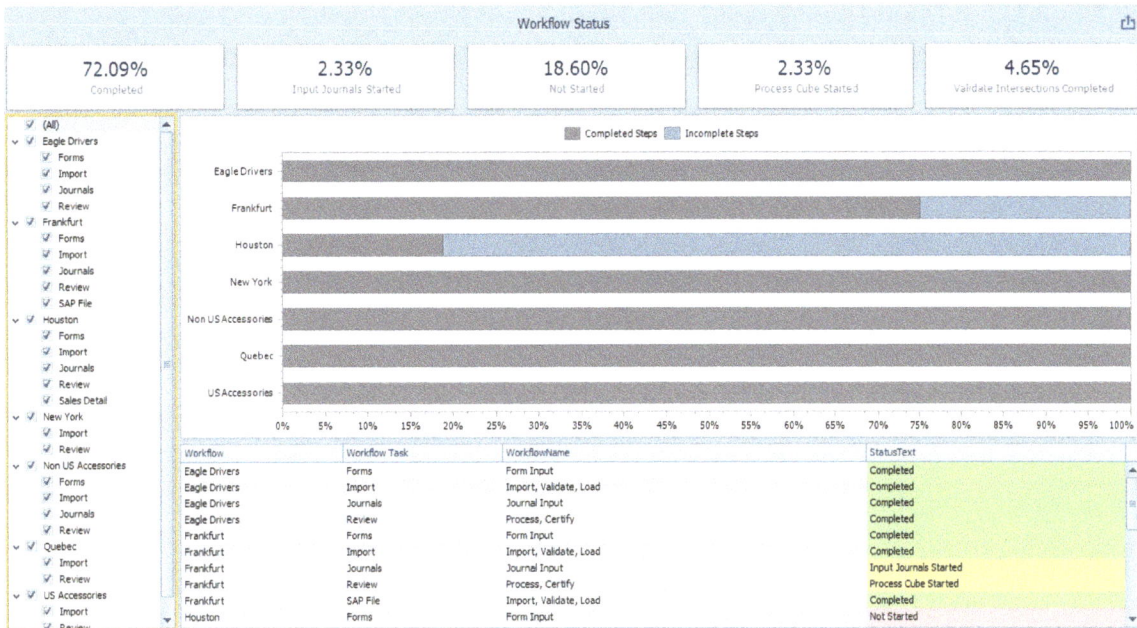

Figure 13.66

Navigate to the Dashboard Group and click Create Dashboard.

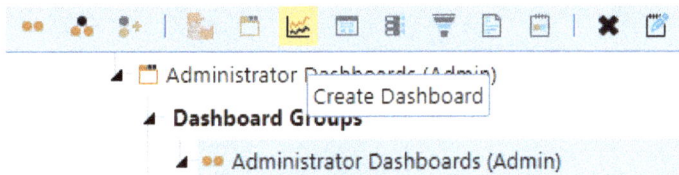

Figure 13.67

Navigate to the Dashboard named 3b_WorkflowStatus_Admin and select the Dashboard Components tab. Click Add Dashboard Component. Start typing in biv to see the applicable Components appear, select the BI Viewer Component we created previously, and click OK. Then save the Dashboard.

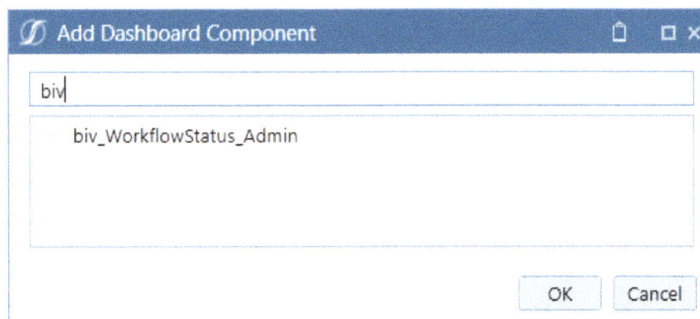

Figure 13.68

Vital Signs

Administrators are responsible for monitoring the application's health. This means checking for errors and system messages that may impact Users and data quality. OneStream has a MarketPlace solution called **Close Manager** – a solution that consists of various application monitoring Reports and Dashboards to support Administrator functions. Instead of recreating the solution, we can simply create an embedded Dashboard Component to display the solution on our Administrator Dashboard.

The Close Manager solution is shown below; we shall create an embedded Dashboard that will display the **Vital Signs Dashboard** in our Dashboard.

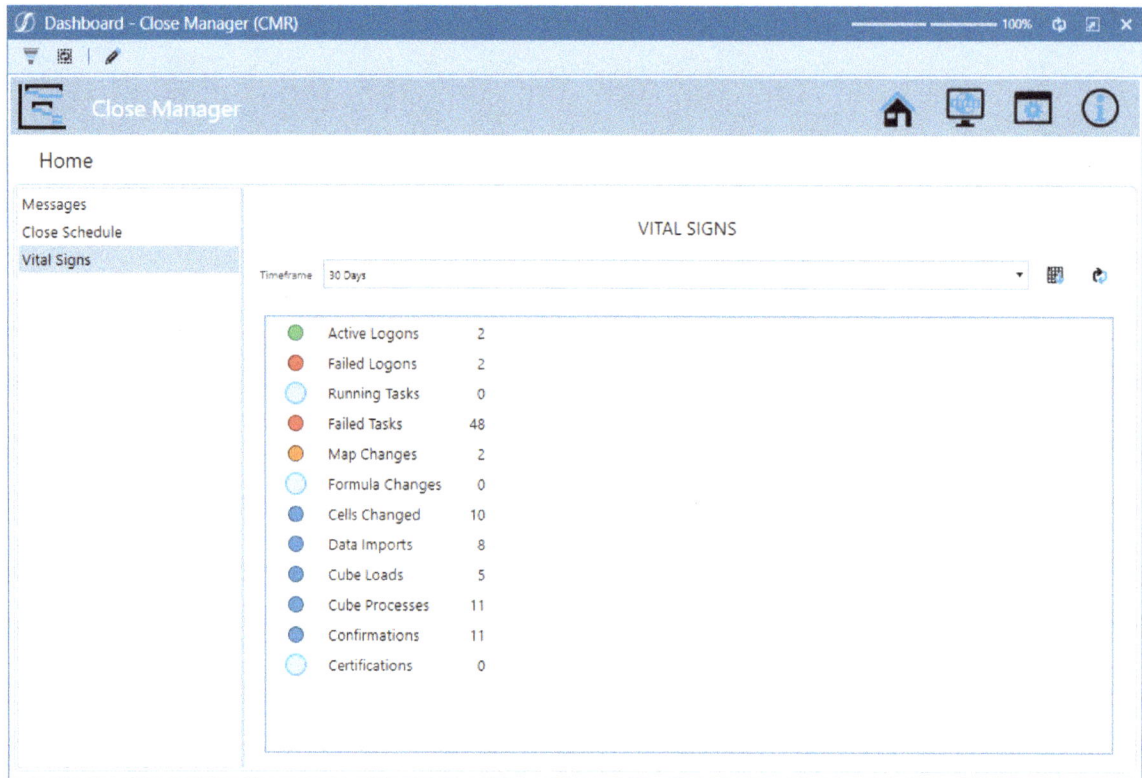

Figure 13.69

Navigate to Components and click Create Dashboard Component.

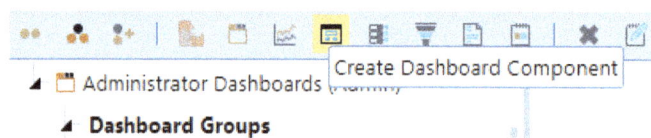

Figure 13.70

Select Embedded Dashboard from the dialog and click OK.

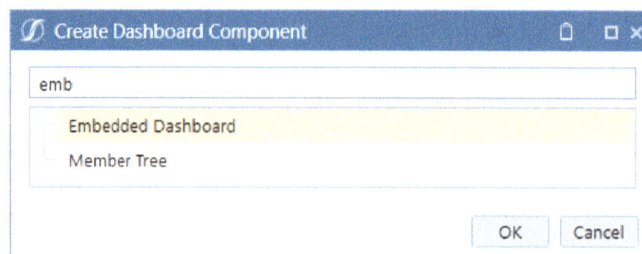

Figure 13.71

Name the Component emb_VitalSigns_Admin and click the Edit button.

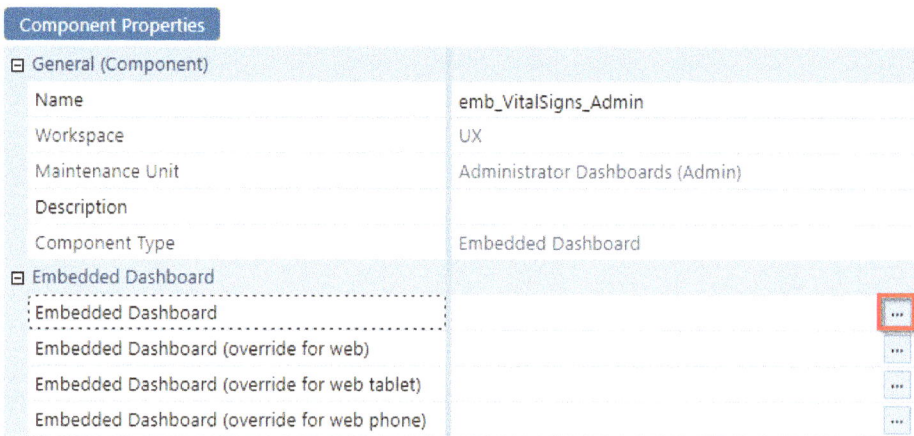

Figure 13.72

Type VitalSign into the object lookup dialog and select 0_VitalSignPanel_CMRV, then click OK.

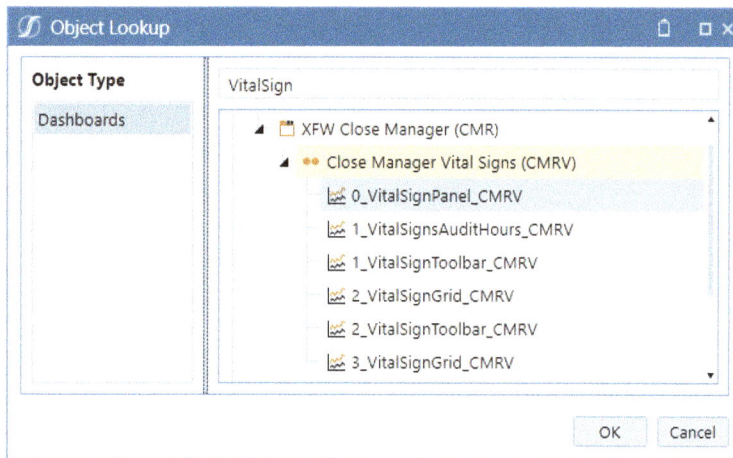

Figure 13.73

Navigate to the Dashboard named 3c_VitalSignsPanel_Admin, select the Dashboard Components tab, then click Add Dashboard Component.

Figure 13.74

Type Vital in the search bar and select the embedded Component we created. Click OK and save the Dashboard.

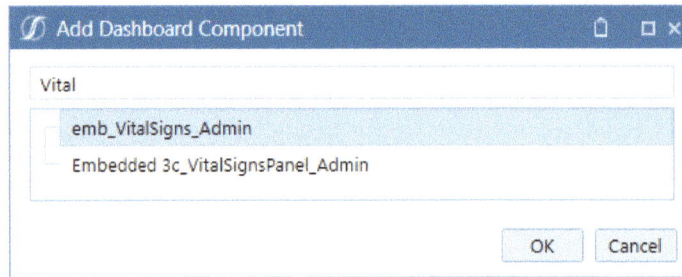

Figure 13.75

Navigation Buttons

Administrators manage the application, which means they handle various functions and need to quickly access different areas within the solution for a number of reasons. As such, Administrator Dashboards are extremely powerful because they provide a landing page for Administrators to access their role-based functions from a central location.

Buttons can be placed on Dashboards to open pages and dialogs, and run a variety of jobs; they are the most powerful Component because of their flexibility. This exercise involves creating various buttons to enhance the Administrator experience to give you ideas for your own application.

Select Parameters and click Create Parameter.

Figure 13.76

Name the parameter btnformat_Admin and paste the following string into the Default Value:

```
BackgroundColor = Transparent, BorderThickness = 0, Height = 100,
HorizontalAlignment = Center, HorizontalContentAlignment = Center, ImageStretch =
Uniform, LabelPosition = Bottom, MarginBottom = 25, VerticalAlignment = Center,
VerticalContentAlignment = Top, Width = 125
```

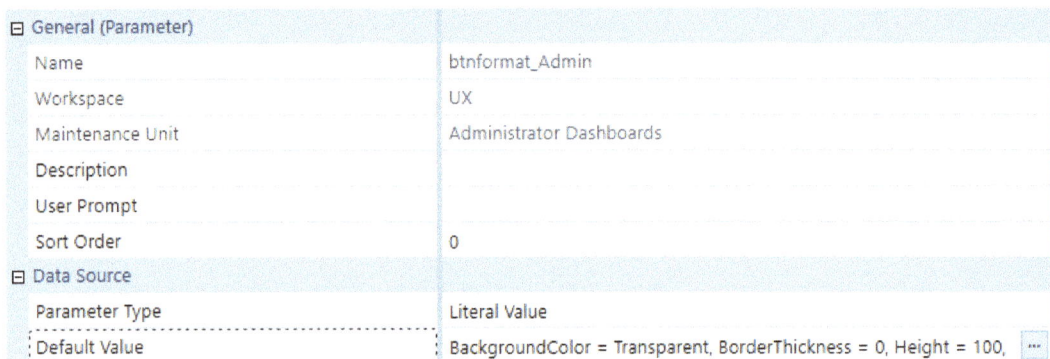

Figure 13.77

Select Files and click Create File.

Figure 13.78

Click the Upload File button from the Content File field and select an image to upload.

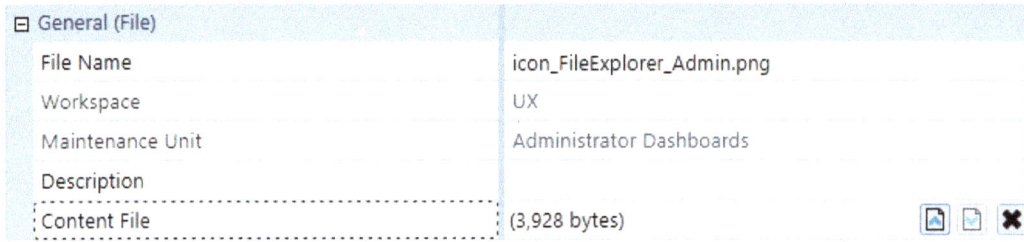

General (File)	
File Name	icon_FileExplorer_Admin.png
Workspace	UX
Maintenance Unit	Administrator Dashboards
Description	
Content File	(3,928 bytes)

Figure 13.79

Select Components and click Create Dashboard Component, then select Button and click OK.

Figure 13.80

Name the button btn_FileExplorer_Admin and set the following properties.

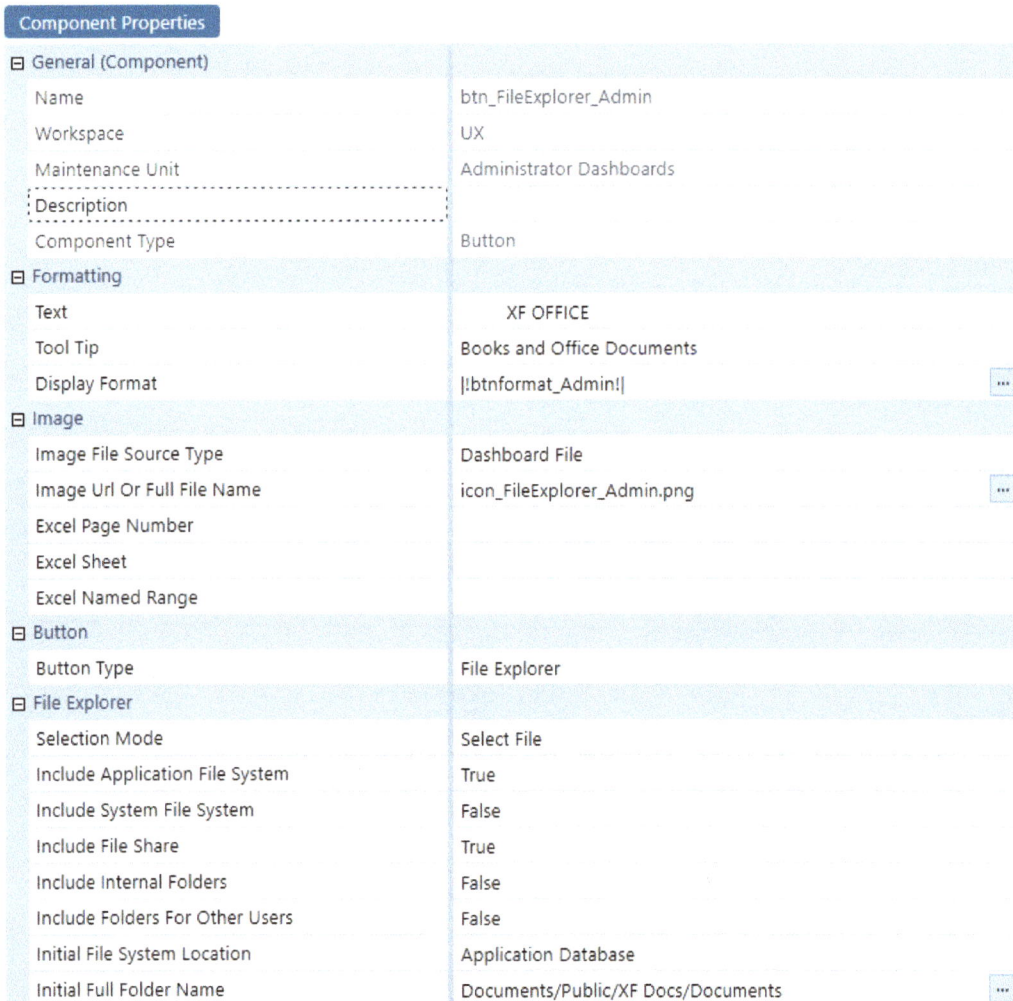

Component Properties

General (Component)	
Name	btn_FileExplorer_Admin
Workspace	UX
Maintenance Unit	Administrator Dashboards
Description	
Component Type	Button
Formatting	
Text	XF OFFICE
Tool Tip	Books and Office Documents
Display Format	|!btnformat_Admin!|
Image	
Image File Source Type	Dashboard File
Image Url Or Full File Name	icon_FileExplorer_Admin.png
Excel Page Number	
Excel Sheet	
Excel Named Range	
Button	
Button Type	File Explorer
File Explorer	
Selection Mode	Select File
Include Application File System	True
Include System File System	False
Include File Share	True
Include Internal Folders	False
Include Folders For Other Users	False
Initial File System Location	Application Database
Initial Full Folder Name	Documents/Public/XF Docs/Documents

Figure 13.81

293

Chapter 13

Select Files and click Create File.

Figure 13.82

Click the Upload File button from the Content File field and select an image to upload.

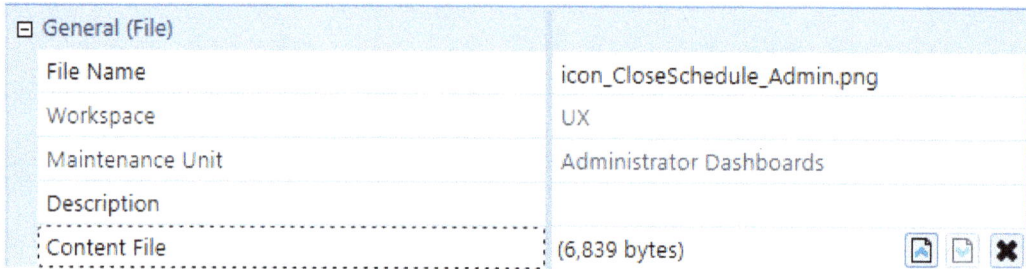

Figure 13.83

Select Components and click Create Dashboard Component, then select Button and click OK.

Figure 13.84

Name the button btn_CloseSchedule_Admin and set the following properties.

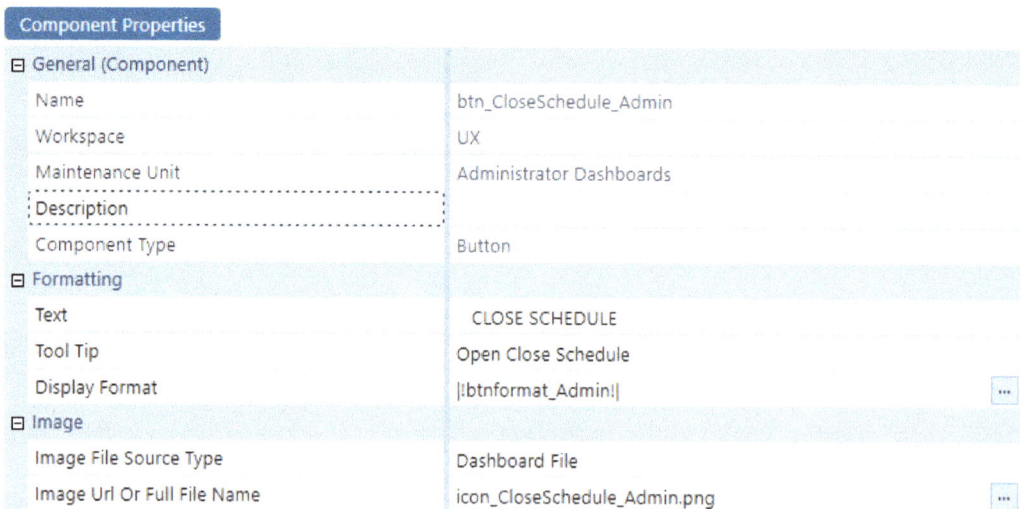

Figure 13.85

Set the User Interface Action to Open Dialog and insert the Dashboard 0_CloseSchedule_CMRSCH in the field shown below.

User Interface Action		
Selection Changed User Interface Action	Open Dialog	
Dashboards To Redraw		...
Dashboards To Show		...
Dashboards To Hide		...
Dashboard To Open In Dialog	0_CloseSchedule_CMRSCH	...

Figure 13.86

Repeat the steps in Figures 13.82-13.86 for four more buttons; the buttons we will need include:

Name	Text	Dashboard to Open In Dialog
btn_GuidedReporting_Admin	REPORTING	0_Frame_V_GRT2W
btn_HelpDesk_Admin	SUPPORT	0_Frame_HDK_OnePlace
btn_ACM_Admin	ACM	0_Frame_ACM
btn_Automation_Admin	AUTOMATION	0_Frame_Aut_AWS

Figure 13.87

Navigate to the Dashboard named 3a_NavigationButtons_Admin, select the Dashboard Components tab, and click Add Dashboard Component. Select the buttons and save the Dashboard.

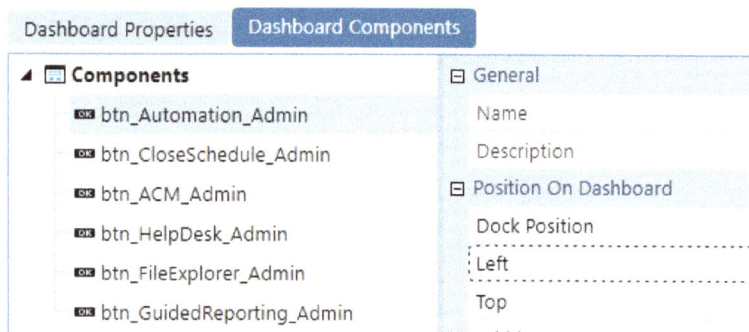

Dashboard Properties	**Dashboard Components**	
▲ 🖼 **Components**		⊟ General
🔳 btn_Automation_Admin		Name
🔳 btn_CloseSchedule_Admin		Description
🔳 btn_ACM_Admin		⊟ Position On Dashboard
🔳 btn_HelpDesk_Admin		Dock Position
🔳 btn_FileExplorer_Admin		Left
🔳 btn_GuidedReporting_Admin		Top

Figure 13.88

Select the Dashboard named 0_Frame_Admin and click View Dashboard.

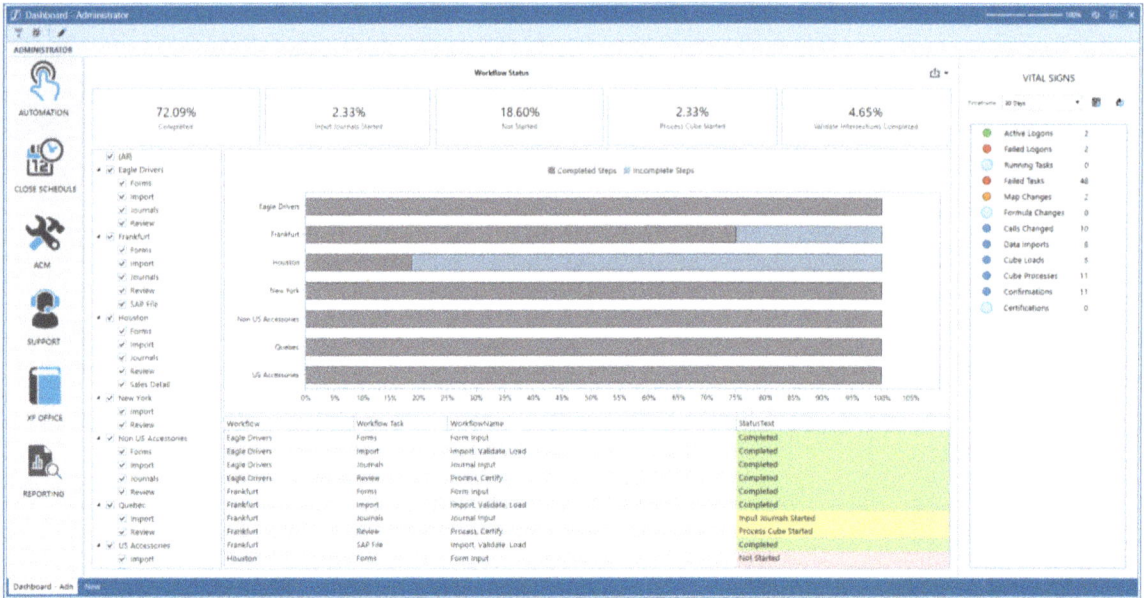

Figure 13.89

Automation opens OneStream's **Close Manager System Automation Solution**.

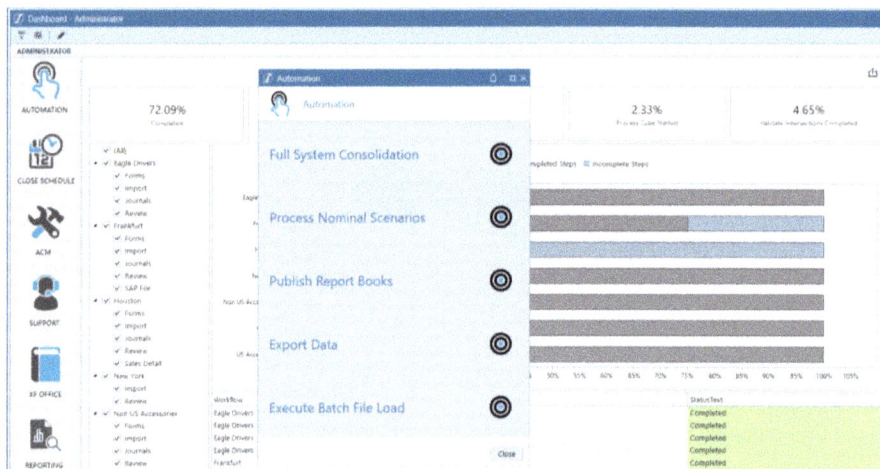

Figure 13.90

Close Schedule opens OneStream's **Close Manager Close Schedule Solution**.

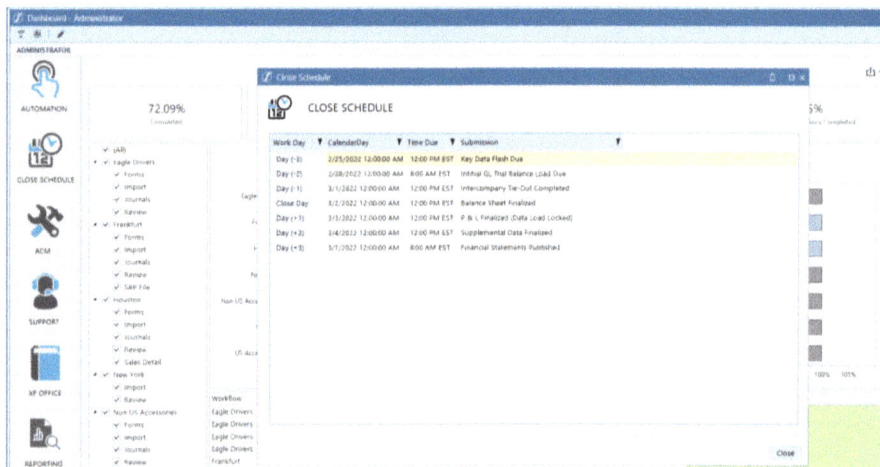

Figure 13.91

ACM opens OneStream's **Application Control Manager Solution**.

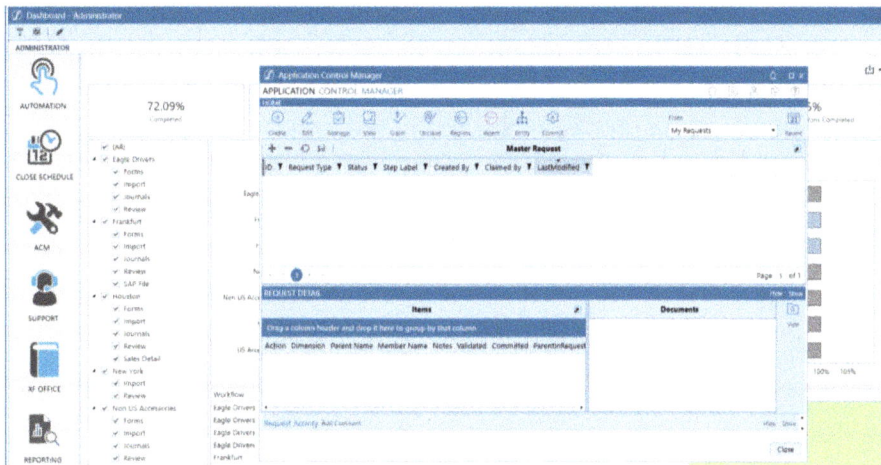

Figure 13.92

Support opens OneStream's **Help Desk Solution**.

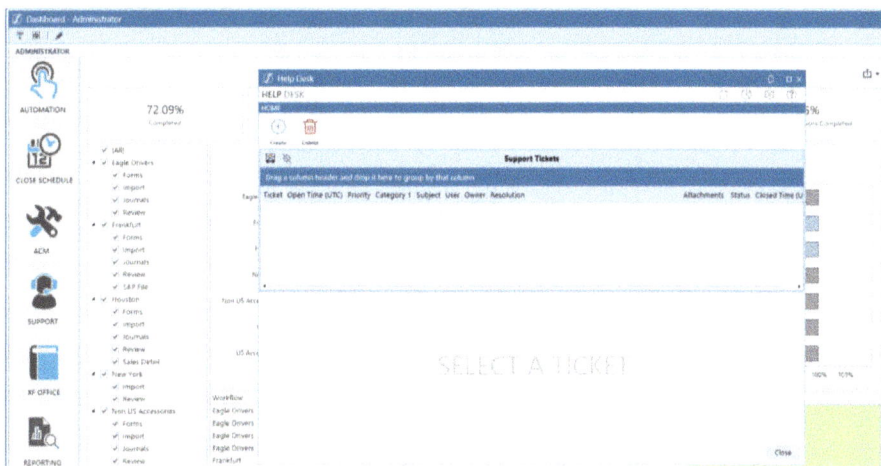

Figure 13.93

XF Office opens OneStream's **File Explorer**.

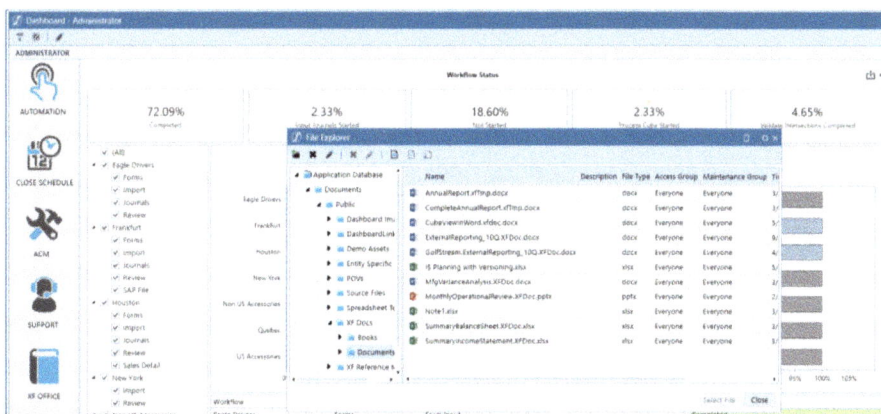

Figure 13.94

Reporting opens **Guided Reporting**.

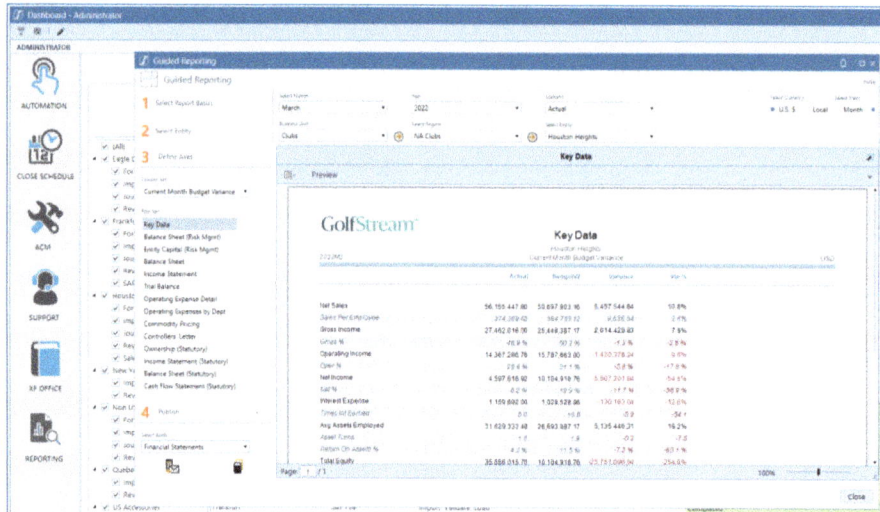

Figure 13.95

Conclusion

In this chapter, we built an Administrator Dashboard with navigation buttons to open a variety of OneStream Dashboards, a BI Viewer that offered a visual way to view Workflow status, and an embedded Dashboard that shows how you can easily leverage existing Dashboards throughout an application.

The MarketPlace solution **Standard Application Reports** contains 70+ Reports that are incredibly useful on their own, but these can also be copied and modified to produce additional Reports tailored to your organization's needs. Hopefully, this has your juices flowing for ideas of what to build for your Administrator Dashboards! Happy building!

14

Dashboards for Budgeting, Planning, and Forecasting

In the preceding chapters, we have learned how to design and build Dashboards to provide User Experiences appropriate to various processes and communities in our organization, including intuitive and attractive home pages, highly functional administrative Dashboards, and Executive-level reporting and analysis views.

Now, we will bring many of these concepts together and – with a few additional design considerations and configuration techniques – we will assemble a powerful, flexible, and easy-to-use front end for the members of our team that do the heavy lifting of the Budgeting and Forecasting processes.

Our Planning Screen Functional Requirements

When thinking through the overall structure of this Dashboard, let's keep in mind that our primary goal is to give our End-Users a clean, intuitive, and consistent User Experience. The Planning process is seldom 'simple' – and the more complex our organization becomes, the less simple this process is likely to be. That said, with a well-thought-out standard screen layout and clear, intuitive navigation, we can simplify the process of producing the plan, no matter how many 'moving pieces' it contains, and we can avoid the visual clutter and User confusion that arises when we fall into the trap of trying to fit everything (or even just a little too much) on a single screen.

Like most organizations, our plan can be broken up into a handful of separate but related parts. For this example, let's assume that the Users of this Dashboard will be focusing on three major components of the plan: Revenues, Expenses, and various Assumptions used to perform Calculations.

Although many Users will be responsible for the Revenue and Expense plans for our various regions, products, and cost centers, the Planning process for any one region or product or cost center will be essentially the same as any other. We can leverage this commonality in the design of our Dashboard. As much as we can, we will try to make every screen look and feel the same for the User, and even though the Revenue Planning process may be very different from the Expense Planning process, certain broad concepts will be identical.

Let's start with navigation and Workflow. No matter which specific part of the plan we are working on, we will always want to be able to 1. easily navigate to another part of the plan, and 2. mark the part of the plan we are working on as 'complete' when we are done.

To provide simple one-click navigation, we will include a panel along the left-hand side of the screen with a button for each of the major functional parts of the plan. We will also include a top-level 'Overview' button that will allow us to review a summarized view of the full plan at any time, with all of the details pulled together.

To keep track of which parts of the plan are completed and which are not, we will leverage OneStream's Workflow functionality. Each of the major sections of the plan (Revenues, Expenses, etc.) will be configured as steps in the Workflow Profile for the Budget Scenario Type. On our Dashboard, we will include two buttons in the upper-right corner of the screen – one to mark the current Workflow step complete, and another to revert that step if necessary.

We can even tie the navigation and Workflow concepts together by configuring each navigation button to reflect the completion status of its respective step. Since these buttons will be visible at all times on the left-hand side of the screen, having the buttons turn green as each step is marked complete will let us know – at a glance – where we stand in the overall process and what we still need to finish up.

Leveraging Dashboard Business Rules

Several of these design ideas are not out-of-the-box – that is, rather than simply relying on the standard functionality of a Component (such as a button), we will need to 'teach' that button to perform very specific tasks that OneStream's engineering team might have never guessed we would dream up.

Fortunately for us, the OneStream platform provides us with the ability to create Business Rules that can perform virtually any logic we require for our specific implementation. When working with Dashboards, we have three broad categories of rules:

1. **Dashboard Data Set Rules**, which can be used to collect, manipulate, and enrich sets of data. These rules are often used to retrieve data from sources such as SQL tables and organize this data in a format that is easily used by a Dashboard data adapter to feed a chart or BI Viewer Component.

2. **Dashboard XFBR String Rules**, which are often used to dynamically generate the configuration of an object based on certain specified conditions. For example, in this exercise, we will use an XFBR String Rule to control the color of our navigation buttons to give an easy visual guide to which button is currently selected (with a grey background), and which of our buttons represent tasks that have been completed (with a green background).

3. **Dashboard Extender Rules**, which are the workhorses of the Dashboard Business Rules. With Extender Rules, we can make our Dashboards do nearly anything. Extender Rules are often used to perform relatively complex tasks when a User performs a specific action within a Dashboard, such as clicking a button, changing the selected Member in a combo box, or reloading the Dashboard. We will use an Extender Rule to complete or revert Workflow steps when the User clicks the relevant buttons, but these rules can also be used to update the values of parameters, launch data management jobs, dynamically generate and execute SQL scripts, and much, much more!

Designing Our Dashboard Layout

We can now begin laying out our Planning Dashboard. As before, our Planning Dashboard design will start as a wireframe sketch. As we often do, across the top of the screen, we will include a header bar with our logo, the title of our Dashboard, and the two Workflow buttons.

Down the left-hand side, we will have our navigation pane, with each of our major functional areas (and Workflow steps) represented by a large button. This leaves a large section of the screen available for the actual content required to complete each step in the process. Each of these steps will have its own specific content – Forms to fill out, charts to review, Calculations to run, etc. These functionally-specific screens will be configured as their own Dashboards, and will be displayed as **embedded content** in the body of our Planning Dashboard, with the header and navigation panes providing a consistent frame.

With these ideas in mind, we can sketch out our initial design like this (Figure 14.1):

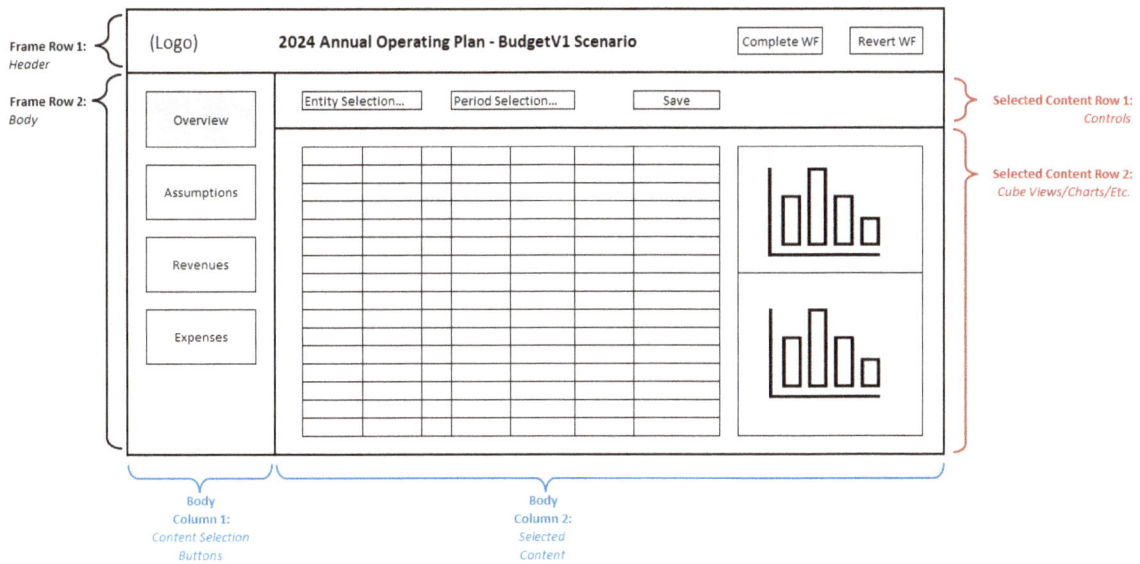

Figure 14.1

Building Our Planning Dashboard

As in previous exercises, we will begin by mapping out the various nested Dashboard panels that will make up the whole screen, and we will get started by creating a Dashboard Maintenance Unit and several Dashboard Groups to keep them organized.

We will have one Dashboard Group (00 Planning Dashboard) that will hold the main Dashboard, another (01 Planning Common) that will hold the header and navigation Dashboards, and several more (e.g., 02 Planning Overview) that will be dedicated to each of our main content sections (Figure 14.2).

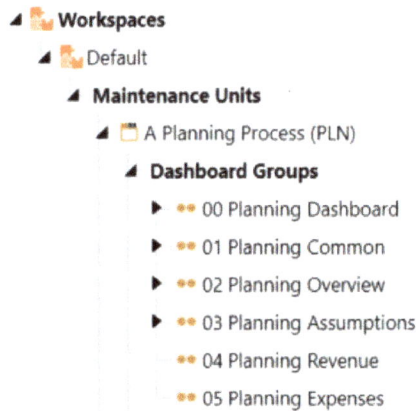

Figure 14.2

The main Dashboard will form the overall frame. This will be a simple one-column grid with two rows, each containing an embedded Dashboard that we will create in the next steps (the header and the body).

All we need to do is create a Dashboard named 00_Planning_PLN in the 00 Planning Dashboard Group and set this Dashboard's Row 1 height to 70 (which will accommodate our header). We will nest embedded Dashboards comprising the header, navigation pane, and various User-selected Content Dashboards within this main frame, using our usual naming convention to give each embedded Dashboard a clear and logical name. Altogether, our Dashboards will fit together like this:

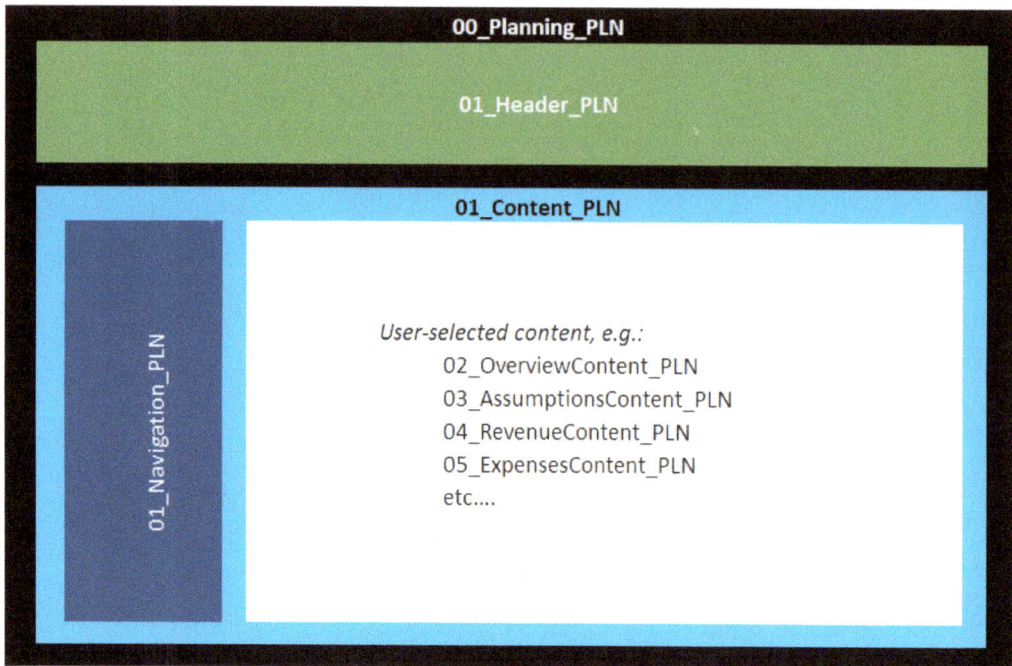

Figure 14.3

We can see that 01_Header_PLN (shown above in green) and 01_Content_PLN (shown above in light blue) are embedded as the two rows in the main Dashboard 00_Planning_PLN (shown above in black).

01_Navigation_PLN (shown above in dark blue) is embedded as the first column in the two-column grid Dashboard 01_Content_PLN. The second, larger column will eventually contain whichever content-specific Dashboard is appropriate for the button the User has clicked in the navigation pane.

For now, we can create and assemble these Dashboards, and in the sections that follow, we will configure and attach the required Components for each Dashboard. See Figure 14.4 for a summary of these Dashboards and their structure. We will create the various content-specific Dashboards as 'placeholders' for now – we will revisit their structures later.

Dashboard Name	Type	Rows	Columns	Row1 Height	Column Widths			
					Col 1	Col 2	Col 3	Col 4
00_Planning_PLN	Grid	2	1	70	*	n/a	n/a	n/a
01_Header_PLN	Grid	1	4	*	250	*	175	175
01_Content_PLN	Grid	1	2	*	190	*	n/a	n/a
01_Navigation_PLN	Vertical Stack Panel	n/a	n/a	n/a	n/a	n/a	n/a	n/a
02_OverviewContent_PLN	Uniform							
03_AssumptionsContent_PLN	Uniform							
04_RevenueContent_PLN	Uniform							
05_ExpensesContent_PLN	Uniform							

Figure 14.4

Configuring the Header

The header will contain several Components – the logo, a label for the title, and the two Workflow buttons. We will create this as a one-row grid with four columns, with one column for each Component, and name it `01_Header_PLN`.

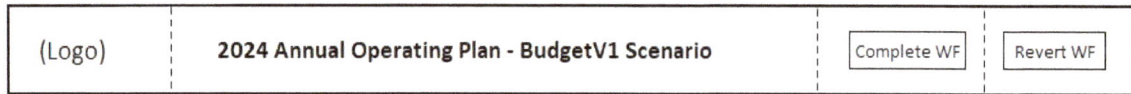

(Logo)	**2024 Annual Operating Plan - BudgetV1 Scenario**	Complete WF	Revert WF

Figure 14.5

The Logo

The logo will be configured very much like the example on our landing page (see Chapter 11). However, on this screen, we want to feature the logo much less prominently, so instead of a height of 60 pixels, we will set the height to 30.

The Title

For the title, we will use a label Component and leverage the substitution variables `|WFTime|` and `|WFScenarioDesc|` to make the title automatically reflect the Year and Scenario we are currently working on.

Component Properties	Data Adapters	
⊟ General (Component)		
Name	lbl_Title_PLN	
Workspace	Default	
Maintenance Unit	A Planning Process (PLN)	
Description		
Component Type	Label	
⊟ Formatting		
Text (use {1}, {2} for Data Table Cells)	|WFTime| Annual Operating Plan - |WFScenarioDesc| Scenario	
Tool Tip		
Display Format	HorizontalAlignment = Center, LabelFontSize = 28, LabelTextColor = Black	
⊟ Data Table Cells From Adapter		
Number Of Data Table Cells	0	

Figure 14.6

The Workflow Buttons

For the two Workflow buttons, we will use icons to give the Dashboard a nice 'polished' look. These icons are image files that we will import to our Dashboard Maintenance Unit, just like we have done in previous exercises. When configuring our two buttons, we select the Image File Source Type as Dashboard File and enter the name of our picture in the Image Url or Full File Name setting.

⊟ Image		
Image File Source Type	Dashboard File	
Image Url Or Full File Name	img_WFcomplete.png_PLN	

Figure 14.7

For these two buttons to do their jobs, we will take advantage of OneStream's remarkably powerful Business Rules Engine. In our sample application, we have created a Dashboard Extender Business Rule named `AAA_SimpleWorkflow`. This rule contains two functions: `WorkflowComplete` and `WorkflowRevert`.

The rule can be called from any button on any Dashboard attached to any Workflow Profile, and will do exactly what it sounds like: the `WorkflowComplete` function will mark the current Workflow step as Completed, and the `WorkflowRevert` function will revert it.

You may have seen similar Business Rules in action when using OneStream MarketPlace Solutions. For example, People Planning, Capital Planning, Account Reconciliations, and many other solutions include similar logic. The rules included with those solutions can be relatively complex. The fundamentals of how they work, though, are straightforward.

Dashboard Extender Business Rules

Although the details of writing Business Rules are outside the scope of this book, let's take a look at our `AAA_SimpleWorkflow` rule to get a sense of how they work.

(For a much deeper dive into Business Rules, I highly recommend Jon Golembiewski's excellent book OneStream Finance Rules and Calculations Handbook, available from OneStream Press.)

Like all Dashboard Extender Business Rules, our rule first checks what Type of function is being called – here, it's a `ComponentSelectionChanged` event (highlighted line A). This means the rule was triggered by a User 'doing something' with a Dashboard Component – in this case, a button was clicked.

Then, the rule checks for the Function Name passed to the rule by the button – in this example, either `WorkflowComplete` or `WorkflowRevert` (highlighted line B).

Finally, the rule uses the Business Rule API function `SetWorkflowStatus` to either complete or revert the Workflow as appropriate (highlighted line C).

```
Select Case args.FunctionType                                                    [A]

    Case Is = DashboardExtenderFunctionType.ComponentSelectionChanged

        'WorkflowComplete: User clicked "Complete Workflow" button, so mark this step as complete    [B]
        If (args.FunctionName.XFEqualsIgnoreCase("WorkflowComplete"))

            BRApi.Workflow.Status.SetWorkflowStatus(si, si.WorkflowClusterPk, StepClassificationTypes.Workspace, _
                                WorkflowStatusTypes.Completed, "Workflow Completed", "", _
                                "Dashboard Button", Guid.Empty)                    [C]

            Dim selectionChangedTaskResult As New XFSelectionChangedTaskResult()
            selectionChangedTaskResult.WorkflowWasChangedByBusinessRule = True
            Return selectionChangedTaskResult

        ' WorkflowRevert: User clicked the "Revert" button, so mark this step as NOT complete
        Else If (args.FunctionName.XFEqualsIgnoreCase("WorkflowRevert"))

            BRApi.Workflow.Status.SetWorkflowStatus(si, si.WorkflowClusterPk, StepClassificationTypes.Workspace, _
                                WorkflowStatusTypes.InProcess, "Workflow Reverted", "", _
                                "Dashboard Button", Guid.Empty)

            Dim selectionChangedTaskResult As New XFSelectionChangedTaskResult()
            selectionChangedTaskResult.WorkflowWasChangedByBusinessRule = True
            Return selectionChangedTaskResult

    End If

End Select
```

Let's take a closer look at line C. This rule reads:

```
BRApi.Workflow.Status.SetWorkflowStatus(si, si.WorkflowClusterPk,
StepClassificationTypes.Workspace, WorkflowStatusTypes.Completed,
"Workflow Completed", "", "Dashboard Button", Guid.Empty)
```

This may look confusing, but once you break it down, the syntax is not too hard to understand. The line begins with:

- BRApi, which means that we are calling a function that is part of OneStream's Business Rule API.

- Workflow, which means we will use functionality that is part of the application's Workflow Engine.

- Status, which is the thing we want to update.

- SetWorkflowStatus, which is what we want to do – in this case, set it to Completed.

The SetWorkflowStatus function needs some information to perform its job, and that information is included in the various parameters within the parentheses. The object si is managed by the OneStream application and contains a great deal of useful system information. The other parameters make sense if you think about what we are doing – the function will need to know which Workflow we want to mark complete (this is the WorkflowClusterPK), what Type of Workflow step we are completing (Workspace), what we want its new status to be (Completed), and various informative text parameters that will be writing to the audit log.

To call a Dashboard Extender Business Rule from a button, the syntax looks like this:

```
{RuleName}{FunctionName}{Paremeter1 = 123, Parameter2 = "ABC", etc.}
```

Our functions do not need any passed parameters, so for our Complete Workflow button, we just need to set the Selection Changed Server Task property to Execute Dashboard Extender Business Rule, and enter {AAA_SimpleWorkflow}{WorkflowComplete}{} on the Selection Changed Server Task Arguments property.

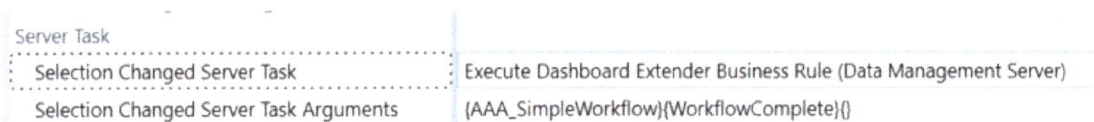

Server Task	
Selection Changed Server Task	Execute Dashboard Extender Business Rule (Data Management Server)
Selection Changed Server Task Arguments	{AAA_SimpleWorkflow}{WorkflowComplete}{}

Figure 14.8

The last step in configuring our Workflow buttons is to set the Selection Changed User Interface action to Refresh. Later on, we will be configuring our navigation buttons to have green backgrounds if their related Workflow steps are complete – this setting will ensure those buttons repaint to show their correct colors when the Workflow buttons are clicked.

With our four header Components created, we can now add them to our 01_Header_PLN Dashboard. If we give that Dashboard a test run, after a little fine-tuning of font sizes, column widths, etc., our header now looks like this:

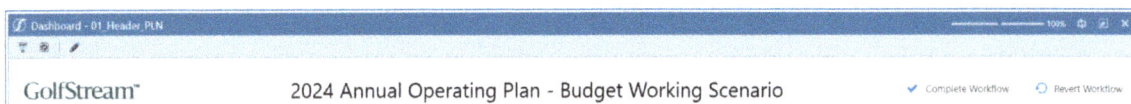

Figure 14.9

Configuring the Navigation Pane

The navigation buttons on the left-hand side of the screen will reside in a simple Vertical Stack Panel Dashboard.

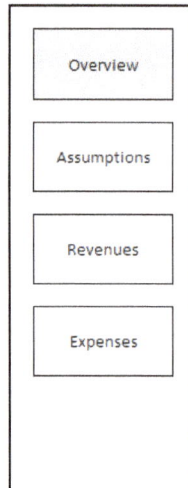

Figure 14.10

The Navigation Buttons

Each of these buttons (and any others we may add later) are configured in the same way.

Each button will use an XFBR Business Rule to control its formatting, will use a Bound Parameter to store the name of the Content Dashboard that will be associated with the button, will change the Workflow as appropriate to the button, and will refresh the Dashboard so the button's associated content will be displayed after the button is clicked.

Figure 14.11 shows the configuration for a typical button – we will discuss each of these settings individually.

Component Properties	
General (Component)	
Name	btn_Assumptions_PLN
Workspace	Default
Maintenance Unit	A Planning Process (PLN)
Description	
Component Type	Button
Formatting	
Text	Assumptions
Tool Tip	
Display Format	XFBR(PLN_ParamHelper, FormatButton, wfStep = [Assumptions]),
Image	
Button	
Button Type	Standard
Action	
Bound Parameter	prm_PlanningContent_PLN
Parameter Value For Button Click	03_AssumptionsContent_PLN
Apply Selected Value To Current Dashboard	True
Save Action	
Selection Changed Save Action	No Action
Selection Changed Save Arguments	
POV Action	
Selection Changed POV Action	Change Workflow
Selection Changed POV Arguments	WFProfile=[Equipment Plan NA.Assumptions], WFScenario=[BudgetWorking], WFTime=[|WFYear|]
Server Task	
Selection Changed Server Task	No Task
Selection Changed Server Task Arguments	
User Interface Action	
Selection Changed User Interface Action	Refresh

Figure 14.11

Dashboard XFBR String Business Rules

For each button's display format, instead of using the traditional text string of formatting parameters (e.g., `Bold = True, BackgroundColor = Blue`), we will use a Dashboard XFBR String Business Rule we have created called `PLN_ParamHelper` (see below). This rule will dynamically assemble a formatting string based on the Workflow step associated with the button. If a button's Workflow step has been completed, we will make the button green. If the button is associated with the Workflow step we are currently using, we will make the button blue. If neither of these conditions are true, we won't change the buttons color at all, so it will be displayed in its default color (white).

Here's the full rule that performs this logic and returns a formatting string appropriate for the current status of the button calling the rule:

```
If args.FunctionName.XFEqualsIgnoreCase("FormatButton") Then

    ' Retrieve the name of the requested Workflow Step (e.g., "Revenue") passed in by this button
    Dim wfStepForBtn    As String        = args.NameValuePairs("WFStep")                           A

    ' Set the basic formatting string options
    Dim buttonFormat    As String        = "FontSize = 16, HorizontalAlignment = Center, Width = 120, Height = 60,
                                          MarginBottom = 20, MarginTop = 20, "                     B

    ' Get the name of the currently active Workflow information, and its top-level parent
    Dim wfname          As String        = BRApi.Workflow.Metadata.GetProfile(si, si.WorkflowClusterPk.ProfileKey).Name
    Dim wfparent        As String()      = wfname.Split(".")

    ' Get the workflow information for the workflow step passed in by the button.
    ' If the requested step is "Review" we want to use the 'Top Level' workflow (e.g., "Budget Workflow"); otherwise, we want
    ' the name of the parent level workflow combined with the requested workflow step (e.g., "Budget Workflow.Revenue").
    Dim wfToCheck       As WorkflowUnitClusterPk        = si.WorkflowClusterPk

    If wfStepForBtn.XFEqualsIgnoreCase("Review") Then
        wfToCheck.ProfileKey = BRApi.Workflow.Metadata.GetProfile(si, wfparent(0)).ProfileKey
```

```
Else
      wfToCheck.ProfileKey = BRApi.Workflow.Metadata.GetProfile(si, wfparent(0) & "." & wfStepForBtn).ProfileKey
End If

Dim wfStatusForBtn  As WorkflowInfo       = BRApi.Workflow.Status.GetWorkflowStatus(si, wfToCheck, False)
```
C

```
'Get the numerical indexes of the requested workflow step and the currently active workflow step
Dim currentWFindex As Decimal            = args.SubstVarSourceInfo.WFProfileIndex
Dim buttonWFindex  As Decimal            = BRApi.Workflow.Metadata.GetProfile(si, wftocheck.ProfileKey).Index

'If the step is complete, change text to white and the background to green
If (wfStatusForBtn.AllTasksCompleted) Then
      buttonFormat = buttonFormat & "TextColor = White, BackgroundColor = Green, Bold = True"
```
D

```
'If this is the button for the selected workflow, change text to white and the background to blue
Else If currentWFindex  = buttonWFindex    Then
      buttonFormat = buttonFormat & "TextColor = White, BackgroundColor = XFDarkBlueBackground, _
                     BorderColor = XFDarkBlueBackground, Bold = True"
End If
```
E

```
'Pass back a string with the appropriate button format settings
Return buttonFormat
```
F

```
End If
```

Let's take a closer look at the most important lines in this rule and see what they are doing.

When this rule is invoked by a Dashboard button, the button will pass in the name of the Workflow step that would be selected if that button were clicked – we store that in a string variable named `wfStep` (line A):

```
Dim wfStepForBtn As String = args.NameValuePairs("WFStep")
```

Then, we set the basics of the button's display format in a string variable called `buttonFormat` (line B):

```
Dim buttonFormat As String = "FontSize = 16, HorizontalAlignment =
Center, Width = 120, Height = 60, MarginBottom = 20, MarginTop = 20, "
```

After retrieving relevant information about the currently active Workflow Profile as well as the Workflow Profile associated with the button being formatted, we use the BRAPI function `GetWorkflowStatus` to retrieve the current status of the this button's Workflow step (line C):

```
Dim wfStatusForBtn As WorkflowInfo =
BRApi.Workflow.Status.GetWorkflowStatus(si, wfToCheck, False)
```

If the button we are currently formatting is for a Workflow step that has been completed, we will set the background color for that button to green and its text to a bold white font (line D):

```
buttonFormat = buttonFormat & "TextColor = White, BackgroundColor =
Green, Bold = True"
```

If this button's Workflow step has not been completed, but this is the button associated with our currently selected Workflow step, we will set the button's background color to blue (line E):

```
buttonFormat = buttonFormat & "TextColor = White, BackgroundColor =
XFDarkBlueBackground, BorderColor = XFDarkBlueBackground, Bold = True"
```

Finally, the rule returns the complete formatting string back to the Dashboard button, so it will have the correct size, font, background color, and any other formatting options we might be using the rule to control (line F):

```
Return buttonFormat
```

To apply this rule to our buttons, we just set the Display Format to `XFBR(PLN_ParamHelper,` `FormatButton, wfStep=[Expenses])` with the `wfStep` parameter set as appropriate to the button (Figure 14.12).

⊟ Formatting	
Text	Expenses
Tool Tip	
Display Format	XFBR(PLN_ParamHelper, FormatButton, wfStep = [Expenses]),

Figure 14.12

Setting the Button's Bound Parameter

Each button will also set the value of a Bound Parameter to the name of the Dashboard we want displayed in the body of our main Dashboard when that button is clicked. We will first create this parameter as an Input Value Type, name it `prm_PlanningContent_PLN`, and set its Default Value to the name of one of our Content Dashboards (Figure 14.13). We will actually flesh out those Dashboards in a later step, but for now we can enter the name we plan to use (e.g., `02_OverviewContent_PLN`).

⊟ General (Parameter)	
Name	prm_PlanningContent_PLN
Workspace	Default
Maintenance Unit	A Planning Process (PLN)
Description	
User Prompt	
Sort Order	0
⊟ Data Source	
Parameter Type	Input Value
Default Value	02_OverviewContent_PLN

Figure 14.13

Now, for each of our navigation buttons, we will set the Bound Parameter to `prm_PlanningContent_PLN`, and enter the name of the Content Dashboard we plan to associate with each button in the Parameter Value for Button Click setting (e.g., `05_ExpensesContent_PLN`).

⊟ Action	
Bound Parameter	prm_PlanningContent_PLN
Parameter Value For Button Click	05_ExpensesContent_PLN
Apply Selected Value To Current Dashboard	True

Figure 14.14

Setting the Button's POV Action

Next, we want each button to change the currently selected Workflow as appropriate. In Figure 14.15, we can see that clicking the `btn_Expenses_PLN` button will set our Workflow Profile to Equipment `Plan NA.Expenses`, our Workflow Scenario to `BudgetWorking`, and our Workflow Time to the current Workflow year.

(In this simple example, we have hard-coded some of these settings – in a fully configured application, we would most likely use parameters for the top-level Workflow name (Equipment Plan NA) and the current active Budget Scenario.)

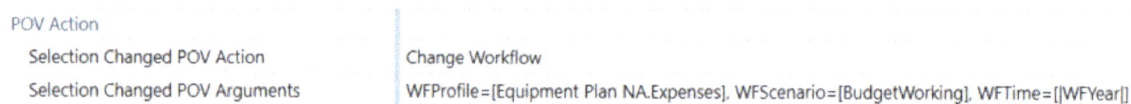

POV Action

Selection Changed POV Action   Change Workflow

Selection Changed POV Arguments   WFProfile=[Equipment Plan NA.Expenses], WFScenario=[BudgetWorking], WFTime=[|WFYear|]

Figure 14.15

Finally, we will set the Selection Changed User Interface Action to Refresh, so any changes to button formatting and the displayed content will immediately appear on our screen after clicking the button.

User Interface Action

Selection Changed User Interface Action   Refresh

Figure 14.16

Now that we have our buttons configured, we simply add them to the vertical stack panel Dashboard named 01_Navigation_PLN in the order we want them to appear.

Embedding Our Content Dashboards

The final step in configuring our Planning process navigation Dashboard is to include the selected Content Dashboard in the large space filling the right side of the screen. Whenever we click one of our navigation buttons, it stores the name of its associated Content Dashboard in the parameter named prm_PlanningContent_PLN, and we will use this stored text to dynamically change the content of our Dashboard by creating an **Embedded Dashboard Object**.

Embedded Dashboards

Each time we create a Dashboard, the application automatically creates an Embedded Dashboard Object. These act as pointers when we are nesting one Dashboard inside another. We can also create our own; instead of having it point to a specific named Dashboard, we can use a parameter to make this embedded Dashboard present different content (depending on the current value stored in that parameter).

Figure 14.17 shows our embedded Dashboard Component – notice that for the Embedded Dashboard property, we have used our prm_PlanningContent_PLN parameter.

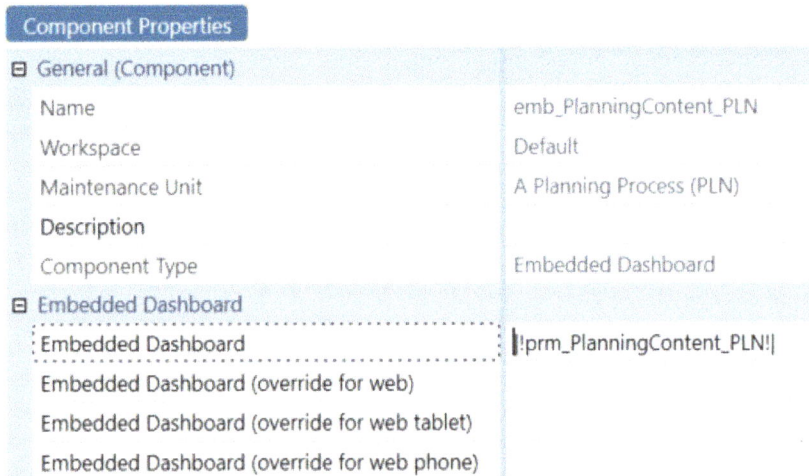

Figure 14.17

We will now add this Embedded Dashboard Component as the second Component on our 01_Content_PLN Dashboard, so whatever Dashboard name is currently stored in the Planning Content parameter will appear in the large space to the right of our navigation panel.

Attaching Our Dashboard to Our Workflow Profile

Now that we have the core functionality of our Dashboard complete, we can attach it to the Workflow Profile for our Budget process.

As seen in Figure 14.18, the Assumptions step has the Budget Scenario Type configured with the Workspace Name of Workspace. This simply means that when this step is selected, the User should be presented with the Dashboard identified in the Workspace Dashboard Name setting – in this case, it is set to our main Planning Dashboard 00_Planning_PLN.

The Revenues, Expenses, and Parent-level Equipment Plan NA Workflows are configured in the exact same way, with the exact same Dashboard; the way we have configured our buttons, the main Dashboard will show the content appropriate to the Workflow step.

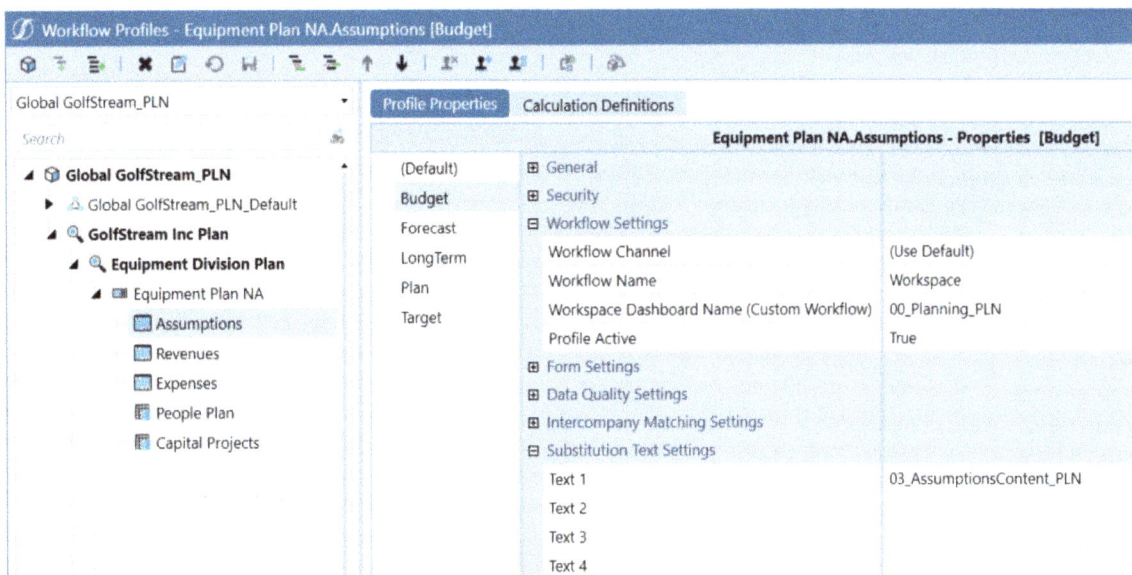

Figure 14.18

Executing a Business Rule When a Dashboard is First Opened

Notice that we have also included the name of the associated Content Dashboard in the Text 1 field for each Workflow step. We will use this to synchronize the content displayed if a User manually selects a Workflow step through the standard OnePlace interface instead of using our Dashboard's navigation buttons. To make this work, we will add one last change to our 00_Planning_PLN Dashboard.

When the Dashboard is opened for the first time, we will use the Workflow's Text 1 value for whatever Workflow step is currently active. This will essentially simulate a 'click' on the button that points to that step.

We will set our 00_Planning_PLN Dashboard's **Load Dashboard Server Task** to Execute Dashboard Extender Business Rule (Once), and the arguments for that task to {PLN_SolutionHelper}{SelectContent}{selectedContent=|WFText1|}

Action (Primary Dashboard Only)	
Server Task	
Load Dashboard Server Task	Execute Dashboard Extender Business Rule (Once)
Load Dashboard Server Task Arguments	{PLN_SolutionHelper}{SelectContent}{selectedContent=|WFText1|}

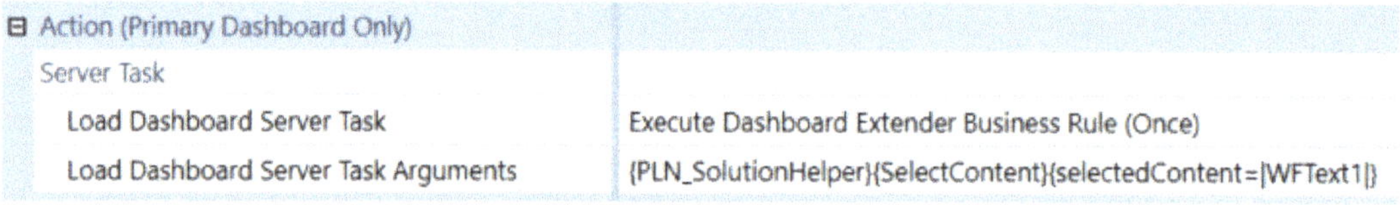

Figure 14.19

This will pass the Text 1 value for the current Workflow step to a very simple Dashboard Extender Business Rule that will be run when the Dashboard is first opened. The rule looks like this:

```
Select Case args.FunctionType

    Case Is = DashboardExtenderFunctionType.LoadDashboard

    'When loaded, dashboard will pass |WFText1| value, which contains the appropriate content dashboard for the
    workflow step. This will be written to the prm_PlanningContent_PLN parameter, which is used by the embeddded
    dashboard component emb_PlanningContent_PLN.
    Dim selectedContent As String = args.NameValuePairs.XFGetValue("selectedContent")
    brapi.Dashboards.Parameters.SetLiteralParameterValue(si,False, args.PrimaryDashboard.WorkspaceID, _
                                        "prm_PlanningContent_PLN", selectedContent)

End Select
```

All this does is retrieve the Workflow's Text 1 value (the name of the Content Dashboard associated with that Workflow), and save that value to the prm_PlanningContent_PLN parameter (which tells our embedded Dashboard Component what to display).

If we now open our Planning Workflow, we will see our Dashboard displayed, with the button for the selected Workflow step highlighted in blue (Figure 14.20).

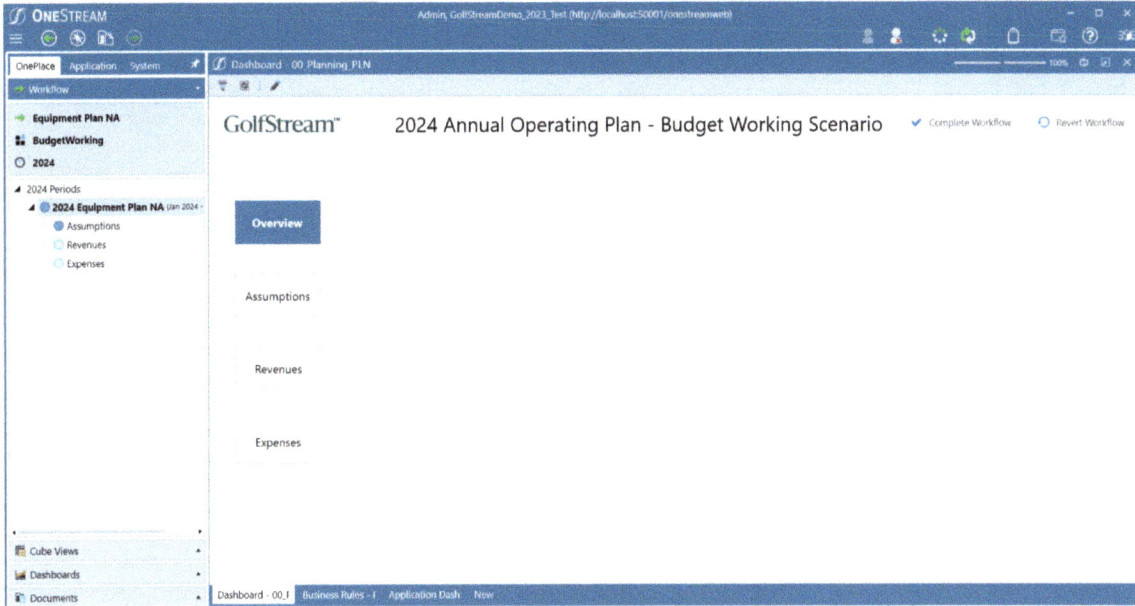

Figure 14.20

If we click on one of the buttons, the Workflow step tied to that button is automatically selected:

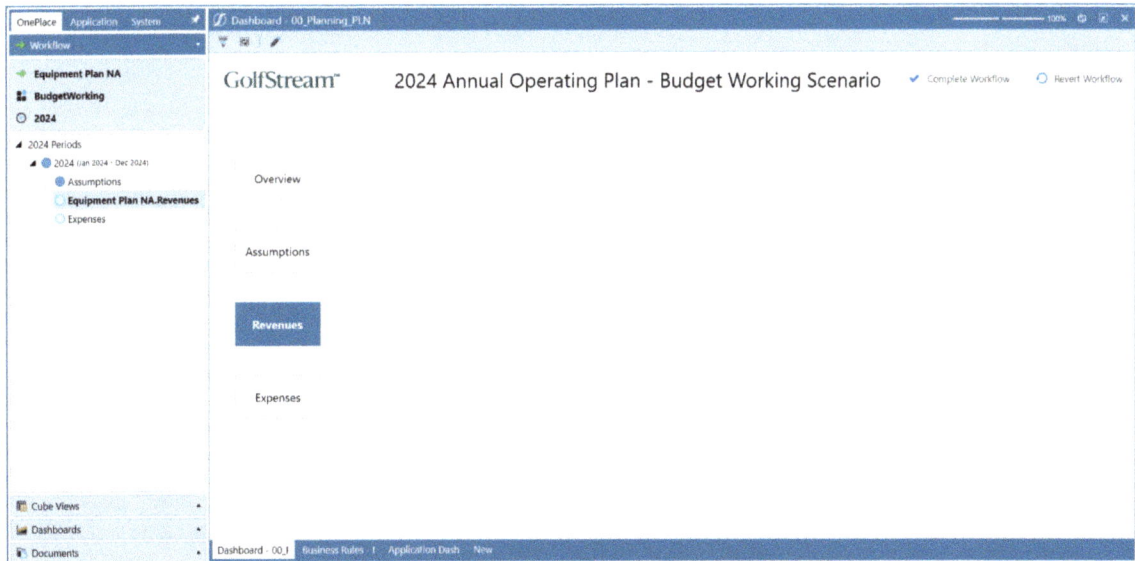

Figure 14.21

If we click the Complete Workflow button, that Workflow step now shows completed, and the button turns green:

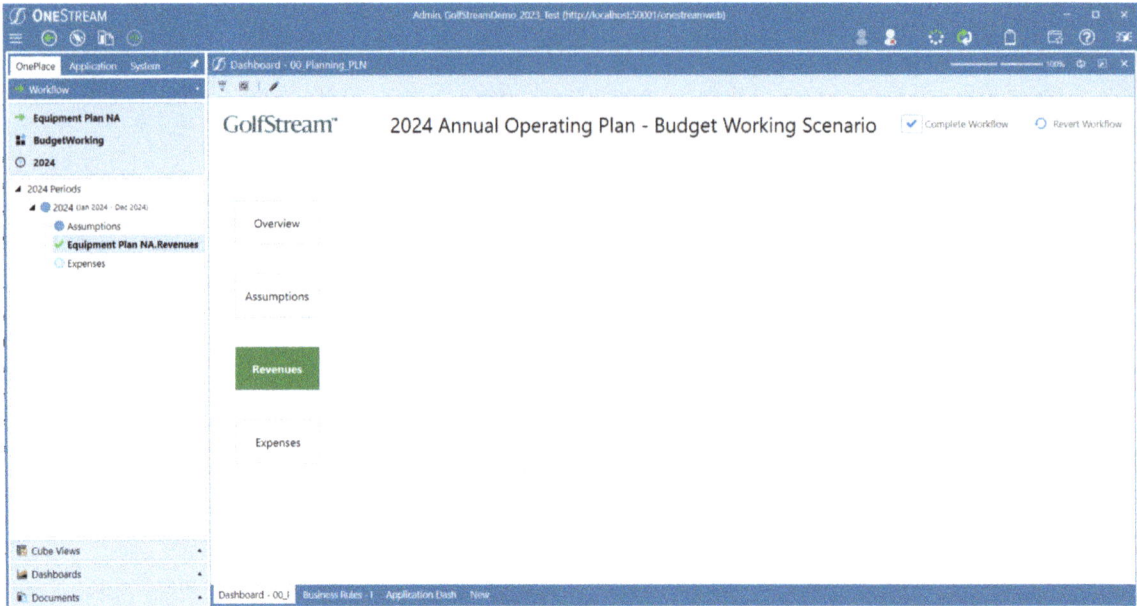

Figure 14.22

It looks and works great! End-Users will be presented with this clean, easy-to-use interface, seeing only the buttons and content they need to complete their Planning process. They can keep the OnePlace panel pinned closed, and never worry about remembering how to navigate through the comprehensive set of application controls displayed there – they will only see the buttons they care about.

Now, all we need is some Planning content to fill in that big white space!

Building Our Budget Overview Dashboard

Now that we have the framework for our Planning Dashboard complete and attached to the Workflow Profile, it is time to create the content that will be displayed for each of the steps in the process.

Most of our Content Dashboards are likely to display Cube Views to perform data entry, but for our top-level Workflow step, we would like to see 'the big picture'. In other words, when the Overview button is clicked, we will show the User a summary Income Statement, with a column showing the current active Budget values, as well as variances from the current year's Forecast, last year's Actuals, and a column for the User to enter some text commentary.

Since our Users are likely to be working on plans for multiple Entities, we will include a combo box at the top of the screen to select which Entity they are currently viewing, and we will provide a couple of nice charts on the same screen to give a clear visual of the current state of the Budget.

In a wireframe sketch, our Overview Content Dashboard might look like this:

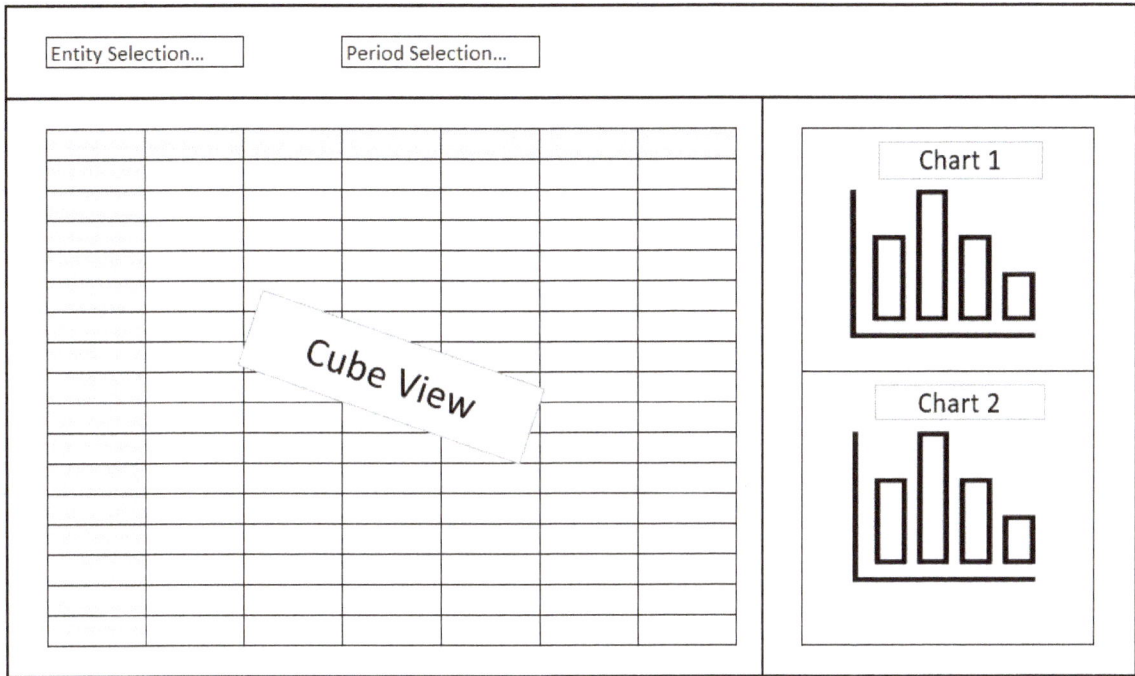

Figure 14.23

Earlier, we made a simple placeholder Dashboard named `02_OverviewContent_PLN`. It is time to revisit that Dashboard and make it look and behave like our design.

The first step will be to change the configuration of the `02_OverviewContent_PLN` Dashboard to a grid with two rows and one column. The first row will be for the combo boxes and save button; the second row will hold the Cube View and charts.

For the first row, we will create a simple horizontal stack Dashboard to hold our combo boxes and save button. We will call this Dashboard `02_OverviewControls_PLN`.

For the second row, we will create another grid Dashboard with one row and three columns – the first column will hold our Cube View, the second column will be a movable splitter, and the third column will hold our charts. We will call this Dashboard `02_OverviewDetails_PLN`.

Finally, to stack two charts in the right-hand column, we will create a fourth Dashboard – this one will be a grid with one column and three rows, one for each chart and a moveable splitter between them. We will call this Dashboard `02_OverviewCharts_PLN`.

To summarize, here are the configurations for the various embedded Dashboards for our Overview content; we will need:

Dashboard Name	Type	Rows	Columns	Row Height			Column Width		
				Row 1	Row 2	Row 3	Col 1	Col 2	Col 3
02_OverviewContent_PLN	Grid	2	1	70	*	n/a	*	n/a	n/a
02_OverviewControls_PLN	Horizontal Stack Panel	n/a	n/a	n/a	n/a	n/a	n/a	n/a	n/a
02_OverviewDetails_PLN	Grid	1	3	*	n/a	n/a	1000	Splitter	*
02_OverviewCharts_PLN	Grid	3	1	*	Splitter	*	n/a	n/a	n/a

Figure 14.24

We will assemble these embedded Dashboards as follows:

`02_OverviewContent_PLN` will contain `02_OverviewControls_PLN` and `02_OverviewDetails_PLN`.

315

`02_OverviewDetails_PLN` will contain `02_OverviewCharts_PLN` (and a Cube View Component we will configure later).

Combo Boxes

Now, let's add the Components we need to our Controls Dashboard. The two combo boxes will be configured the same, except for the Text and Bound Parameter properties. Our application already has Member List parameters for these two Dimensions – we will be using those standard lists, but if you are starting from zero, you might need to create your own. They are very simple to create – just create a parameter in the Parameter Type property, select Member List, and then fill out the Form with the Cube, Dimension Type, Member Filter, etc., as needed. Here's how our sample application has the `prm_Entity_PLN` parameter configured:

General (Parameter)	
Name	prm_Entity_PLN
Workspace	Default
Maintenance Unit	A Planning Process (PLN)
Description	
User Prompt	
Sort Order	0
Data Source	
Parameter Type	Member List
Default Value	EUS01
Display Member	Description
Cube	Global GolfStream
Dimension Type	Entity
Dimension	Equipment
Member Filter	E#NAE.DescendantsInclusive

Figure 14.25

Our `prm_Time_PLN` Member List parameter is configured like this:

General (Parameter)	
Name	prm_Time_PLN
Workspace	Default
Maintenance Unit	A Planning Process (PLN)
Description	
User Prompt	
Sort Order	0
Data Source	
Parameter Type	Member List
Default Value	|WfYear|
Display Member	Description
Cube	Global GolfStream
Dimension Type	Time
Dimension	Time
Member Filter	T#WFYear.DescendantsInclusive

Figure 14.26

For our combo boxes, we will create Components named `cbx_Entity_PRM` and `cbx_Time_PRM`, with the Bound Parameter settings for each assigned to their respective Member Lists.

We will set appropriate Text for each (e.g., Entity: and Time:), and set the Selection Changed User Action to Refresh. For the display format settings, after a little trial and error, these settings seem to look nice:

- Height = 50
- HorizontalAlignment = Center
- LabelPosition = Top
- MarginRight = 20
- VerticalAlignment = Top
- Width = 200

After adding these two combo boxes to our 02_OverviewControls_PLN Dashboard, if we run our main 00_Planning_PLN Dashboard and select the Overview button, here's what we see:

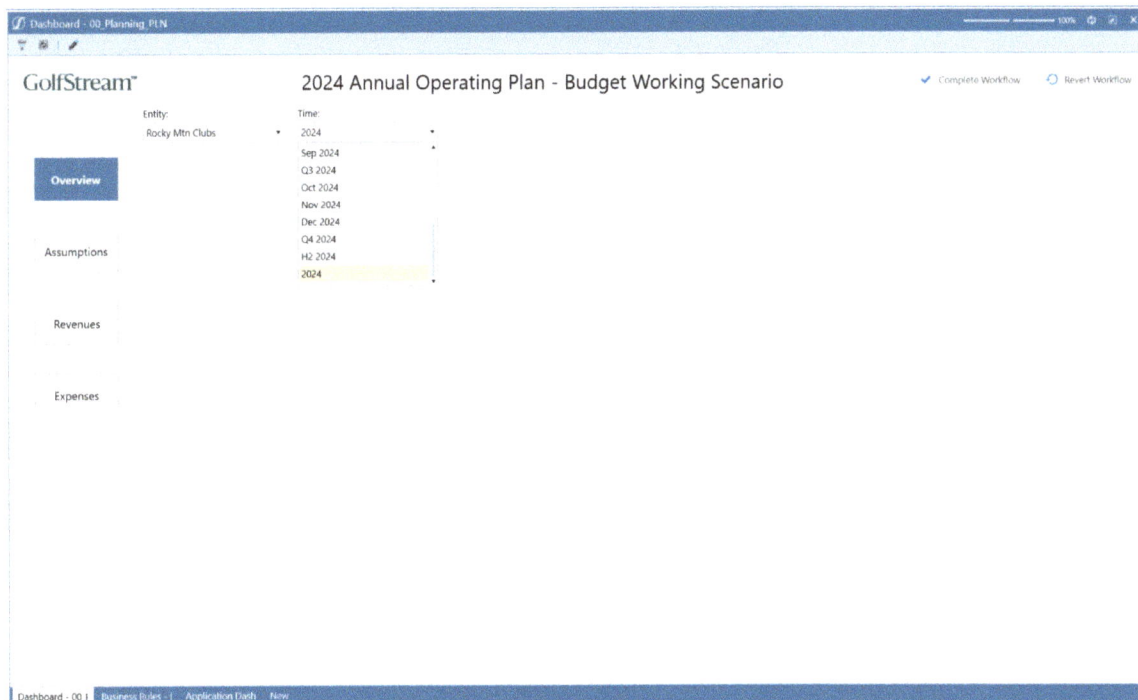

Figure 14.27

Cube Views

Next, let us add our Cube View. We have configured a Cube View for this Dashboard containing the rows and columns we want for our high-level Budget overview, and we have used the prm_Entity_PLN and prm_Time_PLN parameters in its Point of View.

All we need to do now is create a Cube View Dashboard Component, select this Cube View for the Cube View setting, and attach it to the 02_OverviewDetails_PLN Dashboard as the first Component (ahead of the Charts Dashboard, which will fill column two).

With the Cube View added, running our main Dashboard now looks like this:

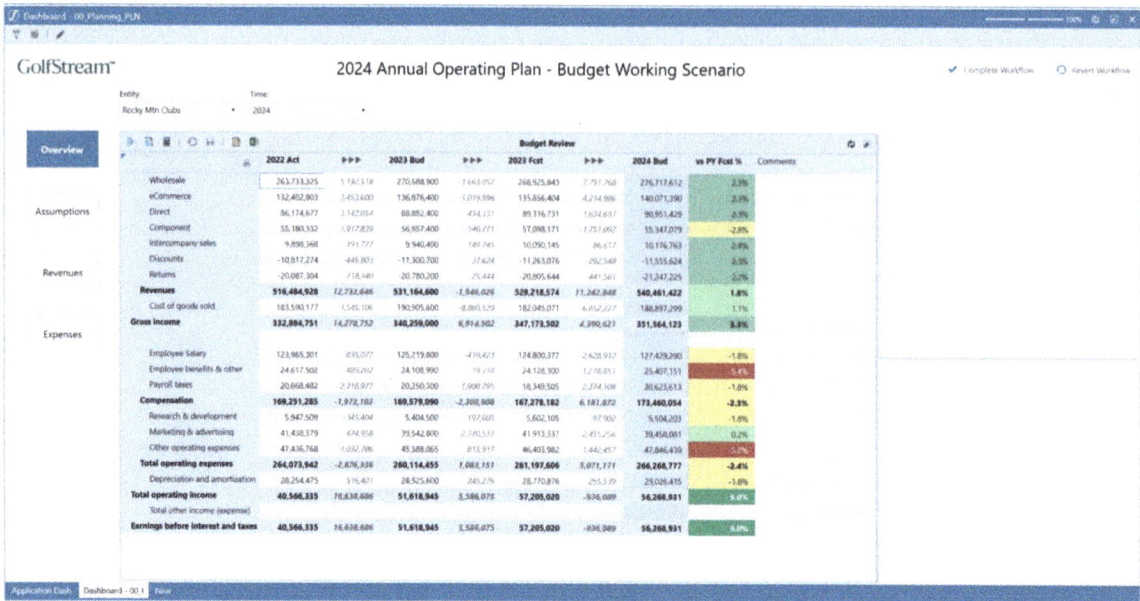

Figure 14.28

Now it is really starting to look like our original vision!

Charts

Let's add our charts. For the top chart, we will display a nice waterfall chart showing the changes in Revenue, Cost of Sales, Operating Expenses, etc. The leftmost bar in this chart – the 'starting point' for our waterfall visualization – will be last year's Actual Net Income. From there, we will walk through the changes from last year to this year's current Forecast, and then we will walk through the changes we expect to see based on the current version of next year's Budget.

Here is what our Cube View looks like – last year's Actual Net Income is in the first column, variances from last year to this year's Forecast are in the next five columns, then those equivalent variances from this year's Forecast to next year's Budget are in the following five columns. Our budgeted Net Income for next year is in the final column (Figure 14.29):

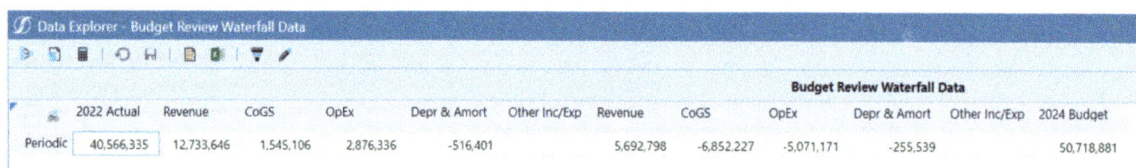

Figure 14.29

Like the Income Statement Overview Cube View, this Cube View uses the `prm_Entity_PLN` and `prm_Time_PLN` parameters to set its Point of View, so these two Cube Views will always be in sync.

To get this data to our chart, we will create a **Dashboard Data Adapter**. To configure this, all we need to do is set the Command Type property to Cube View, and then select this Cube View in the Cube View property – the rest of the parameters can be left to their defaults.

General (Data Adapter)	
Name	dat_OverviewWaterfallData_PLN
Workspace	Default
Maintenance Unit	A Planning Process (PLN)
Description	
Data Source	
Command Type	Cube View
Cube View	Budget Review Waterfall Data
Data Table Per Cube View Row	True
Include Title	False
Include Header Left Label 1	False
Include Header Left Label 2	False

Figure 14.30

Now, we will create the actual Chart Component. Note that when creating a new Component, you actually have two choices for charts: Basic and Advanced (Figure 14.31). Basic charts are VERY basic – this chart type is only included for backward compatibility with very early releases of OneStream. You will always want to choose Chart (Advanced).

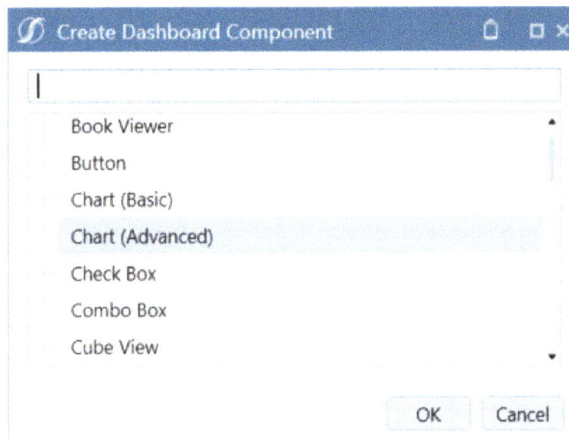

Figure 14.31

OneStream's Chart Component provides tremendous flexibility with layout, style, formatting, and more. Because there are a lot of options, Chart Components have a lot of settings. At first, it can seem a little intimidating, but if you only focus on the settings that are important for the chart you are creating, they are really quite simple to configure.

For our waterfall chart, we will only need to make a few choices – the vast majority of the properties can be left to their defaults. Here's what we need to set for this chart:

Section	Property	Setting
Chart	Enable Animations	FALSE
	Show Border	FALSE
Legend	Show Legend	FALSE
Crosshair	Crosshair Label Text Format	Change in {A}: ${V:N0}
Chart Y-Axis	Text Format	{V:$#,##0,,)m
Series Properties	Type	Waterfall
	Model Display Type	Basic
	Show Markers	FALSE
	Bar Width	0.9
Waterfall Series Properties	Include Subtotals	TRUE
	Subtotal Indexes	5
	Subtotal Labels	TY Forecast
	Subtotal Bar Color	XFLightBlueText

Figure 14.32

Most of these settings are self-explanatory (and many of them are really just up to your personal preferences). The Crosshair Label Text Format and the Y-Axis Text Format settings define how numbers will be displayed – if you hover your mouse over the property name, a tool tip will appear with some helpful guidance on the syntax (Figure 14.33):

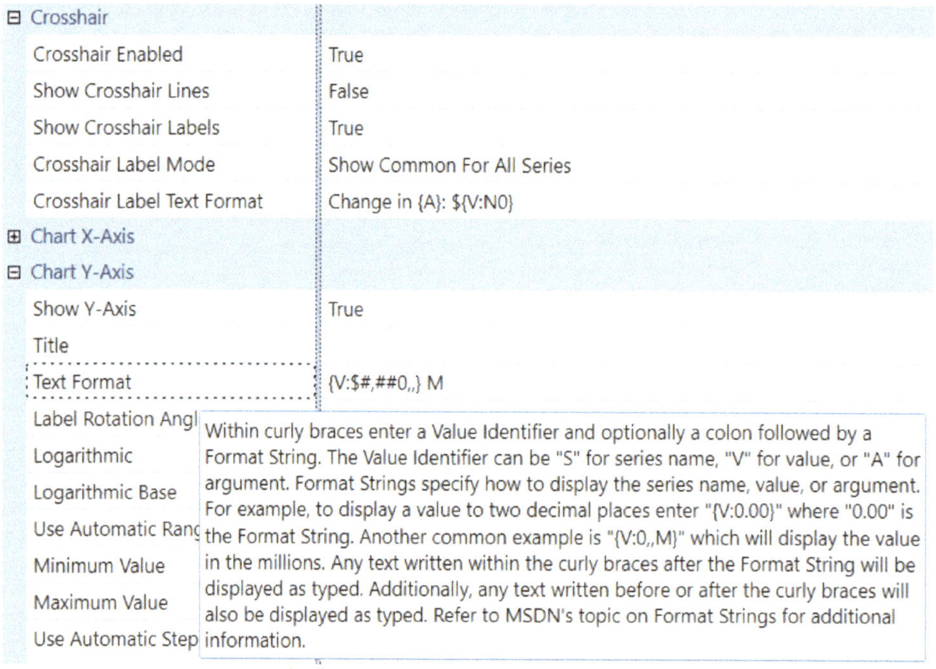

Figure 14.33

Obviously, the **Model Type** setting of waterfall is the most important property for this chart; when it is selected, various other properties appear that are only applicable to waterfall charts.

For this example, we are going to have three 'total' bars on our chart: last year's Actual, this year's Forecast, and next year's Budget.

Since we have the intermediary value for this year's Forecast, we have set Include Subtotals to True. This intermediary total is not actually included on our Cube View – only the starting value, the ending value, and all the variances we want to see are included. The waterfall chart will calculate this intermediary value for us – we just need to tell the chart how many of the variance columns should be included in this subtotal.

In our example, there are five variance columns for each Scenario, so we have set the Subtotal Indexes property to 5. The chart will sum up the starting value and the first five variance columns and draw a subtotal bar with the resulting amount. The Subtotal Label property lets us define the text under that bar, and the Subtotal Bar Color property sets the bar's color.

With these properties set and our dat_OverviewWaterfallData_PLN data adapter added to the Data Adapters tab, we can now add this chart to our 02_OverviewCharts_PLN Dashboard.

When we run the main Dashboard now, we see this:

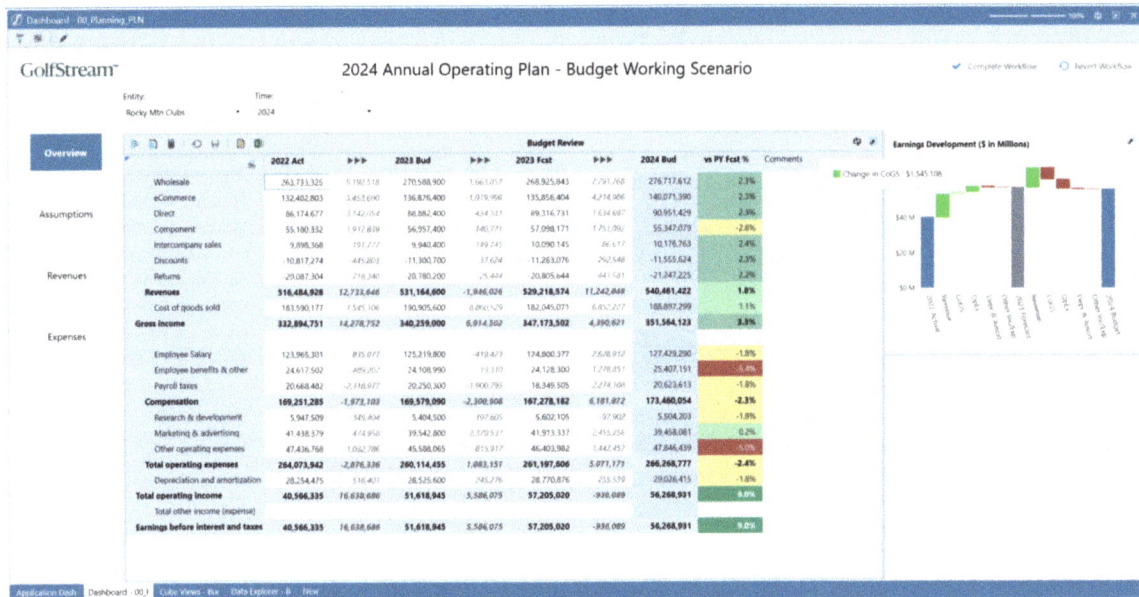

Figure 14.34

Notice that if we hover our mouse over one of the bars, the crosshair label appears using our specified text format.

Now, we will add a second chart to the Dashboard. This will be a simple bar chart showing the budgeted operating expenses. The Cube View that will supply the data looks like this:

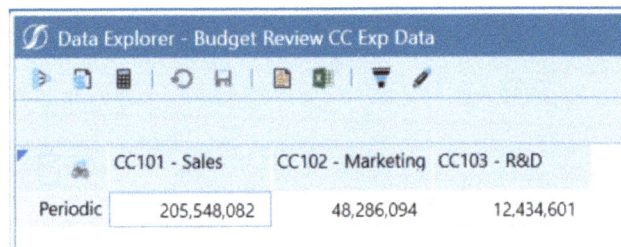

Figure 14.35

As we did previously, we will create a Dashboard data adapter with the Command Type set to Cube View and the Cube View property set to this Cube View's name. Again, we can leave everything else at their default settings.

For our Cost Center Expenses chart, we will create a Chart (Advanced) Component and configure it using these settings:

Chapter 14

Section	Property	Setting
Legend	Show Legend	FALSE
Chart	Swap Axes	TRUE
	Enable Animations	FALSE
	Show Borders	FALSE
Crosshair	Crosshair Label Text Format	{A} - {S}: {V:$#,##0}
Y-Axis	Text Format	{V:$0,,.0}m
	Label Rotation Angle	45
	Show Grid Lines	TRUE
Series Properties	Type	BarRangeSideBySide
	Model Display Type	Basic
	Bar Width	0.7

Figure 14.36

With our `dat_OverviewCCExpData_PLN` data adapter attached to the chart's Data Adapters tab, we can add this chart to our `02_OverviewCharts_PLN` Dashboard, and when we run the main Dashboard, we see this:

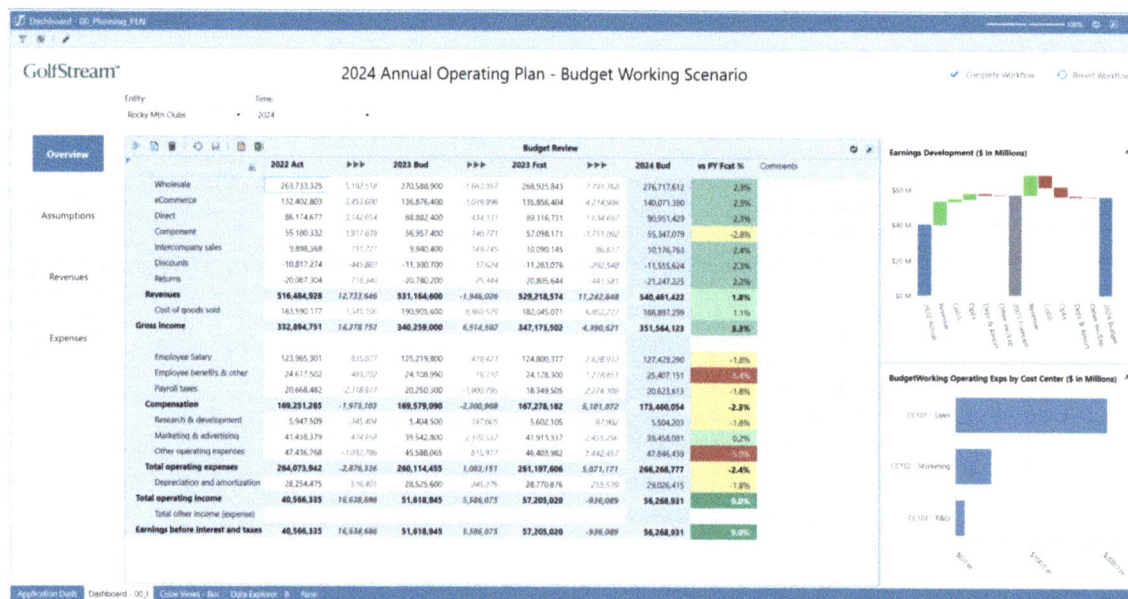

Figure 14.37

This is looking great! Just to fine-tune it a little, though, let's add a line above the waterfall chart – that continuous white space above the chart looks a little 'off'.

To add a line there, all we need to do is make a very simple change to the `02_OverviewCharts_PLN` Dashboard. This is currently configured with three rows – the top chart, a movable splitter, and the bottom chart. If we change it to four rows, with the first row as a Line row Type and the third row as the Movable Splitter, it will look like this – a small detail, but just that easy to adjust:

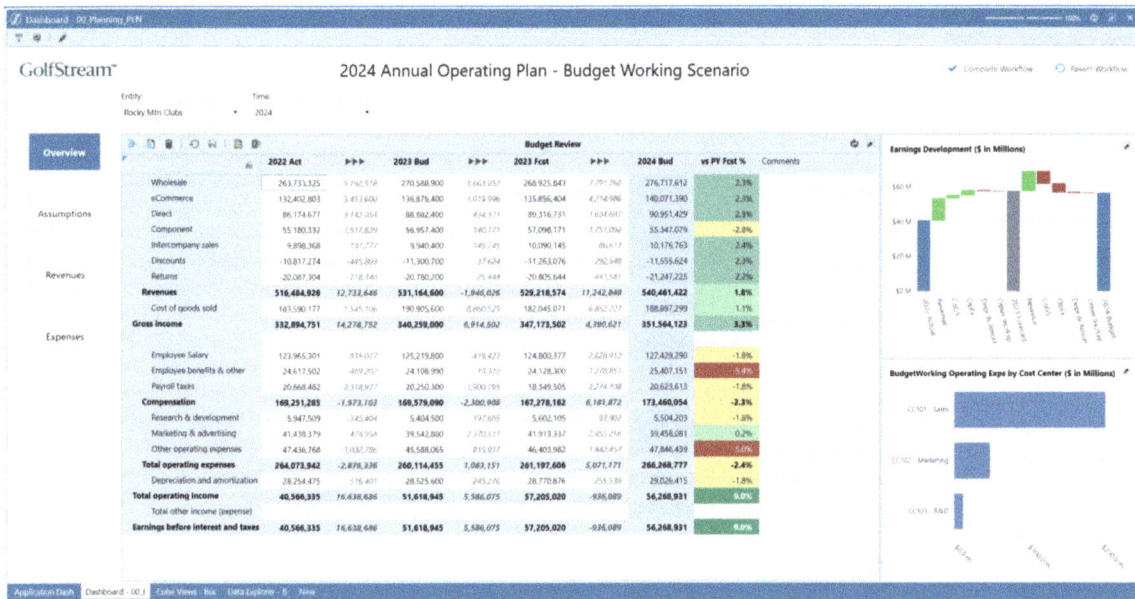

Figure 14.38

Dialog Boxes

One more thing. There is a lot of very useful information conveyed by that waterfall chart, but sometimes a User might want to take a closer look. We can help with this by adding another, larger version of this chart. We can even have this larger version open in its own window when a User clicks on the chart.

First, we will configure the chart. It will be almost identical to our existing waterfall chart, so we can simply copy and paste the current chart and rename the copy.

The only change we will make to this second version of the chart is to add labels to each of the bars showing the net change represented by those bars. To do this, in our new copy of the chart, we will change the Show Point Labels to True.

We would also like to accompany this version of the waterfall chart with a Cube View clearly showing the variances making up this chart, and even provide a place for Users to enter commentary on those numbers. We can now create a Dashboard named 02_OverviewWaterfallDialog_PLN, set its Layout Type to Grid, and set the Rows to 3 and the Columns to 1. The first row will hold our chart, the second row will be a movable splitter, and the third row will hold our Cube View, so we add these Components to the Dashboard.

On the original waterfall chart, there is a setting called Selection Changed User Interface Action. We will set that to Open Dialog, and in the Dashboard to Open in Dialog setting, we enter the name of our dialog box Dashboard 02_OverviewWaterfallDialog_PLN.

Now, when we run our Dashboard, clicking one of the bars in the waterfall chart opens a new window, showing us the chart with each bar labeled with the net change it is contributing to the total variance, and our explanatory Cube View on the lower half of the window. With a little trial and error, we can use the Display Format settings on our dialog Dashboard to adjust the size of the window to fit the content – DialogHeight = 700, DialogWidth = 1050 seems to work nicely – and adjust the Row Height for Row 3 to about 250 pixels to make a well-sized frame for our Cube View.

After these adjustments, here is what we see when we click on the waterfall chart – very nice!

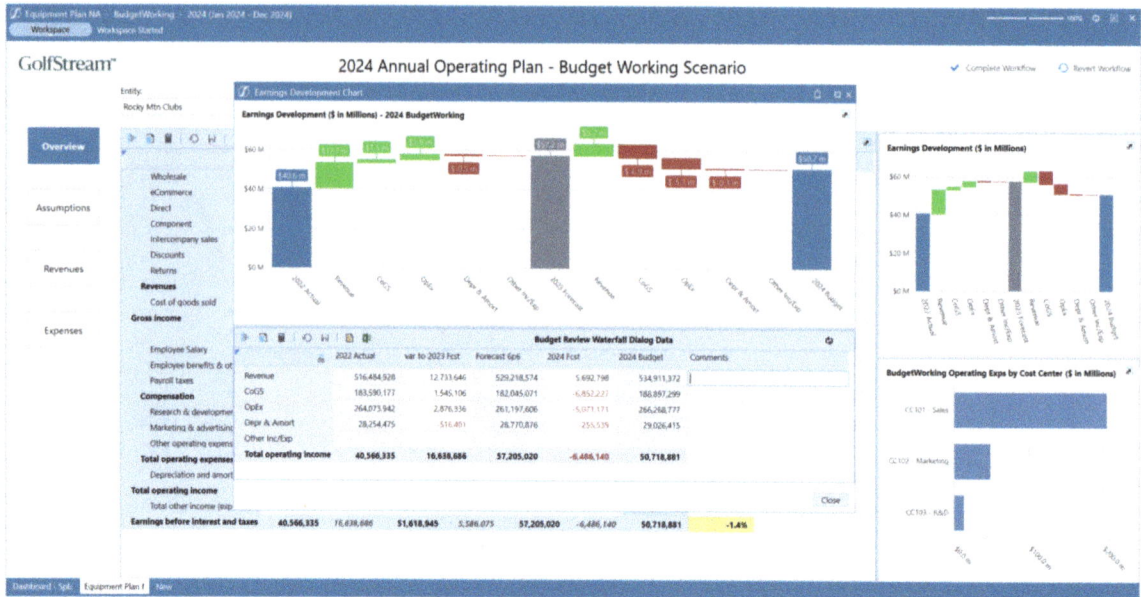

Figure 14.39

Our Overview Content Dashboard is complete! Now, using the same techniques, we can easily configure the Assumptions, Revenues, and Expenses Dashboards.

Building Our Assumptions Dashboard

As part of our Planning process, we will derive much of our revenue and cost of sales using driver-based Calculations. This both simplifies the process for the End-User and helps ensure consistency across the broader plan. If an assumption has changes – say, the expected average selling price for one of our products – we only need to change that assumption once. Every value that is dependent on that number throughout the plan will automatically update.

The Assumptions step in our process lets us update these values (or review them, depending on our responsibilities and security settings). In this example, we will be planning Wholesale Average Selling Prices and Cost of Sales assumptions by Entity and Product Category. All that is needed is a simple Form to collect these prices and rates, and combo boxes to select which Entity and Product line we are working with.

Just as we did with our Overview content, we can start by modifying the simple placeholder Dashboard we created earlier to accommodate a panel with our controls at the top, and our Cube View in the body of the Dashboard. To do this, we will change Dashboard 03_AssumptionsContent_PLN to a grid layout with one column and two rows. We will set the first row to a height of 70 to hold our controls panel, and leave the second row and the column settings to their defaults.

To hold the controls for this Dashboard, we will create another simple horizontal stacked panel Dashboard, name it 03_AssumptionsControls_PLN, and add it as the first Component on the 03_AssumptionsContent_PLN Dashboard. Since we already have an Entity combo box that we created for the Overview content, we can just reuse this and add it as the first Component on the Controls Dashboard.

This Dashboard will also need a combo box to select the Product Category. Just as we did earlier for the Entities and Time combo boxes, we will first create a list parameter, selecting the appropriate Dimension and Member Filter to provide the list of products to our combo box. Then, we can copy and paste the Entity combo box, change the new object's name to cbx_ProductCategory_PLN, and update the text and Bound Parameter settings as appropriate. We can now add this to our 03_AssumptionsControls_PLN Dashboard as the second Component.

The Save and Calculate Button

When our Users update their plans, we would like to provide them with a simple one-click button to save any data they have changed, and recalculate the part of the model they are working with. To do this, we will create a button Component and name it btn_Save_PLN. To give our Users a clear visual indication of what this button does, we will import an image of a shiny modern diskette and attach it to our button as the image source file.

Now, we need to tell the button what to do when it is clicked. The first thing we want to happen is to save any data the User has entered or updated. To do this, we just change the Selection Change Save Action to Save Data For All Components. With this option, a single click will save all data that has been entered, even if the Dashboard is displaying multiple Cube Views on the same screen.

After saving the data, we want the model to automatically recalculate so we can see the results of our changes. To make this happen, we will change the Selection Changed Server Task to the Calculate setting, and use the Selection Changed Server Task Arguments setting to tell the button what part of the model we want to calculate. This property has a [...] button that will display a dialog box showing various examples of the syntax that this property is looking for (Figure 14.40).

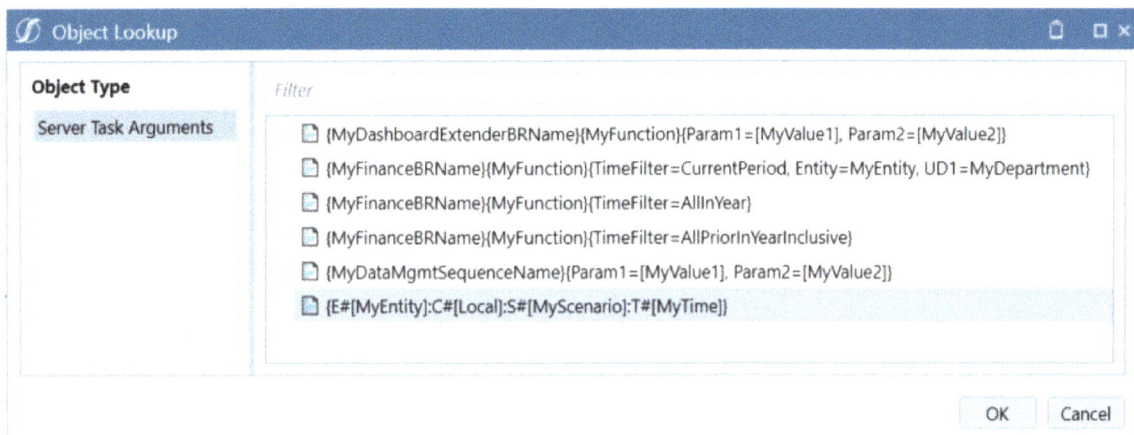

Figure 14.40

The first few examples show the syntax to use when running a Business Rule or a data management sequence. The final example in the list is the one we want – all we need to do is specify the Member Filter defining the subset of the model we want to calculate. If we select this example and click OK, this sample text will be entered into the property.

When we perform this Calculation, we only want to do it for the Entity we are currently working with – which is conveniently available to us via the parameter used by the Entity combo box. Similarly, we only want to calculate the Scenario we are currently working with, and we want to calculate any period in the year we are working with that may be impacted by our changes. Both the current Workflow Scenario and the Workflow Year are always available to us via system variables. When we replace the sample code with our requirements, it looks like this:

```
{E#[|!prm_Entity_PLN!|]:C#[Local]:S#[|WFScenario|]:T#[|WFYear|M12]}
```

Finally, we will set the Selection Changed User Interface Action to the Refresh setting, so after the data is saved and the Calculation is run, the screen will refresh to show us the results.

That is all we need to do – our button is ready to do its job. We can now add it as the third Component on the 03_AssumptionsControls_PLN Dashboard.

The last step in configuring our Assumptions Content Dashboard is to create a Cube View Component pointing to our Product Assumptions Cube View and add it to the 03_AssumptionsContent_PLN Dashboard as the second-row Component, filling the body of the screen.

Now, when we run our main Dashboard and click the Assumptions button, here is what we see:

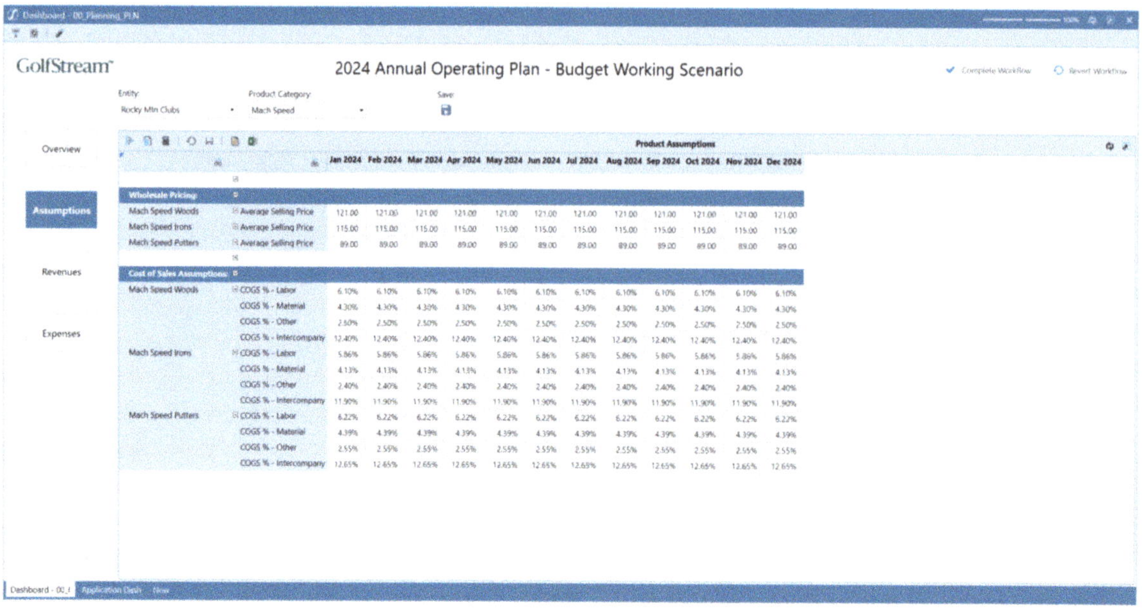

Figure 14.41

Building Our Revenues Dashboard

Our Revenues Content Dashboard will be structured very similarly to our Assumptions content. Besides the name of the Cube View displayed, the only difference between the two is that our Revenues are planned at the Region and Customer Category levels, as well as Entity and Product. Our Cube View includes our Products as rows in the Form, so – for our Dashboard – we will need combo boxes for the Entity, Region, and Customer Category Dimensions.

As with our Assumptions Dashboard, we can simply reuse the existing `cbx_Entity_PLN` Component, and for Region and Customer Category, we can go through the same steps as all our other combo boxes. For each of these Dimensions, we first create a list parameter with the desired Dimension and Member Filter, then clone one of our existing combo boxes, replacing the text and Bound Parameter as appropriate.

Again, just like we did with the Assumptions Content Dashboard, we will start by modifying the simple placeholder Dashboard we created earlier to accommodate a panel with our controls at the top, and our Cube View in the body of the Dashboard. To do this, we will change Dashboard `04_RevenuesContent_PLN` to a grid layout with one column and two rows, set the first row to a height of 70 to hold our controls, and leave the second row and the column settings to their defaults.

We will then create another simple horizontal stacked panel Dashboard, and name it `04_RevenuesControls_PLN`, add the required combo boxes and the save button to this Dashboard, and add this Controls Dashboard as the first Component on the `04_RevenuesContent_PLN` Dashboard.

Finally, we will create another Cube View Component, this time pointing to our Revenue Planning Cube View, and add it as the second Component on the `04_RevenuesContent_PLN` Dashboard.

When we are finished, clicking our Revenues button shows us this:

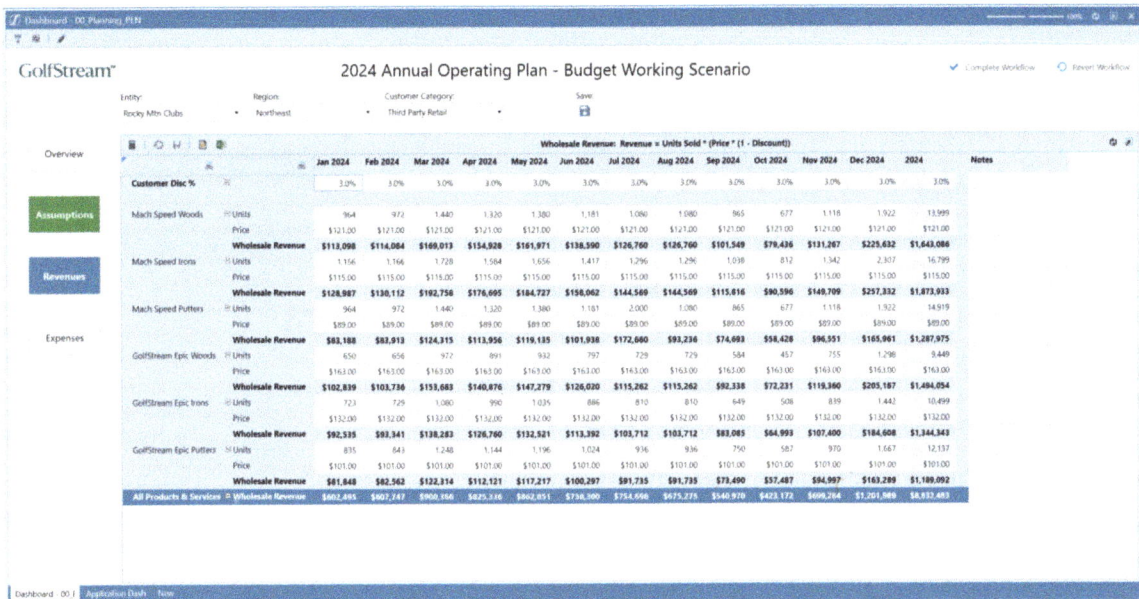

Figure 14.42

Notice also that the Assumptions button is green. That is because we clicked Complete Workflow after completing that Form, and our XFBR Rule is doing its job nicely.

Building Our Expenses Dashboard

Our final Content Dashboard will again follow a similar pattern to its predecessors.

For our expenses, we plan by Entity, Region, and Cost Center. Since we already have combo boxes for Entity and Region, we will create one more list parameter for our Cost Center Dimension and Member Filter, and use this as the Bound Parameter on a clone of one of our existing combo boxes.

We will again restructure our existing 05_ExpensesContent_PLN Dashboard to be a grid-type Dashboard with two rows and one column, and the first row 70 pixels high. Then, we will create a Dashboard named 05_ExpensesControls_PLN, add our three required combo boxes and the save button to it, and add this Controls Dashboard as the first Component of Dashboard 05_ExpensesContent_PLN.

Tabbed Dashboards

For our Expenses plan, we have two very different Cube Views that we need to complete – one for Compensation Expenses and one for Non-Compensation Expenses. We will have both of these appear in the body of the Dashboard, but we will have them in separate tabs.

To accomplish this, we will create a Dashboard named 05_ExpensesDetails_PLN, and set its Layout Type to Tabs. With this Type of Dashboard, each Component you add will appear on a different tab; in our example, each tab will have a Cube View, but we can also use tabs to display entire Dashboards of their own.

On the Display Format dialog for this Dashboard, there is a setting for TabControlStyle. There are several options available, including Classic, No Border, and Rounded Corners. We will choose the last one on the list – Rounded Corners.

As we have done before, we will now create two Cube View Components, one each for our Compensation and Non-Compensation Expense Cube Views.

> **Note**: With these Cube View Components, be sure to enter a meaningful name for the Description property – this is the text that will appear on the tabs.

Chapter 14

Finally, we add our two Cube View Components to the `05_ExpensesDetails_PLN` Dashboard, add the Details Dashboard as the second Component of our `05_ExpensesContent_PLN` Dashboard, and we are done.

When we run our main Dashboard and click the Expenses button, here is what we see:

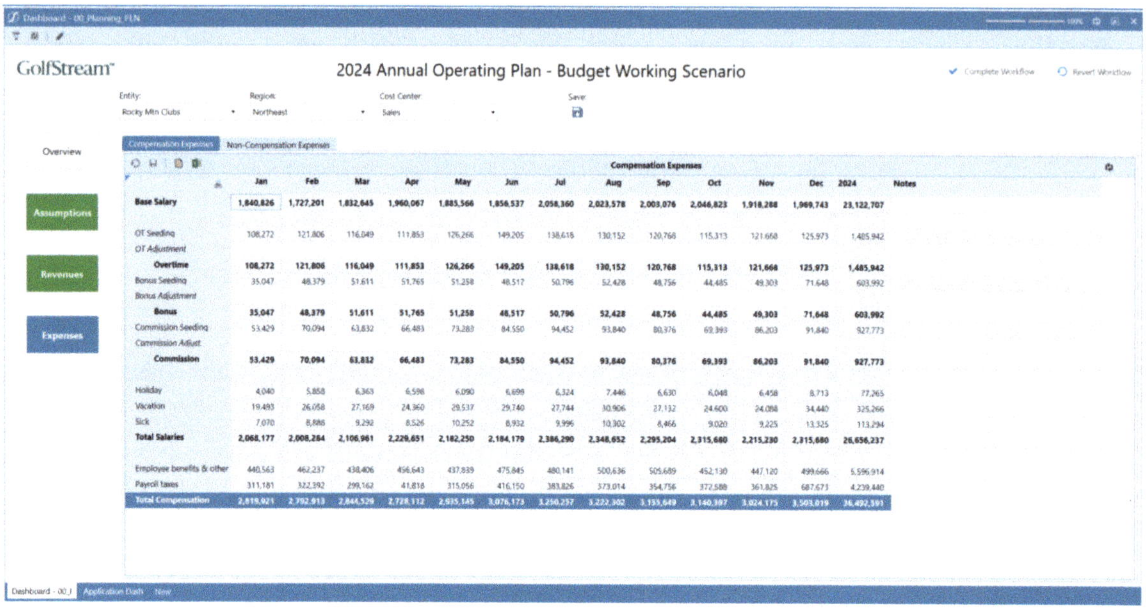

Figure 14.43

Clicking the second tab reveals the Non-Compensation Expenses Form:

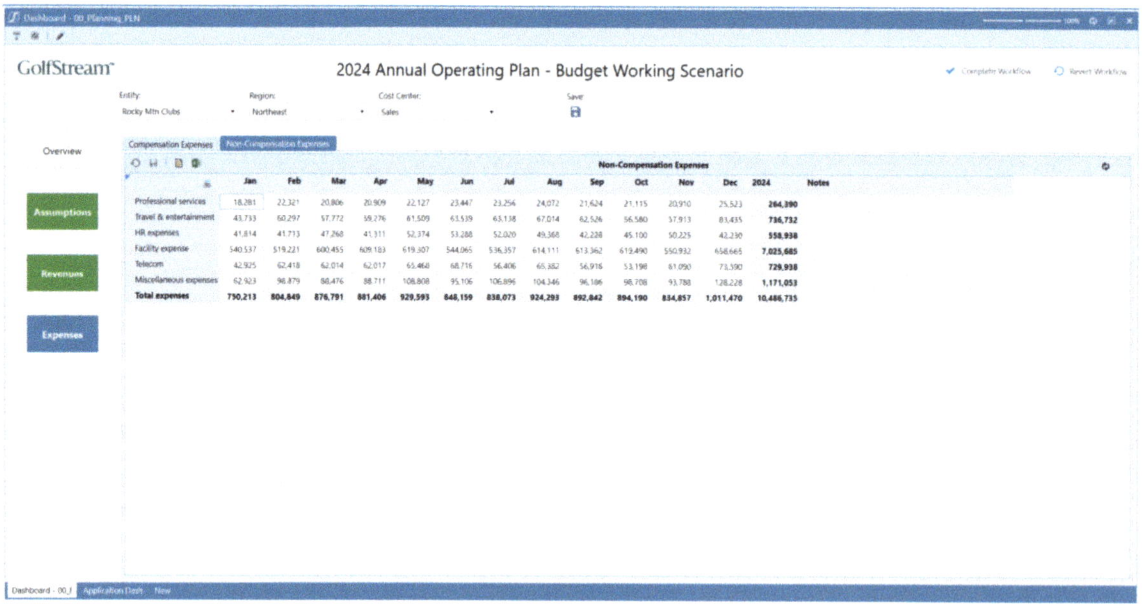

Figure 14.44

Our Planning Dashboard is complete!

Let's take a step back and review the End-User Experience we have just established for members of our organization's Planning community. When they sign on to OneStream, they will be greeted by the landing page we created in Chapter 11:

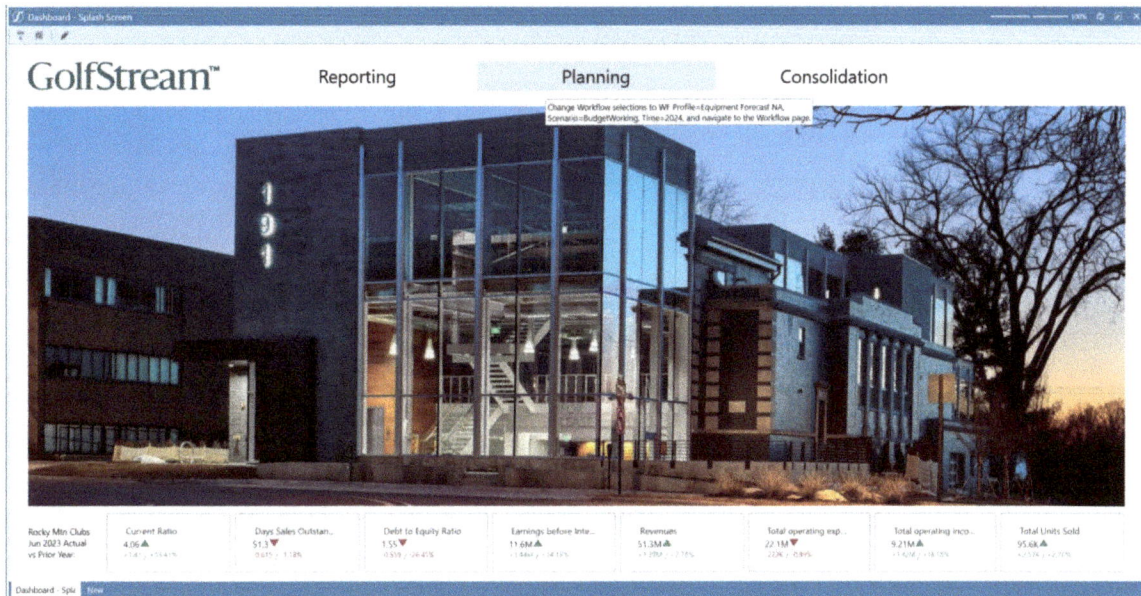

Figure 14.45

Clicking the big Planning button at the top of the screen will take them straight to the correct Workflow and the current in-progress version of next year's Budget. There, they will be greeted by a clean, informative, and easy-to-navigate Budget Overview Dashboard:

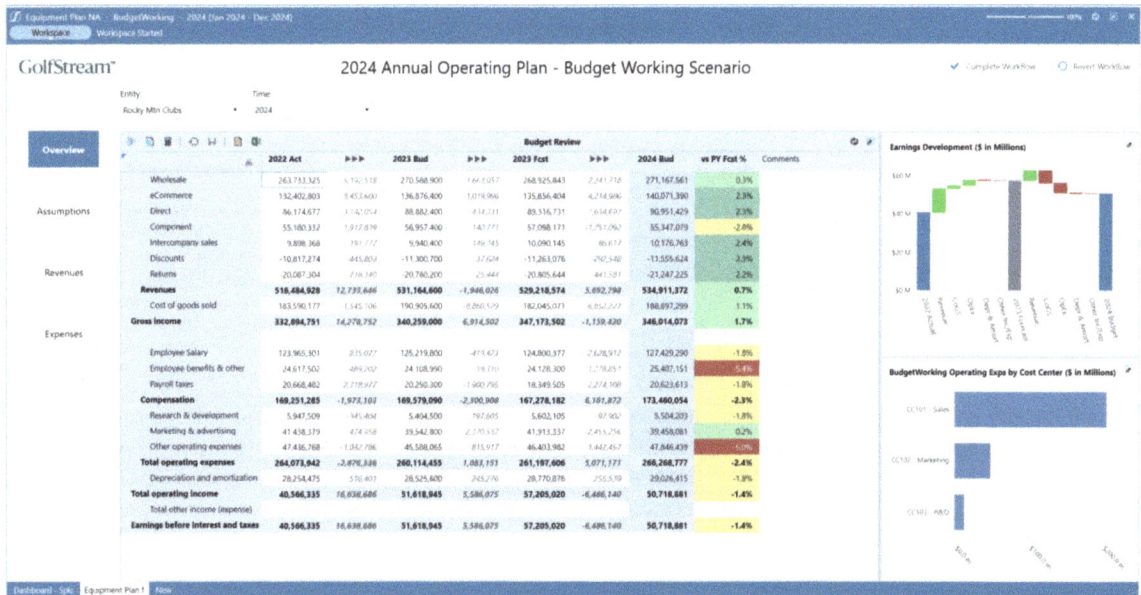

Figure 14.46

Clicking through the clearly marked navigation buttons on the left-hand side of the screen, Users will be taken directly to the Forms they need to fill out, each with drop-down boxes for the Dimensions appropriate to their content, and each with a Save button that will both commit their changes to the model and recalculate the Entity, Scenario, and Year they are working on.

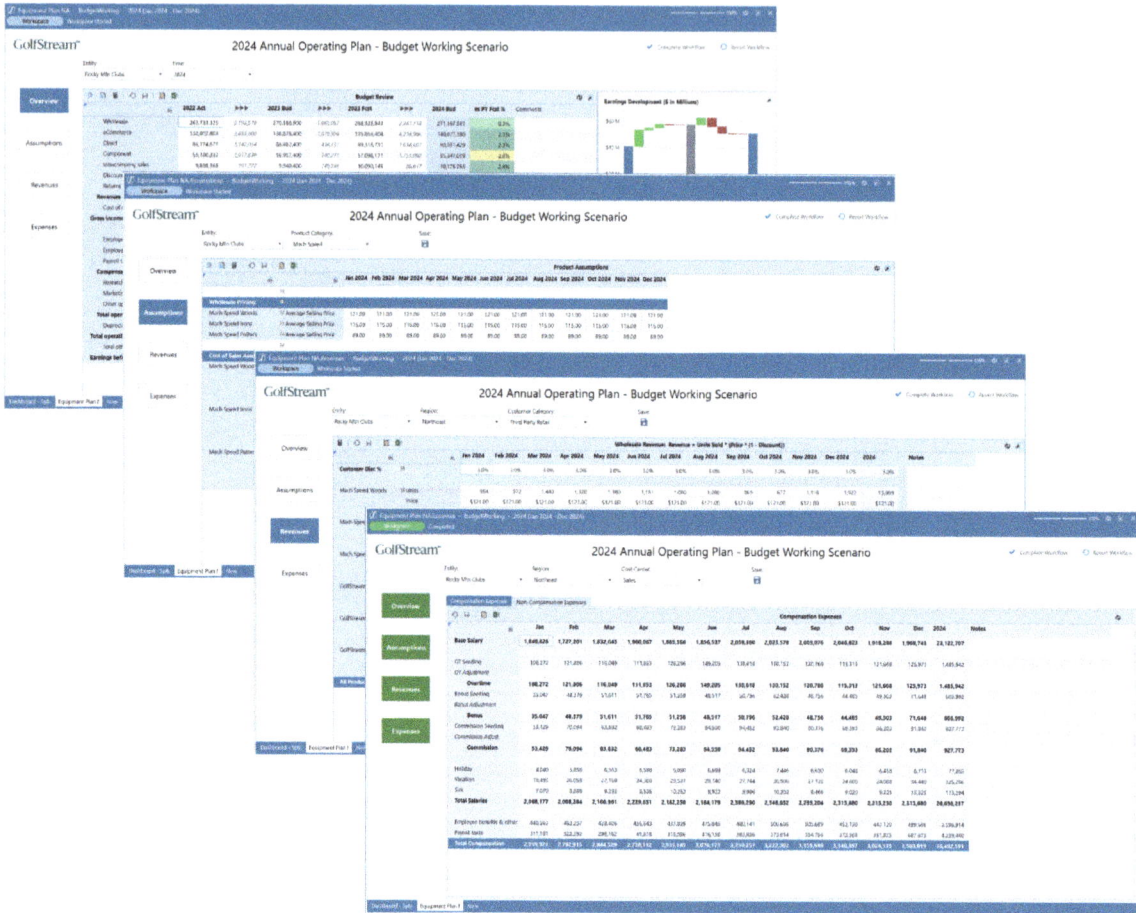

Figure 14.47

At any step in the process – with one click – our Users can return to the Overview page to review the impact their changes have on the full Income Statement. Once satisfied, they can mark each step as 'complete' and be confident that none of their required tasks have been missed. And they can also be confident that they have established a solid, achievable plan for the coming year!

Conclusion

This chapter was all about – as the name suggests – Dashboards for Budgeting, Planning, and Forecasting! We covered a lot of ground, including header configurations, navigation panes, embedding Dashboards, and even a look at Dashboard Business Rules.

Later, we saw how Dashboards could be attached to Workflow Profiles, before building example Assumptions, Revenues and Expenses Dashboards. And with that, we find this book drawing to a close. Just one final chapter to go…

15

What Have We Learned?

We started this book with one mission in mind: to craft the best User Experience in the OneStream application. This is not always an easy challenge because we have so many different User types.

We know about the flexibility of OneStream, of course, and our application could have been implemented for many different reasons and must continue to grow as the business evolves. Your Planning application may pivot to include Consolidations, for example, or it may grow to encompass Operational Planning, or perhaps some solutions found in the MarketPlace, such as People Planning. Building a User Experience for all these situations requires a design that can pivot and accommodate different directions.

But the versatility of our application is not the only hurdle we have to cross. What about the Users? Yes, you have heard so much about all the types of Users we need to address! From the person keying into a Form, to the Administrator running Calculations, to the Executive searching for quick ratios, we have a lot of Users to consider, and each of them will behave differently. On top of that, as OneStream continues to grow, the software has flexed to handle Users who span multiple industries, each of whom have their own unique requirements. We must all do our part to stay up to date with what the software can do and what our community has found to be the most effective practice!

One thing that we did not touch on much in this book is overall application design and performance. You may or may not be interested in this given your position, but the first thing that can greatly hurt the User Experience is poor application performance. I would be remiss not to mention the underlying items that every application designer should be accountable for and their impact on the tools we have discussed. Having an application with proper metadata and Workflow design – that puts the Data Unit first – is a must, therefore. If your foundation is not solid, the other items we learned about in this book will not be able to shine. If you are someone who is starting to design applications, I would recommend looking at:

1. The Designing an Application Course on Navigator (OneStream's online learning portal)

2. The OneStream Foundation Handbook

3. Being an active part of ONECommunity

These three resources are a major help to anyone wishing to take their knowledge to the next level and truly understand how the application 'ticks'. If you are more interested in reporting tactics and techniques, I would recommend using ONECommunity as you get stronger and have more questions. We cannot cover everything in our materials, but what makes up the OneStream Ecosystem is the creative and passionate people who work together to fight new challenges and uncover new ways to work in the software. ONECommunity is a very flexible tool, and there is a lot you can learn to do with it.

Now that this book is drawing to a close, let's take a little time to review some of the items we have covered.

The Moving Pieces

After we discussed the different types of Users that we must cater for, we learned how we can craft the best User Experience for them by specifically looking at our reporting tools. A lot of these tools can also be used to calculate or bring data into the system as well. These options are Cube Views,

Excel Add-in/Spreadsheet, Extensible Documents, Report Books, and Dashboards. No matter what we choose, we must always consider the design of our metadata and the location of our data when crafting Reports.

Cube Views

First up, Cube Views – our simple way to pull data residing in the Cube. Cube Views are easy to get started with and can be incorporated into many areas of the OneStream application. Typically, they will be your best way to handle most of your financial reporting requirements because they respond well to these challenges:

1. They are easy to build and maintain.

2. They can be heavily formatted.

3. They are *typically* the most performant option.

4. They can be easily accessed across the application.

5. They can be viewed in multiple formats (Data Explorer Grid, Microsoft Excel, OneStream Spreadsheet, PDF Report).

Excel Add-in/OneStream Spreadsheet Tool

Then, we covered the Excel Add-in/Spreadsheet tool. This a fan favorite for many of our clients either because they have worked with other add-ins in the past, or they just love working with Excel! The Spreadsheet tool is a nice way to bring the Excel Add-in into the software; as a Consultant, I was often on different versions than my client, and it allowed me to maneuver and train End-Users quickly. I have also incorporated Spreadsheet into Dashboards and Forms in the past to give a more interactive option for Users. The benefits we discussed for Excel Add-in/Spreadsheet are as follows:

1. Allows you to grow your population of builders.

2. Multiple options as to how you want to query data.

3. Greatest flexibility with formatting and Calculations.

Dashboards

We then introduced Dashboards, the reporting tool that we spent a great deal of time discussing in this book, alongside many examples. Dashboards are so much more than a reporting tool; they are something that implementors will often use to create a *dynamic* User Experience in the application.

Like Cube Views and the Excel Add-in, they are often used for reporting data and data entry, but more than that, they provide great flexibility with their reporting options and how they can run tasks.

Dashboarding is something that is undergoing several changes in the product currently, and I would keep your eyes peeled for the latest releases. With 7.3, we introduced the concept of Workspaces, which changes how we see the page and how items are organized within Dashboards. From version 8 and beyond, there will no doubt be many other new features and enhancements added to the Dashboarding Engine. As this concept develops, it will force us to extend our perception of Dashboards and their capabilities. But for now, here are the key benefits of working with this tool:

1. Dashboards allow you to integrate multiple reporting/data entry options.

2. They are necessary when querying non-Cube data.

3. They can run 'jobs' (e.g., Consolidation, Calculation, Translation, Business Rules, etc.).

Extensible Documents

A lesser-known tool, Extensible Documents, was also briefly discussed in this book. Extensible Documents allow you to create a PowerPoint, Excel, and/or Word document that can display real-time OneStream data, Cube Views, Charts, or Excel Reports, and which can even refresh based on User selection.

Extensible Documents tend to be used for specific purposes; that is why I recommend giving them a try so you know when they can get you out of a pinch. They are also a great way to collect and integrate your other reporting options.

Report Books

In the spirit of integrating reporting options, we also have Report Books. Report Books are excellent if you are trying to create financial or managerial reporting packages. And, as you have learned, they are very easy to build. So, here are some reasons to use Report Books:

1. You can add flexibility to your reporting options.

2. They can be 'shipped' via email to Users through the Parcel Service solution.

Out-of-the-Box Basics

Besides our reporting tools, what other items in the software can we take advantage of to drive the User Experience? These items are not mutually exclusive, which is why we are also trying to promote an application design where all items are carefully thought through.

Because of this, we wanted to explore what gets brought to the User through the OnePlace Navigation Pane. This comes down to some of the tools that require no configuration, our Workflow design, and where our reporting tools (or, more commonly, data entry options) can be plugged into the User Experience. Many of us can forget that our End-Users rarely have access to items outside the OnePlace Pane, so we want to curate a flow that ties all the things we created into something that drives the best experience for them. Therefore, we broke this chapter down into the three areas of OnePlace: Workflow, Cube Views and Dashboards, and Documents.

Workflow in OnePlace

Workflow is the crux of your OneStream application and the place where you can build your User Experience. Therefore, the Workflow sometimes takes the longest amount of time to get right in any OneStream implementation; it is a new concept for most people and it is built around the population of Users. So, you must let them interact with it to get it right.

If people struggle with the concept of Workflow, I first explain it as the responsibility structure of your End-User population. You want to build something that is intuitive for your End-User to move through the tasks they need to complete. If that does not quite clear the cobwebs, I go in with, "It's how you get data into OneStream." Yes, there are some exceptions to this rule, but start there to build out the pieces in your mind on what you will need for your Workflow. Therefore, we break our Workflow down into three items (or ways) to bring data into OneStream:

1. Import

2. Forms

3. Adjustments

Let's start first with Import. Not all End-Users will be importing data and this key fact is something you want to consider when designing your Workflow. Because of that, let's ask ourselves *who* is importing data and *what* would be helpful for them to see. OneStream is full of helpful tables that are interactive and which allow you to see the source data that is brought to Stage (or not if you use Direct Load or BI Blend, see the Design and Reference Guide, OneStream Foundation Handbook, or "Designing an Application" Course on Navigator if those terms made your head spin!).

The next way to collect data is through Forms. We spent a lot of time discussing data entry Cube Views and Dashboards, and interacting with Forms is something that MOST of your End-Users will play a role in. Because of this, this step is extremely flexible, and you will want to choose the method and a design that will make the data collection process as seamless as possible. Spell it out for them; make it so obvious that they know what to click and what to input at every point. If they need to put in comments or make an attachment, use your background color or a clever way to name your rows to make this very clear. If they need to run a Calculation, decide if you want this to be something the User should control or not. If they should, a nice prominent button will do the trick.

The final way to collect data through the Workflow is through Adjustments, or what we commonly rename them to: Journals. This is used a little bit less often (typically reserved for post-close adjustments to Actuals loaded into the system) and is not something that all Users will see in their Workflow. Every client is different, though.

Adjustments are commonly employed because of the ability to approve or reject them. Thus, someone can prepare the entire Journal and not post it, therefore not impacting Cube data. In general, they do offer more security settings on the Workflow page, and that may be another reason to consider them. Journals do tend to be misunderstood, though, so I like to take a little time to explain them to my client so they know what they may (or may not) want. Personally, I love the Excel templates that can be found on the MarketPlace for posting Journals – a great way to submit a lot of data easily.

Outside data collection, there are many other things that can be crafted in your Workflow:

1. A 'Process' step to allow your End-User to run Calculations, Translations, Consolidations, or any other data management sequence.

2. Confirmation Rules to employ appropriate checks that your User should clear. This is where I ask my Admin, "Do you have anything where you always have to chase people down to submit or fix?"

3. Analysis sections where you can place Cube Views or Dashboards to help your Users along the way.

4. Review nodes where a different type of User (perhaps a Controller) might review the dependent Workflow Profiles under them.

5. Certification – something required on every Workflow Profile – to sign off on the work the User has done. This can be adapted to a wide variety of requirements, from questionnaires to quick certify.

Workflow is a hefty topic and something that requires a lot of careful consideration when it comes to design. Knowing what is available to you is key. As we moved through this book, we spent a lot of time discussing our reporting options, and Workflow is the shell that underpins how these items will be brought to the User. Because of this, I cannot stress the importance of a good Workflow design enough. We didn't get into it that much in this book, but if you are a Consultant hoping to learn more, I strongly advise looking at the "Designing an Application" course. We have a lovely panel from our Architects if you want to hear some of their stories!

Cube Views and Dashboards in OnePlace

I will not recap too much on Cube Views and Dashboards because we spent a lot of time on these two topics. In general, we can create a repository of your common Cube Views and Dashboards within the OnePlace tab. This is handy for your Users to always access. Personally, I like to display them throughout the Workflow to show Users exactly *what they need, when they need it.*

Documents

This item might seem obvious to most, but it is very much underutilized in the field. I have one piece of advice to give you on this section, and it is this… there are security properties in the File Explorer icon that you configure for the documents section – USE THEM!

You are going to end up storing Report Books, Dashboard images, Extensible Documents, etc., in the Documents page. You may or may not want your User accessing these items, accessing them here (specifically), or editing them.

You can also store quick reference cards, End-User training material, or POVs. I like to use this space not just to store all my stuff, but anything that can help acclimate my Users. Therefore, you want to use security to ensure you don't clutter up the space that you created to make lives less stressful.

Reviewing Building Cube Views

Now, what is a book on the OneStream User Experience without some deep discussions on Cube Views? We spent four chapters discussing, building, and designing Cube Views to give you as many ways to use these simple but intricate artifacts to satisfy your many requirements. Along the way, I hope you developed an appreciation for the Cube View and its versatility!

Cube View Concepts

We started off by focusing our discussion on the different ways that Cube Views can be used in our application:

1. As Reports

2. In Report Books

3. In Extensible Documents

4. For data entry

5. In Dashboards (as Components and data adapters)

6. A Cube View connection in the Excel Add-in/Spreadsheet

Reviewing Cube Views as Reports

First, we took Cube Views as lone objects and focused on how they can be built into Reports. We listed out some tips to follow when designing your Report for maintenance and flexibility:

1. Utilize the Application Properties Standard Reports tab as much as possible.

2. Set all common formatting as parameters.

3. Aim for consistency across Reports.

4. If you use Cube View Extender Rules, ensure your code is commented.

5. Make your Reports dynamic by prompting for Dimensions. This can often reduce the number of Reports you think you need.

6. Utilize row and column sharing where possible.

7. Utilize Member Expansions as much as possible. Resist the urge to pick individual Members.

8. Explore creating dynamic Calculations in UD8 for common expressions, as opposed to rewriting the same formulas within your Cube Views.

Reviewing Cube Views and Report Books

Then, we discussed how Cube Views can be added to Report Books. This is where we take the most neatly-formatted and legible Reports and tie them all together into a package for internal and external stakeholders to view. Although Report Books didn't get their own chapter, we didn't want to leave you hanging! This is where we went through how to build a Report Book using existing Cube Views if this is something you are new to in OneStream.

Reviewing Cube Views and Extensible Documents

Extensible Documents, like Report Books, don't always get the attention they deserve. This is our way of incorporating live OneStream data, Cube Views, Dashboard Reports, or Excel Add-in Reports into our various Microsoft tools.

Here, we learned how to add a Cube View into an Extensible Document. You may do this if you have a cover letter for a Report Book or a PowerPoint presentation that refers to a nicely formatted data grid. Perhaps we need this grid to be dynamic, based on some selection (parameters), and updated as data changes.

Cube Views for Data Entry

Then, we focused on enabling an existing Cube View for data entry. When designing data entry within OneStream, you can choose if you want to collect data through Forms or Journals. Most of the time, we see people picking Forms, and these can be built through Spreadsheets, Dashboards, or Cube Views. But as we saw, no matter which option you choose, we will likely need to create a Cube View to get started.

Can you recall how we made a Cube View available for data entry? There are three things we needed to adjust:

1. Set Cube View Can Modify Data to True. This property can be found on the Common properties under the General Settings of the Cube View.

2. Choose the appropriate Origin Member. Remember, either BeforeAdj or Forms.

3. Ensure the Cube View is pulling all Base Members.

Cube Views as Dashboards

We ended up going heavily into Dashboards for the rest of the book, so this section stayed a little light. Cube Views are a really simple way to bring data into our Dashboards, either as a Dashboard Component themselves or as a data adapter.

First, we introduced the concept of using a Cube View as a Dashboard Component. Remember, a Dashboard Component is the type of item that we visualize on the screen when we are running our Dashboards. These can be charts, logos, buttons, combo boxes, or (of course) Cube Views!

Then we talked about Cube Views added to Dashboards as a data adapter. A data adapter is what feeds your various Dashboard Components with data. So, while Dashboard Components are the visual aspects of our Dashboards, data adapters are a bit more 'behind the scenes'. Our two options here were Cube View MD Data Adapters or Cube View Adapters.

Cube Views Connections in Excel Add-in/Spreadsheet

Finally, we discussed how Cube Views can be incorporated into our trusty Excel Add-in (or the Spreadsheet tool). Creating a Cube View connection in Excel is much more powerful than simply exporting a Cube View. This provides a live connection into Excel and can be refreshed to ensure you are seeing the latest information in case the data or the Cube View has changed. This is a great tool to use if you are going to make a Spreadsheet Form template or if you want to give Users the option to submit a Cube View Form in Excel.

Fundamentals of Cube View Design and Build

After we discussed how versatile our Cube Views can be, we sat down and discussed the basics of building one. One important lesson we wanted to learn was to take extra care that our Cube Views are easy to maintain, and other Cube View builders can jump in at any point to share the load. Thinking ahead – by locking down a repeatable process – we can make any implementation simple and future maintenance more palatable.

Building your First Cube View

After discussing Cube View Groups and Profiles, we started building. So, what do we need to have a functioning Cube View? We will want to build these three items first to see what data the Cube View is querying:

1. A Cube View POV

2. Cube View rows

3. Cube View columns

As we know, we usually don't just place one Member in our row and one in our columns. This is where our Member Expansions came into play. Member Expansions are a great way to query many Members at one time. This reduces your build time with any Cube View but also reduces your time maintaining the Cube View. It is *so* important to consider reporting when building your metadata design. See Figure 15.1 for an example.

Figure 15.1

But as we know, sometimes we must incorporate some more difficult Member Expansions to meet our requirements and keep our Cube View tied to our Dimensions. We referred to our Samples and Member Expansions tab to help us build some of these. But the one we spent a lot of time on, and which is very commonly used in the field, is Where clause expressions. Where clauses can tack onto your Member Expansions to provide additional logic in a pinch. This is where we could filter further on Text Properties, Account Types, Intercompany, and so much more!

Dynamic Cube Views

Alright, we have started to feel confident about building the bones of a Cube View. But what can we do to really set our entire project up for success? One great trick is to implement sharing rows/columns and Cube View templates. Both are great ways to essentially cut down the amount of time spent building Cube Views so you can re-use pieces that might be consistent. On top of that, now you can centrally control any future updates! These concepts feed into each other because the prevalence of row and column sharing will require you to make templates.

Next, we talked about how to keep our Cube View dynamic using Parameters and Substitution Variables. We rarely see a Cube View (honestly, if ever!) that is totally static across all its Dimensions. There is usually some sort of User interaction that is required (a selection, maybe, or defaulting off something else) to ensure our Cube View twists and turns to every User's every wish!

Performance Considerations

We know how to build a Cube View and how to streamline our maintenance but – as we know – one of the things that can ruin a User Experience is bad performance. Here, we remember our Data Unit and discussed the following options when thinking about performance and Cube Views:

1. Recognize the impact of dynamically-calculated data.
2. Watch the amount of aggregated data present.
3. Apply suppression where necessary.
4. Utilize Cube View paging.

Cube View Formatting

Formatting a Cube View is something that can become a bit of an art form, and it can get very intricate. Here, we covered some of the basics, but don't take this as a challenge to learn every single formatting property! Just take things day by day or requirement by requirement.

To get started, we need to cover our Cube View formatting order of operations. Let's recall:

1. Application Properties get overridden by the…

2. Cube View Default formatting gets overridden by the…

3. Column formatting gets overridden by the…

4. Row formatting gets overridden by the…

5. Column overrides gets overridden by the…

6. Row overrides

Application Properties

Application Properties is the first item we will want to set and discuss shortly after (or during) any design session. These are commonly forgotten about when implementing OneStream, but there are many important areas to discuss. I recommend reviewing each property and familiarizing yourself with what is available.

Your Dimensions tab, where you can set your User-Defined descriptions, is available when building Cube Views, drill down, and across many places through the Workflow data collection process. Remember, this is a User-friendly way to label your User-Defined (UD) Dimensions because this will be a new concept for every new User in OneStream.

And, of course, the Standard Reports tab. This tab is where you are going to set your general page formatting, but it is also where you alter the header bars and colors you see on the PDF versions of your Reports.

Cube View Formatting

Once we have our application properties set, we are ready to build some Cube Views. We may need to ask ourselves, what version of the Cube View are we trying to format? We know Cube Views are versatile and can be featured in many areas of the application; when it comes to digesting our Cube Views, we can view them in three different main formats:

1. Data Explorer Grid

2. Excel-exported version

3. Printed PDF Report

Therefore, we can format each of these three exports separately. You will also notice each one will have some unique properties. But this is not the only place you can see different formatting; the options between the header formatting and cell formatting will also be different, as shown in Figure 15.2.

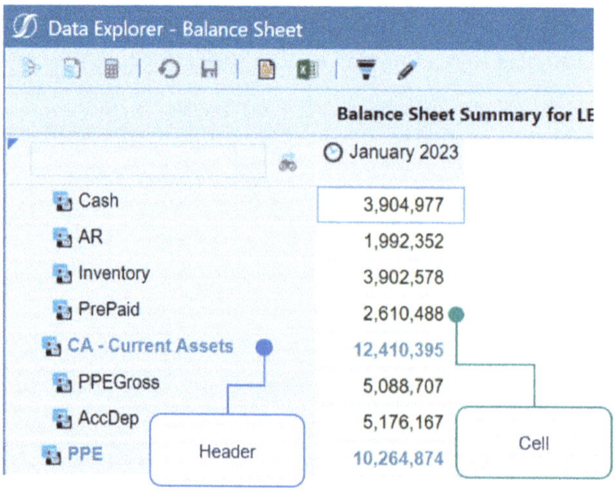

Figure 15.2

There are many formatting options you can work with for your Cube Views. Because of this, we typically recommend discussing your formatting *ahead of time* with key stakeholders and then setting formatting parameters. Typically, we keep our Literal Value Parameters organized in one clearly labeled Maintenance Unit. The best thing about using parameters is if you ever need to update your formatting, you can simply update the parameter as opposed to redoing all your Cube Views.

You can apply your Literal Value Parameters to all your necessary rows and columns within a Cube View, or you can easily utilize conditional formatting. In our hands-on chapter (Chapter 9), we used conditional formatting to quickly format the entire Cube View on the default header and footer using the naming convention applied to the row and column name. This taught us an important and recommended strategy: *use your row name effectively*. Figure 15.3 shows how we applied suffixes that would trigger the conditional formatting to apply differently.

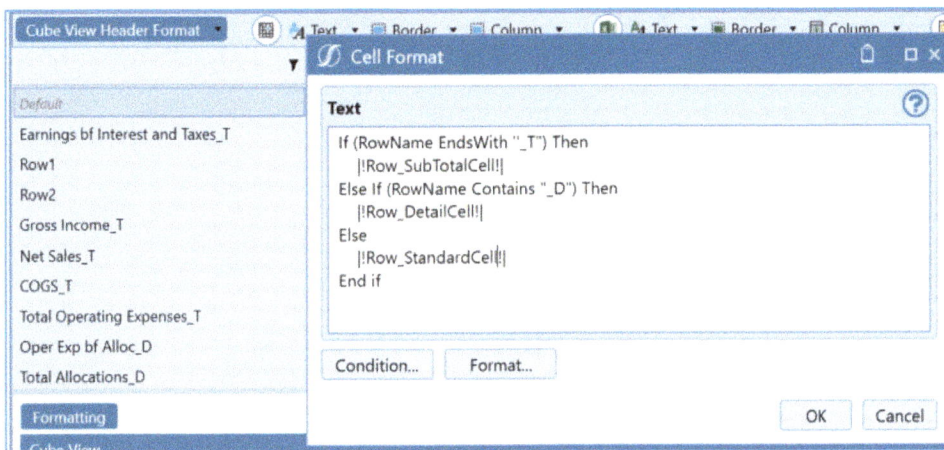

Figure 15.3

If you need even more intricate formatting, row and column overrides can also be applied. These were the last two items in our order of operations. This can be done for formatting as well as applying a new Member Filter. Essentially, with overrides, you are trying to home in on a specific cell. Commonly, we do this if we want to undo the behavior that the rows override the columns. And, of course, remember that this also is triggered by the name of your rows and columns. You can apply a list or a range to activate your overrides.

If all these options don't quite get you there when it comes to formatting, you can also explore using a Cube View Extender Rule that can be written inline on the Cube View itself or on the Business Rules page. Typically, we use them to get specific control over the headers, footers, and logos of our Report, but you can really grab anything here. Just remember, this only applies to the PDF version of your Cube View. Also, if rules are not your strong suit, we have plenty of snippets to get you started and help you out.

Building Your Own Cube View

We ended our time with Cube Views with a short chapter on building our very own Cube View. We wanted to put a few exercises into this book to make things a bit more interactive for you since what better way is there to learn than being hands-on? Our final Cube View ended up looking a little something like Figure 15.4 (we formatted the Data Explorer, Excel, and PDF versions of these Reports).

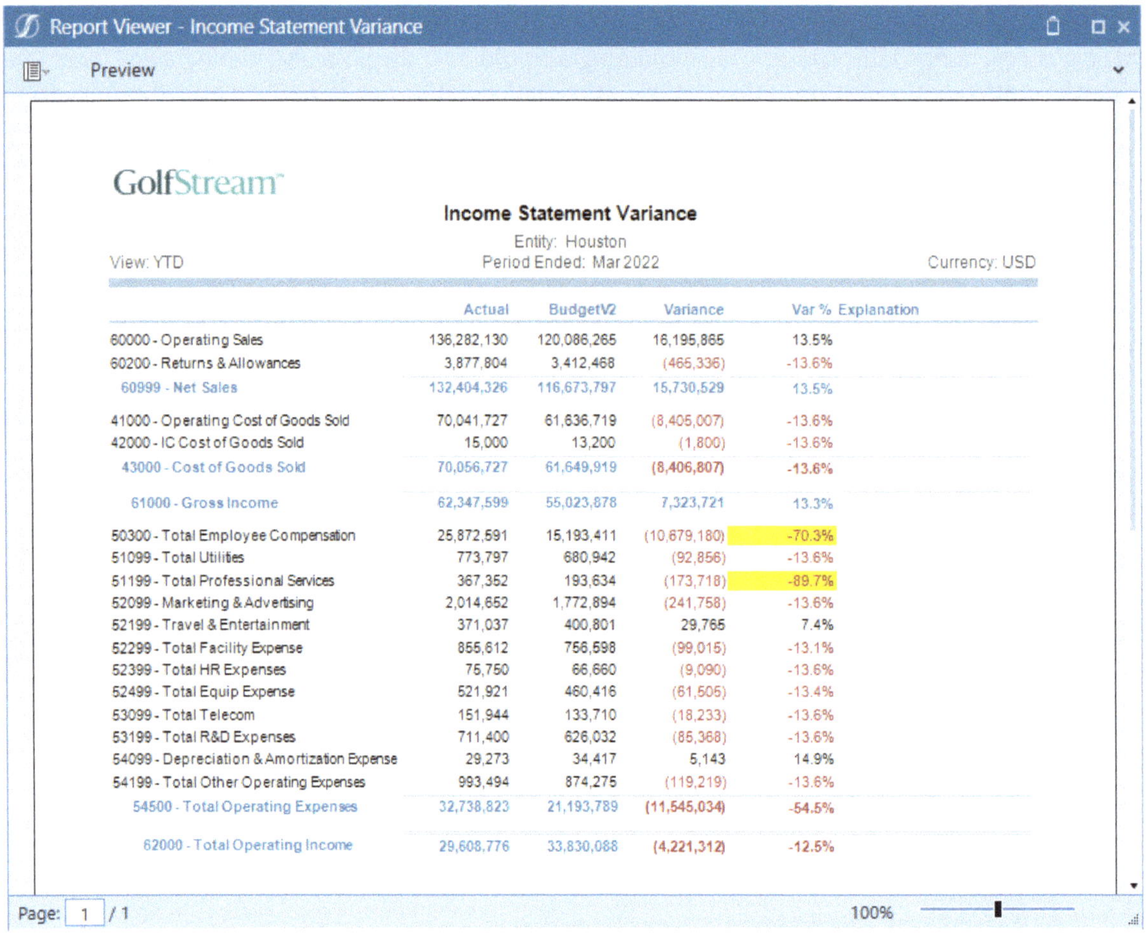

Income Statement Variance

Entity: Houston

View: YTD | Period Ended: Mar 2022 | Currency: USD

	Actual	BudgetV2	Variance	Var %	Explanation
60000 - Operating Sales	136,282,130	120,086,265	16,195,865	13.5%	
60200 - Returns & Allowances	3,877,804	3,412,468	(465,336)	-13.6%	
60999 - Net Sales	132,404,326	116,673,797	15,730,529	13.5%	
41000 - Operating Cost of Goods Sold	70,041,727	61,636,719	(8,405,007)	-13.6%	
42000 - IC Cost of Goods Sold	15,000	13,200	(1,800)	-13.6%	
43000 - Cost of Goods Sold	70,056,727	61,649,919	(8,406,807)	-13.6%	
61000 - Gross Income	62,347,599	55,023,878	7,323,721	13.3%	
50300 - Total Employee Compensation	25,872,591	15,193,411	(10,679,180)	-70.3%	
51099 - Total Utilities	773,797	680,942	(92,856)	-13.6%	
51199 - Total Professional Services	367,352	193,634	(173,718)	-89.7%	
52099 - Marketing & Advertising	2,014,652	1,772,894	(241,758)	-13.6%	
52199 - Travel & Entertainment	371,037	400,801	29,765	7.4%	
52299 - Total Facility Expense	855,612	756,598	(99,015)	-13.1%	
52399 - Total HR Expenses	75,750	66,660	(9,090)	-13.6%	
52499 - Total Equip Expense	521,921	460,416	(61,505)	-13.4%	
53099 - Total Telecom	151,944	133,710	(18,233)	-13.6%	
53199 - Total R&D Expenses	711,400	626,032	(85,368)	-13.6%	
54099 - Depreciation & Amortization Expense	29,273	34,417	5,143	14.9%	
54199 - Total Other Operating Expenses	993,494	874,275	(119,219)	-13.6%	
54500 - Total Operating Expenses	32,738,823	21,193,789	(11,545,034)	-54.5%	
62000 - Total Operating Income	29,608,776	33,830,088	(4,221,312)	-12.5%	

Figure 15.4

Here, we made a simple Income Statement Cube View. We started by setting our:

1. Cube View POV
2. Headers/Footers
3. Name/Description settings

We showed this in the Advanced tab but, remember, you can choose to work in any tab that gets the job done. I personally like to mix and match.

We then moved into our rows and columns. This will make up the meat of the Cube View and is typically where the action happens. First, we started with our rows, a place where we normally spend the majority of our time. We applied a consistent naming convention to note which items were detail rows and which ones were total rows. This is a great way to keep yourself organized as well as improve the readability of your Cube View setup if you are not the only person who has to maintain it.

On our columns, we took this time to introduce some potential variance Calculations. We have a few options for using Calculations in Cube Views, but here we applied GetDataCells. We called out the Member name specifically, but you can also write GetDataCell Calculations that are based on the specific column name. Remember, there are samples for these included in the application, in our handy Member Filter Builder pop-up. We had an entire chapter on Cube View formatting, and I am sure you have learned that with great flexibility comes great power. We also know that our formatting can be applied to the data cell grid, PDF, and Excel-exported versions of the Cube View. Depending on your company's style and the Cube Views used, you may spend more time in one of these than any of the others. We set up:

1. Cube View default formatting
2. Literal Value Parameters

3. Conditional formatting

4. Cube View Extender Rules

Instead of going into the individual rows and columns of our Cube View to apply intricate formatting, we did this all through conditional formatting on the default header and cell of the Cube View. This is a handy trick you can take with you to easily format your Cube View and a creative way to think of conditional formatting.

Finally, we added some navigation links into our Cube View. Navigation links also make it easy to create drill paths that guide Users through various visualizations of their data. This means that Users can move seamlessly from one visualization to another without having to navigate through multiple screens or menus. This creates a more fluid and intuitive User Experience that encourages better data exploration and discovery.

Dashboards

We talked a lot about Cube Views, and this is a common place for many people when they start working in OneStream. But we have also learned that this book is about so much more than simply creating Reports; it's about designing a User Experience in OneStream. And while we know there is a stoic side to reporting, User Experience challenges us to broaden our goals and add elements of style and interactivity into our design. Dashboards are what really grab the attention!

Most people don't need much convincing when it comes to the value of Dashboards. They are typically the thing that people wish they had more of, and are enthusiastic to implement. Dashboards are great because:

1. They create excitement and people want to see them in their applications.

2. They solve certain reporting requirements:

    a. If non-Cube Data needs to be queried/submitted.

    b. If an interactive element is required.

    c. If your existing reporting tools are not quite getting you there.

3. They cultivate the best User Experience possible:

    a. Data Entry

    b. Analysis

    c. Admin tasks and information

But Dashboards can be intimidating, so where do we start? This is an interesting question because I think anyone can build a Dashboard. We highlighted a few key skills that you should work on developing if you are new to Dashboards:

1. Can break down the anatomy of a Workspace.

2. Able to create at least five Dashboard Components.

3. Can build each of the data adapter types.

4. Able to embed Dashboards.

Breaking Down Workspaces

Application Dashboards are built in the Dashboards page on the Application tab, while System Dashboards are built in the Dashboards page on the System tab. But when you get to that page, 'Dashboards' are not the first item you see. You get hit with something called 'Workspaces' and probably a lot of other things!

We had to start at the top and ask ourselves, what is the purpose of Workspaces and why is the software moving in this direction? Workspaces were created to provide the following benefits:

- Isolation between Dashboards. This allows developers to work on the same Dashboard in a sandbox environment.

- Greater flexibility for developers. Better control amongst team members for changes, testing, and overall design.

- Allowing same-name items to exist in separate Workspaces. This reduces the likelihood of naming conflicts, especially when importing/exporting them from other applications or sources.

- Sharing Workspace objects with other Workspaces provides the opportunity to re-use objects rather than having to copy them.

From now on, this will have to be the first item that we create when building Dashboards. Think of it as a great way to lay out *all the items you need* to build the User Experience of your dreams. This concept is pivotal because it is meant to remove us from the mindset of "I am going to this page to build Dashboards." You may have seen that what we create in OneStream can be so much more powerful than a quintessential Dashboard. This is just the beginning!

Then we wanted to tackle our Components. As mentioned, this is any item that you can visually see on your final Dashboard: your charts, pivot grids, buttons, combo boxes, video players, Reports, and the list goes on and on.

Your data adapters, parameters, files, and strings are the unsung heroes of Dashboards. You may not be able to see them, but they bring your various Components to life. We spent a lot of time recapping parameters already, and we didn't touch too much on strings and assemblies.

Data adapters are used to flood your Components with data either from the Cube or application/external tables. We went through and created a few of them in Chapter 10. Files may not be used as commonly but are widespread when building Components such as a Book Viewer (for OneStream Report books), Spreadsheet, or File Viewer.

Be Able to Build at least Five (or Ten) Components

One of the things I said everyone should know is how to build around five (or ten) Dashboard Components proficiently. There are more than that, but this will be a great way to get yourself well-rounded. I will give you my top ten based on what I have found to be the most helpful in my career. The top five are the most important.

1. Buttons
2. Combo boxes
3. Grid View
4. Charts (advanced)
5. Cube View

But there are plenty of other Dashboard Components that you can learn to build. I also work with Labels, Book Viewer, BI Viewer, Reports, and pivot grids. No matter what you decide, just take them one at a time.

Building Different Types of Data Adapters

We learned about some key Components that get us building Dashboards. But we also saw that some of these items required a data adapter. I have a rule – if you can get the data adapter working, you can get the Dashboard working. Many of the Components do not require that much configuration and really 'sing' on their own. But if their data is clunky, they cannot function! There are five types of data adapter:

1. Cube View
2. Cube View MD
3. Method

4. SQL

5. BI Blend

I personally recommend learning them all, but the Cube View, Cube View MD, and SQL data adapters are what you will probably use the most often. It really boils down to one thing: are you trying to query data that lives in the Cube or not?

Embedding Dashboards

At this point, we understood how to build items individually, but how do we bring them together? As we decide on our Dashboard layout and place our Components, we found out that sometimes having a lot of Components is tricky to design. So, we started embedding Dashboards into other Dashboards. Here, things might start to get more complicated, but it is not something that should scare us. It enables us to break down a complicated solution into small pieces.

Embedded Dashboard Components nest one Dashboard inside another. Figure 15.5 revisits this:

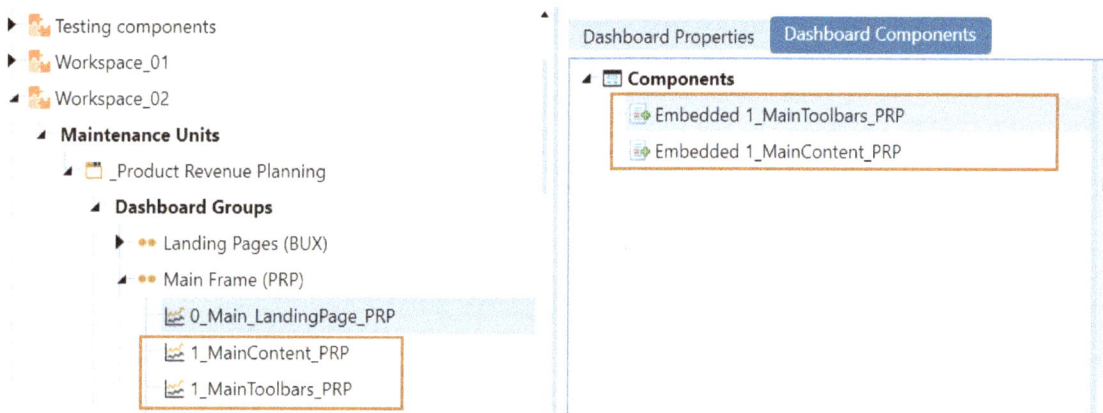

Figure 15.5

Embedded Dashboard Components are automatically created every time a Dashboard is generated. You can take advantage of them without having to do anything!

Before we start embedding Components, we should point out that our Dashboard design mode is going to be our best tool for helping to pull apart more complicated Dashboards. This way, we can simply point, click, and edit.

As you saw, things can get a little crazy, so a good naming convention pattern will keep us organized. Figure 15.6 illustrates a simple pattern that we follow, containing prefixes that highlight the Dashboard hierarchy, a solution code to keep this group of Dashboards organized together, and a good description that describes how each Dashboard is being used.

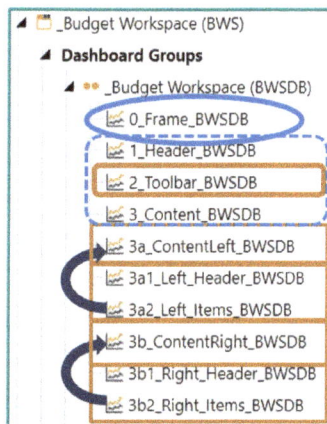

Figure 15.6

Building a Splash Screen Dashboard

We then moved to our heavy hands-on section of the book. The first Dashboard we looked at creating was a Splash Screen Dashboard.

This type of Dashboard will serve as the landing page our Users see when first signing on to the application. By setting this Dashboard as the User's home page, it will provide a welcoming and attractive introduction to proceedings, as well as offer 'big button' one-click navigation to our Users' most frequently-used Workflows and reporting assets.

Something like this is a great way to improve every User's experience in the application. Remember, this is something that potentially ALL Users will be exposed to, so our audience is a bit broader. Our goal is to provide the functionality that the User requires and a space that is clear and efficient. We should strive for something attractive, easy to follow, and performant. On this issue of performance, remember that if this is your User's home page, you don't want it to take too long to load.

Here, we employed a tactic many people use when starting any Dashboard design – sketching out. You can use whatever tool you are most comfortable with to achieve this, and it will undoubtedly get revised and refined as the actual Dashboard gets built out, but it *will* help you stay organized.

Then, we wanted to lay out the various Components we will need to bring our Dashboard to life, and where they will reside on the screen. To organize these objects, we will use a Dashboard of Type Grid as the 'main' Dashboard, with three rows and one column. One of the most powerful and useful concepts in OneStream Dashboards is the ability to embed them. In the end, our result was an attractive and simple Dashboard that looks something like this (Figure 15.7).

Figure 15.7

Notice that the screen is not too busy, even though we included items such as:

1. A big picture that required a bit of formatting.

2. Linkable icons along the top that navigated our User to the correct location.

3. Quick ratios and KPIs along the bottom that are interactive but do not take too long to load.

Building an Administrative Dashboard

Our splash screen was something that we had to think about for all Users. Now, we are moving into something that is geared specifically toward Administrators. An Admin Dashboard creates a special-purpose home page for someone who needs to know what is going on with the application, run certain tasks, and potentially check on their User population. Again, we are thinking of our End-User and what they need to do. The nice thing about crafting these Dashboards is that an Administrator is familiar with OneStream, so this is something Administrators and the implementation team can design and work on together.

These Dashboards are typically intended to serve as a one-stop shop for Administrators to access application vitals, metadata changes, data errors, and other functionality that they require in order to efficiently administer the application. At the end of this chapter, we created a Dashboard that looks something like Figure 15.8.

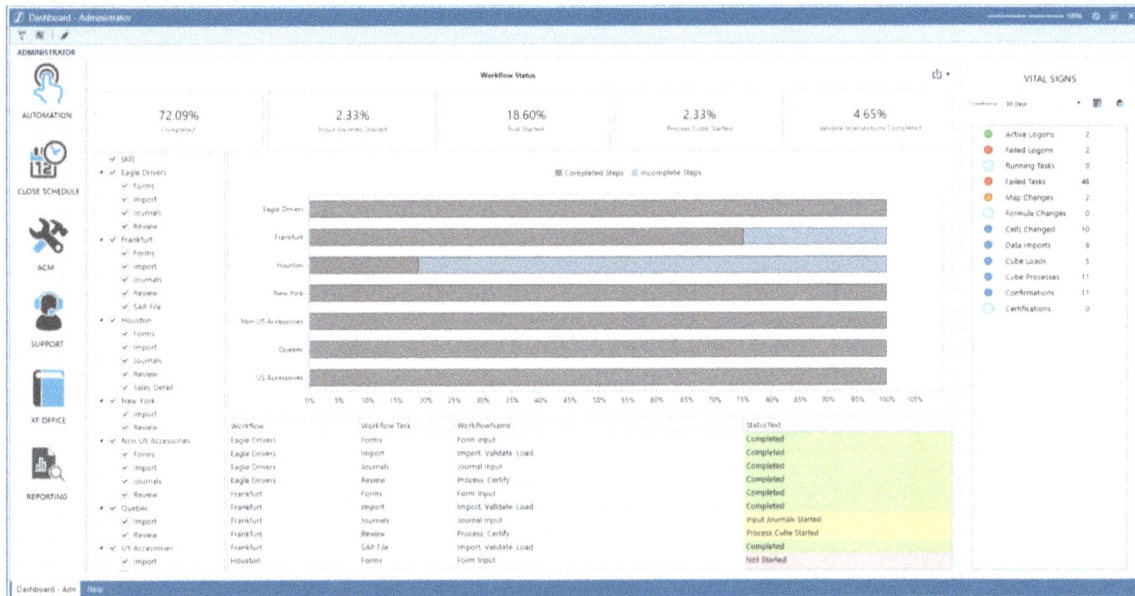

Figure 15.8

Notice this one is very different:

1. We have a pane going down the left-hand side that navigates the Administrator to key areas they may need to explore, or tasks they need to perform.

2. The center panel gives them information on their various Workflow statuses using the BI Viewer (paired with a Method Query data adapter).

Building an Executive Dashboard

In a similar fashion, we then looked at building a Dashboard for Executives. Executives and Managers need quick and clear information regarding their organization's performance. This exercise highlighted the importance of parameterizing Dashboard Components for filtering and quick navigation. Again, we have our User population directly in the name of the Dashboard.

Some common things Executives need are clear KPI metrics and other business-specific data to streamline financial operations. Effective Dashboard design involves more than just a clean layout, however. When creating Dashboards, it's crucial to consider the message you want to convey. It's also essential to understand *who* your Users are and *what* information they need to see. Consider whether there are specific actions that need to be taken based on the results displayed, or if the Dashboards are for informational purposes only.

We used the following Components to create the Dashboard in Figure 15.9:

- Labels with conditional formatting and tool tips

- Dialog buttons

- Combo box

- Radio buttons
- Cube Views
- Line Chart
- Waterfall Chart
- Bar Chart
- Data Explorer Report

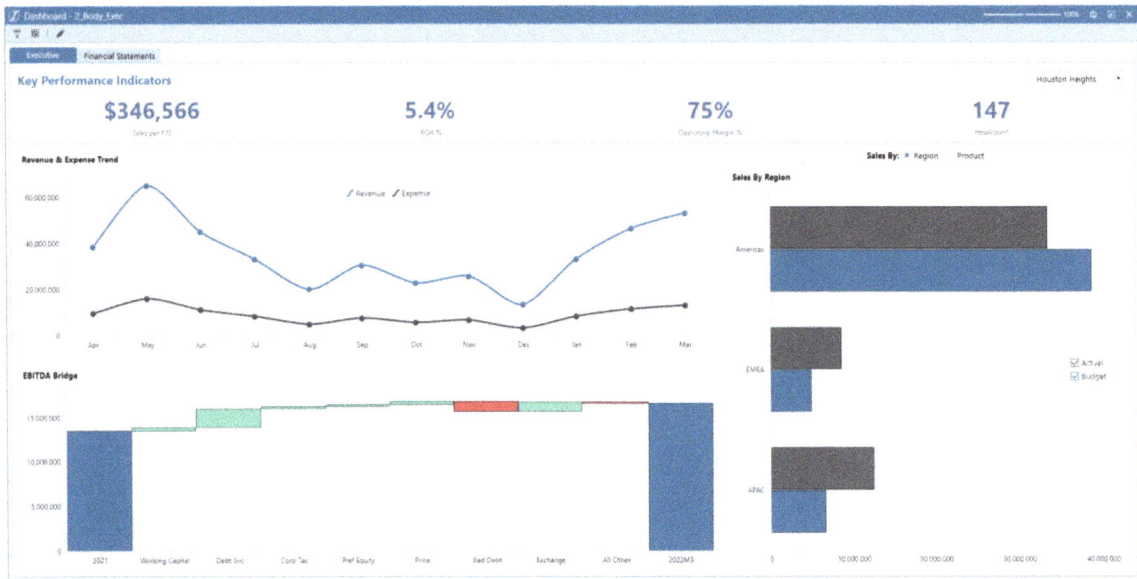

Figure 15.9

Dashboards for Budgeting, Planning, and Forecasting

This was our final hands-on item, and we really tried to tie in as much as possible (plus go a little deeper in a few areas). This was an interesting Dashboard to create because we are dealing with our Users responsible for Budgeting, Planning, and Forecasting. While this helps us to understand our audience, you will find that this process is different for all companies, so designing something around the User process will be key.

In this case, we were incorporating something with an element of data entry, so we had to think of the Workflow. We wanted to ensure that what we create allows the User to easily navigate to another part of the plan, and mark the part of the plan we are working on as 'complete' when we are done. To refresh your memory, check out Figure 15.10 to see the many faces of what we created.

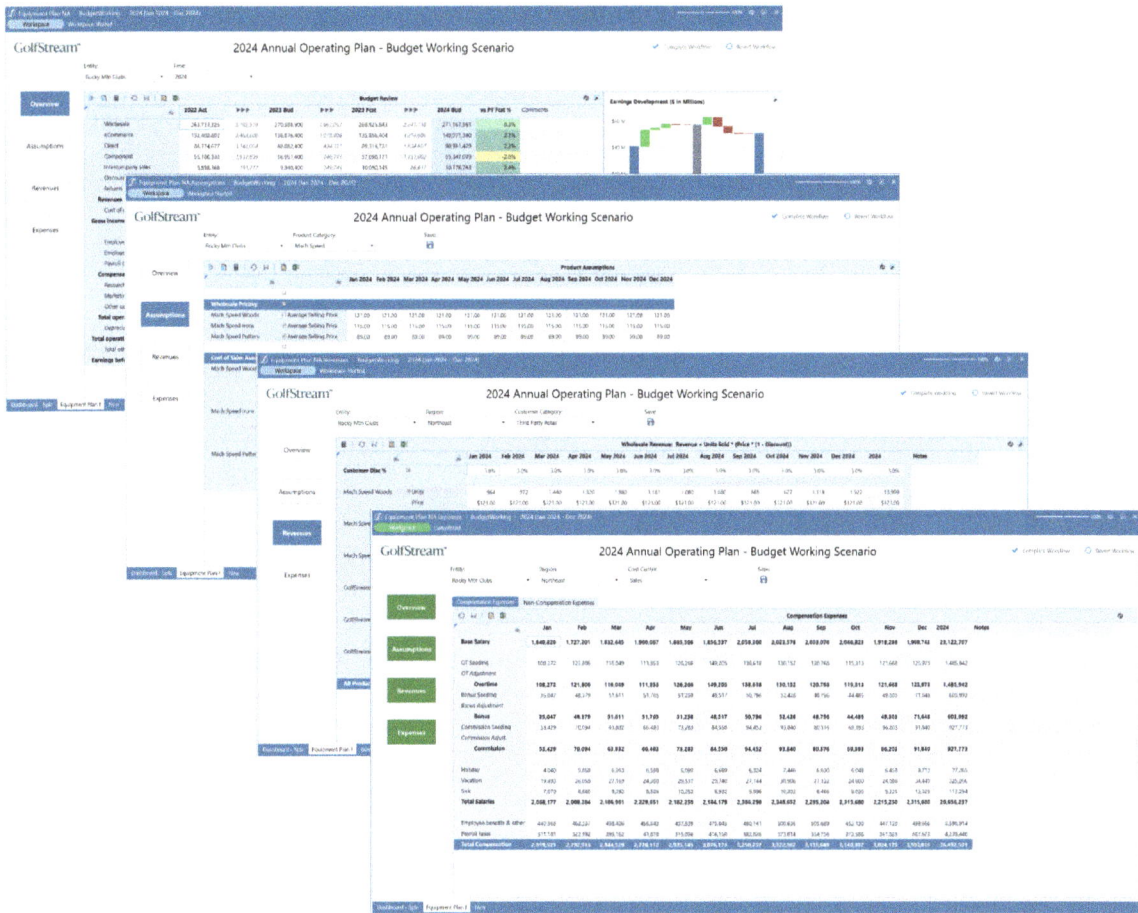

Figure 15.10

1. A panel along the left side of the screen with a button for each of the major functional parts of the plan. We also included a top-level 'Overview' button that will allow us to review a summarized view of the full plan at any time, with all the details pulled together.

2. To keep track of which parts of the plan are completed and which are not, we will leverage OneStream's Workflow functionality. We included two buttons in the upper-right corner of the screen – one to mark the current Workflow step complete, and another to revert that step if necessary.

3. On the left-hand side of the screen, we tied the navigation and Workflow concepts together by configuring each navigation button to reflect the completion status of its respective step.

4. On the right-hand side, we included some helpful information for the User to see when completing their plan using charts, as well as embedding conditional formatting into our Cube View.

There were a lot of moving aspects in this item, but as you will notice, it wasn't a particularly busy Dashboard. The User could easily see what they needed to do and enjoy a clean working space. Because of some of the moving pieces, we did incorporate some Business Rules. It is important to balance our use of Business Rules, ensuring that we provide something that will not hurt performance, but which also makes Dashboard maintenance easy later on. Three rules we used were:

1. Dashboard Data Set Rules, which can be used to collect, manipulate, and enrich sets of data.

2. Dashboard XFBR String Rules, which are often used to dynamically generate the configuration of an object, based on certain specified conditions.

3. Dashboard Extender Rules, which are the workhorses of the Dashboard Business Rules.

As you can see, we had many moving elements in this Dashboard, but it gave the User all the information they needed and quick access to expedite their journey. If Users are already learning to work within OneStream, why not make it easier for them with an easy-to-follow Dashboard? Of course, ensure you always think about the person who is left to maintain the Dashboard. Because of this, we always want to keep the design simple, with well-named items and nicely commented rules.

Conclusion

This brings us to the very end of our book. The three of us came together to write something based on what we have seen work – in the variety of situations we have been exposed to – within OneStream. Each of us has played different roles in the company, but we have always had the goal of creating applications that drive the best User Experience we can. No matter what role you play, if you keep the practice in mind, you will be successful when creating your own items.

Of course, your journey doesn't end here! After all, our intention with this book was to lay out your options and inspire you to get out there to come up with things that help you and your User community. As we know, no application will look the same, and the flexibility of the tool should make you excited – not afraid – to jump in and try something different. Indeed, this practice doesn't just apply to our reporting tools but to every facet of OneStream. If you never build a Cube View in your life, but you create artifacts in OneStream, keep your User in mind – whether it is driving a new process, being mindful of maintenance, or optimizing performance. Nothing is built in a vacuum.

What makes OneStream special is not only the product, but also the community of people that come together to share their knowledge and experiences with it. We have quickly learned that one person cannot know it all, and that should not be anyone's goal. What makes you get better is flexing and forming to the new requirements that you are faced with. If something seems new to you, it is likely new to many others, so – as you get stronger – don't forget to invest back into the OneStream Community by sharing your experiences and what you have learned along the way. Join our conferences, attend new training, participate in ONECommunity, and be a support system to those around you.

And one final point. Our product is always shifting to reach new markets and improve the experience for its Administrators, Users, and implementors. Our resources will help you to stay up-to-date and try new things, and one area where we see a lot of growth is in Dashboards itself, with the introduction of Workspaces. This is changing how we think, opening new possibilities, and even making some items easier to create. The overarching principles in this book do not change, though, so grow with the software and try your hand at the new features as they are rolled out!

Index

Index

Index

Index

OneStream Foundation Handbook

The Definitive Reference to Design, Configure and Support Your OneStream Platform.

OneStream is a modern, unified platform that is revolutionizing corporate performance management. This proven alternative to fragmented legacy applications is designed to simplify processes for the most sophisticated, global enterprises. Hundreds of the world's leading companies are turning to OneStream to help with reporting and understanding financial data.

In this practical guide, The Architect Factory team at OneStream Software explains each part of an implementation, and the design of solutions. Readers will learn the core guiding principles for implementing OneStream from the company's top team of experts. Beyond offering a training guide, the focus of this book is on the 'why' of design and building an application.

- Manage your Implementation with the OneStream methodology
- Understand Design and Build concepts
- Build solutions for the Consolidation of financial data, and develop Planning models
- Create Data Integration solutions that will feed your models
- Develop Workflows to guide and manage your end-users
- Advance your solutions with Rules and Security
- Take advantage of detailed Data Reporting using tools such as Analytic Blend, Advanced Excel reporting, and Dashboarding
- Tune Performance, and optimize your application

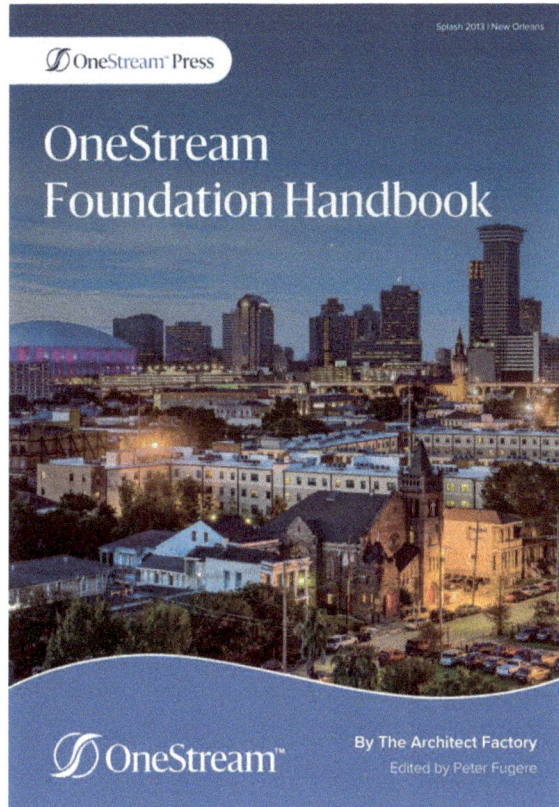

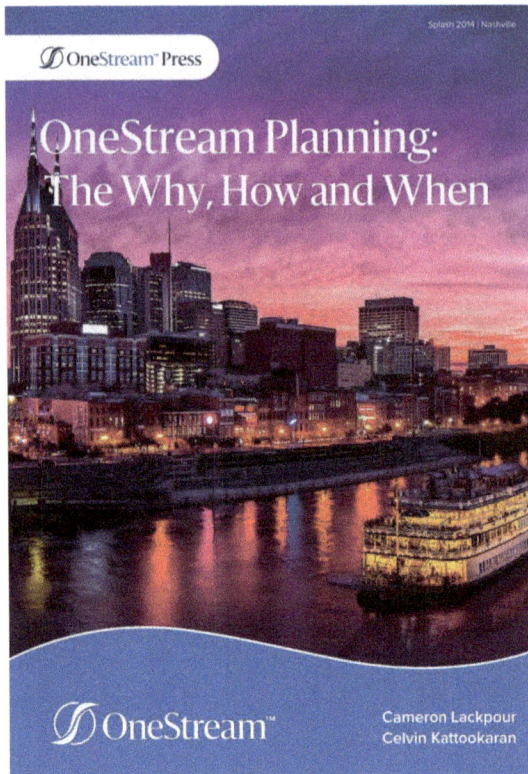

OneStream Planning: The Why, How and When

OneStream is a world-class Intelligent Finance Platform that handles the complex planning, consolidation, reporting and other requirements of mid-sized to large enterprises. Whether in retail, financial services, manufacturing or other industries, the OneStream platform provides the means to integrate multiple data sources and utilize a wide range of tools and methodologies to improve business processes and performance. Through OneStream, organizations benefit from unified, real-time, enterprise-wide planning and forecasting.

Aimed at OneStream Planning practitioners, administrators, implementors, and power users alike, as well as Financial close and consolidations practitioners, *OneStream Planning: The Why, How and When* is the first standalone book in the performance management space to cover the power and potential of Planning in OneStream. Drawing from real-world deployments, the book is rooted in easily understood business use cases, and explains approaches (with code) through a comprehensive exploration of the solution. All this is offered within a framework of top functional and technical practice as informed by the authors' decades-long consulting and application development experiences.

- Which should I do – Import or Direct Load, Consolidate or Aggregate?
- How do Data Buffers really work; what is Eval and why should I care? Which approach is fastest and does it really matter?
- Why Multiyear Scenarios should never be Yearly
- Can Thing Planning run in the Spreadsheet? (It can.)
- Combining REST API and Analytic Blend
- Slice Security down to the very tiniest slice
- Pivot Grid or Large Pivot Grid, that is the question
- A book filled with clear use cases
- Exhaustively tested and verified solutions, and extensive source code
- Undocumented features and functionality covered, along with functional and technical good practices

OneStream Finance Rules and Calculations Handbook

Hundreds of companies have turned to OneStream to solve complex planning, consolidation and operational reporting needs. OneStream's unique ability to provide a multitude of solutions across dozens of industries is largely due to its dynamic Finance Engine which provides the capability to add industry- and company-specific business intelligence to data. Employing the full power of the Finance Engine allows companies to extend the platform and fully exploit the power of their investment.

Aimed at everyone from novices to seasoned veterans, this handbook—by OneStream Distinguished Architect Jon Golembiewski—will break down the Finance Engine and outline how to write Finance Business Rules and Calculations. Its insights will help propel OneStream applications to the next level.

- Fundamentals of the Finance Engine
- Detailed breakdown of the Cube and Data
- A look under the hood of the api.Data.Calculate function
- Techniques for tackling complex calculation requirements
- How to use the Custom Calculate function to make calculations dynamic
- How to write calculations for optimal performance
- How to troubleshoot calculations
- How to solve and avoid common errors and pitfalls
- Real-world calculation examples with detailed explanations
- A full application with all referenced code examples is available to download

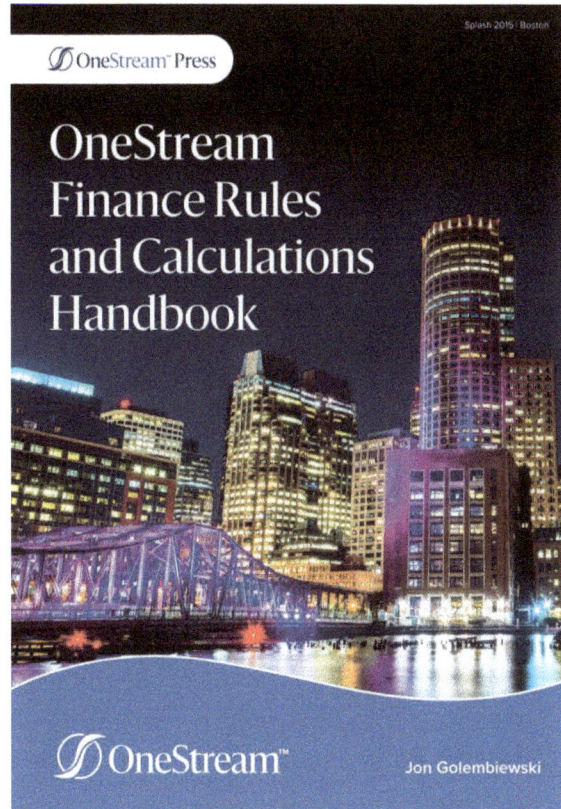

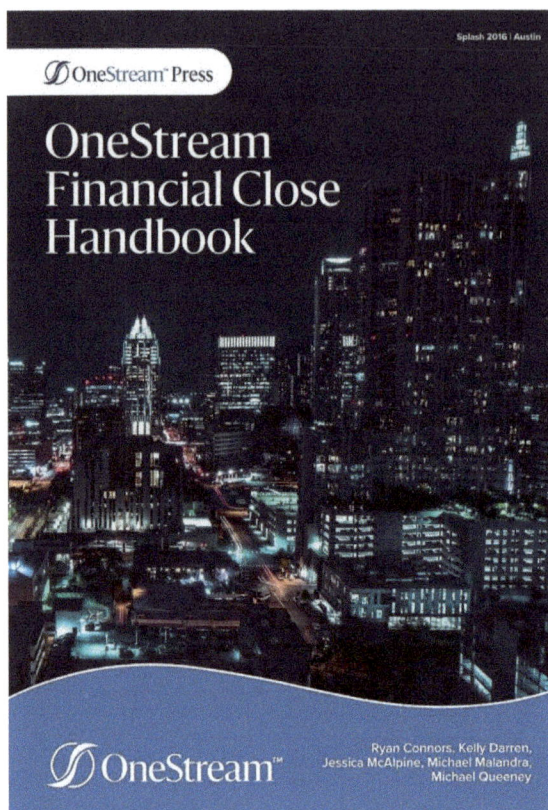

OneStream Financial Close Handbook

OneStream provides a market-leading Intelligent Finance Platform that reduces the complexity of financial operations. It unifies corporate performance management (CPM) processes such as planning, financial close & consolidation, reporting and analytics through a single, extensible solution.

The OneStream Financial Close Handbook – written by expert authors – is a practical book for implementors, administrators, and end-users, that dives into the Financial Close with a specific focus on the Account Reconciliations and Transaction Matching solutions.

The Account Reconciliations solution is a complete package that plugs into the Financial Close Workflow to leverage data that already resides within the consolidation application, whilst Transaction Matching helps accounting teams automate the collection and matching of large numbers of transactions across multiple sources.

With these solutions, OneStream Financial Close delivers the four key pillars of a good reconciliation process: Visibility, Standardization, Efficiency and Control.

In this book:

- Get a better understanding of the Financial Close process, and how OneStream delivers a streamlined, automated solution.
- Learn how to implement Account Reconciliations through detailed project phases, and accompanying case studies.
- Get to grips with the administration of Account Reconciliations, including settings, security, and auditing.
- Deep dive into the Account Reconciliation Solution from the End User's perspective, including how to prepare a Reconciliation, the sign-off and approval process, and overall reporting and monitoring capabilities.
- Learn what Transaction Matching is, plus how to build, test, and implement OneStream's highly automated system.
- Understand how to administer Transaction Matching through global options, access control, match sets, data sets, rules, and more!

www.ingramcontent.com/pod-product-compliance
Lightning Source LLC
Chambersburg PA
CBHW041621220326
41598CB00046BA/7428